GRAVEN STONES

Inscriptions from Lower Accomack County Virginia

Including Liberty and Parksley Cemeteries

— *Third Edition* —

*Jean Merritt Mihalyka and
Faye Downing Wilson*

HERITAGE BOOKS
2007

HERITAGE BOOKS
AN IMPRINT OF HERITAGE BOOKS, INC.

Books, CDs, and more—Worldwide

For our listing of thousands of titles see our website
at
www.HeritageBooks.com

Published 2007 by
HERITAGE BOOKS, INC.
Publishing Division
65 East Main Street
Westminster, Maryland 21157-5026

Copyright © 1986, 1987, 1992 Jean Merritt Mihalyka
and Faye Downing Wilson

Third Edition - revised and corrected

Other books by the author:

Colonial Deaths: Northampton County

Loose Papers and Sundry Court Cases, 1628-1731, Volume 1

Loose Papers and Sundry Court Cases, 1732-1744/5, Volume 2

*Loose Papers and Sundry Court Cases, April 1744 to July 1761, Volume 3
Northampton County, Virginia*

Marriages: Northampton County, Virginia, 1660-1854 (Third Revised Edition)

All rights reserved. No part of this book may be reproduced or transmitted in any form or by any means, electronic or mechanical, including photocopying, recording or by any information storage and retrieval system without written permission from the author, except for the inclusion of brief quotations in a review.

International Standard Book Number: 978-1-55613-551-3

CONTENTS

Introduction	v
Alphabetical List of Grave Sites with abbreviations	ix
Numerical List of Grave Sites	xix
Miscellaneous Abbreviations	xliv
Map	xlv
Graven Stones	1
Addendum	309
Index	311

INTRODUCTION

In 1980, *Gravestone Inscriptions In Northampton County, Virginia* was published and seems to have become a useful reference. It was felt that it would be worthwhile to have a similiar volume for the county just to the north. Accomack County, originally part of Northampton County, was created in 1663. It is approximately twice as large and, as part of the two county peninsula, has been isolated from the rest of Virginia by the Chesapeake Bay. This isolation may account in part for the great number of family burial plots which remain scattered throughout the county. Because of the county's size, the compilers decided to limit their survey to the lower half; Pungoteague and Lee districts [1]. However, before this decision was made the stones in the large public cemeteries - Parksley and Liberty - in the town of Parksley in Metompkin District had already been recorded. Since the work was completed, it seemed reasonable to include the material in this volume.

During the late 1930s, Sally Kellam Buchanan, Mrs. F.F., served as Director of the National Youth Administration for Accomack County. Keenly interested in genealogy and local history, aware that many private grave plots were disappearing, and needing projects for her NYA program, Mrs. Buchanan organized groups of young people to copy data found on the old markers. The resulting compilation was placed in the Accomack County Clerk's Office and is referred to in this work as "1940 record". Coverage of plots and accuracy in copying was not consistent but the undertaking is not to be discredited. Some of the approximately 2,000 stones then recorded have disappeared during the intervening forty or fifty years. It has served as a springboard for our recent work and has proved a valuable guide in many instances.

The some 15,000 entries in this volume have been gleaned from 408 burial sites. Nine are large public cemeteries, twenty-five are churchyards, and the remainder are private family plots. On the Eastern Shore of Virginia some burials were made in church graveyards even in the 17th century. By the last decade of the 19th century public cemeteries were established. However, by far the most usual custom was for interment in a plot on the family plantation or on the farm where one lived or worked. The practice lasted well into the first part of this century and is done occasionally to this day. Since there is no native stone on the Eastern Shore, most of the earliest graves were unmarked; some perhaps indicated with a ballast stone or hand-hewed wooden cross. The latter, of course, soon rotted into the sandy soil. Prior to the American Revolution only the more prosperous families were able to import stones from other colonies or from England. Thus the tombstone record of all but a tiny fraction of those early generations are lost to us. By the 1800s, itinerant stonecutters began to travel rural areas, carrying gravestones carved with symbols and verse, ready for the name and dates of the recently deceased. Many stones erected in the last half of the 19th century bear the name of stonecutters in Norfolk, Baltimore, or Philadelphia.

Thus of the thousands of people who have lived and died in the lower half of Accomack County from colonial times, relatively few can be identified by an existing marker. In view of this fact, it seems incomprehensible that any individual would deliberately destroy a graven stone. Of course, to do so is against the law. Nevertheless, the compilers have heard repeatedly (usually from farm hands) that "Mr. So and So had us git up that plot and cart them stones to the gut". Over the years the private plots have been encroached upon as the surrounding field was tilled; the horse and plow often chipping the very stones. Now tractors and large eqipment reek even more damage. All too often a site has been plowed over, a ditch dug, and the stones buried therein. On the other hand, and fortunately for the genealogist-historian, many farmers do cultivate carefully around a site, some even maintain the area, while others have the graves moved to a public cemetery (or encourage family members to do so). Numerous burial grounds were found in woods. Here stones fall and sink deeper into the soft mulched earth with each passing season. Trees spring up, branches cover, and roots strangle markers. Frequently one is alerted to its existence only by those tell-tale signs of a graveyard: ground myrtle, jonquils, and lillies in the Spring, crape myrtles, and a cedar tree.

It is hoped that the great care taken in recording will assure accuracy. Nevertheless some mistakes are bound to surface. Many plots were revisited two or three times to recheck a name, a date, or perhaps just a numeral. Often courthouse records, family bibles, and reference volumes [2] were consulted to assist in correctly reading a stone. Numerals probably cause the greatest problems. When the crossbar of a "4" was cut lightly, the elements often obliverated the faint line. The number then appears to be a "1". Weathering frequently makes "3", "5", and "8" very difficult to distinguish. Lower case letters can usually be determined by the position in the name, but capital letters when used as initials are far more difficult to decipher. In addition, many markers were made of sandstone which erodes or of poor quality stone which flake. If the compilers could not possible arrive at a solution, the problem figure has been indicated with a question mark.

In more than one instance stones had to be dug from under perhaps a foot of soil, or freed from the tangle of briars and vines which required clearing with bush-ax and lopper. One soon learns to use "spacing" and footstones as guides for finding a possible buried headstone. The small stones marking infant burials have been recorded. Considered of little value to the genealogist at one time, this data serves to complete a family chart, and often helps to clarify marriage and death sequences.

All names have been listed alphabetically to make the volume easier to use as a reference. It is acknowledged that relationships are lost when one cannot read all of the names of those interred in a family plot. The problem can be overcome by referring to the NUMERICAL LIST OF GRAVE SITES in the Preface. Included in each entry is the surname of each person buried at that site. Thus knowing both surname and site name, cross referencing can be used to reconstruct family relationships. Far better, of course, is a visit to the burial plot when possible.

Surnames of similar spellings have been filed together under the most usual spelling; i.e., Dalby (Dalbey, Dolby). Often a cross reference has been listed; i.e., Dolby - see Dalby. When there are two or more entries of the same name, the oldest is listed first. Within entries various abbreviations have been used which are explained in a list in the Preface. If no stone is in the plot but data has been obtained, "n.s." is shown and the source for the information is given. When no dates appear on the marker, "nd" is noted. Very frequently the 19th century markers give the age at death. 54/10/2 is used in the text and translates as: age 54 years, 10 months, and 2 days; 0/0/22 indicates that an infant died when 22 days old. The initials on a footstone are included only when no headstone could be located. If the name of the spouse is not given on the stone but could be ascertained, it has been placed within parentheses; i.e., John Brown (h/o Amy Lou). If Amy Lou's name appears as an entry in the text, only her initials are used; i.e., John Brown (h/o A L). Any information which has been supplied by the compilers has also been parenthesized. Unless an individual was killed in action, military service is noted only if prior to the 20th century. The stones for both white and black burials have been recorded. If known, the sites of black burials are indicated in the NUMERICAL LIST. Many graves in the black cemeteries are unmarked. Therefore those involved in black genealogy may find it of value to consult the records of the following funeral directors: Humbles, Accomac., VA; Giddens, Painter, VA; and Wharton, Accomac., VA.

It has taken almost five years to locate and record the tombstones in the lower two Accomack districts. It has been an undertaking of pleasure and satisfaction. Miles were covered in that little Toyota over highway and byway, by foot over fields, across marshes, and through brambles. Aggravating were mosquitoes, snakes, and red ants (they bite). Thorns, cockle burrs, windburn, sunburn, and unexpected rainshowers! Above all was the frustration of, "Why hadn't someone copied the existing stones one hundred years ago?" and, "How could anyone destroy the stones which have managed to survive?". None of the above could take away from the delight, however, of finding a quiet and peaceful little graveyard in the middle of a green field, a burying ground covered with periwinkle and masses of daffadils under old trees at the far end of a yard, or a single stone standing in a carpet of shatters deep in a pine woods. There was gratification, indeed, in recording a stone which seemed doomed for destruction. It was easy to work in the large cemeteries, but the favorites were the hard to find, almost forgotten small plots, which are steadily disappearing - the victims of time, weather, and man.

It is not possible to list the dozens of folks who helped the compilers in this undertaking. Special appreciation must be shown, however, to Mrs. E.G. Drummond who had the foresight to rescue the original card file from Mrs. Buchanan's estate. The Accomack-Northampton District Planning Commission loaned a large map of the county and Mrs. Anne Sayers of the Northampton County Real Estate and Mapping Office gave advice on its reproduction and detailing. Many, many people gave directions to and information about plots. The following personally took the compilers to various sites: Glenn Atkinson, Sr.; Teagle Bonniwell; Fenn Bott; John K. Branch; Pete Bulman; Carl Bundick; Glenn Custis; Alvah Evans; Chuck Evans; the Dorsey Fletchers; Richard Hofmaster; Carroll Justis, III; Joseph Kamp; Edward Kellam; Helen Mountcastle; Ethel D. Mulally; R.E. Nelms; the George Nicholsons; Margaret Oldham; the James Shrieves; Mrs. William Thornberg; Edward Truitt; C.I. Waterfield; and the Reverend W.B. Watson. E. Spencer Wise was especially helpful in supplying data for specific sites, as were Gladys Bayly; James Belote; Inde Budd; Juanita Bundick; Mary F. Carey; Richard Downing; Pierce Eichelberger; Belle Fears; the James Foxes; G.F. Hogg; Ray Landan; Sarah M. Lewis; Mildred Nock; Hilda Powell; Rooker Powers; Gladys Sherwood; Suzanne Taylor; Nora Turman; Eleanor Upshur; and Carlisle Williams. Upon several occasions Betty Bunting, Grace Badger, Charlotte Merritt, and Lila H. Schmidt assisted in recording.

We must not overlook Dr. Eugene E. Mihalyka who helped alphabetize and file hundreds of cards, patiently waited for many late dinners, supplied the cost of gallons of gasoline, and really seemed to look favorably on this five-year preoccupation.

Faye D. Wilson
Eastville, VA

Jean M. Mihalyka
Cherry-Core
Cheriton, VA

1. Recording in the upper half of Accomack County is in progress by Mary Frances Carey, Mrs. W.C., Jr., New Church, VA. The gravestones on Tangier Island, a part of the upper half of Accomack County in the Chesapeake Bay, were recorded in 1978 by F. Wilson and J. Mihalyka. Copies of this compilation of some 750 inscription are in the following libraries: Virginia State, DAR, and Eastern Shore Public.

2. In the text, the researcher is frequently referred to Whitelaw, Ralph T. *Virginia's Eastern Shore*. Virginia Historical Society. Richmond, VA 1951.

ALPHABETICAL LIST OF GRAVE SITES
with abbreviations used in text

Numerals following names refer to the NUMERICAL LIST OF GRAVE SITES and to the corresponding map numerals.

Abra	Abrams grave	389
Addi	Addison plot	250
AmeG	Ames grave	71
AmeH	Ames-Hacks N	133
Amep	Ames plot	72
Ames	Ames-Hyslop	75
Ande	Anderson Place	33
	Andewey - see Fairview	
	Andrews Place - see Parker plot	
Anth	Anthony Bell plot	61
Arli	Arlington	256
Atla	Atlantic View	44
Ayre	Ayres lot	12
Ayrm	Ayres mon	395
Ayrp	Ayres plot	5A
Badg	Badger bur gr	200
Bads	Badger-Savage	213
Bagc	Bagwell cem	252
Bagg	Bagge bur gr	106
Bagm	Bagwell mon	287
Bagw	Bagwell plot	367
Baig	Baily graves	38
Bail	Bailey Cem	209
Bayb	Bayberry Farm	26
Bayg	Bayley bur gr	275
Bayl	Bayly cem	348
Bays	Bayside cem	384
BayV	Bay View	24A
Beac	Beach cem	103
Bead	Bead Farm	331
Belb	Bell bur gr	52
BelF	Bell-Floyd	53
Belg	Bell grave	29
Bell	Belle Vue	168
Belo	Beloat Place	303
Blen	Blenheim	223

BMea	B Mears gr	306
Bogb	Boggs bur gr	263
Bogg	Boggs Place	268
Bowm	Bowman's Folly	332
Brad	Bradford-Burton	49
BraH	Bradford-Hyslop	97
Brap	Bradford plot	115
BraW	Bradford-White	203
BTSa	B T Savage gr	170A
Budb	Budd bur gr	371
Budd	Budd cem	300
Bulb	Bull bur gr	199
	Bull Farm - see Parker plot	
Bull	Bull-Pennyville	88
Bulp	Bull plot	188
Buls	Bull site	6
Bunt	Bunting Place	110
BunW	Bundick-Warner	375
Burb	Burton bur gr	164
	Burckard bur gr	296
above site has no abbreviation - filed with Onancock Cem		
Burf	Burford plot	353
Burg	Burton graves	193
BurJ	Burton-Jones	170
Burt	Burton's	163
Cary	Cary grave	352A
	Cedar View - see Old West Place	
Chab	Chance bur gr	165
Chan	Chandler cem	271
Chap	Chandler plot	32
Chas	Chandler site	357
Chbg	Chandler bur gr	237
Ches	Chestnut Vale	187
Chri	Christian plot	336
Clif	Clifton	362
Clov	Clover Hill	381
Coal	Coal Kiln	5
Coar	Coard Place	382
	Cokesbury - see Poulson cem	
Coke	Cokesbury Ch	286
Colg	Colonna graves	135
Colo	Colonna bur gr	131
	Colonna fam bur gr - see Waterfield Farm	
Coop	Cooper grave	100
Cope	Copes Place	185
Crad	Craddockville Meth	30
Crad-s	Craddockville Meth-s	31
Croc	Crockett plot	234
Crop	Cropperville	333
Cust	Custis bur gr	258A
Cutl	Cutler bur gr	136
CutS	Cutler-Stewart	35

Dahl	Dahl's Swamp	245
Davi	Davis-Mears	62
DavL	Davis Lot	54
Deep	Deep Cr Plantation	386
Dixf	Dix farm	330
Dixg	Dix grave	93
DoeC	Doe Creek	391
Doug	Doughty grave	228
Doup	Doughty plot	76
Down	Downing bur gr	117
Dowp	Downing plot	102
DrDi	Dr Dix Farm	378
DrMC	Drum'town Meth Ch	340
Drub	Drummond bur gr	264
DruD	Drummond-Doughty	36
Druf	Drummond fam cem	318
Drug	Drummond graves	341
Drum	Drummond plot	244
Drup	Drummond fam plot	319
Drut	Drum'town Bap	344
Dunt	Dunton plot	112
East	East cem	201
Edge	Edgehill cem	339
EdmB	Edmonds-Braxton	13
Edmg	Edmonds bur gr	114
Edmo	Edmonds plot	39
Edwa	Edwards plot	305
Elli	Elliott-Floyd	181
Elmo	Elmore Lot	196
EtDo	E T Downing plot	69
Evab	Evans bur gr	134
Evan	Evans plot	227
Ever	Evergreen	235
Expe	Experiment Farm	34
Faif	Fairfield	224
Fair	Fairview Ln	294
Faiv	Fairview	85
Fing	Finney grave	212
Finn	Finney, A W	376
Fino	Finney, old site	273
FinP	Finney Place	272
Fitz	Fitzgerald bur gr	320
Fith	Fitzhugh bur gr	290
Flet	Fletcher Fr	60
Flob	Floyd bur gr	15
Floy	Floyd plot	169
	Folly (The) - see TheF	
Fore	Forest Grove	77
Fore-old	Forest Grove-old plot	78
FoxB	Fox-Burton	321
FoxP	Fox-Poolman	370
Free	Freeman plot	282

GarL	Garrison Lot	50
Garr	Garrison plot	40
Gask	Gaskin's Ch	260
Gask-old	Gaskin's Ch-old	259
Gasp	Gaskins plot	302
GenW	Gen West Place	138
GeoH	Geo H Bell bur gr	55
Geor	George's Point	274
Gill	Gillett cem	352
	Glebe (The) - see TheG	
	Grinnolds Place - see Clover Hill	
Grot	Groton cem	327
Gsit	"G" site	394
Guin	Guinea	81
Gulf	Gulf Stream	104
Gunt	Gunter plot	393
Guyb	Guy bur gr	232
Guyc	Guy cem	208
Guyp	Guy plot	90
Hagr	Harmon grave	146
Hale	Haley bur gr	176
Hall	Hall grave	398
HaPh	Harman-Phillips	155
	Harmon Place	154

above site has no abbreviation because graves were moved to Wach Cem

Hapl	Harmon plot	161
Harg	Hargis plot	324
Harm	Harmon bur gr	118
Harp	Harrison plot	270
Harr	Harrison cem	242
Hart	Hart plot	262
Hedr	Hedra Cottage	24
Herm	Hermitage	29A
Hero	Heron Hill	183
Hgra	Hart graves	364
HicG	Hickman-Gravenor	380
Hick	Hickman-Killmon	119
Hill	Hills Farm	392
Holb	Hollybrook	150
Holf	Hollybrook Farm	25
Holl	Hollies Ch	151
Holm	Holmes gr	361
Home	Home Place	162
HTri	Holy Trinity	87
Hutc	Hutchinson-Harbarton	230
Hutg	Hutchinson graves	126
	Hutchinson Place - see Chestnut Vale	
Hysl	Hyslup-Nock	101
Hysp	Hyslup plot	98
	Hyslup site	27
Jaco	Jacob bur gr	18

	Jacob Warner Place - see Bundick-Warner	
Jame	James bur gr	48
JamP	James Place	171
JnoP	Jno Phillips plot	198
JnoS	Jno S Bundick cem	192
JoCu	Joynes-Custis cem	241
Johc	Johnson cem	373
John	Johnson gr	346
JoyB	Joynes-Bayne	283
JoyC	Joynes Cem	297
Joyn	Joynes bur gr	217
Joyp	Joynes plot	74
Kebg	Kellam bur gr	28
Kegr	Kelly grave	159
KelB	Kellam-Bell	57
KelG	Kellam-Groton	328
Kell	Kellam-P'teague	129
Kelp	Kellam plot	308
Kels	Kelso bur gr	233
Kenn	Kennahorn gr	240
Kepl	Kelly plot	311
Kerr	Kerr Place	288A
Kilb	Killmon bur gr	239
Kill	Killmon-Broadway	261
Kilm	Kilmontown	206
Kilp	Killman plot	229
Lawr	Lawrence cem	207
LeaW	Leatherbury-Waters	266
LeCa	LeCato-Bell	46
Leve	Leven James plot	257
Lewi	Lewis bur gr	390
Libe	Liberty cem	400
Lill	Lilliston graves	316
Lils	Lilliston site	354
Ling	Lingo plot	79
Linb	Lingo bur gr	99
	Locust Grove - see Parker Place	
LocM	Locustville U Meth	178
Locu	Locustville	180
Lofl	Lofland cem	238
Logr	Logan gr	309
McLa	McLane plot	124
Majo	Major Doughty plot	145
MajF	Major Farm	84
	Major Wise Place - see Wise plot	
Mapl	Maple Dale	82
Mapg	Mapp graves	214
Mapp	Mapp bur gr	105
Marb	Martin bur gr	210
Mari	Marino	399
Marp	Martin plot	94
Mars	Marshside	109

Mart	Martin-Hatton	205
Maso	Mason bur gr	202
Masp	Mason plot	145A
MattW	Matthew-Wyatt	13A
MeaA	Mears of A	310
MeaB	Mears-Bird	113
Meac	Mears cem	312
MeaD	Mears-Downing	120
Meag	Mears graves	70
Meap	Mears plot	147
Mear	Mears bur gr	121
	Mears Wharf - see Poplar Cove	
Meav	Meadville	280
Metr	Metro Mem	366
	Michael's Hill - see Mitchell's Hill	
Mile	Miles-Groton	323
	Millner Place	322
Mist	Mister cem	211
Mitc-e	Mitchill's Hill-e	149
Mitc-w	Mitchill's Hill-w	148
Mont	Montrose	300A
Mooc	Moore cem	374
Moor	Moore bur gr	220
	Moore Farm - see Vaux Hall	
Mori	Morino	399
Morr	Morrison Hill	64
MtCu	Mt Custis	335
MtHo	Mt Holly cem	292
MtHo-s	Mt Holly-s cem	293
	Mt Hope - see Joynes bur gr	
MtNe	Mt Nebo Ch	254
MtNe(E)	Mt Nebo Ch (E)	254
MtOr	Mt Oregon	172
MtPl	Mt Pleasant	20
MtWi	Mt Willis	116
Myrt	Myrtle Grove	139
Neda	Nedab cem	325
Negr	Negro bur gr	253
NewM	New Mt Zion	9
Nick	Nickawampus Fr	166
Nock	Nock bur gr	68
Nocp	Nock plot	3
Oakg	Oak grove	158
Oatl	Oatlands	278
OlBe	Old Beloat Place	304
OlCu	Old Custis Tract	388
OldA	Old Ashby plot	190
OldB	Old Bell plot	2
OldC	Old Custis graves	365
OldF	Old Finney fr	167
OldH	Old Homestead	47
Oldl	Old Floyd bur gr	16

OldN	Old Nock Place	157
OldP	Old Parker prop	215
OldW	Old West Place	83
OlHa	Old Harmon graves	334
OlHp	Old Harmon plot	152
OlNp	Old Nock plot	157A
	Old Scott Fr	267
OlWa	Old Walker plot	197
Onan	Onancock cem	295
PaBo	Parker-Bobtown	216
Padd	Paddy plot	251
Papl	Parks plot	372
Parb	Parks bur gr	369
ParC	Parker-Core	204
Parg	Parker grave	189
	Parker Place	222
Park	Parksley cem	401
Parp	Parker plot	130
Parr	Parramore cem	186
Phil	Phillips gr	265
	Phillips Place	11
Pitt	Pitts bur gr	144
PopC	Poplar Cove	277
PopG	Poplar Grove	140
Poug	Poulson grave	58
Poul	Poulson cem	289
Powe	Powell plot	7
Powl	Powell lot	42
Ptea	P'teague Meth Ch	123
Quin	Quinby Cem	45
Rave	Ravenswood	174
Rayf	Rayfield plot	276
Read	Read bur gr	143
	Read plot	231
Rewp	Rew plot	219
Rich	Richardson grave	191
Rile	Riley plot	360
Rodc	Rodgers cem	249
Rodg	Rodgers-Boggs	247
RodP	Rodgers-Poulson	279
Roge	Rogersville	142
Ropl	Rodgers plot	132
	Rose Cottage – see Old Finney Fr	
Ross	Ross' Run	317
Runn	Runneymede	337
Rura	Rural Felicity	315
Samp	Sample plot	23A
StGe	St George's	127
StJa	St James	347
StJo	St Joseph's	17
StLu	St Luke's	326
StPa	St Paul's	128

Sava	Savage plot	65
Savb	Savage bur gr	96
Savg	Savage grave	153
SavH	Savage-Harmon	205A
Savl	Savage burial	358
SavN	Savage-Northan	383
Savs	Savage site	182
Savv	Savageville	258
Scag	Scarburgh graves	226
Scam	Scarburgh marker	225
Scbg	Scott bur gr	396
ScoB	Scott-Bishop	356
Scot	Scott Hall	284
Seve	Seven Gables	343
Seym	Seymour-Ross House	350
SeyS	Seymour-Snead	285
Shab	Shabby Hall	177
Sher	Sherwood cem	298
Shie	Shield plot	173
Shil	Shiloh	86
	Silver Stream - see Topping Lot	
Shir	Shirley	137
SmiC	Smith's Chapel site	43
Smip	Smith plot	243
Smit	Smith's bur gr	80
	Snead fam plot	281
Snea	Snead's	67
Snug	Snugly	221
Step	Stephens plot	313
	Stevenson bur gr	355
Stew	Stewart cem	184
Stoc	Stockley plot	63
StoM	Stockley-Mears	160
Stub	Sturgis bur gr	23
StuP	Sturgis-Painter	10
Stur	Sturgis plot	22
Swag	Swanger graves	179
Syca	Sycamores	141
Sylv	Sylvan Retreat	91
Tave	Tavern Lot	351
Tayg	Taylor grave	269
Tayl	Taylor Farm	41
	Taylor-Hacks Neck - see Sycamores	
Teac	Teackle House	108
TheF	The Folly	329
TheG	The Glebe	21
	Thomas Fr - see Leven James plot	
ThoC	Thorny Crest	51
Thor	Thoro Mears	73
Thos	Thos H Bell plot	59
Tipt	Tipton Farm	37
Topp	Topping lot	246

Trad	Trader plot	122
Tunn	Tunnell cem	379
	Tunnell plot - see Shabby Hall	
Turf	Turlington fam plot	194
TurJ	Turlington-Jester	125
Turl	Turlington bur gr	56
Turn	Turner plot	8
Turp	Turlington Place	156
Twyf	Twyford graves	349
Unde	Underhill Pt	236
Vale	Vale of Shavez	25A
Vaux	Vaux Hall	218
Wach	Wachapreague Cem	111
Wacb	Wach bur gr	107
Walf	Walker farm	92
Walk	Walker bur gr	314
Walp	Wallace plot	66
Wals	Walston cem	342
	Walter gr	19
Wapl	Waples Place	359
Warb	Ward bur gr	307
Ward	Ward fam cem	14
Warp	Ward plot	195
	Ware House - see Joynes bur gr	
Warw	Warwick	4
Wate	Waterfield Farm	89
Wats	Watson cem	299
Watt	Watts Island	387
Wepl	West Place	385
Wesg	West graves	255
Wesl	West Lot	95
West	West bur gr	288
Wess	Wessells plot	368
Whie	White bur gr	301
Whit	White plot	1
WhiB	White-Bayley	291
	Wilkins bur gr	345
Wilb	Willet bur gr	397
Wilg	Willis grave	14A
Will	Willow Bank	175
Wise	Wise cem	363
Wisp	Wise plot	377
	Woodbourne site	338

NUMERICAL LIST OF GRAVE SITES

The name of the plot in which the burial can be found is indicated after each entry in the text. All plots are listed here, each having been assigned a number. That number is used to identify the location of the plot on the accompanying map. Recorded with each entry are precise directions for finding the site which include the general area in the county, mileages, and route numbers. Also for each site are listed the surnames of all families buried in that particular plot. Such is not done, of course, for the large public cemeteries and churchyards.

Belle Haven Cemetery (inc Feb 1901) - recorded in *Gravestone Inscriptions in Northampton Co., VA*, J.M. Mihalyka, comp. Published by VA State Library, 1980.

1. White Plot - in Upshur's Neck, 3.2m S of R606 in Quinby to the west of R605. Follow farm lane for about .4m to wooded area along Machipongo Creek. Turn S along creek. Burial site is at least .5m at southern end of field a few yards into woods. (White)
2. Old Bell plot - (Bell's Neck) to end of R603; then .5m on farm road toward point. Plot to the W. Once a large burial plot with very old slate markers. (Bell)
3. Nock plot - (Bell's Neck) 2.1m from R600, to the W of R603 in lane for .4m. In field to the right. (Nock)
4. Warwick - 1m S of Quinby (junction of R605 & R182), to the E of R605. Two plots; one to the N side of the driveway, one to the S side - both W of the main house. (Boisnard; Eickelberger; Quinby; Upshur)
5. Coal Kiln - .1m S of the junction of R607, take dirt road to E off R600 for .4m. Plot is .1m to the N in field. (Dunton; LeCato; Moore; Smith)
5A. Ayres Plot - .4m S of the junction of R607 (Coal Kiln) to the W of R600 beside the road. (Ayres)
6. Bull site - .5m S of Mappsburg to the W of R600. No stones remain in clump of trees in middle of field. Ref: 1940 record. (Bull)
7. Powell plot - .2m S of R182 (Mappsburg), to the W of R600. Well behind house; very overgrown. (Ames; Ashby; Dunton; Jackson; Mapp; Nottingham; Powell)
8. Turner plot - (Mappsburg) .7m E of R600, to the S of R182; .4m in field (Kellam; Turner)

9. New Mt Zion - (E of Painter) New Mt Zion African Baptist Church. Est. 1881, rebuilt 1947. 1m E of R13, to the S of R607. Churchyard extends to a new section to the west behind houses (copied April 1982).
10. Sturgis-Painter - .7m E of R13 near Painter to the S of R607; .1m in field. (Sturgis)
11. Phillips Place - .2m N of R601, to the E of R600 (just into Accomack Co.), .3m in lane to house. This rather large plot is recorded in *Gravestone Inscription in Northampton Co., VA*, J.M. Mihalyka, comp. 1980. (Chandler; Dunton; LaCato; Nottingham; Robins)
12. Ayres Lot - .1m E of R13 to the S of R601. Numerous black burials. (Ayres; Harmon; Robinson; Rogers; Smith; Taylor; Thomas; Williams)
13. Edmonds-Braxton - to the W of R13 across from junction of R603 (Belle Haven Station). Behind Kellam Distributing Co. office building. Also 6 or more unmarked graves. (Edmonds; Braxton)
13A. Matthews-Wyatt plot (Belle Haven Station just N of county line) - to the E of R13 across RR tracks c50 yards into woods, .1m S of R603. Once a large family burial ground. (Abdell; Brown; Churn; Matthews; Smith; Turner; Wyatt)
14. Ward family cemetery - in Belle Haven Town Square at junction of R602 with R178. (Lewis; Ward)
14A. Willis grave - .1m S of R178, to the E of R602 (Belle Haven Cemetery Rd.). Behind house. Stone is enveloped in the base of large tree. (Willis)
15. Floyd burial ground - .5m N of Belle Haven (junction of R181 & R178) to the W of R609, .5m in lane to S of shed on slight hill. (Floyd)
16. Old Floyd burial ground - .5m N of Belle Haven (junction of R181 & R178) to the W of R609. In lane for .8m to woods (passing to the left the Floyd burial ground near shed). Straight back in woods on a knoll. Once many stones; only one located. Old Byrd's Sawmill area. (Floyd)
17. St. Joseph's - St. Joseph African Methodist Episcopal Church (1920 site). 1.1m N of the center of Belle Haven on R609 at the junction of R607; in the SE corner. This burial ground is poorly kept; many unmarked graves (copied Feb. 1982).
18. Jacob burial ground - (near Shields) .5m E of R178 to the S of R613 .3m in farm lane to the left in field. (Jacob; Kellam; LeCato; Martin; Wise)
19. Walter grave - behind site of old stone at Shields (intersection of R613 & R178). Moved to Fairview Lawn. (Walter)
20. Mt. Pleasant - just W of Occahonnock Creek Bridge on R178, turn S in private lane for .5m. To the right of house beyond the lawn; within brickwall. (Bull; Bradford; Douglas; Duncan; Kellam; Shield)
21. The Glebe - from R615 into Davis Wharf turn E into lane at top of hill; almost to the Wharf. (Ames; Davis; Goffigon; Mears; Rue)
22. Sturgis plot - (Scarborough Neck) .2m W of R615 to the S of R612, in private lane for .5m. Plot to the left near lane. (Hutchinson; Mason; Sturgis; Wright)

23. Sturgis burial ground - (Scarborough Neck) .35m W of R615 to the S of R612; .4m in dirt lane to the left. Indications of many unmarked graves in this old plot. (Ames; Mason; Parkes; Sturgis)
23A. Sample plot - .3m N of R612 to the W of R615 (Davis Wharf Road). (Moore; Sample)
24. Hedra Cottage - (Scarborough Neck) 1.6m W of R615 from R612, turn S onto R611 for .3m. Take lane to the right for .4m. Plot across field to the right in heavy thicket. (Custis; Nottingham; Scarborough; Smith)
24A. Bay View (Scarborough Neck) .7m W of R615 on R612, turn left onto hard surfaced road for .4m. Turn right onto lane for .1m to house. Grave to south. (Bayne)
25. Hollybrook Farm - (Scarborough Neck) 1.35m W of R615 to the N of R612; .5m in lane to NW of house. (Boggs; Bull; Goffigon; Kellam; Royal)
25A. Vale of Shavez - 2.4m W of R615 to the N of R612 (Scarborough Neck Rd.); c.8m in farm road to site of former house. A recording of the stones (which have not yet been located) is among the Thos Teackle Upshur Manuscript Collection, vol. 2, pp. 401-2 in the Swem Library, College of Wm. and Mary. His work was done during the first decade of the 1900s. (Coward)
26. Bayberry Farm - (Craddock Neck) 1.5m W of R615 on R614. Continue due W on hard surface road for .9m to house; then turn E along creek for .2 mile to point. Two plots: Allen is beside woods road; Hyslop is deeper in woods to the S. (Allen; Hyslop; Tawes)
27. Hyslop site - (Craddock Neck) 1.1m W of R615 to the S of R614. 1m in farm lane. Graves which were to W of old house near creek in the Hyslop family burial ground were moved in 1936 to Belle Haven Cemetery. See *Gravestone Inscriptions in Northampton Co., VA.*
28. Kellam burial ground - (Craddock Neck) 1.1m W of R615 to the S of R614. 1m in farm lane to E in wooded area. (Kellam)
29. Bell grave - (Craddock Neck) .4m W of R615 to the S of R614 in lane for .6m to the W of field on edge of woods. Other stones bulldozed years ago. (Bell)
29A. Hermitage - 1.1m W of the intersection with R178 (at Craddockville), turn right off R 165. In dirt road for .9m. Graveyard in field to the left in clump of trees. (Bailey/ Bayley; Neely)
30. Crad. Meth. - Craddockville United Methodist Church, built 1871. At junction of R615 with R178N, Craddockville. Graveyard behind church building. (Ayres; Berry; Callahan; Hickman; Killom; Mason; Martin; Smith; Thomas; West; Winder)
31. Crad. Meth.-s - at junction of R615 with R178N, in Craddockville; SE corner. This is the site of Craddockville United Methodist Church from 1850-71. (Bull; Custus; Guy; Jones; Kellam; LeCato; Lingo; Melson; Parks; Winder; Young)
32. Chandler plot - (Craddockville) .1m N of the junction of R615 with R178N. On E side of R178N. (Chandler; Colona; Elmore; Mason)
33. Anderson Place - .5m S of Craddockville on R178S, turn left into lane for .5m. Site well to E of house in a thicket. (Wynder)
34. Experiment Farm - (W of Painter) .1m from R614, to E of R617 in field. (Ames; Mears)

35. Cutler-Stewart - (between Middlesex & Shields) .25m W of R609 to the N of R614; .05m in field. (Cutler; Stewart)
36. Drummond-Doughty - .2m N of R614 (at Middlesex) to the W of R609. Across field and along the N side of woods; plot is just insdie the woods. Evidence of many graves; only 3 stones found. (Drummond; Doughty)
37. Tipton Farm - (W of Painter) .2m N of R614 (at Middlesex) to the E of R609 .1m in lane to left of house. (Tipton; Sturgis)
38. Baily graves - (W of Painter) .8m S of R614 (Middlesex) to the E of R609 in farm road for .8m. Across field to the E in woods. Once a very large Black burial ground. Only 2 marked graves remain. (Baily)
39. Edmonds plot - (in Painter) in the SE corner of junction of R1202 with R182. (Bell; Edmonds)
40. Garrison plot - at intersection of R600 & R182 (Mappsburg) on the NW corner in field NW of house. Numerous unmarked graves. (Thought to be the original site of Garrison's Chapel later moved to Painter). (Bell; Garrison; Glenn; Goffigon; Harrison)
41. Taylor farm - (at Mappsburg) .4m N of R182, to the W of R600; .05m into field. (Bradford; Marston: Nock; Stringer; Taylor)
42. Powell lot - 1m E of Mappsburg (.4m E of the Quinby Bridge) to the N of R182; about .2m in field. (Floyd; Powell)
43. Smith's Chapel site - .1m from R605 to the S of R606 (between R773 & R748). This was the church graveyard of Smith's Chapel before the church was moved nearer to the center of Quinby. (Pilchard; Turner)
44. Atlantic View - (in Quinby) .3m S of junction of R182 on E side of R605. Only 1 stone remains of the very old & large Bradford Burial Ground which was a good distance to the east of the old Wm. Bradford home. Stones were pushed into the marsh; a tragic loss. (Bradford)
45. Quinby Cemetery - .1m from R605, on R773 in Quinby. This community cemetery is well kept, but does have a good many unmarked graves. In the southwest corner is the old LeCato burying ground (copied Feb. 1982).
46. LeCato-Bell - .05m N of Quinby (junction of R182 with R605), to the E of R605 behind house in a field. Once a fairly large burial plot on the Bell property. Only 1 stone remains. Information supplied by Rooker Powers & Gladys Bayly of Quinby. (Bell; LeCato; Ward)
47. Old Homestead - (in Quinby) .1m N of R182 to the E of R605 behind house .1m in hedge row. (Bundick)
48. James burial ground - .25m N of Quinby (junction of R182 & R605), to the E of R605; .2m in lane to the SE of house. (Barnes; Eickelberger; James)
49. Bradford-Burton - .6m N of Quinby (junction of R182), to the E of R605. S of house in thicket. (Ashby; Bradford; Burton; Elliott; Kelly; Wallace)
50. Garrison Lot - 1.2m N of Quinby (junction of R182 with R605), to the E of R605. To the SE of house in field. (Garrison)
51. Thorny Crest - 1.45m N of Quinby (junction of R182 with R605), to the E of R605. To the SE of house. (Fet-terman; Fleming; Smith)

52. Bell burial ground - 1.5m S of R622 (Old Trower) to the W of R605. Stones lie flat in grass to the south of house. (Bell; Downing)
53. Bell-Floyd - 1.8m N of Quinby, to the E of R605. Behind house to the SE. (Bell; Bradford; Floyd; Kellam)
54. Davis Lot - 2m N of Quinby (junction of R182 with R605), to the E of R605. To the NE of house behind barn. (Davis)
55. George H. Bell burial ground - 2.4m N of Quinby (junction of R182 with R605), to W of R605 in yard behind small, old house. (Bell; Downing; Edmunds; Welch)
56. Turlington burial ground - 2.75m N of Quinby (junction of R182 with R605), to E of R605, .2m in lane. SE of house near marsh. (Bell; Downing; Stockley; Turlington)
57. Kellam-Bell - (at Old Trower). SW corner of junction of R622 with R605. To S end of house. (Bell; Bradford; Kellam)
58. Poulson grave - (at Old Trower) .2m W of R605 to the S side of R622 in woods but close to road. (Poulson)
59. Thomas H. Bell plot - (at Old Trower) .7m W of R605 to the S of R622, go into woods following old road. Turn E & follow remains of an older road across marsh (head of Machipongo Creek). Go only at low tide. Upon reaching a wooded spit of land, turn S & walk a good distance. Grave plot is almost to the point near ruins of old brick house in thick woods. (Bell; Bradford; Marston; Mears; Rose)
60. Fletcher Farm - Old Trower. 1m W of R605 to the N of R622. Follow farm road at least 1m through woods to ruin of old house. Plot to right side of front yard. Data for unmarked graves supplied by Hilda H. Powell, Quinby & Mildred B. Nock, Wachapreague from ledger kept by her father, Abel J. Bell, merchant of Old Trower. (Fletcher; Hickman; Scott)
61. Anthony Bell plot - (Old Trower). 1m W of R605, to the S of R622; .05m in lane to plot. (Bell; Isdell; Mears)
62. Davis-Mears - 1.1m W of R605 at Old Trower to the N of R622 beside road. (Davis; Mears; Miller)
63. Stockley plot - (N of Frogstool) .1m N of R743, to the E of R600 in field. (Coleburn; Stockley)
64. Morrison Hill - (S of Frogstool) .8m S of R622 to the W of R600. (Davis; Ensor; Fletcher; Floyd; James; Johnson; Mears; Nock; Powell)
65. Savage plot - (just N of Red Hill) .2m N of R621, W side of R600. This plot & the Wallace plot are in field behind houses, about 100 feet apart. (Christian; Savage; Sturgis)
66. Wallace plot - (just N of Red Hill) .2m N of R621, W side of R600. This plot & the Savage plot are in field behind houses, about 100 feet apart. (Wallace)
67. Snead's - Snead's African Methodist Church; organized 1881. In SW corner of the intersection of R600 & R621. Some graves are across R600 (copied Jan. 1983).
68. Nock burial ground - (S of Red Hill) .5m S of R621 to the W of R600, .5m in farm road to SW of old house in field. (Nock; Turner)
69. E. T. Downing plot - (between Painter & Keller) .3m E of R620, to the N of R621; about .4m across field near woods. (Downing; Mathews)

70. Mears graves - (Ames Ridge N of Painter) .45m E of R13 to the E of R620 in field. (Mears)
71. Ames grave - .1m N of R620 to the E of R13 (across from Central High School). Part-way in field. (Ames)
72. Ames plot - (Painter) .4m E of R619 to the N of R620, .2m in lane; plot to left of house. (Ames; Elliott; Taylor)
73. Thoro Mears - (NW of Painter) .7m N of R620 to the W of R619, .1m in field. Probably more stones covered by heavy thicket. (Ames; Mears)
74. Joynes plot - (NW of Painter) 1.5m N of R614 to the W of R609; .2m into field. (Joynes; McKowan; Twiford; Young)
75. Ames-Hyslop - (N of Painter) 1.3m N of R614 to the W of R609, .3m into field. (Ames; Hyslop; Twiford)
76. Doughty plot - (SE of Pennyville) 1.1m N of R614, to E side of R617. Behind house. (Doughty; Frost; Guy)
77. Forest Grove - (SE of Pennyville) 1m N of R614, to the W of R617. At S end of house. (Doughty)
78. Forest Grove-old plot - (SE of Pennyville) .9m N of R614 to W of R617; .4m of farm lane into field. (Behind the main Forest Grove house.) (Doughty; Fowler)
79. Lingo plot - (NW of Experiment Station-Painter) in field in NW corner of the junction of R732 with R614. (Lingo; Mason)
80. Smith's burial ground (black) - (between Craddockville & Boston) .75m S of R730 to the E of R178; .3m in dirt lane. Plot in NE corner of field beside woods. Numerous names; also some unmarked.
81. Guinea - (between Craddockville & Boston) .7m S of R730 to the W of R178 beside road. Black burials; numerous, most unmarked.
82. Maple Dale - .6m N of Craddockville Church on R178, turn W into R724, .6m to the end of road. Plot to N of old house on edge of creek. Large burial plot; only 2 stones remain. (Kellam)
83. Old West Place - (N of Craddockville) 1.2m W of R178 to the S of R616, .3m in shell road; plot to N of house. (Also known as Cedar View.) (Gascoyne; Rowles; West)
84. Major Farm - (Craddock Neck) 1.5m W of R615 to the N of R614; .7m in dirt lane to the E in woods. (Major)
85. Fairview (Andewey Plantation) - (near Boston) .2m S of R732E to the W of R178, turn onto R732W. Drive 1.3m to house, behind which is a large shaft erected in 1929 bearing data "of those buried here & those related". See Whitelaw:658-60. The compilers are indebted to E. Spencer Wise for a list found in the "Hack Manuscripts" of the inscriptions on the original tombstones before they were covered over by the newer monument. (Hack; Henry; Kellam; Knight; Read)
86. Shiloh - Shiloh Baptist Church; organized 1875. Oldest of the 3 churches named Shiloh (black). 2.4m N of Craddockville to E of R178N (copied Dec. 1982).
87. H. Trinity - Holy Trinity African Baptist Church. Est. 1905. (N of Boston) .3m S of R617 to the W of R178 beside road. (Copied 1979.)

88. Bull-Pennyville - .2m E of R178 (Pennyville), to the N of R617. According to Dick Doughty of Panther, VA, c1948 a new owner of the farm, wanting to build a racetrack, "looked the other way" and paid workers $100 to remove the stones. They were dumped deep in a woods owned by Doughty who has offered them to the families involved. (Ayres; Bull)
89. Waterfield Farm - (SE of Pennyville) 1.4m N of R614 to the W of R617; in field about .4m. Also known as the Colonna family burying ground. (Colona; Doughty; Holt; Jones; Onley; Stewart; Watson)
90. Guy plot - .9m S of junction of R178 (at Pungoteague) to the W of R609. In wooded area .3m into field. (Downing; Guy; Miles)
91. Sylvan Retreat - .6m E of intersection with R178 (just SE of Pungoteague), to the S of R609. In farm lane for .4m; plot to W of house in yard. Stones lay flat partly covered by grass. Also called G.E. Bull Farm. (Andrews; Ker)
92. Walker Farm - W of Painter at the junction of R619 with R180; SW corner. (Walker)
93. Dix grave - (NW of Painter) 1.6m N of R620 to the W of R619, .15m in field. One stone dug from 18 inches below surface; others probably buried deeper. (Dix)
94. Martin plot - (NW of Painter) 1.1m N of R620, to the E of R619 beside road. (Kellam; Martin)
95. West lot - (S of Keller) .1m from R13 to the S of R620 in field. (West)
96. Savage burial ground - (E of Keller) .9m S of R696 to the W of R622, .1m in field. (Savage)
97. Bradford-Hyslup - .1m S of R180 (at Grangeville) to the W of R600; to the N of house in garden. Hyslop plot in same yard. (Bell; Bradford; Drummond; Hyslup)
98. Hyslop plot - (Grangeville) .1m S of R180, to the W of R600, in front yard. Bradford-Hyslop plot in same yard in garden to the N side. (Hyslop/Hyslup)
99. Lingo burial ground - .3m S of R180 (Wachapreague Road at Grangeville) to the W of R600. Plot is about 100 feet from road in field but stones have been destroyed. (Ref: 1940 data & Lingo Bible). (Lingo)
100. Cooper grave - .01m W of R600 (at Trower), to the N of R622 in field. One Cooper who ran a mill near Grangeville buried here over 50 years ago. No stone.
101. Hyslup-Nock - (Trower) at intersection of R622 & R600, .15m into farm on SW corner. To S of ruins of house. 2 plots, one to the W of the other. (Beach; Chance; Hyslup; Kellam; Nock)
102. Downing plot - .05m W of R600 (at Trower), to the N of R622. Plot was near site of old house, lately known as the Rev. T. J. C. Heath farm. (Stones destroyed; 1940 data). (Downing)
103. Beach cemetery - 1.6m W of R605 to the S of R180. Take section of old Wachapreague Road which ends within .2m. Walk across field to wooded area in which are the remains of the Bradford house. Cemetery is to E of house. Heavy undergrowth. (Beach; Bell; Bradford; Coleburn; Fentress; Walter)
104. Gulf Stream - .2m N of Old Trower (junction of R622 with R605), to the E of R605 in lane for .2m. To the SE of garden behind house. (Bell)

105. Mapp burial ground - .65m N of Old Trower (junction of R622 with R605), to the E of R605 in lane for .2m. To the S in field. (Bulman; Doughty; Mapp)
106. Bagge burial ground - .65m N of R622 (Old Trower) to the E of R605 in lane for .2m. Plot to the N in wooded area bordering yard of house. (Bagge)
107. Wach. Bur. Gr. - Wachapreague Burial Ground; turn S off Main Street (R180) in Wachapreague onto West Avenue (R1716) for 2 blocks. Turn W onto R1719 for .15m. Very old burying ground to W of road on small rise of ground. (Ashby; Fox; Kellam; Mears; Parker)
108. Teackle House - (in Wachapreague) at the corner of R1709 & Brookyln Street. Behind house. (Read; Teackle)
109. Marshside - .5m N of R180Y to the E of R624 (an extension of Church Street in Wachapreague). Across field toward creek. (Fletcher; Holt; Mapp)
110. Bunting Place - .2m N of junction of R624, to the E of R605 (just S of Wachapreague Cemetery). In farm road for .6m. Cemetery behind house in pasture, toward Nickawampus Creek. (Bunting)
111. Wach. Cem. - Wachapreague Cemetery (est. c1908), .9m N of R180 to the E of R605. A well-kept community cemetery; a good number of unmarked graves, however (copied March 1982).
112. Dunton plot - .1m N of R624 to the W of R605 beside road (between Wachapreague & Chancetown). (Dunton; Willis)
113. Mears-Bird - .9m E of R600 to the N of R736 (Old Wachapreague Road); .3m in lane to edge of front yard. 2 plots: Bird family within wall; Mears family to the S. (Bird; Kellam; Mears; Turlington)
114. Edmonds burial ground - (NE of Grangeville) .3m E of R600, to the S of R736 (Old Wachapreague Road), .2m in lane to S of house. (Edmonds)
115. Bradford plot - (N of Grangeville) .2m N of R736 to the E of R600 beside road. (Belote; Bradford; Brown; Powell)
116. Mt. Willis - .2m N of R180 (at Grangeville) to the W of R600 beside road. (Mears; West; Willis)
117. Downing burial ground - .5m W of R600 (at Grangeville) to the S of R180). In yard E of house. (Coleburn; Downing)
118. Harmon burial ground - (between Keller & Wachapreague) .1m E of R696, to the N of R180. Behind house to NW. Many unmarked graves; once a very large family plot. (Bell; Harmon; Nock)
119. Hickman-Killmom - E of Keller, .2m N of R622 to the E of R696, .2m into field. (Charnock; Hickman; Killmon)
120. Mears-Downing - .3m E of R13 (at Keller) to the N of R696 beside road. (Downing; Mears)
121. Mears burial ground - .05m E of R13 in Keller; to the S of R696, .1m into field. (Bivens; Byrd; Clowes; Mears)
122. Trader plot - .3m E of Pungoteague (R178N) to the S of R180E behind house in thicket on edge of field. (Ashby; Savage; Trader)
123. P'teague Meth. - Pungoteague Methodist Church (1888 site), .1m from R178N to the S of R180E (copied Jan. 1982).
124. McLane plot - .05m S of R180E, to E of R609 (Back Street - Pungoteague). (Jones; McClain; McLane; Mears)

125. Turlington-Jester - .05m W of R178 (center of Pungoteague) to N of R180W. (Jester; Kelley; Turlington)
126. Hutchinson graves - just S of St. George's Church, Pungoteague, to the W side of R178 in field. (Hutchinson)
127. St. George's - St. George's Episcopal Church (1676). To the W of R178N just N of the village of Pungoteague (copied Jan. 1982).
128. St. Paul's - St. Paul's African Methodist Episcopal Church. Built 1886. Just N of St. George's Episcopal Church on R178N, Pungoteague. Churchyard is poorly kept; only a few of the many graves are marked. (Copied Feb. 1982.)
129. Kellam-P'teague - .1m S of center of Pungoteague to the W of R178 behind house in box bushes. (Bayly; Blackstone; Coward; Kellam)
130. Parker plot - .1m N of the junction of R609 with R178 (S end of Pungoteague) to W of R178 into farm lane, .8m in lane to Old Carroll Waterfield house. Plot to the N in heavy thicket. Poor condition. Also known as Andrews Place or Bull Farm. (Andrews; Davis; Davezac; Galt; Joynes; LeCato; Parker; Upshur; West)
131. Colonna burial ground - (Hacks Neck) .7m from R178 (center of Pungoteague) to the S of R180W; .4m in farm lane. Plot beside house. (Colonna; Nicolls)
132. Rodgers plot - (Hacks Neck) .9m W of R178 (center of Pungoteague) to the S of R180W into lane for .7m. Plot to W across field along edge of woods. (Some footstones bear initials & date of death monogramed by Richard Rodgers.) (Read; Rodgers)
133. Ames-Hacks Neck - .9m S of R180W to the S of 630S in lane for .3m. Plot to E in yard. (Ames)
134. Evans burial ground - (Hacks Neck) 1.4m S of R180W to the S of R630S, into dirt lane for .15m. Plot in field to W of house. (Evans)
135. Colonna graves - (Hacks Neck) 1.6m S of R180W, to the end of R630S in dirt lane to the south for .2m. Graves to the E across field. Some Nock graves moved to St. George's Cemetery. (Colonna)
136. Cutler burial ground - (Hacks Neck). From R178 (center of Pungoteague) drive W on R180W, continuing on R631, then R633 for 3.8m. Turn S in farm lane for .6m; then W across field for .3m. Plot is to the N near creek. (Byron; Cutler; Martin)
137. Shirley - (Hacks Neck)> From R178 (center of Pungoteague) drive W on R180W, continuing on R631, then R633 for 4.2m. Turn S in lane for .4m. Plot is to NW of house on edge of lawn. (Adair; Hack; Lucas; Scherer)
138. Gen. West Place - (Hacks Neck) 3.9m W of R178 (center of Pungoteague) W on R178W, continuing onto R631 turn N into farm lane. Walk behind old house, cross small gut, proceed to pine woods. Follow along the E side of the creek edge to a point on Butcher's Creek. Plot is in thick brambles just into pine woods. (West)
139. Myrtle Grove - (Hacks Neck) .7m W of the junction of R180 (Harborton Road) turn N off R631 into farm road. Go 1m; road dead ends before 2 wooded areas. Graves are about 50 feet into the western section near field edge. (Kellam)

140. Poplar Grove - (Hacks Neck) 1.6m W of R178 (Center of Pungoteague) turn N off R180W. In lane for 1.3m. Plot behind house to the E. Once a large graveyard; few stones remain. Taylor family members moved to St. George's in early 1900s. (Bayly; Parker)
141. Sycamores - (Hacks Neck) 1m W of R178 (center of Pungoteague) to the N of R180W. In lane for 1.5m. Plot to the right of house on edge of field. (Ames; Doughty; Henderson; Hornsby; Mears; Slocum; Taylor; Turner)
142. Rogersville - (Hacks Neck) .7m W of R178 (center of Pungoteague) to the N of R180W. In from road for .3m, behind house to the W of barn. (Hoffman)
143. Read burial ground - between Bobtown & Pungoteague to the W of R178, .3m N of the junction of R609. In dirt road for .7m; plot on S side of road. Once a large plot; now grass covered with no stones. (Read)
144. Pitts burial ground - .9m N of Pungoteague to W of R178N; .2m in lane behind house. (Mears; Pitts; Watson; West; Wescott)
145. Major Doughty plot - (NW of Keller) .6m E of R178 to the N of R609 in field. (Doughty; Young)
145A. Mason plot - identified in 1940 data as located on the Ben Mathews Place between Pungoteague & Holly's Church. Unable to locate. (Mason)
146. Harmon grave - (NW of Keller) .8m E of R178 to the N of R609. One grave (black) beside house. (Harmon)
147. Mears plot - (NW of Keller) .3m N of junction of R609 with R620, to the E of R620 in front of house. (Bell; Mears; Stevens)
148. Mitchell's Hill-w - W of Keller at intersection of R609 & R620. This section is on the NW corner. (Also known as Michael's Hill.) (Bowden; Gardner; Mears; Parker; Stevens)
149. Mitchell's Hill-e - W of Keller at intersection of R609 & R620. This section is on the NE corner. (Also known as Michael's Hill.) (East; Hickman; Mears; Stevens)
150. Hollybrook - (between Keller & Bobtown) just SW of intersection of R609 & R620. NE of house in garden. (Battaile; Rogers)
151. Hollies - Hollies Baptist Church 1.1m W of Keller on R620, to N side of road. Oldest burials are behind the church to the NW. Newer burials to the E of church. (Copied March 1982.)
152. Old Harmon plot - (just N of Keller Fairgrounds) .5m S of R734 to the W of R626, in farm lane for .7m. In wooded plot near site of old house. (Harmon)
153. Savage grave - (just N of Keller Fairgrounds) .5m S of R734 to the W of R626 in farm lane for about .6m. Across field to the right. Once a large burial plot; now only one stone. (Savage)
154. Harmon Place - (near Keller Fairgrounds) .6m S of R734 to the W of R626. Graves moved from yard of old house to Wach. Cem. Ref: Sarah Mapp Lewis, Melfa, VA. (Harmon)
155. Harman-Phillips - (just N of Keller Fairgrounds) .55m S of R734, to the W of R626 beside road. (Harman; Phillips)
156. Turlington Place - (SE of Melfa) to the E of R626, .2m N of junction with R734. Badly overgrown in middle of field. Stones damaged; once large plot. (Bull; Copes; Nock; Trower; Turlington)

157. Old Nock Place - (SE of Melfa) to the E of R626, .1m N of junction with R734. No stones remain in this large plot. (Ref: 1940 data.) (Nock)
157A. Old Nock plot - (SE of Melfa) .1m W of R600 to the S of R624; .05m in field. Some graves moved to Oak Grove Cem. (Nock; Trower)
158. Oak Gr. - Oak Grove Methodist (Burton's Chapel) Churchyard. Present building erected 1871. At the junction of R624 & R600; SE corner. (Recorded Dec. 1981.)
159. Kelly grave - (just N of Oak Grove Church) junction of R624 with R600. In field in NE corner. (Kelly)
160. Stockley-Mears - .4m S of Oak Grove Church (at R624) to the E of R600 behind house in field. Poor condition. (Mears; Stockley)
161. Harmon plot - E of Oak Grove Church, .6m E of R600 to the S of R624 in center of field. (Harmon)
162. Home Place - (E of Oak Grove Church) .4m E of R600 to the N of R624 turn in farm lane for .6m. Plot in field to SE. (Belote; Bundick; Kellam; Killmon; Savage; Turlington)
163. Burton's - Burton's United Methodist Church; established 1801. Present buidling erected 1897. One of the oldest black churches on the Shore. (Chancetown, southeast of Melfa), .1m W of R605; then .05m W of R754 to the left side of dirt road. Large, well-kept burial ground with some rather old stones; many graves unmarked. (Copied Mr. 1984.)
164. Burton burial ground - (S of Chancetown) .5m N of R624 to the E of R605, .2m in lane; plot to N in field. Once a large burial site; poor condition. Also stones for several servants between house & barn. (Burton; Spiers)
165. Chance burial ground - (near Chancetown) .6m E of R605, plot to the N of R645 in field. (Chance)
166. Nickawampus Farm - (near Chancetown) .6m E of R605 on R645. Turn N on dirt lane (lane then veers E) .6m. Graves to S of house in yard along creek. (Chance; Heath)
167. Old Finney Farm - SE of Locustville, 1m E of R605 at end of R644; .4m in field lane. Now known as Rose Cottage. (Bunting; Finney)
168. Belle Vue - from Locustville, 7.1m E on R647; S on R646 for .7m; then E for 3.1m on dirt road. To right in field. (Bayly; Parramore)
169. Floyd plot - from Locustville, 7.1m E on R647; S on R646 for .05m. Behind house to the E. (Bloxom; Floyd; Phillips)
170. Burton-Jones - from Locustville, 7.1m E on R647; N on R646 for .3m - to the E in middle of field. (Burton; Hollis; Jones)
170A. B.T. Savage grave - .2m W of junction with R787 (road to Burtons Shore), on the S side of R647, .15m along edge of field. Grave is just inside a wooded strip between the field & the marsh. (Savage)
171. James Place - .4m from R605 (N of Locustville), then N off R647 into farm lane for .6m. Plot to N in field. (James; Parker)
172. Mt. Oregon - (E of Daughtery - in Custis Neck), 1.3m E of R605 to the N of R648; .8m in farm lane. Stones to W of house. (Coleburn; Fosque)

173. Shield plot - 1.2m E of R605 (at Daugherty), turn N off R648 into private field road. Go .7m to house. Plot is to the W in wooded area. Once a much larger plot. (Bunting; Ward)
174. Ravenswood - .8m E of R605 (at Daugherty), turn S from R648 into private farm lane. Go 1.6m to house; plot within iron fence near barn. (One very large stone face down.) (Custis)
175. Willow Bank - .5m N of R647 (between Daugherty & Locustville) to the E of R605; .8m in lane. Behind house at the end of garden. (Gunter; Young)
176. Haley burial ground - .1m N of R647 (between Daugherty & Locustvile) to the E of R605 in field. (Cropper; Haley)
177. Shabby Hall - .7m N of center of Locustville to the E of R605, well back in field. (Tunnell)
178. Locustville U. Meth. - Locustville United Methodist Churchyard. On R605 in Locustville. Once a large burial yard. (Copied Jan. 1982.) (Crowson; James; Wright)
179. Swanger graves - .2m N of the center of Locustville to the W of R605 in yard to back & left of house. (Swanger)
180. Locustville - .15m N of center of Locustville to W of R605 in yard behind house. (Burton; Kellam)
181. Elliott-Floyd - in Locustville at junction of R647 to the N of R605 in yard behind house. (Copes; Elliott; Floyd)
182. Savage site - .1m S of center of Locustville to the W of R605 beside road. (Savage)
183. Heron Hill - .3m S of junction of R647 in Locustville, to the W of R605. Formerly called Cloverdale. (Ashby; Bloxom; Kellam; Savage; Townsend)
184. Stewart cemetery - .25m SE of R605 (at Locustville) to the W of R647, well into field toward creek. Only 1 stone remains. (Stewart)
185. Copes Place - .3m SE of R605 (at Locustville) to the W of R647, well into field toward creek. Moved to Mt. Holly; new stones set. However, original stones remain at this site. (Copes)
186. Parramore cemetery - .5m SE of R605 (at Locustville) to the W of R647 in dirt lane for .4m. Plot to N of house in field. (Parramore; Reed; Satchell; Walker)
187. Chestnut Vale - .6m N of R605 (W of Locustville) to the W of R789; .2m into middle of field. Plot nearly destroyed. Farm also known as the Hutchinson Place. (Read)
188. Bull plot - (E of Melfa) .3m W of R605 to the S of R644 in field. Area has been cemented with stones embedded. (Bull; Hopkins)
189. Parker grave - (E of Melfa) .4m E of R672 to the N of R644. Back in field. Tree roots probably cover several stones. (Parker)
190. Old Ashby plot - (E of Melfa) .4m N of R644 at the end of R672. In pasture in front of house. Once a large burial site. (Ashby)
191. Richardson grave - (NE of Melfa) .2m N of R644 to the E of R672. Follow lane into woods, down hill, across stream & up hill to field. Approximately halfway to power lines, cross field to the west. Plot is well into woods. Once a large burial site; now only one stone remains. (Richardson)
192. Jno. S. Bundick cemetery - (NE of Melfa) .4m NE of R639, to the E of R625, .1m in lane. To the S of house beyond barn across field. (Belote; Bundick; Duncan; Mason; Ward; White)

193. Burton graves - (E of Melfa) .35m E of R639 to the N of R672 back in field about .4m. (Turlington family plot is just to the SW in same field.) Once a large plot; now only 2 stones. (Burton)
194. Turlington family plot - (E of Melfa) .4m E of R639 to the N of R672, in farm lane for .4m. Lovely family plot still in use under old cedar trees. (Kellam; Turlington)
195. Ward plot - (NE of Melfa) .9m E of R639, to the SE of R672. Follow old farm road across field, through woods to clearing. Large plot to the N side of wooded area beyond. (Richardson; Ward)
196. Elmore plot - in Melfa; .3m S of the junction of R639 with R626. On front lawn. (Elmore)
197. Old Walker plot - (in town of Melfa). Turn N off R626 to end of Virginia Avenue (R1103). Walk across ditch & wooded strip into field. Plot is midway in field; to the W near woods. (Harmon; Turlington; Walker)
198. Jno. Phillips plot - (NE of Melfa) just N of R672, to the W of R639, .2m in field. (Belote; Mason; Phillips)
199. Bull burial ground - (N of Melfa) .2m S of R639 to the E of R13. Across railroad tracks to S of house in middle of field. (Bull; East; Jones; Phillips)
200. Badger burial ground - .5m N of R639, turn E from R731 onto R625. (Texico Town). Go .1m & turn in dirt lane for .2m. Burial ground to the E end of house. (Badger; Martin; Ward)
201. East cemetery - (between Melfa & Onley) .4m N of R639 to the E of R609 far back in field. (East; Gibb; Parker; Smith)
202. Mason burial ground - .3m W of R13 (at Police Station between Melfa & Onley) to the NW of R639 in middle of field. (Mason; Parker)
203. Bradford-White - (N of Melfa) .2m S of R639 to the W of R13. In lane; plot was moved from meadow near house to Fairview Lawn Cemetery. (Bradford; White)
204. Parker-Core - (NW of Melfa) .2m S of R639 to the E of R609. Well back in field. (Core; Harrison; Parker; Wimborough)
205. Martin-Hatton - in Melfa, at the end of W. Phillips Street (R1115). (Badger; East; Hatton; Martin; Phillips)
205A. Savage-Harmon - in the 1940 data this site was indicated as being at Melfa. Unable to locate. (Savage)
206. Kilmontown - (SW of Melfa Airstrip) 1.2m S of R626 to the W of R609. Behind house in middle of field. (Kilmon)
207. Lawrence cemetery - .5m S of R626 on R818 at Melfa Airstrip. Walk E crossing airfield, over a ditch & up through a wooded rise into an open field. Plot is to the S in a narrow wooded area. (Hickman; Kilmon; Lawrence; Turner)
208. Guy cemetery - .9m W of R13 (at Melfa) to the S of R626 about .1m in field. Just E of the Airstrip Road. (Guy; Jones)
209. Bailey cemetery - fairly large private black burial ground for the Bailey family. (NW of Melfa Airstrip). Plot is behind house on the SE corner of the junction of R627 with R609. (Copied Apr. 1982.) (Bailey; Harris; Needam; Parker)
210. Martin burial ground - (W of Melfa) 1m W of junction with R609 to the N of R627, .2m in dirt lane to W of house. (Martin)

211. Mister cemetery - .9m N of Bobtown to the E of R178 in farm lane. Plot in field destroyed by previous owner. Unable to verify data obtained in 1940. (Ayres; Mister)
212. Finney grave - (NE of Bobtown) .4m E of R718, to the N of R627; beside road. (Finney)
213. Badger-Savage - (NE of Bobtown) .3m E of R718, to the S of R627; .1m in field. (Badger; Savage)
214. Mapp graves - .4m N of Bobtown (intersection of R718 & R620) to the W of R718. Stones no longer in yard; recorded c1940. (Mapp)
215. Old Parker property - NE corner of intersection of R620 & R718 at Bobtown. Behind house. (Mason; Parker; Watson)
216. Parker-Bobtown - this plot was recorded in 1940 as at "Bobtown-Store". Bobtown is on R178 at the junction of R620. The store, which stood on the SW corner has been moved; no plot could be found. (Parker)
217. Joynes burial ground - .6m W of R178 (at Bobtown) to the S of R620. S of present house well into woods overlooking Warehouse Creek. Farm also known as Mt. Hope or Warehouse. (Ames; Joynes; Mister; Scott; Winder)
218. Vaux Hall - 1m N of Bobtown to the W of R178. (Just S of R628E), .9m in private road to house; plot in back garden. Also known as the Moore Farm. (Kellam; Moore)
219. Rew plot - .4m W of junction of R637 (Mt. Nebo), turn S off R634 into lane for .3m. Plot is at end of yard W of the house. (Coard; Rew)
220. Moore burial ground - (Bobtown) .4m N of R628 (Country Club Road) almost to the end of R629 (Boggs Wharf). E of house in yard. (Moore; Taylor)
221. Snugly - (Bobtown) .35m N off R628 (Country Club Road) to the end of R629. Graves in woods to the E of the house to the right. (Boggs Wharf) (Mister)
222. Parker Place - old name: Locust Grove. At end of Yoe's Neck. Stones moved to Onancock Cemetery. (Goffigon; Parker)
223. Blenheim - 1.5m W of R178 (at Bobtown), turn N from R628W into farm lane for .7m. Pass main house & continue W beside creek to point. Plot to the S in field. (Parker; Smith)
224. Fairfield - (Mt. Nebo area) .8m SW from junction of R637 with R634. Turn S off 634 in private lane for .3m. Plot is to the left of front yard in wooded area. (Scarburgh; Teackle)
225. Scarborough marker - on SE corner of junction of R634 with R638. About 12 yards from corner on edge of bank. (Scarborough)
226. Scarburgh graves - (Evans Wharf) to the W of R638, .15m from the junction of R634; about three-quarters way across large field. 2 large imported flat slabs lay side by side. Whitelaw (p. 808) indicated this as the probable burial site of Charles & Elizabeth Scarburgh. No inscriptions on stones.
227. Evans plot - (near Harborton) .1m from R180W, to left side of R2602. To the right of house. (Adams; Dize; Evans; Kelehear; Ross)
228. Doughty grave - (in Harborton) .05m from Dock Road to W of R180W in yard. Only 1 grave. (Doughty)

229. Killman plot - .1m from Dock Road to E of R2601 in Harborton; behind house. (Killman; Sparrow)
230. Hutchinson-Harborton - (in Harborton) to the W of intersection of R260 & Dock Street on hillside. (Beasley; Bull; Hutchinson; Marsh; Martin)
231. Read plot - (Hacks Neck, Smithville area) .65 mile N of R631, to the E of R630N beside road in NW corner of heavy wooded section. Only footstones remain. New headstones placed in St. George's Cemetery. (Read)
232. Guy burial ground - (Hacks Neck, Smithville area) .6m N of R631, to the W of R630N beside road in heavily wooded area. (Dize; Guy; Mister)
233. Kelso burial ground - (Hacks Neck, Smithville area) at end of R630N, about .2m W on edge of creek in thicket. (Kelso)
234. Crockett plot - (Hacks Neck, Smithville area) at end of R630N, to left of road near creek. (Crockett; Evans; Fisher; Rayfield)
235. Evergreen - (Hacks Neck) 2.3m W of R178 (center of Pungoteague) (following R180W, then R631) turn N onto R632 (Smithville Road) for .8m. Turn W into lane for .2m. (Hatton; Kellam; Muir)
236. Underhill Point - (Prospect Neck) .9m W of the junction of R717 to the end of R636. In undergrowth to W between road & Underhill Creek. (Smith)
237. Chandler burial ground - (Prospect Neck) turn left off R717 onto R636; proceed .6m. Turn left into private lane for .3m. Family burial ground is to left of house at end of yard in woods near edge of Underhill Creek. (Chandler; Evans; Turner)
238. Lofland cemetery - (SW of Cashville) turn W onto R745 (Sandpiper Cove Road) from R638. Go .5m to end; continue on farm road to point. Plot to the S near the road. (Lofland)
239. Killmon burial ground - .2m W of R638 (W of Cashville) to the S of R717, turn in farm road & drive .2m to end. Turn into lane to right which goes around field, then into woods, & on to old house on point. Plot is a good distance to E of house on a wooded point near creek. (Crockett; Drummond; Hoffman; Killmon)
240. Kennahorn grave - (W of Cashville) .4m E of the junction of R637, turn N off R638 into long farm lane. This Revolutionary soldier's grave is to front of house on W side of lawn. (Kennahorn)
241. Joynes-Custis cemetery - (SW of Cashville) .2m W of junction with R638, turn S off R717. In dirt lane for about .1m. Plot to the E in center of field. (Custis; Joynes; White)
242. Harrison cemetery - (SW of Cashville) .4m W of junction with R638, turn N off R717. In dirt lane to old house. Plot to the right at end of yard. (Chandler; Custis; Harrison; Scott; Smith)
243. Smith plot - (between Cashville & Mt. Nebo) .1m slightly NE of junction of R717 to the N side of R638. On edge of old school grounds near road. (Andrew M E Chapel just to the E.) (Smith)
244. Drummond plot - .5m E of the junction with R717 (but W of Cashville), to the S side of R638. In pasture in front of house. (Boggs; Drummond)

245. Dahl's Swamp - to the S of R638 just W of the junction of R642 (E of Cashville). A good distance across fields & woods. Also, access from R638 between Andrew Chapel & Crockett Town. No stones; data by Mr. James Belote. (Jackson)
246. Topping Lot - to the S of R638 just W of the junction of R642 (E of Cashville). A good distance across fields & woods into Dahl's Swamp. Once high land & a large family plot. Stones now gone. Mr. James Belote supplied some data. Original house known also as Silver Stream. (Finney; Mears)
247. Rodgers-Boggs - (W of Cashville) .4m E of junction with R637, turn N off R638. In farm lane for .1m. Plot is to the E across wide field in heavy woods. (Boggs; Joynes; Rodgers)
248. error made; there is no site #248. JMM
249. Rodgers cemetery - .1m E of junction of 637 (Crockett Town) to the S of R638 in field. (Boggs; Rodgers; Strang; Taylor)
250. Addison plot - (between Cashville & Mt. Nebo) .05m E of junction of R637, to the S of R638 in field. (Addison)
251. Paddy plot - black (across from Mt. Nebo Church) .1m slightly NW of the junction of R634 to the S of R637; S side of several houses. (Carr; Paddy; Snead; Stratton)
252. Bagwell cemetery - .2m W of junction of R637 (near Mt. Nebo Church), to the S of R634 beside road. Private black burial ground. (Bagwell; Carr; Henderson; Loftland)
253. Negro burial ground - (Mt. Nebo) to the S of junction of R634 with R637 across field into woods. Once a large Negro burying ground. Now in thick woods; many rusted markers; only a few readable.
254. Mt. Nebo Church - Mt. Nebo African Baptist Church - 1891, .1m slightly NW of junction of 634 to the N side of R637. Several graves to the E of building; most to the W side. (Copied Apr. 1983.)
255. West graves - (black) in front yard to the S of R637, .7m from the junction of R634 (Mt. Nebo). (West)
256. Arlington - .5m E of the junction of R634 (Mt. Nebo-Slutkill Neck), take dirt road to the S of R637; .4m to house. Plot to the back & W of yard. (Arlington; Eichelberger; Finney; Hart; Heath; Mason; Riley)
257. Leven James plot - (S of Savageville) 1.1m W of R718 to the S of R626 (Mt. Nebo Road) turn into shell road. Go .5m to old house to the W. Plot in field to right of house. (Also known as the Thomas Farm.) (James; Waterfield; Wescott)
258. Savageville - the the W of R718 at the junction of R639 (in Savageville). In garden to the SW of mobile home. (Savage)
258A. Custis burial ground - location indicated on 1940 card as "Savageville". Unable to find site in 1984. (Custis)
259. Gaskin's Church-old - the site of the original Gaskin's African Methodist Chapel founded in 1873, .2m W of R718 (just N of Savageville) to the N side of R640. Some very old graves remain marked. However, this is a large cemetery with well over 200 unmarked graves. (Copied Sept. 1985)
260. Gaskin's Church - Gaskin's Chapel African Methodist Church moved to this site in 1951, .3m N of Savageville (junction of R639) to the E of R718; to N & rear of church. Many unmarked graves. (Copied Sept. 1983)

261. Killmon-Broadway - 1.3m N of Cashville (R638) to the right of R641, just beyond old house in yard near road (now heavily overgrown) (Barnes; Killmon)
262. Hart plot - (Broadway) 1.1m N of center of Cashville (R638) to the W of R641. Beyond house & yard about 50 feet into thick woods. (Hart)
263. Boggs burial ground - from R638 (W of Cashville), turn N onto dirt road R635. Go .7m & turn right into lane to house (about .4m). Burial ground to the right of old house beside Matchatank Creek. (Boggs; Colonna; Underhill; Waters)
264. Drummond burial ground - on R635, go .4m from the junction of R638 (W of Cashville). Turn E into private lane for .3m. Plot is to the N of large home along Matchatank Creek. (Drummond; Killman; Parker; White)
265. Phillips grave - .6m from R638 turn left off R641 (Cashville-Broadway Road) onto R733. Go .5m to house on Matchatank Creek. Grave in front yard; once a large family plot. (Phillips)
266. Leatherbury-Waters - W of Cashville, turn N off R638, .6m E of the junction with R637 into farm lane for .4m to house. Plot is to NE of house in heavily wooded area just beyond a small pond close to Matchatank Creek. Once known as Old Scott Farm. (Leatherbury; Underhill; Waters)
267. Old Scott Farm - (W of Cashville) turn N off R638, .6m E of junction with R637 into farm lane for .4m. Grave was on edge of yard before you reach the house. Moved to Mt. Holly. (Scott)
268. Boggs Place - W of Cashville turn N off R638, .6m E of the junction with R637 into farm lane for .2m. Cemetery is to the left across field beside Matchatank Creek. (Boggs; Crockett; Killmon; Moore; Olive; Rodgers)
269. Taylor grave - just N of R638 (at Cashville) to the E of R641, take dirt lane running beside the Broadway Baptist Church. Continue .45m to creek. Plot slightly to the left by cedar trees. (Taylor)
270. Harrison plot - to the S side of R638, .3m E of Cashville (at junction of R641). Burials to the E of house beside shed. (Crosley; Custis; Harrison)
271. Chandler cemetery - to the N side of R638, .3m E of Cashville (junction of R641). Burials are to the W of house beside large box bushes. (Boggs; Chandler; Drummond)
272. Finney Place - .3m E of Cashville turn N off R638 onto dirt road (R641). Drive .4m to house to the W. Burial ground is behind house. (Finney; Hopkins)
273. Finney, old site - between Onancock & Cashville, .1m E of junction of R642, to the N of R638. In private lane to 2 homes. To the E of the home on the right, just inside a small point of woods near creek. Beside the 1 marked grave there are 5 large, smooth stones (ballast?). 2 have initials. (Finney)
274. George's Point - on Finney's Creek (E of Cashville), .2m N of R638 to the E of R642. Walk .1m through woods to Point near gut. (Finney)

275. Bayley burial ground - (Bayley's Neck in Prospect Neck) 1.3m N of R638 to the E of R643 in field near head of a gut. The Bayley family allowed numerous neighbors & servants to be buried here. Some graves have been moved; few stones remain. (Bayley; Drummond; Scott)

276. Rayfield plot - E of Cashville turn off R638, into Bayley's Neck on R643. Go 2.1m (turning onto dirt road at end of the hard surface road). Graves are to the left between road & creek. (Rayfield)

277. Poplar Cove - (NW of Onancock) .05m from the end of R653 (Poplar Cove Wharf - also known as Mears Wharf). In yard beside road. (Carmine; Parker)

278. Oatlands - (NW of Onancock) .8m W of R654 to the S of R653. In private road .7m to house. Plot to the W on lawn. (Fletcher; Parker; Topping; Van Kesteren)

279. Rodgers-Poulson - (NW of Onancock) 1m W of R658 to the S of R653. In dirt lane for .7m. Plot behind house to SW toward creek. (Carmine; Edwards; Mears; Poulson; Rodgers)

280. Meadville - from R638 (between Onancock & Cashville) turn N onto R778 for 1m to end of road. Plot to W of house. (Finney)

281. Snead family plot - (Old Harmanson Farm) from R638 (between Onancock & Cashville) turn N onto R778 for .6m. Leaving R778 continue on stone road to house. The stones from this burial ground have been moved to Onancock Cemetery. (Joynes; Snead; White; Wright)

282. Freeman plot - to the N of R638 (W of Onancock) at the junction of R637, take dirt lane for .3m to house. Plot to the W in field. (Freeman)

283. Joynes-Bayne - in Onancock at W end of Meadville Drive, 1 block from Mt. Prospect Avenue. Behind last house on the right. (Bayne; Joynes; Pearce)

284. Scott Hall - (in Onancock) on the S side of Market Street across from Cokesbury Church. There are 2 plots behind the house. (Bagwell; Corbin; Ker; Leatherbury; Riley; Snead; Teackle; Wise)

285. Seymour-Snead - (in Onancock) .05m S of Market Street to the E of Ames Street, 2 adjoining plots to the left of house. (Miles; Riley; Seymour; Snead)

286. Cokesbury Ch. - Cokesbury United Methodist Church. Founded 1788. Present building 1854. Market Street in Onancock to the W of the town square. Numerous graves marked only with rocks; some rather old stones.

287. Bagwell mon. - monument in memory of Gen. Bagwell. To the N of Market Street, Onancock on Town Square.

288. West burial ground - in Onancock on King Street at junction of East Street (at the Town Square). Behind house near creek bank. (Rew; Russell; West)

288A. Kerr Place - Market Street, Onancock. Home of the E. S. of VA Historical Society. (West)

289. Poulson cemetery - (N of Onancock) .3m from R658 to the S of R1028, turn in dirt road for .2m. Plot is to the E among newer houses. (also referred to as Cokesbury.) (Bayne; Coe; Fletcher; Guy; Goffigon; Hopkins; Poulson; Revell; Robinson; Smith; Taylor)

290. Fitzhugh burial ground - Fitzhugh burial ground in Onancock, .05m from Holly Street to N of Johnson Street. In yard behind house. (Fitzhugh)
291. White-Bayley - in Onancock, to the W side of College Street to the S side of the High School. Once a much larger family burial plot. (Bayley; White)

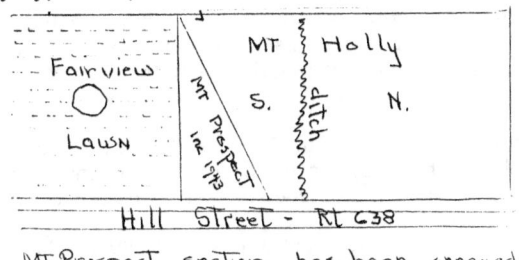

292. Mt. Holly - Mt. Holly Cemetery (incorporated July 1892) .2m S of Market Street, Onancock to W of R 638 (Hill Street). This cemetery adjoins Fairview Lawn to the S. (Copied June 1983.)
293. Mt. Holly-s - Mt. Holly Cemetery; S end beyond ditch & adjoining Fairview Lawn Cemetery. Copied June 1983.
294. Fairview Ln. - Fairview Lawn Cemetery. (Est. 1948.) .4m S of Market Street, Onancock to W of R638 (Hill Street). This cemetery adjoins Mt. Holly Cemetery to the N. (Copied May 1983.)
295. Onancock - Onancock Cemetery. (incorporated April 1892.) 1.1m S of Market Street, Onancock to W of R638 (Hill Street). (At junction of R718.) (Copied June 1983.)
296. Burckard burial ground - this family plot originally adjoined the Onancock Cemetery. The cemetery has grown around the plot, or the stones have been moved to their present location in the northern section of the cemetery. (Ames; Belote; Burckard; Turner; Warrington; Williams)
297. Joynes cemetery - .5m E of R718 (SE of Onancock) on the S side of R638. Fairly large black burying ground; many unmarked graves.
298. Sherwood cemetery - (N of Onancock) .6m W of R316 (from Tasley) to the N of R648. Midway in field. (Sherwood)
299. Watson cemetery - N of Onancock .5m W of R316 (Tasley) to the S of R648 in middle of field. (Ayres; Watson)
300. Budd cemetery - .3m N of R648 in Tasley to the E of R178. Beside road; plot in thick brambles. (Budd; Campbell; Mears)
300A. Montrose - .4m W of R13 (Onley) to the S of R179. Unmarked graves in NW corner of lawn. (Burials said to be sister & infants of Alfred T. Scott. Ref.: Mrs. Catherine N. Richardson - Onancock, VA 23417.) (Lewis; Scott)
301. White burial ground - on R639 about three-quarters mile from Savageville toward Melfa. Plot has been destroyed. Unable to verify 1940 data. (White)
302. Gaskins plot - (black) between Onley & Melfa - just W of R609 to the S of R640 beside road. (Gaskins)

303. Beloat Place - (S of Onley) .6m N of the junction of R625 to the E of R731. In lane, plot is in garden SE of house. (Beloat; Carmine)
304. Old Beloat Place - (S of Onley) .6m N of the junction of R625 to the E of R731. In lane to house. Plot is NE about .5m across field near woods. (Bebloat; Beloat)
305. Edwards plot - this plot was recorded in 1940 as "S of Onley". Unable to locate. Dates on cards fit with court records. (Edwards)
306. B. Mears gr. - .2m E of junction of R609 (NE of Onley) to the S of R650 in middle of field. Only 1 stone; evidence of other graves. (Mears)
307. Ward burial ground - 1.3m E of the railroad tracks in Onley to the S of R789 (just beyond junction of R647), .3m in very bad farm road. Plot is just inside the woods to the E of double power lines. (Ward; Waterfield)
308. Kellam plot - E of Onley; .3m N of R789 to the W of R715 in middle of field. (Harman; Kellam)
309. Logan graves - (black) E of Onley, .05m E of R715 to the N of R647 in yard near road. (Several graves unmarked.) (Logan)
310. Mears of A. - (E of Onley) .2m W of R715 to the N of R647 behind house. (Mears)
311. Kelly plot - E of Onley, .3m W of R715 to the N of R647, .1m into field. (Kelly)
312. Mears cemetery - .9m S of R648 (W of Daugherty), to the W of R715. In farm lane about .5m just beyond irrigation pond in field to the N. (Bull; Mears; Williams)
313. Stephens plot - 1m S of Bus. R13, to E of R609 (Acc-Onley Road) just into field. Iron fenced. (Stephens)
314. Walker burial ground - .8m S of Bus. R13, to E of R609 (Acc-Onley Road) in middle of field near ruins of house. (Eichelberger; Herch...; Hornsby; Townsend; Walker)
315. Rural Felicity - 1.25m E of Bus. R13 (in Accomac) to the S of R605. Behind house in field. (Boisnard)
316. Lilliston graves - .8m N of R648 (at Daugherty) to the E of R605. Beside back porch of small house near road. (Bloxom; Lilliston)
317. Ross' Run - .4m N of R648 (at Daugherty) to the W of R605. Behind house to the N lawn. (Barker; Bayley; Bull; Matthews; Ross)
318. Drummond family cemetery - (black) .4m W of Daugherty to the S of R648 in field near road. At least 10 unmarked graves, also. (Drummond; Lackey; Parker)
319. Drummond family plot - (black) .35m W of Daugherty to the S of R648 beside road in clump of bushes. These burial are from the same family as those listed in the graveyard above. (Drummond; Garrison)
320. Fitzgerald burial ground - .3m N of R648 (at Daugherty), to the E of R605, .2m in lane; plot is SE of house (Parker Place) across field in edge of woods. (Fitchett; Fitzgerald; Justice; Rew)
321. Fox-Burton - .2m E of R605 to the N of R648 in field beside road; just E of Daugherty. (Burton; Fox)
322. Milliner Place - (in town of Daugherty) just E of R605 to the S side of R648. Graves from this yard were moved to Edgehill Cemetery. No stones. (Milliner)

323. Miles-Groton - (W of Daugherty) .3m S of R648 to the E of R715, .2m acorss field to the S end of site of old house. (Fosque; Groton; Miles)
324. Hargis plot - E of Daugherty (in Custis Neck) .4m from R605 to the S of R648, .2m into field. (Hargis)
325. Nedab cemetery - (black) (N of Locustville) 1.3m N of R647 to the W of R605. In yard beside road. (Allen; Bailey; Domon; Drummond; Harris; Nedab; Toye)
326. St. Luke's - (black) (N of Locustville) 1.2m N of R647 to the E of R605, across field in edge of woods. Large plot with many unmarked graves. Cemetery for St. Luke's A M E Church, Daugherty. (Copied Dec. 1983.)
327. Groton cemetery - N of Locustville, 1m N of R647 to the W of R605 at least .5m back in field towards woods. (Groton; Kellam; Watson)
328. Kellam-Groton - (N of Locustville) .6m N of R647 to the W of R605, about .4m in field. (Bunting; Groton; Kellam; White)
329. The Folly - 1.1m S of Bus. R13 (in Accomac) to the E of R605; 1.2m in dirt lane to house. Graves in front lawn to the left. (Bradford; Custis)
330. Dix Farm - (Joynes Neck) 1.6m E of Bus. R13, to the S of R652, .7m in dirt lane. To the SE of house, on creek bank. One stone; evidence of many more burials. (Twiford)
331. Bead Farm - (Joynes Neck) 1.7m E of Bus. R13, to the S of R652 about .8m across field. Iron fence encloses plot in woods on bank along gut. Name on gate - Coxton. Only 1 footstone remains: W.T.M.
332. Bowman's Folly - (Joynes Neck) 2.4m E of Bus. R13 (N of Accomac) to the end of R652. S in private lane for .4m. Plot to right across front lawn toward creek. (Cropper; Duffield; Gibb; Joynes; Pettit; Scarburgh)
333. Cropperville - (Joynes Neck) 2.4m E of Bus. R13 (N of Accomac) to the end of R652. Through gates in private lane to house. Grave in garden. (Smith)
334. Old Harmon graves - (in Bayly's Neck N of Accomac) 2.2m E of R13 to the S of R662. Less than .05m in dirt road, turn E on dirt lane for .4m. Plot is to the N in field. (Harmon)
335. Mt. Custis - (in Baylys Neck, NE of Accomac) 2.5m E of R13 to the N of R662; .5m in private lane. One grave in front of house. The Bayly family plot is to the NE end of pasture near creek. (Ambler; Bayly; Browne; Custis; Hansford; Melvin; Miller; Stokes; Tidball; Tiffany)
336. Christian plot - SE of Pastoria, 1.3m E of R13 to the S of R664; .3m in lane. Plot behind house near creek. (Christian)
337. Runneymeade - (in Bayly's Neck, N of Accomac) 1m E of R13 to the S of R662; .3m in lane. Plot in NW corner of yard. (Cooper; Hope; Mabie; Parramore)
338. Woodbourne site - 2m S of the junction with R13 to the E of Bus. R13. House was used as a Federal Hospital during Civil War. Burial plot about .7m behind house in field; Union soldiers said to be buried. No stones. Tradition holds that the plot was used after the War for animal burials in contempt for the Union forces.

339. Edgehill - Edgehill Cemetery (incorporated Apr. 1902) .5m E of Bus. R13 (N end of Accomac) to the S of R652. (Copied Sept. 1983.)
340. Drum'town Meth. Ch. - no stones remain in Drummondtown Methodist Churchyard established 1789 in Accomac; N side of R605 just E of R1503. The data for several graves is taken from a 1940 record. (Lewis; Ritter; White)
341. Drummond graves - .15m from R605 in Accomac on the E side of R1503. In wooded area near creek well behind the large brick Fletcher house. (Drummond)
342. Walston cemetery - .15m from R605 in Accomac to the E of R1503 (Back Street) behind house in garden to the S. (Walston)
343. Seven Gables - (in Accomac) NE corner of R1502 (Cross Street) & R1503 (Back Street). Behind house in box garden. (Ailworth; Walston; Young)
344. Drum'town Bap. - Drummondtown Baptist Church. Organized 1871; rebuilt 1912; .2m N of center of Accomac to the E of R605 (Bus. R13) at junction of R1503. (Groton; Hopkins)
345. Wilkins burial ground - to the N of Bus. R13 at the junction of R609 on the SE side of Accomac. Graves moved to Edgehill Cemetery when Health Dept. acquired the farm. (Waddy; Wilkins)
346. Johnson grave - in NW corner of yard of house at NW corner of R605 & R1503 in Accomac. Stone badly damaged. (Johnson)
347. St. James Ch. - only a few stones remain in St. James Episcopal Churchyard in Accomac; N side of R605, just W of R1503. (Doughty; Kellam; Oldham)
348. Bayly cemetery - .1m from R605 in Accomac to th W of R1503 behind the Episcopal Rectory. (Bayly)
349. Twyford graves - .1m from center of Accomac to the S of R764 where county building now stands. Stones gone; cards made from 1940 record. (Twyford)
350. Seymour-Ross House - in Accomack .5m S of center of Town (i.e. R1502) to the E of Bus. R13. Behind house in box garden. (Custis; Fisher)
351. Tavern Lot - (center of Accomac) .5m to the S of R1502 behind small house. Once the back yard of the Upper Tavern. Modern building now on site. (Adair; Dix; Pielee; Wilson)
352. Gillett cemetery - .2m N of center of Accomac, to the W of R605 (Bus. R13); N of house in garden. (Blackstone; Cropper; Gillett; Lilliston)
352A. Cary grave - in Accomac. Unable to loacte; data from 1940 card. (Cary)
353. Burford plot - .2m from center of Accomac to N of R764; behind house in garden. (Burford; Coleburn; Revell)
354. Lilliston site - (between Accomac & Greenbush) .4m W of R764 to the N of R660. In clump in field. (Lilliston)
355. Stevenson burial ground - (SW of Greenbush) 2.9m E of R658 to the N of R660. Plot is behind house in clump to the W end of yard. No stone. Information from Garland Evans, Greenbush.
356. Scott-Bishop - (between Bayside & Greenbush) .3m W of R658 to the N of R660 beside road. Probably had numerous stones. (Bishop; Scott)

357. Chandler site - .9m E of junction with R658 (Bayside Road to Onancock), just E of Merry Branch to the N of R657 turn in farm road. Follow through farm for 1.6m to site on left. One large stone marked "Chandler" only. A burial plot to the right on edge of woods has been recently "pushed up".
358. Savage burial - E of the junction of R660 (N side - Deep Creek Road) & R658 about .3m in field. Once a fairly large black burial ground. (Savage)
359. Waples Place - 1.1m W of intersection with R658 toward Deep Creek, to the S of R657. In lane for .6m to house on Chesconessex Creek. Graves in front yard. Only footstone legible. (S.U.S.)
360. Riley plot - 1.2m W of R654 (toward S Chesconessex) to the N of R655. Plot is .1m across field towards creek. (Riley)
361. Holmes grave - (S Chesconessex) .6m E of R649 to the N of R655. In yard to W of house; evidence of more graves; only 1 marker. (Holmes)
362. Clifton - (S Chesconessex) .5m E of R649 to the N of R655. In garden to the NE of house. (Marsh)
363. Wise cemetery - (S Chesconessex) .5m E of R649 to the S of R655. This is a beautifully restored graveyard of the Wise family on the original plantation site. Some stones have been set in the brick wall, as well as some memorial placques. (Guilette; Outten; Wilkins; Wise)
364. Hart graves - E of village of Deep Creek .05m N of R657 to the W of R824. Beside road, trashy plot. (Hart)
365. Old Custis graves - .3m E of R658 to the S of R660 (N side of Deep Creek), .3m across field in edge of woods very near creek. (Custis)
366. Metro. Mem. - (Bayside) Metropolitan Memorial A M E Churchyard. Founded 1870. Rebuilt 1914, .2m N of R660E to the W of R658. (Copied Dec. 1983.)
367. Bagwell plot - .1m N of R659 (at Greenbush), E side of R316 across railroad tracks in middle of field. (Bagwell)
368. Wessells plot - N of Accomac .9m NW of R13 to the SW of R663; .2m into field. (Wessells)
369. Parks burial ground - (N of Accomac) .6m N of R13 to the E of R662 in field. (R662 is a dirt road shortly after leaving R13.) (Melson; Parks)
370. Fox-Poolman - (just N of Accomac) about .5m W of R13, to the S of R663. This plot containing some very old stones was bulldozed to clear land. Data recorded in 1940. (Bull; Fox; Poolman; Preston)
371. Budd burial ground - (N of Accomac) to the E of R13 at the intersection with Bus. R13; about .2m back in field on the N side of the branch. (Budd; Core; Wright)
372. Parks plot - (SE of Pastoria) .8m E of R13 to the S of R664; plot to W of house. (Parks; Russell)
373. Johnson cemetery - (SE of Pastoria) 1.3m E of R13 to the N of R664; in lane for .1m. Plot in front yard to the S. (Johnson; McCready; Onley)

374. Moore cemetery - (SE of Pastoria) .7m S of the junction of R661 to the end of R665; continue on dirt road for .2m. Plot across field to the W on edge of marsh. (Hickman; Moore; Savage)
375. Bundick-Warner - (Pastoria) .3m E of R13 to the S of R661; .6m in dirt lane. Two plots: Bundick in pasture to W of house; Warner in yard behind house. (Bundick; Warner; Wise)
376. Finney, A. W. - (E of Pastoria) .4m E of the junction with R665 to the S of R661 in field. (Finney)
377. Wise plot - (E of Pastoria) NE corner of R661 & R665. Stones fallen; dense undergrowth. Known as the Major Wise Place. (Wise)
378. Dr. Dix Farm - (Pastoria) .1m S of R661 to the E of R13; about .3m through field to site of old house. In wooded area along the N edge. (Dix; Wright)
379. Tunnell cemetery - (Pastoria) .1m N of R661 to the E of R13; .2m into field. (Tunnell)
380. Hickman-Gravenor - (Pastoria) 1.1m W of R13, to the S of R661 (turn left when R661 comes to a "T"). In dirt lane .01m. (Gravenor; Hickman; Onley)
381. Clover Hill - (between Pastoria & Chase Crossing) .6m E of R316 to the S of R661; .4m in lane to house. Two plots on farm - 1 in field behind house to the SE; the other is in the back field about .3m into farm. (Bull; Grinnalds; Melson; Middleton; White)
382. Coard Place - .7m W of R316 (at Greenbush) to the S of R763, .1m in lane; plot behind house. (Coard)
383. Savage-Northan - (black) (Bayside) .8m N of Metropolitan A M E Church to the E of R658; beside road. (Johnson; Northan; Savage)
384. Bayside cemetery - (black) at Bayside (also called White Rabbitt) .3m N of Metropolitan A M E Church, to the W of R658. Small community cemetery .1m back in field. Numerous unmarked graves.
385. West Place - 1.2m W of junction of R658, to the N of R657. In road through woods for about .4m to open field. Brick ends of the West House are across field to the left, bordering Deep Creek. Graveyard was to W end; only part of 1 stone remains. (West)
386. Deep Creek Plantation - S side of Deep Creek 1.8m W of junction with Bayside Road to the N of R657. Turn in private lane for .2m. Once a very large plot behind house to the NE in garden. Only several very old stones remain with initials only; could be Wise or West.
387. Watts Island - in Tangier Bay; now washed away. Photographed on 27 Nov. 1969 by Mr. Ray Landon, Onancock, VA. (Parker)
388. Old Custis tract - 1.9m E of R658 to the S of R660 (N side of Deep Creek) .3m in lane to N of house near creek. (Recently known as Mimosa Farm.) (Custis; Turner)
389. Abrams grave - on the S shore at the head of Doe Creek, approximately 100 yards from waters edge. Only 1 grave remaining; indications of a larger plot. (Abrams)
390. Lewis burial ground - (Doe Creek) 1.3m W of the junction of R658 with R661 (the Oakes - N of Bayside). At the end of R661 turn left into private lane for .4m. Walk in woods road to the left for about .3m to plot in woods near banks of Doe Creek. (Lewis; Melson; Thomas)

391. Doe Creek - (W of Greenbush) .7m W of the junction with R658, to the S of R661. Follow old woods road for about three-quarters mile almost to creek. Once a large burial plot, now deep woods. (Drummond)
392. Hills Farm - (W of Drummond's Mill Pond) .3m W of junction with R658 (the Oakes), to the N of R661. In private lane for .7m. Burial plot is a good distance in front of house to the E just inside woods. (See White-law:980-2.) (Bayly)
393. Gunter plot - (W of Greenbush) just W of the junction with R658, to the N of R661, about .3m in dirt road to old house. Plot is in clump of trees to the NW. (Ayres; Gunter; Lewis)
394. "G" site - N of the junction of R661 & R658 (Bayside Road to Onancock) is a large wooded plot about .5m back in field. Indications of numerous burials; only 2 foot-stones found: E.G. & J.G.
395. Ayres monument - (W of Greenbush) .1m E of the junction with R661 to the S of R658. Take farm road passing cut-over area on left; across large open field; then walk well into the center of woods known as Pea Ridge. This very old site (35 feet square) held many burials. Now only 1 monument, erected in this century, gives a de-tailed lineage of the Ayres, Drake, & Drummond families. (See Whitelaw:986.)
396. Scott burial ground - (W of Greenbush) .3m E of the junction with R658 to the N of R661. Across field to ruins of old house in large wooded area. Graves in heavy woods well to the W end of site. (Scott)
397. Willett burial ground - .1m N of the junction of R661 with R658 (Drummond's Mill) to the W of R722, 3m in farm lane to house. Behind house, across field, in a pine woods. (Melson; Willett)
398. Hall grave - Old Ref. (1940) states near Drummond's Mill, W of Greenbush. Unable to locate. (Hall)
399. Marino - (N of Drummond's Mill) .9m N of junction with R661 to the E of R658. In farm road for .3m to ruins of brick house; plot to W end. Stones have been set in a cement paving for preservation. (Barnes; Lewis; Melson)
400. Liberty - Liberty Cemetery (incorporated Oct. 1902) SE section of town of Parksley, 2 blocks S of R176 to the W of R763. (Rechecked 1984.)
401. Parksley - Parksley Cemetery. (Incorporated Sept. 1906.) NE of town; about .5m N of R176 to the W of R678. (Rechecked 1984.)

MISCELLANEOUS ABBREVIATIONS

Abs	Absolum	N	north
b	born	nd	no date on stone
b&d	born and died	NE	northeast
Benj	Benjamin	nee	born
bur gr	burial ground	ns	no stone in plot
Bus.R	business rt	NW	northwest
c	about	prob	probably
Capt	Captain	Pvt	Private
cem	cemetery	R	route
Ch.	Church	Richd	Richard
Chas	Charles	Robt	Robert
ch/o	child of	S	south
Col	Colonel	Saml	Samuel
Cpl	Corporal	SE	southeast
CSA	Confederate States of America	s/o	son of
		Sr	Senior
d	died	SW	southwest
Danl	Daniel	Thos	Thomas
d/o	daughter of	USA	United States Army
DAR	Daughters of the American Revolution	W	west
		Wm	William
E	east	w/o	wife of
Edmd	Edmund	wid/o	widow of
Edwd	Edward		
Eliz	Elizabeth		
f/o	father of		
fam	family		
Gen	General		
Geo	George		
grf/o	grandfather of		
grm/o	grandmother of		
h/o	husband of		
inf/o	infant of		
Jas	James		
Jno	John		
Jos	Joseph		
Jr	Junior		
Lt	Lieutenant		
m	miles		
Margt	Margaret		
m/o	mother of		
mar	married		

Location of Survey
Commonwealth of Virginia

N
Accomack Co.
Northampton Co.
Virginia's
Eastern Shore

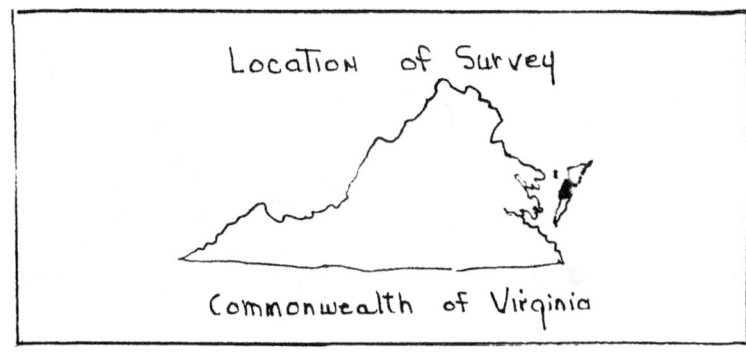

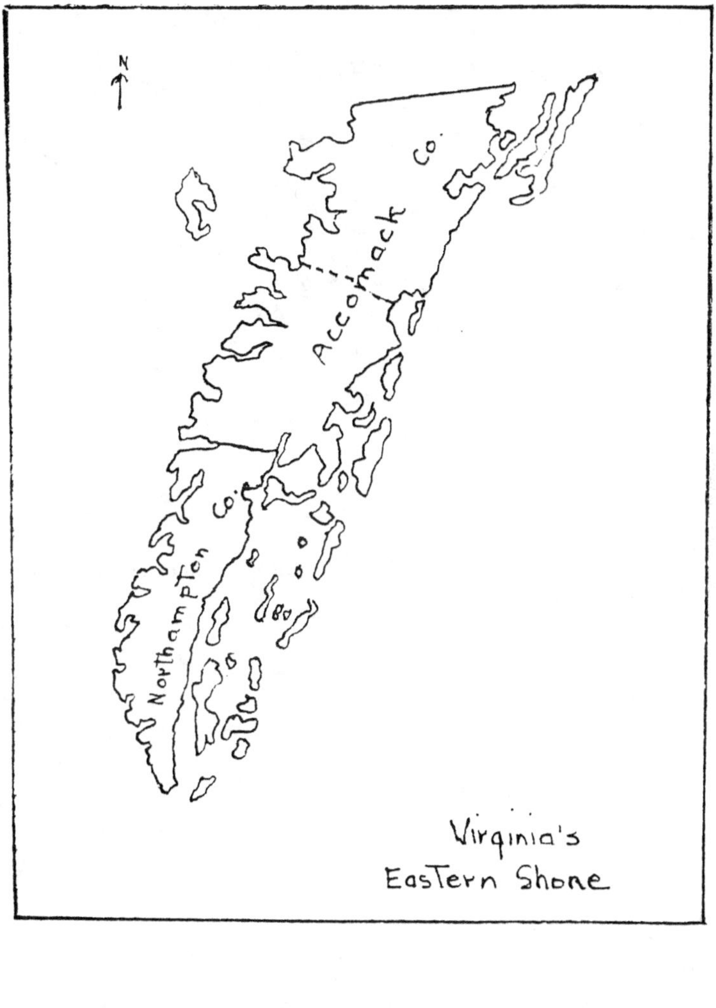

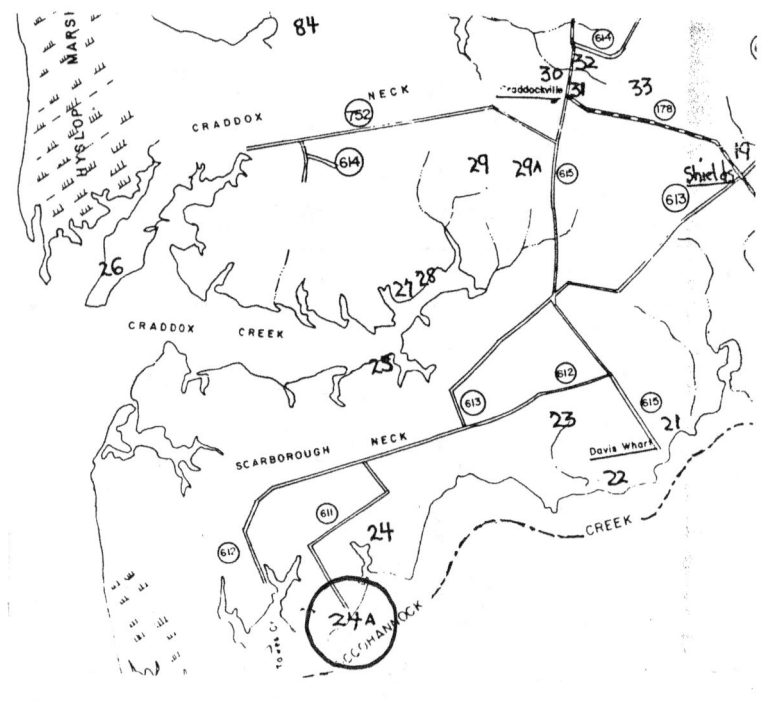

Add cemetery 24A (circled) to the fold-out map accompanying this book.

CEMETERY INSCRIPTIONS

ABBOTT, Hattie Gillespie w/o J A 1884-1974 Park
Indie Downing w/o S L 1900-1973 Park
James A h/o H G 1875-1938 Park
Samuel L h/o I D 1900-1976 Park
ABNEY, Rev H A 1894-1978 Gask
Mary M 1897-1976 Gask
ABRAMS, Mary S d/o Saml J & Mary H 2 Apr 1848-15 Jan 1853 Abra
ACKLEY, Augustus h/o Grace 1854-1931 Park
Grace w/o Augustus 1857-1922 Park
Harry C h/o R N 1881-1952 Park
Herman Augustus h/o M M 1 Jan 1887-12 Mar 1962 Park
J Wallace h/o M R 1856-1935 Park
John T h/o M M 1827-1909 Park
Margaret Mears w/o H A 10 Apr 1882-31 Mar 1962 Park
Marietta M w/o J T 1828-1914 Park
Mary R w/o J W 1860-1954 Park
Rose N w/o H C 1882-1963 Park
ADAIR, Edwin L 7 Jan 1852-14 Jan 1881 Tave
Frances E w/o G H; d/o Dr Geo & Frances Scherer d 21 Oct 1852; age: 25 yrs Shir
John W 29 Apr 1827-6 Mar 1882 Tave
Margaret L 1 Aug 1827-12 July 1883 Tave
ADAMS, Alonzo J 25 Dec 1889-12 Feb 1975 MtHo-s
Annie A (w/o W L) 1875-1952

ADAMS (continued)
StGe
Daniel J 1858-1934 StGe
Edwin Foote (h/o P M) 28 July 1880-12Jan1935 StGe
Effie L w/o WmL 7 Feb 1872-28 July 1902 Evan
Elizabeth M 27 Aug 1882-7 Dec 1906 Edge
Gladys T (w/o J H) 1916- Fair
Harry T 8 Aug 1892-18 May 1924 Park
Henry D h/o M A 1847-1925 Park
Howard H h/o M P 1891-1971 StGe
J Wilmer Jr 15 Mar 1904-26 Feb 1915 StGe
James C h/o M A 10 Aug 1812-2 Feb 1880 Libe
John H (h/o G T) 1904-1979 Fair
John Henry (h/o M E) 1875-1934 Wach
Joseph Wilmer (h/o J A) 13 July 1854-30May 1937 StGe
Julia Anna w/o J W 13 Aug 1861- 23 Mar 1941 StGe
Lawrance S d 25 Oct 1918; age: 27 yrs (killed in France) StGe
Mabel P w/o H H 1895-1972 StGe
Margaret W 1874-1953 StGe
Mary A w/o J C 9 Feb 1822-9 July 1890 Libe
Mary A w/o H D 1860-1942 Park
Mary Emma (w/o J H) 1878-1964 Wach
Maurice T 24 Oct 1894-13 Jan 1974 StGe
Mildred T 25 Aug 1897-24 June 1899 Evan
Oswald J 1854-1917 Edge

1

ADAMS (continued)
Pearl Marsh (w/o E F) 30 Jan 1881-2Feb 1967 StGe
Rosa J w/o Wm D 1883-1952 Fair
Ruth M 11-23 July 1925 MtHo-s
Thomas J 23 May 1863-2 Mar 1920 Libe
William D (h/o R J) 1880-1949 Fair
William L (h/o A A) 1869-1954 StGe

ADDISON, Ann R w/o Jas H 17 Aug 1808-21 Mar 1898 Addi
Anne E E 20 May 1837-9 Feb 1907 Addi
Annie B 1891-1953 Snea
George W 23 Nov 1839-28 Apr 1922 Addi
Herbert G 2 Feb 1895-18 June 1926 NewM
Isaac 1915-1974 NewM
Major d 11 Apr 1948; age: 57 yrs Snea

ADKINS, Charles H (w/o M S) 1880-1962 Onan
Delos D 1900-1944 Park
Derek D 2 May 1936-12 May 1974 Park
Harry L Jr 1905-1973 Fair
Mary S (w/o C H) 1881-1942 Onan

AGATHOIN, Beth 1893-1961 StGe
Dion George 27 Apr 1857-17 Feb 1920 StGe
Ella B 1871-1962 StGe
George L 1900-1965 StGe
Lester I (h/o M E) 1900- StGe
Mary E (w/o L I) 1901-1975 StGe

AILWORTH, George C h/o Ida W 29 Nov 1860-24 Jan 1905 Edge
James J 4 Aug 1810-20 Jan 1850 (clerk at Acc Court for 43 yrs) Edge
James J s/o Jas J & Sally T 2 Oct 1849-13 Sept 1865 Seve

ALBRIGHT, Robert B 1909-1964 Wach

ALLEN, - d/o W W & S C b&d 12 Apr 1906 Park
Alfred L 1896-1952 Burt
Amy C 1894-1922 Onan

ALLEN (continued)
Annie E 1897-1963 Burt
Annie L (w/o W C) 1889-1975 Fair
Atha V w/o E T; d/o Geo H & Sallie Hart 4 June 1882-4 Jan 1899 Onan
Blanche M w/o Horace 17 Jan 1888-12 Feb 1922 StLu
Charles L 15 Oct 1867-29 June 1929 Onan
Charles L s/o Chas L & Emma S 11 June-28 Sept 1901 Onan
Charlie R s/o Chas L & Emily S 8 Apr 1883-20 July 1890 Onan
Cheste 1900-1945 Neda
Dale M 1938- Fair
Dorothy 1923-1978 Gask
Earl Dulany 30 Aug 1895-15 Dec 1902 Onan
Edgar Plumb s/o I B & Mary A 2 Mar 1857-10 May 1885 Bayb
Edward T h/o A V 11 May 1867-22 Mar 1920 Onan
Ethan Edgar s/o Ira N & Emma M 29 Feb 1880-12 Mar 1881 Bayb
Evelyn 1915-1957 NewM
George F 1907- Fair
Harry Deweary h/o N P 18 Nov 1898-9May 1963 Edge
Henry L (h/o N D) 25 Apr 1905- Onan
Herman E 1890-1982 Onan
Ira Billington 6 Dec 1816-10 Apr 1886 Bayb
Jennings Hubard 9 Apr-5 Aug 1885 Onan
Jessie M 1910- Fair
John A h/o M E 1887-1952 Park
John Berkley s/o Rev Jno & Henrietta d 21 Oct 1856; age: 1/0/24 Coke
John D 1862-1946 Onan
L Fletcher h/o N V 1878-1943 Libe
Larry B 1939-1981 Fair
Luther T h/o N C 1888-1973 Onan
Margaret E w/o J A 1895-1971 Park
Margaret M 1902-1977 Edge

ALLEN (continued)
Marie E 1906- Onan
Mary E w/o Wm R 31 Aug 1857-30 Aug 1947 Edge
Mildred M w/o W L 1903- Edge
Missouri J 30 Aug 1862-13 Sept 1910 Onan
Myrtle W w/o S B 1906- Park
Nancy C (w/o L T) 1889- Onan
Naomi D w/o H L 17 Aug 1905-22 Nov 1980 Onan
Nellie Parramore w/o H D 18 Aug 1907-7 Nov 1958 Edge
Nora V w/o L F 1889-1942 Libe
Ray 1888-1945 Onan
Robert T 17 Jan 1925-25 Sept 1975 Fair
Rose W 1869-1934 Edge
Sallie E w/o Thos; d/o Henry & Mary Saulsbury 26 Feb 1870-23 Mar 1893 Onan
Sarah C w/o W W 3 Mar 1865-17 Jan 1928 Park
Stephen B h/o M W 1905-1964 Park
Tryphena E d/o Rev Jno & Henrietta d 28 Oct 1856; age: 3/3/0 Coke
Vernon 1926-1977 HTri
W W h/o S C 16 Mar 1859-28 Apr 1915 Park
William d 29 May 1969; age: 59 yrs StLu
William B h/o J M; s/o Jas & M E 12 May 1850-9 June 1912 Wach
William L h/o M M 1894-1971 Edge
William R h/o M E 7 July 1859-23 Mar 1942 Edge
Willie C (h/o A L) 1891-1963 Fair

AMBLER, Betty Custis d 1922 MtCu

AMES, - child/o Jas F & S S d 10 Aug 1843 TheG
- s/o L O & Lillie S 9 Feb-12 Mar 1899 StGe
- d/o Warner & E F 22-25 Feb 1909 MtHo
A M w/o S M 19 Dec 1802-10 Aug 1833 Ames

AMES (continued)
Albertine K 18 Sept 1893- StGe
Alexander 15 May 1852-24 June 1904; age: 52/1/9 Gask-old
Alfred O d 19 Oct 1962; age: 76 yrs Gask
Annie Edmonds w/o S W; d/o Benj W & Emma S (Mapp) Mears 28 Oct 1865-5 Oct 1956 StGe
Annie P d/o Leonard H & Jennie S 10 Dec 1864-28 Oct 1866 Joyn
Annie Thomas 1870-1922 StGe
Aratha J d/o Jas F & S S d 15 May 1843; age: 1/8/10 TheG
Benjamin F s/o J F & M S 6 July 1843-2 May 1914 MtHo
Rev Benjamin Thomas h/o J A 7 Jan 1821-27 Sept 1881 MtHo
B(etsey) w/o S M d 14 Oct 1825 Ames
little Catherine nd StGe
Chancie L 5 June 1895-29 July 1960 StPa
Chancie L 5 Jan 1920-16 June 1963 Gask
Charles H 26 Nov 1858-10 Aug 1917 StGe
Charlie Tankered s/o J F & M S 25 Sept 1865-1 Mar 1870 MtHo
Christine 1898-1968 StPa
Cordelia 31 July 1876-5 Aug 1924 HTri
Earl S 1936-1980 Gask
Edward Almer h/o L E T 1856-1939 MtHo
Edward H s/o Benj H & Nancy 19 Oct 1806-4 Mar 1864 Expe
Effa Julia d/o J F & M S 27 Oct 1858-10 Feb 1862 MtHo
Elijah M h/o V E 14 June 1845-30 Dec 1915 StGe
Ella 1866-1951 Wach
Ella E 1871-1944 StGe
Elsie M (w/o J R) 15 May 1881-29 Sept 1968 StJo
Emma S 1905-1983 Gask
Ethel w/o Warner; d/o Dr E B & V B Finney 2 Oct 1881-22 Feb 1909 MtHo
Eva S 1878-1972 MtNe

AMES (continued)
Eva V d/o E M & V E 3 July 1876–29 Aug 1916 StGe
Floyd T h/o O S 15 Nov 1896–20 Feb 1972 MtHo
Frances Fletcher 28 May 1900–13 May 1982 Edge
Garland s/o A W & Nottie A 25 Mar 1885–16 June 1887 Powe
George d 10 Feb 1963; age: 75 yrs Gask-old
George 1889–1967 Quin
George L, MD 3 Sept 1867–28 July 1902 StGe
George R 1908–1978 Gask
George T d 9 July 1873; age: 31/3/10 AmeH
George T 1 Nov 1902–2 July 1978 NewM
Georgia T 4 June 1857–18 July 1881 Syca
Glenwood 1911–1982 Gask
Gracie W 1911–1979 Burt
Helen Margt Reed (w/o O K) 2 Nov 1907– Fair
Herbert G 1900–1965 StGe
Hilda Mae 1906–1955 JoyC
Howard S 1919–1968 Shil
Isabella S w/o Jos B; d/o Zadok & Sallie Ames 4 Apr 1841–22 July 1898 AmeG
J Robert s/o J R & E M 4 July 1910–7 Mar 1972 StJo
Jack 1903–1962 Wach
James J S s/o S M & A M 15 June 1828–20 Oct 1833 Ames
James P 19 July 1858–21 Aug 1887 Thor
James S 19 Jan 1828–7 May 1895 Thor
Jesse R (h/o E M) 15 May 1880–1 Nov 1952 StJo
John A h/o P G d 6 Aug 1843; age: 50/8/28 MtHo
John F h/o M S 5 Mar 1819–26 Apr 1887; age: 68/1/21 MtHo
John H h/o M T 19 Jan 1845–22 Apr 1885; age: 40/3/3 Mt Ho
John Henry s/o J H & M T 8 Dec 1882–22 July 1883 MtHo
Joseph F s/o Benj & Nancy 2 Apr 1818–15 Oct 1850 (leaving

AMES (continued)
a widow & 2 children) TheG
Julia Ann w/o Rev B T 20 Oct 1825–21 June 1912 MtHo
Juliet Grace Heath w/o R T 1855–1932 MtHo
Junious nd Gask
Laura J d 26 Apr 1938; age: 26 yrs Burt
Lecretia 1889–1975 Burt
Lena Elva Trower w/o E A 1871–1952 MtHo
Leonard H 26 Sept 1831–19 Dec 1912 StGe
Leonard H s/o Leomard H & Jennie S 18 Mar–26 June 1858 Joyn
Leonard O (h/o L S) 1869–1923 StGe
Levin G 1872–1919 StGe
Levin J h/o R C P 1849–1922 MtHo
Lillian S (w/o L O) 1868–1948 StGe
Lillie T 1892–1979 Shil
Louis s/o Leonard H & Jennie S 6 May–30 Aug 1875 Joyn
Louisa Taylor w/o R T 15 Sept 1822–8 June 1912 Syca
Mamie d 11 Jan 1962; age: 72 yrs Snea
Margaret w/o Richd d 31 May 1834; age: 52 yrs Amep
Margaret w/o Levin S 14 May 1811–23 Sept 1863 AmeH
Margaret 1891–1962 Gask
Margaret Hylda 11 Feb 1899–10 Feb 1981 MtHo
Margaret S w/o J F 19 July 1822–26 Feb 1894; age: 71/7/7 MtHo
Mary B 1908–1959 Shil
Mary Collins w/o Robt 20 Oct 1916–3 Aug 1937 Gask-old
Mary E 10 June 1860–28 June 1923 Gask-old
Mary Kate 1905–1979 NewM
Mary S 1923–1964 Gask
Mary T w/o J H 29 Aug 1848–29 Dec 1923 MtHo
May E d/o Leonard H & Jennie S 28 Feb 1880–28 May 1881 Joyn

AMES (continued)
Olive Smith w/o F T d 30 Jan 1958 MtHo
Orris S 12 Mar 1868-21 Sept 1937 MtHo
Orvis Kingsley (h/o H M R) 28 Dec 1893-20 Feb 1974 Fair
Polly G w/o J A d 20 Nov 1841; age: 42/20/17 MtHo
Rachel nd Gask
Ralph T 15 Jan 1896-3 Apr 1965 NewM
Richard h/o Margt 11 Apr 1776-20 Nov 1834 Amep
Richard F 24 Mar 1834-13 Aug 1915; age: 81/4/20 (Confederate soldier) Amep
Richard T h/o L T 10 May 1819-28 Apr 1883 Syca
Richard T h/o J G H 1848-1922 MtHo
Richard W h/o S E 9 July 1827-26 Mar 1899 Edge
Roosevelt 1924-1962 Gask
Rosa F d 1 Feb 1939; age: 20 yrs NewM
Rossie L 1928-1963 Gask
Roxanna C Parker w/o L J 1858-1922 MtHo
Roy b&d 1980 Metr
Sallie J 1884-1946 StJo
Samuel H 1890-1956 Snea
Samuel Hall s/o Saml W & Annie (Mears) 12 June 1890-19 Apr 1891 Mear
Samuel Williams h/o A E; s/o Leonard Hall & Virginia S Joynes Ames 25 Aug 1862-29 Apr 1940 StGe
Sarah d/o R W & S E d 3 June 1851; age: 1/6/25 Edge
Sarah E d/o J A & P G d 26 Jan 1838; age: 20/10/13 MtHo
Sarah S w/o Jas F d 11 Nov 1843; age: 23/4/30 TheG
Shadrack M (h/o B & A M); s/o Thos & Tabitha 21 Apr 1781-30 Jan 183(5?) Ames
Sidney 1891- Snea
Stanley D 1 Dec 1890-1 Aug 1968 StGe
Stewart 1906-1975 StJo

AMES (continued)
Stran E 1880-1948 StJo
Susan E w/o R W 18 Sept 1825-25 May 1904 Edge
Susie M d/o S W & A E 10 Jan 1888-30 July 1969 StGe
Thomas Robert Howland s/o O K & H M R 22 Feb 1930- Fair
Vandalia E w/o E M 21 Oct 1846-13 Jan 1929 StGe
Virginia H w/o WmE 5 Aug 1865-15 Sept 1899 (moved from Burckard bur gr) Onan
Virginia S 23 Dec 1839-3 Oct 1913 StGe
W H s/o S M & Betsey 5 Apr 1812-22 Mar 1855 Ames
Walton E 1908-1971 Snea
Warner h/o E F; s/o R T & J G H 25 Mar 1879-7 Apr 1938 MtHo
William 1853-1934 Wach
William 1894-1959 Burt
Rev William F d 18 Oct 1852; age: 20/6/16 (in the 2nd yr of his ministry) Coke
William K d 8 Aug 1923; age: 59 yrs StJo
Willie LeCato 1864-1946 Burt
ANCARROW, James R 1895-1952 MtHo
ANDERSON, Earl H h/o P A Stitely 1902-1931 Libe
Ezekiel 1902-1970 JoyC
Mary L 7 Mar 1915-20 Apr 1966 JoyC
S D 3 Apr 1894-12 July 1956 Snea
Samuel 1887-1977 JoyC
Sylvanus 1916-1969 JoyC
William d 10 Feb 1963; age: 64 yrs JoyC
ANDREWS, Anna Maria 30 Nov 1738-13 Feb 1815 Parp
Flora I w/o M F 1884-1951 Libe
Jacob h/o Margt 8 Nov 1701-21 Feb 1770 Sylv
Lottie E w/o Wm J 1869-1940 Libe
Margaret T (nee Joynes) 11 Nov 1724-29 Sept 1784 Sylv
Mullineau F h/o F I 1876-1943

ANDREWS (continued)
Libe
Robert 24 Apr 1761-14 Feb 1803 Parp
Ruth E 1897-1964 Libe
William 26 Aug 1733-4 Apr 1777 Parp
William J h/o L E 1865-1946 Libe
ANNIS, - 2 inf daus & inf s/o W S & B B nd Park
Alma S 1918- Park
Archie J h/o L M 1900-1942 Park
Bertie B w/o W S 1891-1979 Park
Bertie S 1894-1946 Libe
Christie L 29 Jan 1922-6 Sept 1982 Libe
Daisey Ewell 1885-1905 Park
Delia T w/o G D 1910-1981 Park
Elizabeth M w/o H D 1899- Park
Forrest 6 Apr 1909-10 Aug 1982 Libe
Fred V 1915-1961 Libe
G Dewey h/o D T 1898-1968 Park
Harold D h/o E M 1894-1976 Park
Harvey 1894- Park
Irene 1925-1984 Libe
J William h/o M J 1875- Park
John D s/o J S & M G W 22 Feb 1902-25 Jan 1957 Libe
John Savage h/o M G W 13 Aug 1876-29 Nov 1911 Libe
Lane C h/o M S 1889-1977 Park
Laura Mable d/o Sylvestor F & Shirley F b&d 24 Dec 1969 Libe
Lillian S 11 May 1912-26 Oct 1979 (photo on marker) Wach
Lillie M w/o A J 1900- Park
Margaret J w/o J Wm 1877-1923 Park
Mary Ann 26 July 1837-31 Dec 1916 (erected by one to whom she was more than a mother. Geo A Sturgis) Park
Mary C 1891-1938 Park
Melisha G Wessells w/o J S 11 Mar 1883-28 Oct 1973 Libe

ANNIS (continued)
Merrill L 12 June 1916-22 Mar 1945 Park
Minerva S w/o L C 1899-1954 Park
Mitchell 2 Nov 1924-19 Apr 1982 Libe
Paul D 1913-1980 Park
Ruth E 1901-1928 Libe
Ruth T 1901-1976 Park
Samuel J 1884-1969 Park
Sherwood T 1928-1956 Park
Vernon 1892-1970 Libe
Warren S h/o B B 1882-1965 Park
Will Roy 1904-1941 Park
Willard T 1930-1949 Park
ANTHONY, Anna w/o Louis 1876-1954 Quin
Dorothy W (w/o G W) 1911- Quin
George W (h/o D W) 1912-1979 Quin
James Henry 1885-1956 NewM
Louis h/o Anna 1870-1939 Quin
Maude Parks 1906-1977 Park
ARBUCKLE, Edward 15 Mar 1829-10 Nov 1889 StGe
Margaret B 26 June 1829-17 May 1894 StGe
ARLINGTON, John s/o Jno & Sophia 10 Aug 1800-17 Jan 1851; age: 50/5/7 Arli
John (b Wm W Finney) 26 Dec 1820-28 Oct 1887 Arli
John T F s/o Jno & Mary S 30 Jan 1869-5 Oct 1871 Arli
Mary d/o Jno & Mary S 24 Aug 1862-26 Sept 1867 Arli
ARMISTEAD, Andrew D 29 July 1835-9 Feb 1897 StGe
ARRIGO, Elizabeth 1901-1966 Park
ARTHUR, Robert Peebles 3 July 1892-28 Oct 1923 MtHo-s
ASGOOD, Georgianna 1904-1966 Shil
ASHBY, Alice T w/o Wm; d/o Joshua & Polly Burton d 27 Sept 1848; age: 19/1/19 Brad
Albert G w/o E A 9 Aug 1811-17 May 1889 Powe

ASHBY (continued)
Anna M 1897-1978 Shil
B Stuart 22 May 1890-4 Oct 1918 Edge
Bailey S h/o L C 1857-1940 Edge
Elizabeth w/o Jas & d/o Ruben Joynes d 17 July 1824; age: 49 yrs Hero
Elizabeth d 16 Sept 1834; age: 15 yrs OldA
Elizabeth A w/o A G d 23 Sept 1835; age: 20/2/8 Powe
Esther Belle w/o A G 18 Aug 1824-23 Mar 1896 Powe
Herbert nd Burt
Howard J (h/o S V) 22 Nov 1907- MtHo
James d 10 Jan 1857; age: 70 yrs Hero
Joseph 1929-1968 Shil
Joseph Lee 1936-1976 Fair
Lizzie C w/o B S 1860-1921 Edge
Maggie E d/o R C & N E 13 Dec 1874-29 July 1892 MtHo
Margaret w/o Thos 1 Oct 1777-7 May 1837; age: 60 yrs Wacb
Margaret & her inf child; w/o Geo; d/o Bartholomew & Patience Taylor 6 Feb 1784-28 Apr 1824 Trad
Margaret d 1 Aug 1830; age: 41 yrs OldA
Martha 1914-1933 Edge
Mary d 15 Aug 1817; age: 32 yrs OldA
Matilda w/o Jas; d/o Peter Hack d 31 July 1819; age: 78 yrs Hero
Minnie K 1911-1977 Snea
Nonie P 1891-1968 Burt
Norvilla E w/o Robt C 2 Sept 1846-8 Nov 1883 MtHo
Pierce s/o B S & L C 9 May 1892-11 Oct 1955 Edge
Richard T s/o R C & N E 4 July 1870-21 Sept 1871 MtHo
Rose(y? - letter broken) d 2 July 1840; age: 50/0/0 Coke
Rozety 7 Mar 1800-11 Mar 1844 Wacb

ASHBY (continued)
Ruth 1921-1977 HTri
Sally V (w/o H J) (nee Phillips) 20 July 1906-12 Nov 1967 MtHo
Sarah w/o Jas; d/o Chas Bayly d 20 Jan 1833 Hero
Sarah A C 29 Jan 1817-11 Mar 1901 OldA
Sarah T 1882-1931 Edge
Thomas 26 Dec 1771-29 Nov 1856 Wacb
Willie C 1909-1970 Snea
ASHMEAD, J W 1853-1925 StGe
ASHWORTH, Melton F Sr h/o M C 1913-1979 Edge
Mildred C w/o M F Sr 1911-1971 Edge
ASKEW, Martin Cecil 28 Jan 1955-26 May 1974 Fair
ATKINS, CharlesH 26 Aug 1838-26 Apr 1911; age: 72/8/0 Onan
ATKINSON, - s/o J G & M B 15 Sept-24 Sept 1910 Holl
Eunice G (w/o W T) 1888-1965 MtHo-s
Herman Arthur 15 Apr 1908-27 Aug 1932 StGe
Rev John 13 Aug 1820-24 Dec 1899 Onan
John Glen (h/o M B) 1876-1945 Holl
Mollie B (w/o J G) 1875-1966 Holl
Sarah F d/o W P & Eva Mae 1943-1945 Holl
Sarah Frances d/o J G & M B 25 Oct 1903-25 Dec 1916 Holl
Wm T (h/o E G) 1883-1945 MtHo-s
AUTH, Elizabeth M w/o J W 12 Aug 1912-4 Feb 1984 Libe
Jack W h/o E M 8 Aug 1906 Libe
AYDELOTTE, Alvin J (h/o J A) 1877-1948 Quin
Edward J (h/o G D) 1903-1960 Fair
Gladys D (w/o E J) 1908 Fair
Julia A (w/o A J) 1883-1947 Quin
AYRES, - inf/o C T & B J nd

AYRES (continued)
Onan
- inf/o J E F & B U nd Libe
Alfred 1935-1983 Gask
Alfred G 18 Feb 1883-16 Dec 1956 Edge
Alice J 1905-1983 Gask
Alma L w/o J F 6 Jan 1920- Libe
Andrew D (h/o E V) 15 Sept 1874-30 Nov 1937 MtHo-s
Andrew D h/o E J 1901-1966 Fair
Benjamin Thomas s/o L R & S M 1858-1862 Gunt
Bertha B (w/o G W) 1871-1939 Onan
Bertha M (w/o C G) 1893-1974 Fair
Bessie 1916-1984 Libe
Bessie D 1898-1983 Ayre
Bettie Upshur w/o J E F 17 Apr 1862-3 May 1925 Libe
Beulah J w/o C T 1879-1947 Onan
Bobby Lee 31 Mar-20 Oct 1944 Libe
Bobby Lee 29 Aug 1945-26 Sept 1946 Libe
Brooks M 20 Aug 1919-18 Apr 1969 Fair
Carrie 1888-1975 NewM
Charles R 31 Jan 1866-6 Sept 1936 MtHo
Charles T h/o B J 1870-1959 Onan
Charles T h/o S T 1887- MtHo-s
Charles U 31 Jan 1878-28 Sept 1947 Edge
Charlie G (h/o B M) 1886-1960 Fair
Charlotte C 1922-1980 Ayre
Clifton 1828-1971 JoyC
Daisy C d/o R S & E A 1869-1955 StGe
Denise D 1952-1953 Ayre
Edmund h/o Kasiah Johnson d Jan 1834 (see Whitelaw:986) Ayrm
Edna J w/o A D 1908- Fair
Edward J h/o M P 1870-1941 Edge

AYRES (continued)
Edward T h/o M S 20 Apr 1860-2 Apr 1912 Onan
Eliza J w/o L D 1 Mar 1837-3 Dec 1909 MtHo
Elizabeth A (w/o R S) d 26 Dec 1904; age: 74 yrs StGe
Ella Jane Elizabeth 1862-1895 StGe
Elsie T (w/o L W) 1906-1979 Fair
Elton 25 Apr 1895-3 Oct 1964 NewM
Ernest T 1924-1979 Ayre
Estella V (w/o A D) 1 Oct 1877-27 Apr 1954 MtHo-s
Evelyn d/o C T & B J 5 Sept 1910-1 Mar 1920 Onan
Everett J s/o J L & H S 27 July 1884-30 Aug 1885 (moved from Hollies) Fair
Fairy d Sept 19?? (last 2 numerals are missing from stone); age: 29 yrs NewM
Florence H 1882-1945 Edge
Frances R 4 Sept 1831-15 Sept 1908 Wats
Frank s/o Edwd & Mary 26 Sept 1880-15 June 1899 Onan
Franklin 1914-1983 Libe
George 1884-1945 MtHo-s
George W (h/o B B) 1867-1952 Onan
Georgie E (w/o L O) 27 Mar 1874-28 Feb 1946 MtHo
Georgie Lee 1892-1968 Onan
Harriet Wilkins Derby 8 Feb 1883-10 Jan 1961 Edge
Hattie S w/o J L 10 Feb 1860-9 July 1924 Fair
Helen Adams d 7 Feb 1901 StGe
Irma B 1926-1955 NewM
J Fulton h/o A L 24 Sept 1916- Libe
Jacob L h/o H S 23 June 1849-19 Sept 1923 Fair
James E h/o A A 1884-1953 Park
Rev James E F h/o B U 18 Aug 1854-19 June 1934 Libe
James Edward s/o Jno R & Mary A 8 Sept 1897-2 Sept 1898

AYRES (continued)
Crad
James H 1884-1940 Ayre
James K 19 Oct 1833-10 Apr 1917 StGe
James W 1894-1964 NewM
John h/o Mary Hill dc1702 (see Whitelaw:986) Ayrm
John Cropper s/o J H & M C D 30 Dec 1899-5 Jan 1926 Edge
Dr John Hack h/o M C D 12 July 1865-8 Dec 1932 Edge
John Hack II s/o B D & N B 28 Dec 1930-25 Jan 1931 Edge
John Henry 2 June 1903-18 July 1982 Gask
John T s/o T R & S A 3 Nov 1854-8 Aug 1879 Onan
John T s/o Littleton D & Eliza J 15 Dec 1866 (56?)-19 Apr 1892 MtHo-s
John T d1959 NewM
John W 26 Nov 1857-26 June 1905 StJo
John William Gillet h/o M L B; s/o Jas Kellam & Sally Upshur Hack Ayres 1865-1940 Onan
Leah W May 1799-Feb 1882 StGe
Lee Roy 1905-1973 Libe
Lelia T w/o P J 1921- Libe
Lester Paul s/o C C & Bertha B 21 Nov 1909-15 Mar 1910 Onan
Levin R (h/o S M) 16 Jan 1819-30 Dec 1891; age: 72/0/16 Gunt
Levin R h/o M F 1862-1944 Libe
Littleton D h/o E J 6 Aug 1833-18 Apr 1907 MtHo
Lloyd W (h/o E T) 1907-1979 Fair
Lola 1896-1980 NewM
Lottie B w/o R L 19 Feb 1894-6 Oct 1969 Libe
Loudry O (h/o G E) 19 Aug 1872-15 Dec 1934 MtHo
Louise 1892-1967 NewM
Lula C w/o R L 1886-1963 Libe
Luvenia 1945-1960 NewM
Mamie P w/o E J 1882-1956 Edge
Manie S w/o E T 21 Oct 1865-7

AYRES (continued)
June 1890 Onan
Mary Adair 1 July 1831-26 Mar 1918 Edge
Mary Charlotte Derby w/o J H 21 Feb 1874-1 Aug 1967 Edge
Mary F w/o L R 1874-1947 Libe
Mary Gillet d/o J W G & M L B 24 Feb 1900-6 Dec 1903 Onan
Mary H d/o T R & S A 9 Dec 1864-1 Jan 1865 Onan
Mary Louis w/o J W G; d/o Henry & Adelaide (Rogers) Battaile 1866-1941 Onan
Mary R d/o Jno R & Mary A 4 Mar 1885-9 Mar 1887 Crad
Mildred B 26 May 1893-6 Sept 1980 Edge
Minnie B d/o E T & M S 21 Oct 1889-1 Jan 1892 Onan
Nancy w/o Thos 15 Oct 1792-17 Aug 1874 Onan
Odie Anna w/o J E 1890-1953 Park
Olin T 1893-1908 Onan
Page Bradford 22 May 1922-1 Jan 1971 Libe
Percy Carroll 14 Sept 1896-25 Sept 1973 StGe
Phoebe B w/o W S 1881-1928 Edge
Polly 13 May 1823-13 July 1876 (unable to verify) Mist
Prentis J h/o L T 1917-1977 Libe
R J Feb 1801-Feb 1872 StGe
Rachael 1900-1980 NewM
Richard S (h/o E A); s/o Jno & Margt 16 Mar 1833-17 Jan 1885 StGe
Richard W 1874-1932 Edge
Rodgers L h/o L B 7 Mar 1893-7 Oct 1948 Libe
Rosa D d/o Jno R & Mary A 9 Oct 1894-28 June 1896 Crad
Roy Lee h/o L C 1885-1953 Libe
Ruth Wessells w/o T C 1893-1968 Libe
Sallie d 26 Jan 1953 NewM
Sallie T w/o C T 1890-1978 MtHo-s
Sarah A w/o T R 25 Dec 1828-17

AYRES (continued)
June 1919 Onan
Sarah F w/o W J 2 Nov 1840-23 Oct 1933 Edge
Susan M w/o L R 10 Aug 1833-5 Jan 1913 Gunt
Thomas h/o Nancy 27 Mar 1792-20 Sept 1855 Onan
Thomas C h/o R W 1895-1954 Libe
Thomas R h/o S A 4 Feb 1818-18 Sept 1892 Onan
Thomas Stockley 10 Oct 1888-18 Mar 1949 Fair
Upshur 1881-1967 StJo
Ursula T d/o T R & S A 18 Apr-18 May 1873 Onan
William H s/o T R & S A 28 Nov 1859-7 Nov 1861 Onan
William J h/o S F 31 Dec 1831-20 July 1901; age: 69/6/19 Edge
William S s/o W S & P B 1910-1934 Edge
William Samuel Sr h/o P B 1 Sept 1866-3 Apr 1919 Edge
William Samuel Jr s/o W S & P A 28 Mar 1909-11 Mar 1910 Edge
Willie Clay d 22 Novd 1940 StGe
Wilmer Adams s/o P C & H A 9 Feb 1927-21 Feb 1937 StGe
B, L B footstone only Holl
BADGER, s/o L F & A J d 1 Oct 1907; age: 0/0/6 Quin
Anna Hallett d/o T H & Anna V 1 Aug 1941-19 July 1943 MtHo
Anna Vaughan 8 June 1906-9 Mar 1975 MtHo
Arenia w/o Isaac d 12 Oct 1891; age: 55 yrs StPa
Arinthia J w/o L F 26 Mar 1879-30 Jan 1964 Quin
Daniel James s/o L F & A J 3 Sept 1912-5 Sept 1981 Quin
Doris L w/o I H; d/o Oveless E & Bernice (Thomas) Ewell 2 Sept 1913-19 May 1977 Quin
Ire Love 9 Oct 1914-4 Jan 1971 MtHo-s
Isaiah H (h/o D L) 1909-1981 Quin

BADGER (continued)
L Joses 17 May 1916-1932 Quin
Levin & Elizabeth, his wife (unable to read) Quin
Levin F h/o A J 9 Mar 1871-11 Dec 1936 Quin
Margaret A d/o Wm S & Rosa 14 June 1819-6 Mar 1844; age 24/8/22 Mart
Mary w/o Nathl; d/o Thomas & Letty Robins 8 Oct 1784-11 May 1831; age: 46/7/3 Badg
Mary L 22 Dec 1829-12 Jan 1903 BadS
Nathaniel h/o Mary 21Oct 1777-19 Jan 1846; age: 69yrs Badg
Paul A s/o L F & A J 10 Sept 1911-22 May 1928 Quin
BAGGE, Samuel d 9 Oct 1774; age: 47 yrs Bagg
BAGWELL, Annie H w/o E T 1879-1960 Edge
Christina w/o Isacah; d/o Andrew Newton & Cathrine (Goldie) of Scotland 29 Oct 1758-11 July 1839 Bagw
Dorothy J w/o H W 1903-1979 Park
Gen Edmund R (CSA; member VA Legislature; VA Commissioner at Phila Centennial Exh) 2 June 1840-13 June 1876 Bagm
Edmund Robinson h/o M D 2 June 1840-13 June 1876 MtHo
Edward T h/o A H 1878-1950 Edge
Eugenia Taylor 1894- MtHo
Gara W w/o J N 10 Dec 1874-26 Jan 1942 MtHo
George P 1891-1982 MtNe
Harold W h/o D J 1892-1968 Park
I William II 1881-1954 MtHo
Isaiah s/o Isaiah & Sarah 13 Sept 1760-8 Oct 1839 Bagw
Col Isaiah N d 17 Sept 1862; age: 49/11/8 MtHo
Isaiah William h/o S R 23 Jan 1855-22 June 1905 MtHo
J Newton h/o G W 8 July 1877-9 Feb 1947 MtHo

BAGWELL (continued)
James T 11 Dec 1925-18 July 1974 MtNe
Josephine B w/o P S 1902-1982 Edge
Julius N Jr 1932-1960 Gask
Leah H w/o I N 29 Oct 1815-21 Apr 1890 MtHo
Margaret Douglas w/o E R 30 Jan 1846-14 Sept 1916 MtHo
Margaret F 1848-1949 MtNe(E)
Margaret G w/o Wm; d/o Abel & R Gascins Teackle 26 May 1793-3 Dec 1864 Bagw
Oscar H 1908-1937 Libe
Preston S h/o J B 1901-1957 Edge
Roberta 1912-1980 MtNe
Roscoe Lee 17 Apr 1896-29 Sept 1971 Bagc
Rosey S w/o I N; d/o Jno B & Rosey D Revill 21 July 1819-7 Jan 1842 MtHo
Roy h/o Mary T 1908-1978 Gask
Sally Hamilton (Wise) w/o Thos P 1804-1887 Scot
Sarah R w/o I W; d/o Jas & Annie B Edwards 16 Feb 1859-2 Aug 1918 MtHo
Thomas Poulson 1805-1866 Scot
Vernon H Sr h/o Annie 1881-1964 Bagc
William h/o M G; s/o Isaiah & Christina 7 Dec 1790-26 Dec 1841 Bagw
William Samuel s/o I N & R S 3 Nov 1841-3 July 1842 MtHo

BAILEY (BALEY, BAYLEY, BAYLY)
- d 1964 JoyC
baby b&d 1975 Bail
Abel Powell s/o E J & P E J P 5 Jan 1840-18 Sept 1843 Herm
Addie Lee 1913-1972 Burt
Alberta d 9 May 1964; age: 78 yrs JoyC
Alma C w/o J H 1907- HTri
Ann w/o Thos; d/o Richd Drummond (see Whitelaw:980 for her ancestry) 26 Feb 1742/3-8 Sept 1801 On her left lies her Father, Sister & 6 of her

BAILEY (continued)
children. Her 2nd son was lost at sea. She left 3 sons and 2 daus Hill
Anne May d/o T H & E H M 1840-1860 MtCu
Annie (w/o Dulaney) 1898- Onan
Annie w/o Moses d1951 Bail
Ben 1875-1955 Snea
Bertie V 1898-1967 Shil
Carrie J 1896-1981 MtHo-s
Catherine C w/o Wm P; d/o Dr Jno R & Elizabeth E Wise 15 Nov 1831-4 Apr 1860; age: 28/4/20 Kell
Charles E h/o L M 1880-1948 Park
Col Charles H s/o Jno J & Sally 9 Feb 1817-16 Jan 1855 Whit
Charlotte 2 Mar 1785-18 July 1871 OldW
Claude 1900-1975 Bail
Claude W 2 Feb 1923-221 Sept 1975 Bail
Columbia 1891-1973 Gask
Desdemonia 1932-1978 JoyC
Dulaney (h/o Annie) 1889-1954 Onan
Ebbie B 1889-1979 MtHo-s
Edmund 17 Apr 1741-22 Oct 1796 Herm
Edmund s/o Thos & Ann; h/o Rachel d/o John Upshur of Northampton Co 27 Aug 1763-18 Nov 1805 Hill
Edward h/o L G 1829-1913 MtHo
Edward J s/o E J & P E J P 10 May 1837-27 Dec 1843 Herm
Egbert G (h/o M S) 1805-1896 Popl
Elizabeth Dennis d 5 Nov 1824; age: 13 yrs Bayl
Elizabeth M Boggs w/o T S 1827-1916 (moved from Bayley bur gr) Onan
Ellen Lilliston w/o J J Sr 29 Nov 1872-16 Feb 1951 MtHo
Emma 1910-1960 Snea
Emma K w/o T J 1890-1952 Onan
Esther Burton d/o Thos & Mary Parramore 27 Dec 1798-12 Feb

BAILEY (continued)
1821 Bell
Evelyn Harrison May w/o T H; d/o Judge Jno Fitzhugh & Margt Field May 6 June 1819-10 Sept 1897 MtCu
Fannie 1915-1982 MtNe
Florence C 3 May 1892-29 Nov 1965 MtHo-s
George P 30 Sept 1902-11 Nov 1909 MtHo
George Thomas 30 May 1896-31 Mar 1963 Gask
Georgie C d/o T S & E M B 27 Jan 1864-12 June 1951 Onan
Grace James 1889-1970 MtHo
Harriet d 30 June 1900 Shil
Henry Custis eldest s/o Col T M & M P C 26 Dec 1802-8 Oct 1821 (erected by his bro Thos H Bayly) MtCu
Henry D 1897-1960 Shil
Holly 1896-1952 Burt
Jacob Jr 1928-1971 Bail
Jacob M 1899-1981 Bail
James 1870-1954 JoyC
James E 1905-1954 Fair
James H 28 Dec 1838-20 Jan 1916 Bayg
James H h/o A C 1906-1977 HTri
James Henry s/o T S & E M B 1857-1919 Onan
James S s/o Ralph & Fannie 1910-1911 Onan
Jennie A 1883-1952 NewM
Jennie S 18 Dec 1873-15 June 1912 Bayg
John h/o Mary Ann d 7 July 1913; age: 74 yrs Shil
John 1958-1979 Bail
John J Jr 1908-1952 MtHo
John Justis Sr h/o E L 2 Sept 1986-25 Dec 1940 MtHo
John T d 26 Jan 1925; age: 52 yrs Shil
John W 14 July 1881-20 Apr 1912 Snea
John W 1894-1932 MtHo-s
John W 1917-1976 HTri
Johnie 1892-1970 Burt
Johnnie 1914-1982 MtNe

BAILEY (continued)
Joshua T 1919-1970 NewM
Josiah L s/o Jas H & Mary E 11 Oct 1862-1 Aug 1894; age: 31/9/20 Bayg
Lillian 1 Dec 1888-22 Mar 1971 Fair
Lillie M w/o G E 1897- Park
Lola M 1900-1962 NewM
Lovey G w/o Edwd 1830-1900 MtHo
Magdalene 1898-1964 Gask
Maggie 1898-1954 HTri
Margaret w/o Wallace d 18 July 1893; age: c57 yrs Shil
Margaret McMath (w/o W H) 5 Apr 1907- Onan
Margaret Pettit Cropper 1st w/o Col T M; d/o Gen Jno & Margt Pettit Cropper 15 May 1784-3 Dec 1824 leaving 2 sons & 4 daughters by whom this stone is erected MtCu
Margaret S 1st w/o E G 17 May 1808-25 Mar 1870 Popl
Margaret S 1906-1978 HTri
Margie Ann 1880-1969 StPa
Margie H 1885-1939 MtHo
Martha d 31 May 1966; age 70 yrs Burt
Mary Caroline d/o Chas H & Edna 23 Jan 1852-19 July 1855 Whit
Mary E 1855-1904 JoyC
Mary Susan (w/o P H) 1837-31 Mar 1908 Baig
Minnie Ames Kellam 26 Apr 1871-17 Dec 1936 MtHo
Moses h/o Annie d1939 Bail
Myrtle 1900-1971 Gask
Nina Revell 1886-1961 MtHo
Obedia d 17 Nov 1958; age: 74 yrs JoyC
Oscar 1890-1976 Gask
Oscar Jr 1918-1959 Gask
Otho 1904-1970 JoyC
Otis Lee 1946-1965 HTri
Pansy G w/o Jno; d/o Elsie G Turner 1903-1978 MtNe(E)
Pearl Upshur 3 Feb 1894-5 Oct 1974 Bail
Peter H (h/o M S) 27 Oct 1837-8

BAILEY (continued)
May 1903 Baig
Miss Polly 1793-4 June 1870 Ross
Purnell E 22 May 1913-20 Nov 1967 Gask
Rachel U d 14 Sept 1832; age: 17 yrs Bayl
Ralph 1936-1958 JoyC
Richard D d 28 Jun 1828; age: 17/8/16 Bayl
Richard D d 29 Aug 1836; age: 8 yrs Bayl
Ruben 1924-1955 Burt
Sadie P 22 Aug 1848-24 Aug 1914 Edge
Sally D w/o Richd D 5 Mar 1784-1 Mar 1865 Bayl
Samuel L 29 Jan 1924-15 Apr 1973 Bail
Samuel S 4 Sept 1872-12 May 1948 MtHo-s
Sarah 1920-1968 Neda
Spenser 1900-1968 JoyC
Tasso s/o E J & P E J P 25 Mar-3 Apr 1842 Herm
Thomas h/o Ann; s/o Edmund & Rose (Fisher) Bayly; grand s/o Edmund Bayly; gr grand s/o Richard Bayly of Craddock 14 Mar 1737/8-(1808) Hill
Thomas s/o Thos W & Sarah E 13 Dec 1850-14 Mar 1893 Hedr
Thomas Henry h/o E H M; s/o Thos Monteagle & Margt Pettit (Cropper) 11 Oct 1810 at MtCu-22 June 1856 (see Whitelaw:1062) MtCu
Thomas I s/o E G & M S 19 Dec 1843-21 Dec 1862; age: 19/0/2 Popl
Thomas J h/o E K 1888-1967 Onan
Thomas J s/o T J & E K 6 May-12 Sept 1915 Onan
Col Thomas M, 3rd s/o Thos & Ann (Drummond) (see Whitelaw:982) 26 Mar 1775-7 Jan 1837 mar: 24 Mar 1809 - Margt P Cropper d/o Gen John mar 21 Dec 1826 - Jane O Addison wid/o Col Kendall Addison;

BAILEY (continued)
d/o Saml Coward Hill
Thomas S h/o E M B 1830-1886 (moved from Bayley bur gr) Onan
Thomas S h/o V L W 1867-1950 Onan
Thomas S Jr 25 Mar 1900-27 Dec 1981 Onan
V Lee Weaver w/o T S 1866-1924 Onan
Vandalia w/o Jno T 1 May 1864-25 May 1913; age: 49/0/25 Snea
Virginia T w/o Arthur R 18 Jan 1888-28 Dec 1916 HTri
W Thomas 1858-1932 MtHo
Wallace h/o Margt d 29 Aug 1893 Shil
Wallace 1897-1969 HTri
Walter Wescott 5 Apr 1893-5 Nov 1947 Bail
William 1895-1977 Gask
William H 1902-1970 Shil
William Henry (h/o M M) 2 Feb 1902 Onan
William Pettit, 5th s/o Thos M & M P C 14 June 1820-26 Aug 1848 mar - Elizabeth d/o Wm Parramore. Died leaving a daughter 4 days old; attended Wm & Mary College & Univ of VA. Was a lawyer. MtCu
Willie s/o Moses & Annie d1923 Bail
Willie Mae 1912-1977 Shil
BAITY, John B h/o L F 5 Dec 1876-28 July 1950 Edge
Louisa Fay w/o J B 14 Apr 1896- Edge
BAKER, A Lewellyn 31 Aug 1872-3 Apr 1950 Park
Betty G 1912-1979 Park
Clara 1885-1959 Park
Edward h/o L G 1876-1945 Park
Edward T h/o G P 1904- Park
G Wash 1905-1977 Park
Gertrude P w/o E T 1904- Park
Ida J 1885-1970 Park
Leonard T 1896-1950 Park
Lillie G w/o Edwd 1885-1962 Park

BAKER (continued)
Matilda 12 Nov 1800-1 Nov 1888 Park
Mattie R w/o Wm J 1878-1954 Park
Minnie C 1898-1981 Park
Nancy Cooper 1960-1980 Fair
R Ross 29 Aug 1913-22 Nov 1977 Park
Samuel Lafayette 29 Jan 1867-2 July 1939 Park
Samuel White 30 Apr 1902-8 May 1945 Park
William 1895-1969 Gask
William A 13 Apr 1840-21 Dec 1917 Park
William J h/o M R 1874-1953 Park
William T 1887-1952 Park

BALIS see also BAYLIS
John J (h/o O M) 1897-1963 StGe
Olga (w/o J J) 1897-1966 StGe

BALL, A Preston h/o M B 1910-1975 Park
Ambrose Markley h/o Thelma Bonnivil 12 July 1890-12 June 1977 Edge
Andrew F 1894-1953 Park
Arthur J h/o D P 1885-1954 Park
Dollie P w/o A J 1886-1957 Park
Mary C w/o N D 1860-1921 Park
Mollie B w/o A P 1908- Park
N Drummond h/o M C 1858-1941 Park

BALLARD, Elizabeth 1878-1962 HTri
James T 28 Jan 1878-14 Apr 1957 HTri
Lucas N 17 Mar 1924-5 Aug 1972 Shil
Walter Brooks 8 July 1922-21 Nov 1982 MtHo

BARBER, Jane T Lilliston w/o W A Sr 12 May 1911- Edge
Thelma 1927-1981 Wach
William Albert Sr h/o J T L 22 Feb 1901-8 July 1974 Edge

BARCROFT, Monnie 1894-1971 Holl

BARKER, Sarah 2nd w/o Geo W; nee Scott d 1858 Ross

BARNES, - d/o F J & Sadie D b&d 13 Oct 1903 Mori
- s/o C E & R S b&d 1920 Park
- inf/o W P & L B b&d 1937 Fair
A Frank 15 Jan 1859-21 Nov 1915 Libe
Addie W 1893-1968 Edge
Alfred B h/o R C 6 July 1877-14 Aug 1933 Park
Alfred J h/o M A 30 Sept 1835-13 Nov 1912 Park
Althea S d/o G W & E S 28 Mar 1886-17 Oct 1906 Onan
Amanda Mears (w/o E H) 1870-1951 Onan
Annie F d/o F J & Sadie D 5 Jan 1889-13 Dec 1902 Mori
Annie M 1876-1954 Onan
Arinthia J w/o A R 1848-1934 Libe
Arthur R h/o A J 1846-1925 Libe
B Carson h/o D E 1884-1951 MtHo
Beckie T w/o H P 1879-1954 Onan
Bertha J 1894-1981 Onan
Bessie M w/o R E Sr 1882-1970 Edge
Bessie M w/o G T 1888-1951 Libe
Betty S 1855-1925 Onan
Birdie (w/o Golden) 1896-1918 Onan
Blanche 1916-1982 Libe
Brooks P h/o T M 13 Oct 1904-28 Apr 1983 Park
Burnetta J w/o Wm J 1852-1941 Libe
Byron B h/o N M 1887-1953 Park
Caroline E w/o G D 7 Mar 1877-17 Feb 1937 Park
Carrie Guy 29 Dec 1891-27 Dec 1982 MtHo
Carroll 1895-1962 MtHo-s
Carson H 1893-1983 Park
Charles J h/o M E 16 Dec 1869-4 July 1930 Libe
Charlie E h/o R S 1898- Park
Clara D d/o L R & Margt d 0/1/2 (nd) Libe
Clifford L h/o F P 1885-1972

BARNES (continued)
Park
D Eva w/o B C 1883-1963 MtHo
Daisy B w/o G W 1879- Libe
Daniel Webster s/o R F & I B 1938-1939 Park
Dorothy F G 29 June 1906-25 Feb 1982 Park
E Thomas 1921-1963 Libe
Eddie b&d 1891 Libe
Edith F 1890-1960 MtHo-s
Edward H (h/o A M) 1886-1954 Onan
Elizabeth w/o Wm; d/o Jno & Eliz Garrison 4 Feb 1805-19 Sept 1867 Jame
Elizabeth S w/o O J 1870-1939 Libe
Ella Marrow w/o F J 1873-1954 Libe
Ellsworth 1891-1976 Onan
Elsie R w/o J P 1900- Park
Ethel T w/o G P Jr 8 Sept 1893-18 Oct 1961 Libe
Ethel V 1897-1981 MtHo-s
Evelyn Estelle d/o J G & M E 3 May-27 Sept 1892 Libe
Evelyn V w/o G L 1881-1954 Libe
Evaline T w/o G W 1833-1920 Libe
Everette F s/o F J & Sadie D 3 Jan-13 Jan 1896 Mori
F James II 27 Aug 1905-11 Apr 1978 Park
Fletcher 1878-1894 Libe
Fletcher J h/o E M 1867-1925 Libe
Florence P w/o C L 1891-1976 Park
Frances J w/o S L 1914- Onan
Frank J h/o S D 14 Apr 1865-1 Dec 1954 Libe
Garland F 1905-1962 Libe
Gaylon H 1894-1961 Libe
George 1842-1902 Onan
George C s/o F J & Sadie D 24 Dec-29 Oct 1900 Mori
George D h/o C E 18 Sept 1865-8 Nov 1943 Park
George F 1893-1941 MtHo-s
George G 1881-1969 Libe

BARNES (continued)
George H 1911-1980 Libe
George L h/o E V 1881-1950 Libe
George P Sr h/o V T 17 May 1861-13 May 1918 Libe
George P Jr h/o E T 3 Mar 1895-20 July 1955 Libe
George T h/o B M 1886-1959 Libe
George W h/o E T 1834-1884 Libe
George W 13 Apr 1836-1 Aug 1907 Libe
George W h/o D B 1878-1954 Libe
Golden (h/o Birdie) 1893-1918 Onan
Grover S 18 Oct 1892-23 Apr 1954 Libe
Hance L 1895-1944 Park
Hanson P (h/o B T) 1875-1943 Onan
Hanson P Jr 1909-1960 Onan
Harrison F 1905-1965 Wach
Harvey J 15 Mar 1879-30 Mar 1938 Park
Hattie C 1904-1976 MtHo-s
Herbert h/o K M 1895-1968 Park
Hettie L w/o W F 1877- MtHo-s
Irene Bloxom w/o R F 1914- Park
Iris Jane 1922-1968 Edge
Isabella T w/o Geo W; d/o Thos & Caroline Killmon 25 Feb 1854-25 Apr 1882 Kill
Isabelle Copes 21 Dec 1901-15 Apr 1969 MtHo
Isaiah T s/o Jno & Sallie 1 May 1858-8 Mar 1895 Libe
Jacob D h/o M A 1877-1940 Libe
Jacob S s/o GW & E T 14 Mar-14 Apr 1874; age: 0/1/0 Libe
James A 14 Aug 1855-18 Apr 1920 Park
James G h/o M E 24 Jan 1870-7 Jan 1954 Libe
James W 1846-1932 Libe
John h/o Sallie; s/o Arthur & Fannie 10 Nov 1809-17 Dec 1867 Libe
John h/o Sallie 25 Sept 1820-17

BARNES (continued)
Dec 1878 Libe
John Arthur 17 Apr 1899-4 Jan 1970 Libe
John B h/o M A 1 May 1845-13 Mar 1926 Libe
John Columbus h/o S J; s/o Jno & Sallie 28 Jan 1850-10 Apr 1923 Libe
John F 1875-1948 Libe
John P h/o E R 1898-1962 Park
John Riggs s/o J P & E M 1925-1943 Park
John W h/o N C 13 Oct 1878-10 May 1945 Park
John W h/o L T 27 Feb 1893-15 Oct 1954 Libe
John W Jr 13 Jan 1919-27 Aug 1977 Park
Josephine A d/o G W & E T 23 Oct 1858-10 Apr 1862; age: 3/5/17 Libe
Julia C d/o P C & N B 1909-1915 Libe
Katharine M w/o Herbert 1899-1973 Park
Laura F d/o G W & E T 14 Oct 1861-20 Dec 1874; age: 12/2/6 Libe
Leanora W 21 Dec 1889-31 Aug 1971 Onan
Leila R w/o W S 25 Aug 1891-18 Oct 1953 Park
Lemuel P h/o M N 4 Jan 1887-11 Sept 1944 Libe
Lillian T w/o J W 8 Nov 1898-9 Jan 1934 Libe
Lillie Chesser 24 Feb 1885-18 July 1983 Park
Llewellyn B w/o W P 1913- Fair
Louise B 1913-1980 Park
Louise P w/o W S 1913- Libe
Lula Bundick 1887-1967 Libe
Lydia S w/o Wm F; d/o G W & H E East 18 Sept 1865-20 June 1884 MtHo
Maggie A 1843-1933 Libe
Manie A w/o J D 1869- Libe
Manie E w/o C J 20 Feb 1872-10 June 1946 Libe
Manie J w/o O T 25 Feb 1874-12 Jan 1938 Park

BARNES (continued)
Margaret A w/o J B 8 Dec 1848- Libe
Margaret N w/o L P 17 Mar 1889-20 May 1946 Libe
Mary A w/o A J 8 Oct 1842-15 Jan 1918 Park
Mary Elizabeth 14 Nov 1918-20 Jan 1934 Libe
Mary J 1850-1926 Libe
Mary S w/o W C 4 Oct 1862-1 May 1901 MtHo
Mary W (w/o M W) 1916- Fair
May Belote 24 June 1881-30 July 1960 MtHo
Milfred W (h/o M W) 1914-1972 Fair
Minnie 1934-1969 Wach
Minnie E w/o J G 25 Oct 1872-4 Dec 1961 Libe
Muriel D w/o P W 1899-1984 Libe
Nancy C w/o J W 11 Dec 1884-23 Jan 1942 Park
Naomi D 1888-1961 Libe
Neal 1886-1893 Libe
Nellie 19 Dec 1895-20 Nov 1903 Libe
Nola B w/o P C 1882-1962 Libe
Nora M w/o B B 1898-1980 Park
Norman R 14 Oct 1898-29 Sept 1925 MtHo-s
Oliver J h/o E S 1869-1943 Libe
Oscar T h/o M J 9 Nov 1869-12 Aug 1941 Park
Oscar T 21 Feb 1883-29 Apr 1948 Libe
Otho S 11 Feb 1828-10 Aug 1918 Onan
Paul A Jr s/o Paul & Maude b&d 1936 Park
Paul G 10 Feb 1910-20 Jan 1977 Fair
Phillip C h/o Nola B 1882-1956 Libe
Preston 1907-1976 Park
Preston W h/o M D 1891-1960 Libe
R Forrest h/o I B 1914- Park
Revel J 1867-1868 Libe
Robert E Sr h/o B M 1884-1961 Edge

BARNES (continued)
Ruth C w/o A B 17 Feb 1885-29 Mar 1907 Park
Ruth S w/o C E 1899-1980 Park
Sadie M (w/o W T) 1891-1969 MtHo
Sallie w/o Jno 11 Dec 1810-30 June 1901 Libe
Sallie w/o Jno 28 Jan 1823-17 Dec 1904 Libe
Sallie E 1879-1965 Libe
Samuel C d 11 July 1917; age: 60 yrs Libe
Sarah A w/o W F 1878-1958 Libe
Sarah D w/o F J 21 Feb 1867-4 May 1948 Libe
Sarah J w/o J C; d/o Maj & Betsy Lewis 15 Mar 1849-12 July 1923 Libe
Sharron M s/o O T & M J 13 Aug 1900-26 Sept 1902 Park
Sidney L h/o F J 1911-1977 Onan
Steve R 1911-1977 MtHo-s
Susie P 22 Jan 1863-4 Dec 1944 Libe
Thelma M w/o B P 3 Mar 1913- Park
Tommie 1871-1876 Libe
Vesta 1 Sept 1905-10 July 1917 Libe
Virginia T w/o G P Sr 14 Jan 1866-20 Dec 1920 Libe
W C h/o M S 28 Mar 1860-21 May 1941 MtHo
W Frank h/o S A 1873-1939 Libe
W Samuel h/o L R 2 May 1891-9 May 1940 Park
W Thomas (h/o S M) 1888-1951 MtHo
Walter S h/o L P 1905-1983 Libe
Wesley Miller 29 Feb 1920-2 Oct 1920 Libe
Wesley R s/o L R & Margt d 0/1/1 nd Libe
William A s/o G W & E T 14 Mar 1856-4 Mar 1872; age: 15/11/20 Libe
William F h/o H L 1859-1936 MtHo-s

BARNES (continued)
William J h/o B J 11 June 1848-2 Mar 1919 Libe
William P h/o L B 1910-1963 Fair
Wilson (inf in Ellsworth Barnes plot) nd Onan
BARNHILL, Regina N 13 Oct 1924-27 Sept 1970 Onan
BARTON, Albert M 12 Dec 1898-14 Oct 1971 Park
Daisey S 1897-1968 Burt
BARULSEN, Carolena 11 Apr 1887-14 Jan 1981 MtHo
Harold 16 Dec 1889-20 Aug 1971 MtHo
John Egbert 14 Apr 1898-28 Mar 1918 MtHo
Lola M 1894-1972 StGe
Nellie T 3 Nov 1865-1 Nov 1927 MtHo
Capt Olaus 17 Nov 1861-13 Mar 1947 MtHo
BASSETT, Clyde 1922-1981 Gask
BATTAILE, Adelaide M w/o Henry; d/o Geo S & M J Rogers 10 Oct 1838-6 May 1881; mar 19 Dec 1861 Holb
Estelle b&d 1968 Onan
Estelle Conway 9 Sept 1878-8 July 1968 Onan
Francis W 28 Feb 1870-25 Jan 1909 Onan
George S d 28 Dec 1885; age: 23 yrs Holb
Henry w/o A M 29 July 1830-23 Feb 1910 Holb
Susan Rogers w/o Henry 4 Feb 1849-5 Mar 1929 Holb
BAUM, Edwin C h/o S E 24 Feb 1872-16 Apr 1928 Libe
Margaret J w/o Chas S 12 May 1870-15 July 1917 Libe
Martha S 1851-1929 Libe
Sarah E w/o E C 9 Feb 1876-14 June 1933 Libe
BAUMGARDNER, Robert H 27 July 1916-28 Jan 1982 MtHo-s
BAYLEY, see **BAILEY**
BAYLIS, see also **BALIS**
Clarence M (h/o M M) 1902- Fair

BAYLIS (continued)
Marjorie M (w/o C M) 1905-1980 Fair
BAYLOR, Ann Doughty 1879-1942 MtHo
BAYLY, see **BAILEY**
BAYNE, Colmore S h/o E S; s/o Lt Wm & Mary (Fenley) 23 Apr 1774 in Pr Geo Co MD-6 May 1816 (erected by gr grdaughter - Henrietta D Ayers Sheppard - 1923) Poul
Colomore S s/o Walter & Sally 25 June 1800-11 Dec 1834; mar: Eliza A R d/o Matthew & Eliza Harmanson 30 Nov 1825. Two inf children are deposited on his right. BayV
Edward Walter s/o W D & H E R 12 Apr 1828-20 Sept 1836 JoyB
Elizabeth Smith w/o C S; d/o Peter Hack d 6 Apr 1812; age: 36/0/12 Poul
Harriet E R w/o W D; d/o Col Jno G & Ann Joynes 3 Dec 1805-6 Apr 1838 JoyB
John Joynes s/o W D & H E R 25 Sept 1821-1 Feb 1832 JoyB
Sally Ann d/o W D & H E R 4 June-13 July 1832 JoyB
Walter Drummond s/o W D & H E R 24 Mar-27 Apr 1827 JoyB
BEACH, Cynthia 10 Oct 1953-24 Sept 1954 NewM
Elizabeth B w/o Jno S 6 Jan 1801-14 July 1887 Beac
George W h/o L N 6 Aug 1859-12 Nov 1938 MtHo
Geraldine T 1911-1969 Snea
John S (h/o E B); s/o Kendall & Rosy d 28 Mar 1854; age: 57/7/23 Beac
Kendall (h/o Rosa) nd (d 1815) Beac
Lina M 1916-1977 Burt
Lizzie N w/o G W 24 Sept 1869-25 Apr 1943 MtHo
Maggie 1890-1973 Burt
Norman L 1915-1978 Burt
Rosa (w/o Kendall) d 22 Apr 1837 Beac
Virginia E w/o WP 1 Jan 1834-

BEACH (continued)
11 Nov 1886 Hysl
Virginia R 22 Feb 1893-7 May 1908 MtHo
William P (h/o V E) 15 July 1830-2 Nov 1893 Hysl
BEACHBOARD, Jno H h/o L M 17 Feb 1873-13 Sept 1944 MtHo-s
Lena M w/o J H 16 Oct 1875-24 Feb 1962 MtHo-s
BEAKLEY, Amelia Boggs 1900-1963 MtHo
BEASLEY, Addie T w/o G C 1874-1947 MtHo
Alfred G 19 Feb 1861-12 Nov 1921 MtHo
Benjamin Ray 1893-1952 MtHo
Betty C w/o C R Sr 4 Nov 1917- Park
Burleigh 29 Nov 1886-7 Oct 1953 MtHo
Coley Jr b&d 1939 Park
Coley R Sr h/o B C 22 Jan 1913-7 June 1984 Park
Emma Guy 14 Nov 1888-23 Apr 1970 MtHo-s
Ernest Rogers h/o G A 1902-1963 Park
Frank S Sr 29 Aug 1882-18 Nov 1970 MtHo-s
Fred S h/o G B 1870-1950 MtHo
G Colie h/o A T 1872-1946 MtHo
Garland W 1938-1944 Libe
George T 1867-1936 Libe
Gertie Allen w/o E R 1903-1984 Park
Gertie B w/o F S 1874-1959 MtHo
Gladys Davis 1910-1946 MtHo-s
Harvey L Sr 21 June 1902-6 Nov 1980 Wach
Harvey L Jr 27 Sept 1932-17 Oct 1976 Wach
John H 14 Aug 1911-11 Sept 1942 MtHo-s
John R 1875-1963 MtHo
John Riley s/o Wm & Mary H 25 May 1886-12 Jan 1903 Hutc
Joyce M 13 July 1934-6 May 1981 Edge
Julia Anna b&d 1958 Onan

BEASLEY (continued)
Laura M 1869-19554 Libe
Leonard F 1898-1959 Libe
Margaret d/o Mary (Milliner) 1927-1974 MtHo
Marguerite M w/o Wesley 23 Mar 1901-4 Apr 1938 MtHo
Mary C 1868-1952 MtHo
Mary Elizabeth d/o E R & G A 1947-1962 Park
Mary S (w/o O D) 1905-1971 MtHo
Michael Kenneth s/o K J & M B 2 Sept 1960-15 Sept 1962 MtHo-s
Oscar D (h/o M S) 1893-1973 MtHo
Patricia Ann b&d 1944 Park
Peggy Jean b&d 1942 Park
Richard G b&d 1949 Park
William s/o Jno & Leanna 15 Jan 1842-9 July 1890 Hutc
William H 1888-1949 Park
William Henry s/o Burleigh & Addie d 26 May 1930 MtHo
William Oswald s/o Wm & Mary (Hutchinson) 14 Mar 1878-1 Nov 1893 Hutc
BEATO, Pablo dc1938 JoyC
BEAUCHAMP, Annie H w/o R J 13 Aug 1893-2 Dec 1978 Park
Cordelia B 1915-1960 NewM
Cordie 1863-1955 NewM
Grace E d/o R J & A H 1915-1938 Park
Margaret w/o W K 1856-1929 MtHo
Reuben J h/o A H 14 June 1890-22 Feb 1980 Park
William K h/o Margt 1863-1934 MtHo
BEAUDRY, Sallie J 1898-1979 Libe
Thomas E 23 Aug 1885-20 Apr 1948 Libe
BECKET, (BECKETT),
Abbie A 1878-1937 NewM
Charles C h/o M F d 11 Apr 1928; age: 74 yrs Gask-old
Charlie Moses 1898-1967 Shil
Emory 27 Sept 1927-20 Sept 1971 Gask

BECKET (continued)
Frank d 31 Mar 1964 Gask
George Henry 1930-1948 NewM
Hazel M 1891-1968 Snea
Henry F h/o Maggie S 4 July 1861-6 Feb 1921; age: 59/7/2 StPa
James 1928-73 Gask
John 1898-1977 Gask
LeRoy T 1894-1973 Gask
Mary 1896-1981 Gask
Mary F w/o C C d 11 Mar 1919; age: 49 yrs Gask-old
Rachel w/o Moses d 28 Oct 1923; age: 56 yrs Shil
Sallie w/o Saml d 14 Jan 1899; age: 76 yrs Gask-old
BEERS, Isabel G w/o W Wm 1908-1974 Park
W William h/o I G 1902-1977 Park
BEGNELL, Helen C d/o J A & K H 15 Oct 1895-4 July 1898 Onan
John A h/o K H 23 May 1871-27 Oct 1924 Onan
Kate Hurst w/o J A 11 Nov 1866-6 Dec 1958 Onan
BELL, Abel A 22 Nov 1845-18 May 1926 Anth
Abel Jones (h/o S B) 30 Dec 1870-28 Feb 1942 Wach
Abigail d/o Nathl & Mary d 20 Dec 1737; age: 10/3/22 OldB
Allan D (h/o E D) 1900-1955 Onan
Alonzo R (h/o M L) 1880-1936 Onan
Ann w/o Anthony d 8 Feb 1848 Anth
Anthony h/o Ann 22 Oct 1789-8 July 1864 Anth
Bernie Lee (h/o K L) 1896-1966 Holl
Bertha Lilliston w/o R V 1909-1968 Edge
Bertie Mears w/o G W 16 Nov 1879-9 Oct 1947 Oakg
Bessie d/o L J & B C 14 Dec 1858-29 July 1859 Edge
Bettie C w/o L J 10 Apr 1828-6 Feb 1884 Edge

BELL (continued)
Bettie J w/o Geo W; d/o Jno S & E B Beach 2 Apr 1833-17 June 1872 Beac
Bettie M w/o D T 1890-1974 Quin
Birdie d/o Jas F & Maggie 17 Mar 1890-30 Mar 1891 Meap
Burnice A s/o A A 8 Oct 1885-20 Mar 1892 Anth
Burwell O (h/o S E); s/o Gilbert & Katherine 2 Feb 1846-1 Nov 1872 Anth
C Calvin (h/o E C) 1902-1962 Fair
Charlotte 12 Nov 1807-26 Mar 1895 Belb
Clara d/o Jas F & Maggie 27 Aug-20 Oct 1893 Meap
Cordie Lee (w/o H H) 4 Oct 1887-13 Jan 1965 MtHo
David T (h/o B M) 1883-1963 Quin
Druscilla M (w/o E L) 1894-1979 Wach
Edna H (w/o E T) 1904- Fair
Edward J (h/o M A H) 1830-9 July 1864 Harm
Edward L (h/o D M) 1889-1963 Wach
Edward William 13 Dec 1930-30 Apr 1980 Park
Eleshe w/o Nathl Jr 13 Sept 1724-29 Aug 1745 OldB
Elise Quinby 1899-1970 Onan
Elizabeth w/o J S 21 Mar 1821-13 Apr 1908; age: 87/0/23 Anth
Elizabeth D (w/o A D) 1882-1964 Onan
Ellen Leonard d/o B L & K L 31 May 1919-7 Jan 1920 Holl
Elton 1908-1957 Burt
Emily S w/o W T; d/o Jno & Eliza K Smith 22 May 1819-8 Dec 1844; at her feet lay her 2 infants Belg
Emma E Davis w/o A A 23 Feb 1848-11 Oct 1917; age: 69/7/11 Anth
Emma Kate w/o G E 23 Jan 1866-1 Aug 1961 Quin

BELL (continued)
Emmie Fluhart (w/o G T) 29 Dec 1908- Quin
Estelle B 1866-1939 Wach
Esther Nock 25 Oct 1899-27 Oct 1950 Fair
Evelyn Bundick 1899-1966 Onan
Everette T Sr (h/o E H) 1907-1970 Fair
Fannie W (w/o W B) 1880-1965 Edge
Forest L (h/o S C) 14 Aug 1897-1 Feb 1966 Onan
G Aline d/o A R & M L 27 Dec 1916-17 Feb 1919 Onan
Garland J (h/o N C) 1 Aug 1899-10 Aug 1964 Onan
Geodiah J s/o Lorenzo D & Alice Ann Stewart Bell 5 Mar 1851-21 Oct 1852; age: 1/7/16 Belb
George Edward h/o E K 3 June 1860-5 Oct 1942 Quin
George H (h/o M R) 14 Oct 1796-5 Jan 1860 GeoH
George Thomas (h/o E F) 27 Nov 1904-28 Apr 1976 Onan
George W h/o B M 22 Jan 1859-11 Jan 1926 Oakg
George W (h/o M S) 1874-1929 Wach
George W T h/o R J 1866-1943 Onan
Harry S (h/o V C) 22 Feb 1900-24 Aug 1973 Quin
Horace h/o Eliza Mears ns LeCa
Hugh H (h/o C L) 4 Aug 1883-15 Mar 1942 MtHo
J Herbert (h/o L A) 1875-1938 MtHo-s
James F 1860-1936 Holl
James H 10 Mar 1805-19 Aug 1840; age: 35/5/9 Belb
James M 1921- Holl
James S (h/o Elizabeth); s/o Wm & Rachel 4 Aug 1816-4 Dec 1886; age: 70/4/0 Anth
James W s/o Wm H & Margt d 3 Mar 1850; age: 23/1/0 Turl
John 1903-1921 Edge
John B s/o Geo W & B J d 19 Oct 1852; age: 2/0/7 Beac
John E h/o Lucretia 2 Feb 1846-

BELL (continued)
6 Aug 1914 Edge
John E h/o M E ns LeCa
John H 24 Mar-13 June 1890; age: 0/2/19 Thos
John S s/o Wm & Rachel d 16 Feb 1894; age: 79/0/26 Thos
John T 1857-1934 Holl
Juanita C w/o W H 1923- Wach
Katherine w/o Gilbert 18 Oct 1818-19 Feb 1883 Anth
Kathryn L w/o B L 1898- Holl
Keturah w/o Anthony (formerly wid/o Jas Glenn); d/o Isaiah & Adah Garrison 19 Oct 1790-13 Mar 1872; age: 81/4/26 Garr
Lettie Susan w/o Saml d 14 Feb 1953; age: c80 yrs Snea
Levin T s/o L D & Alice A broken stone Gulf
Lorenzo J h/o B C 16 Sept 1827-17 Sept 1861 Edge
Louis F 15 Dec 1851-4 July 1880 BraH
Lucretia w/o J E; d/o Geo & Nancy Bundick 12 Sept 1830-13 Mar 1906 Edge
Lucy A w/o J H 1858-1945 MtHo-s
Maggie M 1872-1958 Holl
Mahala A 1826-18 Jan 1879 BraH
Margaret w/o Wm H d 20 Nov 1873; age: 71 yrs Turl
Margaret w/o Lorenzo D; d/o R H & A B Mapp 28 Sept 1810-20 Apr 1900 Mapp
Margaret A w/o Thos H 27 Nov 1819-12 Nov 1876 (unable to verify) Thos
Margaret A w/o W W 24 June 1828-20 Dec 1911 Wach
Margaret A Harmon w/o E J 18 Oct 1828-2 Dec 1908 Harm
Margaret Douglass Blackstone w/o Wm P 29 Apr 1862-18 July 1900 Gill
Margaret R w/o Geo H; d/o Wm & Elizabeth Welch d 1 Nov 1857(52?); age: 53/5/24 GeoH
Margaret R d/o Geo H & M W d 27 Mar 1841; age: 6/3/20 GeoH

BELL (continued)
Margaret S w/o G W 1877-1948 Wach
Mary Ester w/o Jno E; d/o W R & J C M LeCato ns LeCa
Mary J w/o Edwd J; d/o Jas H & Charlotte Bell 24 Jan 1833-20 June 1860; age: 27/4/26 Belb
Mary R Tyler w/o W P 1870-1960 Edge
Mary Scarbrough 1(8?) Dec 1691-27 May 176_ (worn) OldB
Mary V 30 May 1873-13 Sept 1915 Edge
Nancy d/o Wm & Rachel d 10 Oct 1876; age: 75/3/5 Thos
Nannie L w/o W H 1908- Wach
Nathaniel Sr 3 Oct 1689-19 Dec 1745 OldB
Nellie C (w/o G J) 1 Oct 1913- Onan
Rachel w/o Wm; d/o Jas & Lucretia Bradford 9 Nov 1785-17 Feb 1862 (unable to verify) Thos
Rachel J w/o G W T 1867-1955 Onan
Ralph V h/o B L 1904-1954 Edge
Robert J (h/o S M) 31 Jan 1843-24 July 1904 Onan
Robert Lee 1 July 1895-9 Nov 1897 Edge
Robin h/o Sallie; s/o Geodiah & Leah 17 Oct 1817-8 July 1860 KelB
Ruth Keaton (w/o W E) 20 Feb 1876-18 Oct 1947 Onan
Sallie w/o Robin H d 18 July 1887; age: 70 yrs KelB
Sallie L 29 Aug 1804-15 July 1857 Edmo
Sally d/o Jediah & Catherine d 24 Aug 1850; age: 49/8/9 Gulf
Sarah Ann d/o Geo H & M R d 9 Nov 1836; age: 7/4/1 GeoH
Sarah Byrd w/o A J 1874-1952 Wach
Sarah C (w/o F L) 12 Sept 1901- Onan
Sarah E w/o B O; d/o Robin & Sally A Bell 25 Mar 1848-20 Feb 1923 Anth

BELL (continued)
Sarah Henry 15 Jan 1835-2 May 1902 Anth
Sarah P 24 Mar 1808-20 June 1880 Edge
Savage H 18 Nov 1815-29 Nov 1892 BraH
Susan M (w/o R J) 15 Sept 1841-15 Jan 1919 Onan
Thomas H (h/o M A) Dec 1818-10 Oct 1882 Thos
Virginia M E d/o Walter W & Margt A 28 Dec 1858-14 Jan 1865 Turl
Vivian C (w/o H S) 6 June 1900-13 Dec 1932 Quin
Wade H (h/o J C) 1921-1969 Wach
Walter W (h/o M A) 26 July 1830-25 Sept 1908 Wach
Walter West s/o G W T & R J 1896-1936 Onan
William E (h/o R K) 24 Apr 1876-3 Oct 1956 Onan
William P B 23 June 1892-25 Sept 1920 Edge
William Parramore h/o M R T; s/o L C & B C 1860-1935 Edge
William H (h/o Margt) 5 Aug 1798-29 July 1865 Turl
William T 1889-1957 Park
Willie B (h/o F W) 1893-1961 Edge
Willie H (h/o N L) 1900-1970 Wach
BELLOWS, Laura 1892-1974 Quin
BELLS, Cordie Evans 1st w/o N T Evans 1870-1970 Onan
BELOATE, see BELOTE
BELOTE, (BELOAT, BELOATE), inf d/o L T & Katie H 29 Sept 1899-1 Jan 1900 Holl
- 1938-1964 Edge
baby girl b&d 20 Mar 1969 Wach
Agnes E 1921- Fair
Alfred T 1927-1973 MtHo-s
Alice Lee w/o W T 1863-1904 MtHo
Altan P 14 Sept 1904-6 Nov 1955 MtHo-s

BELOTE (continued)
Anna C (w/o F H) 1850-1929 Onan
Annette Corbin (w/o R L) 1923- Onan
Annie E 1889-1968 Fair
Avery 22 Jan 1901-6 Jan 1971 Holl
Bertha T w/o J N 1881-1966 Onan
Bessie 1884-1943 MtHo
Bettie L (w/o G T) 1 Oct 1884-7 Jan 1922 MtHo
C Forrest 1899-1900 MtHo
Carla R b&d 1975 Onan
Carrie E d 7 Jan 1929 MtHo
Carroll C 1885-1942 Onan
Catherine Gladstone w/o J H 23 Mar 1912-26 June 1964 MtHo
Cecil F h/o E T 1921-1975 MtHo
Cecil G (h/o G H) 10 Nov 1895-16 June 1966 StGe
Charlie T (h/o H C) 31 Jan 1880-9 July 1962 Fair
Clinton L (h/o H M) 1908-1975 Onan
Columbus East 1875-1941 Wach
Dora W w/o L W 1881-1952 MtHo
Edna B w/o J D 30 June 1846-4 Dec 1912 Onan
Edna F (w/o U Q) 1893-1968 Fair
Edward A 16 Jan 1838-4 June 1921; age: 83/4/19 MtHo
Edward Cleveland 20 Oct 1888-18 Mar 1967 Holl
Edward J 1892-1967 Brap
Edward Thomas (h/o V C) 17 Feb 1909-2 Mar 1967 Holl
Eliza B (w/o J H) 8 Jan 1829-5 Feb 1902 Belo
Elizabeth w/o J G 10 Mar 1814-3 Apr 1901 MtHo
Elizabeth T w/o C F 1915-1979 MtHo
Ellen W (w/o W A) 1887-1964 MtHo
Elton Heath h/o A B Taylor 28 Aug 1889-10 Dec 1918 Onan
Emily S (w/o J H) 1843-1931 Onan

BELOTE (continued)
Emma S 19 Mar 1859-27 Dec 1884 MtHo
Ernest H h/o R M 18 Sept 1871-22 Feb 1928 MtHo
Everette J 7 Dec 1857-6 Feb 1922 MtHo
Fred H (h/o A C) 1854-1929 Onan
Garland P 1884-1976 Fair
George T (h/o B L) 13 Nov 1868-13 Dec 1926 MtHo
Grace H (w/o C G) 27 Sept 1900- StGe
Grace Richardson 1888-1944 Onan
Guynn L h/o M S 25 July 1863-21 Jan 1921 MtHo
Harold F h/o M K 1892-1971 Onan
Harriette L w/o S R 22 Feb 1873-19 Apr 1961 MtHo
Harvey C h/o Pearl 4 Feb 1887-11 June 1943 Onan
Hattie C (w/o C T) 23 Dec 1884-24 June 1965 Fair
Helen Mae 27 Sept 1907-21 Jan 1921 Holl
Hettie S (w/o J B) 1890-1972 Fair
Hilda L d/o V D & N L 9 Feb-18 Apr 1906 MtHo
Hilda L 9 Aug 1906-16 Aug 1978 Holl
Hortense M (w/o C L) 1914-1958 Onan
Irma T 1924- MtHo-s
(Bebloat), Isaiah K s/o Jas & Eliza 8 Feb-8 Aug 1855 OlBe
J H 19 Dec 1871-23 Jan 1939 MtHo-s
J Norman h/o B T 1880-1948 Onan
James H (h/o E B) 30 May 1829-19 Dec 1890 Belo
James H (h/o E S) 28 Dec 1840-11 May 1905 Onan
James H h/o C G 17 Sept 1909-2 Apr 1971 MtHo
James L h/o M T 4 Apr 1830-19 Feb 1899 MtHo
James R Jr 8 June 1919-4 Aug

BELOTE (continued)
1944 MtHo
James Robert 22 Feb 1899-20 Aug 1949 MtHo
Jessie B (h/o H S) 1884-1959 Fair
John 10 Dec 1885-29 Mar 1941 MtHo-s
John Everett 1909-1910 Onan
John W 9 Apr 1847-14 May 1893 Holl
John W s/o Wm J 21 Oct 1836-4 June 1865; age: 28/7/3 (leaving a wife & 2 children) JnoP
Joseph G w/o Elizabeth 29 Aug 1813-13 Mar 1896 MtHo
Josephine Somers 21 Dec 1894-27 Dec 1976 MtHo
Julia L 1887-1975 Onan
Julius D h/o E B 5 May 1838-9 June 1905 Onan
Kate H (w/o L T) 12 Mar 1879-10 Feb 1925 Holl
Kezziah w/o Wm H 19 June 1807-29 Nov 1848 OlBe
Kirby s/o J L & M T 18 Sept 1873-10 Sept 1876 MtHo
L Rogers Sr (h/o W B) 1899-1973 Fair
Lee W h/o D W 1879-1950 MtHo
Lena Lee 3 Feb 1892-28 Sept 1976 Holl
Leonard Grayson s/o L W & M V 22 July 1894-14 Aug 1901 MtHo
Leonard W h/o M V 18 Nov 1868-7 Jan 1922 MtHo
Levin B 12 Feb 1812-9 Oct 1898 Holl
Levin T h/o K H nd Holl
Lewis S 8 May 1842-6 Dec 1885 MtHo-s
Linda Kay 20 Nov 1941-20 July 1942 Holl
Margaret F (w/o W L) 1913- Quin
Margaret W (w/o V M) 1925- Fair
Marion 1882-1961 MtHo
Marvin D s/o Wm T & A L 1901-1904 MtHo
Mary Anna (w/o W L) 1867-1932

BELOTE (continued)
MtHo
Mary C 1864-1950 MtHo-s
Mary K w/o H F 1893- Onan
Mary T w/o J L 11 Jan 1836-13 Aug 1889 MtHo
Minnie K 23 Sept 1872-15 Dec 1953 Fair
Missouria A w/o Herbert T 16 Feb 1862-9 Mar 1898 Home
Mollie S w/o G L 15 Feb 1866-11 June 1903 MtHo
Mollie V w/o L W 18 Dec 1870-20 Dec 1926 MtHo
Nina M (w/o W L) 1901-1975 Edge
Nona L w/o V D 1889-1969 MtHo
Norman E 26 July 1898-19 Apr 1961 Holl
Pearl w/o H C 22 Feb 1890-4 May 1960 Onan
Polly w/o Jno 31 Mar 1801-11 July 1886 JnoS
Polly K (w/o W H) 1886-1942 Holl
Prentiss s/o L T & Katie H 10 Dec 1902-16 Feb 1905 Holl
Ray L 1907-1978 MtHo-s
Rennie M w/o E H 8 Nov 1877-3 Dec 1947 MtHo
Robert Lee (h/o A C) 1909-1981 Onan
Ruth D (w/o T R) Jan 1892- Onan
S 3 Nov 1807-21 Feb 1852 JnoP
S Ran h/o H L 4 Aug 1859-1 Feb 1934 MtHo
Sadie J 24 Aug 1870-27 Sept 1947 MtHo
Sadie P 22 July 1883-25 June 1965 MtHo
Sanelle R (w/o W H) 1911- Onan
Sarah A w/o Levin B 15 Jan 1821-1 Oct 1895 (moved from Burckard bur gr) Onan
Sarah C (w/o T U) 15 Aug 1878-20 Nov 1955 MtHo-s
Sidney W 1881-1978 Onan
Southey L (h/o V S) 1888-1972 Holl
Stella S w/o U J 25 Mar 1875-15 Mar 1919 MtHo

BELOTE (continued)
Susan H 1889-1941 MtHo
Susan S 30 Aug 1840-23 Jan 1903 MtHo
T P 1831-1922 MtHo
T Ray (h/o R D) 14 Nov 1890-12 Mar 1972 Onan
Teackle U (h/o S C) 15 June 1875-27 Dec 1959 MtHo-s
Upshur J h/o S S 1873-1948 MtHo
Upshur Q (h/o E F) 1897-1962 Fair
V Duncan h/o N L 1881-1945 MtHo
V Strude (w/o S L) 1892-1964 Holl
Vernon 1910-1979 Onan
Vernon Jr 1952-1969 Onan
Vernon M (h/o M W) 1923-1970 Fair
Viola Catherine (w/o E T) 22 Oct 1908- Holl
Walter A (h/o E W) 1883-1963 MtHo
Walter L (h/o M F) 1897-1965 Quin
William H h/o Kezziah 26 Apr 1804-22 Apr 1861 OlBe
(Bebloat), William H s/o Jas & Eliza 19 Oct 1853-14 Aug 1855 OlBe
William H (h/o P K) 1885-1930 Holl
William H (h/o S R) 1912-1978 Onan
William J 11 Sept 1811-9 Feb 1872 JnoP
William L (h/o M A) 1867-1926 MtHo
William L (h/o N M) 1898-1966 Edge
William T h/o A L 20 July 1866-23 Apr 1934 MtHo
William Tankard 1 Nov 1885-25 Oct 1918 Onan
Willie B (w/o L R Sr) 1904-1981 Fair
Willie Lee 1899-1973 Wach
BENFIELD, Carrie G 1898-1954 Libe
LeRoy 1914-1975 Edge

BENNETT, A Boggs h/o A K 1889-1972 MtHo
Allie K w/o A B; d/o J A & G W Kilmon 8 Nov 1893-24 Feb 1920 MtHo
Benjamin B 1818-1900 Libe
Bettie Ann 1865-1954 MtHo-s
Catherine J 1820-1904 Libe
Colie R 29 Jan 1893-2 Nov 1965 Fair
Donna Lynn 19 July 1968-22 Feb 1969 Fair
Elwood C (h/o N L) 1904-1980 Holl
Eva K (w/o J F) 1879-1936 StGe
George-Anna d/o G W Scott 15 July 1852-12 Nov 1930 StGe
Gladys w/o Glenwood 1910-1976 Onan
Glenwood (h/o Gladys) 1913-1970 Onan
Harmanson T 1887- StGe
Hayward H 4 Mar 1919-16 Sept 1982 Fair
Henry R 1849-1940 Libe
James 1902-1970 Holl
Jeanette 1855-1935 Libe
John F (h/o E K) 1881-1972 StGe
John F 3 Jan 1913- (awarded the Carnegie Medal) StGe
Joseph Elwood 1942-1962 Holl
Leonard A Sr 1863-1947 MtHo-s
Leonard A (h/o N G) 1889-1973 MtHo-s
Lizzie T 1881-1957 Holl
Maggie S w/o W T 1872-1967 MtHo-s
Nannie 1873-1959 MtHo-s
Nellie G (w/o L A) 1892- MtHo-s
Nellie L (w/o E C) 1913- Holl
Otho 1900-1953 MtHo-s
R Allie 1898-1964 Holl
Russell F 1921-1945 Holl
Tank W 1886-1948 StGe
Teagle T 1873-1927 MtHo-s
Thomas H 20 Nov 1851-19 Aug 1925 StGe
Vera M 1893-1977 StGe
Wm T h/o M S 27 Apr 1862-27 Mar 1949 MtHo-s
BENSON, Annie W nd (Mary E;

BENSON (continued)
Wm T on same stone - nd) Oakg
Etheridge Teakle (h/o V I) 6 July 1919-30 Aug 1977 Fair
George Teackle h/o I L 17 Mr 1859-9 Feb 1921 Oakg
George William s/o H W & P B 17 Nov 1920-24 Jan 1923 MtHo
Hugh W h/o P B 22 July 1889-24 July 1951 MtHo
Ida L w/o G T 5 Dec 1862-25 Oct 1910 Oakg
James S d 16 July 1854; age: 69 yrs Quin
James S 4 Oct 1816-9 Dec 1876 Oakg
Mary G nd (Annie W Benson; Wm T on same stone - nd) Oakg
Mary Gertrude d/o G T & I L 1 Oct 1895-24 June 1896 Oakg
Pollie B w/o H W 20 July 1891-21 Mar 1961 MtHo
Samuel d 19 Jan 1855; age: 66/2/26 Oakg
Virginia Beach d/o H W & P B 3 June 1916-1983 MtHo
Virginia Ironmonger (w/o E T) 16 Mar 1923- Fair
William T nd (Annie W Benson; Mary G on same stone - nd) Oakg
BENTON, G B h/o R L 12 Sept 1929-16 Feb 1979 Libe
Ruby L w/o G B 25 Feb 1926- Libe
BERNARD, Joseph Alfred h/o M S 1884-1951 Park
Joseph Elias 1916-1964 Park
Mary Susie w/o J A 1888-1923 Park
BERRY, inf/o J W & E S W b&d 22 Feb 1908 Edge
Annie S nd Park
Comet nd Park
Edwin C 1920-1943 Park
Elizabeth A w/o J N 13 Oct 1850-8 Apr 1926 Park
Elizabeth S W w/o Jno W 17 Nov 1873-22 Feb 1908 Edge
George L 1904-1972 Park

25

BERRY (continued)
George R h/o R L 1882-1966 Park
George W nd Park
Howard H 1907-1972 Park
Ida M w/o R J 1870-1936 Park
James T 27 May 1931-23 Oct 1978 Park
John H (h/o S E) 1887-1973 Fair
John W h/o M C 1879-1949 Edge
Marian A 1915-1916 Park
Mary J nd Park
Mary W w/o W A 1904- Park
Mattie Coard w/o J W 1875-1948 Edge
R James h/o I M 1862-1955 Park
Rosa L w/o G R 1887-1966 Park
Sarah E (w/o J H) 1890-1967 Fair
Scarborough T (w/o W O) 1863-1934 MtHo-s
Weldon A h/o M W 1904-1970 Park
William Cicel s/o R H & Fannie E d 22 Oct 1890; age: 0/15/9 Crad
William O h/o S T 1859-1946 MtHo-s
BETTS, Sarah Emma w/o Rev Chas N; d/o W R & S J Lewis 20 Feb 1861-25 May 1934 Onan
BEVANS, see also BIVINS
Noah B 1913-1967 Park
BEVERLY, Blanche 1887-195_ Burt
BEW, Melvin Hezikiah 2 June 1897-21 July 1978 Onan
BICKETT, see also BECKETT
Otho 1902-1977 JoyC
BIGGS, William 1868-1955 Snea
BIRCH, Mannie 16 Sept 1891-22 Dec 1963 Park
Morandolph Moe 19 Apr 1897-7 June 1977 Fair
Vircie 12 Aug 1891-17 May 1943 Park
BIRD, see BYRD
BISHOP, Annie C 1877-1903 Park
Annie W w/o J J 1880-1953 Libe
Bettie D b&d 1903 Park
Brantley L 16 May 1921-25 June

BISHOP (continued)
1960 Libe
Frank D h/o M B 1912-1970 Park
George s/o Geo J & Susan d 13 June 1894; age: 19 yrs ScoB
George J d 26 June 1910; age: 70 yrs Libe
Harry J 9 Sept 1893-23 Nov 1981 Libe
James J h/o A W 1871-1944 Libe
Little Jim 1907-1944 Libe
Margaret K w/o P R 1914- Libe
Maud M d/o J B & Annie 22 June 1906-18 July 1907 Libe
Maude V 1901-1903 Park
Merrill B w/o F D 1916- Park
Paul R h/o M K 1914- Libe
Susan w/o Geo J; d/o Major & Polly Annis 11 July 1840-15 Feb 1892; age: 52 yrs ScoB
Susie D 19 Sept 1914-29 Feb 1977 Fair
W J Bryan 14 May 1897-28 May 1977 Libe
William J Bryan 25 May 1919-16 Sept 1936 Libe
BIVINS, (BIVENS), see also BEVANS
Cecil N 1900-1983 Burt
Elizabeth w/o Severn 5 Jan 1823-24 May 1899; age: 76/4/19 StPa
Henrietta w/o Chas 9 Mar 1863(65?)-5 Aug 1891 Shil
Peter 8 Mar 1843-23 Oct 1919 Faithful colored servant in Mears family for 51 yrs Mear
Severn (h/o Elizabeth) heavy stone face down StPa
BLACK, Fred H (h/o M S) 23 Nov 1872-6 Dec 1965 Fair
Mylie S (w/o F H) 25 Dec 1888-17 Aug 1968 Fair
BLACKSTONE, Elizabeth Dickinson w/o Jno J; d/o Wm & Henrietta Gillett 5 Nov 1825-26 Aug 1893 Gill
Grover 9 July 1883-15 June 1956 Edge
Henrietta Elizabeth d/o Jno J & M D 3 May 1842-15 Jan 1886

BLACKSTONE (continued)
  Gill
Margaret Douglass w/o Jno J; Wm & Henrietta Gillett 30 Nov 1821-14 June 1846 Gill
Rose Dix 18 Oct 1834-7 May 1913 Park
Sarah A w/o T W; d/o Dr F C A & Eliza Kellam 1 Nov 1841-20 Sept 1887 Kell
Sarah P Walston w/o T W 1 July 1868-1 Nov 1939 Edge
Susan Thomas 26 Aug 1837-26 Mar 1914 Park
Thomas s/o Thos Wise & Ann (Dix) Blackstone 24 Aug 1832-28 June 1898 Kell
Thomas W h/o S P W 4 Apr 1860-11 May 1940 Edge
Thomas W Jr s/o T W & S P W 14 May 1895-28 Sept 1928 Edge
William G s/o Jno J & M D 11 Oct 1840-6 June 1845; age: 4/7/25 Gill
BLACKWELL, Charles H (h/o M S) 1900-1971 Edge
Grover R b&d 1941 Edge
James Paul Jr 17 Feb 1935-20 Sept 1969 Park
Minnie S (w/o C H) 1902-1969 Edge
Roland H b&d 1943 Edge
BLADES, Annie T w/o D C 1906- Park
Dewey C h/o A T 1901- Park
BLAKE, Geneva P 1900-1967 Burt
Llewellyn A 11 May 1837-7 Feb 1914 Wach
BLANKENSHIP, Linda W (w/o W F) 1911-1979 Onan
William F (h/o L W) 1907-1978 Onan
BLANKS, Elise 25 Dec 1887-6 June 1966 Park
BLINCOE, Emily Johnson 31 Mar 1880-18 Mar 1973 Edge
BLOXOM, (BLOXSOM),
  Anna L w/o Wm B 1910-1978 Park
Annie B w/o H T 1883-1967

BLOXOM (continued)
  Edge
Bailey B h/o M B H 27 Nov 1886-7 Aug 1943 Edge
Carrie T w/o E B 1912-1979 Edge
Catherine w/o Jas (b1847) d 16 Jan 1894 (unable to verify) Lill
Charles H (h/o G C) 1893-1968 Quin
Charlie B h/o D B 1893-1967 Park
Charlie T h/o E W 1894-1977 Park
Clarence W Jr 19 July 1917-6 June 1944 Park
Custis W 1841-1924 Park
Daisey B w/o C B 1897-1966 Park
David H 20 Aug 1840-31 Jan 1917 Park
Dennis h/o Henrietta 7 Aug 1787-16 Mar 1859; age: 72 yrs Park
Dorsey D 4 June 1898-13 Aug 1923 Park
Earl S h/o E P 1890-1951 Park
Edith Bull 1919-1956 Park
Edna P w/o E S 1891-1979 Park
Edward B s/o J S & Eva M 24 Nov 1907-12 June 1908 Edge
Edward B h/o C T 1911- Edge
Edward H 6 June 1864-6 Aug 1929 MtHo
Elizabeth S w/o Geo 2 Dec 1809-20 Aug 1897 Park
Estelle W w/o C T 1918- Park
Eva L 1882-1954 Edge
Ezekiel A 26 Sept 1860-18 Oct 1929 MtHo
Geneva C (w/o C H) 1893-1971 Quin
George h/o E S 18 Nov 1809-8 Aug 1882 Park
George C h/o P F 1883-1915 Park
George W 24 Nov 1907-11 Dec 1971 Edge
Georgie James 26 May 1866-17 Jan 1952 MtHo
Helen w/o W A Jr; d/o Jno T & May H Carmine 27 July 1896-

BLOXOM (continued)
21 May 1924 Edge
Henrietta w/o Dennis 7 Feb 1798-22 July 1892 Park
Herbert T (h/o A B) 1880-1974 Edge
James h/o Catherine d 18 Jan 1894 (unable to verify) Lill
James J h/o M L 14 Apr 1868-25 Sept 1936 Park
Jewell J 12 Jan 1902-19 Mar 1983 Fair
Joe Elliott s/o J M & L E 12 Aug 1894-29 Dec 1940 Edge
John M h/o L E 2 Nov 1864-23 Mar 1924 Edge
Lillian L d/o W H & M A 18 July 1861-2 Nov 1879 Park
Lou E (w/o J M) 3 Feb 1869-24 Dec 1953 Edge
Maggie S 1846-1924 Park
Maggie S w/o Wm T 1874-1965 Park
Maggie Sue d/o W A Sr & M K 16 Sept 1887-29 Apr 1892 Hero
Margaret D w/o M F 1900- Park
Margaret Kellam w/o W A Sr 5 Aug 1850-30 Sept 1930 Edge
Mary Ann w/o W H 1840-1929 Park
Melvin G 1911-1972 Park
Mildred B Hickman h/o B B 10 Mar 1905-14 Oct 1978 Edge
Millard F h/o M D 1896-1971 Park
Millard F Jr 1923-1984 Park
Minnie L w/o J J 1 Nov 1876-15 May 1872 Park
Miranda Thomas w/o W H 1872-1960 Park
Nettie A w/o R F 1903- Park
Pearl S w/o S H 1918- Park
Pearlie F w/o G C 1885-1971 Park
Ray Hamilton s/o W A Sr & M K 27 July 1890-5 May 1892 Hero
Roy F h/o N A 1900-1979 Park
Revell J 23 Nov 1906-10 Mar 1982 Fair
Robert Lee Jr 15 Nov 1956-12 Nov 1957 Fair
Sallie A w/o E G H d 9 Apr 1895;

BLOXOM (continued)
age: 66/3/3 Floy
Samuel H h/o P S 1907-1975 Park
Sarah E w/o Sewell 1863-1946 Park
Sewell h/o S E 1862-1942 Park
Stanley W 1894-1952 Park
Thomas M 30 Apr 1843-7 Dec 1871 Park
Thomas S 1903-1980 Edge
Thomas Teackle s/o W A & M K 6 May 1879-1 June 1928 Edge
W H h/o M A 7 Feb 1836-3 June 1904 Park
W H h/o M T 14 Jan 1868-18 Aug 1927 Park
Wesley A Jr h/o Helen 16 Apr 1876-19 Jan 1941 Edge
Wesley Anderson Sr h/o M K 8 Aug 1841-28 Apr 1916 Edge
William B h/o A L 14 Mar 1910-18 Apr 1981 Park
William E 20 Oct 1873-28 Aug 1917 Edge
William P s/o L & Pearl 10 Jan 1900-20 Aug 1908 Wach
William T h/o M S 1868-1938 Park
BOCKLET, Margt B (w/o W B) 3 June 1887-29 Oct 1977 Fair
William B (h/o M B) 1 Apr 1888-5 Jan 1980 Fair
BODELL, Carl 16 Sept 1850 Lulea Sweden-30 May 1915 Harbarton VA (Music professor: Hollins 1898-1905; Sullins 1905-1915. Died at piano.) Onan
BOEHM, Samuel R h/o S E 9 Nov 1840-6 Jan 1919 Edge
Sarah E w/o S R 15 Feb 1854- Edge
BOGGS, A Grayson (h/o R N) 1890-1954 Onan
Amelia E C w/o J C 30 Apr 1840-21 Jan 1918 Onan
Ann Elizabeth (w/o F T) 16 Jan 1833-31 Jan 1907 Onan
Annie F w/o J C 1903- Gask
Annie Sue Reaston w/o T L 16 Nov 1889-1 Feb 1970 Onan

BOGGS (continued)
Arthur W s/o H J & E S 26 Nov 1843-22 Sept 1853; age: 9/9/27 Bogg
Benjamin Lee s/o J W & L A 8 Apr 1867-23 Oct 1871; age: 4/6/15 Onan
Bessie (w/o Harry) 1883-1949 MtHo-s
C Starr h/o M A 1886-1951 Onan
Calvin S (h/o M N) 16 May 1848-12 Oct 1926 Onan
Carroll H 1899-1967 Burt
Catharine Angelica 1st w/o J E; d/o Jno W & Elizabeth Chandler 3 Dec 1842-4 Aug 1882 Onan
Charles s/o Robt & Martha 27 Oct 1812-6 Dec 1876 Bogb
Charles H s/o H W & M S 4 Dec 1886-18 May 1960 Onan
Charlie 1897-1976 Shil
Cillie 1891-1941 JoyC
David 1888-1962 Shil
E Paul 1888-1950 Onan
Edward 1886-1968 Shil
Edward Thomas s/o C S & M A 31 Jan-1 Feb 1920 Onan
Edward W inf/o Wm H & Esther 18 Nov 18_-27 July 1869 Drum
Edwin Mapp 1859-1920 Onan
Elijah T s/o J E & C A 29 July 1866-11 Mar 1892 Onan
Elizabeth Augusta d/o C S & M A 13 Oct 1915-19 July 1918 Onan
Elizabeth P w/o Jas; d/o Levi & Euphamey Rodgers 6 Oct 1791-26 Apr 1859 Rodg
Elizabeth R d/o H W & M S 10 June 1896-6 July 1982 Onan
Elizabeth S w/o H J; d/o Wm & Rachael Rodgers 14 May 1821-22 Sept 1902 Bogg
Ella S 2nd w/o J E 1857-1943 Onan
Elma F s/o Jos C & Amelia E C 19 Dec 1875-12 Apr 1876 Bogb
Elmira only d/o Jos C & Amelia E 22 Apr 1865-29 Sept 1874; age: 9/5/7 Bogb

BOGGS (continued)
Emma Laura 5 Feb-19 Feb 1925 Onan
Emma T 1st w/o L T 30 Jan 1847-3 Aug 1903 Onan
Emma T d/o Henry & Margt 4 Apr-10 Aug 1905 Bogg
Emma V 2nd w/o L T 15 Sept 1847-6 Mar 1910 Onan
Emory S w/o J P 1881-1922 Onan
Ernest U (h/o S M) 1893-1967 Onan
Esther E w/o W H; nee Bull 9 Feb 1845-27 Nov 1900 Holf
Ethel L (w/o J E) 1916- Onan
Francis T (h/o A E) 30 Nov 1832-6 Apr 1906 Onan
George 1855-18 Mar 1924 Shil
George C h/o L F 13 Feb 1890-29 Jan 1957 Onan
George Douglas s/o Thos D & Susan A 22 Feb 185_-17 Mar 1862 Bogb
George U 1867-1943 MtHo-s
Grace M 1899-1957 Onan
Harry (h/o Bessie) 1872-1943 MtHo-s
Harry 1905-1980 Shil
Henry J h/o E S; s/o Arthur & Susanna 26 Jan 1814-20 Aug 1858 Bogg
Henry R h/o K R 1857-1930 Onan
Henry W h/o M S 19 July 1865-8 Jan 1943 Onan
Hester A w/o L R; d/o Geo S & Catherine C Mapp 17 June 1832-15 Nov 1899 Rodc
J Edwin (h/o E L) 1917-1965 Onan
James (h/o E P); s/o Jno S & Margt 26 July 1787-27 Mar 1855 Rodg
James 1913-1980 Gask
James E h/o C A & E S 1840-1913 Onan
James E 1888-1958 Gask
James E 1890-1980 Shil
Jennie E d/o Wm H & Esther 17 Apr-4 May 1870 Drum
John 1880-14 Dec 1951 Shil
John Clifton 1901-1967 Gask

BOGGS (continued)
John P h/o E S 1882-1964 Onan
John T 7 July 1836-7 July 1902 Onan
John W E s/o J E & C A 10 Sept 1871-5 Sept 1874 Onan
John William w/o L A; s/o Jos P & Susan E 26 June 1834-20 June 1872; age: 37/11/24 Onan
Joseph C h/o A E C 20 Dec 1833-27 Dec 1920 Onan
Joseph C h/o A F 1897-1978 Gask
Joseph L s/o T L & A S R 17 July 1918-29 Aug 1920 Onan
Joseph P (h/o S E); s/o Francis & Agnes 23 Dec 1802-23 Sept 1873; age: 70/9/0 Bogb
Kate J w/o Louis F 19 June 1846-1 Apr 1896 Chan
Kate R w/o H R 1858-1948 Onan
Laura A w/o J W 8 Nov 1838-2 Sept 1919 Onan
Laura A d/o L R & H A 14 Feb-3 Oct 1873 Rodc
Laura William d/o G W & L A 12 Apr-10 July 1872; age: 0/2/28 Onan
Leah M w/o Jno R; d/o Francis & Agnes Boggs 16 July 1810-16 July 1885 Onan
Lella R w/o Jno W 25 Oct 1880-26 Aug 1906 Onan
LeRoy F 2 Jan 1875-16 Dec 1925 Onan
Levi R h/o H A 6 Jan 1825-5 Nov 1911 Rodc
Lewis F 8 July 1844-2 Jan 1928 MtHo-s
Lillie C 1881-1967 Shil
Lisa Y d1961 Snead
Littleton T h/o E T & E V 2 Sept 1838-31 Aug 1924 Onan
Louis 1911-1974 Gask
Lucille K 30 July 1885-28 Feb 1939 Onan
Lucy 1907-1957 Shil
Lucy Finney w/o G C 23 Feb 1892-29 May 1933 Onan
Luther N h/o M B 4 Oct 1846-20 July 1925 Onan
Manie N (w/o C S) 10 Jan 1853-1

BOGGS (continued)
July 1924 Onan
Margaret Ann d/o Jos P & Susan E 4 Feb 1837-6 Sept 1842 Bogb
Margaret D 1862-1928 Onan
Margaret E d/o G C & L F b&d 4 Nov 1920 Onan
Margaret Sarah w/o H W 10 May 1863-17 Oct 1927 Onan
Mary A d/o Francis & Agnes 29 Oct 1804-12 June 1886; age: 81/7/13 Bogb
Mary D 1880-1919 MtHo-s
Mary McMath 25 Feb 1883-3 Apr 1946 MtHo-s
Maude K 1890-1981 MtHo-s
Minnie A w/o C S 1891-1948 Onan
Mollie B w/o L N 9 Dec 1856-11 Nov 1890 Onan
Myra L 30 Mar 1877-16 Jan 1964 Onan
Nanie 1860-1958 Shil
Peter T 2 Jan 1830-28 Mar 1908 Gask-old
Reginald J h/o V N 2 Sept 1870-6 Feb 1946 MtHo
Ruth Nottingham (w/o A G) 1896-1970 Onan
Sabra M (w/o E U) 1892-1971 Onan
Sallie Ann d/o Jos P & S E 20 Dec 1842-9 May 1864 Bogb
Sallie M 1899-1972 Gask
Samuel J Jr 3 Dec 1929-20 June 1978 HTri
Sarah A 15 June 1800-3 May 1882 Gask-old
Sarah A 1866- Gask
Sarah Ann w/o Southey B d 2 Dec 1902; age: 52 yrs Gask-old
Sarah E d/o R J & V N 7 Sept-1 Oct 1900 MtHo
Susan A w/o Thos D; d/o Wm D & Margt Chandler 10 June 1819-11 Apr 1893 Bogb
Susan E w/o Jos P; d/o Thos & Nancy Underhill 4 Dec 1810-13 July 1881 Bogb
Thomas D (w/o Susan A); s/o Francis & Elizabeth 8 Mar

BOGGS (continued)
1812-9 Mar 1869 Bogb
Thomas Littleton h/o A S R 18 Sept 1888-26 Sept 1970 Onan
Thomas Steele s/o Thos D & S A 30 Jan 1856-15 May 1874 Bogb
Victoria 1900-1967 Shil
Virginia N w/o R J 14 Feb 1872-10 July 1915 MtHo
William H h/o E E 14 Oct 1836-26 Oct 1907 Holf
BOISNARD, Esther w/o Jno; d/o Edwd & Margt Robins 1762-1797 (stone gone; Ref: Whitelaw) Rura
Nancy w/o Jno; d/o Wm & Sarah Parsons d 4 Apr 1806; age: 52 yrs Rura
Louis s/o Jno & Sarah 9 Jan 1784-4 Oct 1808 Rura
Sarah d 10 Dec 1785; age: 26 yrs Warw
BOLDEN, Elijah d 3 Feb 1961; age: 50 yrs Metr
Sarah L 1915-1982 Metr
BOND, Annie E w/o G McI 13 Apr 1836-10 Apr 1915 Libe
George McIllhiney h/o A E 30 Dec 1827-25 Mar 1901 Libe
George Thomas 10 Jan 1901-23 Sept 1955 Libe
John L h/o M A nd Edge
Margaret A w/o J L nd Edge
Mary Dickerson 1880-1946 Libe
William S B 20 Apr 1846 (at Fallston, Harford Co MD)-13 Oct 1905 Libe
William Thomas 1872-1946 Libe
William Thomas Jr 9 Jan 1916-15 Feb 1947 Libe
BONN, Henry d 4 Nov 1963; age: 58 yrs NewM
BONNAWELL, Robert d1920 Wate
BONNIWELL, (BONAWELL, BONAVILLE, BONEVILLE, BONNAVILLE, BONNEVILLE, BONNIVIL, BONNEWELL, BONNIWELLS, BONWELL),
s/o G T & V A b&d 8 Aug 1918 Park

BONNIWELL (continued)
Agnes C (w/o J V) 1907-1981 StGe
Alice (w/o Jesse) 1875-1949 Wach
Augustis s/o G T & E S 28 Oct 1871-8 Mar 1887 MtHo
Augustus D 1887-1918 (killed in France) StGe
Benjamin T h/o C K 1863-1940 MtHo-s
Bertha M 1st w/o E C d 12 Oct 1910; age: 27 yrs MtHo
Bettie W (w/o J T) 1883-1949 StGe
C Wertenbaker Sr (h/o M N) 28 Oct 1881-21 Oct 1941 StGe
Byron O 1900-1974 Fair
Cecil F (h/o V H) 1899-1959 StGe
Charlotte K (B T) 1856-1940 MtHo-s
Cordie A (w/o W H) 1863-1933 StGe
E C h/o B M & Maggie d 11 Nov 1921; age: 49 yrs MtHo
Earl (h/o R C) 1892-1979 StGe
Edward Allen s/o W E & Marguerite E 1939-1952 Park
Elizabeth S w/o G L 1913-1978 MtHo
Ella H (w/o J W) 1888-1980 StGe
Emma S w/o G T 2 Feb 1843-25 Jan 1916 MtHo
Faith Reid 1947- StGe
Fred B 1895-1962 StGe
Garnett Lee h/o E S 1913- MtHo
George A h/o G E 12 July 1896-23 Dec 1953 MtHo
George C (h/o S E M) 2 May 1874-16 Aug 1941 StGe
George E h/o H S 1881-1954 Park
George T 27 Sept 1853- MtHo
George Thomas h/o V A 16 June 1890-12 Feb 1966 Park
Grace E w/o G A 4 Oct 1895- MtHo
Grace E 22 Jan 1914-23 May 1929 StGe
Gustave R 15 Dec 1921-30 Sept

BONNIWELL (continued)
1967 StGe
Hester A (w/o J W) 1858-1924 StGe
Hester S w/o G E 1895- Park
Ida C w/o R W 13 May 1873-19 Dec 1946 StGe
Inez E (w/o W T) 1891-1973 StGe
J Thomas (h/o M A) 12 Apr 1835-3 June 1917 StGe
J Vernon (h/o A C) 1906-1970 StGe
J W (h/o H A) 1858-1933 StGe
James T (h/o B W) 1880-1953 StGe
Jesse (h/o Alice) 1871-1967 Wach
John D h/o P H 1883-1960 Edge
John Eric 24 Nov 1914-6 Mar 1974 (WW II; Korea) Park
John W (h/o E H) 1882-1955 StGe
Joseph B (h/o V A) 1883-1928 Onan
Lula Coates (w/o O L) 1903- StGe
Lynwood N 1914-1958 MtHo
Madeline 1916-1959 Fair
Maggie 2nd w/o E C d 3 Feb 1924; age: 37 yrs MtHo
Manie E d/o E C & Maggie 7 May-7 Sept 1920 MtHo
Margaret d 26 Oct 1867; age: 85/0/0 Coke
Margaret A w/o J T 14 Mar 1836-6 Jan 1922 StGe
Margaret Nelson (w/o C W Sr) 22 Apr 1884-14 Oct 1972 StGe
Marian Mason w/o W S 23 Sept 1874-23 Aug 1957 Edge
Marie 1923-1974 StGe
Marie Perdew 1923-1974 StGe
Narene B (w/o W H) 1904- StGe
Otho L (h/o L C) 1898- StGe
Polly H w/o J D 1881-1959 Edge
R W (h/o I C) 18 Oct 1868-19 July 1953 StGe
Rev Ralph Ed 1949- StGe
Ralph S 1920- StGe
Robert H (h/o V H) 1902-1975 Edge

BONNIWELL (continued)
Rosalie C (w/o Earl) 1892-1963 StGe
Ruth S 1897-1971 StGe
Sarah E Mears w/o G C 1876-1939 StGe
Sarah Kathleen d/o G T & V A 28 June 1919-23 Aug 1920 Park
Velma H (w/o C F) 1902- StGe
Vera Anna w/o G T 5 Oct 1895-5 Feb 1975 Park
Versa H (w/o R H) 1892-1966 Edge
Virgil E 1897-1960 Wach
Virginia A (w/o J B) 1891-1969 Onan
Virginia Hortence d/o G A & G E 2 Aug-27 Nov 1920 MtHo
W L 25 Dec 1879-16 Apr 1948 MtHo
Wayland H (h/o N B) 1900-1965 StGe
Wilber Robin 14 Feb 1899-24 July 1958 MtHo-s
William H (h/o C A) 1860-1927 StGe
William Saml h/o M M 25 Jan 1875-9 Jan 1968 Edge
William T (h/o I E) 1887-1956 StGe
BOOLE, see also **BULL**
Charles L 16 Mar 1916-25 July 1941 MtHo-s
Clara Bundick (w/o W J) 1 Apr 1898-17 Apr 1967 Quin
Fannie A (w/o J A) 8 Aug 1893-10 Dec 1939 MtHo-s
J Allen Sr (h/o F A) 3 June 1887-21 Mar 1965 MtHo-s
Walter J (h/o C B) 4 Mar 1894-9 June 1976 Quin
Waymon L 11 Feb 1914-7 Apr 1941 MtHo-s
BOONE, Nell S w/o Walter 7 Feb 1897-13 Dec 1960 Park
Walter, MD h/o N S 22 Feb 1893-1 Jan 1943 Park
BOOTH, Charles h/o E C d 12 Sept 1886; age: c65 yrs Edge
Elizabeth C w/o Chas 9 June 1829-3 Dec 1887 Edge
John W 1858-1914 Edge

BOOTH (continued)
Lotta Scott (w/o R L) 21 Oct 1913-2 July 1982 MtHo-s
Martha w/o Thos d 7 Jan 1920 Edge
Richard Lee (h/o L S) 18 Aug 1915- MtHo-s
Capt Thomas h/o Martha 15 Sept 1861-20 Apr 1928 Edge
William O d 12 June 1936; age: 77 yrs Edge
BORUM, Alvin P 1907-1976 MtHo-s
Blanche F w/o G B 1871-1957 MtHo-s
George B h/o B F 1866-1928 MtHo-s
John T h/o T B 1896-1969 MtHo-s
Thelma B w/o J T 1906-1981 MtHo-s
BOSS, Charles W 1898-1944 Park
BOTT, James S h/o S W 3 Dec 1886-10 Dec 1947 Edge
Sallie W w/o J S 20 Jan 1888-1 Apr 1947 Edge
BOUFFORD, A L Omer (h/o E U) 1914-1978 Holl
Elsie U (w/o A L O) 1908- Holl
BOULTER, Alberta E w/o J P 1872-1936 Wach
Charles 11 Mar-16 Mar 1918 Libe
Joseph P h/o A E 1868-1938 Wach
BOWDOIN, (BOWDEN),
Amanda W w/o Jno R (MD) d 19 Oct 1883; age: 54/7/0 Park
Bettie W 1864-1945 Park
George H (a friend of W C & M S Stevens) 1882-1951 Mitc-w
John H 1906-1976 Park
John Phillip Jr (Jay) 1963-1975 Park
Dr John W 1855-1939 Park
Madeline S 1911-1955 Park
Peter 13 Jan 1837-7 Apr 1913 Onan
Elton C (h/o M S) 1878-1938 Wach
Maggie S (w/o E C) 1882-1968 Wach

BOWMAN, Susan J 1872-1958 Park
BOYCE, Alvin D h/o Vercie Boyce Johnson 19 Aug 1889-19 Sept 1951 Park
Alvin D 23 Oct 1929-13 Feb 1977 Park
Bonnie Ellen d/o A & E 14 Nov 1952-22 Apr 1953 Park
Harry J 22 Apr 1910-6 Apr 1968 Libe
J Norman 1884-1927 Park
James L 19 Mar 1911-13 Oct 1967 Libe
Robert D s/o A D & Vercie 1925-1926 Park
BRADFORD, twins b&d 1915 Quin
d/o C K & Sylvia b&d 1955 Edge
A Roland (h/o L B) 27 Aug 1880-26 Mar 1951 Quin
Anna sis/o Rev Geo d 2 Aug 1886; age: 80 yrs Holl
Annie Maria w/o Wm T 1863-1956 Edge
B Thomas 1842-1917 Edge
Benjamin E s/o J E & S A 15 Dec 1864-16 Feb 1921 Brap
Betsy wid/o T H; mother/o Rev Geo Bradford d 29 July 1874; age: 93 yrs Holl
Betsy Ann 1966-1967 Wach
Clarence W (h/o M E M) 1887-1955 Holl
D Duncan 1878-1938 Brap
Dennis T 1893-1949 Edge
Edward S 1883-1952 Quin
Mrs Elcy wid/o T A 12 Jan 1763-29 Mar 1825; age: 62/2/17 Brad
Emily A 20 Feb 1826-4 Dec 1905 Edge
Emily J w/o Jno d 2 Nov 1897; age: 64 yrs BraH
Ezra h/o R J d 28 June 1880; age: 65 yrs BraW
Fannie S w/o L T 14 Oct 1861-26 Feb 1936 Tayl
Florrie E 15 July 1892-10 May 1974 Edge
Frank 1855-1938 Holl
Fred Thomas (h/o M K) 1869-1940 MtHo-s

BRADFORD (continued)
Rev George s/o Thos Hall & Elizabeth 13 Mar 1811-29 Dec 1888 Ordained a Baptist Elder in 1841. Baptised 29 Dec 1838. He served as Pastor to most of the churches in the Acc Association & many in MD & NC, & never changed his membership from the Pungoteague Church. Holl
George Thomas s/o Wm T & A M 15 Aug 1887-26 May 1892 Edge
George W h/o M C 1883-1941 Onan
Grace 1909-1976 Wach
J William 1884-1966 Fair
Capt John mariner of Accomack Co 14 June 1742-24 Feb 1771; age; 29 yrs TheF
John s/o Abel & Sarah 24 Mar 1809-12 Oct 1870 BraH
John E h/o S A 6 Dec 1843-17 Sept 1912 Brap
John Edwin 1917-1971 Quin
John H 1st h/o S A Sherwood 10 Jan 1830-13 Apr 1897 MtHo
John Martin 17 May 1911-28 Apr 1964 MtHo-s
John W 16 Oct 1835-16 Apr 1905 KelB
John William 1864-1920 MtHo
Joseph L s/o L T & Fannie 1 May-8 May 1887 Tayl
Katy w/o Arthur; d/o Wm & Rachel Bell d 19 Sept 1882; age: 77/1/6 Thos
L Fisher s/o Jno & Jane (Hyslup) 18 Mar 1856-23 Dec 1882 BraH
Lee C h/o R M 1911-1974 Libe
Levin T (h/o F S) 10 Dec 1862-14 Nov 1891; age: 29 yrs Tayl
Lillian B (w/o A R) 1894-1981 Quin
Maggie C w/o G W 1879-1937 Onan
Margaret Sarah 30 June 1846-4 Mar 1930 Holl
Mary E Mears (w/o C W) 1895- Holl

BRADFORD (continued)
Mary Kellum (w/o F T) 1878-1967 MtHo-s
Mary S 31 Jan 1859-4 Oct 1908 Edge
Mattie w/o E S 1894-1964 Quin
Pearl 1902-1976 StJo
Rachel Ann 29 July 1859-13 Oct 1918 Quin
Rachel J w/o Ezra d (19 Apr 1887 ?); age: 58/10/0 BraW
Robert Lee (h/o S B) 1 Apr 1885- Quin
Rosser C s/o L T & F S 14 June 1884-10 Apr 1905 Tayl
Ruth M w/o L G 1909- Libe
Sadie (w/o U T); d/o Geo W & B J Bell 15 July 1853-31 May 1943 Beac
Sadie Bell (w/o R L) 22 May 1889-21 Feb 1967 Quin
Sallie A w/o Wm T; d/o Hulton & Susan Kellam 2 Nov 1830-31 Dec 1912 MtPl
Sarah A w/o J E 9 Apr 1845-20 Apr 1921 Brap
Thomas A (h/o Elcy) 6 Mar 1764-8 July 1818; age: 54/4/2 Brad
Thomas H s/o Wm S & Sallie A 26 Sept 1862-21 Sept 1890 MtPl
Twillie (s/o Frank) 1890-1908 Holl
Upshur Teackle (h/o Sadie); s/o Jno & Jane (Hyslup) 31 Aug 1859-20 Oct 1934 Beac
William of Acc Co d 4 June 1769; age: 44 yrs Atla
William Abbie s/o G W & M C 20 Oct 1901-21 Aug 1919 Onan
William H 1927-1974 Wach
William T (h/o S A) 16 Apr 1834-13 Nov 1894 MtPl
William Thomas h/o A M 1853-1934 Edge
BRADLEY, Adrian C (h/o D C) 1899-1961 Fair
Atwill J 25 Aug 1889-25 Aug 1954 Gask-old
Bettie S (w/o I S) 1895-1977 Holl
Dorthea C (w/o A C) 1895-1963

BRADLEY (continued) Fair
Ira S (h/o B S) 1894-1970 Holl
BRADSHAW, Beatrice Newton 1904- Onan
Ella Dean 1863-1927 Onan
Stanley 10 Apr 1916-24 Sept 1979 Edge
William A 1879-1944 Onan
BRADY, Hildrey 1915- Libe
Vyrl H 1908- Libe
BRASHEARS, Robert L Sr 20 Nov 1911-19 Oct 1972 Fair
BRAUER, Wilhelmine (w/o W T) 1899-1968 Fair
William Thomas (h/o Wilhelmine) 16 Feb 1900-9 Feb 1976 Fair
BRAXTON, Margaret A w/o Jas 23 Oct 1844-18 Feb 1908 Gask-old
Viola B 30 June 1900-22 Feb 1920 EdmB
BREENE, James Edmond s/o Danl & Nancy b&d 2 Aug 1945 Fair
BRIM, Edward 1909-1969 Metr
Maggie 1885-1965 Metr
Malachi 1942-1975 Metr
Thomas d 11 Dec 1964; age: 44 yrs Metr
BRIMMAGE, Rachel N 1898-1977 NewM
BRITT, Eloise B 2 Feb 1924-27 May 1979 Park
BRITTINGHAM, Charles A h/o M D 4 Nov 1891-28 Mar 1939 MtHo
Elsie S (w/o O B) 1885-1961 MtHo-s
Granville W s/o J A & M E 22 Mar 1872-26 Sept 1940 Wach
John A (h/o M E) 22 June 1837-1 Dec 1912 Wach
John R (h/o V R) 1880-1959 StGe
M Elizabeth w/o J A 16 Mar 1845-1 Aug 1923 Wach
Mildred D w/o C A 1899-1942 MtHo
Oscar B (h/o E S) 1876-1969 MtHo-s
Valentine R (w/o J R) 1882-1969

BRITTINGHAM (continued) StGe
BRODIE, Mabel Watson 1913-1958 NewM
BROUGHTON, Edgar B 1888-1961 MtHo
Lillian Jacob (w/o W R) 5 Jan 1885-1 Nov 1975 MtHo
inf dau Mary nd MtHo
Norris M 2 Dec 1893-3 Oct 1958 MtHo
Rebecca McMath w/o W T 1862-1938 MtHo
William Roy Sr (h/o L J) 5 Oct 1884-20 July 1972 MtHo
William Thomas h/o R McM 1853-1943 MtHo
BROWN, (BROWNE),
Alma F w/o C B 1904-1982 Libe
Anna Drummond w/o T H B; d/o Jas Henry & Elizabeth Broadwater Fletcher 4 Dec 1849-2 Jan 1926 MtCu
B Hezekiah 1872-1951 Libe
Bernice M (w/o L H) 1908- Fair
Birdie B d/o J E & S A Bradford 16 Sept 1874-5 Apr 1904 Brap
Calvin 1875-1963 Holl
Carroll B h/o A F 1898-1945 Libe
Chancey 1919-1956 Snea
Charles Dickens 27 Feb 1927-24 Oct 1980 Park
Charles L (h/o M S) 1882-1921 Quin
Clifford L 1910-1922 Quin
Effie P w/o O L 3 June 1896-22 Oct 1973 Libe
Elizabeth 1902-1976 MtHo-s
Fletcher eldest s/o T H B & A D F 26 Dec 1873-24 Nov 1922 MtCu
Frances Cathrine Winder 1859-1950 MtHo
Frances L 1912- Quin
Francis Harvey 1856-1938 MtHo
Freddie J 1904-1961 Fair
Rev George M 1881-1955 NewM
Harold 1899-1938 Brap
Hattie G (w/o S E) 1879-1965 MtHo-s
Helen Virginia 8 Aug 1900-3 Apr

BROWN (continued)
1927 MtHo
John A (h/o L M) 7 Aug 1915-23 Jan 1932 Onan
John R h/o L G 1879-1974 Park
John T s/o C W & V E 12 Feb 1876-21 Sept 1903 Holl
Joseph L h/o M W 10 May 1890-16 Nov 1980 Edge
Katherine Powell 18 Feb 1871-17 Feb 1953 Holl
Larry H (h/o B M) 1898-1974 Fair
Lola G w/o J R 1880-1955 Park
Lorie C 1925-1979 Libe
Louise M (w/o J A) 23 May 1899-5 July 1921 Onan
Mamie w/o Warren 1902- Oakg
Margaret 1907-1981 Quin
Margaret d1924 Oakg
Margaret Bayly eldest ch/o Dr P F & S C 23 Jan-19 Oct 1841 MtCu
Marion Davis 16 Sept 1898-5 Nov 1925 MtHo
Maude Wescott w/o J L 8 July 1893-22 Oct 1982 Edge
Minnie S (w/o C L) 1882-1964 Quin
Norman A Sr 1899-1966 Park
Norris C 1910-1976 Fair
O Landon h/o E P 3 May 1896-22 Apr 1966 Libe
Orris Applethwaite s/o Dr P F & S C 8 Aug 1842-28 Sept 1898 (served in John Brown Insurrection - 1859 & surrendered with the cruiser *Shenandoah* - 6 Nov 1865) MtCu
Orris Devreaux s/o T H B & A D F 16 Apr-26 July 1883 MtCu
Dr Peter Fielding s/o Jno Eaton & Ann Elizabeth 6 Nov 1813 at Windsor nr Wmsburg-30 Nov 1880 at Drummondtown, Acc VA MtCu
Sally Cropper w/o Dr P F; d/o T M & M P C Bayly 22 Dec 1813-1 Jan 1857; mar: 14 Nov 1839 MtCu
Sheppard E (h/o H G) 1872-1947 MtHo-s

BROWN (continued)
Sidney K 1902-1959 Fair
Sue P 1927- Libe
Thomas H Bayly s/o Dr P F & S C 8 Feb 1844-27 Aug 1892 MtCu
Warne L d1956 StLu
Warren h/o Mamie 1902-1963 Oakg
BRUMAGE, Minnie J 25 July 1887-9 Aug 1916 Holl
BRYANT, s/o Rev R O & N J b&d 27 Nov 1927 Edge
Lelia D 30 Oct 1896-21 Sept 1982 MtHo-s
Lula M (w/o W J) 1898-1930 MtHo-s
Roger J 14 Sept 1915-9 Jan 1971 MtHo-s
William J (h/o L M) 16 Sept 1892-1 Sept 1971 MtHo-s
BUCKLE, Joan d/o S H & Polly 1929-1951 Onan
Polly w/o S H 1897- Onan
Stewart Henry h/o Polly 1894-1971 Onan
BUDD, inf twins b&d 27 May 1914 StGe
inf d/o D W & R S b&d 1939 Park
Allen T 1919-1983 Edge
Anna S w/o T E 10 Mar 1856-1 Apr 1929 Libe
Annie D w/o Wm T 1882-1962 Park
Annie L w/o T H 4 May 1869-26 Dec 1942 Quin
Bettie S Bloxom w/o G W d 31 Dec 1915; age: 40 rs Edge
C Dean d 1975 Fair
Charles I Sr (h/o G A) 1890-1961 StGe
Charles I Jr 10 Jan 1916-20 Mar 1964 StGe
Charlie R h/o E L 1885-1958 Park
Clara P w/o J F 1 Aug 1881-17 Dec 1969 Edge
Dorsey W h/o R S 1900-1951 Park
Edward H h/o L B 1886-1947 Libe

BUDD (continued)
Elizabeth w/o Wm d 16 July 1847; age: 64 yrs Budd
Ella w/o M T 1908- Libe
Ethel L w/o C R 1890-1960 Park
Eva Thomas w/o J Wm 1878-1954 Edge
Evie M w/o N R 10 Apr 1892-17 Aug 1975 Libe
Frank d 14 May 1962 MtHo
George-Anna (w/o C I Sr) 1889- StGe
George N 9 May 1863-13 July 1934 Edge
George Thomas s/o Thos H & Annie L 14 June-8 Oct 1887 Budd
George W 20 Feb 1847-10 Feb 1924 (erected by G W Budd Jr) Budd
George W d 8 Nov 1953 MtHo-s
Grace A (w/o J T) 1885-1955 Edge
Harold J h/o L F 1894-1966 Park
Helen D (w/o L E) 1889-1971 Edge
Henrietta d/o Wm & Elizabeth d 18 Feb 1891; age: 76 yrs Budd
Irving T b&d 18 Jan 1911 StGe
India w/o T H 1 Jan 1858-18 Nov 1883 Budd
Indie M w/o R C 1923- Fair
J Walter 1900-1968 Fair
James Arthur h/o L K 26 Sept 1904-8 Mar 1963 Edge
James F s/o Wm S & S A 13 June 1848-13 June 1870; age: 22 yrs Budd
James F h/o C P 15 Dec 1873-9 Nov 1958 Edge
James F h/o V L & M D 1882-1957 Park
John Carson 4 June 1893-1 Oct 1960 MtHo
John T 1849-1939 Budb
John T (h/o G A) 1880-1921 Edge
John William h/o E T 1864-1944 Edge
L Katherine w/o J A 10 Mar 1906-14 Dec 1964 Edge
Laban James 3 Feb 1854-27 Jan

BUDD (continued)
1936 Budb
Lizzie Sue 1885-1976 MtHo-s
Lloyd E (h/o H D) 1884-1941 Edge
Lottie F 1898- Park
Louis T 26 July 1910-15 Mar 1971 Edge
Louise M 23 Mar-27 Mar 1923 Libe
Lula B w/o E H 1894-1969 Libe
Manie K (w/o W S) 1879-1966 Onan
Manning T h/o Ella 1910-1952 Libe
Margie D w/o J F 1883-1978 Park
Martha Dix 1867-1947 Park
Mary A w/o W F 3 Dec 1856-7 July 1911 Park
Matilda d/o T T & Sally 28 Jan 1859-7 Oct 1870 Budb
Missouri F 20 July 1852-12 Aug 1888 Budd
Newell R h/o E M 13 Apr 1884-27 Apr 1934 Libe
Ralph T 18 Dec 1898-22 Sept 1978 Libe
Randall F h/o R P 24 Oct 1915-14 Dec 1974 Park
Raymond C h/o I M 1921-1978 Fair
Roxie S w/o D W 1907- Park
Ruth 6 Apr 1923-27 Dec 1946 StGe
Ruth P w/o R F 1920- Park
Sally w/o T T; d/o Denis & Nancy 14 Apr 1825-10 Jan 1889 Budb
Sarah A w/o Wm S 8 Nov 1820-4 Aug 1896 Budd
Sarah F d/o Geo & Missouri 17 Dec 1870-15 Sept 1872 Budd
Susan A w/o W H 27 Dec 1842-9 Oct 1903 Edge
Susan Ann 6 Oct 1845-9 Aug 1930 Budb
Thelma b&d 1915 Libe
Thomas E h/o A S 22 Oct 1850-17 Mar 1921 Libe
Thomas H (h/o A L) 29 Sept 1857-11 Oct 1941 Quin

BUDD (continued)
Thomas H Bennett 13 July 1912-4 Aug 1914 StGe
Thomas T h/o Sally; s/o Jno & Sally 3 Mar 1820-25 Feb 1860 Budb
Virginia 20 Apr 1851-30 Apr 1930 Budb
Virginia Lee w/o J F 24 Mar 1886-28 Apr 1911 Park
W F h/o M A 18 Sept 1852-29 Mar 1935 Park
William 6 Oct 1779-30 Nov 1848; age: 69 yrs Budd
William Bagwell 28 June 1877-11 Apr 1901 Budd
William H h/o S A 7 Feb 1841-20 Feb 1923 Edge
William S h/o S A 12 Mar 1812-13 May 1874; age: 62/2/1 Budd
William S (h/o M K) 1875-1944 Onan
William T h/o A D 1877-1960 Park
William T Sr 1882-1952 Libe
William T 1906-1968 Libe
William Tiffany 16 May 1908-26 Apr 1909 Edge
BUEHLER, Harry J 1909-1982 Park
BULL, see also BOOLE,
inf s/o Henry Frank & Henrietta nd Clov
inf children/o J T & Emma H nd MtHo
d/o J S & F L b&d 8 Dec 1893 Holf
s/o Leonard T & Manning W 5 Nov 1907-3 July 1908 Holf
d/o W E & S J b&d 5 Sept 1891 Fair
d/o Wm H & L M b&d 1906 Park
s/o Wm H & L M b&d 1908 Park
A Sidney h/o E S 17 Apr 1873-25 May 1939 Park
Alfred S 16 Dec 1852-31 Dec 1927 MtHo
Alice B d/o Wesley & Sallie 22 Sept 1890-16 Aug 1891 (unable to verify) FoxP
Alice L w/o J R 29 Apr 1854-2

BULL (continued)
Feb 1923 MtHo
Amanda A w/o H L 11 May 1862-18 Aug 1914 Quin
Annie G 16 Sept 1867-9 Oct 1925 Bulb
Armenia Edith w/o J E 3 Jan 1875-2 May 1949 Edge
Asa T h/o F M 1886-1944 Park
Avery Franklin h/o M L 1898-1976 Libe
Beach 1888-1966 MtHo
Benjamin Frank 1874-1956 Holl
Benjamin Franklin h/o B P 1848-1904 Holf
Benjamine T 7 Apr 1858-29 Sept 1929 Bulb
Bettie W d/o J T & H E 3 Dec 1860-28 Apr 1874 Bulb
Betty Parker w/o B F 1848-1890 Holf
Birtie L w/o W C 12 Oct 1878-4 May 1896 Park
Blanche S w/o Wm F Sr 1888-1970 Libe
C Coleburn 1894-1948 MtHo
Calvin B Sr 1946-1980 Park
Carrie B w/o F S 2 Oct 1892-Park
Carrie L C 1882-1928 MtHo
Cora L w/o W C 1881-1972 Libe
Carroll R h/o Va T 1877-1966 Fair
Cattrine Turner 1857-1947 MtHo
Charles M (h/o M L) 1891-1964 StGe
Delmas R 1908-1937 Holl
E E h/o E S 1862-1948 Park
E Parks 22 Dec 1915-4 Dec 1980 Park
E Russell (h/o H B) 1902-1954 Edge
Edna Mears 1886-1967 Holl
Edward C s/o W F & B S 21 Oct 1909-17 July 1910 Libe
Edward C 1911-1931 Libe
Edward S h/o S S 25 Jan 1821-8 Aug 1856 Holf
Edward T s/o Edwd T & M E 6 Mar 1876-25 Sept 1897; age: 21 yrs Buls
Elecia R w/o J D 13 Aug 1867-

BULL (continued)
19 Apr 1947 Edge
Eli W h/o M S Apr 1844-Mar 1917 MtHo
Eli W s/o E W & M S 18 Dec 1891-23 Mar 1892 MtHo
Elijah F (h/o Louisa) d 16 Nov 1914; age: 74 yrs Park
Elijah T 1892-1966 HTri
Elizabeth w/o G W 27 Apr 1838-18 Feb 1922 Park
Elizabeth B d/o E F & Louisa d 5 Apr 1877; age: 19 yrs Park
Elizabeth Carol d/o C R & V T 1933-1934 Fair
Elizabeth R w/o G E; d/o S M & E R Turlington 18 Sept 1835-16 July 1910 Turp
Elizabeth Susan w/o E E 1865-1935 Park
Ella S d/o W W & S E 24 June 1874-31 Jan 1919 MtHo
Eloise Cake (w/o J R) 1910- StGe
Elsie Wescott w/o S J 23 May 1882-9 Sept 1917 MtHo
Emma P w/o A F 31 Dec 1894-6 Dec 1920 Park
Estella Satchell w/o A S 23 Oct 1873-23 May 1963 Park
Esther E inf d/o J S & F L 7 Jan-10 Jan 1884 Holf
Eugene 1923-1945 MtHo-s
Fannie d/o J S & F L b&d 14 Oct 1891 Holf
Fannie L w/o J S 4 July 1862-14 Dec 1893 Holf
Flonnie M w/o A S 1889-1962 Park
Florence M d/o Wesley & Sallie 21 July 1888-29 Apr 1892 (unable to verify) FoxP
Florence V 1876-1967 Park
Floyd Duncan s/o J R & A L 7 Sept 1890-1 Mar 1894 MtHo
Floyd S h/o C B 4 Sept 1890-20 Nov 1979 Park
Frank S (h/o K B) 1904-1951 MtHo
Fred 1882-1955 Shil
Garland F 17 Oct 1915-6 Apr 1969 Park

BULL (continued)
George (Bud) 4 Jan 1889-2 Aug 1948 Park
George E (h/o E R) 21 Nov 1836-1892 Turp
George Edward (h/o S A) 16 Nov 1872-19 Aug 1941 Crad-s
George H s/o T S & Mary E 2 June 1900-1 June 1919 Holl
George W h/o Eliz 8 May 1833-8 Feb 1907 Park
George W 22 Feb 1856-23 Jan 1897 Holf
George W 1870-1952 Park
Gertrude Kilmon 16 Dec 1881-15 Mar 1934 MtHo
H Frank h/o H G 1869-1941 Park
H Lee h/o A A 12 May 1862-18 Sept 1937 Quin
Harriet E w/o J T; d/o Smith Phillips 6 Sept 1836-23 May 1907 Bulb
Harry C s/o Jno T & J A d 1 Apr 1892; age: 7/11/7 Bulp
Hazel B (w/o E R) 1906-1975 Edge
Henrietta G w/o H F 1871-1943 Park
Henry C (h/o E M); s/o Thos S & Pollie 18 Apr 1845-23 June 1865; age: 20/2/5 Holf
Henry Edward 17 Aug 1897-6 Sept 1952 Edge
Henry R h/o P H; s/o Elisha & Esther 12 Oct 1836-25 Aug 1877 MtHo-s
Henry R (h/o L F) 1872-1946 MtHo-s
Herman Fristoe 22 Dec 1895-15 Oct 1957 Edge
Jack Pheobus 2 Feb 1928-3 Dec 1972 Park
James Barton 16 Nov 1908-2 Jan 1943 Park
James D h/o E R 24 Mar 1854-25 Feb 1922 Edge
James H 1895-1963 MtHo
James Heath s/o S T & V E 6 Dec 1875-11 July 1876 Holf
James R h/o A L 1 Oct 1854-10 Oct 1908 MtHo
James Robert s/o Thos & Harriet

BULL (continued)
E 6 July 1854-20 Apr 1900 Hutc
James Robert (h/o E C) 1900-1976 StGe
James Russell b&d 1978 Edge
James S h/o M D 1905- Park
Jennie L d/o E W & M S 10 Jan-12 Mar 1878 MtHo
John Edward h/o A E 4 Mar 1875-7 Jan 1939 Edge
John T h/o J A 11 Sept 1846-14 Mar 1894 Bulp
John T 1927-1972 Shil
John Thomas 26 Nov 1878-1 July 1958 MtHo
John W 16 Oct 1864-21 June 1924 Bulb
Joseph S h/o F L 11 June 1850-6 Apr 1923 Holf
Joseph S 1895-1948 Fair
Joseph T (h/o H E) 16 Nov 1826-27 Jan 1887 Bulb
Joseph V s/o Sydney J & Susie J 5 Jan 1911-22 Oct 1914 MtHo
Josephine Hutchinson 1869-1928 Hutc
Julia A w/o Jno T 28 Mar 1851-4 Apr 1912 Bulp
Kate Turlington 25 July 1890-19 Feb 1977 Onan
Kathrine Rose w/o L J 1869-1961 MtHo
Kitty N d/o Thos W & Lizzie 20 Jan 1858-17 May 1873 Bull
Lafayette Harmerson s/o S T & V E 6 Dec 1875-11 July 1876 Holf
Lena E d/o W W & S E 8 Oct 1884-18 Oct 1907 MtHo
LeRoy James h/o K R 1869-1947 MtHo
Lillian d/o L J & K R 27 Oct 1891-14 Aug 1892 MtHo
Lola N w/o W L 12 June 1876-16 May 1928 Onan
Lottie E 19 Nov-25 Nov 1905 StGe
Louis P h/o M E 1896-1945 Edge
Louise M d/o J R & A L 30 Oct 1899-5 Mar 1900 MtHo

BULL (continued)
Lula F (w/o H R) 1874-1943 MtHo-s
Lula M w/o Wm H 1884-1965 Park
Lydia S d/o W E & S J 20 Aug 1894-3 Jan 1895 Fair
Lydia Susan d/o W E & S J 19 Jan-29 Aug 1897 Fair
M E Missouri w/o H C; d/o Wm C & ? M(iers?) 8 Nov 1817-? Dec 1866 (stone badly worn) Holf
Madeline B w/o R B 22 Dec 1902-2 Aug 1982 Park
Madeline D w/o J S 1906-1978 Park
Mae T (w/o S C) 1877-1935 Onan
Maggie 1881-1974 Shil
Maggie A w/o S W 1875-1951 Park
Malisha Joynes w/o T C 5 May 1874-15 Jan 1920 MtHo-s
Marcie Parks w/o Geo 9 Sept 1887-10 Feb 1972 Park
Margaret 1919-1977 HTri
Margaret B (w/o R J) 1903- MtHo-s
Margarette S w/o E W Dec 1847-Dec 1922 MtHo
Mary 1897-1963 Shil
Mary d1979 MtHo
Mary A w/o Jas D d/o J M & S A Ross d 28 June 1856; age: 26 yrs Ross
Mary A w/o Shepherd T; d/o Geo A & Ann Kellam 12 Dec 1852-27 Nov 1872 MtPl
Mary Ann w/o Wm; d/o Jas & Mary Mears 27 Oct 1827-29 Nov 1857 Meac
Mary E w/o Edwd T d 29 July 1900; age: 63 yrs Buls
Mary E 1876-1943 Holl
Mary E w/o L P 1923-1944 Edge
Mary F d/o J R & Susan 24 Dec 1852-4 Feb 1876 MtHo
Mary Lynn 1876-1951 MtHo
Mary Rogers 1879-1946 Holf
Maude L (w/o C M) 1895-1966 StGe
Maude Lee w/o A F 1906 Libe

BULL (continued)
Mirt Wise 1870-1925 MtHo
Missouri M 1851-1924 MtHo
Missouri T d/o W W & S E 4 June 1877-26 Sept 1911 MtHo
Morris 1903-1960 Onan
Nancy d 30 May 1899; age: 69 yrs Edge
Norman C 1917-1971 (bur Gettysburg Natl Cem) Libe
Oakley K 1899-1943 Park
P Barton h/o M B 15 Mar 1901- Park
Parker 5 Apr 1861- HTri
Paul G s/o Soula G & May E 29 Aug 1900-20 Apr 1901 Bulp
Polly H w/o H R d 29 Aug 1923; age: 90/6/0 MtHo-s
R Barton h/o M B 15 Mar 1901-28 Nov 1983 Park
Reggie H s/o S W & M A 31 Mar-11 Sept 1895 Park
Richard H 1899-1969 Fair
Robert S 1877-1933 MtHo
Roy James (h/o M B) 1903-1965 MtHo-s
Sadie A (w/o G E) 8 Nov 1874-25 June 1953 Crad-s
Sallie E w/o W W 1853-1936 MtHo
Sallie Elizabeth 24 Nov 1899-19 Aug 1977 Edge
Sally nd MtHo
Sarah Walter (w/o W E) 20 Dec 1863-28 Mar 1950 Fair
Shafter nd MtHo
Sheppard T h/o V E 9 Nov 1848-21 Jan 1912 Holf
Sidney J (h/o S J) 1887-1968 MtHo-s
Soula C (h/o M T) 1876-1942 Onan
Southey W h/o M A 1873-1942 Park
Stonewall J h/o E W 2 Dec 1863-11 June 1939 MtHo
Susan Reeston w/o Jas R; d/o Mitchel & Susan (Byrd) Chandler 4 Mar 1825-12 Sept 1885 MtHo
Susan S w/o E S 12 Apr 1825-29 June 1900 Holf

BULL (continued)
Susie J (w/o S J) 1886-1973 MtHo-s
Thomas C h/o M J 25 Sept 1865-26 Mar 1924 MtHo-s
Veeda E Shrieves w/o A F 26 Nov 1904-31 May 1932 Libe
Vetreal nd MtHo
Victoria E w/o S T 20 Jan 1845-2 Jan 1932 Holf
Victoria Goffigon 9 Oct 1913-16 Sept 1914 Holf
Virginia T d/o E S & S S 11 Oct 1846-18 July 1869 Holf
W C h/o C L 1875-1937 Libe
Warner 1902-1968 Onan
Wesley W h/o S E 1851-1929 MtHo
Wharton F 1895- MtHo-s
William Edward (h/o S W) 8 Feb 1854-16 Oct 1915 Fair
William F Sr h/o B S 1882-1943 Libe
William F Jr 1921-1970 Libe
William H h/o L M 1882-1977 Park
William L h/o L N 29 May 1874-18 June 1943 Onan
Willie Mathews 19 Sept 1920-25 Mar 1983 Park
BULLOCK, Wiley 1915-1975 Fair
BULMAN, Durwood M 1907-1964 Wach
Elizabeth B (w/o L S) 1896-1980 Wach
Elizabeth S (w/o P R) 1887-1974 Wach
Flavius Josephus (h/o J H) 1 Dec 1858-8 Dec 1928 Wach
Jessie Hume w/o F J 20 Jan 1875-13 Mar 1918 Wach
Leon S (h/o E B) 1892- Wach
Leroy C 27 Nov 1830-28 June 1890 Mapp
Muscoe R h/o T S 23 Aug 1856-9 Sept 1927 Wach
Percy R (h/o E S) 1888-1965 Wach
Theresa S w/o M R 31 Mar 1862-8 Apr 1939 Wach
BUNDICK, inf s/o W W & N L nd Park

BUNDICK (continued)
inf s/o J T & Henrietta b&d 1917 Park
baby girl d 12 Nov 1967; age: 0/0/1 Burt
Albert nd JoyC
Albert Hudson d 12 Sept 1923 StGe
Alfred J (h/o E S) 26 Jan 1832-2 Apr 1919 Edge
Amie 1901-1955 NewM
Andrew D (s/o D C & E L) 1917-1983 Libe
Andrew S s/o Jno & Sallie 28 May 1894-4 Mar 1914 Libe
Annie w/o J H; d/o W E & R S Lilliston 13 Apr 1909-19 Dec 1884 Edge
Annie B (w/o J T) 1890-1971 Quin
Annie Lou w/o J H 30 Nov 1920- TheG
Annie W 1854-1901 Libe
Beatrice E w/o C O 1918- Edge
Benjamin R s/o Jno & Bettie 30 June 1881-13 Oct 1882 OldH
Berdie G w/o R S 1881-1963 MtHo
Bettie L (w/o J F) 4 July 1854-8 Mar 1936 Quin
Betty Ruth w/o E T 1924-1961 Park
Billy R 1924-1936 Park
Blanche S w/o C T 1916-1973 Libe
Brantley W h/o J P 1912- Park
Carroll O h/o B E 1906-1969 Edge
Cecil A 11 May 1909-2 Feb 1976 Edge
Cecil M h/o M S 1904- Libe
Charles T h/o H T 1891-1964 Park
Clinton T h/o B S 1913- Libe
Colombus W h/o M E 1868-1959 Park
Daisey M w/o W L 26 June 1879-25 Feb 1949 Edge
Dame A w/o R J 8 Sept 1845-5 Mar 1910 Park
Dora E 1901-1978 Libe
Dorothy d/o C T & H T 16 Dec

BUNDICK (continued)
1915-12 Nov 1920 Park
Dulanie C h/o E L 1889-1978 Libe
Edward C h/o M L J 7 Mar 1875-27 Nov 1929 Park
Edward J 1875-1954 Park
Edward T h/o B R 1906- Park
Elizabeth 1906-1957 JoyC
Elizabeth S (w/o A J) 6 Nov 1837-12 July 1912 Edge
Elizabeth Sarah S d/o Jno S & A C 12 Oct 1812-12 Oct 1836; age: 24 yrs BunW
Ernest G h/o W S 1903-1978 Edge
Ernest M (h/o V D) 1890-1957 Quin
Essie L w/o D C 1893-1964 Libe
Ethel C 1889-1973 Park
Etta B w/o J D 1883-1933 Park
Etta L 16 Nov 1884-28 Feb 1976 Edge
Eunice H w/o G E 1917- Park
Eva D (w/o J T) 1876-1946 Onan
G Elwood h/o E H 1908-1978 Park
George A 1908-25 June 1976 MtHo-s
George E (h/o O E) 1867-1952 MtHo-s
George H 1884-1913 Libe
George S s/o J D & E B 15 July 20 Nov 1908 Park
Hamner Dunkley w/o J Wm 1903-1977 Onan
Hampton K h/o M B 1903-1943 StGe
Harry L d 26 May 1948; age: 66 yrs MtHo
Helen T w/o C T 1892- Park
Henrietta w/o J T 1880-1917 Park
Henrietta M w/o O L 1884-1947 Edge
Izona B w/o J L 1885-1970 Libe
J H 1880-1932 MtHo
J Hamilton h/o A L 27 Feb 1923-21 Mar 1980 TheG
J Thomas h/o Henrietta 1882- 1957 Park
James A 31 May-8 Sept 1902

BUNDICK (continued)
Edge
James Eldred (h/o M E) 1858-1944 Wach
Jane w/o Jno S d 28 Apr 1855; age: 79/3/19 JnoS
JoAnne d/o C M & M S 1935-1943 Libe
John of W h/o L F 15 Apr 1832-16 Aug 1913 Park
John B h/o M E 19 Jan 1810-28 May 1888 OldH
John D h/o E B 1880-1948 Park
John F (h/o B L) 7 Aug 1854-4 Apr 1904 Quin
John S h/o Ann C - she m2 S Taylor; s/o John A & Elizabeth 1 Feb 1785-2 May 1821 (married 9 yrs, leaving adored wife & 2 daus) BunW
John S h/o Jane d Aug 1861; age: 80/3/0 JnoS
John T (G?) 5 Mar 1840-6 May 1914 Libe
John T (h/o E D) 1873-1925 Onan
John T (h/o A B) 1886-1953 Quin
John T Jr 17 May 1921-10 Feb 1955 Edge
John Thomas h/o S T 22 Feb 1892-5 Sept 1943 Edge
John W h/o S B 1881-1939 Park
John William h/o H D 1904-1950 Onan
Joseph L h/o I B 1882-1972 Libe
Juanita P w/o B W 1918-1983 Park
Kate S w/o W T 15 Aug 1849-10 Mar 1915 Onan
Laura V w/o R W 1898-1954 Park
LeRoy W 3 Mar 1905-12 Nov 1928 Onan
Lora Neville w/o Thos 6 July 1875-24 Aug 1908 MtHo
Louise S Ewell 1917-1976 Edge
Lovey F w/o Jno of W 15 Feb 1838-16 Dec 1919 Park
Maefield S w/o C M 1911-1973 Libe
Mamie L J w/o E C 9 May 1885-29 Jan 1977 Park

BUNDICK (continued)
Manie D (w/o W H) 1867-1932 Quin
Margaret E w/o J B; nee Floyd d 1 June 1883; age: 55/8/8 OldH
Margaret Matilda d/o J B & M E d 17 June 1852; age: 0/7/0 OldH
Margaret S w/o E T 26 Mar 1844-7 Jan 1896 Home
Margaret Savage 1893-1955 Fair
Martha A w/o W S 25 Dec 1852-11 Feb 1928 MtHo
Martin Gillett 1880-1958 Park
Mary A C d/o Jno S & A C 1 Apr 1814-7 Jan 1848; age: 33/9/6 BunW
Mary B (w/o H K) 1905- StGe
Mary E w/o Thos 1 Aug 1844-3 July 1913 Park
Mary E 1848-1935 Park
Mary Ellen w/o J E 1863-1939 Wach
Mary S d 14 Mar 1958; age: 70 yrs Bays
Mary Thomas w/o Wm T 1888-1964 Libe
Mason L Sr 1906-1982 Edge
Missouri E w/o C W 1871-1948 Park
Nancy Lee w/o W W 12 Feb 1865-1 Mar 1929 Park
Nancy Payne (w/o W T) 1836-8 June 1930 Quin
Ocea E (w/o G E) 1873-1946 MtHo-s
Oscar L h/o H M 1883-1959 Edge
Oscar Lee h/o V S 1887-1967 Libe
Otho 1897-1974 JoyC
Pearl Mears 1897-1918 Quin
Ralph W 3 Dec 1920-26 Nov 1944 (VA, 319 Inf WW II) Libe
Ray T 1877-1926 Park
Richard J h/o D A 13 Sept 1847-20 Feb 1932 Park
Richard J Jr s/o R J & D A 1 Apr 1880-3 Nov 1941 Park
Richard S h/o B G 1877-1954 MtHo
Robert 1900-1963 NewM

BUNDICK (continued)
Robert E 28 Jan 1891-23 Feb 1920 Edge
Robert Lee 1903-1943 Libe
Roy W h/o L V 1894-1970 Park
Ruth E w/o W T 1926-1979 Edge
Sallie D 22 May 1861-1 Sept 1932 Park
Sallie F w/o J G 21 Apr 1859-16 July 1905 Libe
Sallie T (w/o J T) 1896-1958 Edge
Shirley Simpson (w/o Ervin Linwood) 25 Feb 1938-23 Apr 1975 Fair
Sidney L 1879-1905 Libe
Susie B w/o J W 1890-1933 Park
Sylvia M 1925- Edge
Thomas h/o M E 9 Nov 1836-12 Sept 1924 Park
Vernetta S w/o O L 1888-1962 Libe
Victoria A 22 Dec 1909- Park
Virginia D (w/o E M) 1893-1964 Quin
W W h/o N L 19 Dec 1865-16 May 1915 Park
Wendel P 1945-1979 Park
William A 1873-1940 MtHo
William H (h/o M D) 1867-1952 Quin
William L h/o D M 7 Feb 1866-3 Mar 1938 Edge
William S h/o M A d 18 July 1906; age: 62 yrs MtHo
William T h/o K S 15 Feb 1847-9 Dec 1908 Onan
William T 6 Dec 1867-24 Feb 1938 Park
William T s/o Jno & Sallie 13 Dec 1875-3 Nov 1900; age: 24/10/20 Libe
William T 11 Oct 1893-15 Jan 1914 Quin
Wm T s/o O L & H M 16 July 1916-7 May 1918 Edge
William T h/o R E 1919- Edge
William Thomas (h/o N P) 1845-3 July 1919 Quin
William Thomas h/o M T 1882-1975 Libe
Willye S w/o E G 1904- Edge

BUNTING, Albert 1921-1982 Snea
Alonza L h/o E Y 1868-1940 Park
Annie P w/o W R; d/o Jas K & Elizabeth Shield 15 Aug 1827-17 Dec 1891 Shie
Betty C 1887-1978 Snea
Blanche 1900-1974 Snea
Catherine T w/o Solomon 11 Nov 1801-7 Jan 1868 OldF
Edward W h/o S T 1867-1942 Wach
Ellen Mears w/o J W 1902-1968 HTri
Elma H (w/o E C) 1910- Fair
Elmer C (h/o E H) 1908-1980 Fair
Emily Y w/o A L 1867-1946 Park
Eunice R w/o M L 1924-1974 HTri
Fern Ayers w/o H E 1906-1981 Wach
G Lambertine 1849-1930 Quin
George S s/o Thos C d 30 Sept 1851; age: 15/10/14 Bunt
Harry Edward h/o F A 1898-1961 Wach
James L 1947-1978 HTri
Rev James W h/o E M 1901-1954 HTri
John A nd Shil
John E 1897-1959 Shil
Junior 1919-1921 MtHo
Lahera T d/o Thos & Harriet P 8 Sept 1854-26 Sept 1863 KelG
Lester J 1919-1982 Snea
Mary B 1863-1948 Quin
Mary E 1908-1967 NewM
Milton L h/o E R 1923- HTri
Norman 1911-1982 Shil
Quay s/o G L & M E 10 Mar 1898-15 Feb 1923 Quin
Rachel G d/o Thos & Harriet P 7 Jan 1856-23 Sept 1863 KelG
Rose Campbell 1910-1928 MtHo
Sallie T w/o E W 1871-1957 Wach
Sallie W 1833-1925 Park
Soloman (h/o C T) d 11 July 1850; age: 64/7/21 Bunt
Susanah C d 7 Oct 1830; Age: 51

BUNTING (continued)
yrs Bunt
Thelma T 1899-1979 Park
Thomas C (s/o Soloman) 8 Mar 1812-1 Oct 1877 Bunt
William L 1893-1968 Park
William R h/o A P 15 Mar 1830-24 Jan 1909 Shie
BURCKARD, Alice J d/o Augustus & Sarah 11 Apr 1882-23 Dec 1886 (moved from Burckard bur gr) Onan
Augustus W s/o Augustus & Sarah 3 July 1870-19 Mar 1892 (moved from Burckard bur gr) Onan
John T s/o Augustus & Sarah E 18 Jan 1873-17 July 1874 (moved from Burckard bur gr) Onan
S A footstone only (moved from Burckard bur gr) Onan
BURDGE, Brian P 3 Feb 1957-20 Aug 1977 Fair
Evelyn W 14 Dec 1920-27 May 1978 Fair
BURFORD, Alfred Coleburn h/o H J 1912-1973 Park
Beulah C w/o J I 1881-1970 Burf
Helen Jenkins w/o A C 1921- Park
John I h/o B C 1875-1942 Burf
John W s/o J I & B C 1905-1971 Burf
BURGESS, Margaret Bell 1882-1963 Onan
Robert Lee 1886-1955 Onan
BURKE, Henrietta H (w/o W E) 1893-1975 Fair
Pearl Cropper 1914-1962 Park
William E (h/o H H) 1890-1978 Fair
BURKHEAD, Jerry C 19 Oct 1946-8 Feb 1968 Park
Junius J 22 June 1895-12 Feb 1983 Park
BURKINS, H Carroll 1895-1956 Libe
BURROUGHS, Cecil Fox 24 Apr 1894-21 Jan 1981 MtHo
Ralph A 6 Oct 1890-26 Jan 1954 MtHo-s

BURTON, baby girl b&d 1931 MtHo
Addie C 5 Mar 1887-13 Dec 1976 Wach
Albert Floyd h/o M E 1858-1927 Wach
Alexander O 1863-1936 MtHo
Alice 1913-1980 Shil
Annie C 1938-1966 Burt
Charles H (h/o M T) 18 June 1884-20 Oct 1964 Ptea
Charles S h/o G B 22 May 1877-9 Dec 1964 Wach
Charles S 1913-1914 MtHo-s
Charles Shields 1856-1931 Wach
Charlie H 1902-1968 NewM
Claude 1900-1982 NewM
Daisey 1877-1949 Burt
David 20 Oct 1889-19 Dec 1908 JoyC
Edith S w/o W F 1914-1970 Wach
Edward T Sr h/o M J 10 June 1860-21 Nov 1932 Burt
Edward T Jr h/o H A 1890-1975 Burt
Edward T 1922-1981 NewM
Effie M 1880-1966 MtHo
Elizabeth M 1914- MtHo-s
Emma L J 1901-1979 Snea
Gertrude B w/o C S 27 Feb 1882-12 Dec 1952 Wach
Gloria June Chase 1929- Park
Grace M 1886-1966 MtHo
Haddassah 1875-1945 MtHo
Hallie A w/o E T Jr 1890-1967 Burt
Harold H s/o E T & H A 14 May 1923-7 Aug 1938 Burt
Harry F h/o M A 1886-1966 MtHo-s
Harry F Jr 1913-1953 MtHo-s
Harvey L 8 Feb 1882-24 Jan 1955 Wach
Herbert s/o W C & Helen B 13 Oct 1910-15 Dec 1918 Edge
Herbert T s/o H F & M A 8 Dec-23 Dec 1914 MtHo-s
Ira F h/o S C 1882-1931 Wach
James 1879-1953 Burt
James Henry 1883-1956 Snea
James W (h/o Maria) 2 June

BURTON (continued)
1844-17 Aug 1913; age: 69/2/15 Burb
James W 1919-1973 Burt
Jennie C w/o E T 24 Sept 1866-9 Apr 1885 Burg
Jennie M w/o J T 14 Dec 1854-10 Nov 1916 MtHo
John Ashby s/o Jno J R & Sallie M d 28 Sept 1858; age: 0/9/1 Brad
John E 6 Mar 1869-18 Feb 1926 NewM
John Edward s/o E T & H A 10 May 1917-7 Aug 1938 Burt
John J R (h/o Sallie M); d/o Joshua & Polly d 10 Oct 1865; age: 34/1/21 Brad
John M F s/o Jno J R & Sallie M d 31 Aug 1862; age: 0/8/28 Brad
John R Sr h/o M S 1890-1961 Wach
Joshua (h/o Polly) 8 Dec 1783-15 Feb 1859; age: 77 yrs Brad
Joshua T h/o J M; s/o Wm & Margt A 14 May 1853-15 July 1912 MtHo
Joshua T B 1855-1909 MtHo-s
Junita Bundick 1934-1951 StGe
Kristine Sande 1949- Edge
Laura L w/o W J 6 Dec 1855-19 Jan 1886 Wach
Lizzie S d/o Chas F & Mary E 14 Aug 1896-18 July 1897 FoxB
Lloyd S s/o Obedience & Mary 24 Feb 1860-16 Oct 1893 Burb
Lolita Boggs (w/o V S) 1885-1960 Fair
M Page 1896-1965 MtHo
Mabel E 25 Aug 1892-25 Aug 1972 Onan
Maggie 1894-1958 Snea
Margaret 14 Mar-16 Mar 1899 BurJ
Margaret A 3 Mar 1820-12 May 1898 BurJ
Margaret S 1879-1939 MtHo-s
Margaret S w/o J R Sr 1886-1959 Wach
Margaret S 1891-1963 MtHo

BURTON (continued)
Maria w/o J W 10 Mar 1843-9 June 1908 Burb
Mary Anne w/o H F 1889-1946 MtHo-s
Mary D 1899-1980 NewM
Mary E w/o Chas F 8 Dec 1857-21 Jan 1904 FoxB
Mary E w/o A F 1868-1948 Wach
Mary Jane w/o E T Sr 24 Oct 1865-3 Mar 1940 Burt
Maude T (w/o C H) 4 Sept 1889-10 Aug 1973 Ptea
Minnie V 1882-1951 MtHo
Morris W s/o H F & M A 3 Dec 1918-27 Feb 1919 MtHo-s
Mortimer J 1888-1964 MtHo
Obedience s/o Saml & Mary 22 Mar 1838-5 Apr 1905 Burb
Otho Elwood s/o J T & J M 3 July 1878-28 Nov 1886 MtHo
Otho Lee s/o M J & Margt S 29 Feb 1912-4 June 1913 MtHo
Peggy Ann 1925-1950 Wach
Polly w/o Joshua; d/o Thos & Alica Bradford 27 July 1786-18 Nov 1832; age: 66 yrs Brad
Ralph G 1891-1955 MtHo
Rennie S 1859-1950 MtHo-s
Richard Coard 1946- Edge
Sagasta 1898-1972 NewM
Sallie M w/o Jno R 14 Oct 1834-3 Mar 1904 Locu
Sallie T w/o Garrison nd Oakg
Sarah d 16 Apr 1882; age: 47 yrs Burt
Sarah Core w/o I F 1888-1978 Wach
Sarah Jane d/o E T & J C 8 Apr 1885-3 May 1886 Burg
Sarah Swanger w/o W A 1860-1947 Edge
Sue Fisher (w/o T K) 16 Dec 1900-14 Feb 1977 Fair
Thomas Kellam Sr (h/o S F) 17 Oct 1897-28 June 1968 Fair
Veris B w/o Walter 1907-1962 Burt
Vernon Swanger (h/o L B) 1883-1956 Fair
W Heber 1882-1939 MtHo-s

BURTON (continued)
Walter h/o V B 1902-1968 Burt
Webster 1905-1978 Burt
William Ashby h/o S S 1859-1942 Edge
William Copes 27 July 1903-15 Dec 1948 Wach
William F h/o E S 1906-1978 Wach
William F 19 Feb 1820-23 Aug 1894 BurJ
William J h/o L L 5 Apr 1846-11 Apr 1915 Wach
William T 2 Apr 1896-28 Sept 1941 MtHo
William T s/o Wm T & Gertrude 18 May-15 Nov 1919 MtHo
BUTLER, Carrie 1889-1978 Gask
Donald C 2 Aug 1918-5 Apr 1962 Onan
Frank Llewellyn Jr 5 May 1897-10 Feb 1972 Onan
Grace H 1899-1952 Onan
Henry Luther 5 Oct 1886-19 Apr 1946 Onan
Nannie M 1903-1958 JoyC
BUTTS, Estelle Louise 1893-1973 Gask
BYRD, (BIRD),
A James (h/o S C) 27 Feb 1860-25 May 1937 Mear
Aaron S 1884-1968 Park
Abel J (h/o S A) 16 Jan 1825-16 Feb 1885 MeaB
Annie West d/o A J & Sarah Mears Bird (5th line of Wm Bird of Westover, VA) 20 July 1869-18 July 1933 MeaB
Austin J Jr (h/o B L) 1894-1973 Fair
Bertha V 1896-1971 Smit
Bessie L (w/o A J) 1894- Fair
Bettie M w/o W S 24 Jan 1844-22 May 1924 Park
C M 1875-1964 MtHo-s
Carrie S w/o G T 1868-1963 Wach
Charles L h/o M V 6 June 1849-21 Jan 1925 Park
Charles Wise MD s/o Chas L & Va (Bundick) 9 Sept 1886-14 Sept 1933 mar: Sallie Camp-

BYRD (continued)
bell Johnston - 8 June 1910 Edge
Daisy Euginia d/o A J & S A 12 Feb 1863-16 Jan 1923 MeaB
E Cora w/o A J; d/o Benja W & Emma (Mapp) Mears 6 Aug 1868-23 Apr 1926 Mear
E Roy h/o M A 1876-1940 Park
Edward P h/o M E S 1845-1925 Park
Ella D w/o L J 24 May 1867-19 May 1922 Park
Emma Sarah 1881-1957 MtNe
Ethel G (w/o J M) 1889-1970 Fair
Era L d/o A J & E C 23 Mr-23 June 1890 Mear
George E 7 Mar 1934 Smit
George T h/o C S 1866-1932 Wach
Georgiana H d/o Abel J & Sarah A d 3 Feb 1853; age: 5/9/12 MeaB
Harriet Parker 1850-1934 MtHo-s
Henry R 1892-1943 Oakg
Henry R s/o Henry R & Sudie F 18 Jan 1919-27 Mr 1919 Oakg
J Clifford Jr 21 Sept 1918-11 Nov 1974 Park
J Milton (h/o E G) 1888-1963 Fair
Jane 1868-1940 Park
Jessica Ann d 19 Feb 1970 Park
John Abbott 1889-1936 Park
John H 21 July 1853-24 Dec 1885 MeaB
John T h/o M N M 5 Aug 1856-28 Feb 1899 Park
Lela C (w/o M F) 1 July 1880-31 Mar 1964 Ptea
Levin J h/o E D 26 Dec 1864-13 Nov 1940 Park
Lillie R w/o W L 1875-1952 MtHo
Mabelle M 1894-1977 Park
Maggie N Mason w/o J T 1866-1921 (bur Charlottesville VA) Park
Mahlon F (h/o L C) 14 Apr 1872-22 May 1929 Ptea
Margaret E S w/o E P 1845-

BYRD (continued) Park
Marion U 2 May 1893-7 Nov 1969 Park
Marvin L 1 Sept 1923-10 July 1974 Ptea
Mary C w/o Jno 26 Dec 1827-22 Dec 1912 Onan
Mary V w/o C L 17 Sept 1855-2 Mar 1912 Park
Mattie Gray 1880-1959 Park
Maude A w/o E R 1879-1942 Park
Milton Levi s/o Wm & Rona 1 June 1924-9 Mar 1926 MtHo
Nancy J 27 Oct 1824-22 Aug 1911 Park
Norman F 4 Nov 1902-31 Jan 1976 Ptea
Ocia 1888-1956 JoyC
Polly P w/o Staton F 1869-1950 Park
Prentice C 30 Mar 1918-13 Feb 1960 Ptea
Rachel w/o Henry; d/o Peter & Anna Snead 10 May 1840-14 Mar 1889 Gask-old
Richard P 4 Mar 1813-4 July 1881 Park
Robert Lee 15 Sept 1926-25 Feb 1960 Snea
Sarah A w/o A J 10 May 1828-25 May 1912 MeaB
Sarah T 1882-1974 MtHo-s
Stanley Milton s/o W L & Rosa L 25 Mar 1909-6 Jan 1919 MtHo
Tabbie K 1882-1974 MtHo-s
W Scott h/o B M 8 Oct 1847-16 July 1919 Park
William E s/o A J & S A 1 Mar 1858-23 Sept 1945 MeaB
William L h/o L R 1869-1945 MtHo
BYRON, Anna sister/o Isabel Cutler 1874-1968 Cutl
CAHALL, Joseph Laws s/o Dr Lawrence M & Elizabeth A (Cannon); grson/o Gov Wm Cannon b at Bridgeville DE 9 Aug 1859-d at Georgetown DE 28 June 1937 (Secr of State of

CAHALL (continued) DE 1905-1909) Onan
CAIN, James L 3 Oct 1914-29 Jan 1969 MtHo
CALLAHAN, Rev Griffen h/o Susan, the d/o Luke & Susanna (Christian) Luker 1759-22 Aug 1833 Oakg
Griffen W h/o L A 1803-1841 Oakg
Leah A w/o G W 22 Sept 1805-21 Feb 1895 Oakg
CALLAWAY, Granville (h/o M F) 1919-1965 Wach
Marie F (w/o G L) 1921- Wach
CALLOWAY, Rebecca Holland 25 May 1951-6 June 1974 Edge
Wendy L d/o R H 14 Nov 1973-6 June 1974 Edge
CAMPBELL, A C h/o M S 1856-1929 MtHo
Aaron R 1905-1981 Park
Archibald 20 Nov 1753-17 June 1852 (one of founders of Old Friendship Church; Revolutionary soldier) MtHo
Arron J h/o L M 1904- Onan
Belvia L w/o J W 18 Apr 1902-17 Nov 1982 Park
Claude L h/o S W 1884-1958 MtHo
Core E 1881-1945 MtHo
David 1928-1962 Snea
Edwin Francis 6 June 1942-14 Oct 1969 MtHo-s
Frank A h/o S W 1832-1883 MtHo
Frank A h/o H E 11 Oct 1862-21 Mar 1932 MtHo
George W (h/o M K) 1907-1971 MtHo-s
Hennie E w/o F A; d/o J C & Mary Bunting 22 Jan 1861-24 July 1892 MtHo
John B 20 Mar 1855-29 Aug 1888 Budd
John W h/o B L 17 Aug 1901-1 Feb 1981 Park
John W Jr 24 Oct 1924 Park
Josephine Travis 27 Sept 1881-5 Mar 1945 Onan
Joshua H 28 May 1876-23 Oct

CAMPBELL (continued) 1961 MtHo
Julia w/o T M 23 Feb 1878-25 Aug 1900 MtHo
Lowery N 3 Sept-4 Sept 1957 MtHo
Lucy M w/o A J 1903-1946 Onan
Margaret S w/o A C 1856-1929 MtHo
Mildred K (w/o G W) 1909-1973 MtHo-s
Rose A (w/o W F) 1880-1974 MtHo
Sarah W w/o F A 1836-1930 MtHo
Susan W w/o C L 1889-1981 MtHo
Thomas M h/o J A 4 Aug 1874-8 Mar 1926 MtHo
William F (h/o R A) 1875-1930 MtHo
CAMPER, Alton P 1905-1940 MtHo-s
Marjorie P 1893-1968 MtHo-s
Nannie E (w/o W B) 1870-1942 MtHo-s
Selma T 1889-1958 MtHo-s
William B (h/o N E) 1861-1931 MtHo-s
CAPETILLO, Osiel b&d 15 June 1954 Edge
CARDWELL, Mervin 1884-1965 Snea
CAREY, Thomas J Sr 1884-1978 Libe
CARLOS, Mary Mitchell 1876-1958 Quin
CARLSON, August 18 Sept 1886-10 Mar 1973 Fair
CARMINE, father 22 Nov 1825-29 Apr 1878 Onan
mother 16 Mar 1827-21 May 1892 Onan
Anna Thornton w/o E T 1880-1974 Wach
Annie 27 Oct 1852-4 Aug 1875 Onan
Earle M 1904-1967 Fair
Edward T h/o A T 1877-1945 Wach
Eliza A w/o Geo E 21 Mar 1860-17 Dec 1901 RodP

CARMINE (continued)
Elizabeth F w/o Jas; d/o Chas Fitzgerald 26 Oct 1802-6 Aug 1870 (stone badly broken) Belo
Henry Coe 30 Aug 1877-16 Apr 1938 MtHo-s
Henry D h/o R A W 22 Aug 1833-24 Feb 1893 MtHo
Henry Douglas 1900-1971 MtHo-s
James h/o E F 11 Mar 1798-25 Nov 1868; age: 70/8/15 MtHo
John H 1913-1934 Wach
John James (h/o M H) 1870-1945 MtHo-s
Laura S 1867-1926 Park
Lena C 25 Sept 1875-17 Jan 1969 MtHo-s
Lillie May d/o Geo E & E A 1 May 1882-8 Jan 1900 RodP
May Helen (w/o J J) 1870-1955 MtHo-s
Rachel E (w/o S E) 1888-1930 MtHo-s
Rebecca Anne Watson w/o H D 12 Oct 1839-1 July 1909 MtHo
Roy E 1906-1931 Wach
Sidney E (h/o R E) 1887-1962 MtHo-s
Sidney E Jr 1931-1959 MtHo-s
'Spunker' ns (ref: Rufus Parker) PopC
CARPENTER, Burleigh E h/o Hazel Kilmon; s/o Burleigh & Annie East 26 May 1922-29 July 1965 Fair
CARR, Bernice 1897-1968 MtNe
Hezekiah 1892-1973 Padd
Mary S 10 May 1874-6 Mar 1950; age: 76 yrs Gask-old
Robert 1882-1975 Gask-old
Rodney Michael 13 Jan-9 Mar 1968 Libe
Roland B 22 Apr 1922-12 June 1950 Bagc
CARRUTHERS, (CARUTHERS),
Charles H 1883-1961 Quin
George H 3 Mar 1887-7 Apr 1957 Quin
George W (h/o M C) 1849-1926 Holl
Grace S (w/o G W) 1905-1968

CARRUTHERS (continued) MtHo
Gurney W (h/o G S) 1902-1957 MtHo
Kay W 1939-1958 MtHo
Lloyd W h/o M B 1878-1942 Onan
Lula A d/o Wm & Melissa 9 Aug 1879-15 Mar 1892 Onan
Maggie C w/o Geo 20 Mar 1860-6 Aug 1899 Holl
Mary B w/o L W 1884-1937 Onan
Melissa w/o Wm 13 Mar 1848-18 Jan 1924 Onan
Samuel A s/o L W & M L 18 Mar 1907-2 July 1908 Onan
William h/o Melissa 1 Aug 1843-8 Oct 1913 Onan
CARTER, Beulah 1912-1971 Snea
John 1887-1972 JoyC
Laura 1899-1981 Burt
Peter 1908-1960 Snea
Samuel 1896-1968 Shil
Susie L 1899-1943 JoyC
Will 15 Apr 1913-20 Apr 1953 Gask-old
CARY, Tabitha G w/o Purnel P 11 Nov 1811-17 Mar 1899 (un-able to verify) Cary
CASE, Rev Charles d 13 Mar 18(6?)8; age: 66 yrs StPa
CASTILLO, Guadalupe 1972 Onan
CATLIN, Caroline West 1892-1971 Park
CAUSEY, Amelia M 1882-1961 StGe
Amy Augusta 4 Apr 1898-28 Jan 1920 Libe
Elizabeth R (w/o J A) 15 Feb 1894-7 July 1966 Onan
Grace Miller 14 Feb 1869-4 Apr 1935 Libe
Joseph A (h/o E R) 9 July 1888-10 Dec 1957 Onan
Margaret Sue 26 Apr 1851-6 Apr 1936 Libe
Oliver Ernest 12 Oct 1874-10 Jan 1958 Libe
R A 16 Oct 1847-21 Oct 1915 Libe
William James 21 Nov 1878-24

CAUSEY (continued) Mar 1963 Libe
CHAMBERS, baby boy b&d 1949 Quin
Burleigh 1902-1968 Edge
Colie B 1894-1938 MtHo-s
Colie W h/o E P 1871-1932 Wach
Doris W d/o C W & E P 9 Feb 1907-1 Jan 1911 Wach
Elsie P w/o C W 1877-1968 Wach
Etter C 1 Feb 1887-30 Sept 1983 Park
Georgianna W (w/o W A) 2 Aug 1873-13 May 1942 Edge
James H 1890-1954 Fair
Joseph R (h/o M L) 1879-1938 MtHo-s
Maggie L (w/o J R) 1895- MtHo-s
Paul W 1903-1962 Wach
Ralph R 1898-1964 Wach
Richard R 1941-1972 Fair
Rufus B 10 May 1932-29 July 1957 Edge
Sarah M (w/o T C) 1907-1960 Fair
Theodore C (h/o S M) 1901-1951 Fair
William A (h/o G W) 1869-1913 Edge
William C 1927-1945 MtHo-s
CHANCE, A Garner (h/o E H) 1895-1955 Wach
Albert T 31 Jan 1868-5 Oct 1941 Wach
B Thomas 3 Nov 1880-20 Mar 1940 MtHo-s
Banjamin F 25 Feb 1874-27 Nov 1938 Wach
Burley R 25 Mar 1893-28 Aug 1919 MtHo
Claude W 1896-1969 Wach
David A h/o E J 10 Mar 1863-31 Jan 1936 Wach
Elijah h/o S M 1876-1962 Oakg
Emily Heath (w/o A G) 1898- Wach
Emma Jane w/o D A 6 Nov 1864-4 Oct 1951 Wach
Emma Laura w/o J T 22 Feb

CHANCE (continued)
1843-23 Dec 1921 Wach
G C footstone only Chab
George C h/o M A 1882-1949 Edge
George T s/o Elijah & Eliz 14 Dec 1842(47?)-4 Dec 1851 Hysl
J Edward 1871-1951 MtHo
James T s/o J W & M A 15 Oct 1865-4 Dec 1895; age: 30/1/9 Chab
James W h/o M A 2 Mar 1832-2 July 1906; age: 74/4/0 Chab
Jesse B 1 Apr 1881-6 Feb 1940 MtHo-s
John T h/o W A S 1860-1936 MtHo
John W 10 Aug 1885-23 Dec 1907 Edge
Joseph T h/o E L 28 May 1836-3 July 1919 Wach
Josephine w/o Obadiah 1870-1943 Wach
Kathryn A 9 Jan 1859-3 Sept 1939 MtHo-s
Leah A 22 Jan 1834-(3?) Sept 1895 Nick
Mae Corbin 1881-1939 Onan
Mary Ann w/o Jas W 31 Aug 1833-16 Mar 1908; age: 74/6/15 Chab
Mary Ann w/o G C 1886-1943 Edge
Mary Y w/o W J 1909- Fair
Missouri B w/o R V 9 Oct 1901-19 July 1971 Wach
Obadiah h/o Josephine 1867-1938 Wach
Page 1906-1974 Libe
Ray Thomas 1906-1963 Edge
Raymond W 2 Feb 1913-19 May 1969 Oakg
Robert E 1933-1978 Fair
Roland V h/o M B 8 Sept 1893-15 Aug 1963 Wach
Sadie 1877-1961 MtHo
Sallie M w/o Elijah 1880-1951 Oakg
William J h/o M Y 1903-1965 Fair
Willie Anna Savage w/o J T

CHANCE (continued)
1866-1935 MtHo
CHANDLER, inf son & dau/o Thom B & Sarah A nd Libe
A Louise 1869-1946 Park
A Trench Sr h/o K B 1891-1970 MtHo-s
Agnes M 2 June 1847-19 June 1938 Chan
Alice A w/o T J 10 Aug 1870-10 Apr 1953 MtHo-s
Alice L w/o J L 1857-1941 Park
Allie 1888-1980 Metr
Annie G 1895-1946 HTri
Annie W (w/o J A) 1872-1948 Onan
Capt Bagwell h/o Nancy 28 Oct 1811-21 June 1896; age: 84/7/24 Harr
Basil R 15 Oct 1912-9 Mar 1975 Onan
Bennie s/o J W & Maggie 26 Oct 1869-31 Oct 1895 Chap
Bessie w/o E H 31 May 1884-18 Aug 1926 Park
Carrie E (w/o C K) 1857- MtHo-s
Carrye Russell w/o O S 12 Jan 1889-13 Aug 1968 Libe
Catherine S w/o J J 29 Apr 1850-17 Feb 1931 MtHo-s
Charles D 17 Oct 1874-30 Dec 1934 MtHo-s
Charlie K (h/o C E) 1862-1942 MtHo-s
Cordie R w/o J T 1884-1974 MtHo-s
Cynthia A w/o J M 27 July 1846-8 Oct 1915 Libe
Daisy L (w/o E D) 1892-1947 Wach
Dixie L 15 Oct 1914-3 Jan 1968 MtHo-s
Dorsey L 1887-1950 Park
Rev E Gunter s/o T B & S A 27 July 1853-7 Aug 1891 Libe
E Herman h/o Bessie 21 May 1884-12 May 1969 Park
Edith 1904-1959 JoyC
Edith H (w/o V A) 1889-1971 Fair
Edward D h/o K M 1861-1940

CHANDLER (continued)
MtHo
Edward D (h/o D L) 1889-1976 Wach
Edward Delch (h/o J S) 18 Oct 1886-21 Feb 1968 Wach
Elijah 1912-1965 Gask
Elizabeth M w/o E Staples 1914-1960 Park
Emily S 1st w/o T R 8 June 1839-7 Feb 1888 Chbg
Etta T w/o L H 1882-1953 MtHo
Evelyn C 1926-1969 Burt
Forest Davis h/o Evelyn M 24 July 1903-13 Dec 1969 MtHo
Georgie T nd Metr
Gwendolyn 1949-1950 HTri
Hattie C w/o Jas L 23 Apr 1879-15 Mar 1902 Gask-old
J J (h/o C S) 8 Nov 1847-16 Dec 1937 MtHo-s
J Merritt 1878-1953 Edge
J Thomas h/o C R 1884-1957 MtHo-s
James 1912-1979 Metr
James Edward s/o J T & C R 24 May-7 July 1905 MtHo-s
James L (h/o H C) 20 Dec 1875-5 Nov 1904 Gask-old
Jane Scott (w/o E D) 10 Feb 1889-23 Aug 1961 Wach
John 1900-1982 Metr
John A (h/o A W) 1865-1953 Onan
John D 1880-1954 Park
John J h/o A L 1850-1930 Park
John M h/o C A 30 May 1851-24 Mar 1882 Libe
John Newell 29 Dec 1901-6 Sept 1972 Onan
Johnnie d 30 July 1965; age: 0/3/0 Burt
Joseph Merritt Jr h/o M A; s/o J Merritt & Nora (White) 16 Oct 1916-2 Dec 1983 Park
Joseph W h/o M T 12 Feb 1842-26 Apr 1919 Chap
Julia W w/o T J 20 Jan 1826-20 Dec 1925 Onan
Kate M w/o E D 5 Sept 1863-20 Aug 1907 MtHo
Katie B w/o A T Sr 1892-1970

CHANDLER (continued)
MtHo-s
Katie Kelley 1893-1969 Onan
L Mack h/o R A 4 Sept 1872-2 Nov 1938 Onan
L McKenney (h/o M B) 1891-1973 MtHo-s
L Paige 20 Apr 1906-22 May 1937 Onan
Leland F (h/o T N) 19 June 1902 Fair
Leo P 17 July 1916-2 May 1946 MtHo-s
Leony V d/o T R & E S 10 June 1883-16 Nov 1887 Chbg
Liby T 20 Nov 1897-22 Dec 1976 Fair
Lola 1913-1976 NewM
Louise B w/o Nolan 1904-1978 Fair
Loyd H h/o E T 1879-1925 MtHo
M Hill h/o Virginia 14 Feb 1854-15 Dec 1914 MtHo
M Leamon 1893-1910 MtHo
Maggie T w/o J W 26 Feb 1849-12 Oct 1895 Chap
Margaret w/o W D 12 Jan 1792-23 Apr 1856; age: 65 yrs Chan
Margaret B (w/o L McK) 1894-MtHo-s
Maragret B d/o L H & E W 26 Sept 1904-11 Mar 1920 MtHo
Margaret Major 1936-1979 Shil
Margaret S d/o S R & M A d 29 July 1845 Fair
Margaret 1929-1982 Gask
Margaret Sarah 31 Dec 1839-8 Feb 1848 Chan
Martha Arminda w/o J M Jr; d/o Wm Oscar & Eulalie (Martin) Lewis 18 July 1920- Park
Mary A w/o S R 4 Dec 1824-26 Feb 1892; age: 67/2/22 MtHo-s
Mary D w/o R L 1907- Oakg
Mary E d/o J J & C S 23 Nov 1883-19 Aug 1884 MtHo-s
Mary H w/o T M 1867-1933 Chap
Mary K 11 Dec 1907-14 July 1908 Onan
Mary K 1907-1933 MtHo
Mary S w/o T M 14 May 1849-12

CHANDLER (continued)
Feb 1883 Chap
Minnie C w/o W M 27 Oct 1887-22 Feb 1945 Onan
Minnie C d/o W M & M C 13 Feb 1932 Onan
Missouri M 2 May 1900-11 May 1981 Fair
Mitchell E G s/o J M & C A 1 Apr-21 June 1882 Libe
Mitchell H 21 Dec 1902-27 Jan 1966 MtHo
Morris L 1897-1966 NewM
Nancy w/o Bagwell 30 May 1803-29 Oct 1889 Harr
Nora White 1882-1982 Edge
Norris 1911-1966 Metr
Obed S h/o C R 22 Nov 1885-2 Mar 1940 Libe
Olevia E 20 Aug 1878-11 June 1947 MtHo-s
Orphus d 9 Feb 1964; age: 71 yrs Metr
S Randall 1867-1931 Park
Rebecca A w/o L M 15 Dec 1872-19 Nov 1955 Onan
Richard 1905-1983 Gask
Richard L h/o M D 1906-1980 Oakg
Roberta L 1894-1974 JoyC
Sadie B d/o T R & E S 17 Oct 1869-28 Nov 1870 Chbg
Sarah A w/o T B 8 Feb 1831-19 Apr 1911 Libe
Susan d/o S R & M A d 29 Apr 1832 MtHo-s
Sylvester R h/o M A 13 July 1819-29 Feb 1877 MtHo-s
Thelma N (w/o L F) 24 June 1897- Fair
Thomas B h/o S A 1 Feb 1815-1 Feb 1878 Libe
Thomas J h/o J W 13 Apr 1815-16 Mar 1866 Onan
Thomas J h/o A A 30 June 1863-12 Dec 1933 MtHo-s
Thomas M h/o M S & M H 1843-1910 Chap
Capt Thomas R h/o E S 20 Aug 1838-5 Sept 1913 Chbg
Vernon L s/o W M & M C 31 Oct 1903-27 Sept 1904 Onan

CHANDLER (continued)
Vibart A (h/o E H) 1892-1960 Fair
Vibart Asbury Jr 27 Oct 1916-26 May 1975 Fair
Virginia w/o M H 15 Feb 1845-1 Feb 1914 MtHo
Virginia Reese (w/o W F) 1903-1978 MtHo
W Fisher (h/o V R) 1903-1963 MtHo
Wilbert M h/o M C 26 May 1881-23 Jan 1957 Onan
William 1900-1978 JoyC
William D d 10 Feb 1834; age: 39 yrs Chan
William D 21 Apr 1848-15 Oct 1911 Chan
William James Jr 23 Jan 1949-24 June 1973 NewM
CHANEY, Mae Mason Short 1885-1977 Park
CHAPMAN, F Thomas h/o T G 27 May 1918 Park
Thelma G w/o F T 26 Jan 1914- Park
CHARLES, Henry V d 3 Nov 1967 MtHo-s
CHARNOCK, Charles H 2 Mar 1925-22 Apr 1975 Fair
Maggie 1877-1962 Hick
Maggie L 17 May 1892-20 Jan 1968 Fair
Solomon 1872-1958 Holl
William 1872-1952 Hick
CHASE, C Jack h/o L K 1895-1972 Park
Columbus h/o Jewell B 1896-1968 Park
Everett T h/o N E 1890-1957 Park
Henry Laurence h/o N B 11 May 1892-6 Mar 1971 Edge
Iona W w/o J M 1907-1971 Park
J Madison h/o I W 1906-1949 Park
Lillis K w/o C J 1903- Park
Manie K w/o T T 1868-1954 Park
Nannie Bonnivil w/o H L 11 Mar 1900-23 Apr 1983 Edge
Nannie E w/o E T 1892-1944

CHASE (continued) Park
Ruth B 1906-1975 Park
Spurgeon Lee Jr 1 May 1904-18 Nov 1972 Fair
Teagle T h/o M K 1865-1954 Park
Ernest L 2 Mar 1914-15 Aug 1969 Burt
CHERRICKS, (CHERRIX), d/o E L & Maxine b&d 8 Feb 1953 Park
Bertha 22 Sept 1905- Fair
Dorsey 1915-1946 Edge
Fannie R 1871-1944 Edge
Ike N 1944-1945 Edge
Lamon A 22 July 1899-4 Sept 1971 Fair
Louis T h/o M E 1876-1957 Wach
Manie E w/o L T 1883-1958 Wach
CHESSER, John S h/o S H 1886-1953 Park
Josephine F 1887-1975 Park
Michael T 1954-1958 Onan
Pearl C w/o S B 1895-1982 Park
Sallie H w/o J S 1896- Park
Sewell B h/o P C 1890-1966 Park
CHESTER, Elizabeth 30 Jan 1831-6 Jan 1927 Onan
CHEW, Alma G w/o C R 14 Mar 1933- Park
Clifford R h/o A G 11 Sept 1930- Park
CHILDS, Alice Nottingham 8 June 1901-2 Dec 1935 Onan
CHIPMAN, Sally Roache 1891-1962 Edge
CHRISTIAN, George S s/o Symmore & Sarah A 24 Oct 1858-4 Dec 1881 Chri
Mary Julia Savage w/o R T 23 July 1860-19 June 1938 Sava
Ollie 1892-1980 Shil
Rupert T h/o M J S 20 Feb 1861-19 Jan 1896; age: 34/10/29 Sava
Mrs S(arah) A w/o Seymour 1 Oct 1838-11 Dec 1874 Chri
Seymour h/o S A 21 Apr 1836-28

CHRISTIAN (continued) May 1870 Chri
CHURN, Bessie Guy w/o C P 1902- MtHo
Clinton Paige h/o B G 1905-1959 MtHo
Hazel L w/o S L 1893- Libe
John W L h/o M A 1860-1936 Libe
Mary A w/o J W L 1862-1931 Libe
Samuel L h/o H L 1890-1943 Libe
Virginia Susan 1862-1951 MtHo
CLARK, Gladys M 1920-1957 JoyC
H Marshall h/o S P 3 Nov 1907- Onan
Isaac Butler h/o M L W 1961-1936 Edge
Marion Lee Warner w/o I B 1862-1913 Edge
Mary Ella 7 Nov 1870-14 Apr 1946 Wach
Mary Lee (Lyde) 14 Apr 1890- Edge
Mary Lee d/o J B & M E b&d 17 Nov 1921 Edge
Matthew 1901-1981 Snea
Minnie B 1884-1949 HTri
Sallie Perrow w/o H M 12 May 1914-19 June 1966 Onan
CLAYTON, mother (poss w/o Thos G d 7 Apr 1924 Libe
Carry K d/o H K & Gertrude F 14 Feb 1911-6 Mar 1915 Libe
Emma M w/o R W 1899- Libe
Henry T s/o H K & Gertrude F 11 June 1913-20 June 1916 Libe
Lula May w/o A F 7 Apr 1895-2 Aug 1920 Libe
Mary E 1886-1947 Libe
Richard W h/o E M 1891-1974 Libe
Thomas G 4 Jan 1832-13 Aug 1912 Libe
CLIFFORD, Dennis O 1948-1977 Shil
Edith 7 Feb 1886-28 Feb 1959 Shil
George 1901-1965 Shil
Jacob E 11 Sept 1914-11 July

CLIFFORD (continued)
1943 Shil
John H d 9 Feb 1966; age: 66 yrs Shil
William 1895-1955 Shil
William 1906-1968 Shil
CLOVER, Richmond 1889-1937 MtHo-s
CLOWES, Peter J, 2nd h/o Sarah Jane Mears 23 Aug 1805-21 Mar 1883 Mear
Sarah Jane Mears w/o P J 25 Aug 1813-25 Oct 1898; age: 85/2/0 Mear
COARD, Anna A w/o W M 2 Mar 1850-26 Sept 1922 Edge
Annie d 24 Mar 1966; age: 74 yrs Metr
Arinthia M w/o J R 16 Feb 1858-20 Nov 1943 Libe
Arthur R s/o Wm R & E W 10 July 1845-4 July 1911 Coar
Bertha T w/o H F 1884-1972 Edge
Bettie R 1890-1973 Edge
Catherine W 17 Nov 1898-12 Dec 1970 Edge
Dorsey S 6 Nov 1888-5 Mar 1971 Edge
Elizabeth J 6 Jan 1880-28 June 1900 Coar
Elizabeth W w/o Wm R d 27 Sept 1874; age: 66/7/7 Coar
Ernest W 1889-1964 Edge
Esmoranda d/o W M & A A 24 Aug 1874-3 Mar 1877 Edge
Evelyn L 1894-1979 Libe
Fletcher d 17 Jan 1966; age: 84 yrs Metr
Georgg S 1823-1895 Edge
George Wellington h/o W A 6 June 1852-24 Feb 1924 Edge
Harriet A 1833-1912 Edge
Harry Franklin s/o G W & W A 2 June 1892-19 June 1936 Edge
Harvey T h/o L A 23 Dec 1879-4 Nov 1945 Edge
Hezekiah F h/o B T 1880-1945 Edge
Hugh R h/o M B 1888-1961 Edge
John R h/o A M 22 Oct 1850-25 July 1930 Libe

COARD (continued)
John W h/o N B; s/o Wm R & Eliz W 5 Nov 1825-15 Feb 1898 Edge
John W 1890-1968 Libe
Laura Ayres w/o H T 13 Oct 1882-19 July 1961 Edge
Mary B w/o H R 1886-1945 Edge
Mary Josephine d/o Geo U & Ullica 23 Aug 1884-18 Sept 1887 Edge
Merl W 1896-1979 Park
Missouri A d/o Jno W & N B 22 Mar 1852-15 Feb 1915 Edge
Nancie w/o Chas; d/o Richd & Nancy Rew 14 May 1843-23 Apr 1869; age: 25/11/9 Rewp
Nancy B w/o Jno W; d/o Mitchell Chandler 24 Sept 1824-15 Aug 1886; age: 61/10/21 Edge
Neely C w/o O H 1866-1940 Edge
Oliver H h/o NC 1866-1948 Edge
Sallie W (w/o W F) 21 May 1859-15 Feb 1944 Edge
W Dewey 27 Sept 1898-28 July 1934 Edge
William F (h/o S W) 7 June 1857-21 June 1925 Edge
Dr William H 6 Jan 1834-15 Sept 1901 Coar
William M h/o A A 17 Jan 1849-30 Aug 1932 Edge
William R h/o E W 25 Dec 1800-25 Sept 1885 Coar
Willie Anna w/o G W 23 Sept 1856-26 Sept 1924 Edge
COBB, Alonzo (h/o S S) 1870-1970 Onan
Charlie T (h/o E B) 1875-1941 Onan
Elizabeth B (w/o C T) 1881-1964 Onan
Henry Woodward h/o M E 1877-1958 Edge
Ida R w/o J T 1900-1978 Onan
James W (h/o J A) 1850-1911 Onan
James W h/o S A 1868-1967 Onan
Jennie A (w/o J W) 1865-1946

COBB (continued) Onan
John T h/o I R 1892-1963 Onan
Mary Elizabeth w/o H W 1885-1939 Edge
Oscar T s/o J W & S A 21 Feb 1897-13 Aug 1922 Onan
Sarah A w/o J W 1870-1951 Onan
Sarah J w/o W T 20 Apr 1848-10 Nov 1920 Onan
Sudie S (w/o Alonzo) 24 Nov 1875-15 Jan 1949 Onan
William T h/o S J 30 Jan 1844-23 Dec 1931 Onan
COE, Annie Jackson d/o Rev Wm G & Annie M 11 Aug 1863-20 Aug 1864 Poul
COFFMAN, Susie Campbell (w/o W H) 1903-1926 MtHo
W Hobart (h/o S C) 1896-1973 MtHo
COLLINGE, Ronald nd Libe
COLEBURN, (COLBOURN, COULBOURNE),
- d 1931; age: 74 yrs StLu
Addie V w/o J Marshall 5 June 1914-20 Sept 1942 Park
Annie 1912-1981 Gask
E Frances 7 May 1938-18 Jan 1941 Park
Edward Alphonse 18 Feb 1915-9 Mar 1982 Edge
Eliza C w/o Jno F; d/o Rev Peter Williams 28 Oct 1826-15 July 1850 MtOr
Eliza S wid/o Saml 27 Dec 1810-10 Jan 1899 Stoc
George s/o Geo & Mollie (Beach) 27 June 1815-14 Feb 1866 Beac
George T s/o T S & T S 2 May 1829-30 May 1861 MtHo
George T 22 Feb 1858-25 Jan 1935 Down
Harry B 1874-1952 Burf
James E Jr 1919-1979 Edge
James E 23 Mar 1923-26 Oct 1981 Gask
James W s/o Thos & Tabitha 30 July 1834-25 Mar 1905 MtHo
John F s/o Robt & Mary 25 Sept

COLEBURN (continued) 1819-25 Dec 1891 MtOr
John Thomas s/o J F & E C 18 May 1849-13 July 1850 MtOr
Juliet 3 Nov 1818-20 Apr 1904 Down
Madlyn M 1919-1970 Edge
Martha K w/o R P; d/o Jas W & Hannah French Kelley 1872-1950 Edge
Mary w/o Robt d 18 Sept 18__ (stone broken); age: 56 yrs MtOr
Mollie Beach w/o Geo nd Beac
Robert P h/o M K s/o Wm C & Sarah T 1871-1937 Edge
Robert T s/o Robt & Mary badly weathered; unable to read MtOr
Samuel s/o Geo & Mollie (Beach) 12 Mar 1812-2 Mar 1883; age: 70/11/18 Beac
Tabitha S w/o T S 1 Sept 1790-5 Sept 1855 MtHo
Thomas S h/o T S 1 Mar 1785-10 Aug 1840 MtHo
William C nd Burf
COLEMAN, David Lee 1950-1965 Holl
COLEY, Louise B w/o W J 1916- Edge
Walter J h/o L B 1904-1969 Edge
COLLINS, (COLINS),
- 1905-1968 Shil
C Robert nd Coke
Carrie 1931-1980 MtNe
Charles E d 29 Oct 1964; age: 64 yrs Burt
Effie W w/o L W 1870-1939 Park
F R 1906-1983 Fair
George d 23 Dec 1966; age: 53 yrs Shil
George Henry 12 Sept 1898-30 June 1965 NewM
Georgia O 1911-1977 Burt
Jeanette 1874-1974 Park
Jennie 1887-1958 HTri
John Leon 1906-1974 HTri
L W h/o E W 1863-1951 Park
Laura 1904-1972 Shil
Mary d 14 June 1973; age: 85 yrs

COLLINS (continued) MtNe
Mary L 1882-1963 Shil
Milton 9 Nov 1922-4 Oct 1966 JoyC
Rachel 1880-1957 StJo
Robert J 1909-1970 Htri
Stanley 1910-1977 StJo
COLNEY, Susan d/o J C & M C 4 Jan 1860-24 Aug 1863 Onan
COLONNA, (COLONA),
Abel B 14 Oct 1813-12 Mar 1872 Colo
Abel Thomas (h/o M H) 1870-1939 Onan
Abel Thomas b&d 1908 Onan
Alfred J (h/o P K) Dec 1878-15 Nov 1925 Holl
Annie B 10 Mar 1877-1 Aug 1879 Colo
Annie T w/o Arthur E 28 Oct 1843-4 Nov 1879 (unable to verify; 1940 data) Colo
Arthur B 15 Nov 1842-8 Sept 1891 Colo
Beatrice Guy mother/o Richd Lee & Otho Page Parks 1911-1964 Ptea
Benjamin (h/o Elizabeth B; s/o Major & Joice) 10 Feb 1763-2 July 1851 (soldier in Rev War & War of 1812; Major Colonna served in Rev War) Wate
Benjamin A (h/o M R) 1874-1965 Fair
Benjamin S s/o Benj & Eliz 24 July 1820-3 Nov 1861 (unable to verify; 1940 data) Colo
Berlie R h/o L A 1894-1972 Park
Berta W w/o E F 1877-1964 Park
Bertie T 1884-1925 Park
Bessie M w/o L B 1897- Park
Charles B s/o C W & M P d 23 Oct 1917 Park
Charles F h/o V C 1865-1949 Park
Charles W h/o M P 16 Jan 1879-2 Apr 1963 Park
Clifton H 1916- Edge
Daisy M (w/o W T) 1887- Wach
E T h/o N L 7 Jan 1869-16 Nov

COLONNA (continued) 1942 Park
Edward F h/o B W 1874-1958 Park
Edward M 18 Apr 1847-17 Mar 1910 Libe
Edward T h/o R H 1900-1961 Park
Elisha nd MtHo
Elizabeth w/o Benj; d/o Reuben & Molly Beach 17 Oct 1784-18 Jan 1848 Wate
Elizabeth E d/o Benj & Eliz 26 Aug 1815-5 June 1836 Wate
Ernest L 12 Nov 1890-30 Aug 1948 Edge
Fannie Davis d/o Roberta H & H E 18 Apr 1862-24 July 1863 Colg
Fred 1878-1964 Shil
George A 12 Feb 1849-16 Feb 1909 Libe
George C 1885-1958 Park
George S s/o Abel E & Mary 8 July 1847-22 Aug 1856 Colo
George S s/o Benj & Mollie 27 Aug 1858-17 May 1859 Colo
George T 1885-1962 Park
George W s/o Abel E & Mary 29 Dec 1844-6 June 1845 Colo
Gertie B (w/o R L) 1882-1957 Edge
Harry Lee (h/o M L) 1887-1967 Edge
Harry W (h/o L W) 1893-1969 Quin
Herbert L 3 July 1904-29 Apr 1966 Park
Hugh P s/o Benj & Mollie 5 Apr 1856-23 Oct 1863 (unable to verify; 1940 data) Colo
Ida W w/o Wm H 1875-1947 Park
J William (h/o S M) 1910-1963 MtHo-s
James 1900-1955 Shil
James E h/o M W 1868-1948 Park
Jimmy L 7 Jan 1918-7 Oct 1943 Park
John h/o M A d 12 Sept 1903; age: 80 yrs Onan

COLONNA (continued)
John C (h/o N E) 1864-1929 MtHo-s
John E h/o S J 1849-1923 Quin
John R s/o Jno M & Sarah E 23 Feb 1883-11 Oct 1895 Chap
John T 2 Nov 1835-10 June 1887 Chap
John W h/o M V 1860-1923 Edge
John W h/o N B 1908-1960 Park
John Watson 15 Aug 1805-8 Apr 1871 Wate
John William h/o R B 6 May 1867-11 Sept 1946 Edge
John William h/o V L 1882-1970 Edge
Johnie L s/o L H & Mannie E 6 Mar 1885-2 June 1886 Chap
Joseph L s/o L H & Mannie E 14 Jan 1833-20 Sept 1888 Chap
Lizzie R 11 Feb-1 Aug 1875 (unable to verify; 1940 data) Colo
Lottie A w/o B R 1892- Park
Lottie Ailworth 22 Oct 1901-7 June 1980 Edge
Louis B h/o B M 1897-1945 Park
Lucille W (w/o H W) 1901-1965 Quin
Mae Riley (w/o B A) 1878-1966 Fair
Manie P w/o C W 15 Mar 1875-12 Aug 1937 Park
Mannie L w/o E T 1871-1950 Park
Margaret (Jones) 2nd w/o Jno W 6 June 1819-30 Dec 1856 Wate
Margaret E R w/o A B; d/o Arthur & Elizabeth Powell 3 May 1820-27 July 1887 Colo
Margareta A w/o Jno; d/o Thos & Nancy Ayres 14 May 1820-24 July 1906 Onan
Mary L (w/o H L) 1890-1974 Edge
Mary Susan (w/o W M) 1865-1952 Quin
Mary T 1915-1933 Park
Mary V w/o J W 1864-1924 Edge
Merrill A 1915-1975 Fair
Miranda W w/o J E 1872-1946 Park

COLONNA (continued)
Mollie H (w/o A T) 1880-1950 Onan
Nancy H w/o S K 1933- Fair
Nannie E (w/o J C) 1869-1941 MtHo-s
Nellie B w/o J W 1911-1963 Park
Patrick B s/o Benj & Eliz 28 May 1803-13 Mar 1843 Wate
Pearl K (w/o A J) 18 June 1883-13 Mar 1981 Holl
Rachel Blackstone w/o J W 7 May 1869-28 July 1947 Edge
Rachel W w/o W W 1917-1980 Park
Rebecca Robb d 20 Sept 1863; age: 9/0/9 Wate
Rhoby H w/o E T 1901-1979 Park
Robert L h/o S S 1863-1935 Park
Robert Peyton 21 Aug 1901-23 May 1963 Edge
Roger L (h/o G B) 1874-1957 Edge
Sallie Mason 1867-1937 Park
Samuel W s/o Wm & Eliz 2 Jan 1796-9 Oct 1835 Colg
Sarah A w/o Jno W; d/o Francis & Eliz Boggs 2 Apr 1818-3 Oct 1841 Bogb
Sarah J w/o J E 1848-1926 Quin
Shelton T 25 July 1893-2 Oct 1958 Park
Stewart K h/o N H 1931-1981 Fair
Sudie S w/o R L 1868-1945 Park
Susie M (w/o J W) 1909- MtHo-s
Tully nd MtHo
Vara Lewis w/o J W 1885-1978 Edge
Vida Kelly w/o C P 12 Oct 1870-23 Jan 1920 Onan
Virginia C w/o C F 15 July 1876-5 Aug 1904 Park
Walter W h/o R W 1900-1974 Park
William d 11 Mar 1830; age: 61 yrs Colg
William H h/o I W 1864-1939 Park

COLONNA (continued)
William M (h/o M S) 1859-1952 Quin
Capt William T (h/o D M) 1885-1956 Wach
CONNER, Albert T 1901-1980 Gask
Charles H h/o M J 1866-1960 JoyC
Douglas 1897-1957 Gask-old
Elizabeth 12 Oct 1818-8 July 1910 MtHo
Georgie 1901-1981 Gask
Harriett 1845-1919 JoyC
Joseph L s/o C H & M J 1894-1933 JoyC
Mary J w/o C H 1873-1927 JoyC
CONNORTON, Mary C 16 Apr 1899-14 Oct 1931 MtHo
Mary J w/o Chas C 25 Mar 1870-1 May 1899 MtHo
CONQUEST, Charlie 1897-1968 Gask
Edward 6 Mar 1856-26 Aug 1905 Gask-old
Ella nd Gask-old
George 21 Jan 1895-17 Dec 1959 Gask-old
George M 1935-1971 Snea
Herbert 1916-1972 Gask
Hester A w/o Levi R 9 Mar 1859-10 Oct 1916 HTri
Leah J 20 May 1860-6 Aug 1905 Shil
Lisa b&d 1967 Gask
Lucy 1899-1983 Gask
Mary I 1900-1980 Snea
Ray 9 Jan 1924-12 June 1966 Gask
Ronnie Lee 26 May 1952-3 July 1967 Snea
Sylvester M 1918-1981 Gask
CONRAD, Levin S 20 Nov 1951-6 Jan 1976 Onan
CONRADES, inf d/o Wm & Annie nd Onan
Annie w/o Wm 5 Sept 1863-27 July 1894 Onan
Joseph W 17 Sept 1898-12 Sept 1899 Onan
CONWAY, Columbus h/o M S 1872-1928 MtHo

CONWAY (continued)
Margorie K w/o W R 1925-1980 MtHo-s
Mary S w/o Columbus 1871-1938 MtHo
William R h/o M K 1923- MtHo-s
COOLEY, Chandler 1913-1976 HTri
COOPER, Annie N w/o J L 1880-1955 Libe
Charles L 1883-1958 Fair
Frank Edwin h/o S C 1856-1909 Runn
Irvin E h/o J W 1 Aug 1923- Fair
Jean W w/o I E 28 Feb 1923- Fair
John G 11 Aug 1844-11 Dec 1913 Oakg
Joseph E 29 Sept 1924-4 Feb 1977 Onan
Joseph L h/o A N 1875-1942 Libe
Joseph L (h/o V H) 24 Jan 1895-12 Oct 1972 Onan
Kendrick Jr 1979-1981 StJo
Margaret Sturgis 20 Aug 1852- Oakg
Marguerite W w/o R E 1917-1976 Park
Myrtle O d 24 Oct 1948 Onan
Raymond E h/o M W 1906-1979 Park
Victor 1915- Libe
Viola H (w/o J L) 6 Sept 1898-30 May 1971 Onan
William H h/o M O d 24 Oct 1948 Onan
COPES, Ann P w/o T P 7 Sept 1807-7 Nov 1883 (moved from the Copes Place) MtHo
Annie Louise Davis w/o W N 4 Mar 1876-31 Dec 1951 MtHo
Bessie H 31 Jan 1877-21 Jan 1956 MtHo
Catherine A 7 Jan 1849-12 Mar 1916 Park
Ernest W s/o J B & O S 17 Feb-19 Apr 1894 Libe
J H 2 Apr 1828-14 Mar 1912 Edge

COPES (continued)
James E h/o C S C Matthews 4 Nov 1843-17 Feb 1882 Libe
John B Sr h/o O S 21 Aug 1864-3 Feb 1944 Libe
Leah J w/o Wm T; d/o S M & E R Turlington nd stone broken Turp
Lillian M w/o W T 1895-1970 Edge
M K 3 Dec 1838-7 Feb 1911 Edge
Margaret Ann d/o Thos P & Ann P 1 Apr 1855-21 Sept 1858; age: 3/5/20 Elli
Margaret B Lodge w/o P D 10 Feb 1912-26 Nov 1972 MtHo
Margaret Blackstone 12 Jan 1825-16 Nov 1884 Park
Mary J d/o W T & Sue A; grd/o Thos P & Ann P Copes 28 Feb 1871-27 Aug 1942 MtHo
Otella Susan w/o J B Sr 13 Aug 1866-18 Nov 1935 Libe
Peter Davis h/o M B L 10 May 1907-28 Jan 1961 MtHo
Sue A w/o W T 5 Dec 1848-3 Oct 1921 MtHo
Thomas P h/o A P 12 Oct 1812-17 July 1886 (moved from the Copes Place) MtHo
Thomas P 8 Dec 1872-31 Oct 1950 MtHo
William Nock h/o A L D 30 Nov 1874-23 Sept 1956 MtHo
William T h/o S A 7 Feb 1839-11 Dec 1919 MtHo
William T h/o L M 1894-1957 Edge
William Thomas s/o P D & M L 18 Mar 1943-27 Aug 1970 MtHo

COPPAGE, Beulah I 13 June 1882-3 Dec 1927 MtHo-s
Harvey 1904-1978 Burt
Lena M 1892-1962 Snea
Samuel Russell 1896-1973 Burt
Thomas R 1900-1972 Burt

CORBETT, Andrew J 27 Nov 1887-15 Dec 1952 Fair

CORBIN, - 1944-1967 Fair
Amanda F 22 June 1873-27 Feb 1932 Quin

CORBIN (continued)
1932 Quin
Andrew J 16 Dec 1866-10 Oct 1940 Quin
Charles W h/o M S 1839-1900 MtHo
E J h/o E C 25 Dec 1848-26 Aug 1926 Onan
Ellen C w/o E J 11 Sept 1852-14 Aug 1914 Onan
Ethel M (w/o N L) 29 Sept 1892 Quin
George Esq (DAR marker: Col Geo Corbin 1744-1793 Rev soldier) d 28 Sept 1793; age: 49 yrs Scot
George L (h/o M S) 1883-1964 Quin
James Revell d 22 Sept 1793; age: 20 yrs Scot
Leland S (h/o S B) 7 Jan 1887-22 Feb 1973 Quin
Leland S s/o L S & S B 6 Mar-8 Apr 1914 Quin
Mary Dorothy d/o C W & M S 31 Mar 1900-24 Sept 1902 MtHo
Mary S w/o C W 1860-1922 MtHo
Mary S (w/o G L) 1891-1966 Quin
Norman L (h/o E M) 25 Sept 1889-8 Dec 1963 Quin
___ h Revell w/o Geo d 25 Sept 1775; age: 22 yrs Scot
Sallie Budd (w/o L S) 30 Mar 1894-3 Apr 1971 Quin
Stephen Grady h/o Hattie 16 Dec 1892-21 June 1949 Onan
William E 5 Jan 1928-2 Dec 1957 Onan

CORE, inf/o F F & A F b&d 4 Feb 1907 MtHo
Amy F w/o F F 1890-1972 MtHo
Annie E w/o L T 1890-1952 Park
Bernard R h/o E S 1891-1949 Park
Bessie B w/o D C 1891-1973 Park
Bessie E 1879-1894 MtHo
C Frank 1860-1891 MtHo
Doris Lucille b&d 1920 Park
Dorsey C h/o B B 1889-1984

CORE (continued)
Park
Ellen S w/o B R 1898-1973 Park
Emma L d/o Wm T & M C 24 Mar 1844-28 Dec 1909 Park
Emma L w/o J H Sr 1866-1947 Libe
Fred F h/o A F 1885-1968 MtHo
Rev George (h/o H H) 1913-1971 MtHo-s
George T h/o R E 1882-1946 MtHo-s
George W h/o G E 1852-1936 Park
Gertrude E w/o G W 1863-1939 Park
Harvey O 3 Aug 1901-14 Feb 1969 Park
Hatcher M 11 Aug 1886-29 July 1964 Park
Hattie Virginia 6 Nov 1910-28 Mar 1982 Park
Hilda H (w/o Rev Geo) 1913-1972 MtHo-s
J Robert h/o M E 1856-1928 MtHo
James H Sr h/o E L 1868-1954 Libe
James H Jr 1907-1962 Libe
John C h/o M G 1876-1932 MtHo
John W h/o M E 20 Jan 1851-21 July 1914 Budb
Levi R 1867-1938 MtHo
Levin E 23 Feb 1858-19 Sept 1955 Edge
Levin James (h/o M S) 26 June 1889-16 May 1957 Wach
Levin T h/o A E 1880-1956 Park
Maggie A d/o Wm T & Fannie E 29 June 1886-11 June 1908 ParC
Manie G w/o J C 1879-1943 MtHo
Margaret Stiles (w/o L J) 16 Feb 1891- Wach
Marie E w/o Jno W 1 Oct 1856-24 Nov 1915 Budb
Marvin F s/o J W & M E 14 June 1895-23 Oct 1914 Budb
Mary C w/o Wm T 22 Feb 1825-17 Nov 1883 Park
Mary E w/o J R 1856-1921 MtHo

CORE (continued)
Nettie R w/o W T 1868-1955 Edge
Rubie E w/o G T 1880-1943 MtHo-s
Sarah A 18 Oct 1859-21 Oct 1934 Edge
Susan d/o Levin & Susan d 11 June 1831; age: 0/6/0 yrs Edge
Susan C w/o Levin d 9 Nov 1835; age: 34/9/0 yrs Edge
Vernon F s/o F F & A F 3 May 1912-29 Mar 1914 MtHo
Warren J 16 Mar 1884-18 June 1938 Edge
William Leonard 1917-1941 MtHo-s
William T MD h/o M C d 24 Oct 1857; age: 57/10/6 (moved from Core bur gr - Pastoria) Park
William T h/o N R 1859-1943 Edge
William T Jr 1900-1981 Edge
Willy H R s/o Wm & Frances 23 June 1876-20 Dec 1879 ParC
CORNEY, Bertha M 23 May 1884-31 June 1978 Park
CORSON, Ella W 1877-1964 Burt
COSTEN, Bernice B (w/o H R) 1900-1979 Onan
Harry R (h/o B B) 1896- Onan
COSTON, James 1880-1976 StJo
James 1911-1979 StJo
COULBOURNE, see COLEBURN
COULSON, baby b&d 8 Nov 1942 Edge
George Wilson h/o S L 1905-1961 Edge
Sarah Leigh w/o G W 1908-1968 Edge
COURTNEY, Carrie S 1889-1965 Fair
Della R (w/o P R) 23 Nov 1912- Fair
Doris Lee b&d 1930 MtHo-s
Elizabeth S w/o J R 1848-1914 MtHo-s
Ella M 1907- MtHo-s
John R h/o E S 1852-1897 MtHo-s

COURTNEY (continued)
John W 1907-1965 MtHo-s
Margaret Ewell 31 Jan 1906-27 Oct 1977 Park
Preston R (h/o D R) 27 Mr 1909-21 May 1980 Fair
Rachel L 1875-1904 Fair
William S 1875-1951 Fair
COVINGTON, Althea H 1885-1965 Fair
E Howard H 1908-1928 Fair
Edgar E 1884-1964 Fair
Ella A (w/o I J) 1874-1960 Fair
I James (h/o E A) 1871-1959 Fair
Missouri T (w/o Howard W) 1908-1974 Fair
Oten Clay s/o Jas Wesley & Annie (Nowell) 16 Jan 1915-7 Feb 1978 Quin
W Robt 1925-1944 Fair
COWAN, Elizabeth Rogers w/o L T 1884-1966 MtHo
Luther T h/o E R 1884-1974 MtHo
COWARD, Catherine S w/o Saml stone gone; 1940 data Kell
COX, Jay Anderson 7 July 1895-30 Sept 1963 Edge
COXTON, Edna E (w/o W J) 1879-1931 Edge
Malisia w/o T M 1 Apr 1853-27 Apr 1926 MtHo
Thomas A s/o W H & V D 27 Jan 1858-15 Oct 1886 Edge
Virginia D w/o W H 25 Dec 1819-22 Nov 1905 Edge
W J (h/o E E) 1856-1926 Edge
William & Virginia names on gate of iron fence enclosure Bead
William H h/o V D 10 Oct 1834-25 Mar 1908 Edge
William T s/o Thos A & Lelia A 2 Apr-3 Apr 1886 Edge
CRATER, Alice Baity 1 Sept 1872-27 Sept 1952 Edge
CRIPPEN, Logan Jr 1931-1963 JoyC
Mamie 1893-1966 Gask
CROCKETT, Alvin T 1934-1973 Quin

CROCKETT (continued)
Annie C (w/o E C) 28 July 1867-30 Aug 1953 Fair
Annie Louise d/o A J & S E 10 June 1867-27 Dec 1877 Croc
Asa J (h/o S E; s/o Asa Thos & Catherine M) 1822-1907 Croc
Benjamin Franklin h/o E C 16 Dec 1852-29 Dec 1919 MtHo
Betsey 15 Feb 1839-15 Jan 1865 Bogg
Bettie P w/o Jno A; d/o Jno J & Margt Ayres 6 Oct 1854-16 Mar 1896 StGe
Betty D (w/o C E) 1919-1977 Fair
Betty G 1925- Park
C Crosley 11 Jan 1928-18 Mar 1970 Onan
Carlie A (h/o E J) 1894-1971 Fair
Carlton J s/o Malissa B 1913-1968 Quin
Carroll W h/o E R 1911- MtHo-s
Charles S 1903-1972 Onan
Charlie E (h/o B D) 1915- Fair
David B s/o J W & K R 28 Mar 1894-12 Nov 1908 Onan
E Ruth w/o C W 1916- MtHo-s
Edith J (w/o C A) 1897-1979 Fair
Edward C (h/o A C) 9 Sept 1856-25 Sept 1930 Fair
Eliza J 1835-1928 MtHo
Ellen C d/o W & L 1945-1946 Libe
Ellenora Carmine w/o B F 21 Oct 1859-6 Dec 1950 MtHo
Evelyn M w/o J W 1900-1969 Libe
Flora S 9 July 1895-29 June 1979 Fair
George S h/o M S 1865-1919 Edge
George Thomas (h/o I J) 1875-1949 Onan
George W (s/o A J & S E) 1845-1903 Croc
Georgie Vera d/o J A & B P 24 Feb 1886-8 May 1890 StGe
Harry S h/o L W 1884-1963 Wach

CROCKETT (continued)
Helen V 1910-1980 Onan
Henry and his wife, Ann nd MtHo
Henry L 10 June 1844-25 Mar 1911 MtHo
Henry L h/o M J 1883-1946 MtHo
Henry Lee Jr 2 June 1884-9 Sept 1904 MtHo
Ina V (w/o W H) 1908- Fair
Isabell C w/o C C 25 Dec 1880-14 July 1910 MtHo
Iva Jackson (w/o G T) 1884-1946 Onan
Jack L b&d 24 July 1926 Wach
James E s/o A J & S E 25 Mar 1862-25 Oct 1898 Croc
Jesse W h/o E M 1887-1948 Libe
John A h/o B P 1850-1912 StGe
John S 1888-1944 Onan
John W h/o K R; s/o Southey & Rachel 8 Feb 1864-7 Sept 1929 Onan
Julia Campbell 1907-1934 Onan
Kate L w/o W H; d/o E H & Mary Killmon 26 Apr 1864-12 Jan 1885 Kilb
Kate R w/o J W 7 July 1860-1 Nov 1925 Onan
Leone B d/o W & L b&d 1925 Libe
Louis 1927-1982 Onan
Louis G 1910-1971 MtHo
Lucy w/o Weston 1904-1977 Libe
Lula B 1912-1960 Fair
Lula W w/o H S 1879-1958 Wach
Lydia E w/o W M 1885-1974 MtHo
Malissa B 1875-1960 Quin
Margaret S w/o G S 1865-1934 Edge
Margaret Susan d/o Thos H & Nancy S 3 Feb 1844-9 July 1928 Croc
Mary E 7 Feb 1895-31 July 1973 Libe
Marvin L 1896-1964 MtHo
Mary 1963 MtHo
Matilda J w/o H L 1888-1962

CROCKETT (continued) MtHo
Missouri W 1849-1927 MtHo-s
Nancy Smith w/o Thos H 24 Sept 1819-9 Apr 1857 Croc
Polly 1899-1982 Onan
Rachel A w/o Southey 26 Mar 1836-8 July 1930 Onan
Richard Joseph 9 Oct 1925-24 Sept 1941 Onan
Roy M (h/o Valera) 1899-1981 Fair
Sadie S 1890-1967 Onan
Sherman L 1906-1948 Fair
Southey S h/o R A 2 Oct 1817-13 Mar 1905 Onan
Susan E w/o A J; d/o Geo & Esther Turner 7 Dec 1824-9 Mar 1891 Croc
Thomas H (h/o N S; s/o Asa Thos & Catherine M) 9 Dec 1820-25 Nov 1879 Croc
Valera (w/o R M) 1895-1978 Fair
W Harrison (h/o I V) 1893-1970 Fair
Weston h/o Lucy 1898-1971 Libe
William F s/o Thos H & Nancy S 15 Sept 1851-16 May 1925 Croc
William J 16 Apr 1890-17 Apr 1970 MtHo
William M (Bud) h/o L E 1887-1957 MtHo
CROPPER, Amanda w/o Wm 1850-1929 Park
Ann J B adopted d/o Capt Thos B Cropper b Liverpool Eng d 22 Oct 1856 at Drummondtown, Acc VA Bowm
Anna Corbin d/o Jno Jr & Catherine d 13 Oct 1793; age: 1/5/5 Bowm
Catherine wid/o Gen Jno 24 Jan 1772-24 Jan 1855; age: 83 yrs Bowm
Clarence E h/o D S 1887-1952 Park
Cornelia S w/o C W 1876-1934 Edge
Coventon Corbin s/o Sebastian & Sabra d at Washington Aca-

CROPPER (continued)
demy MD 1 Mar 1786; age: 18/4/12 Bowm
Coventon H s/o Gen Jno & Catherine 5 Apr 1812-18 Jan 1873 Bowm
Custis W h/o C S 1874-1950 Edge
Daisey S w/o C E 1888-1965 Park
E Carroll 1910-1968 Fair
George C (h/o M L) 1884-1964 Edge
Gertrude Bloxsom w/o J T 1870-1958 Edge
Gen John h/o Margt & Catherine; eldest s/o Sebastian & Sabra b at Bowmans Folly, Accomack Co VA 23 Dec 1755-15 Jan 1821; age: 65/0/22 officer in Rev War. Left a wife, 7 children, & 10 grandchildren Bowm
John H h/o S A 2 Oct 1820-2 Feb 1894 Hale
John Tankard h/o G B 1871-1961 Edge
Dr John Washington (h/o M A); eldest s/o Jno & Catherine of Accomack Co VA 15 Jan 1804-4 Sept 1837 He was a Methodist the last 11 yrs of his life Bowm
Littleton 1890-1980 Quin
Margaret w/o Jno Jr; d/o Wm & Mary Pettitt of Northampton Co VA d 3 June 1784; age: 29/1/21 Bowm
Mary Ann w/o Dr Jno W ; only child/o Maj Jno & Elizabeth Savage 1 Oct 1814-23 Dec 1837 Bowm
Mary L (w/o G C) 1890-1970 Edge
Sabra w/o Sebastian; d/o Coventon & Barbara Corbin d 28 Dec 1776; age: 38 yrs Bowm
Sabra d/o Gen Jno Jr & Margt d 24 Sept 1779; age: 0/0/6 Bowm
Sabra 2nd d/o Jno Jr & Margt d 27 Oct 1783; age: 2/8/0 Bowm

CROPPER (continued)
Sarah A w/o Jno H 19 Jan 1820-12 Feb 1887; age: 67/0/23 Hale
Sabra Corbin d/o Gen Jno & Catherine d 2 Nov 1791; age: 0/0/12 Bowm
Sarah T w/o Covington H; d/o Wm & Henrietta Gillett 16 Jan 1820-15 Feb 1884 Gill
Sebastian h/o Sabra; s/o Bowman & Tabitha d 20 Mar 1776; age: 45 yrs Bowm
Thomas Bayly s/o Coventon H & Sarah T 3 Aug 1842- 13 Jan 1843 Bowm
William h/o Amanda 1845-1929 Park
CROSLEY, Andrew L 26 Mar 1883-2 Nov 1951 Onan
Augustus (h/o C A) 1849-1933 Onan
Berryman A 1892-1949 Onan
Blanche W 1890- Onan
Calvin 1891-1893 Harp
Caroline A (w/o Augustus) 1857-1937 Onan
Charles H (h/o E L) 1861-1932 Onan
Cora W w/o W C 1874-1937 Park
Dorsey E h/o E S 1889-1944 Onan
Dorsey Elton Jr 1909-1966 Onan
Edward T 1916-1948 Onan
Ella S (w/o G D) 1900-1974 Onan
Emma L (w/o C H) 1869-1956 Onan
Fannie L 28 May 1887-8 Nov 1937 Onan
Emma S w/o D E 1889-1981 Onan
George D (h/o E S) 1889-1950 Onan
Henry E 1895-1946 Onan
Ida Gibbons 1902-1979 Park
James B 3 Mar 1881-7 Oct 1951 Onan
James E h/o S W 1822-1903 Onan
John W 1879-1941 Onan
Lottie E 4 Dec 1890-9 Apr 1974

CROSLEY (continued)
Onan
Margaret Fogle w/o R H 1917-1982 Onan
Mary W Killmon w/o T F 23 July 1854-26 Aug 1919 Onan
Minnie C w/o W C 1874-1908 Libe
Roy H h/o M F 1913-1961 Onan
Roy H Jr 11 Dec 1952-18 Nov 1980 Onan
Sarah W w/o J E 1839-1901 Onan
Sulie Cobb 14 Jan 1881-27 Mar 1981 Onan
Thomas F h/o M W K 23 Jan 1853-8 May 1921 Onan
Upshur H 30 Nov 1878-1 Jan 1937 Onan
Walter C h/o M C 1877-1941 Libe
William T 17 Nov 1876-13 Nov 1927 Onan
CROSWELL, LeRoy h/o M A 13 Feb 1852-20 Nov 1905 MtHo
Mary A w/o LeRoy 2 June 1849-17 Mar 1931 MtHo
CROWSON, Amy Catherine d/o C T & B M 19 Sept 1904-9 Dec 1924 Libe
Anita Jamison w/o E T 2 June 1919- Libe
Bertha M w/o C T 1885-1973 Libe
Charles D Sr h/o E F 1911-1980 Park
Charles Thomas h/o B M; s/o L T & S D R 22 May 1879-8 Apr 1950 Libe
Edwin Levin s/o Lt Col & Mrs B F 20 Dec 1920-3 Jan 1921 Libe
Elizabeth Dunton w/o J H Jr 13 May 1928- Libe
Elmer Thomas h/o A J; s/o J H & L B 4 July 1916- Libe
Estelle F w/o C D Sr 1914-1981 Park
Ethel J w/o L T 12 Oct 1905- Libe
Fred V 5 Apr 1907-21 Jan 1970 Park

CROWSON (continued)
George S w/o S M 1877-1942 Libe
J P h/o S J 1 Dec 1831-12 Jan 1891 LocM
James H 18 July 1867-21 July 1923 Wach
James Henry h/o L B; s/o Levin Thos & Sallie Dennis (Rew) 7 Jan 1882-13 Aug 1962 Libe
James Henry Jr h/o E D; s/o J H & L B 3 Sept 1912-15 July 1973 Libe
John R 1848-1923 MtHo
John Revel s/o L T & S D R 19 July 1892-19 Jan 1965 Libe
Joseph Edward s/o C T & B M 29 July 1914-17 Mar 1915 Libe
Joseph F 5 Nov 1881-21 Feb 1908 Park
Joseph W h/o M S 1853-1926 Park
L Brooks 1915-1955 Libe
Levin T h/o S D R 20 Sept 1849-24 Mar 1915 Libe
Levin T h/o E J 8 Nov 1895-15 May 1974 Libe
Lula Brown w/o J H; d/o Saml Revel & Vianah Justis 6 Apr 1882-28 Feb 1942 Libe
Manie C 7 Jan 1871-30 Nov 1938 Wach
Mary A 21 Aug 1865-1 July 1947 MtHo
Mollie S w/o J W 1858-1927 Park
Orris Lee h/o S M 24 Nov 1874-24 Aug 1952 Park
Paul G 4 July 1905-27 Mar 1922 Wach
Sadie L 16 Dec 1869-21 Aug 1889 LocM
Sallie Dennis Rew w/o L T 31 Oct 1855-14 Apr 1930 Libe
Sallie M w/o G S 1880-1963 Libe
Samuel Hill 1890-1965 Libe
Sarah J w/o Jas P 8 Dec 1832-16 Mar 1913 Wach
Susan M w/o O L 1876-1933 Park
William 5 Feb 1860-9 Mar 1949 Wach

CROXTON, Bessie B w/o N U 1884-1934 Edge
Harold U s/o N U & B B 15 Apr 1914-25 July 1917 Edge
Neely Upshur h/o B B 1878-1953 Edge
CRUMP, Barbara F 1952-1977 NewM
CUGLER, Burleigh 28 Sept-28 Oct 1885 Edge
Byron C s/o S J & S F 14 Sept 1897-9 Oct 1918 Edge
George L 4 Oct 1893-6 Mar 1894 Edge
Lottie b&d 9 Aug 1882 Edge
Parrie G b&d 14 Sept 1894 Edge
Sallie Frances w/o S J 17 Sept 1861-27 Dec 1928 Edge
Samuel J h/o S F 3 Sept 1859-17 July 1924 Edge
William L 1886-1951 Edge
CULLEN, Katherine Mapp w/o W C 8 Oct 1908- Fair
Winter Calvert h/o K M 25 Sept 1908 Fair
CULLOP, Douglas Barnett h/o L D; Rector-Zion Bap Ch 1968-80 22 Oct 1922-20 Mar 1980 Park
Lois Dunford w/o D B 14 Mar 1931-29 Oct 1980 Park
CURTIS, Archie W 1897-1973 Park
Crystal Lynn b&d 1979 Park
Mary B w/o G F 1895-1976 Edge
CUSTIS, on one shaft; no dates - In memory of: Martha Washington Custis the 1st & the 2nd; Francis Yardley Custis the 1st & the 2nd; Peter Robinson Custis both 1st & 2nd; Thomas Custis OldC
inf/o J R & M A d 1886 Park
inf/o T J & S A b&d 13 Jan 1902 Onan
Agnes Martin w/o Floyd R Jr; d/o M B Martin 3 Nov 1922-20 Jan 1964 Edge
Alice Emma d/o W H B & E V S d 21 Dec 1915 Rave
Alicia A D inf d/o W H B & E V S nd Rave

CUSTIS (continued)
Amanda E (w/o W R) 1870-1962 Onan
Ann Drummond inf d/o J W & M P B nd MtCu
Anne Maude w/o Lynwood O 1903-1930 Onan
Annie E 19 June-23 Sept 1895 Onan
Annie L 1867-1929 Crad-s
Annie Lula d/o H W & M V 18 July-1 Aug 1878 OlCu
Arthur B h/o M J 1858-1939 Crad-s
Benjamin F h/o M A 5 Oct 1827-8 July 1893 (unable to verify) Cust
Benjamin R (h/o L M) 1875-1935 StGe
Bertie 1873-1948 StPa
Bessie Smith w/o M N 15 Nov 1888- Onan
Bettie F 3 Sept 1855-1 Jan 1917 Onan
Bettie M w/o T E C 1 Jan 1839-3 Jan 1926 Onan
Birdie M d/o B F & Mary 22 Sept 1852-29 Nov 1879 (unable to verify) Cust
Blanche Ann h/o L J 1893-1972 Gask
Calvin 1884-1951 NewM
Carl 1912-1983 Onan
Catherine Wharton d/o J W & M P B 7 Oct 1841-19 Aug 1892 MtCu
Cecil 1903-1968 Burt
Charlie 1907-1968 Burt
Clarence E 1902-1983 Gask
Clarence Parker 21 Sept 1882-12 Oct 1960 Onan
Cleo b&d 1963 NewM
Clifton E 1921-1957 Holl
Colebourne E 1873-1943 StGe
Cordia B 1878-1972 StGe
Daphne M 1888-1975 Oakg
Eddie Parker s/o Edwd H & Sue W 6 Oct 1875-15 Mar 1887; age: 11/5/9 OlCu
Edmund R (h/o T S W) 22 July 1791-2 Feb 1837 OldC
Edward H s/o Jno & Tabitha d 18

CUSTIS (continued)
Apr 1820; age: 4/8/11 (stone broken) OlCu
Edward P F h/o N S 1859-1930 Onan
Edward R h/o P A; s/o Henry & Tabitha 17 Aug 1817-2 Oct 1891 JoCu
Eleanor Douglas w/o Wm S; d/o Tully R & Mary Wise 22 Jan 1812-9 Mar 1866 OlCu
Elizabeth A P w/o Thos; d/o Wm M & A P Scarborough 7 Dec 1811-1 Apr 1848 Hedr
Elizabeth C w/o F B; d/o Jas & Harriet Drummond 12 May 1834-22 Mar 1914 Onan
Elizabeth Fisher wid/o Wm P; d/o Dr Fenwick & Rosannah Fisher 11 Sept 1797-(1864) no death date on stone she m2nd Hugh G Seymour Seym
Elizabeth G w/o Jacob 1 Apr 1849-11 Mar 1910 Burt
Elizabeth P w/o J W 1873-1955 Onan
Emma S (w/o S O) 1898-1976 Onan
Emma V S w/o Wm H B; d/o Wm & Euphemia M Conquest 1 May 1816-25 Feb 1894 Rave
Estelle H 1904- Holl
Ethel M (w/o F R) 1899-1953 Fair
Eunice 1935-1976 Burt
F St Clair 1887-1968 MtHo-s
Floyd R (h/o E M) 1900-1959 Fair
Floyd R Jr h/o A M 19 Jan 1925 Edge
Francis B h/o E C; s/o Wm & Eliz 21 Jan 1832-5 Sept 1882 Onan
Francis Dean s/o Mary E 23 Jan 1929-15 May 1963 Onan
Francis J s/o Tankard J & Willie 8 Nov 1889-20 Nov 1891 Harr
Francis T (h/o L S) 1864-1915 Onan
George C (h/o L D) 1862-1945 MtHo-s

CUSTIS (continued)
George F h/o M B 1892-1968 Edge
George R Sr 1889-1963 MtHo-s
Gertrude H (w/o L O) 1908- Fair
Harry Fletcher s/o Wm H B & E V S d 16 Feb 1885; age: 28 yrs Rave
Harry Wise (h/o M V); s/o Wm S & Eleanor Douglas Wise 12 Aug 1849-27 Aug 1914 OlCu
Hattie B w/o J W 1905- Gask
Henry 1902-1977 Metr
Lt Col Henry s/o Robinson & Mary 28 July 1743-27 May 1795 (Rev soldier) MtCu
Henry D (h/o P S) 17 Oct 1894-4 Apr 1972 Onan
Herman 1904-1977 Burt
Henry Hopkinson inf s/o W H B & E V S nd Rave
Herman Lee 2 Oct 1894-3 Mar 1962 Burt
Indiana Burley w/o O F 3 Apr 1876-31 May 1970 Onan
Isaac 1900-1953 Burt
Jacob h/o E G 10 May 1845-8 May 1921 (erected by dau Ida) Burt
James W 11 Apr 1811-4 Aug 1878 OlCu
Jane Henry d/o Wm H B & E V S d 28 Sept 1916 Rave
Jeanette 1902- Onan
Jenifer Marshall inf d/o W H B & E V S nd Rave
John s/o Jno & Tabitha d 28 Dec 1837; age: 30/0/5 (dates badly worn) OlCu
John s/o Jno & Catharine d 17 Nov 1848; age: 70/6/15 OlCu
John R (h/o M A) 1860-1924 Park
John Robinson s/o Wm S & E D 26 Feb 1834-21 Dec 1871 OlCu
John Robinson s/o J W & E A 12 Nov 1904-2 Mar 1906 Onan
John T 17 May-20 July 1908 Onan
John W s/o Wm Robinson Custis d 18 Oct 1836; age: 35 TheF

67

CUSTIS (continued)
John W my husband; s/o Thos & Eliz 28 Nov 1833-29 July 1861 Hedr
John W h/o E P 1874-1941 Onan
John W h/o H B 1901-1973 Gask
John William h/o N P 15 Apr 1887-5 Apr 1960 MtHo
Johnny s/o Johnny & Rose 1 Sept 1858-25 July 1859 Hedr
Laura S (w/o F T) 1870-1940 Onan
Lee 1901-1974 Gask
Lena nd Gask
Liebig K 1902-1977 Holl
Lillie D (w/o G C) 1867-1950 MtHo-s
Lloyd James h/o B A 1886-1975 Gask
Lloyd James 9 June 1925-4 Jan 1971 Gask
Lucy M (w/o B R) 1882-1974 StGe
Lyndia E d/o M N & B S 14 Sept 1915-28 July 1917 Onan
Lynwood O (h/o G H) 1903-1980 Fair
Margaret 1917-1980 Onan
Margaret P w/o Jas W; d/o Thos & Margt Bayly 15 Jan 1818-18 Mar 1856 marr: 27 Oct 1840 MtCu
Margaret S 1861-1922 Crad-s
Margaret S 20 Sept 1891-23 Oct 1893 Harp
Margaret Virginia w/o H W 12 Apr 1853-9 Jan 1902 OlCu
Margaret Virginia d/o H W & M V 6 May-18 July 1885 OlCu
Mary A w/o B F 11 May 1831-9 June 1894 (unable to verify) Cust
Mary A (w/o J R) 1860-1948 Park
Mary Elizabeth 1 Dec 1892-16 Feb 1975 Onan
Mary J (w/o A B) 1861-1943 Crad-s
Mattie E w/o W T 1890-1974 Onan
Milton Nock h/o B S 23 Feb 1891-12 Jan 1976 Onan

CUSTIS (continued)
Minnie d 2 Aug 1955; age: 42 yrs Gask-old
Minnie R w/o S A 27 Nov 1895-13 July 1923 Onan
Monnie A d/o Thos J & Monnie E 21 Nov 1886-30 June 1887 JoCu
Nellie Powell w/o J W 14 Dec 1886-23 Aug 1952 MtHo
Nellie Scott w/o E O F 23 July 1877-1 Aug 1966 Onan
Oswald F h/o I B 1873-1947 Onan
Pamelia A w/o E R; d/o Elias D & Margt Joynes 20 June 1820-3 June 1892 JoCu
Pearl S (w/o H D) 16 Nov 1897-10 Apr 1959 Onan
Phoebe S w/o R P; d/o Jno W H & Sarah A Parker 27 Dec 1852-22 Sept 1892 Onan
Prudie Fulcher 8 Jan 1923 in Atlantic NC-26 Jan 1978 Fair
Rebecca N 1927-1970 Snea
Robert Poulson h/o P S 18 Mar 1846-3 June 1909 Onan
S A h/o M P 1896-1956 Onan
Sarah A w/o T J 1875-1948 Onan
Sarah Stockley inf d/o W H B & E V S nd Rave
Sidney C 1919- Onan
Sidney O (h/o E S) 1898-1945 Onan
Solomon 1917-1964 Burt
Soule Campbell s/o W H B & E V S d 29 Dec 1864; age: 17 yrs Rave
Spencer F 1896-1924 Onan
Stella B (w/o W T) 31 May 1885-3 Jan 1981 Crad-s
Susan W 11 June 1841-6 May 1909 OlCu
s/o Thos J & Monnie 10 Jan-16 Jan 1888 JoCu
Tabitha w/o Jno; d/o Ayres & Margt Gillett d 17 Oct 1822; age: 47/6/21 (dates badly worn) OlCu
Tabitha Scarburgh Wise w/o E R 18 Apr 1793-15 Jan 1855 OldC
Tank J h/o S A 1868-1934 Onan

CUSTIS (continued)
Thomas s/o Jno & Tabitha d 21 Dec 1840; age: 38?/11/9 (dates badly worn) OlCu
Thomas 1875-1958 StPa
Thomas E C h/o B M 13 July 1836-12 May 1889 Onan
Timothy S s/o H S & M R b&d 1954 Onan
Vernon A s/o T J & S A 28 Mar-3 Aug 1913 Onan
W H B (brother) nd (in Chandler lot) MtHo
William Conquest s/o W H B & E V S d 29 Sept 1874; age: 24 yrs Rave
William H B h/o E V S; only s/o Major Henry B & Eliz 28 Dec 1814-7 Oct 1885 (erected by his only descendants, Jane H & Alice E Custis - 1902) Rave
William L 1882-1901 Park
William P h/o E F; s/o Jno & Catherine 7 May 1788-6 Nov 1838; age: 50/6/0 Seym
William R (h/o A E) 1870-1946 Onan
William Robinson (Col Bob) s/o Thos d 1839 no stone; ref Mrs Nelson TheF
William Samuel (h/o E D); s/o Jno & Tabitha 14 Oct 1809-8 Feb 1876 OlCu
William T (h/o S B) 30 Sept 1884-7 Dec 1951 Crad-s
Willianna S w/o Tankard J; d/o J E & M A Harrison 5 May 1870-31 Dec 1891 Harr
William T h/o M E 1895-1966 Onan

CUTLER, baby girl b&d 30 June 1968 Wach
infs/o R J & V M: Charlotte; George; Samuel; Charlie nd Cutl
Alice K 25 Apr 1868-9 July 1922 Holl
Allen T s/o Richd J & Alice Curtin 1924-1969 Cutl
Annie M 1928-1932 Wach
Clara C (w/o G W) 1890-1978 Wach

CUTLER (continued)
Colie L (h/o H E) 1917- Onan
Edward G 1869-1942 Cutl
Elijah Tazewell h/o E J; s/o R J & V M 1 July 1858-18 Apr 1932 Cutl
Emma J w/o Elijah T; d/o Wm H & Esther Hardy 30 Nov 1863-12 Nov 1931 Cutl
Fannie B 1923-1927 Wach
Capt Frank J 1857-1936 Cutl
George W (h/o C C) 1881-1957 Wach
Helen E (w/o C L) 1923-1971 Onan
Horace P C s/o E G & Annie W 5 Apr 1902-6 Mar 1963 Cutl
Isabel w/o Tazewell 1885-1969 Cutl
Jesse Crown w/o Elijah T d Aug 1932 Cutl
Jimmie C 1926-1928 Wach
John R 19 Aug 1852-2 Apr 1935 Holl
Mary A w/o Geo W 27 Sept 1829-14 Nov 1913 Park
Mary Taylor w/o Richd J; d/o Elijah W & Margt A Nock 24 Nov 1830-23 July 1906 Cutl
Milton J 1910-1983 Edge
Paul C 1922-1946 Wach
Peter s/o Jno & Polly 7 Sept 1784-7 Oct 1845 Cutl
Richard s/o Jno & Polly 22 Sept 1778-10 Jan 1862 Cutl
Richard J h/o Virginia M & Mary T; s/o P J & Rosanna 27 June 1833-24 Feb 1917 Cutl
Richard J s/o Elijah T & Emma H 1888-1965 Cutl
Rosanna w/o Peter; (nee Finney) 10 Jan 1794-7 Dec 1870 Cutl
Susan A w/o Geo P 26 Sept 1804-17 Aug 1865 CutS
Tazewell (h/o Isabel); s/o E T & E J 5 Jan 1887-20 Dec 1955 Cutl
Tommie N b&d 1932 Wach
Virginia M w/o Richd J; d/o E W & Margt A Nock 22 May 1835-13 June 1876 Cutl
Virginia Y b&d 1930 Wach

CUTLER (continued)
William F 3 Dec 1866-23 Aug 1933 Cutl
William H s/o Elijah T & Emma J 2 Aug 1899-9 Oct 1918 Cutl
D, W L footstone only Hutc
DAFFIN, Philip h/o Elsie M Outten 1921-1978 Fair
DAISEY, Annie L w/o Wm P 1887-1976 Park
Edward L s/o W P & A L 1907-1929 Park
William P h/o A L 1876-1964 Park
DALBY, Handy W h/o H V 1904-1980 Park
Hilda V w/o H W 1907- Park
DALEY, Cornelius F 1893-1951 Fair
DAMLIN, William 1860-1934 Park
DANGERFIELD, Lillian 1919-1981 Gask
DANIEL, Rev (James?) N Jr 1893-1975 JoyC
Margarette F 1907-1955 JoyC
DAUGHERTY, Cheryl Dewes 1951-1977 Edge
Edward T Jr 21 Nov 1902-12 Oct 1959 Edge
Edward Thomas 18 July 1873-17 Apr 1958 Edge
James A 3 Aug 1824-27 Feb 1917 Edge
James Gibson 1925-1969 Edge
James P 1864-1935 Edge
James Purnell Jr 1898-1957 Edge
Kathryn M w/o R F 1903- Edge
Minnie Phillips 21 Aug 1878-25 Feb 1958 Edge
Robert F h/o K M 1891-1961 Edge
Sudie L w/o W B 26 Apr 1864-19 Dec 1947 Edge
William B h/o S L 15 Sept 1861-27 Oct 1929 Edge
DAVENPORT, Ernest Brooks 1909-1938 Onan
James Edward 1920-1942 Onan
Laura Arthur 25 July 1892-1 July 1975 MtHo-s

DAVEZAC, Margaret w/o Dr Augustus Sr d 5 Sept 1847; age: 79/0/8 Parp
DAVIS, inf boy d 1962 Fair
baby boy b&d 1962 MtHo
Albert F h/o V B 1924-1979 Park
Andrew J (h/o M A) 1877-1960 Fair
Annie 1894-1956 Snea
Annie 1913-1978 Burt
Annie M d/o Benj & M S 24 Aug 1873-20 Oct 1911 TheG
B Thomas Jr 1921-1971 MtHo-s
Ben F Jr 28 Sept 1917-2 Mar 1981 Shil
Benjamin 25 Dec 1805-18 July 1880 TheG
Capt Benjamin F 8 Apr 1847-22 Mar 1903 TheG
Benjamin F s/o B F & M R 15 May 1876-25 May 1878 TheG
Bertie C w/o J L 1884-1951 Wach
Betsy T 1896-1959 Bays
Bettie 1873-1948 Snea
Billie B 15 Oct 1902-19 Oct 1980 Fair
Brice Everett 17 Oct 1901-22 May 1972 Fair
Carrie Lee 16 Oct 1921-28 Dec 1976 Snea
Charles 1940-1960 Snea
Charles B 1881-1958 MtHo-s
Charles B Jr 1910-1978 Edge
Charles F 1871-1949 Libe
Charlie d 20 Sept 1961; age: 61 yrs Snea
Charlie B Sr h/o M L 1881-1959 Edge
Charlotte 1919-1921 TheG
Clara R w/o N C 1903-1973 Park
Claude Jr 1953-1974 Metr
Coley H h/o M C 23 Oct 1898-7 Nov 1966 Park
Edna Wise 1893-1972 TheG
Elizabeth C 1868-1944 MtHo-s
Ella F w/o J S 1853-1921 MtHo-s
Florence C w/o G O 1899-1942 Park
Forrest M 1875-1946 TheG
Frank s/o B F & M R 7 Dec

DAVIS (continued)
1878-26 July 1897 TheG
Frankie E 15 Feb 1927-28 Nov 1970 MtHo-s
George A 1909-1968 Burt
George Charlie 1856-1947 Snea
George E (h/o M S) 24 Mar 1850-1 Dec 1911 Morr
George O 19 June 1895-23 Feb 1972 MtHo-s
George O h/o F C 1895- Park
George T 1879-1962 Burt
George W 1869-1952 MtHo-s
Harry Floyd s/o G E & M S 9 Sept 1883-10 Nov 1954 Morr
Harry R s/o B F & M R 27 Feb 1883-3 Feb 1884 TheG
Harvey R 1906-1980 Fair
Hazel V 1908-1963 MtHo-s
Henry Jacob Sr 22 Jan 1925-20 Jan 1977 TheG
Henry S s/o Savage & Peggie 1 Aug 1820-13 July 1859 DavL
Hester A 1835-1893 Davi
India H w/o W D 30 Sept 1877-4 June 1964 Wach
Ira F (h/o M B) 1875-1960 Fair
Isabelle Johnson w/o W M 2 July 1906-30 Apr 1977 Wach
James 22 Mar 1867-22 May 1891 Burt
James Edward 3 Jan 1863-26 Mar 1933 MtHo-s
James V 1952-1983 Metr
Jessie C 1920- MtHo-s
John Henry 1907-1978 Snea
John L h/o B C 1873-1956 Wach
John R 1905-1978 Metr
John S h/o E F 20 Nov 1851-18 Apr 1925 MtHo-s
John S s/o B F & M R 5 Feb-12 Feb 1881 TheG
Leah A d/o Geo T Mapp & Leah 27 Dec 1821-15 Aug 1892 DavL
Lela Ames w/o L N; d/o Jno Stephen & Charlotte (Downing) Ames 15 Dec 1885-10 June 1983 Fair
Levin Nock w/o L A; s/o Geo Edwd & Margt (Nock) 6 Oct 1887-11 May 1971 Fair

DAVIS (continued)
Littleton B 1825-1897 Davi
Lola W 1877-1957 MtHo-s
Louise 1916-1960 Burt
Magadalene 1911-1961 Metr
Maggie 1871-1957 Burt
Maggie 1896-1932 Snea
Maggie E w/o Capt Peter; d/o Richd Thos & Louisa Taylor Ames 9 Apr 1852-16 Dec 1941 TheG
Maggie S (w/o W F) 1873-1956 Wach
Manie A (w/o A J) 1885-1957 Fair
Mannie B 1882-1944 MtHo-s
Margaret B (w/o I F) 1872-1963 Fair
Margaret R w/o Benj F 18 Apr 1852-9 July 1909 TheG
Margaret S w/o Benj 2 Sept 1836-30 July 1911 TheG
Margaret S w/o G E; d/o L W & S C Nock 23 Feb 1856-15 Mar 1929 Morr
Mary C w/o C H 30 Sept 1908- Park
Mary G w/o S J 15 Oct 1856-19 Sept 1946 Edge
Mary P w/o R P 1878-1947 TheG
Maude L w/o C B Sr 1889-1972 Edge
Milcah Ann w/o Benj 12 Dec 1812-24 May 1868; age: 55/5/12 TheG
Milton 1919-1973 Snea
Milton Lee 1892-1962 Shil
Minnie G b&d 1962 Snea
Norman C h/o C R 1890-1973 Park
Peggie Mapp w/o Savage; d/o Howson & Bettie (Thomas) Mapp 7 Mar 1777-6 Oct 1842 DavL
Peter H 21 Sept 1839-21 Dec 1890 TheG
Peter R 21 Sept 1839-21 Dec 1890 TheG
Posie d/o B F & M R 4 July 1891-6 Sept 1892 TheG
Priscilla Hall d 11 Oct 1797; age: 27 yrs Parp

DAVIS (continued)
R Penn (h/o M P) 1872-1954 TheG
Ray Danial 10 Jan 1933-15 Aug 1968 Quin
Rosie d/o B F & M R 4 July 1891-6 Sept 1892 TheG
S Jefferson (h/o M G) 2 Aug 1862-21 Feb 1940 Edge
Savage (h/o P M) 15 Mar 1772-1 Nov 1834; age: 62 yrs DavL
Stanley 15 Mar 1896-1 Nov 1970 Snea
Susan E 1865-1960 Burt
Thomas P h/o W J 1881-1943 Park
Virginia B w/o A F 1915- Park
Will 1889-1969 NewM
William Andrews s/o Martin A & Priscilla 15 Sept-15 Oct 1797 Parp
William D h/o I H 17 Apr 1876-17 Mar 1953 Wach
William H 10 Nov 1895-25 Sept 1970 Wach
William Milton h/o I J 3 Oct 1905-14 Nov 1959 Wach
William T 30 Sept 1918-11 Jan 1981 Snea
William T s/o Henry S & Leah 15 Aug 1844-3 July 1859 DavL
William Van 28 June 1894-3 Aug 1972 Wach
Willie F (h/o M S) 1876-1962 Wach
Winnie J w/o T P 1881-1953 Park
Edith Kellam d/o Jno W & Mary 22 Dec 1881-19 Oct 1906 Hysl
DeCORMIS, Hazel M Jan 1914-Aug 1968 Edge
Dr Joseph L h/o M L 26 Mar 1882-10 Apr 1966 Edge
Mabel Lewis w/o J L 10 Dec 1889-16 July 1964 Edge
DEECHER, Evelyn W (w/o P J) 1922- Onan
Paul J (h/o E W) 1917-1982 Onan
DEITRECK, Gladys M w/o V S Jr 1912- Park
Margaret W w/o V S 1880-1969

DEITRECK (continued)
Park
Virgil S h/o M W 1869-1947 Park
Virgil S Jr h/o G M 1912-1951 Park
DENNIS, Arinthia 1872-1932 HTri
Baker B (h/o M C) 1908-1979 Edge
E Lewis 30 Apr 1910-7 July 1970 Libe
Emily L 1884-1953 Edge
Ernest J h/o O L 10 Apr 1881-17 Dec 1969 Libe
Estelle V (w/o M W) 1884-1970 Onan
Eula F w/o R J 1917- Edge
Grayson Savage s/o R J & E F b&d 1942 Edge
John 1827-4 Mar 1907 HTri
Louisa Ann w/o Dr Geo Robinson of Kingston, Somerset Co MD; d/o Thos R Joynes of Acc Co VA 29 Jan MDCCCXX11 (1822)-10 July MDCCCLII (1852) Bowm
M Wesley (h/o E V) 1872-1937 Onan
Mary 1836-11 Sept 1916 HTri
Mary C (w/o B B) 1910- Edge
Olive L w/o E J 25 July 1885-24 Mar 1962 Libe
Pauline S 1920-1974 Edge
Robert J h/o E F 1916-1968 Edge
DENNISON, Emmillee S b&d 1982 Onan
DENSTON, s/o Ronnie & Yvonne b&d 1968 Fair
Marian W 1898-1915 Park
DENTON, Sue Robertson 30 May 1915-14 Feb 1981 Onan
DERBY, Harriet Alexander d/o Chas Alexander & Charlotte (Basset) 26 Apr 1862-21 Feb 1927 Edge
Landon Basset 15 Sept 1877-11 May 1915 Edge
DERROSSETT, Charles L 4 Feb 1920-29 Nov 1979 Park
DETWILER, David F Sr 1902-1974 Fair

DEVER, Bessie Mason w/o W K 1884-1953 Libe
W K h/o B M 1880-1945 Libe
DICKEN, Georgie Marcylene 7 Dec 1916-31 July 1917 MtHo
DICKENS, Callie Marton 1915-1958 MtNe
DICKERSON, Alice C w/o J D 1876-1965 Park
Edgar H 24 June 1874-21 Aug 1914 Libe
Eleanor d/o Thos & E R 9 Jan 1870-12 Dec 1892 Libe
Eleanor Russell w/o Thos 11 Sept 1836-30 Aug 1913 Libe
J Douglas h/o A C 1870-1955 Park
Lenora F 28 July 1881-11 Apr 1939 Park
Thomas h/o E R 12 Oct 1827-12 Oct 1901 Libe
Thomas J 26 Jan 1856-4 July 1885 Libe
DIGGS, A Linwood 1909-1971 Onan
Charles E h/o L E 1890-1953 Onan
Charles S h/o S J 1882-1965 Onan
Lillie E w/o C E 1891-1962 Onan
S Jane w/o C S 1883-1959 Onan
DISE see DIZE
DISHAROON, J Walter (h/o M H) 8 May 1907-19 July 1982 Fair
Minnie Hinman (w/o J W) 17 Nov 1909- Fair
DIX, Alfred J h/o A E 10 Oct 1854-10 Dec 1897 Park
Alfred J h/o A E 1886-1934 Park
Alfred J h/o Pauline 1912-1968 Park
Alma B w/o Wm T Jr 1912- Park
Annie D w/o Wm W 7 Dec 1878-15 July 1953 Park
Annie E w/o A J 25 Feb 1859-10 May 1920 Park
Annie E w/o A J 1890-1964 Park
Annie L w/o L J 1869-1939 Park
Arinthia T 1858-1940 Libe
Arthur Thomas h/o M S 1894-

DIX (continued) 1967 Park
Asa T MD 1816-1882 (erected by Dr J Morgan Dix, Capt in Medical Corps USA) DrDi
Bessie L w/o B H 3 Oct 1885-29 Sept 1971 Park
Burleigh H h/o B L 22 Aug 1881-18 Oct 1954 Park
Clarence H h/o L T 1892-1940 Park
Claude K 30 May 1917-2 Dec 1944 Park
Daisey W 8 May 1894-17 Apr 1924 Park
Dorsey Thomas 1927-1942 Park
Dorsey W 8 May 1894-17 Apr 1924 Park
Elizabeth W w/o H J 1912- Park
Emma A (w/o P C) 1879-1966 Fair
Emma K (w/o H S) 3 June 1845-9 Nov 1926 MtHo
Everett F h/o V V 1888-1971 Park
George Lee 27 Nov 1882-7 June 1940 Park
Grace G w/o M L 1918- Park
Harvey J h/o E W 1909-1976 Park
Henry S (h/o E K) 23 Feb 1844-6 July 1918 MtHo
James H s/o W T & M J 16 July 1875-19 Jan 1894 Park
James Lee h/o L R 1887-1979 Park
Jeff 27 May 1860-7 Dec 1915 Park
Jefferson L h/o M A 1884-1972 Libe
Jennette G w/o J Wm 19 Feb 1876-19 July 1919 Park
John W 1857-1935 Libe
John William h/o J G 1875-1961 Park
Levi J h/o A L 1865-1937 Park
Lillian R w/o J L 1887-1967 Park
Lola T w/o C H 1892- Park
Lottie A w/o G L 27 Sept 1882-4 Feb 1927 Park
Lydia J w/o Dr A T 1836-1916

DIX (continued)
DrDi
Margaret A w/o Dr A T; d/o Henry & Harriet J Wheeler 26 Aug 1826 in Worcester Co MD-28 May 1854 DrDi
Margaret J w/o Wm T 8 Feb 1845-17 Nov 1920 Park
Margaret E w/o L D d 11 May 1855; age: 20/11/22 Dixg
Martha J d/o A P & Frances M 6 Nov-22 Nov 1942 Libe
Mary Alice w/o J L 1888-1962 Libe
Mary G 16 Oct 1874-13 July 1922; age: 48 yrs Shil
Parke C (h/o E A) 1878-1949 Fair
Maurice L h/o G G 1917-1965 Park
May Savilla w/o A T 1903-1942 Park
Nancy Lee 1922-1984 Park
Pauline w/o A J 1921- Park
Ruby S 1923-1977 MtHo-s
Sarah Ann J d 11 May 1832; age: 28/8/8 Tave
Sudie G w/o Wm T Sr 1889-1979 Park
Virgie V w/o E F 1901- Park
Virginia J 1897-1981 Libe
William T h/o M J 21 May 1843-29 Apr 1920 Park
William T Sr h/o S G 1890-1934 Park
William T Jr h/o A B 1911-1971 Park
William W h/o A D 21 Feb 1877-13 May 1951 Park
DIXON, Elizabeth P w/o W I 1923-1977 Onan
William I h/o E P 1908- Onan
DIZE, (DISE),
Andrew C (h/o H J) 1907- Fair
Annie Louise 1928-1975 Libe
Beatrice P 1913-1975 Onan
Bessie S w/o J W 1876-1950 Holl
Clifton C (h/o I J) 14 June 1894-28 July 1977 Wach
Edward C 1896-1944 Holl
Elmer T h/o S M 1905-1977

DIZE (continued)
MtHo-s
George Nickie 1959-1960 Onan
George W (h/o L P) 1904-1965 Onan
Georgie L (w/o T S) 1879-1976 Fair
Harry W (h/o O H) 1928-1977 Onan
Hazel J (w/o A C) 1909-1972 Fair
Ida J (w/o C C) 2 July 1891- Wach
Irma S 1898-1946 Holl
James S 1874-1924 StGe
Jennie S (w/o J C) 25 Feb 1893-3 Aug 1967 MtHo-s
John C (h/o J S) 20 May 1892-29 Feb 1976 MtHo-s
John W (h/o B S) 1852-1932 Holl
Lena P (w/o G W) 1907- Onan
Mary E w/o Jno W; d/o R P & Margt T Guy d 31 Dec 1887; age: 18 yrs (stone not located; 1940 data) Guyb
Mary W (w/o P H) 1852-1936 StGe
Oledia H (w/o H W) 1921- Onan
Peter H (h/o M W) 1848-1918 StGe
Peter H & Mary W - children of: (ages at death) Archie 19 yrs 1873-1892; Alfred T 6 yrs; Henry 5 days; Charlotte 5 yrs; Annie Jack 14 mon (all on one stone) StGe
Preston W 1912-1970 Onan
Raymond T (h/o S E) 1884-1951 MtHo-s
Sallie E (w/o R T) 1886-1954 MtHo-s
Sally 8 Mar 1919-21 Feb 1976 MtHo-s
Sarah M w/o E T 1907- MtHo-s
Thomas S (h/o G L) 1872-1949 Fair
Warren 1900-1984 Libe
DOBIN, Judy 22 Jan 1849-24 July 1901 Gask-old
DOCTOR, Prudence w/o Hallie 1918-1943 JoyC
DODD, Margaret 1895-1964 Onan

DODSON, James H (h/o K C) 1876-1956 Onan
Katherine C (w/o J H) 1897- Onan
Manie J w/o J Henry; only child/o J S & K S Killmon 5 Jan 1884-17 Dec 1909 Onan
Margaret Kilmon 1869-1953 Fair
DOMON, Annie nd Neda
DONAHOE, E Marlene (w/o P R Jr) 20 Aug 1939-16 May 1964 and inf dau Fair
Paul R Jr (h/o E M) 17 May 1930-23 June 1981 Fair
DONAWAY, Annie Byrd 1856-1949 Park
DOUGHTY, Abel T 4 Oct 1852-20 Aug 1880 Wate
Alexander W s/o Jas C & Eliz 3 Oct 1839-21 Feb 1855 Fore-old
Annie S d/o Edwd & Sarah 27 Apr 1847-28 May 1910 MtHo
Archie S Sr (h/o B W) 8 Dec 1886-1973 Quin
Augtin 1928-1981 Shil
Bessie L d/o S J & M L 1890-1899 (moved from Hog Island) Quin
Bettie V w/o Major R; d/o Jas C & Sophronia Mapp 25 Sept 1862-8 Jan 1882; age: 19/3/13 Mapp
Blanche W (w/o A S) 1890-1959 Quin
Bryce T 13 Dec 1954-25 June 1970 Holl
Beulah Pearl d/o M R & Manie C 14 Sept 1885-27 June 1890 Mapp
Catherine Johnson w/o M R d 21 March 1875; age: about 55 yrs Majo
Charlie F Sr 1901-1968 HTri
Clara L 1887-1976 Edge
Clarence h/o Viva 1890-1939 Edge
Daisy M w/o L T 21 June 1894-8 May 1923 MtHo
E Upshur s/o Major R & Mary (Mapp) 8 Sept 1885-26 Apr 1974 Onan

DOUGHTY (continued)
Elizabeth 10 July 1773-9 June 1848 Doug
Elizabeth w/o Jas C 12 Sept 1812-5 Dec 1840 Fore-old
Elizabeth S w/o G L; d/o Lincoln & Sallie Kellam 21 Aug 1847-26 Apr 1918 Edge
Elizabeth S 1908-1977 Onan
Elva G (w/o L C) 1878-1961 Onan
Fannie 1911-1973 Burt
Garrison 1913-1971 Edge
Garry W d 24 Mar 1959; age: 0/3/5 Burt
George s/o G W & Margt 1865-1888 Majo
George Lloyd h/o E S 27 Sept 1848-9 Mar 1920 Edge
George Lloyd 1884-1953 StJa
George W h/o Margt 1837-1885 Majo
George W 1887-1955 Edge
Georgia Bell w/o J T 1855-1940 Onan
Gus ns Wate
Harry d 23 Mar 1932; age: 75 yrs JoyC
Hattie S w/o R T d 6 Mar 1907; age: 47 yrs Onan
James C (h/o S P) 4 July 1862-28 Apr 1903 Fore
James Colonna 16 May 1816-6 Mar 1887 Fore
James Corbin MD 11 Mar 1891-15 June 1968 MtHo
James H s/o R T & H S 4 Sept 1884-5 July 1885 Onan
James R s/o J C & S P 6 Feb 1887-26 Feb 1890 Fore
James T s/o J C & M S T 16 May 1855-20 Apr 1858 Fore
John 7 Oct 1801-19 Oct 1857 Doup
John B (h/o R A & L S) 18 Dec 1841-2 Nov 1919 Syca
John R 6 Mar 1806-22 Feb 1874 Wate
John Tankard h/o G B 1853-1938 Onan
John W s/o Jno O & Mary C 17 Apr 1837-16 Mar 1893 Doup

DOUGHTY (continued)
Lanett S w/o J B 1847-1931 Syca
Leonidas Rosser h/o S B; s/o Jas Colonna & Margt S T (Johnson) 30 Sept 1858-2 Aug 1935 MtHo
Levin T h/o D M 11 June 1883-9 July 1938 MtHo
Lloyd C (h/o E G) 1876-1965 Onan
Lucile d/o L T & D M 11 Nov 1919-5 Mar 1920 MtHo
Maggie d/o J C & S P 30 Nov 1882-6 Aug 1884 Fore
Maggie F 1919-1932 HTri
Major D h/o M S 8 June 1862-4 Jan 1922 Ptea
Major R 8 Feb 1806-11 May 1861 Majo
Major R 13 Oct 1854-11 Nov 1937 Onan
Major Robertson III s/o Major R Jr & Lillian (Sturgis) 1935-1953 Onan
Mamie 1896-1972 HTri
Manie C w/o Major R; d/o J C & Saphronia Mapp 20 Apr 1864-22 Nov 1891; age: 27 yrs Mapp
Margaret w/o G W 1834-1883 Majo
Margaret Chandler w/o W J 1851-1899 MtHo
Margaret Sarah (Sadie) w/o M D; d/o Robert A & Maggie Drummond 26 Nov 1866-28 Nov 1942 Ptea
Margaret Sarah Thomas (w/o J C) 11 July 1822-28 Oct 1911 Fore
Martha Lowry Lee 1896- StJa
Mary C w/o Jno 21 June 1814-28 Feb 1892 Doup
Mary F w/o Jno W; d/o Wm C & Eliz Ames 5 July 1846-14 May 1872 Doup
Mary J 1892-1970 Shil
Mary L (w/o S J Sr) 1862-1952 Quin
Mary R 10 Aug 1810-1 July 1884 Wate
Maudie F d/o M R & B V 5 Jan-29 June 1882 Mapp

DOUGHTY (continued)
Mildred Milliner 20 Feb 1911-4 Feb 1970 Edge
Minnie Rosser d/o L R & Tannie 29 July 1888-26 Apr 1890 MtHo
Nellie B 1889-1975 HTri
Oswald Dix (h/o Y K) 14 Mar 1850-4 Mar 1910 Onan
Otho s/o M D & Sadie 22 Sept 1887-22 June 1888 DruD
Otis Thomas 1929-1979 Shil
Miss P J 27 Apr 1847-17 Apr 1871 Doup
Pauline B 1920-1975 Holl
Peggy Colonna w/o Jeptha 10 Oct 1786-14 June 1870 Majo
Rebecca A w/o J B d 9 July 1873; age: 26/10/3 Syca
Richard T h/o H S 14 May 1850-22 Jan 1913 Onan
Sallie R 22 Oct 1870-10 Nov 1955 Onan
Sallie Yerby d/o J C & M S T 19 Feb-7 Dec 1865 Fore
Sarah D 1867-1956 Park
Sarah P w/o Jas C 1857-1933 Fore
Sarah W 30 Oct 1842-16 July 1904 Onan
Sheppard J Sr (h/o M L) 1852-1940 Quin
Sheppard J Jr 1896-1970 Quin
Sue Colonna d/o L R & Tannie 8 Oct 1886-15 Aug 1894 MtHo
Susan Britann w/o L R; d/o Wm Corbin & Susan Aydelott Slocomb 15 Nov 1855-12 Nov 1941 MtHo
Susie 1895-1982 Burt
Theodore 1890-1970 Burt
Thomas J s/o Thos J & Margt 31 May 1811-1 Apr 1847 Fore-old
Viva w/o Clarence 1894-1953 Edge
Walter Lee 1 Oct 1889-5 June 1912 Ptea
William s/o Wm & Tabitha 29 Jan 1804-19 June 1837 Wate
William J h/o M C 1847-1915 MtHo
Willie s/o M D & Sadie 29 July-

DOUGHTY (continued)
  4 Aug 1886 DruD
Yula Kellam (w/o O D) 7 Sept 1858-4 June 1948 Onan
DOUGLAS, Helen Rowles (w/o L H) 30 Dec 1891-15 Nov 1980 Fair
  Joseph F d 16 Apr 1910; age: 39 yrs Edge
  Louis Harriman (h/o H R) 25 Dec 1888-23 July 1961 Fair
DOUGLASS, Ralph Benjamin (h/o R B) 6 May 1891 (Alexander City AL)-21 Aug 1972 (Norfolk VA) MtPl
  Renova Beard w/o R B; m/o Do-rothy Douglass Kellam & Rebecca Douglass Mapp 12 July 1893 (Luverne AL)-23 Jan 1951 (Norfolk VA) MtPl
DOWNING, Alice E 11 Sept 1849-3 Nov 1923 MeaD
Alice Hickman (w/o G R) 1898-13 June 1984; age: 86 yrs Holl
Anna E w/o E T; (nee Twyford) 24 Jan 1841-22 May 1888 ETDo
Catherine E d/o J B & Georgie S b&d 21 July 1925 Turl
Edna 1916-1973 Gask
Edward T (h/o A E) 10 May 1830-25 Aug 1887 ETDo
Eliza T w/o J F 25 Feb 1894- Edge
Elizabeth d/o Francis & Betsy 25 June 1809-1 Mar 1879 Down
Elizabeth A w/o J W 7 Mar 1826-31 Jan 1901 ETDo
Elizabeth J w/o F A 24 Oct 1829-26 May 1893 Down
Fay 1889-1940 Mead
Francis A w/o E J 21 Sept 1824-8 Mar 1872 Down
Francis Arthur h/o M W; s/o F A & E J 3 Apr 1869-13 Oct 1942 Edge
Garland Beach s/o Jno B & Polly W 16 Apr 1894-20 Oct 1918 Down
George W s/o J R & Margt 29 Nov 1845-20 May 1864 (killed in Battle of Petersburg; re-

DOWNING (continued)
  mains moved here 20 Oct 1865) Dowp
George W s/o E T & A E 24 Mar 1865-30 Sept 1887 ETDo
Georgie S w/o Jno B 30 Sept 1883-19 Feb 1974 Down
Gilmore R (h/o A H) 1888-1964 Holl
Gladdis 27 Feb-29 Feb 1912 Guyp
Harriet 1897-1975 JoyC
Indie M d/o F A & E J 9 Aug 1863-28 June 1883 Down
Indie Delitha d/o Jno & Polly W 16 May 1883-18 Sept 1884 Down
J G 1871-1937 MeaD
James R h/o Margt; s/o Jno & Esther 15 Mar 1807-24 Mar 1881 Dowp
James R s/o J W & E A 21 Jan-21 June 1861 ETDo
James W (h/o E A); s/o Jno & Mary 12 July 1828-3 Nov 1880; age: 52/3/21 ETDo
John h/o Mary; s/o Jno R & Sally 9 May 1796-7 Dec 1858; age: 62/6/28 ETDo
John 1914-1983 Gask
John Beach s/o F A & E J 4 Feb 1862-22 Oct 1931 Down
John H 1914-1945 MtHo
John Obed s/o E T & A E 21 July 1863-30 Sept 1887 ETDo
John R 30 Mar 1832-27 June 1895 MeaD
Joseph F h/o E T 17 July 1892-8 Apr 1972 Edge
Mamie Wescott w/o F A; d/o Jos J & Betsy E Wescott 22 Apr 1869-24 Sept 1944 Edge
Margaret w/o J R 8 Jan 1810-10 Dec 1892 Dowp
Maria Jane w/o Jno R 23 Apr 1835-9 July 1874; age: 39/2/16 Belb
Mary w/o Jno; d/o Jno & Mary Mears 19 June 1796-19 Oct 1840 ETDo
Mary C d/o Jno R & Maria J 24 Dec 1855-27 Nov 1856; age:

DOWNING (continued)
0/11/2 Belb
Mary S d/o Jno & Susan 11 Dec 1842-8 Sept 1843 ETDo
Omster d 5 Feb 1963; age: 50 yrs Gask
Polly Wharton w/o Jno Beach Downing; d/o T L & A N Trower; mother of Indie, Dorsey, Mildred, & Garland 21 Apr 1864-6 July 1938 Oakg
R Coe (prob s/o J W & E A) b 11 Feb 1863; d age: 0/0/5 ETDo
Sarah J (prob s/o J W & E A) b 6 Mar 1864; d age: 0/0/5 ETDo
Tom 1895-1950 JoyC
William S 15 May 1830-31 July 1904 StPa
DRAKE, Grace Mears 22 Apr 1892-19 June 1941 MtHo
DRUMMOND, Albert 1906-1967 Gask
Andrew G 1886-1974 Metr
Anna F w/o J C 25 Oct 1844-1 Oct 1918 Chan
Annie D (w/o J E) 1888-1946 Ptea
Annie J (w/o F R) 1856-1943 Onan
Annie Mae (w/o H J) 1893- Onan
Annie S (w/o O L) 1899-1977 Fair
Annie Virginia d/o Wm L & Nannie 30 Aug-3 Sept 1895 Holl
Arthur H s/o Robt & S A 20 Oct 1857-8 Mar 1888 Drum
Benjamin F 9 Mar 1856-25 Feb 1909; age: 52/11/14 Onan
Bessie K w/o J H 1885-1967 Onan
Bettie S w/o Jno H 22 May 1853-28 June 1910 Holl
Bowdoin M 26 Sept 1907-19 May 1942 (Coxswain USNR; lost at sea when the SS *Heredia* was torpedoed in the Gulf of Mexico) Oakg
Charles s/o Spencer & Mariam, colored 17 Oct 1861-20 Sept 1886 Druf
Charlie T nd Snea

DRUMMOND (continued)
Christine S 1880-1972 Metr
Cordie E nd Neda
D footstone only Druf
Damas d 27 Mar 1963 Gask
Dasie Lee d/o Louis D & Mary 20 Sept 1883-19 Sept 1885 BraH
Doris B d 2 Feb 1908; age: 1/7/5 Onan
Dorothy C (w/o M E) 1910- Ptea
Edith C 23 May 1873-16 Oct 1907 Onan
Edmund h/o Ellizabeth 3 July 1840-23 May 1907 Druf
Edna Earl 1889-1969 Onan
Edward K h/o M W 1875-1936 MtHo-s
Edward T 1884-1952 Gask-old
Elisha A w/o J R; d/o Thos & Elizabeth Fletcher 7 Nov 1814-21 Oct 1874 Park
Eliza d/o Robt & Margt 6 Aug 1801-6 May 1883 Park
Elizabeth w/o Edmd 6 Sept 1850-10 Aug 1899 Druf
Elizabeth F (w/o H B) 1903-1965 Onan
Elizabeth F w/o Linwood 1911- Gask
Elizabeth R (w/o F D) 1896-1972 Onan
Elizabeth S 23 Aug 1887-17 Oct 1929 Onan
Ella D d/o J E & S A Bradford 14 Apr 1869-15 Feb 1910 Brap
Ella N w/o T J 6 Feb 1875-8 Apr 1948 Onan
Elsie O (w/o H F) 1888-1955 Edge
Emma 1920-1976 Neda
F Simpson 1888-1942 Onan
Dr Fletcher 1847-1922 Park
Forrest M 27 Dec 1910-4 Oct 1935 Oakg
Francis R (h/o A J) 1851-1933 Onan
Frank D (h/o E R) 1887-1963 Onan
G Georgianna nd Gask-old
G Virginia (w/o P A) 9 May 1917- MtHo-s

DOWNING (continued)
George (h/o Susannah) 11 Aug 1722-20 Nov 1766 Drug
George B (h/o M W) 1876-1945 Onan
George H s/o J H & B K 1908-1910 Onan
George J s/o J H & B K 1919-1920 Onan
Georgie C 1894-1952 Onan
H Amos h/o M M 1900-1948 Edge
Hall K h/o S L 20 June 1884-4 Dec 1958 Onan
Harriet w/o Jas; d/o Custis & Eliz Kellam 10 Dec 1809-4 July 1848 Drub
Harriet T 1884-1939 Onan
Harry E 1870-1933 Onan
Henry B (h/o E F) 1901-1969 Onan
Henry C h/o S J 18 Aug 1831-14 Nov 1908 Onan
Henry J (h/o A M) 1883-1971 Onan
Herman F (w/o E O) 1889-1962 Edge
Horace U 1903-1982 Snea
Isaac d 27 Sept 1900; age: 59 yrs (stone missing; 1940 data) Druf
J Ellis (h/o A D) 1883-1956 Ptea
J H (h/o B S) 28 Nov 1831-2 July 1917 Holl
J Raymond s/o Frank & Annie (Bayley) 12 July 1897-15 Feb 1984; age: 86 yrs Onan
James 1910-1966 Gask
James h/o Harriet; s/o Richd & Catharine 13 Dec 1890 (obviously engraving error - should be 1790)-8 Mar 1875 Drub
James B h/o M B 1878-1942 Onan
James C h/o A F 28 Feb 1830-13 Mar 1904 Chan
James Lee 1940-1962 Snea
James R 11 Aug 1909-20 Jan 1962 MtHo-s
James S s/o Louis D & Mary A 15 Apr 1893-15 Jan 1916 Oakg

DRUMMOND (continued)
Janie Mears w/o V W 27 Nov 1884-9 Mr 1971 Oakg
John 28 Dec 1896-12 June 1966 StPa
John A d 10 Apr 1918; age: 51 yrs Druf
John E nd Neda
John H h/o B K 1878-1961 Onan
John R h/o E A; s/o Robt & Sarah A 20 Dec 1811-13 June 1882 Park
John R Lee h/o M E 1863-1948 Onan
John S 1865-1946 Libe
John T s/o Jas & Harriet 4 Aug 1836-15 June 1863; age: 26/10/11 mar: 21 July 1859 Drub
Joseph P h/o R A 1845-1934 Park
Joyce Mae 1951-1969 Gask
Katura B 1896-1967 Onan
Kinley 1 Jan 1899-8 Aug 1947 StLu
Leland W d 5 Apr 1901; age: 0/0/26 Onan
Leroy 1938-1979 Metr
Leven d July 1931 StLu
Linwood h/o E F 1909-1967; mar: 11 Mar 1929 Gask
Lois K 18 May 1909-6 Apr 1910 Onan
Lorenzo d 9 Apr 1965; age: 54 yrs Metr
Louis d 14 May 1966; age: 52 yrs Gask
Louis B h/o M L 1882-1956 Oakg
Louis D s/o Robt & Margt 10 Aug 1804-23 Apr 1879 Park
Louis D h/o M A 27 May 1842-10 May 1913 Oakg
Luther 10 Mar 1924-30 Apr 1954 HTri
Maggie A w/o O A 30 Aug 1866-5 Aug 1926 Onan
Manie W w/o E K 1876-1959 MtHo-s
Margaret Ann b&d 1911 Onan
Margaret Doughty 4 Nov 1880-2 Dec 1934 Onan
Margaret E (w/o S S) 1886-1964

DRUMMOND (continued)
MtHo-s
Margaret E 1930-1971 JoyC
Margaret Mears w/o H A 1899-1938 Edge
Margaret S 2 Oct 1841-5 Jan 1926 MtHo
Margaret W (w/o G B) 1872-1965 Onan
Mariam G w/o Spencer 1827-1915 Druf
Marvin s/o Frank & Annie b&d c1886/7 (ref: Raymond Drummond) Bayg
Mary A w/o L D 17 Aug 1847-1 June 1930 Oakg
Mary Emery w/o J R L 1868-1927 Onan
Mary F w/o J E 15 Jan 1862-23 Mar 1898 Druf
Mary Fletcher d/o J R & E A d 27 Dec 1851; age: 3 dys Park
Mary J w/o Jno E; d/o Jacob & Isabelle Garrison 4 Mar 1866-1 Jan 1889 Druf
Mary O 1859-1940 Libe
Mary R w/o Henry; d/o Carvey & Margt Dunton 20 Apr 1799-3 June 1859 Drub
Mary Stewart w/o Geo Billy 1867-1941 StGe
Maude B w/o J B 1880-1940 Onan
Melvin E (h/o D C) 1909-1965 Ptea
Minnie L w/o L B 1883-1970 Oakg
Minta 20 Jan 1801-2 Jan 1885 Druf
Morris 1902-1975 Onan
Nan w/o W L; d/o E D & Va Tyson Wescott 21 Mar 1860-25 Mar 1914 Holl
Nannie E 1894-1983 Onan
Nazarite 1912-1953 Gask-old
Oliver P s/o Robt & Sarah 15 Nov 1821-24 July 1887 Park
Olivia L 1876-1947 MtHo
Oswald A h/o M A 16 Aug 1860-13 Sept 1926 Onan
Otho L (h/o A S) 1893- Fair
Parker A (h/o G V) 29 May 1919-

DRUMMOND (continued)
25 Oct 1981 MtHo-s
Pauline K d/o J N & B K 1924-1945 Onan
Pearlina J w/o T J; d/o Exckiel & C L Killman 31 July 1855-9 Mar 1891 Kilb
Ray 1904-1909 Onan
Renee 1902-1963 Snea
Richard 1922-1973 Shil
Richard T h/o S T 11 Dec 1816-14 May 1890 Onan
Robert A March 1840-July 1887 DruD
Robert S 22 Sept 1832-11 Sept 1896 Drum
Rose A w/o J P 1855-1934 Park
Rose Ames (w/o W H) 1857-1928 MtHo-s
Sallie J w/o H C 25 July 1838-4 Jan 1934 Onan
Sallie P (w/o W L) 1898-1963 MtHo-s
Samuel D (h/o T M) 1877-1924 Onan
Sarah Ann w/o Robt 28 Feb 1782-3 July 1837 DoeC
Sarah Elizabeth d/o J R & E A 15 Apr 1845-12 Apr 1864 Park
Sarah M d 28 Feb 1898; age: 0/1/10 Onan
Sidney S (h/o M E) 1886-1957 MtHo-s
Spencer, colored 2 Mar 1834-9 Feb 1887 Druf
Spencer F 1865-1937 MtHo-s
Spencer J 3 May 1867-14 June 1937 MtHo
Stella Lee w/o H K 31 Aug 1881-19 Oct 1939 Onan
Steven Wayne 17 Aug-18 Aug 1968 MtHo-s
Susan A w/o Robt S 11 July 1835-26 May 1877 Drum
Susan T w/o R T 25 May 1826-21 June 1919 Onan
Susannah w/o Geo 24 Dec 1729-17 May 1762 Drug
Tabitha S w/o J V 4 June 1865-20 Oct 1927 Onan
Tankard J s/o Capt Jno T & Susan 16 Dec 1861-23 Jan

DRUMMOND (continued)
1865; age: 3/1/7 Drub
Theresa M (w/o S D) 1886-1967 Onan
Thomas J h/o E N 13 Apr 1854-13 Sept 1928 Onan
Tymiker S b&d 1982 Gask
Vernon 1934-1955 Gask-old
Vernon A s/o Ellis & Dulcie A 1913-1926 Ptea
Vietta M d/o C S 1900-1968 Metr
Vinal W h/o J M 5 Dec 1878-19 Nov 1936 Oakg
Virginia S 1884-1966 Onan
W J 26 Sept 1857-18 July 1889 Chan
William 1908-1977 Bays
William Henry (h/o R A) 1860-1933 MtHo-s
Willie 1924-1967 Gask
Willie L (h/o S P) 1896-1954 MtHo-s
DRYDEN, Annie D w/o C M 1896-1983 Libe
Archie N h/o W C 1907- Fair
C Merrill h/o A D 1894-1977 Libe
Kenneth M 1924-1942 Libe
Winnie C w/o A N 1911-1979 Fair
DUDLEY, Lois d/o L E & J E 1 Mar 1916-10 Oct 1918 Libe
DUER, Annie K (w/o R H) 1 Jan 1884-1 Sept 1963 MtHo-s
Dorothy C w/o Harry J 12 Jan 1909-29 Oct 1949 MtHo
R Herbert (h/o V S) 11 Apr 1908-10 Mar 1971 MtHo-s
Robert H (h/o A K) 22 Feb 1874-1 Dec 1937 MtHo-s
Virginia S (w/o R H) 16 Nov 1909- MtHo-s
DUFFIELD, Mary Virginia d/o Chas R & Sarah E 28 June-4 Dec 1854 Bowm
DUKE, Geneva Shreaves 1878-1960 Libe
DUKES, Charlie L h/o I J 1871-1961 Libe
Elizabeth Clampitt (w/o J H) 1905-1967 Fair
Harrison M h/o M M 1876-1929

DUKES (continued)
Edge
Ida James w/o C L 1871-1936 Libe
John E 1939- Fair
John H (h/o E C) 1904- Fair
John T d 8 Oct 1903; age: 53 yrs Edge
Manie M w/o H M 1879-1940 Edge
Mattie d/o J T & Malinda d 1 Nov 1903; age: 16 yrs Edge
Robert S s/o C L & I J 23 June-2 Nov 1904 Libe
Willie 1891-1914 Fair
DUNAWAY, A B DD h/o E S 5 Oct 1842-4 Oct 1924 Edge
Alice Byrd d/o J M & Alice B 23 July 1899-28 Apr 1906 Edge
Elizabeth S w/o A B 2 June 1858-29 Mar 1916 Edge
James Manning 25 Apr 1861-27 Apr 1922 Edge
Mitylene English w/o Rev Thos S 1870-1941 Edge
DUNCAN, Albert E Sr h/o L S 1902-1976 Libe
Alfred T (h/o M R) 1883-1970 Edge
Bettie w/o Jno W; d/o Geo A & Ann Kellam 10 Dec 1858-23 Mar 1889 MtPl
Beulah K 1897-1969 Shil
Elizabeth w/o Jno H; d/o Jno S & Jane Bundick 2 Feb 1816-7 Aug 1877 JnoS
Elizabeth Sarah d/o Jno H & Elizabeth 25 Dec 1850-4 Aug 1877 JnoS
John F 1894-1949 MtHo-s
J(ohn) H (probably) footstone only (beside stone of Elizabeth, his wife) JnoS
John William 26 Feb 1855-4 July 1911 Onan
John William Jr h/o S L 13 Oct 1885-8 Sept 1946 Onan
Laura Lilliston 4 Mar 1848-20 Mar 1937 Edge
Lucile S w/o A E 1902- Libe
M E h/o M F 3 Jan 1862-11 Feb 1928 MtHo-s

DUNCAN (continued)
Mattie Fitchett w/o M E 10 Oct 1865-27 Sept 1935 MtHo-s
Minnie R (w/o A T) nd Edge
Suzanne Lankford w/o J W 10 June 1890-22 Nov 1975 Onan
Thomas Alfred s/o Wm T & Mary (Lang) 27 Jan 1851-31 Dec 1885 Edge
William 1895-1969 HTri
DUNTON, Beckie inf d/o C M & E C 28 May-2 June 1860 Dunt
Berkley W 1917- Holl
Carrie Elizabeth d/o C M & E C 24 Feb 1855-1 Feb 1856 Dunt
Charles d 1 Nov 1964; age: 43 yrs Gask
Charles Michael h/o M V 11 Apr 1881-16 Oct 1940 MtHo
Curtis (Custis?) M s/o Wm & Mary 18 June 1816-30 Jan 1896; age: 79/7/12 Dunt
David A h/o H D; s/o Jacob B & Sallie 9 Dec 1880-8 May 1957 Wach
Dora Marcylene d/o C M & M V b&d 12 Aug 1917 MtHo
Edmond Downing 3 Oct 1909-29 May 1954 Edge
Elizabeth G w/o Custis M 17 June 1827-3 Nov 1869 Dunt
Emily Susan d 14 Dec 1906; age: 82 yrs Powe
Ernest Jr 1911- Holl
Helen D w/o D A; d/o Jas A & Carrie Doughty 28 July 1883-13 Nov 1976 Wach
James Thomas s/o C M & E C 17 Apr 1859-28 Sept 1863 Dunt
Juliet L d/o Geo & Elizabeth Smith d 17 Oct 1836 Coal
Kosciusko (h/o M G) 27 Apr 1840-21 Sept 1906 StGe
Littleton W s/o C M & E C 14 Aug 1853-9 July 1887 Dunt
Marcylene V w/o C M 24 May 1883-16 July 1975 MtHo
Mary G w/o Kosciusko 1860-1930 StGe
Mary S w/o Saml d 28 Apr 1884; age: 65 yrs Coal
Mercer E 1861-1939 Dunt

DUNTON (continued)
Stella P 13 Dec 1883-9 June 1906 StGe
DUTTON, Annie Lee w/o L P 2 Apr 1891-21 Mar 1918 MtHo
Annie Lee d/o L P & A L 20 Mar 1918-20 Feb 1919 MtHo
DYE, Benjamin F h/o M B 12 Feb 1894-26 Dec 1969 MtHo-s
Mary Bull w/o B F 21 July 1896-16 Apr 1981 MtHo-s
EARL, Ray Vernon nd MtHo
EASON, Wessie Nock w/o Rev Saml Washington Eason; mother of Dr Saml Eason; d/o John Edward & Sarah Elliott Nock 7 Nov 1866-11 Dec 1936 Oakg
EAST, s/o H S & Alice b&d 11 Nov 1895 MtHo
Alice Lee w/o H S 10 July 1874-10 Jan 1933 Libe
Alice P 1879-1972 MtHo
Annie M w/o E L 6 Jan 1830-9 Aug 1880 MtHo
Carson Lee s/o Baily B & Maggie L 31 Aug 1902-2 Mar 1920 MtHo
Charles Ray 1910-1978 Edge
Charlotte Anne (d/o S C & R P) 1928-1930 MtHo
Clara L 1896- Edge
Clarence F s/o Baily B & Maggie L 11 Feb 1910-25 Aug 1913 MtHo
Dial James h/o L P 1894-1973 Libe
Dial W s/o P T & S W 23 Sept 1852-3 June 1887 East
Duncan D 1878-1967 MtHo-s
Earl C 1906-1932 MtHo
Edward G (h/o M O) 1898-1981 Onan
Edward L h/o A M 25 Mar 1825-2 Oct 1897 MtHo
Edward L Jr h/o F O 1863-1897 MtHo
Effie J d/o Jas S & Ida V 11 Apr 1895-13 Mar 1906 East
Elizabeth d/o Jas & Rachel 14 Sept 1814-3 Jan 1894 East
Elizabeth L w/o Wm A 16 May

EAST (continued)
1843-23 July 1916 Edge
Elizabeth S 5 Feb 1870-17 Oct 1938 Libe
Elizabeth W w/o Wm S 4 Aug 1829-4 Dec 1893 MtHo
Ellen S (w/o F E) 1 Oct 1883-29 Mar 1969 Fair
Etta Hargis 1878-1961 Fair
Eula P (w/o V B) 1897-1974 Edge
Florence Olivia w/o E L Jr 1852-1934 MtHo
Fred E (h/o E S) 19 Jan 1884-22 July 1969 Fair
Harvey Lee 1879-1959 Fair
Hennie J w/o Dial W 17 Oct 1850-6 Sept 1893; age: 42/10/21 Mart
Herbert B Jr 27 Mar 1936-28 Mar 1964 Fair
G Cleve 1885-1940 MtHo
G Thomas h/o S Y 1863-1937 Edge
George W h/o H E 4 Dec 1840-5 Dec 1935 MtHo
George W 8 Aug 1870-27 Sept 1935 MtHo
H Sydney h/o A L 10 Oct 1872-5 Mar 1961 Libe
Harriet E w/o G W; d/o Jno R & Julia A Bull 20 Mar 1842-11 Jan 1908; age: 65/9/21 MtHo
Herman Lee 22 Aug 1890-5 Nov 1934 MtHo-s
Ida V w/o J S 1860-25 Nov 1913 East
J Howard 1893-1939 MtHo
James D s/o Jas T & Julia A 7 Apr-3 Aug 1865 East
James F w/o M L 1877-1940 Libe
James H (h/o M L) 1862-1936 MtHo
James P s/o P T & S W 17 May 1838-9 Aug 1866 East
James S 1868-1950 Onan
James T s/o Leah H 9 Dec 1828-11 July 1888 East
James T 1896-1976 Onan
John W 1862-1934 MtHo
Julia A 28 Mar 1841-1 Feb 1927

EAST (continued)
East
Lola Pearl w/o D J 23 Aug 1894-15 Feb 1920 Libe
Maggie L (w/o J H) 1869-1963 MtHo
Maggie L w/o J F 1882-1968 Libe
Manie Stevens 1868-1938 Mitc-e
Mary A 1873-1958 Edge
Mary J w/o P W 17 Feb 1849-5 Oct 1923 MtHo
Mary O (w/o E G) 1906- Onan
Otelia J (w/o S H) 11 Dec 1847-16 Oct 1933 MtHo
P B 25 Sept 1861-19 Sept 1928 MtHo
Pearlie P 1881-1955 MtHo-s
Peter T (h/o S W) 16 Feb 1816-28 Feb 1897 East
Peter W h/o M J 27 Aug 1848-14 Aug 1926 MtHo
Richard B s/o Richd & Eliz M C 18 Apr 1830-4 Mar 1880 Bulb
Ruby P (w/o S C) 1909- MtHo
Samuel C (h/o R P) 1909-1972 MtHo
Samuel H (h/o O J) 23 Apr 1856-1 Apr 1906 MtHo
Sarah Lewis 1913-1961 Edge
Severn James 1 Apr 1868-24 Mar 1950 Onan
Susan w/o Peter T d 26 July 1892; age: 32 yrs MtHo
Susan W w/o P T 15 Feb 1819-17 Sept 1887 East
Susannah Y w/o G T 1868-1936 Edge
Susie d/o P T & Susan J 7 Oct 1880-17 May 1890 MtHo
V Burnie (h/o E P) 1897-1954 Edge
Warner L 1906- Edge
William A h/o E L 8 Sept 1835-24 July 1891 Edge
William T 1866-1936 Edge
William T Jr 1892-1969 Edge
William T 1901-1952 Edge
Willie Anna 1866-1949 MtHo
EATON, Alpheus 13 Nov 1861-4 Aug 1926 Libe
Alpheus Jr 8 Dec 1902-4 Feb

EATON (continued)
1979 Park
Elizabeth M 9 Dec 1878-20 Nov 1940 Libe
Frances J 8 Aug 1909- Park
Lillian May 24 Sept 1901-10 Sept 1905 Libe
William A 9 May 1933- Park

EDMONDS, (EDMUNDS),
Alfred B G 1889-1962 Edge
Amelia M d/o J W & T A 1 May-17 June 1845 Edmg
Ann w/o Jas; d/o Jas & Susan Wharton 14 Mar 1777-24 Aug 1837 (57?) Edmg
Ann B w/o Thos 27 May 1803-17 July 1873 Edmo
Carrie w/o Herman 1899-1965 NewM
Cathrine S w/o E D 1897- MtHo
Edward D h/o C S 1892-1961 MtHo
Edward T s/o J W & T A 20 July 1847-11 Dec 1927 Edmg
Elizabeth C w/o Jno W; d/o G H & M R Bell d 11 Mar 1843; age: 19/5/23 GeoH
Ellen Tabitha d/o J W & M G 20 Feb 1894-9 Sept 1976 Edge
Emma D w/o J T 1872-1939 MtHo
Emory A d/o J W & T A 24 Sept 1850-1 Feb 1865 Edmg
Emory E d/o J W & T A 26 Nov 1848-2 Apr 1849 Edmg
Eunice Rogers w/o L S 1885-1933 MtHo
George A 17 Mar 1833-20 Feb 1907 Edmo
George R 22 Jan 1930-16 Aug 1980 NewM
Hermon h/o Carrie 1892-1979 NewM
J Fred MD h/o J D 1896-1981 Edge
James d 9 Sept 1844; age: 70/0/19 Edmg
James William s/o Thos & A B 18 Jan 1839-19 Aug 1899 Edmo
Janie H w/o LeRoy S 9 Sept 1844-18 Oct 1918 MtHo

EDMONDS (continued)
John T h/o E D 1869-1947 MtHo
John W s/o Jas & Ann 19 Mar 1852; age: 40/9/10 Edmg
John Willis (h/o M G) 26 Apr 1846-10 Nov 1914 Edge
John Willis Jr h/o K S 1 Feb 1892-17 Aug 1977 Edge
Joyce d/o Jas & Ann 21 Dec 1813-7 Sept 1822 (stone not located; 1940 data) Edmg
Katherine Spicer w/o J W Jr 30 June 1901-15 Feb 1982 Edge
Julia Dunaway w/o J F 1902-1963 Edge
LeRoy S s/o Thos & A B 6 Jan 1837-29 Feb 1892 Edmo
LeRoy Smith h/o E R 1880-1909 MtHo
May Emery 17 Feb 1899-12 Aug 1978 Edge
May Gunter (w/o J W) 23 Oct 1853-25 Aug 1938 Edge
Meade S 1964-1983 Edge
Perry d 10 Jan 1909; age: 73 yrs EdmB
Sarah A 24 Mar 1816-4 Sept 1856 Edmg
Tabitha A w/o J W 25 Jan 1819-17 Aug 1883 Edmg
Thomas (h/o A B) 23 Nov 1799-14 July 1856 Edmo
Thomas s/o Thom & A B 16 Jan 1836-25 Sept 1839 Edmo

EDMONDSON, Anna K 1906-1979 Shil

EDWARDS, Ailor 4 June 1885-1 Oct 1951 Gask-old
Ann S w/o Jno; d/o Jno Arlington 17 Feb 1793-22 Dec 1850 (unable to verify) Edwa
Annie B Poulson w/o I J 14 Mar 1835-29 Mar 1913 MtHo
Colie C (h/o M M) 23 Oct 1874-1959 Onan
Daisy C w/o J T 28 Mar 1875-21 Sept 1956 Onan
Dora M (w/o E N) 1877-1949 MtHo-s
Easer W h/o I S 24 Nov 1848-30 Nov 1930 Onan
Edna E (w/o W O) 1889-1958

EDWARDS (continued)
Fair
Elder N (h/o D M) 1876-1964 MtHo-s
Eloise M w/o K L 1912- Onan
Elsie A (w/o R E) 1911- Fair
Ester A w/o J H 20 Oct 1838-23 May 1901 Onan
Everette Preston s/o Jno W & Lena J 28 July 1899-20 Aug 1900 Onan
Everette W 1904-1954 Fair
Helen L w/o R L Sr 1907-1977 Gask
Henry T 7 Jan 1928-18 Dec 1974 MtHo
Hester nd Gask-old
I James h/o A B P 30 May 1834-13 July 1874 MtHo
India S w/o E W 15 Nov 1842-22 Aug 1919 Onan
Ira 1906-1976 Gask
Irene P (w/o W W) 1921- Fair
James T h/o D C 3 Nov 1872-31 Aug 1934 Onan
John h/o Ann S d 18 Feb 1832; age: 37 yrs Edwa
John H h/o E A 30 Aug 1839-11 Mar 1920 Onan
John T (h/o J S) 1850-1938 Ptea
John W h/o L J 8 Dec 1878-12 June 1911 Onan
Josephine Smith w/o J T 12 Mar 1854-12 May 1918 Ptea
Kenneth L h/o E M 1910-1960 Onan
Lena J w/o J W 12 Dec 1874-17 Feb 1901 Onan
Loxie M (h/o R G) 1894-1977 Fair
Maggie Marsh (w/o C C) 1882-1945 Onan
Manie E (w/o R C) 1877-1940 Holl
Martha W w/o Eazer W; d/o Jno & Eliza Poulson 17 July 1833-2 Feb 1888 RodP
Myrtle K (w/o R P) 1899- Fair
Norma 1922-1927 MtHo-s
Reginald C (h/o M E) 1880-1966 Holl
Robert E h/o S B 1874-1935

EDWARDS (continued)
Onan
Robert E (h/o E A) 1907-1974 Fair
Rev Robert L Sr 1902- Gask
Dr Rosser P (h/o M K) 1897-1975 Fair
Ruth G (w/o L M) 1898- Fair
Sallie B w/o R E 1886-1960 Onan
Starr b&d 1946 Onan
Sudie P d/o Jno & Esther 17 Sept 1867-27 Dec 1870 RodP
Tilutha 2 May 1902-10 Oct 1946 Gask-old
W Oscar (h/o E E) 1878-1957 Fair
William s/o Jno & Ann 4 Nov 1830-21 June 1849 (unable to verify) Edwa
William 19 Nov 1922-26 Oct 1968 MtNe
William R 2 Sept 1920-18 Nov 1949 Onan
Woodrow W (h/o I P) 16 Nov 1915-29 Mar 1967 Fair
EICHELBERGER, s/o Pierce & Jane b&d 23 May 1968 Quin
- Sr 1870-1929 HTri
Addie B 1875-1944 StGe
Benjamin T (h/o B M) 1852-1937 Quin
Bessie d/o B T & M E 17 Aug 1886-28 Mar 1887 Jame
Bettie M (w/o B T) 1858-1933 Quin
Charles D (h/o E W) 1881-1969 Quin
Charlotte J (w/o W J) 1843-1922 Walk
Dorothy T 28 Aug 1908- Edge
Emma N (w/o G W) 1877-1951 Quin
Emma W (w/o C D) 1877-1963 Quin
George Marvin 27 Jan 1906-20 Sept 1909 Quin
George W (h/o E N) 1879-1969 Quin
Harry L Jr 1913-1975 Fair
J Walter (h/o M J) 7 Nov 1879-17 Feb 1957 Edge

EICHELBERGER (continued)
Mabel J (w/o J W) 17 Oct 1883-19 May 1933 Edge
Maggie 1875-1956 HTri
Mary 16 May 1833-21 Oct 1920 HTri
Mary 10 Dec 1875-10 Aug 1959 Edge
Sarah A d/o Wm & Mary d 1845; age: 3/4/11 Arli
William F s/o Jas & Susan 30 Oct 1807-9 Aug 1875; age: 67/9/10 Warw
William J (h/o C J) 1840-1904 Walk
William J 24 Sept 1908- Edge
EISENSTEIN, Beatrice LeCato w/o Julius nd Quin
Julius h/o B L 1889-1933 Quin
ELBERT, Helen R 1921-1972 JoyC
ELLARD, Phillip d1979 Fair
ELLIOTT, Angelia w/o T G also: Willie Stewart & Thos G Jr nd Holl
Ann B Bull w/o Thos A d 5 July 1828; age: 41 yrs Oakg
Anzele wid/o Wm 16 Sept 1757-7 Sept 1841 Brad
Bianca F 1875-1938 Park
Elcy T w/o Wm; d/o T A & Elcy Bradford d 22 Feb 1822; age: 17 yrs Brad
Elizabeth G w/o Rev J W A 28 Nov 1816-13 Apr 1898 Oakg
Elizabeth Susan w/o G W 5 July 1846-7 Mar 1926 Edge
G Thomas 1886-1965 MtHo-s
Genovia m/o Lillie, Everett, Thos, David, & Harrison 1861-1951 Fair
George William h/o E S 9 Nov 1844-20 Jan 1945 Edge
Grace White w/o Wm S 1915-1982 Park
Irvin K s/o Rufus M & Lena 5 Nov 1905-1 Oct 1908 Park
James H 1882-1966 Burt
John W (h/o N S) 27 Feb 1871-15 May 1932 Holl
John W A (Rev) h/o E G 28 Dec 1813-13 July 1896 Oakg

ELLIOTT (continued)
John William 16 May 1866-5 Mar 1945 Edge
Joseph L b&d 1919 Park
Lena W 1880-1940 Park
Margaret G d 12 Sept 1975 Park
Margaret S w/o Jno W 4 Mar 1851-27 Mar 1899 Holl
Margaret Susan d/o Wm & Susan 21 Oct 1825-1 Sept 1837; age: 11/10/9 Elli
Nola S (w/o J W) 5 Sept 1874-14 Oct 1958 Holl
Ruth J 1910-1911 Park
Sarah M 1887-1974 Burt
Thomas A (Rev) h/o A B d 11 May 1815; age: 33 yrs Oakg
Thomas Garrison 12 Jan 1837-8 May 1910 Holl
Victoria (ggrd/o Richd Ames) nd Amep
W David 22 Oct 1890-25 Jan 1965 Fair
Wesley T (h/o Ina F) 1894-1964 Fair
Wesley T Jr s/o W T & V M 14 July 1917-25 Sept 1921 Holl
William (h/o Anzele) 20 Oct 1754-23 Sept 1836; age: 82 yrs Brad
William s/o Teackle & Margt 29 July 1795-2 Dec 1836; age: 41/4/3 Elli
William Scott h/o G W 1909-1983 Park
ELMORE, inf/o R H & I G 5 May-18 May 1910 MtHo-s
Anna Edmonds (w/o W S) 10 Sept 1904- Fair
George W h/o S B nd MtHo-s
George W h/o I S 15 Oct 1838-12 July 1908 Elmo
Indiana S w/o G W 9 May 1836-27 Aug 1914 Elmo
Ivey G (w/o R H) 1878-1961 MtHo-s
Jean Long 5 June 1927-27 Aug 1971 Fair
John Walker 11 June 1920-13 Sept 1970 Fair
Kermit Q 16 Aug 1907-14 May 1930 MtHo-s

ELMORE (continued)
Margaret P (w/o R O) 1909- MtHo-s
Marjorie Clare 29 Nov 1904-23 Dec 1905 Fair
Richard H (h/o I G) 1870-1947 MtHo-s
Richard O (h/o M P) 1906-1972 MtHo-s
Roberta H 10 Jan 1860-21 Aug 1934 Chap
Sadie B w/o G W nd MtHo-s
Vincent H 1 June 1848-6 Nov 1926 Chap
Walter Stockely (h/o A E) 11 Jan 1903-8 June 1977 Fair
EMINIZER, Roscoe 1887-1982 Wach
ENGLE, Missouri Bloxsom (w/o T W) 1873-1970 Edge
Talton Woodson (h/o M B) 1872-1942 Edge
ENGLEBRECHT, Edwin R 8 June 1916-30 May 1976 Fair
ENGLER, Harry Eugene h/o Jane 1920-1978 Fair
ENGLISH, Darrell 1951-1979 Park
ENNIS, Elizabeth E (w/o G W) 1886- Onan
Francis J 11 Nov 1850-7 May 1920 Libe
George F 14 July 1912-26 Aug 1982 Onan
George W (h/o E E) 1876-1937 Onan
Jesse F h/o L M 20 June 1881-15 Feb 1958 Libe
John T 29 Apr 1877-2 Dec 1952 Libe
Kenneth Wayne 1940-1962 Onan
Lottie Mae w/o J F 10 May 1882-4 Feb 1949 Libe
Margaret T 1 May 1854-22 Feb 1901 Libe
Maud S 1872-1950 Libe
Milford Elwood 26 Jan 1926-19 Nov 1973 Libe
ENSOR, Roberta B w/o Jno B 18 Nov 1865-1 Apr 1892 Morr
ENT, Leila H w/o Walter 1888-1967 MtHo

ENT (continued)
Walter h/o L H 1885-1955 MtHo
ERINSTEAD, baby/o C O & M W b&d 1926 Edge
Charles O h/o M W 1899- Edge
Mae W w/o C O 1902- Edge
ESDALL see **ISDALL**
EVANS, (EVANES),
inf/o C T & E L nd Onan
inf d/o 24 Nov-16 Dec 1901 Onan
Almer T 1864-1943 Onan
Alonzo F (h/o E T) 1868-1960 Onan
Alva M w/o A B 1922- Fair
Alvah B h/o A M 1908- Fair
Annie D (w/o C W) 25 Sept 1901- Fair
Annie E (w/o J T) 1882-1945 Onan
Annie F 1874-1961 Fair
Annie M w/o Elzy 10 Feb 1840-23 Oct 1910 Onan
Arthur C h/o I M 1893-1970 Edge
Arthur H s/o Jno & Va 31 Jan 1887-7 Jan 1919 Onan
B Roger h/o O J 2 Aug 1899-27 June 1974 Park
Barton Lee Sr (h/o J S) 1904-1969 MtHo
Berlin H (h/o W W) 11 Feb 1898-12 Jan 1977 MtHo
Bernard C 1901-1976 Onan
Bertha w/o L K 5 Oct 1879-10 Sept 1931 Edge
Bertha M 1902-1976 MtHo-s
Bessie D (w/o N W) 1905-1964 MtHo-s
Bettie P w/o S H 10 Feb 1882-6 May 1937 Park
Beulah M d/o W T & I M 19 Sept 1891-7 Nov 1915 MtHo
Blanche L 1900-1904 Onan
Calvin W (h/o A D) 17 June 1901-6 June 1968 Fair
Carroll M 10 Oct 1905-11 Sept 1978 MtHo-s
Carroll V (h/o E D) 1897-1963 Onan
Cassie W (w/o G S) 1893-1972 Onan
Catherine w/o W Z 2 May 1830-30 Mar 1909 Onan

EVANS (continued)
Celia M w/o W O 1899- Fair
Charles W 1884-1946 MtHo-s
Charlie T (h/o E E K) 1 Mar 1866-23 Jan 1941 Onan
Clara L w/o J E 1868-1960 Onan
Clarence R 20 Apr 1901-29 Jan 1973 MtHo-s
Coley L (h/o R P) 1901-1974 Fair
Daisey Young w/o H S 1885-1964 Edge
Della H w/o Wm T 1904- Park
Denard W (h/o M S) 10 Oct 1856-11 Sept 1942 MtHo-s
Drummond F 1 May 1906-6 Nov 1973 Edge
E Franklin 1879-1955 MtHo-s
Eddie G 19 May 1893-21 Jan 1918 MtHo
Edith B 1886-1975 Park
Edith T (w/o A F) 1870-1963 Onan
Edna S w/o W C 1859-9 June 1925 Onan
Edward Finney 25 Jan 1938-24 July 1940 MtHo-s
Edward L s/o J W & Va 7 Jan 1875-4 Oct 1876 Onan
Edwin R 1912-1982 Onan
Capt Egbert G 16 Nov 1859-18 May 1910 StGe
Eillis M (h/o R T) 1856-1936 MtHo-s
Elijah h/o Matilda 1 Sept 1820-3 Feb 1894 Onan
Elizabeth J w/o H L 1908- MtHo
Ella H (w/o R G) 1886-1939 MtHo
Eloise M w/o Wm H 1926-1965 Fair
Elzy h/o A M 3 Feb 1834-8 Oct 1909 Onan
Emma B (w/o T C) 20 May 1877-18 Oct 1961 MtHo
Estelle w/o Weaver 1916-1973 Libe
Ethel E Killmon (w/o C T) 19 Mar 1883-7 Apr 1955 Onan
Etta 1898-1910 Onan
Eula C (w/o R L Sr) 1907-1970 Onan

EVANS (continued)
Eva D (w/o C V) 1899-1975 Onan
Eva G w/o J T 1884-1961 Libe
Evelena Crockett 4 Aug 1874-19 Jan 1917 Croc
Fannie M w/o Wm T 1884-1947 MtHo
Frank J 26 Dec 1876-12 Aug 1900 Onan
George 1861-1936 HTri
George B s/o R H & R A 1869-1943 Evab
George D (h/o V F) 1863-1942 Onan
Gertrude M 1885-1968 Edge
Glenn Russell 1949- Libe
Grace Watson w/o R C Sr 1883-1966 MtHo
Granville S (h/o C W) 1894-1964 Onan
Grayson Lee s/o K K & L P 1922-1974 Onan
Harold L h/o E J 1895-1961 MtHo
Harry Sewell h/o D Y 1883-1970 Edge
Herbert N 1903-1946 MtHo
Ida M w/o W T 27 Jan 1865-24 Feb 1924 MtHo
Inez M w/o A C 1895-1964 Edge
Isaac 1834-3 Feb 1913 HTri
Ivy Crowson (w/o N T) 1880-1969 Edge
J A h/o K A 31 May 1867-28 Dec 1936 Onan
J Carroll h/o S E 1870-1938 Edge
Jennings 1911-1976 Onan
Jewel Savage (w/o B L Sr) 1903- MtHo
John A 1902-1962 Onan
John E h/o T A 1846-1885 Fair
John E h/o C L 1872-1927 Onan
John E s/o J E & T A 5 May 1873-7 Oct 1874 MtHo-s
John F s/o R H & R A 21 June 1864-3 Sept 1896 Evab
John F s/o J E & T A 9 Mar 1869-8 Aug 1870 MtHo-s
John F s/o T C & Emma K 12 June 1905-17 Oct 1906 Park
John H 1906-1944 Onan

EVANS (continued)
John T h/o E G 1870-1922 Libe
John T (h/o A E) 1877-1942 Onan
John T 1882-1956 MtHo
John W h/o K A 1848-1941 MtHo
Kate A w/o J A 8 Feb 1873- Onan
Kennie K 1878-1953 Onan
Kessey A w/o J W 16 Aug 1855-13 Aug 1921 MtHo
Kirby Hickman s/o L W & Bettie 18 Dec 1895-18 June 1916 MtHo
Lambert K h/o Bertha 30 May 1879-13 Sept 1936 Edge
Leah P 1891-1974 Onan
Lee Fosque 14 July 1922-29 Aug 1950 MtHo
Lester O h/o L W 1892-1972 Onan
Libe T 1876-1910 StGe
Lillian M 1874-1901 Onan
Lillian W w/o L O 1899-1931 Onan
Lloyd W (h/o M E) 1867-1950 MtHo
Lloyd W 17 Oct 1924-12 Feb 1971 MtHo
Lockwood Fosque s/o Jos F & Rose D (Chandler) 6 Jan 1900-16 Apr 1903 Chbg
Margaret Kelso 28 Oct 1849-19 May 1929 Onan
Marvin Keener 31 Mar 1889-18 May 1910 StGe
Marvin L s/o L K & Bertha 7 Feb 1915-4 Jan 1916 Edge
Mary A w/o T A 18 Jan 1832-10 Oct 1910 Onan
Mary C 28 Sept 1841-12 Dec 1933 MtHo-s
Mary E (w/o L W) 1870-1957 MtHo
Mary S (w/o D W) 2 July 1860-18 Feb 1940 MtHo-s
Mary Susan 14 July 1859-4 Feb 1932 StGe
Matilda ? (stone broken) w/o Elijah 22 May 1824-1 Feb 1894 Onan
Matilda F w/o S T 1877-1965

EVANS (continued)
Park
Maude d/o T C & Emma 22 Oct 1900-19 July 1904 Park
Minnie E d/o Elzy & A M 22 Oct 1863-21 Dec 1913 Onan
Minnie H 1893-1956 MtHo-s
Noah h/o Tabitha d 19 Feb 1917; age: 78 yrs MtHo
Noah T (h/o I C) 1877-1950 Edge
Noah Thomas h/o Cordie (Bell) 1860-1938 Onan
Norman W (h/o B D) 1895-1947 MtHo-s
Octavia E 1865-1952 Onan
Olaus Bowdoin (h/o P H) 8 Apr 1886-24 Apr 1951 StGe
Olive J w/o B R 20 Dec 1897-29 June 1960 Park
Oscar Rossa s/o Almer T & Elizabeth 3 Mar 1887-11 Mar 1888 Evan
Pearl Hutchinson (w/o O B) 1 Oct 1891-11 Mar 1960 StGe
Phoebe S d/o J W & Va 12 Dec 1880-5 July 1898 Onan
Rachel T (w/o E M) 1867-1952 MtHo-s
Raleigh Lee Sr (h/o E C) 23 Apr 1897-13 May 1976 Onan
Ralph V s/o Geo B & S H 1901-1919 Holl
Riley L h/o R I 1894-1965 MtHo
Robert C Sr h/o G W 1879-1970 MtHo
Robert G (h/o E H) 1875-1944 MtHo
Roberta d/o O B & P H 2 Sept 1915-5 Jan 1918 StGe
Rhoda A w/o R H 1 July 1837-27 Mar 1908 Evab
Richard H (h/o R A) 14 Sept 1830-19 Mar 1901 Evab
Richard L s/o R H & R A 4 Jan 1876-20 Sept 1896 Evab
Roxy Inez d/o L K & Bertha 1 May 1911-28 Jan 1914 Edge
Ruth I w/o R L 1905-1981 MtHo
Ruth Mears 1915- Quin
Ruth P (w/o C L) 1904- Fair
Sadie Ann (w/o W L) 1879-1949 MtHo

EVANS (continued)
Sadie H (w/o Geo B) 19 Oct 1874-28 May 1952 Holl
Sallie D Crockett w/o Vernon 1917-1942 Wach
Samuel H h/o B P 10 May 1884-10 July 1974 Park
Samuel H 1898-1969 Wach
Sarah E w/o J C 1872-1914 Edge
Severn J s/o Wm & Sallie 23 Mar 1849-17 Aug 1888 Evan
Severn T h/o M F 1872-1949 Park
Sue C 1884-1946 MtHo
Tabitha w/o Noah d 3 Apr 1918; age: 76 yrs MtHo
Thadeous C (h/o E B) 16 Oct 1875-3 Apr 1933 MtHo
Thomas A h/o M A 26 Apr 1829-25 June 1896; age: 67/1/29 Onan
Tryphena A w/o J E 1851-1924 MtHo-s
Vincent A 1912-1977 MtHo-s
Virginia E 28 Dec 1855- Onan
Virginia F (w/o G D) 1864-1948 Onan
W Z h/o Catherine 10 Mar 1812-19 June 1894 Onan
Wallace S 4 Dec 1870-28 Jan 1927 MtHo
Walter Hobson 25 June 1896-18 Dec 1967 Onan
Walter W 1889-1956 MtHo-s
Warren S 1 Aug 1895-5 Nov 1958 Edge
Weaver h/o Estelle 1916-1954 Libe
Willard O h/o C M 1897-1954 Fair
William 1814-1889 Evan
William D s/o Wm & Sallie 3 Nov 1868-6 Oct 1912 Evan
William Henry 15 Dec 1926-30 Aug 1969 Fair
William J 1911-1976 Onan
William L 1864-1920 MtHo-s
William L (h/o S A) 1877-1957 MtHo
William Rollins s/o T A & M A 22 May 1859-17 Feb 1921 Onan

EVANS (continued)
William T h/o I M 1867-1952 MtHo
William T h/o D H 1904-1974 Park
Willie s/o N T & Cordie 10 June 1891-10 Nov 1911 Onan
Willie H 28 July 1881-19 Aug 1912 Onan
Willie W (w/o B H) 1914- MtHo
EVENSON, Ernest W 1902-1958 b Biddulph, England Quin
EVERETT, Carrie Wills w/o W C 1882-1935 StGe
William C (h/o C W) 1879-1944 StGe
EWELL, sons/o J R & A G L b&d 27 Oct 1886 Libe
d/o H A & B D Aug-Oct 1922 Libe
inf b&d 1940 Park
Addie L 1880-1944 Park
Alfred S h/o I R 30 Sept 1848-9 May 1933 Park
Alfred T h/o C S 1869-1945 Libe
Amanda B w/o W W 1919- Park
Anna Lee Miles 5 Jan 1872-19 May 1958 Park
Annie May w/o E A 1889-1976 Park
Arinthia G L 1st w/o Jno R Sr 6 May 1862-7 Jan 1892 Libe
Augustus B 1866-1947 Park
Augustus D F h/o S S 24 July 1838-20 Feb 1901 Park
Austin E 1899-1940 Park
Beatrice E d/o C H & S G 17 Sept 1906-25 Jan 1907 HTri
Bessie D w/o H A 1894-1983 Libe
Bettie Rew w/o Wm L 3 Feb 1876-9 July 1939 Libe
Bernice E 1887-1957 Park
Beulah P w/o M T 1912- Park
Billy K 1920-1922 Libe
Carrie S w/o A T 1874-1922 Libe
Charles B h/o M I 1863-1940 Park
Charles H h/o S G 1876-1942 HTri
Charles N s/o C H & S G 25 Jan 1903-28 Oct 1905 HTri

EWELL (continued)
Cora L 4 May 1890-13 Sept 1981 Park
Edward A h/o A M 1883-1951 Park
Elizabeth w/o G P 18 Aug 1813-23 Dec 1887 Libe
Elizabeth C w/o G T; d/o Gilly & Catherine Young 9 May 1824-1 Nov 1852 Park
Fay Parker d/o M T & B P 1935-1943 Park
Flossie I w/o W S 1899-1980 Libe
George B h/o M P 1896-1969 Park
George P h/o Elizabeth d 15 Jan 1859; age: 50/11/7 Libe
George S 1865-1936 Libe
George T h/o E C 24 Sept 1819-1 Aug 1904 Park
George T s/o G P & Elizabeth d 15 Dec 1845; age: 10/10/27 Libe
Gorman W 1907-1948 Libe
H Fletcher h/o R D 1874-1945 Libe
Harry A h/o B D 1898-1969 Libe
Herbert V h/o M R 1903-1965 Park
Ida S w/o R E 1902-1971 Park
Indiana R w/o A S 23 Aug 1857-17 Dec 1905 Park
J Preston 1901-1944 Park
J Webster h/o M C 1891-1971 Libe
James D h/o S C 15 Sept 1859-5 Apr 1939 Libe
Joel T 17 Feb 1872-18 Oct 1939 Park
John O h/o M A 22 July 1836-24 Feb 1915 Park
John R Sr h/o A G L & S P 1856-1940 Libe
John R Jr 1909-1968 Libe
John T h/o S D 1878-1956 Park
John W s/o J R & A G L 28 Oct 1887-27 July 1888 Libe
Joseph b&d 1915 Libe
Laura C w/o S T 1842-1891 Libe
Lucy d/o J R & S P 20 Sept 1896-30 Oct 1897 Libe

EWELL (continued)
Mabel G d/o J R & S P 21 Nov 1902-14 Nov 1911 Libe
Mallie C w/o J W 1891-1961 Libe
Manie E 1885-1960 Libe
Margaret A w/o J O 24 Aug 1847-15 Jan 1928 Park
Marian I w/o C B 1873-1946 Park
Marie P w/o G B 1898-1967 Park
Mary R w/o H V 1903-1972 Park
May N 1875-1960 Park
Merrill T h/o B P 1908-1954 Park
Milton T s/o H F & R D 27 July 1905-22 Feb 1920 Libe
Mitchell 1904-1984 Park
O Miles 1907-1952 Fair
Oliver T (h/o V J) 11 Nov 1871-3 Aug 1927 MtHo-s
Oscar L 17 Sept 1868-6 May 1921 Park
Polly w/o Geo; d/o Mark & Amey Ewell 26 Apr 1794-28 Apr 1851 Libe
Preston B s/o J R & S P 13 Nov 1900-25 Nov 1920 Libe
Robert E 1856-1915 Park
Robie D w/o H F 1883-1959 Libe
Roy E h/o I S 1894-1973 Park
Ruth S 23 Apr 1917-1 Sept 1968 Park
Sallie P 2nd w/o J R Sr 1867-1958 Libe
Sallie P d/o J R & S P 18 July 1905-21 May 1906 Libe
Samuel 28 Apr 1838-28 Apr 1905 HTri
Sarah G w/o C H 1877-1962 HTri
Sarah Sue w/o A D F 27 Dec 1840-4 Oct 1915 Park
Sewell D 1914-1977 Libe
Solomon T h/o L C 1839-1901 Libe
Sulie C w/o J D 16 June 1865-10 May 1924 Libe
Susie D w/o J T 1880-1947 Park
Thomas d 16 Aug 1956; age: 70 yrs StLu
V Wilson 1913-1958 Edge
Virginia J (w/o O T) 20 Jan

EWELL (continued)
1885-29 May 1932 MtHo-s
Virginia T w/o Wm L 1866-1948 Park
W R missing in the Civil War Libe
Walden S h/o F I 1899-1978 Libe
Walter W h/o A B 1907-1969 Park
William L h/o V T 1864-1901 Park
William L h/o B R 5 May 1865-28 Mar 1941 Libe
William L 1886-1965 Park
Willie S 1897-1908 Park
FANTON, Eunice C w/o Wm H 1900-1975 Libe
Noah W h/o S F 30 Mar 1854-27 Mar 1925 Park
Sallie F w/o N W 27 Sept 1856-25 June 1934 Park
Willian H h/o E G 1897-1975 Libe
FARLOW, Edward A (h/o M E) 1880-1956 Quin
Mary E (w/o E A) 1888-1964 Quin
FARMER, Sarah B (w/o W H) 1869-1945 MtHo-s
William H (h/o S B) 1901-1969 MtHo-s
FARNELL, Milton W 1908- Park
FARNEN, C William h/o E M 1903-1977 Park
Edith M w/o C Wm 1907-1981 Park
FARWELL, Langdon F 15 Aug 1904-7 Mar 1974 MtHo-s
FEDDERMAN, see also FETTERMAN,
William H 12 Dec 1838-3 Feb 1866 Onan
FEGER, Charles W 1923-1975 Libe
FELTON, Harry 1906-1977 Shil
Virgie H 1896-1977 Shil
FENTRESS, Bennett d Oct 1895; age: 68 yrs Beac
George Albert h/o M K; s/o Geo L & Sadie (Bell) 21 Feb 1878-20 Dec 1927 Edge

FENTRESS (continued)
George L d 8 June 1879; age: 31 yrs Beac
Mamie Kimmerle w/o G A 21 Sept 1880-1 Dec 1975 Edge
FERGUSON, Barbara S (w/o W T) 1928- Wach
Bertha M (w/o W E) 1897-1969 Wach
Debbie d/o W T & B S b&d 23 June 1959 Wach
Frank A h/o S V 1861-1945 Wach
Preston W 1905-1941 Wach
Sudie V w/o F A 1869-1947 Wach
William E (h/o B M) 1895-1962 Wach
William T h/o B S 1926-1976 Wach
FETTERMAN, Bessie W w/o C S 1890-1979 ThoC
Charles S h/o B W 1885-1964 mar: 6 Dec 1913 ThoC
FICK, Charles L h/o M V 1870-1924 Edge
Margaret V w/o C L 1878-1960 Edge
FIGGS, Clarence A h/o K W 22 July 1889-7 June 1944 Park
Clyde P h/o D E 1901- Libe
Doris E w/o C P 1904-1966 Libe
Elijah A h/o M E 1839-1920 Park
Harold M h/o Frances F Figgs Rhodes 1878-1952 Park
Hettie T 1879-1963 Park
Kate W w/o C A 29 Nov 1896-9 July 1976 Park
Louise B w/o T G 22 July 1874-19 Dec 1943 Park
Mary Estelle w/o E A 1855-1940 Park
T Glenn h/o L B 6 Sept 1859-19 Aug 1937 Park
W Alwood 17 Jan 1914- Park
FINNEY, A W Jr s/o A W & M A 16 Feb 1860-17 Aug 1934 Finn
Alfred W h/o M A 23 Oct 1832-5 Apr 1901 Finn
Alice Snell w/o E O 6 Nov 1884-1 Feb 1953 Onan

FINNEY (continued)
Andrew Gordon s/o E O & M S 17 June 1829-13 June 1895 Onan
Ann w/o Henry F d 4 July 1822; age: 20/0/17 Fino
Annie w/o J S 14 Mar 1875-5 Dec 1907 Park
Annie N w/o H O 17 Aug 1859-29 Apr 1937 MtHo
Annie P w/o F G; d/o Jas A & Carrie V Doughty 1881-1962 Wach
Annie Wise 6 June 1881-31 Mar 1914 Onan
Bertie w/o A W 22 Aug 1863-9 Feb 1905 (moved from Finney, A W Plot near Pastoria) Edge
Bertie R 1885-1968 Gask
Bettie A 2 Mar 1845-13 Apr 1924 Onan
Charles Parkes h/o E S; s/o Thos W & Sarah 22 Nov 1837-3 Dec 1897 FinP
David s/o Col Jno & Margt 21 Mar 1818-16 Oct 1826 Meav
David Bowman s/o E O & M S 7 Mar 1840-3 May 1894 Onan
Darnichel L 1921-1982 Gask
E S 6 Jan-20 Sept 1861 Oldi
Edward B 20 Mar 1820-22 Mar 1911 Onan
Dr Edward Bowman h/o V B 9 Apr 1836-24 Nov 1913 MtHo
Edward Oswald h/o M S; s/o Col Jno & Margt 14 Oct 1802-12 Mar 1872 Onan
Elizabeth d/o Col Jno & Margt 4 Jan 1805-3 Oct 1847 Meav
Elizabeth H w/o L W 1890-1949 Park
Emily A (w/o J T) 1922- Wach
Emma S w/o C P; d/o Jos P & Susan E Boggs 3 Nov 1844-2 July 1869 FinP
Ernest Oswald h/o A S 31 Aug 1873-2 Jul 1959 Onan
Ernest Oswald s/o E O & A S 16 Sept-26 Sept 1916 Onan
Estella C 1904-1971 Gask
Frank G h/o A P; s/o Jno T & Bettie A 1888-1971 Wach
Garland E 1883-1967 MtHo

FINNEY (continued)
George Barnes h/o M L 22 Feb 1862-9 June 1938 Edge
George T 14 June 1876-17 Dec 1940 MtHo
Gertrude W (w/o R G) 1881-1940 MtHo
H Schley 1898-1961 Libe
Henry 1880-1957 MtNe
Henry O h/o A N 5 Apr 1856-25 Oct 1920 MtHo
Isadore R 1904-1950 Fair
James Alfred 1 Apr 1901-4 Nov 1972 Edge
Col John h/o Margt; s/o Jno & Ann 15 Jan 1778-23 Oct 1848 Meav
John A s/o Col Jno & Margt 25 Apr 1807-16 Oct 1825 Meav
John H 1899-1970 Gask
John H h/o S R 1899-1972 Gask
John S h/o Annie 30 Oct 1864-8 Oct 1924 Park
John Smith s/o Wm & Rosey 28 June 1820-28 Aug 1840; age: 20/2/0 Geor
John T 21 Sept 1831-25 Nov 1906 Onan
John T (h/o E A) 1917-1971 Wach
John Thomas (h/o S A); s/o T W & Sally 24 Dec 1826-4 Feb 1905 FinP
Kate 1892-1971 Libe
Lankford d 25 Nov 1938; age: 75/8/5 JoyC
Leah nd Gask
Leah Corban d/o Thos W & Sarah 29 Nov 1828-18 Dec 1858 FinP
Leonard W h/o E H 1887-1960 Park
Lewis C H s/o Col Jno & Margt 20 Jan 1822-21 May 1884 Meav
Mabel Van Pelt 1st w/o Rev J C Van Pelt 1875-1957 MtHo
Madeline B 1925-1969 Gask
Margaret w/o Col Jno 25 Feb 1782-29 June 1845 Meav
Margaret B d/o Col Jno & Margt 12 Jan 1809-1 Dec 1883 Meav

FINNEY (continued)
Margaret Mapp w/o Wm B 17 May 1831-23 Feb 1911 Onan
Margaret Susan w/o E O 2 Oct 1809-3 Mar 1870 Onan
Margaret Susan 1853-1936 MtHo
Mary A w/o A W 6 June 1833-17 Apr 1890 Finn
Mary H d/o Col Jno & Margt 24 Dec 1810-4 Dec 1881 Meav
Mary M (w/o T E) 1901-1945 Onan
Matilda 1875-1956 MtNe
Maude S d/o J S 6 Sept 1899-12 Oct 1904 Park
Mollie Lang w/o G B 4 Sept 1863-13 June 1950 Edge
Dr O B s/o Col Jno & Margt 2 July 1819-22 July 1900 Meav
Otha T 1901-1964 Shil
Pearl Boggs (w/o W S) 28 Oct 1868-23 Aug 1944 Onan
Randolph G (h/o G W) 1884-1968 MtHo
Robert Oliver 18 Sept 1929-2 Dec 1972 Fing
Rosey (Ann Arlington) 16 Mar 1791-9 July 1861 Arli
Rufus d 21 Feb 1954; age: 25 yrs StLu
Sallie w/o Walter R 19 Aug 1796-15 June 1837 Arli
Sallie 1904-1957 JoyC
Sarah w/o Thos W; d/o Thos & Elishea Fletcher 10 Sept 1797-10 Aug 1886 FinP
Spencer Drummond s/o Thos W & Sarah 18 Dec 1834-16 Dec 1863 FinP
Stella Mae 1936-1959 Gask
Susan A (w/o J T) 13 July 1842-11 Feb 1928 FinP
Susie R w/o J H 1900-1974 Gask
Swanee T 1891-1982 MtNe
T F large, smooth stone; initials only Fino
Taylor E (h/o M M) 1878-1955 Onan
Thomas W d 1875 (stone gone; ref: Jas Belote) Topp
Thomas Watts (h/o Sarah) 7 Sept 1784-4 Oct 1873 FinP

FINNEY (continued)
Upshur 1878-1961 Gask
Virginia Bowdoin w/o Dr E B 1846-1914 MtHo
W large, smooth stone; initials only Fino
William s/o Wm & Euphumey 10 Mar 1783-6 Apr 1853 (leav-ing 2 daus who erected this monument) Geor
William s/o Col Jno & Margt 4 Oct 1815-20 Dec 1858 Meav
William B s/o Col Jno & Margt 11 Oct 1816-10 Dec 1859 Meav
William B (Bogy) d 9 Sept 1886 (ref: E Spencer Wise) Geor
William D s/o G B & M S 1 Sept 1891-10 June 1905 Edge
William H 1910-1950 Park
William Henry s/o Thos W & Sally 25 Oct 1821-10 Nov 1871 FinP
William Spencer (h/o P B) 4 Feb 1864-1 Oct 1912 Onan
FISHER, Adam (w/o S L) 1922- Fair
Arinthia J w/o H K d 1983 Park
Edith w/o S F 1930- Libe
Dr Fenwick (h/o Rosannah) d 3 Feb 1816; age: 54 yrs Seym
Fred 1879-1957 Burt
G S (h/o T W) 7 Apr 1830-16 Mar 1884 Croc
Herman K h/o A J 1893-1960 Park
Lillie Gray 1875-1969 Park
Madelyn D 1925-1966 Fair
Martin h/o M R 1870-1921 Libe
Mary R w/o Martin 1876-1959 Libe
Rosannah w/o Dr Fenwick 2 Nov 1762-7 Dec 1821; age: 58/10/5 Seym
Samuel L (h/o A M) 1921- Fair
Sherwood F h/o Edith 1928-1981 Libe
Dr Sydney Henry s/o Dr Fenwick & Rosannah 19 Apr 1787-lost at sea in May 1818; age: 31 ys Seym
Tabitha W w/o G S 28 Dec 1832-9 Oct 1879 Croc

FISHER (continued)
Dr Thomas R s/o Dr Fenwick & Rosannah 19 Jan 1792-28 Mar 1820; age: 28/2/9 Seym
Virnetta N w/o Jas A 1876-1966 Onan
FITCHETT, s/o J G & Lillian b&d 30 Apr 1913 Fitz
Clarence 1921-1975 Gask
Dudley 1881-1962 NewM
Essie (w/o Saml) 1 Mar 1905-3 Oct 1973 Fair
Gloria Kellam w/o Wm 10 Apr 1930- Fair
J Clarence (h/o L F) 1888-1957 Edge
Lillian F (w/o J C) 1896-1978 Edge
Louis A (h/o M S) 1898-1978 Fair
Margaret S (w/o L A) 1903-1967 Fair
Samuel (h/o Essie) 2 June 1902-10 Dec 1965 Fair
Samuel P 12 May 1847-24 Dec 1908 MtHo
Samuel T 2 Jan 1871-30 Jan 1909 MtHo
Susan A d 1 July 1894; age: 54/3/13 Edge
Thomas 1889-1933 HTri
William h/o G K 17 Apr 1928-17 Dec 1982 Fair
FITZGERALD, s/o T H & A S b&d 24 Mar 1894 Fitz
d/o A H & Verra L b&d 5 Jan 1918 Edge
s/o H L & S H b&d 1945 Edge
Alburt s/o T H & A S 5 May 1893-31 Oct 1912 Fitz
Amanda S w/o T H 2 Sept 1881-28 Nov 1930 Fitz
Anna W 1858-1930 Libe
Arthur H 10 Feb 1886-22 Dec 1923 Edge
Catherine M (w/o F L) 25 Sept 1904-22 Sept 1978 Fair
Cornelia D 1861-1916 Libe
Edgar T 1884-1952 Libe
Elizabeth C (w/o J S) 1853-1931 MtHo
Florence 1883-1957 Fair

FITZGERALD (continued)
Forrest L (h/o C M) 10 Sept 1903- Fair
H Newton 1882-1950 Libe
Harvey L (h/o S H) 1890-1963 Edge
Henrietta P w/o T H 20 June 1854-16 Feb 1883 Fitz
Herbert L 1877-1928 MtHo
Hezekiah 1845-1910 Libe
James A s/o Jas S & Betty C 14 Oct 1873-6 June 1881 Fitz
James Albert h/o M A 12 Oct 1887-13 Sept 1917 MtHo
James S (h/o E C) 1850-1924 MtHo
James S s/o T H & A S 27 May 1888-7 May 1893 Fitz
Lloyd F 1897-1898 Libe
Lonie E 1883-1969 MtHo
Margaret A w/o Thos; d/o Stephen & Jane Hopkins 6 Apr 1822-5 June 1903 Onan
Mary Ann w/o J A 10 Dec 1888-18 Sept 1966 MtHo
Ruth L 1900-1981 Libe
Sarah 1831-1928 MtHo
Sarah E 1895-1978 Libe
Sarah H (w/o H L) 1917-1966 Edge
Thomas F s/o T H & H P 29 Dec 1878-2 Oct 1897 Fitz
Thomas H 2 Oct 1852-3 Nov 1943 Fitz
Thomas J 1857-1936 Libe
William Lee Jr b&d 1965 Fair
FITZHUGH, Henry Aylett s/o Dr T & M L d 19 June 1869; age: 0/6/20 Fitz
Maria L w/o Dr T d 7 Jan 1869 Fitz
FLANNAGAN, Cora Ann 1839-1968 StPa
FLEMING, Frank E s/o Wm & Mary Susan 6 Aug 1880-18 Apr 1903 ThoC
William F s/o W T & Mary E d 14 June 1897; age: 57 yrs ThoC
FLETCHER, Annie 9 May 1839-25 June 1906 NewM
Benjamin R L (h/o I E) 1888-

FLETCHER (continued)
1972 Quin
Bettey sister/o Geo ns dc1925 Flet
Bettie J w/o G A 1882-1962 Park
Betty sis/o Geo d 15 Oct 1931; age: 84 yrs Flet
Betty A Mears w/o Geo d 3 May 1933; age: 77 yrs Flet
Corbin D h/o K P 22 Aug 1833-28 Jan 1865 serving as a surgeon in Conf Army Poul
Daisie K (w/o W H) 1878-1956 Fair
Capt Dave bro/o Geo d 9 May 1933; age: 84 yrs Flet
David F 30 Mar 1888-7 Mar 1959 Park
Doris B 15 Jan 1905- Park
Doris Patricia d 18 Feb 1935; age: 0/4/0 Flet
Douglas D s/o Jno T & Sarah T 8 Feb 1847-6 May 1930 Onan
Edgar D (h/o S D) 1872-1934 Onan
Eliza C w/o T E 1849-1935 Onan
Elizabeth w/o Stephen 11 July 1773-23 Apr 1837; age: 64 yrs Mars
Elizabeth James d/o J H & J R 18 July 1894-4 Aug 1895 Edge
Furlton Merce (h/o H M) 12 Apr 1890-28 Mar 1963 Quin
George A h/o B A M d 20 June 1934; age: 79/9/0 Flet
George A h/o B J 1880-1933 Park
George A Jr s/o G A & B J 23 Dec 1907-4 May 1931 Park
George A Jr d 2 Aug 1933; age: 52 yrs Flet
Hattie M (w/o F M) 1892-1974 Quin
Ida Elizabeth (w/o B R L) 1895-1968 Quin
Jack J s/o G A & B J 7 May 1912-7 Jan 1957 Park
James Henry Jr h/o J R; s/o J H & Eliz (Broadwater) (judge of 31st Judicial Circuit of VA) 20 May 1858-12 Feb 1922 Edge
Jennie w/o J H Jr; d/o Robt &

FLETCHER (continued)
Hardenia Rodes 23 July 1860 (in Albemarle Co)-7 Jan 1947 Edge
John s/o Geo & B M ns Flet
Capt John bro/o Geo d 27 Nov 1935; age: 89/11/2 Flet
John s/o Geo & B M dc 1923; age: 21 yrs Flet
John L 1923-1981 Gask
Kate Poulson w/o C D 6 July 1834-7 July 1864 Poul
Lucy T w/o F L Sr 1881-1968 Park
Mary S w/o Wm F 1856-1937 Park
Northrop nd Fair
Pamula b&d 1958 MtHo-s
Parmelia J d/o Geo A & Althetia 8 May-8 June 1882 Morr
Sarah 1896-1955 Shil
Sarah Elizabeth d/o T E & E C 6 June 1884-18 Jan 1917 Onan
Susan C w/o Douglas D; d/o Jno W H & S A S Parker 6 July 1849-2 June 1898 Oatl
Susie D (w/o E D) 1877-1955 Onan
Thomas E h/o E C 1847-1931 Onan
Viola May 5 Jan-21 Dec 1927 Quin
Wade H (h/o D K) 1878-1960 Fair
William F h/o M S 1857-1952 Park
William N 14 Nov 1890-18 Jan 1957 Park
FLICK, C D h/o E L 1840-1920 Edge
Emma Lilliston w/o C D 1831-1914 Edge
FLOYD, A N 24 Sept 1830-16 Apr 1950 Quin
Bettie E 1833-1905 Floy
Catherine S w/o Fredrick 13 Apr 1831-10 July 1860 Elli
Chancey 1912-1983 Gask
Colie 1924-1980 Gask
Elijah (h/o Rachel Garrison) 5 Sept 1793-1 May 1837 Flob
Elijah W 21 Nov 1828-10 Feb

FLOYD (continued)
1836; age: 7/3/19 Flob
Elizabeth M w/o J G; d/o Thos & Esther W Sturgis 3 Nov 1834-18 Mar 1914 Onan
Ella d/o Fred & Catherine S 3 May 1854-17 July 1855 Elli
Ella Dennis w/o G F 3 Apr 1873-21 Dec 1940 Elli
Emma S d/o T F & M E 7 Apr 1844-12 Aug 1845; age: 1/4/5 BelF
Fernon B 15 July 1920-11 Feb 1948 Gask-old
Francis M 11 June 1861-24 Mar 1923 Burt
George E s/o T F & M E 31 July 1845-25 Nov 1872 Wach
George Fred MD (h/o E D) 8 Feb 1859-28 Aug 1935 Elli
George H 24 Nov 1818-25 Mar 1841; age: 22/4/4 Flob
George R 1906-1980 Gask
Isaac 15 May 1911-25 Aug 1969 Gask
James B 23 Feb-6 Nov 1817; age: 0/8/13 Oldl
James G h/o E M 31 Jan 1831-27 Mar 1911 Onan
Jennings O 8 July 1906-19 Apr 1929 StLu
John h/o M W d 1 Nov 1834; age: 39 yrs Quin
John Berry d 10 Jan 1895; age: 58 yrs Floy
John E 18 Jan 1826-26 Mar 1831; age: 5/2/8 Flob
John William 25 Dec 1855-1 Sept 1923 Burt
Josephine H w/o M E 1894-1972 Gask
Lizzie Glenn w/o Matthew 3 Feb 1789-15 Mar 1837 Morr
Louisa J w/o Jno R 12 Mar 1831-3 Jan 1864 Powl
Margaret E w/o T F d 19 Aug 1884; age: 63/7/10 Wach
Mary A 6 Oct 182?-3 Oct 182(6?); age: 2 yrs (stone broken) Flob
Mary A 3 Feb 1836-19 Sept 1837; age: 1/8/10 Flob

FLOYD (continued)
Matilda Walter w/o Jno; d/o Richd Walter d 28 Feb 1838; age: 35 yrs Quin
Matthew (h/o L G) - Rev soldier 7 Mar 1763-20 Aug 1844 Morr
Milton E h/o J H 1892-1971 Gask
O J h/o S E 1861-1949 StLu
Rachel 18 Dec 1839-17 May 1909 Shil
Rachel R (w/o E W) d 12 Dec 1866; age: 69 yrs Flob
Ralph A 1910-1954 StLu
Richard E 18 June 1833-18 June 1859 Flob
Samuel H 1880-1961 Burt
Sophia E w/o O J 1886- StLu
Susan S d 1 Dec 1881 Floy
Thomas B (h/o Sallie) d 1879; age: 81 yrs Floy
Thomas F h/o M E 1819-1903 Wach
Valicetine 1928-1981 Gask
Will 12 Aug 1886-24 Apr 1962 StPa
William E 8 Feb 1859-14 Nov 1935 Elli
FLUHART, Maggie S (w/o M W) 1890-1965 Quin
Moody W (h/o M S) 1883-1974 Quin
FOGLE, George S Sr (h/o M T) 1888-1941 MtHo-s
John H (h/o S B) 1841-1927 MtHo-s
Margaret T (w/o G S) 1898-1953 MtHo-s
Sarah B (w/o J H) 1847-1926 MtHo-s
FOOTE, Doris W w/o S C Jr 1919- Wach
Edwin J h/o E A 11 Oct 1844-27 Apr 1921 Oakg
Emily A w/o E J 5 Aug 1849-30 Dec 1917 Oakg
Merle S w/o S C 1885-1974 Wach
Samuel C h/o M S 1879-1967 Wach
Samuel C Jr 1917- Wach
FORBES, Franklin H 15 Apr

FORBES (continued)
1911-22 Oct 1966 MtHo-s
Lindsay 1903-1977 Fair
FOREMAN, George Sylvester 5 Oct 1931-12 Dec 1959 MtNe
FOSKEY, Sadie M (w/o W M) 1907-1969 MtHo-s
William M (h/o S M) 1904-1943 MtHo-s
F(OSQUE), W T footstone only Nocp
FOSQUE, A Sarah Powell w/o H S 26 Nov 1879-11 June 1961 Wach
Albert P (h/o A L) 1897- Wach
Alice Lee w/o G B; d/o Jno R & Elecia A Drummond 7 May 1849-16 Dec 1888 Onan
Ann R w/o J M Sr 14 Feb 1800-27 Oct 1873; age: 73/8/13 Onan
Annie L (w/o A P) 1899-1970 Wach
Bettie J 13 Oct 1833-29 Apr 1894 Oakg
Bettie M d/o N T & L L 13 Sept 1862-25 Oct 1867 Onan
Charley T s/o N T & L L 23 Nov 1860-14 Nov 1871 Onan
Clara H w/o W T 1881-1960 Wach
Daisy d/o G B & A L 1 June 1875-8 July 1876 Onan
E W badly weathered; unable to read MtOr
Emma Smith d/o Tom & Clara 23 Jan-24 Feb 1903 Coal
George Benjamin h/o A L 3 Mar 1843-2 Nov 1909 Onan
Dr George Lee s/o G B & A L 21 Jan 1876-29 Nov 1958 Onan
Hugh Smith h/o A S P; s/o W J & S M 3 Sept 1876-23 Oct 1911 Wach
Isabella A 1893-1975 JoyC
James C 18 Oct 1853-4 Mar 1932 Wach
James F s/o Jas & Emma 1865-1934 Mile
Jessie Frank d 7 July 1963; age: 59 yrs MtNe
John M h/o A R 1 Mar 1800-23

FOSQUE (continued)
Dec 1882 Onan
John M 2 July 1830-24 July 1885 Onan
John M (h/o J N) 1869-1942 Onan
John M Jr 1902-1980 Onan
Josie N (w/o J M) 1875-1945 Onan
Lena 1888-1969 Burt
Lillian S w/o R G 1911-1978 Wach
Lizzie L w/o N T 4 May 1834-6 Aug 1890 Onan
Mary A d/o N T & L L 10 Feb 1859-20 Nov 1863 Onan
Mary A 1866-1944 Onan
Nathaniel T h/o L L 17 May 1828-10 Feb 1901 Onan
Nathaniel T 13 Aug 1864-30 May 1902 Onan
Olevia d/o Jesse & Clara 7 Aug 1889-31 July 1906 Gask-old
Robert G h/o L S 1907-1976 Wach
Susan M (w/o W J) 25 Oct 1851-12 Dec 1943 Wach
William J (h/o S M) 22 Apr 1850-2 Feb 1918 Wach
William T h/o C H 1878-1962 Wach
FOSTER, David 5 Dec 1889-15 Aug 1972 Gask
Elizabeth S 1902-1967 Snea
Greta M 1968-1978 Snea
FOWLER, Thomas W s/o Upshur & Joyce 7 Sept 1820-15 Aug 1894 Fore-old
FOX, Alice 1916- Libe
Almer J (h/o Amanda) 1890-1945 Edge
Amanda (w/o A J) 1889-1971 Edge
Betty S w/o H W 16 Oct 1867-22 Mar 1954 FoxB
Edmond G h/o E J 14 June 1858-6 Apr 1921 MtHo
Elizabeth d/o Jas & Nellie 6 Feb 1845-12 May 1876; age: 31/3/6 MtHo
Elizabeth A w/o Zerobabel 1819-1909 MtHo

FOX (continued)
Elizabeth James w/o E G 22 Feb 1864-8 Aug 1932 MtHo
Elizabeth M (w/o F T) 1893-1980 Onan
Elizabeth S w/o G T 14 Aug 1822-2 Sept 1894 FoxB
Ella C d/o G G & S E d 21 Jan 1866; age: 5/5/21 Wacb
Emma E w/o Hezekiah 29 Aug 1898-6 Jan 1976 Onan
Emorys d/o Geo & Susan d 1855 (unable to verify) FoxP
Esther D 2 May 1816-26 June 1889 (unable to verify) FoxP
Etta Copes 20 Sept 1890-15 June 1976 MtHo
Fred T (h/o E M) 1888-1946 Onan
George 21 Aug 1825-16 July 1892 (unable to verify) FoxP
Capt Golden T h/o E S 11 Sept 1821-29 Aug 1877 FoxB
Hezekiah h/o E E 8 Mar 1893-13 Apr 1982 Onan
Hezekiah W h/o B S 4 Mar 1861-10 Feb 1925 FoxB
Indiana E d/o Golden T & Elizabeth S 18 Oct 1851-17 Oct 1867 FoxB
Ired W 8 Oct 1887-12 July 1943 MtHo
James s/o Wm & Polly 3 Mar 1811-29 Nov 1872 (unable to verify) FoxP
James D 9 Feb 1886-11 Apr 1930 MtHo
Lena P w/o W E 1892-1973 Edge
Levin J 24 Feb 1861-14 May 1939 MtHo
Mary J w/o Thos 9 Jan 1807-5 Mar 1876 (unable to verify) FoxP
Neer T 13 Sept 1884-19 Nov 1932 MtHo
Oscar Edward s/o H W & B S 15 Sept 1899-29 Mar 1900 FoxB
Polly w/o Wm 25 Oct 1785-4 June 1852 (unable to verify) FoxP
Sallie Ann w/o T A 1857-1913

FOX (continued)
MtHo
Susan E w/o Geo G 28 Oct 1828-19 Nov 1907 Wacb
Thomas s/o Wm & Polly 25 Sept 1813- 25 Jan 1882 (unable to verify) FoxP
Thomas A h/o S A 1856-1903 MtHo
W Franklin 1923-1936 Park
Warner L 1897-1936 Park
William s/o Golden 9 Nov 1780-27 Apr 1835 (unable to verify) FoxP
William C H s/o Z & E A 1847-1922 MtHo
Wilmer E h/o L P 1902-1953 Edge
Zerobabel h/o E A 1807-1864 MtHo
FRANKLIN, Margaret Upshur Quinby 29 Sept 1865-15 Mar 1953 Warw
FRAZIER, Marian 1900-1966 Metr
FREDERICK, Fred E (h/o N T) 1862-1954 Fair
Nora T (w/o F E) 1873-1961 Fair
FREEMAN, Clara J w/o R E 24 Aug 1853-24 Feb 1876 Free
Ernest 1890-1956 Snea
FRENCH, Cordie E Shea White w/o Wm H 6 June 1867-24 Apr 1924 Edge
FRIANT, Charles H (h/o E A) 1878-1952 Onan
Edna A (w/o C H) 1896- Onan
FRIEZE, Doris Pilchard 1909- Edge
FRITZ, Mary Rose d/o Wm C 21 June-22 June 1952 Fair
William CLay 27 Mar 1924-18 Feb 1973 Fair
FROHMAN, Charles T (h/o R C) 1923-1975 Fair
Rebecca Cooper (w/o C T) 1925- Fair
FROST, Maggie S w/o Jno E 4 Oct 1852-3 Dec 1889 Doup
FROSTROM, Mary Ellen w/o R J (DAR) 1926-1976 Park
Robert Julius h/o M E 31 Jan

FROSTROM (continued)
1924-30 May 1977 Park
FUNKHOUSER, Karen 1967-1969 Wach
Stephen 1963-1964 Wach
FURNISS, Blanch M w/o Vaughn S 28 June 1882-1920 Onan
GAIN, Dorothy W 1896-1956 Shil
G A L T, Doctor Samuel 20 Aug 1763-26 Apr 1796 Parp
Samuel s/o Saml & Anna Maria 7 Sept 1792-1 Oct 1797 Parp
G, E small footstone only Gsit
G, J small footstone only Gsit
GARDNER, infs/o A B & A S b&d 1924 Edge
Ada d/o B F & M A 30 Aug 1901-24 Feb 1902 Onan
Alfred B h/o A S 1882-1968 Edge
Alice S w/o A B 1891-1964 Edge
Alise M (w/o U D) 1910- Onan
Alvah B s/o B F & M A 18 Jan 1915-23 July 1917 Onan
Alvin L s/o J H & B C 20 Dec 1928-4 Jan 1930 Edge
B F 24 Mar 1874-12 May 1924 Onan
Belvin A 1907-1946 Onan
Benjamin F h/o M A 27 Apr 1877-28 July 1959 Onan
Benjamin W h/o V L 2 May 1880-20 Oct 1937 Libe
Bennie T 9 Mar 1897-22 Oct 1970 MtHo-s
Bertie F (w/o J W S) 1901-1975 Fair
Bettie C w/o J H 1898- Edge
Brother s/o G E & H T K d 1 May 1907 Onan
Catherine M 1839-1928 Edge
Charles D (h/o E S) 1876-1948 MtHo-s
Coley W Jr 23 Dec 1918-7 Jan 1981 Mitc-w
Pvt Coley Woodwer Sr (Co F 127th Inf) 6 Apr 1895-18 Oct 1918 killed at Argonne Forest, France Mitc-w
David Reed (h/o E T) 1909-1960 MtHo-s
Edward B 28 Aug 1912-24 Sept 1969 Onan

GARDNER (continued)
Eliza A w/o Jas T 29 Sept 1832-9 July 1899 Onan
Elizabeth S (w/o C D) 1875-1943 MtHo-s
Emma B w/o J E 1903- Park
Estelle T (w/o D R) 1908-1963 MtHo-s
Eva 3 Sept 1859-18 Dec 1942 Edge
Fosque L 10 Apr 1912-27 Jan 1971 Onan
George E h/o H T K 3 June 1863-30 Sept 1939 Onan
Harriet T K w/o G E 18 Mar 1874-31 July 1935 Onan
Helen E 4 Aug 1898-7 May 1962 Onan
Henry B 5 Sept 1900-4 Feb 1971 Onan
Henry E (h/o R B) 23 Aug 1860-25 Oct 1905 Edge
J Will (h/o M L) 1867-1950 Onan
James E h/o E B 1902-1983 Park
James S (h/o L P) 1876-1966 Onan
John h/o J A 11 Dec 1823-14 Feb 1895 Edge
John H h/o B C 1896-1956 Edge
John L 30 Nov 1844-23 Nov 1920 MtHo
John W 18 Sept 1913-17 Feb 1967 Edge
John W S (h/o B F) 1902-1976 Fair
Julia A w/o Jno 9 Mar 1840-10 Aug 1925 Edge
Lelia Bond (Dickey) 1911-1947 Libe
Lena P (w/o J S) 1880-1958 Onan
M A (w/o W F) 27 Jan 1857-27 June 1945 Onan
Maggie S 1877-1936 Onan
Manie A w/o B F 20 July 1878- Onan
Margaret S w/o V F 1907-1958 Edge
Mark T 18 May 1915-18 Apr 1960 Onan

GARDNER (continued)
Mary S w/o W C 1903-1976 MtHo
Merrell s/o G E & H T K d 1 Sept 1906 Onan
Milton R (h/o R M) 1903- Onan
Minnie L (w/o J W) 1877-1966 Onan
Rebecca B (w/o H E) 1866-1954 Edge
Rebecca D 30 Dec 1870-4 Nov 1936 MtHo
Rossie 1900-1919 Onan
Ruth M 9 Nov 1894-2 July 1976 MtHo-s
Ruth M (w/o M R) 1908- Onan
Sarah Pate 1898-1967 Park
Thomas 14 Dec 1850-17 July 1922 Edge
U Drummond (h/o A M) 1910-1955 Onan
Vernon F h/o M S 1908-1958 Edge
Virginia L w/o B W 1884-1957 Libe
W Clarke (h/o M S) 1902-1970 MtHo
William F (h/o M A) 14 Feb 1854-5 July 1929 Onan
William H d 18 July 1906; age: 61 yrs Edge

GARLICK, John Christopher h/o M J 1890-1961 Onan
Margaret James w/o J C 1891-1947 Onan

GARRETT, Eliza Frances w/o Geo W; d/o S S & E B Satchell 13 May 1848-27 Jan 1903 Edge
George R h/o M A 6 Dec 1905-11 Oct 1971 Onan
Martha A w/o G R 27 May 1905-15 Mar 1976 Onan

GARRISON, baby boy b&d 4 Sept 1966 Gask
Abel h/o Margt 4 Mar 1775-2 Nov 1836; age: 61/7/28 Onan
Adah w/o Isaiah nd Garr
Berry F 1840-1919 Holl
Bridget w/o Edmd 6 May 1798-29 Aug 1826 MtHo
Charlie 1921-1976 Gask
Clara E w/o G H; d/o Jno T &

GARRISON (continued)
Arithia Ewell Powell 20 July 1855-10 Jan 1936 Oakg
Clarence G 1927-1969 Gask
Edmund h/o Bridget 10 Mar 1786-14 Oct 1841 MtHo
Edward S 26 Aug 1826-17 Aug 1845 MtHo
Emma Sturgis 1917-1976 Snea
Frances S b 12 ___ ber 18?? - d ? (stone broken) Edge
Frank 1911-1980 Gask
George H 4 Oct 1800-31 July 1812; age: 11/9/27 Garl
George H h/o C E 29 Apr 1839-11 Sept 1889 Oakg
George (I?) s/o G H & C E d 11 July 1892; age: 14/4/23 Oakg
George T h/o L A 14 Jan 1835-13 Nov 1889 Edge
Haywood 10 June 1921-14 May 1962 StPa
Helen 1905-1978 NewM
Isaiah h/o Adah nd Garr
Jacob 26 Dec 1836-6 Oct 1890 Drup
James (h/o Sarah) 18 Apr 1773-1 Oct 1820; age: 47/5/24 GarL
James 1892-1952 StLu
James 1909-1971 Burt
James Richard h/o S P; youngest s/o Jas & Sally 27 Apr 1812-27 Oct 1865 Edge
Janie 1886-1968 Snea
John 1843-27 Nov 1922 StLu
John W 5 Jan 1859-7 Dec 1880 Edge
Lottie Ailworth w/o G T d 24 Feb 1914; age: 64 yrs Edge
Maggie S 1898-1977 StPa
Margaret w/o Abel 10Mar 1789-12 Oct 1841; age: 51/7/2 Onan
Maurice A 1877-1928 Edge
Orren M 1850-1918 Holl
Rheuben B 1886-1976 Snea
Robert 1892-1969 Snea
Rubin Jr nd Snea
Sarah w/o Jas d 13 Nov 1842; age: 66/3/23 GarL
Stanley 1917-1981 Gask-old
Susan Parker w/o J R; d/o Jno & Sallie Tankard 9 Dec 1815-30

GARRISON (continued)
Mar 1860; age: 45 yrs Edge
W A 31 July 1876-14 Oct 1915 Oakg
William L 1946-1962 JoyC
GARVEY, Harriet Cault 1891-1962 Fair
GASCOYNE, Rachel West w/o Henry 2 Apr 1736-18 Oct 1810 OldW
GASKILL, Elmer (h/o N E) 17 Dec 1903-14 Feb 1972 Wach
Naomi E (w/o Elmer) 1899- Wach
GASKINS, Addie B (w/o H J) 1912- MtHo-s
Cora H (w/o E S) 1916-1967 Wach
Elton 1899-1966 Shil
Elwood S (h/o C H) 1919- Wach
George 1864-1934 NewM
George Douglas 1867-1957 Gask
George F s/o Geo & Annie d 22 Aug 1919; age: 14/8/0 StPa
Gertrude J 1891-1981 Gask
Harriett 1888-1956 NewM
Harry J (h/o A B) 1904-1963 MtHo-s
Hilda H w/o J W 1891-1974 Wach
Ira R 1906- Shil
James H s/o E T & Mary 6 Aug 1865-26 July 1874 Gasp
John O s/o Rachel 8 Sept 1853-16 Apr 1872 Gasp
John W (h/o H H) 1896-1968 Wach
John W 1900-1960 HTri
Juanita L 1903- Gask
Leah Susan 1880-1957 MtNe
Leon 4 Feb 1908-19 July 1975 NewM
Mabel 1921-1968 MtNe
Maggie E 1873-1938 HTri
Samantha d 17 Nov 1976 Shil
Samuel B 1902-1978 Shil
Walter C 2 June 1927-3 Feb 1930 Wach
William s/o Rachel 5 Apr 1843-8 Mar 1901 Gask-old
GATLING, Alton H h/o M G 1908-1976 MtHo

GATLING (continued)
Margaret G w/o A H 1911- MtHo
GAUGER, D Manie w/o R A 1918- Libe
Richard A h/o D M 21 Feb 1917-18 Nov 1969 Libe
GEIGER, George Lambert 1845-1920 MtHo
Lillie Bowcock w/o S E Sr 20 Mar 1856-11 Nov 1948 MtHo
Mae Bowcock d/o S E & L B 6 May 1881-10 Feb 1902 MtHo
Sylvester E Sr h/o L B 29 Oct 1847-28 Oct 1906 MtHo
Sylvestor E Jr 1892-1927 MtHo
William Franklin 1879-1935 MtHo
GENERO, Edwin L h/o M W 1912- Park
Mary W w/o E L 1912-1984 Park
GEORG, baby boy b&d 1958 Snea
GEORGE, Ella D 1877-1967 Libe
Helen N d/o Laura C Nock nd Gask
Severn 1911-1979 Gask
GERAMTEZ, Joseph b&d 1962 MtHo
GERICKE, Sharon Parks 1948-1977 MtHo
GERRY, Dora 1885-1944 Onan
GIBB, Catherine Frances d/o Jos W & E W of Acc Co VA 27 Apr 1827-30 July 1890 Bowm
Eliza Washington w/o Jos W; d/o Gen Jno & Catherine Cropper 10 July 1801-6 Nov 1871 Bowm
Henrietta W w/o Thos B C; only child/o Dr Jas O & Sabra C Williams 27 Aug 1839-23 Sept 1902 Bowm
John S s/o Wm & Frances 7 Mar 1804-21 Apr 1885 East
Joseph Washington h/o E W; s/o Wm & Frances 18 Nov 1806-7 Mar 1866 Bowm
Katie W d/o T B C & H W 11 Apr 1861-10 Mar 1879 Bowm
Maria Melson Evans 8 Feb 1910-22 Dec 1981 Edge
Thomas Bayly Cropper (h/o H W) 16 Apr 1838-11 May 1895

GIBB (continued)
Bowm
William Joseph s/o Jos & E W 6 Jan 1833-24 Feb 1912 Bowm
GIBBONS, A Elizabeth d/o Howard & Alma 1920-1946 MtHo-s
Alfred J h/o B W 1857-1930 Park
Alfred James Jr h/o S J 30 Aug 1920- Park
Allen (h/o Ellen) 1907-1964 Fair
Alma w/o Howard 1887-1969 MtHo-s
Alma M w/o B G 1898-1979 MtHo-s
Barry Jr b&d 1976 Fair
Benjamin B h/o C S 1845-1927 MtHo-s
Benjamin G h/o A M 1891-1973 MtHo-s
Bertie S w/o C H 1872-1949 Fair
Betty W w/o A J 1858-1905 Park
Charles A h/o M M 1875-1951 Park
Charles H h/o B S 1868-1963 Fair
Clara S w/o B B 1846-1928 MtHo-s
Ella Fox w/o Wm T 29 Sept 1875-7 Jan 1964 Park
Ellen (w/o Allen) 1913- Fair
Elmer L h/o S H 1892-1968 Fair
Eunice d/o J T & J E 14 Sept 1909-23 Mar 1929 MtHo-s
Grace M w/o J T 1888- Park
Howard h/o Alma 1887- MtHo-s
Ida Virginia d/o C A & M M 12 Apr-21 Sept 1901 Park
James T h/o G M 1886-1971 Park
Jennie B w/o J R 1877-1943 Libe
Jennie E w/o J T 1879-1953 MtHo-s
John Braden 1900-1970 MtHo-s
John R h/o J B 1870-1957 Libe
John R Jr s/o J R & J B 16 July-13 Nov 1915 Libe
John T h/o J E 1876-1948 MtHo-s
Leroy 1893-1968 Libe

GIBBONS (continued)
Manie M w/o C A 1880-1965 Park
Sadie 1891-1981 Libe
Sarah H w/o E L 1890-1967 Fair
Sarah Johnson w/o A J Jr 24 Oct 1905-20 Dec 1977 Park
William F 1876-1957 MtHo-s
William T h/o E F 31 Mar 1878-29 Feb 1952 Park
GIBIAN, Alice A (w/o C W) 1894-1963 Fair
Charles W (h/o A A) 1890-1961 Fair
GIBSON, Charles H 1867-1947 MtHo-s
Maude Borum 13 Oct 1892-28 June 1923 MtHo-s
GIDDENS, (GIDDINGS, GIDDINS), baby b&d 1960 Snea
Alice E 1924-1972 NewM
Clarence 20 Dec 1897-18 Mar 1965 NewM
Emma 1902-1963 NewM
Forrest 1914-1980 NewM
John M s/o Jno & Maggie 31 Jan-23 Sept 1893 Shil
Mary Ann 3 Sept 1912-9 Oct 1971 NewM
Otho 7 Feb 1889-11 Sept 1972 NewM
Otho T 10 May 1897-11 Nov 1976 NewM
Otho W 19 Feb 1921-15 Oct 1967 NewM
Norman W Jr 20 Dec 1931-5 June 1979 NewM
Percy 1891-1963 NewM
Percy N 4 Sept 1923-15 Feb 1977 NewM
GILDEN, Charles E s/o W E & I M 1892-1961 Onan
Evalena d/o W E & I M 20 July 1888-29 Mar 1889 Onan
Indiana M w/o W E 1863-1937 Onan
John B s/o Wm E & Mary E 3 May 1859-16 June 1865 Holl
Lloyd Melvin 19 Dec 1883-28 Mar 1940 Onan
Obed J h/o S E 28 June 1862-28 July 1946 StGe

GILDEN (continued)
Susan E (w/o O J) 19 Feb 1873-27 Apr 1892 StGe
William E 3 Dec 1831-22 Feb 1872 Holl
William E h/o I M 1857-1892 Onan
Willie Carroll 4 June 1886-5 June 1909 Onan
GILKEY, Louise W 23 Dec 1879-23 Feb 1977 Park
GILL, Lewis B h/o M L 1879-1934 Edge
Mary L w/o L B 1875-1958 Edge
Ruth E 1911-1981 Edge
GILLESPIE, Birdie E 1887-1971 Park
Clara L w/o Wm F 1877-1956 Park
Creston M Sr h/o Clara M 1900-1979 Park
George T 13 May 1828-23 Aug 1906 Park
George White h/o L W 1876-1953 Park
George William 2 Apr 1908-20 Mar 1971 Fair
Harry W Sr 1879-1952 Park
John Sr 15 June 1800-26 Apr 1873 Park
John F h/o S W 27 Dec 1859-22 Apr 1949 Park
John W h/o S A 10 Sept 1830-15 Nov 1898 Park
Lela Warren w/o G W 1881-1962 Park
Minnie A w/o T L 1879-1958 Park
S Wallop West (mother) 1855-1924 Park
Sallie A w/o J W 24 Aug 1837-10 Sept 1912 Park
Sallie W w/o J F 4 June 1834-19 Mar 1913 Park
Theodosia E d/o J W & S A d 9 July 1871; age: 15/0/22 Park
Thomas L h/o M A 1876-1951 Park
William F h/o C L 1864-1935 Park
GILLETT, see also **GUILETTE**
Henrietta w/o Wm; d/o Zadock

GILLETT (continued)
& Elizabeth Selby 23 Dec 1796-6 Nov 1868 Gill
Henreetta Douglas d/o Wm & Henreetta 14 May 1818-11 Nov 1822 Gill
Henrietta Selby d/o Wm & Henreitta 30 May 1829-18 Oct 1856 Gill
John W s/o Wm & Henrietta 26 Oct 1823-14 Aug 1896 Gill
M E child/o Wm & Henrietta foot stone only Gill
Mary Selby d/o Wm & Henrietta 11 Oct 1814-10 Oct 1836 Gill
William h/o Henrietta 17 Apr 1777-30 Aug 1837 Gill
GIVANS, C Wesley h/o G P 1916- Park
Gerald Wesley s/o Chas W Jr & Geraldine (Parks) 1942-43 Park
Geraldine P w/o C W 1918- Park
GLADDEN, see also **GLADDING**
Arthur R (h/o C B) 1882-1951 Fair
Cordelia B (h/o A R) 1880-1955 Fair
John W (h/o J P) 1916-1979 Wach
Julia P (w/o J W) 1917- Wach
GLADDING, inf dau/o H F & E F b&d 20 Dec 1929 MtHo-s
Althea S 16 Oct 1876-31 Aug 1920 Libe
Amanda E w/o J W 1843-1924 MtHo
Arthur L h/o S J 1886-1954 Park
Clarence McClellan h/o M K 1885-1964 Park
Elizabeth Fontaine (w/o H F) 1908- MtHo-s
Florence N w/o O T 1857-1935 Park
Florence Y w/o J A 1877-1970 MtHo
Glouster P h/o Chrystle P 1898-1979 Park
Harold Franklin Sr (h/o E F) 1907-1963 MtHo-s
John W h/o A E 1834-1902 MtHo
Julius A h/o F Y 1857-1937

GLADDING (continued) MtHo
Julius A 12 Sept 1905-11 Sept 1980 Park
Lawson J h/o M R 16 June 1879-29 Mar 1954 Park
Lee Core 1886-1927 MtHo-s
Mamie R w/o L J 4 May 1889-21 May 1967 Park
Margie T w/o W J 1902- Park
Mary Knight w/o C McC 1899-1977 Park
Mary M w/o Edwd 10 Oct 1835-13 Feb 1919 Libe
Capt Octavius T h/o F N 1862-1942 Park
Oswald T 1866-1952 MtHo-s
Patrick Thomas 1940-1966 MtHo-s
Phyllis M d/o W J & M T 1923-1924 Park
Sallie J w/o A L 1891-1972 Park
W James h/o M T 1895-1965 Park
GLADSTONE, Annie C w/o E T 5 Mar 1895- Park
Charles F (Dr) 27 May 1880-19 Mar 1968 Onan
Elton T h/o A C 19 Mar 1890-28 Mar 1971 Park
John T s/o T O & Nancy 23 Sept 1890-28 June 1898 StJo
GLENN, Edward O d 3 Apr 1940 Burt
Eliza d 13 Nov 1938 Negr
Irene 1902-1958 NewM
Jack P nd Gask-old
James (1st h/o Keturah Garrison Glenn Bell) 14 Oct 1781-11 Nov 1847; age: 66/0/27 Garr
Mary 1892-1969 Burt
GLOVER, Jimmie Lee 1930-1968 NewM
GODSEY, Ethel J 1903-1949 Edge
GODWIN, baby girl nd Park
Bruce M 24 Nov 1878-13 Feb 1951 Park
Clarence H h/o E B 1888-1952 Park
David King 29 Dec 1934-26 Jan 1984 Park
Demeriah P w/o S A 11 Dec

GODWIN (continued) 1856-24 July 1926 Park
Elsie H 1901- Park
Emma B w/o C H 1886-1964 Park
Franklin B h/o V R 1 Sept 1909-17 Sept 1978 Park
Gregory Scott 17 June 1953-16 July 1973 Park
John W s/o M F & M E 31 Aug 1890-30 Nov 1891 Park
Kenneth J 1956-1957 JoyC
Louise O 20 Oct 1899-25 Aug 1971 Park
M Fitchett h/o M E 29 Aug 1853-21 Feb 1923 Park
Mary E w/o M F 18 Feb 1855-19 Jan 1913 Park
Preston P h/o T D 1914-1983 Park
Rebecca E 1 Sept 1888-28 Dec 1920 Park
Sallie H 1901-1930 Park
Samuel A h/o D P 28 Jan 1848-2 Sept 1929 Park
Samuel A Jr 1896-1935 Park
Susan Jane w/o Wm P 1876-1948 Park
Thelma D w/o P P 1919- Park
Velma R w/o F B 10 Jan 1914-21 July 1982 Park
Vilies B 1895-1981 Quin
William King 10 Apr 1900-28 Aug 1971 Park
William P h/o S J 1876-1949 Park
Wrendo M 1896-1976 Park
GOFFIGON, Annie W w/o Wm P 9 Oct 1883-2 Nov 1925 Wach
Billie (Capt) 1852-1924 TheG
Catherine C T w/o E J 1887-1931 Poul
Edwin J h/o C C T 1873-1935 Poul
Elizabeth V Harrison d 30 Aug 1904; age: 85 yrs Garr
J Almer 10 Mar 1858-31 Oct 1894 Wach
Lucretia A d/o Oba & Polly 4 Oct 1833-14 July 1891 Holf
Susan Ann w/o Wm 28 Aug 1820-23 Feb 1840 (moved from

GOFFIGON (continued)
Parker Pl, Yoe's Neck) Onan
Susan Ann d/o Wm & S A 14 Dec 1839-25 June 1840 (moved from Parker Pl, Yoe's Neck) Onan
W B 22 Nov 1831-26 Mar 1906 Coal
GOIN, Edmond h/o M B 1891-1950 Park
Mary B w/o Edmd 1894-1961 Park
GOLDEN, Matthew J Jr gr s/o Matthew & Kathryn Golden 1916- Edge
Otis 1915-1974 Snea
Ruth gr d/o Raymond S & Sarah B Stant 1920-1975 Edge
GONZOLEZ, A b&d 1980 MtHo
GOONER, Ruth D m/o Dorothy M 1907-1928 Edge
GORDY, Hazel V 1895-1984 Park
Levin C h/o M E 1864-1930 Park
Mary E w/o L C 1868-1935 Park
Winnie H 1898-1971 Park
GOULD, Alma R (w/o J M) 1904-1976 Quin
John M (h/o A R) 1901-1972 Quin
GOURLEY, Ethel T (w/o J A) 1919- Fair
James A (h/o E T) 1913-1977 Fair
GRANT, A C footstone only Edge
Drummond Selby s/o J D & M S 6 May 1905-5 Dec 1906 Edge
Rev Edward S S h/o T J 15 Apr 1823-1 June 1869 Edge
Edward W s/o E S & T S 15 May 1852-19 June 1869 Edge
Elizabeth S d/o J D & M S 22 Feb 1907-23 Mar 1973 Edge
John Drummond h/o S E; s/o Edwd & Tabitha 8 Jan 1847-31 Dec 1909 Edge
John Drummond Jr h/o M S; s/o Jno Drummond & Susan Eliz 6 June 1879-31 Oct 1941 Edge
MaBel Selby w/o J D Jr; d/o Jno Outten & Emma Marshall Selby 5 Mar 1880-23 July 1971 Edge

GRANT (continued)
Mary E d/o E S & T S 8 Sept 1848-31 Mar 1930 Edge
Oswall s/o E S & T S 19 Dec 1854-25 Oct 1881 Edge
Selby s/o J D & M S b&d 19 Aug 1919 Edge
Susan Elizabeth w/o J D 23 Dec 1847-16 May 1923 Edge
Susan Thomas d/o J D & S E 4 May 1882-13 Mar 1941 Edge
Tabitha J w/o E S S 22 June 1822-12 Dec 1872 Edge
Tabitha Nancy 1878-1956 Edge
GRAVENOR, Carrie L 12 Nov 1892-12 Nov 1922 Park
G H h/o P L 1866-1933 HicG
Harry J 28 May 1892-4 Sept 1967 Park
Minnie L d/o G H & P L 28 July 1905-28 Jan 1907 HicG
Polly L w/o G H 1866- HicG
GRAW, Helen (w/o Herbert) 1907-1962 Fair
Herbert (h/o Helen) 1896-1956 Fair
GRAY, (GREY),
Alethea R Murray, 1st w/o H R (m/o Alice & Tom) 4 Apr 1815-13 Apr 1850 (bur in Bastrap LA) Libe
Annie B w/o E B 1884-1963 Park
Bertha Parks (w/o J H) 1896-1971 MtHo-s
Betsy w/o J E d 31 Aug 1894; age: 48 yrs Park
Carl L 1929-1966 Park
Charles S 1872-1965 MtHo
Dimariah Scott, 2nd w/o H R 6 Apr 1818-8 Feb 1903 Libe
Earl J 1894- MtHo-s
Edward B h/o A B 1877-1963 Park
Edward T 1890-1947 MtHo-s
Elizabeth w/o J E 9 Mar 1830-28 Nov 1917 Onan
Ethel L 1877-1906 MtHo
George W 8 Mar 1844-9 Oct 1912 Onan
Harry C h/o S M 1889-1946 MtHo-s
Helen P 1901-1967 Onan

GRAY (continued)
Henry R h/o A R M & D S 12 Oct 1815-26 Sept 1884 (d in Washington DC) Libe
(Henry R plot) footstones only: G A G; J M G; E G G Libe
Hilton M 1903-1980 MtHo
James E h/o Elizabeth 29 May 1827-29 Jan 1900 Onan
James E h/o Betsy d 20 Apr 1887; age: 48 yrs Park
James E s/o T R & S S 2 Oct 1864-14 Nov 1865 MtHo
James T h/o L W 1859-1944 Onan
John Harrison (h/o B P) 1891-1969 MtHo-s
John L s/o J T & L W 1894-1905 Onan
Julia W 1888-1927 MtHo
Katherine M d/o J T & L W 1889-1905 Onan
Laura W w/o J T 1857-1924 Onan
Loletia Kellam 1907-1974 Onan
Mary R w/o T J 1870-1953 MtHo-s
Phon 3 Jan 1900-8 Jan 1908 Fair
Roland Holland 18 Apr 1892-26 Oct 1969 Park
Sallie S w/o T R 14 Apr 1835-9 Aug 1911 MtHo
Sam Sr 1891-1978 Snea
Stewart F 1896-1966 MtHo-s
Susie M w/o H C 1894-1976 MtHo-s
T Frank 2 June 1873-26 Jan 1928 MtHo
Thomas J h/o M R 1860-1920 MtHo-s
Thomas R h/o S S 19 May 1830-19 Oct 1880 MtHo
Walter R (h/o C M) 1909-1965 Fair
William E 1870-1957 Fair
Willie V 1871-1952 Fair
GREEN, (GREENE),
s/o J L & C M b&d 5 Feb 1931 Libe
Arinthia B (w/o J H) 1881-1957 MtHo
Bettie A w/o Albert 5 Apr 1858-

GREEN (continued)
14 July 1921 MtHo
Carrie M w/o J L 5 July 1894-19 Oct 1967 Libe
Carvel P 1922-1978 Park
Clifton P (h/o J R) 1923- Edge
Della w/o S P 1921- Park
Edgar A (h/o M L) 6 Jan 1884-10 July 1939 MtHo-s
Glenwood W 3 Oct 1920-11 Sept 1976 Park
Hazel A w/o L B 1897- Park
Ira T 1910-1929 MtHo
J Elwood h/o R E 1897-1950 Park
J Leas h/o C M 23 Apr 1895-30 Mar 1969 Libe
John H (h/o A B) 1881-1929 MtHo
June R (w/o C P) 1925-1981 Edge
Larry L s/o LeRoy & Lula 1945-1946 Park
LeRoy B h/o H A 1889-1952 Park
Mary E 1907-1977 Libe
Maude L (w/o E A) 20 July 1886-1 July 1963 MtHo-s
Melvin J 1931- 1944 Park
Roscoe J 1903-1974 Libe
Ruth E w/o J E 1900- Park
Samuel P h/o Della 1917- Park
Sherman P w/o W P 1893-1961 Park
Susie B 1903-1977 Libe
William B Sr 21 Mar 1897-23 May 1931 Libe
William E 1947-1976 Libe
Willie P w/o S P 1899- Park
GREGG, George G 1888-1927 Edge
GREGORY, J Adam 1864-1934 MtHo
Julia Ann 1868-1956 MtHo
GRIFFEN, George W 27 Oct 1895-9 Aug 1970 HTri
GRIFFIN, Thomas W Jr 1926-1976 Fair
GRINNALDS, (GRINNOLDS),
Alverta E 22 Jan 1868-7 Sept 1940 Park
Annie Bull 1893-1981 MtHo-s

GRINNALDS (continued)

Annie D (w/o G T) 1884-1976 Edge
Annie Mae d/o S S & A T 18 Nov 1897-29 Mar 1913 Edge
Annie T w/o S S 1858-1936 Edge
Bessie Lee d/o W T & Sudie E 31 Aug 1895-10 July 1918 Libe
Bessie P Pilchard 1888-1982 Edge
Bettie D w/o T C 1859- Park
Carrie L 4 Jan 1870-31 Oct 1889 Park
Daisy W 12 Sept 1879-23 Dec 1946 MtHo
Earl R h/o N M 1900- Libe
Edith S w/o T J Sr 3 Sept 1890-17 Mar 1944 Park
Elizabeth B w/o T J 13 Dec 1829-16 Oct 1919 Park
Estelle w/o Southey 1900-1945 Libe
G Warren 29 Nov 1930-28 Feb 1937 Park
George C 8 Oct 1854-9 May 1925 Libe
George T (h/o A D) 1879-1957 Edge
Henrietta Northam w/o Wm T d 27 Mar 1934 Onan
Ida R 18 Mar 1849-1 Feb 1922 Park
John H (h/o Eveline Mason of Saml) 1 June 1842-2 Mar 1866 (stone gone - 1940 data) Clov
John W h/o M T 14 Feb 1836-17 June 1896 Clov
Katherine S 12 Aug 1872-26 Dec 1952 Libe
Margaret T w/o J W; d/o R A & Henrietta White 11July 1838-20 Oct 1890; age: 52/3/9 Clov
Maria R w/o Southey 1787-1844 Park
Mary E d/o S S & A T 20 Aug 1887-23 Sept 1906 Edge
Maurice L 1891-1963 Edge
Neita M w/o E R 1905-1965 Libe
Nellie Mae d/o E R & N M 1932-1943 Libe
Pauline P (w/o W R) 1909-1982 Edge

GRINNALDS (continued)

Roberta Sarah w/o Jefferson Davis Grinnolds; d/o Geo D & Elizabeth Twyford 20 Jan 1862-16 Mar 1886 (m/o Jefferson Cleveland & Roberta Sara Grinnolds) Park
S U 1894-1974 Edge
Samuel Thomas s/o E R & N M 1937-1943 Libe
Southey h/o Estelle 1892-1975 Libe
Southey C 5 Feb 1902-22 Nov 1968 Libe
Southey Mitchell 15 May 1901-19 May 1915 Edge
Southey S h/o A T 1856-1932 Edge
Thomas C h/o B D 1851-1926 Park
Thomas J h/o E B 22 Jan 1819-12 May 1883 Park
Thomas J Sr w/o E S 1 Jan 1884-18 Feb 1934 Park
W Robert (h/o P P) 1898-1972 Edge
W T 29 Oct 1866-9 Nov 1930 Libe

GRINSTEAD, baby b&d 1926 Edge
Charles O h/o M W 1899-1982 Edge
Mae W w/o C O 1902- Edge

GRISCOM, Robert C 12 Mar 1919-27 Feb 1983 Fair

GROSS, Eva T 2 June 1873-2 Nov 1951 Libe

GROTON, Bessie J w/o R L 1 Aug 1897-1 Mar 1972 Edge
Betty F w/o G T Sr 27 Mar 1881-8 Jan 1972 Park
Birdie S w/o C T 12 May 1894-10 June 1958 Edge
Burleigh W h/o L B 16 Oct 1879-13 Apr 1939 Park
Charlie T h/o B S 10 Nov 1891-23 June 1940 Edge
Clara Teresa Lilliston w/o W T 30 Aug 1872-30 Aug 1925 Edge
Ella S d/o J P & M E G 2 Aug 1868-19 Dec 1883 Onan
Ella Susan d/o J P & M E G 16 Jan 1867-16 July 1868 Onan

GROTON (continued)
Freddie s/o J P & M E G 21 Feb 1864-21 Aug 1872 Onan
George C d 7 July 1870; age: 21 yrs KelG
George T Sr h/o B F 7 July 1875-9 Apr 1939 Park
George T Jr h/o M R 1908-1984 Park
Henry G d 7 July 1870; age: 23 yrs KelG
James P h/o K C 1894-1943 Park
James Purnel h/o M E G 25 Aug 1830-25 Apr 1879 Onan
John M 18 Mar 1884-1 Mar 1920 Park
Kitty C w/o J P 1893-1984 Park
Lafayette W s/o J P & M E G 22 Sept 1862-2 June 1864 Onan
Lafayette Watson 12 May 1865-15 May 1937 Onan
Lena B w/o B W 21 Apr 1880-26 Feb 1952 Park
Maggie d/o J L & Maggie A d July 1872; age: 0/1/0 Onan
Mamie S 27 Sept 1902- Park
Manie S w/o Wm L 16 Jan 1855-21 Feb 1901 Mile
Margaret 9 July 1874-31 July 1956 Onan
Marion F 15 Nov 1915-22 Apr 1977 Quin
Mary A w/o Wm T 3 Feb 1821-21 Feb 1901 Mile
Matilda E Garrison w/o J P 4 Mar 1831-14 Jan 1904 Onan
Maude R w/o Geo T Jr 1910-1953 Park
Mollie M w/o Thos W; d/o Jos & Elizabeth Hopkins d 11 Aug 1882; age: 28 yrs Drut
Mollie Skidmore 1890-1965 Onan
Mollie T d/o Thos & Mollie M 1 Aug-1 Oct 1882 Drut
Robert L h/o B J 8 Sept 1896-22 Aug 1939 Edge
Susan (w/o W D) 25 Dec 1796-14 Feb 1835 Grot
Walter s/o J L & Maggie A d Aug 1869; age: 0/5/0 Onan
William D (h/o Susan) 25 Jan

GROTON (continued)
1790-12 Dec 1862 Grot
William H 14 Sept 1904-9 Aug 1950 Park
William L (h/o M S) 9 Aug 1849-14 Aug 1881 Mile
William T (h/o M A) d 18 Dec 18(5?)1; age: 28/10/27 Mile
William Thomas h/o C T L 25 Dec 1852-8 Apr 1927 Edge
GUILETTE, see also **GILLETT**
Peggy 12 Apr 1736-17 Sept 1808 Wise
GUILDIN, Helen G 1895-1976 Libe
GUILLEN, William P 14 Jan 1892-11 Jan 1946 Edge
GUM, Catherine Johnson w/o G M nd Park
George Massey h/o C J 9 Mar 1903-9 Sept 1971 Park
GUNN, Georgie S 1905-1953 Park
Ida M (w/o R F) 1908-1976 Fair
Roy F (h/o I M) 1906- Fair
GUNTER, Agnes w/o Edwd; d/o Jno & Millie Snead 18 Aug 1801-3 Mar 1877; age: 76/6/13 Gunt
Alfred B s/o B T & E F 1 May 1858-16 Feb 1883 Will
Anne F w/o B T; d/o Jas A & Sue A Fisher 1873-1948 Will
Benjamin F Sr h/o C W 1889-1970 Bays
Benjamin F 1910-1970 Bays
Benjamin T h/o E F Judge of 8th Judicial Circuit of VA 18 Jan 1831-6 Feb 1898 Will
Benjamin T s/o B T & E F 1865-1939 Will
Benjamin T Jr 6 Aug 1902-8 Mar 1980 Edge
Cynthia W w/o B F Sr 1893- Bays
Edward (h/o Agnes) 16 Nov 1802-15 Mar 1853 Gunt
Edward M 23 May 1840-28 Nov 1916 Gunt
Elizabeth Ellen d/o B T & E F 1 Sept 1855-4 July 1901 Will
Ellen Elizabeth d/o Jno & Florence (Custis) 1 Nov 1887-24

GUNTER (continued)
July 1888 Will
Ellen Fisher w/o B T 11 Aug 1831-24 Oct 1878 Will
Flossie 1886-1957 Metr
James 1872-1904 Metr
James F s/o B T & E F 28 May 1862-20 May 1887 Will
John J s/o B T & E F 21 May 1860-1 Oct 1889 Will
John W 1876-1891 MtHo-s
Joseph h/o Rachel 19 Aug 1768-6 Oct 1840 Onan
Levin J 18 Jan 1844-15 Jan 1901 Gunt
Lizzie 1841-1906 MtHo-s
Mary A 1815-1895 MtHo-s
Rachel w/o Jos 17 July 1767-4 Feb 1828 Onan
Solomon T 1886-1970 JoyC
Sue Addison d/o B T & Anne F 4 Sept 1905-21 Jan 1906 Will
Vernice 1917-1983 Metr
W Samuel 1846-1904 MtHo-s
William s/o Jos & Rachel 25 Apr 1805-4 Oct 1822 Onan
William Frederick s/o B T & E F 16 Jan 1864-29 Dec 1888 Will
William Henry 1890-1948 JoyC
GUNTHER, John H 1906-1912 JoyC
GUY, s/o Harold & Winnie b&d 1916 Park
s/o Hildon Jr & Janet B b&d 26 Nov 1942 Fair
baby girl (O S & Ella Guy family) b&d 1956 Onan
Adolph R 1912-1963 MtHo-s
Alice Gertrude d/o J W 8 July 1888-11 July 1897 Guyp
Annabella d/o N T & M E 8 Aug 1922-31 July 1924 MtHo-s
Annie B 1901-1975 MtHo
Annie B w/o W C 1909- MtHo
Annie C w/o B F 1875-1945 Ptea
Annie M w/o C J 1891-1966 MtHo
Arinthia G w/o G B; d/o O S & Elizabeth A Garrison 22 Sept 1838-12 May 1910 Holl
Benjamin F h/o A C 1872-1936

GUY (continued)
Ptea
Bettie M (w/o G G) 1870-1904 Crad-s
Blanche 1902-1920 Onan
Carrie L w/o G W 1 May 1864-31 July 1927 Wach
Charles J h/o A M 1875-1961 MtHo
Charles R (h/o C L) 1881-1937 Ptea
Charlotte w/o H C Jr; d/o Floyd V & Marian Mears Matthews d 20 Nov 1984; age: 65 yrs Park
Charlotte Lee (w/o C R) 1883-1964 Ptea
Clarence L 1898-1965 Edge
Dewey P (h/o L W) 1898-1981 MtHo-s
Edward S s/o Wm & Susan 3 Apr 1841-30 May 1881 Guyc
Edward T h/o L S 20 Aug 1869-10 Sept 1899 MtHo-s
Elizabeth Amanda d/o Thos H & Elizabeth R 4 June 1827-23 Aug 1849 Poul
Elizabeth G w/o W F 1895- MtHo
Elizabeth M w/o S C 1 May 1903-10 Dec 1951 MtHo-s
Elizabeth R 16 Aug 1802-3 Nov 1837; age: 35/2/17 Poul
Ella C w/o O S 1877-1929 Onan
Ella M 1908-1967 Wach
Emma J 21 May 1877-30 Sept 1938 MtHo-s
Ernest G 10 Aug 1880-26 Mar 1912 Guyc
Eva A d/o Wm T & Clara A 21 Feb 1899-27 Jan 1902 Guyp
Evelyn Lee 23 Mar 1912-17 Dec 1915 Ptea
Frances A w/o J T 19 May 1900 MtHo-s
G Clifford (h/o G W) 1899-1973 Holl
George 1919-1920 Onan
George B h/o A G; s/o Geo & Margt 30 Dec 1834-24 Jan 1909 Holl
George G (h/o B M) 1868-1927 Crad-s

GUY (continued)
George T 13 Jan 1883-9 Dec 1924 Wach
George W h/o C L 1858-1933 Wach
Gladys d/o W F & E G 16-17 Apr 1915 MtHo
Gladys W (w/o G C) 1900-1980 Holl
Grace 1898-1919 Onan
Harold C h/o W W 1890-1963 Park
Harold C Jr h/o C M 26 Nov 1919-27 Nov 1975 Park
Harold J s/o Jno W & Margt 29 Nov 1889-24 Nov 1890 Guyc
Hildon Gard (h/o M T) 30 Aug 1895-4 Sept 1981 Fair
J B 7 Dec 1791-1 May 1839 Poul
J Stanley h/o L P 1904-1963 Onan
James A s/o Wm T & S J 10 Sept 1876-20 Jan 1884 Guyp
James E h/o M J 30 June 1847-5 July 1913 Onan
Jerome Travers s/o J T & F A 29 Aug 1922-6 Nov 1926 MtHo-s
John R 20 May 1862-7 July 1944 MtHo-s
John T h/o F A 29 Dec 1895-14 Apr 1974 MtHo-s
John W (h/o M A) 6 Apr 1833-23 Dec 1911 Guyc
Joseph A h/o N G 1869-1938 MtHo
Judson R 10 Aug 1896-30 Oct 1950 Park
Leonard F 4 Aug 1883-4 Nov 1910 Guyc
Leonard G 1915-1952 Onan
Lillian 1896-1918 Onan
Lola P w/o J S 1903-1979 Onan
Loraine W (w/o D P) 1900- MtHo-s
Lottie S w/o E T 5 Nov 1872-17 Oct 1947 MtHo-s
Louis F (h/o M S) 5 Oct 1856-21 Nov 1941 MtHo-s
Louise P (w/o W L) 1923-1977 Wach
Lucele Agnes d/o J W & A O 25

GUY (continued)
Feb 1895-29 Dec 1897 Guyp
Mae 1900-1922 Onan
Maggie A d/o Robt T & Caroline E 1872-1882 Doup
Major bro/o Robt P 1828-1888 (ref Mears) (stone not located) Guyb
Margaret Elizabeth w/o Jno W 18 Oct 1849-29 Apr 1895 Guyc
Margaret S (w/o W B) 1883-1944 MtHo-s
Margaret T w/o Robt P 1832-1923 StGe
Margaret Taylor (w/o H G) 2 Oct 1899- Fair
M(argaret?) W d/o Wm & Susan 4 May 1855-22 Jan 1871 Guyc
Margaret W (w/o R L) 1866-1960 StGe
Maria J w/o J E 21 Dec 1850-20 Apr 1909 Onan
Marrion d/o J W & A O 4-17 Sept 1893 Guyp
Mary A w/o Jno W; d/o Saml & Nancy Rayfield 10 Oct 1829-5 Apr 1868 Guyc
Mary E (w/o N T) 10 Feb 1895-7 Nov 1924 MtHo-s
Mary Elinora w/o J W 8 Aug 1864-30 May 1883 Guyp
Mary S Powell (w/o L F) 23 Oct 1857-1 Aug 1942 MtHo-s
Nanny G w/o J A 1866-1935 MtHo
Norman T (h/o M E) 10 Aug 1891-27 Mar 1969 MtHo-s
Otho S h/o E C 1871-1931 Onan
Pam K 1901- Edge
Percey E s/o J W & Lola A 10 Mar 1903-13 Oct 1918 Guyc
Rachel C d/o Wm T & Sarah J 20 Sept 1870-8 Sept 1871 Guyc
Ray Otho 7 May 1904-10 Mar 1957 Onan
Rhonda Lynn 4 Nov 1965-14 May 1973 Onan
Rickey Lee 1958-1959 MtHo
Robert L (h/o M W) 1867-1951 StGe
Robert P s/o Jno & Elizabeth 19 Oct 1818-20 Mar 1876 Guyb

GUY (continued)
Sarah J w/o Wm T d 22 Apr 1890; age: about 46 yrs Guyp
Sarah J d/o Wm T & S J 28 Oct-16 Nov 1885 Guyp
Selby C h/o E M 8 May 1896-12 Jan 1975 MtHo-s
Selby C Jr 1 May 1921-23 June 1967 MtHo-s
Susan w/o Capt Wm d 16 Dec 1875; age: 61 yrs Guyc
Tabitha, 1st w/o R P; d/o Elisha & Amy Chandler 17 Aug 1821-13 Sept 1864 Guyb
Unice V d/o J W & Lola A 14 Feb-25 Aug 1901 Guyc
Unice Veda d/o J W & Lola A 27 June 1907-28 Oct 1910 Guyc
Upshur Lee s/o G W (or H) & (Emma?) 6 Sept 1881-1 Jan 1887 Guyc
W Carroll h/o A B1906-1981 MtHo
W Fletcher h/o E G 1893-1972 MtHo
Walter B (h/o M S) 1883-1942 MtHo-s
Warner L (h/o L P) 1919- Wach
William h/o Susan 28 Aug 1808-22 Dec 1867 (erected by dau - Elizabeth C Guy) Guyc
William C (s/o W C & A B) 1944-1972 MtHo
William H h/o Julia Guy Parker 1865-1902 MtHo
William Thomas h/o S J & Clara A 7 Mar 1837-10 May 1916 Guyp
Winnie W w/o H C; d/o W J & B W Wessells 1892-1948 Park
H, L E (footstone) (inf) nd Libe
HACK, Adelle 1934-1979 Shil
Ann Q S d/o Peter d 1827 Fair
Anne w/o Peter; d/o Capt Henry & Ann (Kendall) Custis d 3 Aug 1790; age: 65 yrs Fair
Bathyna 25 Dec 1916-25 July 1978 NewM
Cave Jones s/o Peter; h/o Charlotte J Denis nd Fair
Charlotte d/o Geo & Margt 7 Oct 1820; age: 36 yrs Shir

HACK (continued)
Etta 9 Oct 1909-26 Feb 1975 NewM
George d 16 June 1817; age: 74/6/3 Shir
George N d 17 Aug 1786; age: 17/7/0 Shir
Geo T P s/o Thos P & Margt H d 26 Dec 1840; age: 2/4/27 Shir
John 1890-1951 NewM
John N d 18 July 1802; age: 0/13/4 (stone gone; 1940 data) Shir
John William h/o Sabra (d/o Thos Cropper); s/o Peter & Sally B U nd Fair
Joris (George) h/o Anna Varlett (d/o Casper & Judith) bap 20 Mar 1620 (in Cologne, Ger)-d 1665 in VA (see Whitelaw: 658-60) Fair
Leah d 10 Sept 1794; age: 16/5/0 Shir
Maggie 1880-1962 NewM
Margaret w/o Geo d 13 Oct 1823; age: 74/6/0 Shir
Margaret H d/o Geo & Margt 17 Jan 1774-29 June 1849; age: 75/5/12 Shir
Margaret H w/o Thos P; d/o Geo & Frances Scherer d 14 Jan 1853; age: 41/1/11 Shir
Melinda U d/o Peter & Sally B U nd Fair
Molly d/o Geo & Margt d 25 Aug 1828; age: 41 yrs Shir
Peter h/o Matilda (d/o Anthony & Elizabeth Rowles West) d 1717 Fair
Peter h/o Eliz Smith & Sally B Upshur 11 Apr 1754-18 Oct 1844 Fair
Peter h/o Ann Custis d 1 Jan 1802; age: 85 yrs (see Whitelaw: 658-60) Fair
Peter Thomas U h/o Sally T Selby & Harriet Fleming Selby 15 Jan 1795-(no death date) Fair
Purnell 1908-1978 NewM
Sally B, 2nd w/o Peter; d/o Thos Upshur of North Co 14 Apr

HACK (continued)
1767-23 Jan 1819 Fair
Sally T Selby w/o P T U 16 Jan 1806-22 Apr 1824 Fair
Susan 17 Dec 1868-1899 Shil
HACKER, Bernice L 1893-1962 Onan
Frank Herman 1895-1964 MtHo-s
HACKETT, Hester 1871-1961 Gask
Robert D 1898-1958 Gask
Vincent S 1901-1977 Gask
HAFFERKAMP, Annie Laurie w/o H R 1911- Wach
Howard R h/o A L 1896-1969 Wach
HAINES, Maud E 1866-1947 MtHo-s
HALES, James E (h/o M A) 4 July 1881-21 July 1972 MtHo-s
Lois B 1898-1975 Park
Mary A (w/o J E) 16 Nov 1872-2 July 1939 MtHo-s
HALEY, Annie E d/o J R & M E 1 Apr 1868-10 May 1909; age: 41/1/9 Hale
Bessie 1895-1979 Snea
Endie 29 Dec 1873-30 Apr 1933 Hale
Evelyn Justis 1899-1974 Libe
J Robert h/o M E; s/o Wm & Annie 29 July 1829-11 Aug 1875; age: 46/0/12 Hale
James P, 1st h/o R A Waterfield 7 June 1810-28 July 1885 MtHo
John 1885-1970 Snea
John T h/o R E 1850-1926 MtHo
Margaret E w/o J R 19 Mar 1837-7 Feb 1912; age: 74/10/18 Hale
Rebecca E w/o J T 1860-1941 MtHo
Robert P 19 Aug 1862-26 Sept 1922 Hale
Sallie P 1 Oct 1865-23 June 1930 Hale
William J 12 Mar 1861-7 Feb 1918 Hale
HALL, A Fuller h/o R B 12 June 1894-29 Apr 1969 Wach

HALL (continued)
A Jane w/o J D 27 May 1860-28 Sept 1909 Park
Adrian Smith 17 July 1924-20 Nov 1981 Libe
Amanda S 30 Dec 1870-21 Aug 1957 Park
Bettie S 1882-1968 Fair
Beulah A (w/o H J) 1898- Onan
Dr Charles F W 16 Oct 1849-14 Nov 1909 Libe
Capt Edward S h/o M S 1854-1929 Park
Exia W 1906-1980 Metr
George nd Shil
George E h/o M M 1899-1979 Metr
Hallie B 20 Dec 1895-12 May 1973 Park
Harry h/o H J 1901-1966 Park
Harry J (h/o B A) 1902-1980 Onan
Harvey F 13 Dec 1893-12 Feb 1972 Park
Helen Jones w/o Harry 1899-1977 Park
Herman E 1928-1979 Metr
James Alfred 22 May 1841-27 June 1906 Libe
John Bloxom 11 Sept 1926-22 July 1983 Park
John D h/o A J 23 May 1852-22 Oct 1931 Park
John F 1861-1945 Park
L Douglas h/o M T 1899-1977 MtHo-s
Lizzie S 1886-1961 Fair
Margaret S w/o E S 1851-1926 Park
Mary M w/o G E 1899- Metr
Mary P (w/o W E) 1890-1960 Onan
Matthew d 24 Aug 1963; age: 79 yrs JoyC
Mildred T w/o L D 1899-1979 MtHo-s
Missouri w/o Wm H 1857-1937 Park
Ray S 29 Apr 1924-4 July 1977 Metr
Rennie B w/o A F 4 Feb 1904-23 Sept 1979 Wach

HALL (continued)
Robert Jr 1934-1976 Metr
Rose Mellon 1880-1934 Park
Sarah E 3 Nov 1848-7 Jan 1895 (unable to verify) Hall
Virginia D 1860-1921 Edge
Virginia S 1865-1914 Park
Wilford E (h/o M P) 1881-1961 Onan
William C 1842-1893 Edge
William Henry h/o Missouri 1853-1925 Park
HALLOWELL, T J bro/o Anna E Wessells 1873-1941 Park
HAMILTON, John R 25 June 1900-2 Dec 1964 Fair
HAMMETT, James F 22 July 1912-30 July 1972 Fair
HAMMOND, Bettie S (w/o G A) 1888-1960 Fair
George A (h/o B S) 1888-1983 Fair
Nola Mears 26 Oct 1889-31 Jan 1968 MtHo
Winfield Scott 24 Aug 1886-3 June 1943 MtHo
HAMPTON, John Charles 3 Mar 1955-2 Oct 1975 Fair
HANCHEY, Karin U 3 Aug 1940-29 Dec 1963 Fair
Manning (h/o M D) 7 Apr 1905-11 Nov 1981 Fair
Mary D (w/o Manning) 7 Mar 1907-2 May 1958 Fair
Owen 31 Aug 1898-16 Feb 1980 Fair
HANCOCK, Dr Eugene T 1870-1921 StGe
Virginia Lee 3 June 1947-21 Sept 1958 Onan
HANSFORD, Margaret Custis w/o Chas C; d/o Jas W & M P B Custis 1844-8 Jan 1917 MtCu
Richard Wynne s/o Chas C & M C 14 June 1881-22 June 1907 MtCu
HARDAWAY, James A 1907-1965 Edge
HARDING, Maud M w/o R W d 18 July 1909; age: 49 yrs MtHo
Rufus W h/o M M 14 Feb 1856-8 Jan 1923 MtHo

HARDWICKE, Ann Godwin 1925-1963 Park
HARDY, Cora 1879-1971 Snea
James 1919-1979 Snea
HARGIS, A Robert h/o M R 1904- Edge
Albert Lee 12 Feb 1912-16 July 1965 MtHo-s
Alice S (w/o E L) 1876-1946 MtHo-s
Bagwell C (h/o E T) 22 Sept 1869-29 Sept 1923 Wach
Benjamin F 1866-1923 Wach
Bessie B Coxton w/o N U 1884-1934 Edge
Bessie C 1904-1942 Edge
Charles H (h/o M H S) 1872-1934 StGe
Claude R 1909-1974 Edge
Clyde M 29 Apr 1914-24 Oct 1976 Wach
Dell S (h/o V P) 22 Aug 1890-30 Mar 1971 Holl
Edward T h/o M W 1882-1966 Edge
Elizabeth S wid/o Parker 1862-1949 MtHo
Emma K 1877-1938 Wach
Esther B 1899- Edge
Esther T (w/o B C) 1873-1957 Wach
Ezekiel L (h/o A S) 1880-1953 MtHo-s
Fletcher S 1887-1963 Edge
Fred D 1882-1928 Edge
George P h/o H P 7 May 1841-26 Jan 1913 MtHo
Harold U s/o N U & B B C 15 Apr 1914-25 July 1917 Edge
Hester P 1909-1915 Wach
Hester Pettit w/o G P 10 Jan 1844-26 Dec 1905 MtHo
Inez F 1883-1972 Edge
Irving L 27 May 1898-11 Dec 1967 Edge
J William (h/o N L) 27 Aug 1890-28 Nov 1937 MtHo-s
James F h/o M F 21 Sept 1844-9 July 1916 Edge
Jennie C (w/o S R) 10 Oct 1847-5 May 1930 Holl
John 19 Dec 1800-9 Oct 1881;

HARGIS (continued)
age: 80/9/20 Harg
Kathryn I (w/o R E) 1916- Fair
Lelia K Holland (1st husband - Geo E Holland) d Sept 1968 Edge
Manie R w/o A R 1889-1978 Edge
Mary Ann 1850-1940 Edge
Mary Ellen w/o W H 3 Dec 1854-27 May 1918 MtHo
Millie H Shaw (w/o C H) 1867-1960 StGe
Minnie W w/o E T 1882-1967 Edge
Missouri F w/o J F 17 Dec 1848-6 Feb 1921 Edge
Mollie E 1872-1940 Edge
Naomi E w/o P J 12 Feb 1896- Wach
Nathaniel Jr 1861-1936 Edge
Nathaniel Jr 22 Oct 1921- Edge
Neely Upshur h/o B B C 1878-1953 Edge
Nellie L (w/o J Wm) 24 July 1895-11 Oct 1976 MtHo-s
Paul 24 Jan 1880-11 Oct 1918 Onan
Preston J h/o N E 10 June 1892-25 Dec 1960 Wach
Roland E (h/o K I) 1900-1977 Fair
Salley d 18 Mar 1882; age: 89 yrs Harg
Soloman 1849-1935 Edge
Stephen R (h/o J C) 26 Mar 1855-19 May 1926 Holl
Sudie G (w/o W T) 1873-1942 Onan
Susie K 1900-1963 Edge
Thomas 1900-1965 Edge
Viola P w/o D S 4 July 1894-14 July 1965 Holl
William F 1885-1953 Edge
William H h/o M E; s/o Thos & Rachel 24 May 1851-16 Jan 1917 MtHo
William T (h/o S G) 1869-1933 Onan
William T 1886-1966 MtHo-s
Winnie M b&d 1915 Wach

HARMON, (HARMAN),
A Sidney (h/o M M) 1870-1955 Wach
Able R h/o N S 25 Nov 1795-4 Feb 1843 OlHa
Alberta 1905-1979 NewM
Alfred C s/o Jas & Rosa 19 Oct 1846-22 Aug 1855 OlHp
Alfred C W s/o Jas W & Rosa H 3 June 1856-22 Feb 1864 OlHp
Alfred Custis Sr 11 Jun 1895-13 July 1978 Fair
Alfred T 1900-1964 NewM
Angla D 3 May 1954-23 Oct 1955 NewM
Ann B 26 Oct 1766-13 July 1829; age: 62/9/18 Hapl
Anna Josephine w/o J K 20 July 1861-4 Nov 1924 Harm
Annie Ames 1912-1966 Shil
Annie D 1863-1917 Onan
Annie E 1889-1955 Burt
Arinthia Phillips w/o J K 1 Nov 1850-21 Jan 1897 (moved from Harmon Place) Wach
Benjamin 1877-1970 Ayre
Bernie 1905-1976 Snea
Bertha B (w/o H H) 1895-1963 Holl
Bertie Mears w/o J W 12 Aug 1895-13 Feb 1918 (buried with infant in her arms) (moved from Old Harmon Plot) Oakg
Chester 17 Sept 1972-1 May 1907 Snea
Clarence d 8 Feb 1964; age: 71 yrs Gask
Clarence s/o Mary 21 Jan 1950-13 Nov 1976 Hagr
Coley C 1876-1963 Wach
Comfort M d/o Jno & Ann 24 Dec 1800-22 June 1845; age: 44/5/28 Hapl
Cora nd Ayre
Della 1908-1969 StJo
Edward E 5 June 1919-11 Jan 1966 Burt
Elizabeth A 1906- Wach
Eleanor 1913-1973 JoyC
Emary B d/o Jas W & Rosa H 20 Sept 1851-10 Aug 1855 OlHp
Enda A 1882-1958 Wach

HARMON (continued)
Ernest 1909-1981 StJo
Ernest T 29 Aug 1875-29 Apr 1940 MtHo-s
Ethel H 1881-1946 MtHo-s
Eunice H 1901-1959 Fair
Evelyn H (w/o J E) 27 Nov 1881-9 Aug 1962 Onan
Florence 1885-1959 Burt
Florence Andrews w/o L L 18 Jan 1889-29 Dec 1921 Libe
Forrest L h/o L B 1903-1957 Fair
Frantz Knoll s/o L L & F A 17 Oct 1919-15 July 1920 Libe
Fred F 1876-1959 Fair
Fred T h/o M K 1909-1963 Fair
Garnet 15 Sept 1915-13 Apr 1957 Burt
George 1927-1983 Burt
George D 15 Feb 1899-8 Oct 1977 Fair
George J 1902-1973 Shil
George W 1882-1969 Burt
Gladys d/o Mannie 18 Mar 1903-27 July 1930 Burt
Helen M 1906-1916 Fair
Homer 1926-1969 Burt
Howard H (h/o B B) 1894-1951 Holl
Indie d 12 June 1965 Gask
James E h/o Lola 21 Dec 1882-5 Dec 1935 NewM
James H 2 July 1917-15 Aug 1970 NewM
James K h/o Margt nd HaPh
James K h/o A P 15 June 1848-21 Apr 1916 (moved from Harmon Place) Wach
James P Jr b&d 1956 NewM
James W 21 Nov 1820-29 May 1892 OlHp
James W s/o Jno & Nancy 15 Oct 1815-20 Mar 1889 OlHp
James Wesley (h/o L G) 13 May 1890-12 Nov 1970 MtHo-s
Jan Sr 1937-1973 Gask
Joan E 1944-1982 Fair
John s/o Kendall & Rosey 22 Jan 1774-25 Nov 1858 OlHp
John s/o Henry & Comfort d 2 Oct 1842; age: 17/3/27 Hapl

HARMON (continued)
John 13 June 1912-30 Mar 1983 Burt
John E h/o S A 29 Feb 1832-10 Mar 1901; age: 69/0/10 OlWa
John E (h/o E H) 8 Mar 1873-3 Dec 1940 Onan
John E s/o Ken & Maggie 29 Nov 1901-9 Nov 1905 Snea
John H s/o Jno & Ann 3 Oct 1805-2 Sept 1838; age: 32/11/1 Hapl
John T d 8 Jan 1962; age: 77 yrs NewM
John Walker h/o B M & M D 16 Nov 1893-3 May 1977 Oakg
Kendall 18 Sept 1873-25 Apr 1913; age: 39:5:7 Snea
Lafayette N 1861-1950 Onan
Leah 1844-22 Dec 1917 Burt
Lena Grinnalds (w/o J W) 17 Mar 1890-6 Feb 1973 MtHo-s
Liccie A 1895-1961 Burt
Linwood (h/o V E) 1902-1965 StJo
Lola w/o J E 1889-1937 NewM
Lorenzo R 1951-1972 Gask
Louis F 15 June 1923-22 Dec 1977 NewM
Louisa Boyett 5 Apr 1838-17 Jan 1920 HaPh
Louise B w/o F L 1903- Fair
Madeleine K w/o F T 1909-1982 Fair
Maggie 1871-1968 NewM
Manie H 1 Apr 1864-16 May 1882 Harm
Mannie E 1868-1954 Burt
Margaret (by 2nd marriage; 1st husband - Chas Kellam) Jan 1804-17 July 1887 Kelp
Margaret w/o Jas K nd HaPh
Margaret T 1880-1958 Fair
Margaret W 9 Jan 1913- Fair
Martha Mears (w/o O T) 1868-1947 Holl
Mary S w/o Wm J 15 Feb 1842-25 Dec 1936 Burt
Mary S 1900-1958 Metr
Mildred D w/o J W; d/o Jno B & Polly W Downing 27 May 1889-17 Dec 1974 Oakg

HARMON (continued)
Minnie D 1878-1955 Onan
Missouri M (w/o A S) 1883-1969 Wach
Mollie Nock 17 Nov 1899-28 Dec 1935 MtHo-s
Nancy S w/o A R 18 Aug 1801-15 Oct 1836 OlHa
Otho Tunnell (h/o M M) 1865-1957 Holl
Polly Sample 1896-1957 MeNe
Ralph P 5 Oct 1912-3 June 1971 Burt
Reitz L 1911-1969 Libe
Rosey B d/o Jno H & Ann 3 Jan 1791-27 Mar 1855; age: 64/2/24 Hapl
Sallie B d/o Jno B & Marget A d 16 Mar 1892 OlHp
Sally A d/o Jas W & Rosa H 20 Sept 1849-5 Nov 1852 OlHp
Sarah A w/o J E 19 Jan 1838-14 May 1913; age: 75/3/25 OlWa
Siner B s/o Jno H & Ann 8 Dec 1798-23 Apr 1870; age: 71/4/15 Hapl
Tabitha E Dec 1854-Dec 1943 NewM
Thomas J 1916-1967 NewM
Thomas Lee 1942-1961 JoyC
Virginia E (w/o Linwood) 1900-1967 StJo
William B 23 Dec 1830-7 Sept 1900; age: 69/7/14 Hapl
William Duncan 1878-1955 MtHo-s
William J h/o M S 16 Feb 1842-24 Jan 1924 Burt
HARMONSON, (HARMANSON),
Ann Hay Battaile w/o Dr C L 27 June 1864-26 Nov 1898 Onan
Anne C Arbuckle w/o Jno L 2 Oct 1823-16 Jan 1908 StGe
Bessie S Pitts w/o L J 2 Jan 1868-1 Mar 1931 Onan
Dr Charles Lafayette h/o Ann 5 Jan 1858-16 Nov 1901 Onan
George 1884-1964 Shil
Henry 5 Feb 1890-12 Oct 1945 Shil
John C H s/o Dr Chas L & Ann 24 Apr 1895-2 Mar 1897 Onan

HARMONSON (continued)
John H s/o Dr Jno L & Ann Arbuckle 1859-1938 StGe
Dr Jno L h/o A C A 31 Mar 1821-25 Jan 1894 StGe
Katherine A d/o Dr Chas A & Ann 12 Nov 1892-6 Aug 1893 Onan
Lewis James h/o B S P s/o Jas R & Tabitha S 14 Mar 1861-25 Dec 1943 Onan
Lottie 1900-1959 NewM
Vivian S 1933-1982 Shil
William H Jr 21 Nov 1947-26 July 1967 HTri
HARPER, Mary C (w/o W L) 1873-1967 Onan
William L (h/o M C) 1869-1956 Onan
HARRIS, children/o J F & Eva 8 May-25 Aug 1893 Holl
Ada D w/o J E 1919- Fair
Audrey J 1908-1949 Park
Edith 1939-1968 Neda
Etta K w/o Purnell 1870-1933 Oakg
Geneva 1903-1977 Snea
Grover C (h/o M S) 6 Dec 1906- MtHo-s
John b in Montgomery Co PA d July 1912 (member of Capt McNeile's Independent Rangers CSA. Disbanded at Strawsburg VA) StGe
John 9 Sept 1888-9 Mar 1948 Bail
John Davis 1943-1977 Fair
John E h/o A D 1916-1979 Fair
Johhny 1920-1983 Gask
Maggie 1908-1981 Bail
Marie S (w/o G C) 26 Feb 1908-20 Sept 1975 MtHo-s
Mary A 1896-1977 Burt
Mary O d/o J F & Eva 25 Nov 1895-13 Apr 1904 Holl
Mary S 1878-1957 MtHo-s
Matilda d/o Purnell & Etta 22 Sept 1894-9 Nov 1910 Oakg
Maude Mears 23 Nov 1901-18 Oct 1925 Fair
Pearlie d/o Jas & Ellen 20 Apr 1896-12 Mar 1914 StPa

HARRIS (continued)
Purnell h/o E K 1868-1938 Oakg
Susie 1915-1982 Snea
Wylie 1916-1982 Snea
HARRISON, Bertha Sue d/o Thos W & Lizzie S 12 Sept 1904-18 June 1906 Harr
Clara T (w/o J W) 1892- Onan
E Blanche Scott (1st hus - Jno W Scott) 22 Apr 1885-15 Jan 1959 Onan
Edith W (w/o L A) 1880-1937 Onan
Edward L (h/o L A) 30 Dec 1874-13 Oct 1942 Onan
Eliza W 1907- Onan
Elizabeth Coard d/o L L 18 July 1906-1 Feb 1942 Libe
Elizabeth Y w/o W T 1883-1978 Onan
Ellen L w/o W N 1911- Onan
Estelle B (w/o M O) 1900-1971 Fair
Esther 27 Sept 1837-26 June 1915 Fair
F Riley 1904-1937 MtHo-s
Frances A w/o G W 1915 Libe
G Werner h/o F A 1903-1967 Libe
James A s/o J E & M A 27 Feb 1875-6 Apr 1890 Harr
James E h/o M A 28 Oct 1835-28 Mar 1914 Harr
James Rogers 21 Oct 1901-14 Feb 1929 Onan
James T h/o S V 18 Oct 1872-16 Nov 1912 Onan
John B s/o J E & M A 4 Oct 1872-22 May 1878 Harr
John W Sr (h/o C T) 1911-1968 Onan
John W Jr (h/o S L) 1932-1960 Onan
Larry E 26 Sept 1949-2 Aug 1974 Fair
Lee O w/o W H 26 Jan 1877-25 July 1903 MtHo
Lillie A (w/o E L) 6 Jan 1877-22 Nov 1957 Onan
Lloyd A (h/o E W) 1877-1956 Onan
Lloyd R (h/o M F) 1921-1965

HARRISON (continued)
Fair
Lulie Lankford 19 Jan 1879-28 May 1952 Libe
Mabel S (w/o N R) 1910-1951 Onan
Margarete A w/o J E 29 Aug 1842-16 Jan 1918 Harr
Mary B d 4 Mar 1903; age: 86 yrs Garr
Mary F (w/o L R) 1924- Fair
Milton O (h/o E B) 1902-1961 Fair
Myrdith R s/o Jno R & Lena 11 July 1907-25 Jan 1908 ParC
Norman R (h/o M S) 1906- Onan
Odessa L (w/o R N) 1890-1973 Wach
Preston B 14 June 1910-5 Aug 1958 MtHo-s
Reese N (h/o O L) 1891-1956 Wach
Sarah M w/o T C 1 Jan 1842-13 Oct 1910 Harp
Shirley L (w/o J W Jr) 1935- Onan
Sudie V w/o J T 20 Mar 1876-1 Jan 1914 Onan
Thomas C h/o S M 11 Jan 1837-5 Aug 1885 Harp
W Thomas h/o E Y 1882-1971 Onan
Warner N h/o E L 1906-1965 Onan
William F 25 Feb 1924-30 Apr 1976 Fair
William H h/o L O 5 Mar 1834-23 Apr 1918 MtHo
HARRY, Esther Parks w/o Wm T 14 June 1911-12 Oct 1975 Park
William Thomas h/o E P 18 June 1910-7 Dec 1962 Park
HART, (HARTE),
Alice H w/o L W 26 Nov 1885-28 Nov 1919 Onan
Amy Elizabeth d 9 July 1947; age: 67/3/29 Park
Ann S w/o C M 1923- Park
Annie S w/o M T 1879-1960 Park
Baxter 1894-1964 Onan
Bonnie C 1947-1958 Park
Bowdoin W 26 June 1911-28

HART (continued)
June 1969 Park
Calvin R h/o M E 1909-1964 Park
Carroll M h/o A S 17 Jan 1914-9 Dec 1976 Park
Carroll R 18 Feb 1888-22 May 1947 Park
Catherine S w/o R D 1846-1933 Onan
Clara B (w/o R T) 1876-1966 Onan
Clarenda S w/o S L 1888-1980 Libe
Dallas W (h/o M L) 20 Oct 1852-11 Dec 1928 Onan
Daniel Thomas s/o E E & V B b&d 1958 Park
Donnie Brian s/o Garland & E B 1945-1947 Park
Dorothy D w/o L J 1884-1977 Park
Edgar R 1903-1973 MtHo-s
Elwood M h/o P P 1928- Libe
Emma B w/o Garland 1 Nov 1919-1 Apr 1982 Park
Ernest E Sr h/o O H 1899-1976 Park
Ernest E Jr h/o V B 1930- Park
Evelyn N 1907-1976 MtHo-s
Little Florence nd Park
Garland h/o E B 12 Aug 1912-6 Dec 1962 Park
Garland E 1905-1976 Park
Grace B (w/o W E) 1916-1982 Fair
Grace W (w/o L B) 1914- Fair
Gracie L 1913-1974 Fair
Hazel G (w/o W D) 1899-1968 MtHo-s
Helen K (w/o I E) 21 Dec 1898- Fair
Irving E (h/o H K) 16 Aug 1892-30 June 1978 Fair
James S h/o Mary 9 Jan 1802-June... stone broken Hart
Janie M 1880-1967 Park
John W s/o Jno & Mary 8 Dec 1830-6 Dec 1900 Onan
John W b&d 1913 Libe
Joshua T (h/o L F) 1876-1945 MtHo-s

HART (continued)
L C child: nd Park
Laura A J d/o Jas & Susan 21 Sept 1857-4 Dec 1863; age: 6/2/28 Arli
Lenora F (w/o J T) 1887-1945 MtHo-s
LeRoy W h/o A H 1884-1954 Onan
Libren Brooks (h/o G W) 29 Nov 1901-25 Dec 1962 Fair
Linzie B w/o O J 1898-1952 Park
Lloyd Jackson h/o D D 1884-1951 Park
Lottie w/o Jno W 5 Apr 1835-24 Mar 1912 Onan
Louie D 1881-1970 Park
Madeline P 1897- Onan
Maggie K (w/o W L) 1881-1960 Onan
Maggie L (w/o D W) 26 Oct 1868-25 Sept 1927 Onan
Major T h/o A S 1875-1960 Park
Marguerita E w/o C R 1911- Park
Mary w/o J S 5 May 1809-23 Sept 1875 Hart
Mary E 1841-1915 Hgra
Melvin 1913-1984 Park
Nellie Budd 21 Sept 1911-12 Oct 1982; age: 71 yrs Park
Oakley H w/o E E Sr 1902- Park
Otha J h/o L B 1894-1969 Park
Phyllis P w/o E M 1931- Libe
R Dennis h/o C S 1843-1922 Onan
R Tankard (h/o C B) 1870-1944 Onan
Selby P 15 Oct 1848-19 Aug 1923 Park
Stanley 1920- Libe
Staten L h/o C S 1884-1951 Libe
Stewart N 1903-1972 Park
Susie 25 Aug 1883-15 Apr 1916 Onan
Virginia B w/o E E Jr 1933- Park
W Lee (h/o M K) 1877-1944 Onan
Walter 1907-1975 Park
Warner E (h/o G B) 1911-1959

HART (continued)
Fair
William D (h/o H G) 14 Apr 1897-2 Dec 1960 MtHo-s
William Dennis 1838-1883 Hgra
Wrendo C 1906-1918 Libe
HARTIN, Rev W 1901-1970 Shil
HARTLEY, Celeste Boykin w/o E F 17 Dec 1883-13 June 1960 StGe
Eugene Fuller h/o C B 21 Sept 1879-4 Sept 1961 StGe
HARTMAN, Alfred B 1 Jan 1889-1 Oct 1976 MtHo
Audrey Eloise 1920-1922 Holl
Dial Ward (h/o L C) 1886-1945 MtHo-s
Diane b&d 1950 MtHo-s
Dorothy b&d 1914 Holl
Edwin D h/o S J C; s/o A Fred & Florence B (Snow Hill MD) 7 July 1894-6 Dec 1932 Onan
Emma P 1894-1959 Oakg
Fairy Gaye (w/o L H) 1897-1958 Holl
George B h/o L L 23 Aug 1896-7 Mar 1977 Libe
James J 7 Apr 1859-28 Jan 1945 Oakg
John H h/o S H; s/o Chas H & Margt (Ward) 1852-1931 MtHo
Lee 1888-1928 MtHo-s
Lillian Lee 1878-1967 MtHo
Lola Core (w/o D W) 1887-1961 MtHo-s
Louise L w/o G B 18 May 1899-2 Feb 1971 Libe
Luther Hitt (h/o F G) 1896- Holl
Manie E (w/o T L) 1868- Wach
Mannie 20 Sept 1880-3 Sept 1921 Oakg
Margaret R wid/o Chas 6 Aug 1824-24 Dec 1897 Oakg
Margaret E 1883-1961 MtHo
Mary James 3 Oct 1883-27 Oct 1923 Onan
Mitchell E 6 Nov 1924-17 Sept 1978 Libe
Sallie J C w/o E D; d/o S J & J L Hopkins 16 Nov 1891-24 Sept 1968 Onan
Sarah Haley w/o J H 1852-1937

HARTMAN (continued)
MtHo
Thomas L (h/o M E) 1863-1934 Wach
HARVEY, Emma 1900-1981 Gask
HATCH, Anna Cropper Gibb 29 Apr 1865-4 Mar 1917 Onan
Anne Cropper w/o W A of NY; d/o Jos & E W Gibb of Acc Co VA 26 Oct 1830-13 Apr 1887 Bowm
HATNEY, John d 1 July 1964; age: 63 yrs Burt
LeRoy 1919-1969 Shil
HATTON, d/o Wm H & Ella B 18-27 Aug 1890 Mart
Annie W w/o G C 1881- MtHo
Benjamin C (h/o Euphamy) 13 Dec 1833-19 Dec 1908 Mart
Ella B w/o W H 23 Sept 1858-12 Apr 1924 MtHo
Euphamy w/o B C 31 Aug 1833-24 Feb 1901 Mart
George C (h/o A W) 1882-1936 MtHo
George C Jr 27 Feb 1926-10 Mar 1982 MtHo
Hattie B 1889-1947 MtHo
Helen M 1909-1978 Smit
Homer 1908-1961 Smit
James A 1894-1971 Shil
Mamie 25 Sept 1881-27 Feb 1947 Shil
Margaret w/o Walter; d/o Adam & Franconia Muir 6 Mar 1745-16 Jan 1774 Ever
Mary d/o Walter Sr & Margt d 21 Dec 1773; age: 4/0/0 Ever
Mary Belote 5 June 1848-26 Nov 1927 MtHo-s
Omar Jr 1940-1969 Shil
Percy 1893-1950 MtHo
W H h/o E B 1860-1935 MtHo
Walter s/o Walter Sr & Margt 15 Nov 1766-11 Sept 1799 Ever
William Emory s/o B C & Euphamy 5 Mar 1881-22 Feb 1892 Mart
William Henry s/o Wm & Ella B 5 Mar 1888-27 Feb 1892 Mart
HAWK, Margaret T 1922- Fair
Russell J 1928-1978 Fair

HAYDEN, Clarence R 1898-1957 Libe
Harry W h/o I M 1873-1936 Libe
Ida M w/o H W 1878-1951 Libe
HAYMAN, David W 1853-1928 Edge
Ethel Broughton w/o J B 18 Sept 1882-June 1978 MtHo
John Brinkley Sr h/o E B 13 May 1880-11 Apr 1970 MtHo
HAYNES, James A d1890 - pastor of St Paul's AME Church StPa
HAYNIE, John C 1885-1945 Holl
Lillian Beulah 1890-1926 Holl
HAZELL, Fred A 7 Apr 1898-28 Aug 1966 Fair
HEARN, Missouri H 1865-1955 Fair
HEATH, s/o A R & J W b&d 17 Mar 1839 Arli
Ada May 1857-1 Oct 1928 Burt
Ada d 14 Feb 1894 (erected by Kate & Jeff Mears) StPa
Albert Lee 1938-1978 Shil
Alfred M 1905-1974 Wach
Annie L w/o E T 24 Jan 1863-14 Sept 1923 Wach
Ashby 1907-1951 NewM
Charlie 1889-1975 Gask
Dinah 1870-1968 NewM
Edward T h/o A L 8 Jan 1855-6 Sept 1938 Wach
Hattie D 1898-1962 NewM
James C (h/o L T) 5 May 1850-7 Sept 1924 Onan
Jane W w/o Albert R d 2 Apr 1839; age: 23/3/16 Arli
Jesse 1901-1979 Wach
John W 1 July 1850-11 Sept 1908 Oakg
Lena T (w/o J C) 24 June 1859-1 Mar 1950 Onan
Lizzie S w/o Jno W 4 Mar 1843-21 Jan 1897 Nick
Louis D h/o M M 1875-1956 Wach
Maggie R 4 Nov 1845-18 May 1926 Onan
Maggie W 15 Nov 1880-28 Aug 1881 Nick
Mannie M w/o L D 1887-1968

HEATH (continued) Wach
Mary B 1880-1954 Shil
Mary E 1896-1979 NewM
R Thomas (h/o S E) 5 May 1867-6 Feb 1953 Edge
Sam d 21 Jan 1894 (erected by Kate & Jeff Mears) StPa
Sarah R w/o Albert Rouell (2nd hus); d/o Henry & Agnes West Parker 3 Oct 1799-31 Jan 1886 OldP
Sue E (w/o R T) 6 Feb 1872-5 Apr 1949 Edge
Rev Thomas J C h/o W P 4 Oct 1878-14 Nov 1952 Onan
Wayne E 11 July 1941-8 Jan 1978 Shil
Will nd NewM
William 10 May 1835-8 Nov 1915 NewM
Willie O 14 May-16 Sept 1877 Nick
Winnie Parsons w/o T J C 26 Oct 1888-5 Nov 1918 Onan
HEBARD, Rev Edward 22 Nov 1807-28 Sept 1880 Oakg
Edward W s/o J H & H J 9 Jan 1864-8 Feb 1908 Onan
Hester J w/o J H 17 Mar 1845-29 Jan 1932 Onan
Joseph H h/o H J 22 Sept 1838-23 Aug 1912 Onan
Joseph H 1866-1947 Onan
Mary C 1870-1945 Onan
HELMS, Arthur Pierce (h/o Edna) 1917-1972 Onan
Edna (w/o A P) 1921- Onan
HENDERSON, baby boy 12-15 Sept 1932 Edge
Bret 1914-1964 Bagc
Florence C (w/o J R) 1886-1942 Onan
George W 1890-1977 Bagc
John B 1856-1911 Onan
John R (h/o F C) 1878-1938 Onan
Mary C 28 Oct 1804-31 Mar 1845 Syca
Mary S 1835-1893 Onan
HENDRICKSON, Holmes C 1893-1955 Fair

HENNESSY, Jno C 24 June 1897-29 Jan 1974 Fair
HENRY, Bertha L 1894-1977 Gask
Charles T 1887-1957 Gask
Elizabeth w/o Wm B; d/o Peter Hack d 21 Aug 1804; age: 55 yrs Fair
Harvey J 1881-1970 Gask
James s/o Hugh d 20 Feb 1787; age: 28 yrs Fair
Vivian C 1956-1982 Gask
William M B h/o Eliz d 1781 Fair
HENVIS, Edmund W (h/o L K) 1893-1975 MtHo-s
Lorena K (w/o E W) 1904- MtHo-s
HERCH..., inf s/o Robt & Martha (stone broken; footstone J S H) Walk
HERING, Esther Ward 28 Feb 1919-23 Mar 1964 MtHo
HERMANN, Carl S (h/o V B) 1885-1973 MtHo
Virginia Bull (w/o C S) 1908- MtHo
HERMES, Sherman S Jr 11 Jan 1931-26 Apr 1979 Holl
HICKMAN, inf s/o Thos & A J 4-5 Jan 1885 Hick
inf d/o Kenneth & Edith (Fletcher) d c1916 Flet
s/o C F & M W b&d 18 July 1931 Libe
baby girl b&d 25 May 1970 Onan
___h A w/o Richd 9 Sept 1839-11 Feb 1865 (footstone S A H) HicG
Adaline w/o J R 11 Oct 1836- Edge
Albert s/o Kenneth & Edith (Fletcher) d c1916 Flet
Algernon T h/o L M 1882-1961 Park
Ann More (w/o C M) 1922- Onan
Anna B d/o Thos & A J 13 Dec 1885-23 Oct 1889 Hick
Annie Fletcher 20 Sept 1832-1 Oct 1911 Mitc-e
Annie J w/o T S 1852- Hick
Annie L w/o J C 1867-1934 Park

HICKMAN (continued)
Annie L Hope w/o E T 1878-1943 Park
Arthur Lee s/o Thos & A J 16 Dec 1894-27 July 1895 Hick
Betsey w/o R W 16 Nov 1842-13 Feb 1919 Park
Bettie L (w/o R C) 2 Sept 1866-7 Jan 1949 StGe
Blanche B (w/o L D) 1886-1971 Fair
C Blanche w/o G R 1899-1979 Libe
C Kenny (h/o E F) 1889-1962 Fair
Carrie W w/o R H 1902- Park
Charles D (h/o M F) 26 July 1864-17 Feb 1936 Holl
Clarence F h/o M W 1893-1968 Libe
Clarence T 1908-1961 StGe
Claude Douglas 6 Apr 1874-24 Dec 1916 Edge
Claude M (h/o A M) 1918-1969 Onan
Custus D 1912-1959 Fair
E Lee 1870-1940 Edge
Edith F (w/o C K) 1896-1965 Fair
Edward H h/o Ann d 5 Nov 1896; age: 83/7/23 Mitc-e
Edward O'Brion h/o E M 1877-1932 Edge
Edward T h/o S E 10 Aug 1852-2 June 1916 Edge
Edward T h/o A L H; s/o Jno E & Matilda D 1878-1945 Park
Elijah s/o Edwd & Sally 10 Aug 1827-13 Feb 1901 Edge
Elijah W 1868-1930 Park
Elizabeth C 1893-1959 Edge
Elizabeth G w/o S R 1893- Onan
Elizabeth S 1872-1968 Edge
Ella W 1854-1933 Edge
Eudie S 7 Oct 1868-13 Apr 1948 Edge
Eulalia M w/o E O 1878-1957 Edge
Eva May w/o J H 1875-1971 Edge
Fitzhugh Lee s/o G D & M C 1 Dec 1885-20 Sept 1897 Holl

HICKMAN (continued)
Florence S d/o G D & M C 18 Sept 1896-10 Feb 1907 Holl
G Fletcher h/o I G 1895-1969 Park
George 11 Feb 1834-4 Jan 1892 Onan
George 1930-1983 Park
George D (h/o M C) 1862-1947 Holl
George E s/o Geo W & Margt E 28 Feb-22 Nov 1914 Holl
George R h/o C B 1894-1980 Libe
George T (h/o M K) 1867-1941 Holl
Georgie w/o R T d 4 Apr 1904; age: 37 yrs Crad
Hattie Killmon 1881-1961 Holl
Henrietta A (w/o W H) 1871-1934 MtHo-s
Herbert D 25 June 1881-14 Apr 1916 Edge
Ida G w/o G F 1892- Park
India A (w/o J L) 29 July 1866-7 Oct 1957 Onan
Irene A w/o J H 1937- Park
J Hampton h/o E M 1875-1930 Edge
J L (h/o I A) 17 Nov 1868-23 Mar 1903 Onan
J R h/o Adaline 12 Jan 1835-19 Apr 1915 Edge
James Edward s/o E W & V J 3 Mar 1876-4 Apr 1894 Edge
James H h/o I A 1933-1979 Park
James M h/o M J 1863-1949 Onan
James R 1907-1976 Park
Jewel S w/o Wm T 16 Feb 1891-5 May 1964 Park
Jimmy s/o Stanford & Reva 2 Feb 1935-4 Mar 1941 Park
John E 1890-1949 MtHo-s
John T 1891-1957 Fair
John W w/o M W J 1878-1950 Park
Johnnie W s/o S E & L E b&d 20 Mar 1893 Park
Joseph H w/o M J 6 Feb 1837-7 Feb 1911 Crad
Joseph H h/o M M 1890-1974

HICKMAN (continued)
MtHo
Judson C h/o A L 1865-1914 Park
Judson C Jr 1905-1971 Park
L Richard h/o L C 1881-1957 Park
Laura E w/o S E 3 May 1874-12 July 1927 Park
Lee 1924-1966 Wach
Lillian H w/o T B 1900-1981 Libe
Lillian May d/o Robt & Georgie 6 June 1898-26 Oct 1899 Crad
Lizzie 1841-1912 Holl
Lois M w/o A T 1884-1962 Park
Lonnie D (h/o B B) 1883-1958 Fair
Lorraine 1934-1943 Fair
Lucretia 7 May 1832-18 Mar 1895 Onan
Lula C w/o L R 1882-1956 Park
Mabel G d/o J H & M M 15 Dec 1915-17 June 1916 MtHo
Mahlon s/o H J & E M 1 June 1901-5 Aug 1902 Edge
Mamie J w/o J M 1873-1962 Onan
Manie C (w/o G D) 1860-1935 Holl
Margaret W w/o C F 1895- Libe
Mary E w/o W H 1 Aug 1843-16 July 1908 Hick
Mary J 1871-1941 Park
Mary Jennie w/o J H d 21 Apr 1898; age: c65 yrs Crad
Mary K (w/o G T) 1874-1964 Holl
Mary V 1849-1924 Park
Mary W Johnson w/o J W 1887-1930 Park
Melinda F (nee Charnock) 10 Oct 1861-6 Apr 1943 Holl
Mervin T Sr 1903-1984 Park
Milford H h/o S W 1888-1963 Park
Minnie B 1885-1979 Park
Minnie M w/o J H 1890-1936 MtHo
Mollie S w/o R W 1869-1943 Park
Nannie Lee d/o Geo D & Mamie

HICKMAN (continued)
C 11-27 Jan 1898 Holl
Neual L D s/o L D & S B 30 May 1906-3 Oct 1907 Holl
Norman J s/o J M & M J 28 Jan 1909-14 Feb 1921 Onan
Oswald R 1877-1965 Holl
Pearl E (w/o T U) d 1980 Onan
Percy L 21 Nov 1898-12 Aug 1899 Lawr
Randall C (h/o B L) 1 May 1871-29 Jan 1961 StGe
Randall G (h/o R A) 1899-1945 StGe
Rebecca Ames (w/o R G) 1902-1963 StGe
Richard Edward 1906-1976 Edge
Robert H h/o C W 1900-1964 Park
Robert T 25 Feb 1866-13 Aug 1934 MtHo
Robert T s/o R T & Annie M 2 July-17 Oct 1912 MtHo
Robert W h/o Betsey 9 Mar 1841-14 Nov 1927 Park
Robert W h/o M S 1869-1956 Park
Sallie E 18 Apr 1863-28 Aug 1937 Libe
Samuel E h/o L E 1871-1946 Park
Sarah E w/o E T 1846-1922 Edge
Severn C s/o Geo W & Margt E 28 Feb-22 Nov 1914 Holl
Spencer R h/o E G 1889-1959 Onan
Stella W w/o M H 1889-1966 Park
Teakle U (h/o P E) 1881-1951 Onan
Thomas J 1912-1957 MtHo
Thomas S h/o A J 1861-1928 Hick
Tommie B h/o L H 1896-1967 Libe
Ulva P 18 Feb 1896-2 Nov 1976 MtHo
Viola J 17 Mar 1845-22 Feb 1903 Edge
W Fletcher 7 July 1919-22 Feb 1978 Wach
Willard S 1922-1958 Edge

HICKMAN (continued)
Willard T s/o E T & Annie L 1901-1922 Park
William 1921-1962 Wach
William B 19 Oct 1900-3 May 1965 Edge
William H h/o M E 10 Jan 1830-30 Oct 1893 Hick
William H (h/o H A) 1872-1948 MtHo-s
William P s/o E T & S E 6 Mar 1878-23 Sept 1894 Edge
William T 1857-1931 Park
William T h/o J S 12 July 1890-1 Oct 1970 Park
William T Jr 1921-1952 Park
HICKS, Amanda E w/o C K d 27 Aug 1976 Park
Bertha Johnson (w/o G S) 13 Apr 1901- Fair
Charles K h/o A E d 6 Oct 1959 Park
Guy Steele (h/o B J) 14 Aug 1902-28 Apr 1982 Fair
Hattie M 1868-1962 Snea
HIDEN, Ellen w/o J H; d/o Henry & Adelaide Rogers Battaile 16 June 1868-4 Aug 1964 Onan
Joseph H (MD) h/o E B; s/o Rev Jas Conway & Elizabeth Chewning Hiden of Orange Co 6 Jan 1866-10 Sept 1937 Onan
Suzette Rogers d/o J H & N B 10 Oct-12 Nov 1893 Onan
HIGGINS, Elizabeth B d/o M H Jr & M P nd Edge
Emory P 1844-1930 Edge
Harriet B 1850-1949 Edge
Marianna P w/o M H Jr 1824-1881 Edge
Marianna P 1865-1938 Edge
Mary Ann 1816-1894 Edge
Mary Hack w/o M H Sr nd Edge
Mary Hack d/o M H Jr & M P nd Edge
Michael H Sr h/o Mary nd Edge
Michael H Jr h/o M P 1819-1896 Edge
Nathaniel B d 1888 Edge
HIGH, Annie H d 29 May 1966; age: 44 yrs Metr
HILDRETH, Raymond b&d 1981

HILDRETH (continued)
MtHo
HILL, Bunie M 1870-1918 Park
Elizabeth V 1874-1961 Park
Geraldine 1939-1959 MeNe
James nd MtNe
John H 1880-1957 Park
Robert J 1877-1949 Onan
Robert J 1936-1967 MtNe
Ryland M 1909-1962 Park
Sarah Belote w/o J Fred d 7 Apr 1902 MtHo
William 1910-1968 Metr
William Byrd s/o Rev Chas & Susan d 8 Sept 1853; age: 1/0/23 Coke
HILLER, Florence M 1898- MtHo-s
HILLMAN, Annie L w/o R W 1901-1979 Libe
Reginald W h/o A L 1900-1969 Libe
HILTON, James nd Shil
HINES, Harry Cecil 23 May 1917-15 Mar 1977 Fair
Harry E (h/o L P) 1889-1975 Fair
Laura P (w/o H E) 1893-1967 Fair
HINMAN, A Milford 1905-1970 Park
Alma F w/o T L 1885-1970 Park
Annie V w/o G F 3 Apr 1867-19 Oct 1941 Libe
Asher S 1880-1940 Libe
Cora J w/o Jno S d 9 Sept 1902; age: 71 yrs Libe
E Bernard s/o E D & M A 27 Feb 1885-18 Feb 1923 Park
Edward P 1889-1979 Libe
Elizabeth w/o Jno R 1 May 1816-23 Aug 1895 Park
Elizabeth E w/o Wm P 27 Oct 1828-19 Aug 1877 Libe
Elizabeth J w/o L F 26 Oct 1849-3 Aug 1929 Park
Emory D h/o M A 21 June 1863-29 Aug 1936 Park
Estelle E w/o F E 1917- Park
Florence C 1891-1960 Park
Franklin E h/o E E 1918-1970 Park

HINMAN (continued)
George F h/o A V 5 May 1853-10 May 1924 Libe
Irving G 10 July 1887-19 Jan 1946 Park
John R 21 Dec 1840-20 Dec 1901 Libe
L J h/o L L 9 Jan 1872-21 Dec 1941 Park
Laurah L w/o L J 27 Dec 1873-27 May 1938 Park
Louis F h/o E J 7 Oct 1851-6 Aug 1912 Park
Malissa Mae d/o F E & E E 1944-1951 Park
Martha A w/o E D 28 Sept 1865-25 Jan 1939 Park
Mary E w/o Jno S d 26 Apr 1941; age: 71 yrs Libe
Melissa M 1881-1964 Park
Meryle D 21 July 1904-28 May 1955 Park
Mitchell J h/o V H 1898-1965 Park
Nona K 1907- Park
Olive P w/o E B 16 Jan 1893-23 May 1973 Park
Susan J 1844-1934 Libe
Thelma G d/o L J & L L 2 Aug 1911-17 July 1918 Park
Thomas L h/o A F 1879-1942 Park
Virgie H w/o M J 1909- Park
HITE, Samuel J 21 June-18 Oct 1928 Libe
HOBBS, Letty M w/o R J 1905-1954 Park
Raleigh J h/o L M 1902-1983 Park
HOCKENSMITH, Anna F (w/o G I) 1890-1967 Fair
George I (h/o A F) 1887-1951 Fair
HODGES, Sarah W w/o Wm 3 Dec 1818-23 July 1903 Onan
William h/o S W d 2 May 1904; age: 81 yrs Onan
HOENSHEL, Audrey G White 1904-1968 MtHo
HOFFMAN, Annabelle 1915-1962 Snea
Harriet Ann (2nd w/o W G) 1849-

HOFFMAN (continued)
1916 Roge
Dr John G (s/o W G& H A) 1875-1903 Roge
Maggie D w/o J W; d/o E H & Mary Killmon 3 May 1867-18 Jan 1893 Kilb
Maudie A d/o Snead & Margt C 25 Sept 1891-26 July 1897 StGe
Snead 5 Oct 1845-21 Nov 1894 StGe
W Griffin (h/o H A) 1827-1916 Roge
HOKE, Dorothy Mears 1916-1962 Burt
HOLLAND, Addie R w/o G L 1875-1955 Edge
Alice B Cropper (w/o W S) 1854-1923 Onan
Archie D 22 June 1899-24 Nov 1960 Edge
George Everett (h/o L K) 1923-1968 Edge
George Lee h/o A R 1883-1959 Edge
George W h/o H W 1854-1934 Edge
George W h/o M D 1925-1979 Park
Hannah W w/o G W 1858-1915 Edge
Hattie L 1888-1952 Edge
Ida Mae 1881-1957 Libe
James d 29 Jan 1966; age: 85 yrs Metr
John D 1882-1936 Libe
John W h/o S E 30 Nov 1843-4 Oct 1918 Libe
John W Kenzie (h/o M W) 1878-1973 Onan
Lula G w/o W D 6 Feb 1890- Edge
Mildred D w/o G W 1917- Park
Millard F (h/o P C) 1896-1955 Edge
Minnie Ward (w/o J W K) 1882-1970 Onan
Pearl C (w/o M F) 1896-1975 Edge
R Paige 1930-1970 Park
Roley Lee 24 May 1922-28 Sept

HOLLAND (continued)
1976 Edge
Roley T 1885-1935 Edge
Samuel H h/o V C 18 Mar 1857-14 Mar 1914 Edge
Samuel H 1888-1955 Edge
Sarah E w/o J W 3 Feb 1844-23 Jan 1921 Libe
Vernon T 1916-1958 Edge
Virginia C w/o S H 1852-1945 Edge
W D (h/o L G) 4 Sept 1891-4 Jan 1939 Edge
William S 1877-1957 Libe
William Sewell (h/o A B C) 1850-1913 Onan
HOLLAWAY, (HOLLOWAY),
Billie June 1939-1982 Edge
Eliza d 7 June 1964; age: 82 yrs NewM
Gary J b&d 17 Jan 1976 Edge
HOLLIS, Benjamin E 1835-1896 BurJ
Mary S 1847-1922 BurJ
HOLLOMAN, John M 1924-1961 Shil
HOLMES, Duffy 1964-1980 Holm
HOLT, Ann T w/o Jas; d/o Geo T & Leah Mapp 1 Oct 1809-3 May 1836; age: 25 yrs Mars
Capt Eldred R (1st hus/o Elizabeth E Colonna Holt Jones) 18 Jan 1816-13 Oct 1869 Wate
Margaret A w/o Edwd E 11 Dec 1826-14 Aug 1900 StGe
HOOD, Ruth B 19 Sept 1900-1 Feb 1982 Fair
HOOPER, Lewis O 1906-1978 Fair
HOPE, Alfred T 7 Aug 1879-21 Sept 1921 Park
Arinthia C w/o S H 1859-1935 Park
George B h/o M W 1883-1966 Park
George C 1909-1959 Park
James F h/o M A; s/o Wm S & Jane 3 Nov 1856-31 July 1928 Wach
John Bable h/o S G 3 Nov 1873-29 May 1936 Park
John F h/o M E 25 Apr 1851-31

HOPE (continued)
Oct 1915 Park
John T 1880-1930 Park
Lafayette F 2 June 1894-6 June 1967 Park
Louisa Parramore 4 July 1878-24 Feb 1949 (Faithful servant to be put here when dead. Wait!) Runn
Lula K 1889-1945 Park
M Eloise 1917-1939 Park
Maggie A w/o J F; d/o Jas T & Bette G Mapp 28 Nov 1862-13 May 1946 Wach
Mary E w/o J F 22 Jan 1858-8 Sept 1939 Park
Mary Watts 1860-1932 Park
Mary West w/o G B 1888-1976 Park
Maude V d/o J F & M E 20 Aug 1896-9 May 1957 Park
S H h/o A C 1855-1919 Park
Sarah Grace w/o J B 24 Sept 1873-27 Jan 1951 Park
William Laws 1849-1935 Park
William P 1878-1947 Park
HOPKINS, inf/o G E & E S nd MtHo
inf/o Jno R & Bettie S nd Bulp
s/o J J & A A b&d 6 Apr 1898 MtHo
inf/o G E & E S b&d 28 Nov 1908 MtHo
s/o C T & Louise W b&d 5 May 1914 Libe
A Stephen h/o A S 17 June 1888-10 Dec 1943 Libe
Adaline, 1st w/o J J 20 May 1845-27 Aug 1893 MtHo
Addison Finney s/o T S & L A 1900-1971 Onan
Albert A s/o Stephen & Alicia A C 27 Dec 1880-9 Aug 1881 Onan
Alfred J 1900-1961 (moved from Wach Cem) Park
ALfred J L 23 Jan 1886-20 Nov 1890 Onan
Alice d/o E W & B W 1 July 1878-24 July 1879 Onan
Alicia A C 1845-1936 Onan
Amanda A, 2nd w/o J J 7 Apr

HOPKINS (continued)
1864-5 Apr 1898 MtHo
Annie S d/o F P & Josephine 14 Feb 1883-23 Jan 1884 Holl
Annie S w/o A S 24 May 1890-17 Aug 1971 Libe
Arinthia J (w/o I I) 1851-1928 MtHo
Asher D s/o J J & Adeline 27 Nov 1881-6 Sept 1882 MtHo
Bessie 1888-1976 MtHo
Bessie G w/o J L 1902-1980 Edge
Bessie W w/o E W 6 July 1857-31 Oct 1944 Onan
Betsy w/o Jos 22 Oct 1824-29 Apr 1903 Drut
Bettie E 18 Feb 1843-26 Mar 1908 MtHo
Burleigh W 1881-1970 MtHo-s
Charles T h/o L L 17 Apr 1881-12 Oct 1936 Libe
Charles W h/o M J 30 Nov 1848-29 Sept 1924 Onan
Charles William s/o Jno P L & Susan C 5 May-20 Oct 1873 FinP
Cora W w/o H G Sr 1900- MtHo
Cornelia E (w/o W H) 12 Aug 1851-2 Feb 1930 Edge
Doris A d/o G E & E S 28 Nov 1902-2 July 1903 MtHo
Dot J w/o G T 1940- Park
Edward W h/o B W 14 July 1854-12 Dec 1903 Onan
Elizabeth w/o J H 1858-1949 MtHo
Elizabeth (w/o O B) 14 Dec 1867-13 Feb 1960 Onan
Elizabeth Susan 1870-1953 MtHo-s
Ella C (w/o O L) 1897- Fair
Ellison Armistead 1808-1887 StGe
Elmer H 1904-1959 Holl
Eva Sarah w/o G E 1878-1915 MtHo
Evelyn Roberts w/o J P L 13 Oct 1866-29 Jan 1950 Onan
Fannie E w/o O R 1888-1981 Edge
Frank P h/o Josephine 19 Apr

HOPKINS (continued)
1857-4 Jan 1931 Holl
George E h/o E S 1873-1944 MtHo
George H 1890-1959 Holl
George S s/o S D & G E 19 Oct 1888-5 Oct 1889 Onan
Georgie P w/o S D 7 Jan 1862-18 July 1946 Onan
Glenn T h/o D J 1934-1973 Park
Harry Allen 1 Aug 1875-9 Sept 1928 Onan
Hazel T 1888-1937 StGe
Helen 1938-1977 MtHo-s
Herman G Sr h/o C W 1900-1981 MtHo
Ira I (h/o A J) 1848-1923 MtHo
J W M 21 July 1832-26 Oct 1899 StGe
James 1901-1940 Snea
James A 27 Feb 1891-5 Dec 1955 StGe
James F h/o S J 1885-1948 Holl
Jane Deeble 1810-1891 StGe
John H h/o Elizabeth 1845-1923 MtHo
John H h/o U T 23 Sept 1858-4 Oct 1939 Libe
John H h/o Catholene T 1916-1979 Park
John Herbert Lee s/o J H & U T 23 Aug 1882-22 Nov 1886 Libe
John J h/o Adeline & Amanda A 10 Jan 1844-10 Aug 1899 MtHo
John L h/o B G 1892-1955 Edge
John Parker Lee w/o E R; s/o Stephen & Jane (Melson) 6 Apr 1830-2 Dec 1913 Onan
John Parker Lee s/o J P L & E R 1 July 1889-9 Feb 1909 Onan
John R 1868-1929 MtHo
Joseph h/o Betsy; s/o Henry & Polly H 18 Oct 1812-28 May 1892 Drut
Joseph I h/o K F 1850-1928 MtHo
Josephine w/o F P 21 Sept 1859-16 Sept 1951 Holl
Julia T, 2nd w/o C W 1 Jan 1845-30 Dec 1927 Onan
Julia T w/o S J; d/o W R & S J

HOPKINS (continued)
Lewis 26 Dec 1865-25 May 1934 Onan
Keturah E w/o Wm H A d 11 Feb 1866; age: 33 yrs Onan
Kizziah F w/o J I 1856-1925 MtHo
Laura H 4 Mar 1833-9 July 1902 StGe
Laura H Everett (w/o W H) 1885-1963 StGe
Leila Powell w/o S U 1873-1958 Onan
Lena S w/o F W 24 Feb 1872-21 Jan 1903 MtHo
Levin L 8 May 1856-5 Feb 1911 Wach
Lillian D 1893-1977 Holl
Louise L w/o C T 1 Apr 1883-22 June 1966 Libe
Lucille Addison w/o T S 1878-1942 Onan
Madeline S d/o G E & E S 8 Nov 1901-11 July 1902 MtHo
Maggie Finney d/o S J & J T L 4 Dec 1897-10 Aug 1950 Onan
Marcia L w/o Sydney J 28 Apr 1866-23 Feb 1887 FinP
Marcie S d/o S J & Marcie 13 Feb-23 Aug 1887 FinP
Marie S w/o W E 4 Mar 1890-2 Sept 1973 Onan
Mary Johnson 22 Oct 1843-3 Dec 1926 Onan
Minervia J, 1st w/o C W 11 June 1853-22 Mar 1891 Onan
O Lloyd (h/o E C) 1894-1949 Fair
Oscar R h/o F E 1884-1967 Edge
Oswald B (h/o Elizabeth) 29 June 1870-12 Mar 1949 Onan
Pansy R 1912- (moved from Wach Cem) Park
Powell s/o S U & L P 1899-1936 Onan
Ralph Elwood 1897-1969 Wach
Ralph T 1917-1972 Edge
Robert Lee h/o S F 1860-1922 Onan
Robert W 1902- Park
Sallie d/o J P L & S C 20 Sept 1860-25 Sept 1877 FinP

HOPKINS (continued)
Sallie J w/o J F 1884-1961 Holl
Sallie Virginia 1862-1915 StGe
Sarah A w/o Jno I 6 Oct 1822-14 June 1896 MtHo
Sidney J h/o J T; s/o J P L & Susan (Finney) 19 June 1862-5 May 1938 Onan
Spencer D w/o G P; s/o Jno P & Susan C 8 Oct 1864-11 Apr 1891 Onan
Stephen 17 Dec 1792-17 Aug 1870 Poul
Stephen s/o Stephen & Jane 5 Jan 1836-14 Feb 1888 Onan
Stephen Upshur h/o L P 1872-1945 Onan
Susan C w/o J P L; d/o T W & Sallie Finney 3 July 1832-8 Dec 1880 FinP
Susan C d/o J P L & S 24 Jan-10 July 1872 FinP
Susie Fitchett w/o R L 1862-1922 Onan
Thomas Stephen h/o L A 1866-1942 Onan
Tommy s/o F P & Josephine 4 Aug-12 Oct 1900 Holl
Ursula T w/o J H 22 Oct 1858-30 Mar 1933 Libe
Vernon E 1921-1971 Fair
Virginia Willis d/o T S & L A 1905-1964 Onan
Willard Dize 1918-1919 Holl
William Edward h/o Marie Warfield Stinson; s/o E W & B W 14 Apr 1880-3 Sept 1936 Onan
William Ellyson 1861-1923 StGe
William Fitchett s/o R L & S F 30 Sept 1888-6 Mar 1936 Onan
William H (h/o C E) 26 Jan 1841-8 Oct 1911 Edge
William H (h/o L H E) 1887-1962 StGe
William H A h/o K E 12 Aug 1824-15 May 1884 Onan
William H Finney s/o J P L & Susan C 24 Jan-10 July 1872 FinP
HORNER, Louise T w/o P G 1909- Libe
Philip G h/o L T 1909-1973 Libe

HORNER (continued)
Reba Carmine (w/o R O) 10 Sept 1902- MtHo-s
Rupert O (h/o R C) 28 Sept 1900-9 Apr 1970 MtHo-s
Stanley K s/o S K & Katharine b&d 8 Feb 1937 MtHo-s
HORNSBY, baby girl b&d 1908 StGe
baby boy b&d 1923 StGe
Abel Lee (h/o M J) 29 Jan 1865-18 Mar 1940 StGe
Bettie M (w/o J T) 1877-1953 StGe
Clara E 1864-1952 Wach
George W 1885-1973 Wach
James H h/o Elizabeth B 1820-1893 (stone not located - ref: Mears) Syca
John T (h/o B M) 1879-1959 StGe
Major (h/o Susannah) d 15 Aug 1809; age: 53 yrs Walk
Martha J w/o A L 1865-1928 StGe
Melvina (Millie) 1884-1961 Wach
Millie W 1884-1961 Wach
Rosey Townsend d/o Major & Susannah d Jan 1815 Walk
Susannah w/o Major d 30 Mar 1829 Walk
Susannah d/o Major & Susannah 22 Apr 1795-22 Sept 1845 Walk
HORSEY, Adam Mar 1970-May 1982 MtHo-s
Dorothy S 1934-1963 Burt
Eddie d 16 Oct 1970; age: 63/7/0 Burt
Ella 1884-1956 Burt
Leola S w/o N E 5 May 1909-7 Apr 1979 MtHo-s
Norman E h/o L S 10 July 1907-16 Oct 1982 MtHo-s
HOWARD, inf/o R A & Rebecca C b&d 1910 Libe
Alma S 1904- Libe
Annie M 1887-1973 Libe
Carrie J w/o W H 1874-1934 Libe
Edward H h/o S B 1873-1957

HOWARD (continued) Park
Edward H h/o O H 1879-1953 Libe
Elizabeth G 1903-1976 Park
Ella Nora w/o L D 20 Nov 1865-3 Aug 1946 Libe
Evelyn R 1872-1915 Libe
J Milton h/o T E 23 Dec 1890-5 May 1969 Edge
Janet Lynne d/o E J & Jean 14 June-8 Nov 1949 Park
John W 1904-1971 Libe
L Ayres 1915-1945 Libe
Louis D h/o E N 18 Nov 1867-26 Sept 1932 Libe
Mary E w/o Capt Wm H 7 Mar 1845-10 Jan 1909 Libe
Ola H w/o E H 1884-1956 Libe
Rebecca C 1884-1958 Libe
Roland A 1878-1962 Libe
Sadie B w/o E H 1877-1969 Park
Thelma E w/o J M 11 Jan 1909- Edge
Viola B 1908- Libe
Walter S 1902-1974 Libe
Webster H h/o C J 1872-1965 Libe
William H h/o M E 20 Nov 1834-20 Jan 1929 Libe
William H 1870-1971 Libe
HUBBARD, A Joseph 1963 MtHo-s
Margt M 1974 MtHo-s
HUCKSTEP, Charles T 9 Dec 1898-14 May 1971 Park
HUDDEN, Gertrude 1926-1946 Burt
HUDSON, Annie W w/o J T 1898-1960 Gask-old
Edward S s/o Martin & Mary 12 Dec 1910-23 Dec 1934 Wach
Edward W 1904-1980 Wach
Eva T w/o G E 1880-1944 Park
George E h/o E T 1872-1931 Park
Hattie L 1902-1975 Metr
J Thomas h/o A W 1890-19?? Gask-old
Laymond 3 Dec 1903-10 Sept 1958 StPa
Mrs Mary M 1917-1964 JoyC

HUDSON (continued)
Miriam F 1906- Wach
Peggy Anne d/o C C & Velma A 1936-1961 Park
Sadie 1922-1983 Metr
HUFFMAN, Alfred Jr 6 June 1929-23 Mar 1980 Fair
John D 9 Sept 1898-11 Sept 1971 Park
Irene Evans 11 Oct 1904-22 May 1983 Fair
HUGHES, Bertie d/o Eva S Lewis 1901-1978 Park
E Howard 1888-1969 Park
Edgar H 1912-1979 Park
Esma M 1890-1956 Park
Mae J 1911-1980 Park
Ruth M 12 Aug 1909-4 Sept 1978 MtHo-s
HUGHEY, Joseph V 1899-1980 Park
HUME, Andrew E 21 May 1873-10 Sept 1894; age: 21 yrs Wach
Andrew W 1 May 1840-8 Jan 1909 (b Plymouth England) Wach
Elizabeth A 10 Sept 1838-13 June 1894; age: 56 yrs (b London England) Wach
HUNDLEY, Arzie J 12 Oct 1896-7 July 1969 Onan
Brenda S b&d 1952 Onan
Elizabeth C 26 Oct 1897- Onan
Elizabeth H (w/o R L) 1922- Fair
Irene C (w/o J W) 1913- MtHo-s
J William (h/o I C) 1910-1967 MtHo-s
John T (h/o R C) 1872-1938 MtHo-s
Racelia C (w/o J T) 1874-1949 MtHo-s
Ray L (h/o E H) 1916-1983 Fair
HUNT, Etta d 24 Mar 1956; age: 50 yrs Burt
Mannie C 1887-1961 Onan
Mitchell J 4 June 1858-16 Jan 1929 Onan
Tennie E 1862-1932 MtHo-s
HURDLE, - s/o J M & M S b&d 1918 Park

HURDLE (continued)
J Thomas s/o J M & M S 1925-1930 Park
John M h/o M S 1896-1965 Park
Mary S w/o J M 1896-1979 Park
HURLEY, Maude W w/o Vyrd 1891-1982 Libe
Vyrd h/o M W 1886-1971 Libe
HURST, - s/o J W & Joanna b&d 23 Dec 1878 Onan
Alfred J 1875-1934 MtHo
B F 23 Nov 1877-27 Dec 1944 MtHo
Betty Ann 8 Apr 1939-23 Aug 1941 MtHo-s
Blanche L 1898-1928 Libe
Carlton H (h/o M L) 6 June 1896-2 May 1966 Onan
Carrye J w/o H E 1884-1974 MtHo
Catherine d/o Thos & S C 16 Mar 1819-6 July 1850 Onan
Charles L Sr h/o M C 1874-1953 Libe
Charles L Jr 1913-1973 Libe
Elizabeth W w/o G C 1883-1964 Onan
Emory B h/o M L 1875-1954 Onan
Grover C h/o E W 1884-1971 Onan
Harriet A w/o J T 5 Nov 1841-7 June 1909 Libe
Harry E h/o C J 1881-1954 MtHo
Henrietta Read 30 July 1918-31 Aug 1920 Fair
I Mitchell 1906-1952 Libe
Ira (MD) 27 Feb 1880-28 Mar 1937) Fair
Ira Jr 24-30 June 1921 Fair
J Frank 1901-1932 Libe
James T h/o H A 1 Jan 1838-7 Feb 1902 Libe
James T 6 Dec 1896-7 Apr 1923 Libe
Jesse J 1 Dec 1877-3 Oct 1922 Libe
Joanna w/o J W 13 Aug 1854-22 Oct 1938 Onan
John h/o Mary; s/o Thos & Susan 15 Sept 1821-23 Dec 1898 Onan

HURST (continued)
John W h/o Joanna 12 Aug 1852-31 Dec 1930 Onan
Maggie I d/o J T & H A d 8 July 1876; age: 12/8/14 Libe
Manie C w/o C L Sr 1877-1954 Libe
Manie L w/o E B 1877-1957 Onan
Martin L h/o P H 13 Aug 1854-25 Sept 1915 Onan
Mary w/o Jno 5 Nov 1826-6 Feb 1911 Onan
Mary Ellen w/o Wm 7 May 1818-31 Oct 1914 MtHo
Mary Lee (w/o C H) 1905- Onan
Peggie H w/o M L 13 June 1861-1 July 1947 Onan
Sarah 7 July 1817-4 Sept 1849 Onan
Sis E d/o T E & Susan 18 Apr 1879-26 Apr 1914 MtHo
Sue w/o T E 1 Jan 1857-4 Dec 1912 MtHo
Susan C w/o Thos 4 Oct 1789-13 June 1869 Onan
Tabitha 8 May 1815-25 Mar 1870 Onan
Thomas s/o Thos & Susan 10 Aug 1778-6 May 1854 Onan
Thomas h/o S C 3 June 1782-1 May 1850 Onan
Thomas s/o Jno 5 Sept 1857-10 May 1860 Onan
Tullie E h/o Sue 1849-1927 MtHo
William h/o M E; s/o Thos & Susan 4 Oct 1807-30 July 1874 MtHo
William O 5 Aug 1886-16 Aug 1931 MtHo
HUSSEY, Alice w/o Wm F 1879-1960 Edge
William F h/o Alice 1878-1952 Edge
HUTCHINSON, inf d/o J E & A T b&d 18 Nov 1910 StGe
Albert M 27 May 1882-26 Nov 1902 StGe
Ann w/o Zerabable 17 Mar 1771-10 Jan 1848 Hutg
Annie T (w/o J E) 1877-1955

HUTCHINSON (continued) StGe
B Clyde (h/o S M) 15 Apr 1893-1 July 1963 Onan
Benjamin D h/o E S 21 Feb 1864-22 Sept 1927 StGe
C Sydney s/o C R & J R 3 July 1902-16 Oct 1918 MtHo
Caroline E w/o E W 25 Sept 1829-1 Mar 1900; age: 70/6/25 Stur
Carroll D (h/o F M) 1887-1957 StGe
Catherine A w/o Jno T 30 May 1837-19 Nov 1909 Hutc
Colie R h/o J R 2 Jan 1874-1 Aug 1952 MtHo
Dorinda Wise w/o J H; (d/o Levin S & Ann Priscilla Hornsby Ames) 22 Sept 1829-27 July 1921 Hutc
Capt Edward W (h/o C E); s/o Edmd & Eliz 23 Feb 1818-19 Sept 1886 Stur
Elizabeth Davis w/o L S 8 Aug 1906- StGe
Elizabeth H (w/o W L) 7 Apr 1858-12 May 1927 StGe
Emma Fairbanks w/o Jno W 19 Mar 1870-23 June 1907 Hutc
Emma S w/o B D 6 Aug 1867-28 Sept 1923 StGe
Florence F w/o O L 10 Dec 1865-8 Sept 1924 StGe
Frieda M w/o C D 1893-1980 StGe
Hanson P s/o Zerabable & Ann 9 Dec 1814-12 Apr 1855 Hutg
Harriet E 1867-1943 Hutc
Harriet T w/o J W; d/o Levi & Euphaney Rogers 25 Oct 1804-9 Aug 1888 Hutc
J R 1864-1930 Hutc
James A (h/o M L) 22 June 1878-24 May 1922 StGe
James H (h/o D W; s/o J W & H T) 17 Mar 1825-28 Nov 1894 Hutc
Jennie R w/o C R 19 Dec 1876-10 Feb 1966 MtHo
John T s/o J W & H T 23 Dec 1826-16 Apr 1899 Hutc

HUTCHINSON (continued)
John T h/o W M 10 Feb 1910- StGe
John W h/o N G; s/o J T & C A 11 Mar 1862-20 July 1919 MtHo
John W s/o Levi & Dorothy 16 Mar 1798-26 June 1864; age: 66/3/10 Hutc
Joseph E (h/o A T) 1879-1949 StGe
Joseph R s/o J W & H T 24 Sept 1833-17 July 1863; age: 29/9/16 Hutc
Joseph Riley 10 Sept 1920-26 Aug 1941 StGe
Joseph Theodore 6 May 1922-15 Sept 1958 HTri
Josie M w/o O L 26 May 1870-1 Dec 1962 StGe
Lee Core w/o T M 1866-1951 MtHo
Leonard Sturgis h/o E D 4 Dec 1904-7 Jan 1981 StGe
Lucy A d/o J W & H T 1 Aug 1838-14 May 1898 Hutc
Lydia 1909-1939 HTri
Maggie B d/o J A & M L 29 June-20 Oct 1902 StGe
Maggie L w/o J A 10 May 1880-8 Sept 1935 StGe
Manie 1 Feb 1891-18 Jan 1978 HTri
Mary E Catheryn w/o O L 26 Sept 1865-8 Aug 1887 Hutc
May Gilden w/o W E 25 Feb 1882-14 Jan 1972 Onan
Melissa F 7 Aug 1851-27 Mar 1911 Wach
Melvin R 1898-1969 StGe
Missouri B (w/o R J) 15 Nov 1899-2 Sept 1977 StGe
Nellie G w/o J W 1874-1927 MtHo
Oswald s/o J W & H T 20 Sept 1841-23 Sept 1848; age: 7/0/3 Hutc
Oswald L (h/o F F) 9 Aug 1862-26 June 1930 StGe
Raymond M 1918-1966 Fair
Raymond R s/o J W & H T 24 Feb 1829-19 Oct 1901 Hutc

HUTCHINSON (continued)
Raymond R 19 Apr 1889-20 June 1954 StGe
Roger J (h/o M B) 2 May 1900- StGe
Sadie Mears (w/o B C) 24 Feb 1896- Onan
Susan B w/o R R 12 Sept 1845-30 Apr 1922 Hutc
Susan Rebecca (d/o J W & H T) 1846-1925 Hutc
Thomas M h/o L C 1869-1960 MtHo
W Elmer Jr s/o W E & M G 5 July-24 Oct 1905 Onan
Warner s/o T M & L C 4 Nov 1894-5 Feb 1915 MtHo
William Elmer h/o M G 2 Feb 1885-29 Apr 1941 Onan
William L (h/o E H) 7 Aug 1857-4 Mar 1937 StGe
William S s/o J W & H T 3 Aug 1831-21 Oct 1852 (Inhumanly assasinated in Baltimore); age: 21/2/18 Hutc
Willye M w/o J T 27 July 1911- StGe

HYSLUP, (HYSLOP),
inf/o J W & Mollie b&d 14 Dec 1867 Colo
Bettie S w/o L J; d/o Chas T & Mary J Sturgis 18 Oct 1846-15 Nov 1887; age: 41/0/27 Hysl
Betty S d/o F S & M E b&d 1 Jan 1905 Oakg
Clara F w/o G T 1876-1958 Oakg
E Sudie d/o L J & B S 25 Oct 1867-19 Oct 1886; age: 18/11/24 Hysl
Edwin 1902-1941 Oakg
Edwin J Jr 21 Feb 1927-24 June 1977 Oakg
Elizabeth A d/o J W & Mary R 20 Aug 1835-23 Oct 1836 Ames
Frank S h/o M E 1880-1969 Oakg
George T h/o C F 1871-1939 Oakg
George W 20 Sept 1841-13 Mar 1918 Hysp
James s/o Levin & Susan 17 May 1799-13 Sept 1871 BraH

HYSLUP (continued)
Dr James E s/o G W & M S 9 June 1876-18 May 1903 Hysp
John H s/o Jas & Mary 27 Sept 1835-5 Oct 1871 BraH
John M s/o Dr J E & A E 26 May 1902-9 July 1903 Hysp
John W d 28 Nov 1836; age: 32 yrs Ames
John W S s/o J W & Mary R 20 Aug 1835-30 Mar 1837 Ames
Julietta w/o Smith; d/o Jno W & Margt W Kellam 8 Oct 1829-6 Mar 1871 Bayb
Levin J s/o Jas & Mary 21 Feb 1839-4 Jan 1924 Hysl
Lewellyn F K s/o Smith & J S 10-18 Oct 1869 Bayb
Luther Carlton s/o Geo T & Clara F d 22 Aug 1903; age: 4/5/17 Oakg
Maggie S w/o G W 24 Aug 1856-13 Jan 1901 Hysp
Margaret S d/o Smith & J S 9 May 1856-22 Apr 1863 Bayb
Mary w/o Jas 24 Feb 1802-29 Aug 1870 BraH
Mary B w/o L J 16 July 1851-3 Feb 1910 Hysl
Mary E 13 Sept 1860-15 Nov 1949 BraH
Minnie E w/o F S 1880-1962 Oakg
Smith s/o Smith & Sallie 31 Aug 1840-24 May 1885 Bayb
Smith Sr h/o J S d 5 Feb 1873; age: 70 yrs Bayb
Susannah d 16 Sept 1848 BraH
IRONMONGER, Notre Scott 25 Sept 1904- MtHo
IRVING, Claretta H 1891-1967 Fair
ISDELL, Annie L (w/o B L) 1899- Anth
Annie M (w/o G C) 1889-1978 Anth
Bessie M w/o J E 1888-1967 Wach
Blanche L w/o J E 1912- Libe
Burley L (h/o A L) 1894-1951 Anth
Cleave J 4 Sept 1927-3 Jan 1928

ISDELL (continued) Anth
George Cleave (h/o A M) 1888-1980 Anth
J Ernest h/o B L 1910-1968 Libe
James Edward (h/o M S) 1857-1932 Anth
John E h/o B M 1884-1954 Wach
Margaret Susan w/o J E; d/o Jno & Elizabeth Abrams 5 May 1866-16 June 1913 Anth
Raymond T 1 July 1920-9 Jan 1921 Anth
Robert E b&d 1983 Park
Samuel H 1923-1978 Fair
Samuel Henry Sr (h/o S S) 15 Feb 1891-17 Mar 1957 Quin
Sarah S (w/o S H Sr) 1894-1978 Quin
Tanya Lynn b&d 1981 Park
JACKSON, Bessie May 9 Oct 1924-2 Oct 1925 Snea
Hattie 1901-1970 NewM
John 1876-1947 NewM
Joseph 1896-1980 Park
Tom b NC d 1939; (Negro: noted for his white oak baskets) Dahl
JACOB, see also **JACOBS**,
Bettie Custis 1865-1954 MtHo
Charlotte A B w/o Wm E 24 Mar 1827-2 Sept 1911 Jaco
Edward d 24 Aug 1963; age: 73 yrs Shil
Ella May 1867-1933 Onan
Emma J w/o Geo W 11 June 1856-30 June 1890 Jaco
Everett Clay h/o Ella; s/o Wm B & Sarah d 9 June 1904 Libe
Flora Miller w/o T N 1914-1968 Fair
George Washington h/o E J & M A; s/o Wm E & C A B 18 Mar 1850-18 Nov 1930 Jaco
James C 18 Feb 1865-9 Mar 1920 Onan
Jefferson Davis 1861-1944 MtHo
Jefferson Dunton 1902-1916 MtHo
Margaret Wescott 9 Sept 1894-18 July 1979 Edge
Matilda A w/o G W; d/o Jno S & Ann Walter 19 June 1853-21

JACOB (continued) Nov 1938 Jaco
Thomas Nathaniel Jr DDS h/o F M 1907- Fair
Virginia L d/o H T & Emelie 12 Apr 1885-30 Mar 1886 Jaco
William Custis 1 Jan 1890-11 May 1956 Edge
William E h/o C A B 5 June 1825-21 Aug 1886 Jaco
William Walter s/o G W & M A 15 Jan 1893-11 May 1894 Jaco
JACOBS, Annie M 1898-1978 Shil
Ethel M 1944-1954 NewM
Florence E w/o J E 1887-1968 HTri
John E h/o F E 1884-1968 HTri
Lena Savage d 28 Apr 1950; age: (5?)3 yrs NewM
Margaret A erected by F M Sturgis, wife & children with whom she lived for 17 yrs & performed her duties faithfully nd Shil
JAMES, Abel Thomas h/o S H; s/o T H & T A 22 Mar 1860-31 Jan 1917 MtHo
Alfred Garrison h/o G W 24 Nov 1866-22 Jan 1921 Morr
Alfred W 1858-1943 MtHo
Andrew B s/o Alfred G & Annie P 1909-1976 Wach
Annie L 8 Apr 1919-24 June 1977 NewM
Audrey R d/o T R & D D 29 May 1904-17 July 1905 MtHo
Banie F 1859-1942 MtHo
Burley W 1872-1946 MtHo
Chester D h/o Gertrude; s/o Alfred G & Annie 1906-1947 Wach
Cordie S w/o J T 7 Nov 1843-26 Dec 1916 MtHo
Daisey B D w/o T R 9 June 1878-10 Dec 1955 MtHo
Eliza Beloate w/o L S d 12 July 1870; age: c70 yrs MtHo
Elizabeth K w/o L T 20 Apr 1824-8 May 1871 Leve
Emma w/o Ernest 1910-1981 NewM
Emma Sue (w/o H L) 1884-1954

JAMES (continued)
MtHo
Eon 1904-1961 NewM
Ernest h/o Emma 1904-1980 NewM
Eunice E 1893-1961 MtHo
Fannie C w/o W L 21 Sept 1870-3 Apr 1950 Onan
Florence 1889-1978 Burt
Fred T h/o M E 1886-1942 MtHo
Gazel 13 Mar 1916-17 Oct 1972 NewM
George A s/o G T & V S 11 May-24 Aug 1888 Jame
George T s/o G W & Margt 17 Jan 1861-21 Sept 1891 Jame
George Thomas s/o H L & Alice L 12 Nov 1915-12 Apr 1933 Onan
George W (h/o M A) 22 Mar 1827-2 Apr 1905; age: 78/0/11 Jame
Georgie W w/o A G 30 Sept 1863-4 Feb 1904 Morr
Grayson A 1888-1968 MtHo
Howard Lee (h/o E S) 1885-1966 MtHo
Jesse K h/o V T nd LocM
John H 1856-1946 MtHo
John T h/o C S 10 Feb 1825-14 Feb 1912; age: 87 yrs MtHo
John W s/o L S & E B 4 Feb 1834-15 Apr 1866 MtHo
John W 24 Nov 1855-2 Mar 1922 Jame
Keturah 1889-1975 MtHo
Leven T d 11 Dec 1876; age: 54/10/5 Leve
Levin D (h/o M R) 19 Aug 1896- Onan
Levin S h/o E B d 13 Apr 1845; age: 51/1/4 MtHo
Llewellyn 1860-1941 MtHo
Louise 1841-1926 Burt
Lucile d/o A G & G W 10-17 Dec 1899 Morr
M Sarah d/o A G & G W b&d 21 June 1897 Morr
Maggie d/o L T & E K 28 Feb 1855-30 May 1874; age: 19 yrs Leve
Margaret A w/o G W 6 Sept

JAMES (continued)
1830-22 Oct 1886 Jame
Margaret E w/o F T 1886-1963 MtHo
Margaret S 18 Nov 1874-24 Sept 1954 HTri
Mary w/o Thos 24 July 1798-13 July 1881 JamP
Mary A (w/o W T) 1852-1920 MtHo
Mary S 15 Oct 1853-25 Oct 1923 Onan
Mary S d/o W T & M A 11 Dec 1879-14 Mar 1880 MtHo
May Bland w/o R L 1887-1967 Wach
Mildred R w/o L D 21 Dec 1899-10 July 1979 Onan
Milton C h/o Pauline E 1892-1956 Onan
Peter 1845-1930 Burt
Ralph B s/o R B & S P 5 Aug 1905-24 Aug 1906 MtHo
Ralph Bernard h/o S P 1878-1951 MtHo
Robert Lee h/o M B 1864-1932 Wach
Rozzie Bowers s/o A T & S H 17 Aug 1880-9 Dec 1882; age: 2/3/22 MtHo
Ruth d/o F T & M E 31 Dec 1915-5 Jan 1916 MtHo
Sadie W 1876-1972 MtHo
Sarah F 1879-1922 Burt
Sidney S s/o A T & S H d 5 Oct 1887; age: 16 yrs MtHo
Sudie Hopkins w/o A T 20 May 1856-4 Sept 1941 MtHo
Sue (w/o Vernon) 1903- Onan
Susie Parker w/o R B 1880-1957 MtHo
Tabitha A w/o T H b 22 Feb 1830-d age: 73 yrs MtHo
Thomas B s/o Levin T & Eliz M 26 Aug 1857-4 Mar 1912 Onan
Thomas H s/o L S & E B b 25 Oct 1823-d age: 73 yrs MtHo
Thomas R h/o D B D 5 Sept 1873-14 Dec 1934 MtHo
Thomas W 15 Dec 1890-25 July 1930 Onan
Vernon (h/o Sue) 1899-1944 Onan

JAMES (continued)
Virginia T w/o J K nd LocM
William L h/o F C 10 Mar 1867-9 Nov 1939 Onan
William L 4 Mar 1938-25 July 1977 NewM
William T h/o M A; s/o Jno T & Susan E 3 Dec 1847-7 Oct 1893 MtHo
William T 1909-1976 Fair
Wilson W 1910- MtHo
JEFFRIES, Daisy w/o Danl 11 Mar 1880-6 Nov 1929 Wach
Daniel h/o Daisy 1881-1947 Wach
JENKINS, Charles Herbert 3 Dec 1897-13 Mar 1918 Libe
David Atwood 14 June 1899-30 May 1916 Libe
Ella C 1858-1932 MtHo-s
Emma Susan w/o H T 29 Aug 1872-16 Mar 1938 MtHo
Ethel Elizabeth (w/o J T) 4 Apr 1908-28 July 1961 MtHo-s
Florida Ellen (w/o R J) 19 Nov 1895-22 July 1940 MtHo-s
Garland 1901-1981 Park
Harry H 1895-1957 MtHo-s
Henry Theodore h/o E S 30 May 1874-16 Mar 1963 MtHo
Joseph Thomas (h/o E E) 7 May 1895-30 June 1962 MtHo-s
L David h/o M K R 24 Feb 1872-9 Aug 1961 Libe
Lillie M w/o R T 1879-1951 Park
Margaret C 24 Aug 1902- Onan
Margaret Katherine Rew w/o L D 25 Mar 1871-30 May 1903 Libe
Paul 1900-1979 NewM
Richard T h/o L M 1878-1959 Park
Robert James (h/o F E) Apr 1892-15 Feb 1968 MtHo-s
Robert W s/o R T & L M b&d 13 Dec 1909 Park
Theresa R 1884-1981 MtHo
William J 14 Mar 1842-24 Nov 1915 Libe
William T h/o W S 1899-1969 Park
Winnie S w/o Wm T 1897- Park

JERMAN, Lois West w/o Llewellyn D 1898-1928 Park
JERVIS, Louise E 1 Jan 1911-22 Jan 1945 Libe
JESTER, Delmas W Sr 1914-1969 Quin
Elias James h/o A E 1871-1940 Park
Elizabeth w/o Jacob 11 May 1806-27 Mar 1878 TurJ
Jacob (h/o Elizabeth) 11 Mar 1802-15 May 1865 TurJ
Ocea Ellen w/o E J 1879-1942 Park
JOHNSON, s/o H M & A L b&d 1951 Park
baby girl b&d 20 Sept 1965 Fair
A May 20 Dec 1875-20 Dec 1967 Park
A Sidney h/o E S 8 Mar 1870-5 Feb 1936 Park
Abel T 1 May 1824-2 Feb 1886 John
Ada Parks w/o S L Sr 6 Dec 1887-19 Feb 1966 Park
Addie Shreves w/o L B 1878-1954 Park
Addie Whitehurst w/o A W 1865-1941 Park
Addye S w/o Cliff 1884-1975 Park
Agnes d/o A J & M E 2 June-8 Sept 1913 MtHo
Albert C 15 Aug 1897-21 Apr 1974 Park
Albert T 27 June 1887-13 May 1954 Park
Alfred (h/o M M) 1884-1955 MtHo-s
Alfred B 1855-1944 Park
Alfred F s/o J R & E M 3 Dec 1837-14 Oct 1865 Park
Alfred M (h/o N W) 1888-1974 Onan
Alfred W h/o A W 1865-1958 Park
Alice Adams w/o L P 29 Aug 1865-11 Oct 1935 Park
Almer C h/o M E 1886-1965 MtHo
Andrew F 29 Feb 1889-10 Mar 1959 MtHo

JOHNSON (continued)
Ann Lee w/o H M 1915- Park
Annie C w/o W J 13 Nov 1884-4 Feb 1905 Snea
Annie R w/o Wm J 1862-1938 Park
Annie T 21 Mar 1921-1 Nov 1977 SavN
Augustus W h/o D S 1857-1943 Libe
Beatrice T 1915- Park
Bettie W d/o J W & T A 17 Feb 1874-8 June 1882 Johc
Braden W 16 Mar 1885-15 June 1950 Park
Carl L (h/o E E) 1898-1976 Onan
Caroline W Bloxom w/o D H 1842-1919 Park
Carrie Matilda d/o D H & C W 1872-1933 Park
Cary F s/o J W & T A 3 Oct 1877-22 Dec 1902 Johc
Cecil 1890-1895 Park
Charles B h/o V W 1862-1938 Onan
Charles D (h/o M B) 1895-1962 Onan
Cliff h/o A S 1902-1976 Park
Columbus M h/o Virginia & M F 22 Apr 1847-30 Dec 1928 Park
Cora B Matthews w/o J W Jr 1877-1945 Park
Cora T w/o N R 1902- Park
Daisey P 1886-1973 Park
Daniel Fletcher s/o Parker & Gloria 28-29 Oct 1969 Park
Darlene H w/o J L 9 Jan 1953- Park
Dorenda S w/o A W 1863-1921 Libe
Durbin Henry h/o C W B 1840-1920 Park
E S h/o K W 1857-1923 Park
Edgar M 8 Jan 1889-25 Oct 1948 Park
Edith S w/o A S 19 Apr 1879-9 Feb 1965 Park
Edward T 1874-1934 Edge
Elizabeth 1906-1968 Shil
Elizabeth Mitchell w/o J R 15 Aug 1816-22 Aug 1897 Park
Elizabeth S w/o Thos 6 Oct

JOHNSON (continued)
1828-9 Apr 1909 Onan
Ella 1891-1983 Edge
Ella Hutchinson 1879-1975 HTri
Emma V 1920-1975 Snea
Erma E (w/o C L) 1906-1979 Onan
Evelyn M w/o J F 27 Feb 1907- Park
Ezekiel 1870-1955 Snea
Fannie V 1889-1968 HTri
Fletcher Lee h/o L H 1891-1966 Park
Fred B 1874-1950 Edge
George T h/o L K M 23 Apr 1875-17 Jan 1946 Onan
Capt George W h/o M J; s/o Thos & Nancy 11 Aug 1847-17 Dec 1882 Onan
George W h/o P I 1876-1964 Park
George W 1877-1928 Park
H Clinton (Sgt) 1921-killed at Iwo Jima 11 Mar 1945 Edge
Harvey 1904-1969 Gask
Hattie H w/o Wm E 1905-1981 Libe
Henry M h/o A L; s/o Jno D & Laura V 1914- Park
Isaiah h/o Tabitha 1828-1922 Libe
Isaiah T h/o M W C 1842-1917 Park
J C h/o Mary; s/o Jno R 1845-1912 Park
J T h/o M C 12 Sept 1858-6 Sept 1935 MtHo
J Fletcher h/o E M 13 Sept 1898-10 Dec 1977 Park
James D 1879-1964 Park
James H h/o May 8 June 1869-18 July 1912 Edge
James H Jr s/o J H & May 9 Apr-3 Aug 1908 Edge
James L h/o D H 27 June 1935-8 Feb 1983 Park
James L Jr s/o Jas & Betsy 25-31 Aug 1963 Park
James Lee 1919-1982 MtHo
James Luther 1930-1934 MtHo-s
James M 17 Nov 1902-22 Dec 1955 Park

137

JOHNSON (continued)
James S h/o K H 1911- Edge
Janie E 2 Jan 1835-31 Mar 1898 MtHo
Jerusha G w/o T H 11 Oct 1844-10 Nov 1902 Edge
Jewell B w/o R J 1900-1981 Park
John A h/o M N 1900- Park
John Calvin 1892-1964 Park
John D h/o L V 1870-1944 Park
John R h/o E M 8 Feb 1814-16 Mar 1890 Park
John T 19 Nov 1840-30 June 1887 Morr
John W (h/o T A) 14 Oct 1835-5 Jan 1904 Johc
John W Jr h/o C B M 1867-1955 Park
Johnny T 1919-1976 NewM
Julia C 1881-1950 Edge
Kate W w/o E S 29 Dec 1867-8 Dec 1952 Park
Katherine H w/o J S 1909-1983 Edge
Laban P h/o A A 30 Sept 1862-5 Oct 1948 Park
Laura R 1882-1961 Park
Laura V w/o J D 1875-1966 Park
Capt Lee M (h/o S E) 1883-1961 MtHo-s
Lena 1868-1869 Park
Lena F 1877-1970 Park
Lena G 1889-1975 MtHo-s
Leonard B h/o Nannie & L A 1883-1970 Edge
Leonard Brantley h/o A S; s/o D H & C W 1881-1940 Park
Levenia H w/o F L 1891- Park
Levin T (h/o M C) 1899- Onan
Lida K Merrill w/o G T 1872-1932 Onan
Lillie M (w/o T J) 1886-1941 MtHo
Lola A w/o L B 1878-1962 Edge
Louisa A 24 Apr 1855-8 Sept 1949 Park
Louise K 1889-1933 Snea
M Lynwood 27 Apr 1909-7 Dec 1928 Park
Mabel Kelly 1902-1979 Fair
Madeline E w/o A C 1886-1977

JOHNSON (continued)
MtHo
Maggie M (w/o Alfred) 1896-1964 MtHo-s
Maine A 1877-1939 Park
Margaret Bell (mother/o Geo T) 1894-1962 Onan
Margaret J w/o G W 29 Oct 1842-2 May 1902 Onan
Margaret S 1 June 1840-5 July 1908 MtHo
Marian d/o A W & A P d 30 Aug 1895 Park
Martha J (w/o W M) 1863-1945 MtHo-s
Mary w/o J C d 1890 Park
Mary B (w/o C D) 1895-1973 Onan
Mary C w/o J T 16 Feb 1858-14 May 1926 MtHo
Mary C (w/o L T) 1901-1968 Onan
Mary E 1884-1885 Park
Mary E 3 July 1902-28 Dec 1976; age: 74 yrs NewM
Mary F Ashburne, 2nd w/o C M 1862-1945 Park
Mary H 3 Mar 1865-24 May 1960 Wach
Mary Mapp d 17 July 1966; age: 44 yrs Burt
Mary N w/o J A 1901-1975 Park
Mary W Core w/o I T 1847-1891 Park
Matilda A w/o Wm A; d/o Saml & Margt Ames 26 Oct 1832-24 Jan 1893 Warw
Matilda A w/o Ezekiel d 12 May 1905 Snea
May w/o J H 28 Aug 1875-18 Apr 1908 Edge
May d/o J H & May 9 Apr-3 Sept 1908 Edge
Merrill s/o G T & L K M 14 Aug 1903-15 Jan 1905 Onan
Myrtle S 1902-1962 Park
Nancy J w/o Thos d 16 Mar 1869; age: 59/3/0 Onan
Nannie w/o L B 31 May 1890-25 Nov 1916 Edge
Nina W (w/o A M) 1900-1982 Onan

JOHNSON (continued)
Norman L 14 Aug 1919-8 Feb 1975 MtHo
Norman R h/o C T 27 June 1905-27 May 1965 Park
Paul 1900-1969 Snea
Paul 1912-1979 Fair
Pearl I w/o G W 1874-1937 Park
Rachel E 1843-1927 Morr
Ralph D 1905-1960 Edge
Ray Thomas 1917-1970 Park
Rennie D 1882-1950 Park
Richard 8 Nov 1956-15 Aug 1983 Park
Richard J h/o J B 1895- Park
Sallie E (w/o L M) 1884-1950 MtHo-s
Samuel 1898-1965 Gask
Samuel Lee 8 Apr 1897-19 Mar 1973 Libe
Southey 1884-1959 Snea
Stanley C 1882-1932 Park
Stewart L Sr h/o A P 27 Jan 1888-7 Dec 1965 Park
Stewart L Jr 6 June 1922-11 Jan 1934 Park
Susie W 1882-1960 Edge
Tabitha w/o Isaiah 1833-1923 Libe
Tabitha 25 Aug 1865-25 Feb 1939 Johc
Tabitha Ann w/o J W 21 Mar 1839-21 Sept 1936 Johc
Capt Thomas h/o E S & N J 6 Dec 1809-5 Feb 1906 Onan
Thomas G 1929-1946 MtHo-s
Thomas H h/o J G 10 Dec 1838-30 Oct 1909 Edge
Thomas J (h/o L M) 1885-1933 MtHo
Tonya 1959-1981 SavN
Vercie Boyce 26 Aug 1902-14 May 1966 Park
Virginia, 1st w/o C M; d/o Dr J B & Amanda Bowdoin d 17 Nov 1892; age: 44 yrs Park
Virginia L 1884-1946 Park
Virginia W w/o C B 1862-1895 Onan
Walter James s/o A W & D S 8 Apr 1902-6 May 1916 Libe
Warner A 1913-1976 Park

JOHNSON (continued)
Wilbur C s/o L B & Nannie 29 Apr 1911-25 Nov 1916 Edge
William A s/o Jno & Maria 26 June 1832-19 Jan 1893 Warw
William E h/o H H 1894-1963 Libe
William J h/o A R 13 Apr 1840-19 Dec 1926 Park
William J h/o A C 26 Feb 1882-26 Feb 1905 Snea
William L 1881-1944 Edge
William S 1870-1942 Park
Willie S 2 Apr 1882-1 July 1957 Park
Woff M (h/o M J) 1862-1935 MtHo-s

JOHNSTONE, (JONSTON),
Earl L 1906-1978 Edge
Elizabeth Hyslup 30 June 1906- StGe
James Watson Sr 17 Feb 1902-12 Mar 1959 StGe

JOINER, Sophronia Lee w/o J D 1841-1917 Libe

JONES, - 1896-1955 NewM
inf/o (prob W L & A C) b&d 1928 Quin
Abraham h/o M L 1866-1952 NewM
Anna C (w/o W L) 1896-1952 Quin
Annie W 26 Aug 1893-26 Feb 1980 NewM
Auta D h/o V B 1891-1959 Edge
Bernice 1921-1980 Burt
Bertha Taylor w/o R B 1883-1917 Park
Blanche L 1900- Park
Cecelia 1862-1889 Wach
Edward F h/o L M 1875-1964 MtHo
Edward Oscar 14 Mar 1914-15 Sept 1971 StGe
Elizabeth d 23 Jan 1869; age: 93 yrs Guyc
Elizabeth E Colonna Holt (1st hus - E R Holt; 2nd hus - Geo Jones) 1845-nd Wate
Elizabeth H 1919-1982 Gask
Elizah d 16 Oct 1959; age: 71 yrs NewM

JONES (continued)
Ella H w/o P E 1888-1972 Snea
Fred M 1941-1973 NewM
Gabriella Scarburgh Mapp w/o O M 1871-1967 Onan
George Jr 1905-1934 Ptea
George D 1888-1980 NewM
George E (h/o L S) 1870-1945 Quin
Gilberte 23 Jan 1921- Fair
Grace B w/o W E 1914- StGe
Harry S (h/o L B) 1880-1946 StGe
Henrietta E Mar 1887-3 Dec 1902 Onan
Irving C h/o M C 1910-1980 McLa
J Fenton 1890-1978 Fair
James Calvin 14 Feb 1920-28 Jan 1969 StGe
James H 8 Mar 1833-26 July 1910 BurJ
John H 1910-1977 NewM
John Paul 1909-1947 MtHo-s
John Walter (s/o W B & E J L) b&d 6 Mar 1912 MtHo-s
Kate Barnes 1875-1942 Libe
Laura A 14 Feb 1895-11 Nov 1977 NewM
Lena S (w/o G E) 1873-1934 Quin
Lizzie M w/o E F 1882-1946 MtHo
Loyed (h/o M F) 6 Feb 1853-11 Nov 1883 Bulb
Lula B (w/o H S) 1882-1930 StGe
Maggie L w/o Abraham 1870-1941 NewM
Margaret A 21 Oct 1843-15 Mar 1925 BurJ
Margie C w/o I C 1914- McLa
Maria Jane 2 Aug 1822-8 Mar 1897 Crad-s
Marvin F 1907-1983 Fair
Marvin Roland 10 Sept 1922-9 Oct 1964 Fair
Mary d 13 Dec 1938; age: 19 yrs NewM
Mary E 1912-1972 MtNe
Mary F w/o Lloyd 14 Jan 1856-16 Oct 1923 Bulb

JONES (continued)
Melvin S (h/o W M) 1914-1976 Onan
Oswald Meiggs h/o G S M 20 Mar 1863-6 Nov 1931 Onan
Pearl 1911-1971 NewM
Pearl E w/o W R 1888-1967 MtHo-s
Peter 1884-1965 Snea
Peter E h/o E H 1881-1965 Snea
Roy B h/o B T 1885-1959 Park
Roy L 1929-1963 Edge
Samuel T 1842-1898 Libe
Smith d 2 Sept 1952; age: 62 yrs NewM
Sue W 18 Oct 1857-23 Oct 1945 Crad-s
Susie d 10 May 1955; age: 60 yrs NewM
Viva B w/o A D 1899-1977 Edge
Walter B, 1st h/o E J LeCato 7 Sept 1882-18 Apr 1920 MtHo-s
Willa M (w/o M S) 1915- Onan
William D s/o W R & P E d 16 Mar 1913 MtHo-s
Werner 1904-1950 Snea
Wilbur E (h/o G B) 1904-1959 StGe
Willard L (h/o A C) 1897-1977 Quin
William d 8 May 1885; age: 64/7/0 Crad-s
William h/o Viola 1889-1978 NewM
William H 14 Feb 1914-21 Nov 1962 Fair
William R h/o P E 1872-1945 MtHo-s
Willie R 3 Apr 1924-26 Aug 1966 NewM

JORDAN, Rev E M 1841-1914 MtHo
Elliott M 1876-1961 MtHo
Lisa 1960-1973 JoyC
Mattie Walker 1853-1923 MtHo
Sarah B 1880-1977 HTri

JOYNES, inf s/o H W & G E nd MtHo
inf s/o E T & M J b&d 25 Sept 1873 Joyn
Alexander Tankard s/o T A T & S P 17 Apr 1845-5 June 1907

JOYNES (continued)
Alice Stewart d/o T R & S W 29 Sept 1856-19 July 1856; age: 0/9/20 Bowm
Ann w/o Col L S; d/o Jno & Susannah (Custis) Smith 11 June 1756-16 Aug 1815 JoyB
Ann C w/o E D 23 Feb 1818-26 Jan 1875 Joyn
Anne Bell w/o Thos R; d/o Christopher & Anne Satchell 5 Apr 1792-6 Sept 1862 Bowm
'Annie' Lillian Ward w/o C V 4 Oct 1891-13 Dec 1977 MtHo
Bessie J 1880-1980 Gask
Blanche Northam d/o G G & S W N 20 Jan 1886-24 May 1959 Onan
Carroll Vaden h/o A L W 5 Sept 1883-5 Dec 1964 MtHo
Charles E 1903-1970 MtHo-s
Charles L h/o W M; s/o Edwd D Jr & Mary 1877-1943 Joyn
Charlie L s/o E D & A C 9 Nov 1856-drowned 9 Sept 1874 Joyn
Charlotte Bell w/o Levin S; d/o Christopher & Ann Satchell d 11 Oct 1822; age: 34/7/24 Onan
Charlotte Bell d/o T R & A B 2 Jan 1825-24 Mar 1843 Bowm
Charlotte T d/o E D & A C 7 Dec 1854-16 Aug 1855 Joyn
Edward A s/o Thos R & Mary A b&d 26 Oct 1875 Parp
Edward A 2 June 1876-19 June 1878 Parp
Edward D (h/o A C); s/o Wm R & Hetty 11 Sept 1812-18 Mar 1891 Joyn
Edward T h/o M J; s/o E D & A C 29 Aug 1846-1 May 1908 Joyn
Edward T s/o Edwd T & M J 27 Nov 1879-1 Sept 1903 Joyn
Elias D h/o S S; s/o Elias & Margt 20 Oct 1816-26 Nov 1867 (embraced religion in 1845 & joined M E Church) Rodg
Elizabeth F Powell w/o G G Jr;

JOYNES (continued)
d/o Wm P & Eliz C Powell 5 Feb 1895-1 Feb 1954 Onan
Frederick C 1956-1957 MtHo
George Goodwyn h/o S W N 6 Sept 1856-18 Oct 1932 Onan
George Goodwyn Jr h/o E F P; s/o G G & S W N 1 Jan 1896-16 Apr 1969 Onan
Georgie E w/o H W 17 Oct 1876-22 Jan 1959 MtHo
Harriet A w/o T S 30 Sept 1853-20 Mar 1917 MtHo
Harry W h/o G E 12 Sept 1877-16 June 1926 MtHo
Henry T (h/o I D) 1892-1938 MtHo
Herbert G s/o Jno W & Ellen P 20 Dec 1871-14 Aug 1873 Joyn
Ida D (w/o H T) 1889-1979 MtHo
Jane S d/o Elias D & Margt 29 June 1815-4 Jan 1892 JoCu
Jennie L w/o W F 24 Oct 1851-3 May 1915 Onan
John H s/o Wm J & Mary (Doughty) 6 Aug 1876-6 Feb 1937 Holl
John Thomas 30 Sept 1835-15 Apr 1836 JoyB
Keren S 1880-1971 Libe
Leon H 29 Oct 1871-31 Mar 1918 Joyp
Levin S (h/o Ann) 6 Jan 1753-16 Oct 1794 JoyB
Lloyd d 1 Jan 1952 Burt
Mrs Maggie 1897-1936 Gask-old
Margaret w/o Elias; d/o Jno & Sarah Smith 22 Sept 1785-2 Aug 1861 (connected with church - 1810; married - 1811) JoCu
Margaret T d/o Elias & Margt 11 Oct 1819-8 Aug 1898 JoCu
Mary Drummond 1883-1957 Gask
Mary E B d/o Thos R & Mary A 2-19 June 1878 Parp
Mary J (w/o Wm J) 6 Nov 1842-21 Oct 1921 Joyp
Mary J w/o Edwd T 4 Feb 1843-10 Sept 1916 Joyn
Mary d/o Wm W & Ellen Major White 22 June 1876-28 June

JOYNES (continued)
1955 Holl
Maud C d/o Jno S & Ellen P 21 Aug 1874-16 July 1870 Joyn
Pearl H d 1965 Shil
Phillip J 1952-1957 MtHo
Phyllis C 1926-1957 MtHo
Riley S 4 Oct 1858-4 Oct 1918 JoyC
Sabra P w/o T A T 16 Jan 1821-13 Aug 1897 Onan
Sallie Wright Northam w/o G G 1860-1921 Onan
Sarah d 17 Nov 1952 Burt
Sarah d/o T R & S W 16 Nov 1857-24 Mar 1863 Bowm
Sarah E d/o E D & A C 9 Jan 1844-23 Sept 1847 Joyn
Sarah H d/o E D & A C 2 July-1 Sept 1851 Joyn
Sarah S w/o E D; d/o Jas S & Eliz P Boggs 3 Apr 1820-21 Sept 1871 Rodg
Sheryl Ann 1948-1957 MtHo
Susan A d/o Jno & Elisha 13 Apr 1828-7 Sept 1887; age: 59/4/24 Joyp
Thomas R h/o A B 17 Oct 1789-12 Sept 1858 (member of VA Convention 1829-30) Bowm
Thomas R s/o Armistead & Eliz 2 Dec 1827-15 Mar 1894; age: 66/3/13 Parp
Thomas R Jr s/o T R & A B 12 Apr 1829-3 Apr 1868 Bowm
Thomas Ray s/o Thos R & Mary A 1 May 1880-4 Oct 1881 Parp
Thomas S h/o H A 28 Nov 1840-9 Apr 1905 MtHo
Mrs Tully Oct 1798-Mar 1836 Recorded in 1940 in Snead fam plot which was moved to Onancock Cem. This stone is not among those moved. Unable to verify. Onan
Tully A T h/o S P 25 Aug 1815-21 Dec 1890 Onan
Tully Armistead 7 Dec 1848-12 Feb 1930 Onan
Capt William F h/o J L 25 Oct 1846-10 May 1920 Onan
William J h/o M J; (s/o Jno &

JOYNES (continued)
Elisha) 13 Apr 1833-12 July 1904 Joyp
Wilson 7 Jan 1853-13 Mar 1914 Gask-old
Winnie M w/o Chas L 9 May 1882-28 June 1933 Joyn
JUBILEE, Arthur J h/o Estella 3 July 1902-29 June 1945 NewM
Custis 1902-1974 Snea
George 1 Mar 1840-6 Jan 1907 NewM
George T s/o ? 27 Apr 18(75?)-10 Oct 1912 NewM
James M 1903-1974 Shil
Jane d 4 Mar 1911; age: 69 yrs NewM
John W h/o Isabella d 16 May 1916 NewM
Lillie 16 June 1891-18 Sept 1963 Snea
Louis Jr 29 Nov 1900-4 Apr 1974 Snea
Malisia d 4 July 1964; age: 76 yrs Snea
Sadie S 1889-1942 Snea
Schman d 12 Sept 1962; age: 67 yrs NewM
Thomas 1880-1963 Snea
Virginia Nock 1920-1978 Gask
William 1933-1963 Shil
JUDD, Edwin W h/o M M 1911-1977 Libe
Margaret M w/o E W 1912-1978 Libe
JUDEFIND, Stella Scott 14 Dec 1875-8 Aug 1970 Libe
JUSTIS, (JUSTICE),
d/o J P & B S b&d 1 Feb 1881 Park
s/o F P & C S 14-18 Oct 1894 Libe
s/o E C & R B b&d 1918 Park
infants (prob of A F) b&d 1927 Libe
s/o Herman & Elise b&d 1945 Libe
baby boy b&d 1976 Fair
Addie L w/o B F 1897-1980 Park
Addie P w/o A L 1883-1961 Libe
Alfred T (h/o J M) 1889-1942 Edge

JUSTIS (continued)
Alfred T (h/o A C) 1920-1978 Edge
Alice L w/o E B 1864-1954 Park
Alice Louise 14 Apr 1924-8 Oct 1940 Park
Alma C (w/o A T) 1913-1974 Edge
Andrew CC h/o B H 12 Dec 1883-14 Dec 1918 Onan
Andrew F 1888-1946 MtHo
Andrew R 29 Sept 1869-3 Nov 1942 Libe
Annie L 1889-1954 Park
Arinthia S w/o Wm T 25 Dec 1866-20 Nov 1952 Libe
Asbury T 16 Oct 1880-20 Jan 1912 Libe
Asher L h/o A P 1880-1956 Libe
Austin Fletcher 1892-1956 Libe
Beatrice H w/o A C C 8 Apr 1882-20 Jan 1938 Onan
Benjamin W h/o E E 1876-1942 Libe
Bennie F h/o A L 1896-1974 Park
Bertha M w/o I C 1884-1972 Libe
Bertie T w/o S R 1881-1961 Park
Bettie G w/o J W 1886-1941 Libe
Bettie L w/o G R 1884-1969 Libe
Bettie S w/o W F 11 Mar 1863-5 Dec 1905 Libe
Betty Ann d/o B W & W S b&d 3 Jan 1937 Libe
Beulah S w/o R L 1895- Libe
Billy W 15 Feb 1924-17 Sept 1983 Park
Brantley W h/o W S 1901-1969 Libe
Caroline S w/o F P 3 Aug 1860-15 May 1929 Libe
Carrie L d/o E B & A L 19 Sept 1886-12 July 1888 Park
Carvella T w/o T A 1896- Libe
Catherine E w/o G R 1854-1928 Libe
Ceylon G 1897-1959 Park
Charles J 17 Feb 1864-31 Oct 1890 Libe

JUSTIS (continued)
Charles M h/o L T 1895-1957 Park
Charles P h/o L B 1891-1963 Park
Charles T h/o M S 1879-1970 Libe
Clara Mae w/o H F 30 Mar 1891-9 Feb 1959 Park
Cora B w/o I W 19 Mar 1877-27 Aug 1905 Park
Cynthia A w/o I F 22 Mar 1856-5 Sept 1918 Libe
Eddie G s/o Geo R & Eveline C b&d 18 Aug 1884 Libe
Edward B h/o A L 1866-1940 Park
Edward B h/o M S 1923- Edge
Edward Carroll h/o R B 1885-1972 Park
Edward S 1871-1946 Libe
Elizabeth M 18 May 1880-7 Jan 1958 Fair
Ella E w/o B W 1880-1959 Libe
Elwood T 1915-1960 Park
Enid S w/o S N 1917- Libe
Eva E 1873-1956 Libe
Eva P 1895-1983 Libe
Eva S d/o J P & B S 28 July 1877-11 Dec 1880 Park
Evelyn Susan w/o J L 1865-1947 Libe
Flora B w/o F R 1879-1946 Park
Frank C 14 Jan 1888-10 Sept 1904 Libe
Frank L h/o N E 1894-1977 Libe
Frank P h/o C S 18 May 1855-24 Feb 1933 Libe
Frank R h/o F B 1877-1950 Park
George R h/o C E 1851-1940 Libe
George R h/o B L 1880-1942 Libe
George R s/o J W & B G 24 July 1905-24 Sept 1908 Libe
George R Jr 17 Sept 1876-27 Aug 1934 Fair
George S 1929- Edge
Harold F h/o L F 1887-1963 Libe
Harry F s/o Wm T & A S 30 May 1890-30 Apr 1892 Libe

143

JUSTIS (continued)
Harvey F h/o C M 11 Sept 1888-18 Oct 1966 Park
Hazel B w/o L G 1926- Libe
Helon K d/o H F & L F 5-19 Dec 1919 Libe
I F h/o C A 4 June 1855-20 Apr 1923 Libe
Isaiah Crippen h/o B M 1882-1952 Libe
J Columbus h/o M A 1845-1919 Onan
J Edward h/o M T 1882-1956 Park
James Keaton 1907-1962 (buried at sea) Onan
James Lee h/o E S 1864-1940 Libe
Jennie M (w/o A T) 1888-1979 Edge
John P (1st h/o B S Parkes) 1851-1886 Park
John Revel 28 Feb 1887-13 Oct 1959 Libe
John Tom h/o M J 1891-1938 Park
John W h/o B G 1876-1963 Libe
John W h/o S C 1883-1945 Libe
Judson L h/o M C 1864-1936 Libe
Julia A w/o L B 9 Jan 1861-21 May 1930 Park
Lawrence G h/o H B 1921- Libe
Lelia X 17 Mar 1873-12 Apr 1949 Libe
Lena T w/o R L 1874-1941 Libe
Littleton B h/o J A 21 May 1860-22 Mar 1923 Park
Lola S w/o T F 15 Jan 1898-14 Sept 1968 Park
Louise B w/o C P 1894-1977 Park
Lucy C 1885-1957 Libe
Lucy F w/o H F 1889-1977 Libe
Lula T w/o C M 1895-1971 Park
Maggie A 1892-1980 Libe
Malissa C w/o Chas P 24 Mar 1843-17 Feb 1906 Libe
Marcella A w/o J C 1849-1923 Onan
Margaret Ann w/o Jno 1850-1923 Park

JUSTIS (continued)
Margaret C w/o J L 26 July 1864-20 May 1902 Libe
Margaret E (mother) 18 Oct 1827-27 Apr 1889 Fitz
Margaret E 1924- Libe
Margaret Keaton (w/o W R) 1878-1961 Onan
Margaret L 1921-1970 Park
Margaret S w/o C T 1887-1960 Libe
Margie E w/o Fletcher 13 Sept 1896-26 Feb 1923 Libe
Martha A 10 Feb 1856-16 Aug 1930 Park
Martha Jane w/o J T 1894-1958 Park
Martha Thorns w/o J E 1880-1948 Park
Mary A 1832-1905 Park
Mary A w/o Wm J 1869-1956 Libe
Mary E w/o Wm S 3 Mar 1854-2 May 1906 Libe
Mary E d/o Revel & Nancy 20 Dec 1855-12 Aug 1857 Libe
Mary S w/o E B 1928-1975 Edge
Matilda B w/o Wm E 3 Apr 1889- Park
Mattie W w/o S J 1881-1936 Libe
McComas 26 Sept 1856-26 Sept 1929 Park
Melva Mae 1911-1963 Libe
Minnie W w/o N G 1885-1962 Park
Missouri E w/o S R 1862-16 Oct 1936 Park
Mollie Y 1898-1927 Libe
Monty C s/o L B & Mannie S 1942-1943 Park
Myrtle Killmon 1910-1957 Libe
Nancy w/o Revel 29 Sept 1823-16 July 1914 Libe
Nancy R w/o R J 30 Feb 1857-28 May 1883 Libe
Nellie A w/o S W 1916- Libe
Nina E w/o F L 1905-1942 Libe
Noah G h/o M W 1885-1943 Park
Norwood H 8 Nov 1891-10 July 1917 Park
Oakland H s/o H F & C M 20

JUSTIS (continued)
Feb 1914-27 Apr 1938 Park
Oakley S 27 Aug 1923-20 Jan 1984 Park
Oscar T 1891-1964 Park
Patrick S 1949-1979 Park
Pearlie H 1906-1970 Libe
Ralph W 1908-1972 Libe
Raymond L h/o V S 1856-1940 Libe
Reubin L h/o B S 1890-1956 Libe
Revel h/o Nancy; s/o Isaiah & Sally 18 Jan 1820-26 Dec 1881 Libe
Revel J h/o S W 7 Oct 1840-17 Mar 1922 Libe
Revel J h/o N R 10 Feb 1847-25 Oct 1948 Libe
Revell J Jr h/o S E 1882-1946 Libe
Richard Earl s/o E B & M S d 1951 Edge
Robert H 1912-1936 Onan
Robert L h/o L T 1864-1938 Libe
Robert T 1883-1940 Libe
Robert T Jr 17 Aug 1911-9 Feb 1952 Libe
Rose A d 1965 NewM
Ruth Byrd w/o E C 1888-1939 Park
S Lockwood 1905-1975 Libe
Sadie V Sparrow 1879-1951 Libe
Sallie C w/o J W 1884-1966 Libe
Sallie W w/o R J 11 Feb 1842-24 Jan 1923 Libe
Sallie W w/o S J 1863-1939 Libe
Samuel 1868-1923 Libe
Samuel F 14 Sept 1914-21 Oct 1976 Park
Samuel J h/o S W 1861-1944 Libe
Samuel J h/o M W 1877-1942 Libe
Samuel R h/o V T 2 Nov 1838-10 Dec 1924 Libe
Samuel R h/o M E 4 June 1848-23 Apr 1909 Park
Samuel R h/o B T 1878-1921 Park

JUSTIS (continued)
Samuel V s/o T F & L S b&d 21 Sept 1920 Park
Sarah E Annis; nee Marshall 1922-1974 Park
Sarah T w/o Wm M 20 Oct 1870-8 Oct 1928 Park
Stantley N h/o E S 1922-1969 Libe
Stuart W h/o N A 1912-1982 Libe
Sudie E w/o R J Jr 1891-1963 Libe
Thomas A h/o C T 1894-1983 Libe
Tully F h/o L S 25 Aug 1898-13 Aug 1954 Park
Upshur Q 12 May 1904-30 Aug 1952 Fair
Upshur Thomas s/o Geo R & Eveline C 25 Feb 1882-6 Aug 1898 Libe
Vance I s/o T A & Carvella 1934-1938 Libe
Vianah T w/o S R 11 Feb 1849-7 Dec 1925 Libe
Virginia d/o U Q & M E 5 Sept 1900-19 Aug 1901 Onan
Virginia S w/o R L 8 Nov 1862-15 Apr 1910 Libe
W Beatrice w/o S L 1906- Libe
W F h/o B S d 1 Apr 1930; age: 76 yrs Libe
Walter F 1909-1970 Park
William E 1873-1956 Libe
William E h/o M B 9 Feb 1884-5 Feb 1973 Park
William J h/o M A 1867-1923 Libe
William M h/o S T 12 Dec 1861- Park
William Revel (h/o M K) 1878-1947 Onan
William S h/o M E 11 Mar 1858-15 Mar 1924 Libe
William T h/o A S 1 May 1860-25 Sept 1934 Libe
Willie M 1892-1962 Park
Willye S w/o B W 1903- Libe
KAPPES, Charles P h/o E P 1875-1947 MtHo
Elva P (w/o C P) 1891-1967

KAPPES (continued)
MtHo
Nell E 1922-1950 MtHo
KAYTON, Mary Neville w/o Bernard 27 Feb 1895-5 June 1971 MtHo
KEATING, Mary E 1880-1958 Fair
KEATON, H B h/o M A; s/o Thos & Betsy 26 May 1826-7 May 1888 Onan
Capt James T h/o Eleanor D Scarborough; s/o H E & M A 5 Oct 1849-29 Mar 1882 Onan
Margaret A w/o H B 22 May 1828-14 Mar 1900 Onan
Thomas J s/o Capt J T & Eleanor D 2 Feb-5 June 1875 Onan
KECK, Harrie A (h/o N D) 1891-1972 Fair
Noel D (w/o H A) 1894-1969 Fair
KELEHEAR, Thomas d Jan 1892; age: 55 yrs Evan
KELLAM, (KELLUM),
inf/o J R & M F nd Hero
inf/o J R & M F d 20 Aug 1862 Hero
s/o T G & Lula A b&d 23 Nov 1921 Park
Alfred C s/o Hulton & Susan 26 Apr 1829-21 Mar 1856 MtPl
Alfred Robinson s/o J T Sr & B J 1905- MtHo
Alfred S h/o E B 29 Dec 1849-16 Dec 1922 (moved from Heron Hill) MtHo
Allie James (h/o M R) 1904- Quin
Alphonso s/o J R & M F d 27 June 1858 Hero
Andrew J h/o M B 20 July 1853-18 Dec 1921 Edge
Ann w/o E W 3 Mar 1831-19 Feb 1908 Hysl
Annie A w/o Geo A 1 Dec 1829-10 Aug 1914 MtPl
Annie A 1876-1960 MtHo
Annie L d/o T R & Mariah 23 July 1852-16 Mar 1876 Grot
Annie M (Mrs) 1880-1957 Holl
Arthur L (h/o L M) 1888-1967

KELLAM (continued)
Fair
Audrey M 21 Oct 1915-19 Aug 1922 Onan
Auduben W s/o J R & M F d 8 July 1852 Hero
Belford D 1889-1972 StGe
Belle S w/o Edwd O; d/o J T & V A Turner 28 Nov 1858-30 Nov 1885; age: 27/0/2 Turn
Benjamine J h/o K A; s/o Stockley & Comfort (Stringer) 8 Sept 1824-5 June 1903 Onan
Bertie w/o T G 2 July 1872-21 Mar 1923 MtHo
Bessie Jane w/o J T Sr; d/o J R & Alice E Downing 1877-1972 MtHo
Bettie B (w/o F C A) 22 Feb 1845-28 May 1930 StGe
Bettie W 1845-1931 MtHo
Brooks E (h/o E J) 6 July 1905-6 Apr 1980 Fair
Burleigh (h/o L A) 1900-1968 Edge
Carrie M 1895-1980 Holl
Carroll C h/o M M 1884-1938 MtHo
Charles (h/o Margt Kellam Harman) 27 Feb 1798-16 Jan 1850 Kelp
Charlie H 15 July 1889-27 July 1959 NewM
Charlotte G 1909-1980 Shil
Charlotte Jane w/o Wm T 9 Feb 1826-5 July 1915 Holf
Clara L wid/o Colie W Gardner; w/o Harry J 27 Dec 1898-21 July 1923 Mitc-w
Colie A 1856-1912 Holl
Cordelia 18 Nov 1843-22 Jan 1889 Oakg
Cordie A w/o R D 1876-1948 MtHo
Custis W s/o Housen & Eliz d 24 Aug 1855; age: 62/6/12 Hero
Daisy V w/o J B 1882-1979 Onan
Daril d 4 June 1975; age: 44/3/28 HTri
Dorothy M (w/o N W) 1915-1970 MtHo

146

KELLAM (continued)
E(liza) Birdie w/o A S 4 May 1853-26 July 1939 (moved from Heron Hill) MtHo
Eagle 1881-1966 Shil
Edgar S 1870-1968 Onan
Edmund 1838-5 Nov 1920 Burt
Edward W (h/o Ann); s/o Arguell & Sallie 27 July 1831-3 May 1903; age: 71/9/6 Hysl
Elicia R w/o T A 1866-1948 MtHo
Eliza C w/o F C A 11 July 1802-25 Nov 1873 (erected by F C A K Jr) Kell
Eliza Coward d/o Dr F C A Jr & Bettie B 3 Dec 1876-13 Sept 1880 Kell
Elizabeth d/o Custis W & Eliz d 28 Sept 1844; age: 18 yrs Hero
Elizabeth wid/o Howsen d 6 July 1854; age: 85/3/9 KelB
Elizabeth B w/o T H 3 Nov 1793-26 Dec 1835 Ever
Elizabeth J w/o R R 10 Nov 1825-6 July 1894 Jaco
Ella Lee d/o W T & E J d 10 July 1885 (stone missing; 1940 data) MeaB
Ella M w/o W J 1875-1947 MtHo-s
Emma C d/o W T & E J 2 May 1882-16 Apr 1884 (stone missing; 1940 data) MeaB
Emma Jane w/o W T 18 Feb 1854-13 Oct 1936 MtHo-s
Emma S w/o R W T 29 Mar 1853-17 Apr 1922 MtHo
Esther M 1895-1945 MtHo-s
Ethel W 23 July 1883-6 Oct 1935 Holl
Eva Jane (w/o B E) 5 Oct 1903-31 Oct 1975 Fair
Dr F C A h/o E C 1814-Aug 1896 Kell
Dr F C A (h/o B B) 3 Feb 1845-5 Jan 1925 StGe
Florida M w/o S B 1918-1974 Snea
Fred C (h/o M S) 1868-1952 Onan
Fred R 1888-1956 Quin

KELLAM (continued)
Garland U 4 Mar 1933-17 Sept 1948 MtHo-s
Garnett A h/o M W 14 Mar 1890-30 Dec 1950 MtHo
George 1912-1964 Shil
George A h/o A A; s/o Stokley & Comfort 8 Jan 1822-12 Mar 1860 MtPl
George L (h/o I L) 1885-1956 Wach
George T 1898-1943 Snea
Grace A d/o Thos C & Julia C 11 July 1879-1 Nov 1883 Hero
H A W b 1840; d age: 67 yrs Park
Harry J h/o M A 1903-1966 Edge
Harry P s/o Berleigh C & Bessie V 13 Nov 1885-16 June 1886 StJa
Harry S nd Shil
Harvey James s/o A S & E B 6 Apr 1875-29 Sept 1882 (moved from Heron Hill) MtHo
Hattie B 1918-1972 MtNe
Hulton (h/o Susan) 19 Oct 1801-27 Jan 1855 MtPl
Irving Custis s/o A S & E B 2 Dec 1880-16 Feb 1882 (moved from Heron Hill) MtHo
Irving Lee s/o J T Sr & B J 1909- MtHo
Isaac L 1900-1961 Snea
Ivy L (w/o G L) 1895- Wach
J Clarence 1891-1965 Holl
J Fred 1872-1936 Holl
James H 1888-1918 Snea
James Roy 1909-1951 Snea
James S 1920-1921 Snea
James Twilley (h/o L M) 1874-1959 Quin
Jane M K wid/o Jno C; d/o Wm M & E M Scarborough 14 July 1819-4 Dec 1852 Hedr
Jennie 1885-1969 MtHo-s
Jennie T 1870-1920 Snea
John d 17 May 1771; age: 75 yrs Wacb
John s/o Robt & Leah 11 Feb 1819-4 July 1841 KelG
John B h/o D V 1879-1950 Onan
John C (w/o L M); s/o Jno &

KELLAM (continued)
Margt (Hatton) 23 Oct 1792-7 Sept 1845 Myrt
John H 1890-1964 Shil
John L 1902-1929 Snea
John R s/o Custis W & Margt (Richardson) 15 Jan 1819-17 May 1890 Hero
John S s/o Geo & Adah 4 Jan 1817-3 Mar 1868 MtPl
John T Jr s/o J T Sr & B J 4 Aug 1913-28 Jan 1967 MtHo
John Thomas s/o Hanson P & Victoria b 8 Aug 1845 (stone missing; 1940 data) Kebg
John Thomas Sr h/o B J; s/o A S & E B 1873-1947 MtHo
John W s/o Severn & Ann 6 Mar 1789-26 July 1850 Kebg
John W s/o W H & S C 5 Apr 1851-19 June 1913; age: 62 yrs Crad-s
John W MD h/o M E 12 Apr 1856-30 Dec 1922 MtHo
John W s/o E W & Ann 22 Apr 1860-20 July 1887; age: 27/2/28 Hysl
John W 1866-1933 MtHo-s
John W 1894-1969 Shil
John William 29 Nov 1874-31 Mar 1919 Holl
Dr John Wise 2 Nov 1890-14 June 1970 StGe
Joseph M s/o S T & Mary E 29 Dec 1867-25 Dec 1918 StGe
Juanita d/o Nita (Neville) 26 Feb 1910-7 Dec 1913 MtHo
Julia Anna w/o T C 29 Sept 1847-31 Dec 1925 MtHo
Katharine A w/o B J 26 Oct 1836-2 Apr 1926; age: 90/5/6 Onan
Kathryn Reade 31 July 1901-20 Jan 1963 StGe
Leah 6 Mar 1783-4 Mar 1845 KelG
Leah M 10 Apr 1806-26 Feb 1861 Turf
Lee B s/o J R & M W 5 Dec 1860-3 June 1945 MtHo
Lee Parramore s/o Andrew J & Maggie S 21 Oct 1885-26 Feb

KELLAM (continued)
1901 Locu
Leon nd (prob d 1967/8) Shil
Leuvenia 1898-1966 HTri
Lisha A (w/o Burleigh) 1900- Edge
Lizzie M (w/o A L) 1890-1974 Fair
Lloyd h/o M E 1879-1947 Shil
Lloyd W 1905-1976 Snea
Louelen s/o J W & M W 30 Sept 1836-14 Dec 1839 (stone missing; 1940 data) Kebg
Lucille 1894-1983 MtHo
Lucinda w/o Geo C 30 Jan 1833-17 June 1907 HTri
Lula A (w/o T G) 1898- Fair
Lula Mears (w/o J T) 1884-1959 Quin
Luther V s/o West & Susan 14 Oct 1790-20 Aug 1838 Mapl
Lydia M w/o J C; d/o Jas A & Sarah Clayton late of DE 18 Sept 1794-19 Oct 1834 Myrt
M C d/o T T & M A 28 May 1847-11 Jan 1872 Hero
M S w/o S A; d/o J S & Catherine Ames 29 July 1859-8 Sept 1892 Holl
Maggie 1881-1971 Snea
Maggie Burton w/o A J 15 Nov 1863-15 Jan 1925 Edge
Maggie E w/o Lloyd 1884-1946 Shil
Mai J (w/o W F) 1878-1960 MtHo
Major 1884-1944 HTri
Major R s/o J W & M W 14 Sept 1818-14 Sept 1842 Kebg
Mamie Richardson (w/o A J) 1910- Quin
Manie F 1892-1973 HTri
Margaret 1849-1934 Onan
Margaret J Thomas d/o W H & S C 3 Dec 1847-28 Nov 1901 Crad-s
Margaret S (w/o F C) 1875-1941 Onan
Margaret S W d/o J W & M W 10 May 1824-28 July 1836 Kebg
Margaret W w/o J W; d/o Fred-

KELLAM (continued)
  erick & Sarah S Kellam 16 Oct 1791-19 Apr 1868(63?) Kebg
Margaret L w/o Teagle 1897-1943 NewM
Mary 1915-1950 Snea
Mary Boggs w/o L T 1880-1924 Onan
Mary E (d/o Wm T & Jane [Pusey]) 6 Sept 1846-22 Oct 1937; age: 91/1/16 Holf
Mary E w/o S T 20 May 1848-30 June 1906 Marp
Mary E w/o J W MD 17 Oct 1858-6 July 1907 MtHo
Mary F d/o Zorobabel & Ann C 29 Oct 1825-7 Nov 1865 Hero
Mary J w/o Jno J 2 Oct 1860-8 June 1921 Crad-s
Mary Kusian 1880-1942 StGe
Mary M w/o C C 1885-1963 MtHo
Mildred Walter w/o G A 1 Aug 1894-24 June 1982 MtHo
Myrtle A w/o H J 1906- Edge
N Swain 1897-1955 MtHo
Nathaniel J s/o Jas & Patience 21 Dec 1843-21 Dec 1885 Oakg
Norman W (h/o D M) 1914-1979 MtHo
Olivia Frances 1881-1956 HTri
Otho s/o Richd H & Missouri 6 May 1868-13 Sept 1898; age: 30/4/7 Mapl
Otho J d 31 July 1948 Holl
Patience w/o Jas; d/o Geo & Rachel Fisher 22 Sept 1805-18 July 1887 Holl
Polly w/o T P 4 Oct 1825-26 Mar 1864 Home
Posie E w/o S R 1894-1956 MtHo
R Duncan h/o C A 1874-1923 MtHo
Racilia C d/o W T & Susan N (Copes) 15 Oct 1876-25 Jan 1967 MtHo
Ralph Downing s/o J T Sr & B J 1900- MtHo
Revel R h/o E J 18 Oct 1816-28 May 1889; age: 72/7/10 Jaco
Robert 1906-1967 Gask

KELLAM (continued)
Robert W T h/o E S; s/o Thos R & Tabitha M 4 Feb 1849-5 July 1914 MtHo
Roxanna d/o Henry & Mary E 16 Oct 1897-17 Apr 1906 Snea
S Thomas 27 July 1862-16 May 1915 MtHo
Sallie 1845-1913 Holl
Sallie B Upshur w/o Col Thos; d/o Peter & Sallie B U Hack d 1874-5 Fair
Samuel B h/o F M 1913-1975 Snea
Sarah w/o Jno d 18 Mar 1772; age: 26 yrs Wacb
Sarah C w/o W H 1 Oct 1823-3 Oct 1899 Crad-s
Shadrack T s/o Shadrack & Eliza Pansy 7 Apr 1839-11 Mar 1921 StGe
Sheppard S 12 May 1834-30 Mar 1900 StGe
Smallwood 1904-1974 Shil
Spencer R h/o P E 1892-1968 MtHo
Stonewall Jackson s/o J R & B W d 3 Oct 1868; age: 0/4/24 Hero
Sudie B 1867-1954 Quin
Susan w/o Hulton 5 Jan 1806-8 Sept 1850 MtPl
Susan Arinthia d/o Thos H & Susan Ann 24 June 1846-20 July 1855 Ever
Susie Belote 3 July 1899-1 Oct 1941 MtHo-s
Tabitha Ann Marian Groton w/o T R 3 Dec 1817-3 Sept 1886 Grot
Tankard G h/o Bertie 19 June 1870-1 Apr 1940 MtHo
Tankard G (h/o L A) 1898-1978 Fair
Teagle Smith Jr 1920-1978 Shil
Thomas A h/o E R 1855-1925 MtHo
Thomas C h/o J A 12 Aug 1847-22 Feb 1908 MtHo
Thomas Hatton h/o E B; s/o Jno & Margt 6 July 1790-25 Sept 1841 Ever

KELLAM (continued)
Thomas R h/o T A M G 15 Sept 1816-9 Nov 1896 Grot
Thorogood s/o J W & M W 26 Mar-2 Apr 1834 (stone missing; 1940 data) Kebg
Thomas B s/o Custis W & Eliz d 23 Oct 1844; age: 17/7/6 Hero
Thomas P h/o Polly 29 Jan 1816-31 Dec 1874 Home
Ulton F (h/o Frances Nottingham Sterling) 1897-1935 Holl
Wilber F s/o J R & Bettie W 21 Dec 1869-21 June 1870 Hero
William C 1855-1939 Quin
William E 1831-1912 MtHo-s
Dr William F (h/o M J) 1880-1943 MtHo
William H (h/o S C) 6 Nov 1823-7 Aug 1907 Crad-s
William J h/o E M 1877-1950 MtHo-s
William L 1891-1962 MtHo-s
William P s/o Jno C P & Mary T 6 July 1864-9 Nov 1866 Vaux
William P Moore s/o Thos H Jr & Susan P (Moore) b nr Pungoteague-1842 d Accomac-1886 bur Confederate section; Hollywood Cem, Richmond VA ref: Mears
William S 8 Feb 1817-12 May 1898 Oakg
William T h/o C J 20 Oct 1821-19 Nov 1857 Holf
William T h/o E J 29 Dec 1850-16 Sept 1926 MtHo-s
Willianna Kellam w/o A H 20 Nov 1853-5 Oct 1935 StGe
Willie T 1885-1946 Quin
Willie L s/o Jas & Bittie 15 Apr 1893-17 Apr 1896 Turn
Zerobabel d 21 June 1791; age: 70 yrs Wacb

KELLY, (KELLEY),
Abel G h/o M A 12 July 1831-8 May 1918 Onan
Archie J 22 Dec 1889-24 July 1940 Edge
Beatrice D d/o M C & I V 1911-

KELLY (continued)
1926 Park
Betty Eva w/o J Custis 7 Mar 1866-14 June 1928 StGe
Braden D s/o C W & S E 25 Nov 1890-15 Apr 1908 Onan
Dr Charles A h/o G P 1903-1973 Park
Charles G (h/o E M) 1875-1954 MtHo-s
Clarence W s/o C W & Sudie E 25 Sept 1889-17 July 1903 Onan
Claude W 1878-1948 Edge
Effie M (w/o C G) 1874-1955 MtHo-s
Elic J (h/o M F) 1904-1952 Edge
Elizabeth C w/o G W 12 Aug 1841-24 Sept 1919 Edge
Elizabeth Washington (w/o M K) 2nd d/o Jos W & Eliza W Gibb 28 Nov 1828-12 Aug 1900 Onan
Ella w/o Jos Custis; d/o J H & R W Mears 1889-1978 StGe
Emily w/o Jas 16 Dec 1844-20 Apr 1918 Park
Emma C d/o Wescoat & Eliz 1 Mar 1834-15 June 1845 Kepl
G Fred h/o S J S 26 July 1864-17 Oct 1937 Onan
George W 9 Jan 1826-24 Dec 1886 Edge
Gertrude T 1882-1953 Libe
Guelda P w/o C A 1909- Park
Hallie 1913-1954 Shil
Hattie Marvin 9 Dec 1879-28 Jan 1915 Onan
Henrietta d/o G F & S J 15 Oct 1893-25 Mar 1896 Onan
Henry M 1894-1980 TurJ
Ida V w/o M C 26 Oct 1877-6 Dec 1938 Park
Irene B 1916- Park
J Custis (h/o B E) 26 Feb 1864-6 Apr 1939 StGe
John of S S 31 Aug 1781-13 Dec 1833 Kegr
John Wise 26 Aug 1873-3 July 1945 Edge
Lillie H w/o O A 1873-1961 Onan

KELLY (continued)
Lula M 1891-1936 Park
Lynwood T 1911-1983 Park
Mabel F (w/o E J) 1910- Edge
Margaret A w/o Obed 2 Sept 1804-24 Feb 1834 Brad
Margaret A d/o Wescoat & Eliz 18 Oct 1817-10 Aug 1838 Kepl
Martin C h/o I V 9 Apr 1875-17 Jan 1948 Park
Martin K (h/o E W) 21 Jan 1824-30 May 1879 Onan
Martin T 1889-1966 Park
Mary A w/o A G 8 Jan 1836-8 Sept 1900 Onan
Oscar A h/o L H 1871-1955 Onan
Sallie J Scott w/o G F d 15 Feb 1952 Onan
Sarah H 22 Oct 1889-24 Jan 1951 MtHo-s
Susan G d/o Wescoat & Eliz 7 Mar 1828-10 Sept 1840 Kepl
Thomas J 1863-1933 Park
Virginia B 1925-1977 HTri
Wescoat (h/o Eliz) d 25 June 1877; age: 87 yrs Kepl
Wesley A 1902-1973 Edge
William J 1867-1929 Onan
KELPIN, baby/o A J & E D nd Edge
Andrew Jackson (h/o E D) 1880-1937 Edge
Elizabeth Davis (w/o A J) 1886-1971 Edge
KELSO, Ann, 1st w/o Jno; (d/o Benj M & Charlotte Evans) 5 Apr 1828-30 Jan 1875 Kels
Charlotte A d/o Jno & Ann 15 May 1864-18 Oct 1867 Kels
George F s/o Jno & Ann 8 Sept 1861-10 Mar 1933 Onan
Hugh S s/o Rev Hugh B & Maude 27-28 Jan 1901 Onan
Capt John h/o S J 1818 in Scotland-17 May 1903 Onan
John A s/o Jno & Ann d 18 Jan 1864; age: 18/9/5 Kels
Joseph P s/o Jno & Ann d 18 Jan 1864; age: 6/8/14 Kels
Mollie May d/o Jno & S J 20 Jan 1882-17 July 1897 Onan
Susan J w/o Jno 15 July 1845-20

KELSO (continued)
July 1922 Onan
KENNAHORN, William 20 Nov 1747-30 Nov 1840 (soldier in War of 1776) DAR marker Kenn
KENNARD, inf/o Philip & L A 25 Mar 1852-5 Oct 1855 Edge
L A w/o Philip d 6 Feb 1853; age: 32 yrs Edge
Mary L d/o P & L A 3 July-27 Aug 1848 Coke
KENNEDY, Stella S 1909-1973 Fair
KENT, M Irving s/o T I & M S 5 Jan-5 Feb 1900 Libe
Mary S w/o T I 4 Oct 1862-23 Jan 1925 Libe
Thomas Irvin h/o M S 5 Jan 1853-28 Sept 1912 Libe
Thomas Irving Jr 13 Mar 1901-22 July 1902 Libe
KENYON, James H (h/o M E) 1915-1964 Wach
Mary E (w/o J H) 1923- Wach
KER, Agnes Drummond w/o Jno S; d/o Geo & Eliz (Revell Horsey) Corbin d Feb 1814; age: 39/1/0 Scot
Edward H h/o M A; s/o Jno S & Agnes D d Jan 1826; age: 29/5/0 Scot
(George) Beside Sarah Ker's stone is an identical large flat stone (approx-7'x5') with no inscription. This could have been placed at her death for her husband, George. Possibly inscription was never done or his burial was elsewhere. Sylv
Rev J F A 1901-1973 Metr
John Shepard Esq s/o Edwd & Margt d Sept 1806; age: (3?)8 yrs (stone erected by his son Edwd Horsey Ker) Scot
Margaret Ann w/o E H; d/o Richd & Sarah Bayly) d 10 Nov 1821; age: 18/6/10 Scot
Sarah, 2nd w/o Geo; d/o Geo & Sarah Parker 5 Nov 1776-19 Oct 1822 Sylv
KIEFER, William J Sgt USAF

KIEFER (continued)
Vietnam 2 July 1947-7 Apr 1973 Libe

KILLMON, (KILLMAN, KILLOM, KILMON),
d/o H W & F A b&d 1914 Fair
inf/o H W & F W b&d 23 Oct 1915 Park
inf/s b&d 1922 Onan
inf/s b&d 1926 MtHo-s
inf/o H W & F W b&d 17 Feb 1926 Park
s/o Alvah & Grace b&d 1958 Park
Adolphus B h/o L C 1873-1905 Onan
Alma Ray w/o S R 11 May 1881-24 Apr 1952 Park
Alonzo M (h/o O B) 1870-1963 MtHo-s
Amanda C (w/o W D) 1884-1967 Onan
Amanda S w/o L M 1876-1961 Holl
Andrew J h/o B A & B C 17 Dec 1856-27 Jan 1940 Onan
Anna Grace 12 May-15 Oct 1913 Park
Annie D w/o A J 18 Nov 1867-29 Jan 1921 Holl
Annie M w/o J H 9 June 1860-16 Dec 1912 Lawr
Annie M w/o C F 1886-1949 Onan
Annie M (w/o O G) 1893-1962 Onan
Annie R (w/o W L) 1895-1982 Onan
Annie R 1901-1966 Onan
Arinthia w/o J R 1 Aug 1876-2 Aug 1955 Park
Arinthia T w/o Littleton H; d/o Arthur & Annie M Barnes 23 Nov 1857-8 Aug 1885 Kilm
Arthur B s/o Edwd & Margt 11 June 1855-26 Oct 1887 Hick
Arthur J (h/o A D) 1855-1945 Holl
Arthur R h/o M R 1884-1956 MtHo
Asher W h/o O P 11 Feb 1880-9 Sept 1963 Park

KILLMON (continued)
Ashton b&d 1904 Holl
Avlyn E w/o E H 1893-1970 Park
Barry Lee 16-24 July 1964 Onan
Basil S h/o M B 1893-1969 MtHo
Belvin Lester s/o L J & C S 27 Nov 1893-2 May 1911 MtHo
Bessie Lee 1897-1930 Park
Bessie S (w/o C B) 1899-1981 Onan
Bettie A, 1st w/o A J 13 Oct 1859-30 Aug 1918 Onan
Bettie C, 2nd w/o A J 1866-1932 Onan
Beulah w/o Noah 1893-1956 Park
Blanche K w/o W C 1889-1982 Onan
Brooks 1887-1888 Holl
C Bradley (h/o R H 1889-1961 MtHo-s
C Snow h/o E T 1874-1938 Onan
Calvin H 22 Dec 1915-6 Apr 1974 MtHo-s
Carson E 1890-1961 Fair
Catherine 1930-1983 Onan
Catherine L w/o Ezikel 1 Nov 1817-12 Dec 1907 Kilb
Cecil B (h/o B S) 1891-1966 Onan
Charl T s/o J H & Mary 11 June 1892-21 July 1893 Crad Meth
Charles F h/o A M 1882-1953 Onan
Charles J (h/o L G) 1894-1966 Onan
Charles L (h/o Bessie K) 1866-1930 Holl
Charles Lynwood 3 Mar 1923-14 Dec 1973 Onan
Charles M (h/o W P) 1895-1950 Fair
Charles O 26 Mar 1918-22 Apr 1954 Holl
Clarence T 1906-1967 Onan
Claude F 1867-1942 MtHo-s
Clinton Kyle 21 June 1975-17 Dec 1975 Onan
Cora S w/o L J 1875-1952 MtHo
Cordelia Lee d/o Jno W & Eliz E 15 Sept 1862-13 Sept 1864 Drub
Corinthia Francis d/o J R & C P

KILLMON (continued)
30 Nov 1919-27 Oct 1921 Park
D Vinston h/o M W 1917- Park
Daniel J 1920-1962 MtHo
Dorothy d/o Harmanson & Jennie 2 Jan-13 Aug 1905 MtHo
Early Clay h/o S T 15 May 1886-12 Dec 1972 Fair
Edgar H h/o A E 1893-1976 Park
Edward 6 Nov 1793-18 Dec 1883 Kill
Edward (h/o Margt) 12 Feb 1824-12 Dec 1895 Hick
Edward 1919-1922 Onan
Effie Turlington 23 Feb 1895-13 May 1914 Home
Elba C 1895-1978 Fair
Elizabeth 31 Dec 1817-10 Feb 1907 Bogg
Elizabeth A 17 July 1836-14 June 1925 Holl
Elizabeth E w/o I W; d/o David & Rachel Evans d 9 July 1890; age: c70 yrs Kilb
Elmer G 1882-1960 Onan
Elton L h/o F F 1911- MtHo
Emma L w/o L T 1900-1970 MtHo
Emma R 25 Dec 1879-31 Oct 1958 MtHo-s
Emma Susan w/o G W 17 Jan 1864-23 July 1923 Onan
Emmitt B 1886-1944 Onan
Emory Clyde 8 July 1923-11 Apr 1924 MtHo
Ernest H (h/o V E) 24 Oct 1894-18 Mar 1962 Fair
Eron R s/o J D & M L 16 Jan 1891-16 July 1892 Holl
Esther A w/o S L 11 Apr 1864-22 Oct 1929 MtHo-s
Ethel T w/o C S 1875-1960 Onan
Ethelyn E (w/o M E) 1896-1977 Fair
Eula W w/o H H 1888- Libe
Eunice E w/o L A 1863-16 Nov 1919; age: 56 yrs MtHo
Eunice M w/o Chas M 23 Mar 1900-17 Nov 1925 Onan
Eva B 1891-1967 Park
Eva G 1878-1947 Onan
Ezekiel (h/o C L) 4 Dec 1814-16

KILLMON (continued)
Mar 1902 Kilb
Ezekiel James s/o Chas & R A 17 Jan 1841-24 Jan 1901 Onan
Faith K (w/o M L) 1900-1971 Holl
Fannie A w/o H W 23 Feb 1887-26 Feb 1970 Fair
Fanny w/o Patrick; d/o Jas E & Lillian (Boggs) LeCato 27 Jan 1899-27 Dec 1984 Onan
FLora F w/o E L 1913-1961 MtHo
Flora W w/o H W 1894-1958 Park
Frank G (h/o I A & S E) 14 Feb 1848-nd (In this plot: unmarked graves of 4 children; 2 adults) Ptea
G Norvel 1892-1952 Ptea
Garrison 1887-1962 Onan
George B h/o M H 1 Jan 1859-7 Nov 1900 Onan
George W 2 Dec 1839-4 Feb 1907 MtHo
George W h/o E S 1870-1962 Onan
Georgeana w/o H T 1853-1936 Park
Georgia White w/o J A 1866-1925 MtHo
Glenwood 1911-1970 Park
Grace L 1889-1938 MtHo
Harry Edward (h/o K M) 25 Apr 1903-28 Dec 1980 Fair
Harry H h/o E W 1885- Libe
Hazel E 1906-1969 Fair
Henrietta (w/o H E) 1904- Onan
Henry E (h/o Henrietta) 1901- Onan
Henry L 28 Jan 1861-24 Feb 1893 Onan
Henry T h/o Georgeana 20 Sept 1845-22 Aug 1929 Park
Henry W h/o M G 1866-1949 Onan
Henry W h/o F A 19 Oct 1885-15 Aug 1951 Fair
Henry W h/o F W 1890-1965 Park
Indie A w/o F G 3 Oct 1853-3 Oct 1893 Ptea

KILLMON (continued)
J Frank 1889-1961 MtHo
J Harmanson h/o M J 1873-1941 MtHo
J Lloyd 1882-1965 Libe
J Monroe (w/o M J) 4 July 1908-8 Aug 1981 MtHo-s
J Robert 1903-1976 MtHo
J Will 1884-1960 Park
James of James 1 Apr 1830-10 Dec 1887 Holl
James A h/o G W 1861-1946 MtHo
James Berry 25 Aug 1916-27 Jan 1971 Fair
James E 1868-1946 Holl
John h/o M J 1851-1940 Onan
John D (h/o M L) 1862-1940 Holl
John D s/o J D & M L 11-17 June 1894 Holl
John H s/o Edwd & Jane (June) 2 May 1828-8 Feb 1871 Kill
John H (h/o M S) 1 Aug 1828-23 July 1890 Holl
John H h/o A M 22 Aug 1857-5 Feb 1913 Lawr
John R h/o Arinthia 12 June 1872-21 Oct 1929 Park
John T 1898-1953 Park
John W h/o M J 25 Mar 1855-18 Nov 1922 Park
Joseph S (h/o K S) 15 Jan 1857-30 June 1927 Onan
Juanita H 29 Apr 1920-19 Aug 1974 MtHo-s
Julia A 1861-1943 Onan
Kate S (w/o J S) 16 Nov 1851-5 Oct 1919 Onan
Kate S (w/o T J) 24 Mar 1867-5 July 1943 Holl
Kathryn Morris (w/o H E) 29 Oct 1906- Fair
Kissier E w/o Wm Sr; d/o Geo & Rachel Fisher 19 Oct 1807-11 Nov 1866 Kilm
L Booker h/o S F 1894-1972 Onan
L Jackson h/o S F 1868-1932 Onan
L Thomas h/o E L 1898- MtHo
L Woodson h/o M H 1876-1957 Holl

KILLMON (continued)
Laurence H (h/o M L) 16 May 1894-3 Dec 1980 Onan
Leah Virginia w/o C F 27 Jan 1863-21 Oct 1921 Onan
LeRoy J h/o C S 1870-1931 MtHo
Lillian C w/o A B 1875- Onan
Lillian G (w/o C J) 1900- Onan
Littleton H (h/o M S) 1884-1966 Fair
Lorenza D h/o R C 1838-1925 Onan
Lorenzo H h/o V J 1 Oct 1889-14 Jan 1981 Park
Luther A h/o E E 1854-17 Dec 1918; age: 64 yrs MtHo
Lloyd M h/o A S 1874-1947 Holl
Louise M 1902-1951 Holl
Loulie F 1874-1971 Holl
Lucile M 7 Apr 1906- Edge
Lybrand J (h/o S M) 1847-1896 Kipl
Mabel W w/o R B 7 Apr 1917- Fair
Malinda A w/o Wm T; d/o Ephrim & Mariah Byrd 8 Oct 1810-29 Oct 1870 Kilm
Manie A w/o N P; d/o J T & Sophia Melson 20 Oct 1848-5 Sept 1906 Edge
Mannie G w/o H W 1872-1971 Onan
Margaret w/o Edwd 20 Jan 1818-21 Mar 1897 Hick
Margaret F 17 May 1862-12 July 1913 Holl
Margaret H w/o G B 2 June 1862-10 July 1930 Onan
Margaret H w/o L W 1881-1951 Holl
Margaret J w/o Jno 1853-1936 Onan
Margaret J w/o J H 1876-1945 MtHo
Margaret S w/o Jno H; d/o L & C Savage 23 May 1835-1 Sept 1857 Holl
Margaret S w/o Jno H 26 Nov 1847-29 Feb 1940 Holl
Margie L (w/o J D) 1873-1948 Holl

KILLMON (continued)
Marie B (w/o P W) 1897-1974 Holl
Martha R w/o A R 1884-1960 MtHo
Marvin E(h/o E E) 1897-1976 Fair
Mary E d/o J D & M L 10-18 Mar 1892 Holl
Mary J w/o J W 1865-1936 Park
Mary S (w/o L H) 1886-1952 Fair
May Lewis (w/o L H) 29 Feb 1892-4 Jan 1978 Onan
Merrill R s/o C F & A M 29 Sept 1917-15 Feb 1926 Onan
Milton G 1894-1970 Holl
Milton H 18 July 1941-21 Feb 1942 Park
Milton L (h/o F K) 1898- Holl
Mollye M 8 Nov 18__-25 May 1970 Onan
Myrie W w/o D V 1920- Park
Myrtle B w/o B S 1897- MtHo
Myrtle J (w/o J M) 21 Oct 1913- MtHo-s
N Polk h/o M A 17 July 1833-11 July 1916 Edge
Nettie Doris d/o L B & S F 1926-1927 Onan
Noah h/o Beulah 1893-1982 Park
Nora B 1884-1971 Libe
Olivia B (w/o A M) 1876-1955 MtHo-s
Oscar G (h/o A M) 1892-1965 Onan
Oscar L h/o R R 1873-1948 Onan
Otelia Price w/o A W 1882-1934 Park
Other 15 July 1895-22 Dec 1964 Park
Otho 1877-1963 Park
P Lee (h/o T S) 1886-1970 Holl
Page W (h/o M B) 1895-1943 Holl
Patrick W 28 May 1850-17 Feb 1899 Holl
Pearl M 1894-1972 MtHo
Peyton H 1 Sept 1895-1 Oct 1955 MtHo
Philip Kennie 22 Sept 1888-21 Apr 1947 Ptea
Preston W 3 Feb 1898-25 May

KILLMON (continued)
1933 Park
Randolph M 1904-1924 MtHo-s
Rhoda R w/o O L 1875-1955 Onan
Rita Adell d/o A R & M R 30 Apr-10 July 1907 MtHo
Robert M 1900-1968 Holl
Rose 1879-1956 Park
Rose Ann w/o Chas 2 Apr 1812-21 July 1888 Onan
Roy B h/o M W 19 Feb 1915-13 Feb 1981 Fair
Ruth C w/o L D 17 Sept 1835-2 Jan 1904 Onan
Ruth H (w/o C B) 1892-1968 MtHo-s
Sally Taylor w/o E C 11 June 1891-5 Nov 1978 Fair
Samuel R h/o A R 30 Sept 1874-25 May 1957 Park
Samuel T 10 June 1861-17 Feb 1925 Park
Sarah E w/o F G 5 Mar 1872-29 Apr 1950 Ptea
Spencer L h/o E A 28 Aug 1864-28 Sept 1939 MtHo-s
Sulie H d/o Jno E & Maggie A 9 May 1878-28 Sept 1880 Kill
Susan F w/o L J 1872-1938 Onan
Susan M w/o L J 1846-1926 Kipl
Susie F w/o L B 1900-1971 Onan
T J (h/o K S) 1 Aug 1853-15 May 1934 Holl
Tabbie S (w/o P L) 1891- Holl
Thomas 6 Dec 1827-(4 July 1891 stone broken - 1940 data) Kill
Thomas J 1882-1954 Onan
Vaden E w/o W J 1888-1926 MtHo-s
Viola E (w/o E H) 1901- Fair
Virginia w/o Edwd 2 May 1800-28 Aug 1875 Kill
Vivian J w/o L H 7 Jan 1894-1 Feb 1971 Park
W Carson h/o B K 1889-1971 Onan
Walter D (h/o A C) 1881-1953 Onan
William h/o K E; s/o Edwd & Tabitha 15 Apr 18801-25 Aug 1873 Kilm

KILLMON (continued)
William David s/o Jno W & Eliz E 24 Sept 1859-27 Sept 1864 Drub
William Harry 1877-1900 Holl
William J h/o V E 1890-1949 MtHo-s
William T (h/o Annie L) 19 Sept 1831-5 Dec 1906 Holl
William T s/o Noah & Beulah 1938-1941 Park
William Warren 1914-1941 MtHo
Willie T s/o W T & Annie L 20 Apr 1896-31 July 1908 Holl
Winfield L (h/o A R) 1893-1968 Onan
Winnie P (w/o C M) 1898-1952 Fair
KIMMERLE, Catharine A w/o Jno T 184_-1890 Edge
John T h/o C A 30 Sept 1826-22 Feb 1903 Edge
Thomas J s/o Jno T & C A 1863-1881 Edge
KING, David Allen 11 Mar 1943-1 Sept 1971 Fair
Etrula Kellam 1909-1968 HTri
Etta Dodson (w/o W A) 1906-1960 Onan
Mary S w/o V H 1892-1975 Burt
Matilda K 1852-1923 Holl
V Harrison h/o M S 1887-1968 (marr: 9 Sept 1910) Burt
Walter Bundick 18 Aug 1910-22 Sept 1982 Fair
William A (h/o E D) 1890-1938 Onan
KIPLING, W M 15 June 1915-8 May 1983 Fair
KIRCOFE, Rev George William h/o V C 5 Aug 1847-19 Aug 1919 Onan
Virginia Catherine w/o G W 25 Oct 1842-25 Mar 1922 Onan
William Norris 16 Sept 1885-25 June 1898 Onan
KISER, Aleen Melson d/o Ray Pendleton & S Earnestine (Mears) 16-19 July 1936 Onan
Vicki Earlene 7 Feb 1962-6 Mar 1981 Park
KLEIN, Neta M 1906-1951 Park

KLINE, John G Jr 1927-1979 Wach
KNIGHT, Clara M w/o D J 1913- Park
Denard J h/o C M 1902-1972 Park
George s/o Thos d 10 Sept 1776; age: 25 yrs Fair
Mary R (w/o W N) 1902- Onan
William N (h/o M R) 1897-1962 Onan
KNOX, Augustus 18 Nov 1891-20 Aug 1959 JoyC
Dewey 1926-1979 Gask
Elmer J 1923-1965 JoyC
Frank Sr 1903-1979 Burt
James Evans 1872-1956 StPa
KOCSIS, Helen Parsons 1921-1982 Edge
KOEBERNIK, Mazie 1911-1982 Wach
KOENIG, Mary Ashby w/o Adolph D 25 Oct 1885-25 Sept 1924 Edge
KOERNER, Bernice L w/o H K 1904-1974 Park
Howard V h/o B L 1916- Park
KOSKEY, Catherine Finney 1901-1959 Park
John A (h/o M E) 1868-1943 MtHo-s
Marvin A 1901-1954 MtHo-s
Mollie E (w/o J A) 1881-1962 MtHo-s
KRALLER, John E 14 July 1916-20 Mar 1979 Park
KRAZINSKY, Adaline B w/o M W 1902-1977 Park
Michael W h/o A B 1894-1980 Park
KROGER, Emma 1883-1962 MtHo
KROMER, Lottie B 1916-1983 Park
KROMMES, Earl W 1 Aug 1910-30 July 1972 Libe
KURTY, Sue d/o N J W & E E LeCato 16 July 1872-26 June 1911 Quin
KUSIAN, A T L 1840-1920 StGe
Emma Johns 1842-1910 StGe
LACKEY, Katherine D 1876-1957 Druf

LaFAYE, Maria Kellam w/o Edwd J 21 Oct 1875-16 May 1971 Edge
LAIRD, Mollie w/o Willis 1919- Onan
Willis h/o Mollie 1907-1962 Onan
LAKE, Peggy 1927-1966 Onan
LAMBDEN, Julia F 1852-1944 Onan
Samuel J 4 Aug 1825-25 Aug 1912 Onan
LAMBERT, Theresa M 7 Feb 1930-20 May 1976 NewM
LANCASTER, Margaret C w/o S B 26 Feb 1905-8 Oct 1983 Fair
Stanley B h/o M C 25 Jan 1903- Fair
LANDES, Kate 1872-1906 MtHo
Stewart W 1895-1910 MtHo
LANDING, W T 10 June 1845-30 June 1929 Park
LANDON, (probably children/o J W & L F) James; William; Winnie nd Wach
John W (h/o L F) 1871-1957 Wach
Laura F (w/o J W) 1875-1958 Wach
LANE, inf/o Chas & Anne V b&d 14 May 1900 Wach
Anne E (w/o C S) 1875-1942 MtHo-s
Charles S (h/o A E) 1875-1955 MtHo-s
Henrietta d/o Chas & Anne V 1 Jan-10 Feb 1909 Wach
Henrietta W w/o H S 17 Oct 1844-9 Dec 1896 Wach
Horace S h/o H W 30 Nov 1846-2 June 1919 Wach
Ida M 10 Dec 1886-17 Oct 1965 Libe
Laurie Lee 1963-1965 MtHo-s
LANG, Catherine F w/o Henry 29 Aug 1836-8 Mar 1904 Edge
Henny A 1891-1951 Edge
Henry h/o C F 1 Mar 1824-5 Dec 1905 Edge
James E h/o S M 1868-1952 Edge
Jay E h/o Ernestine 13 July

LANG (continued) 1903-17 Nov 1968 MtHo
Nannie J w/o Wm H 1863-1929 Edge
Nathaniel Joseph (h/o V P) 19 Dec 1864-23 Sept 1939 Edge
Sallie M w/o J E 1867-1947 Edge
Virginia Parkes (w/o N J) 24 Dec 1865-29 May 1935 Edge
William H h/o N J 1859-1934 Edge
William J 1916-1960 Edge
LANGSDALE, Bettie G d/o J H & E S 8 Sept 1840-14 Mar 1855 Onan
Elizabeth S w/o J H; d/o Abel & Margt Garrison 29 Dec 1821-30 Oct1871 Onan
John H h/o E S; s/o Henry & Eliz 3 June 1807-27 Aug 1855 Onan
John H Jr s/o J H & E S 12 Dec 1852-5 Apr 1874 Onan
Maggie H d/o J H & E S 7 Feb 1843-25 Dec 1870 Onan
Margaret R w/o Jno H; d/o Abel & Margt Garrison 23 Jan 1806-26 June 1837 Onan
Priscilla d/o J H & E S 31 July 1844-17 June 1867 Onan
Susan Ann d/o J H & E S 22 Nov 1846-25 Feb 1924 Onan
LANKFORD, Bessie Lillian 10 Nov 1912-10 Apr 1984; age: 71 yrs Park
Carl T h/o G C 1887-1939 Edge
Gene R 10 Mar 1926-13 Aug 1981 Park
Gertrude w/o C T 1886-1980 Edge
Jerome J 1860-1922 Edge
Julia M 1950-1951 Park
Lemuel T s/o S T & M E 1880-1955 Libe
Leona E 1891-1924 Edge
Lillie Rew 1864-1951 Park
Mary E w/o S T 24 Dec 1853-11 July 1929 Libe
Orris Arnold Jr h/o T P 1918-1984 Park
Preston T 1906-1979 Park

157

LANKFORD (continued)
Robert T 20 Sept 1915-9 Apr 1930 MtHo
S T h/o M E 15 Apr 1853-8 Oct 1935 Libe
Thelma Parks w/o A A 1920-1975 Park
Willard F 4 Feb 1921-23 Oct 1983 Park
LARSEN, Clarence J (h/o H C) 7 Sept 1891-13 Sept 1965 Fair
Hazel C (w/o C J) 24 Jan 1896-1 Oct 1970 Fair
LaRUE, Jacob D h/o M C 1870-1938 Park
Mary C w/o J D 1873-1947 Park
LASSITER, Frances Marshall (w/o S T) 1889-1965 Fair
James 1914-1983 Fair
Sherrill T 1879-1969 Fair
LATHAM, A G 1870-1943 MtHo
Annie M w/o Jos A 4 Feb 1849-24 Sept 1898 MtHo
James Leslie s/o J A & A M 6 May-6 July 1888 MtHo
LATHBURY, John A h/o L B 1898-1974 Quin
Lillie B w/o J A 1905-1979 Quin
LAWRENCE, John h/o M S 29 Jan 1833-29 Mar 1902 Lawr
John K s/o W & Margt 30 Aug 1864-16 Nov 1866 Lawr
Margaret S w/o Jno 12 July 1835-12 Mar 1891 Lawr
William H s/o Jno & Margt 29 Aug 1868-29 Aug 1871 Lawr
LAWS, Herbert Newton h/o Bertha Reeves 1884-1941 (a minister of the church in Diocese of So VA) StGe
Joseph G s/o Zorobabel & M L 30 Nov 1843-15 Mar 1885 Onan
Mahala J w/o Z C 3 May 1808-30 Nov 1843; age: 35/6/27 Onan
Susie S 1903-1978 Snea
LAWSON, Eddie Jr b&d 1962 Snea
Elizabeth G (w/o W T) 1896-1976 Quin
Ella B (w/o G W) 1874-1962 Quin

LAWSON (continued)
George W (h/o E B) 1866-1938 Quin
Nettie M (w/o R L) 1902- Quin
Robert Lee (h/o N M) 29 May 1897-27 Nov 1969 Quin
William T (h/o E G) 1893-1969 Quin
LEATHERBURY, Bettie B w/o E R 12 Mar 1834-2 July 1922 MtHo
Edward R MD h/o B B 29 Jan 1825-1 Mar 1913 MtHo
Emorie P 1873-1949 MtHo
Eva 9 July 1871-18 Dec 1952 MtHo
George C s/o P A & L A d 20 June 1874; age: 0/0/10 Onan
Dr George P Jan 1829-Oct 1867 LeaW
George P Sr d 3 Feb 1855; age: 62/4/3 (Methodist since 1843) LeaW
Hortense K 1875-1961 MtHo
J Chauncey W 1878-1955 MtHo
Leah Annie w/o Rev P A 5 Mar 1831-30 Apr 1896 Onan
Margaret C 1839-1905 MtHo
Perry A h/o L A 17 Mar 1817-13 Mar 1897 Onan
Sarah 19 Oct 1863-14 Feb 1878 MtHo
Sarah 19 Oct 1868-14 Feb 1878 Scot
Thomas B DDS 15 Aug 1867-6 Jan 1926 MtHo
Zipporah w/o P A 11 Apr 1819-25 July 1865 Coke
LeCATO, baby boy b&d 1964 Onan
little Alfred d 9 Feb 1853; age: 6 yrs Quin
Alfred Browne h/o V F 7 June 1859-25 Sept 1905 Quin
Annie F w/o Littleton 20 Apr 1817-6 Nov 1834 Coal
Annie Sue d/o J E & L L 1 Dec 1894-2 Mar 1897 Crad-s
Annie Winder 1882-1937 StGe
Bernard only child/o G W & M J 1 June 1875-17 May 1925 Quin
Bertha D 1888-1968 Onan

LeCATO (continued)
Bettie A w/o J M 24 Nov 1849-6 Aug 1905 Crad-s
Bettie Ann 24 Nov 1893-6 Oct 1936 Onan
Clara 30 Jan 1856-11 Oct 1938 Burt
Clara nd (d prob 1967) NewM
Cordelia E d/o W R & J C ns LeCa
Cordie E Smith w/o L T d in Jacksonville FL 11 Jan 1881; age: 43 yrs Coal
Edwin (Ned) F 31 July 1860-19 Oct 1891 (d in Chicago) Quin
Edwin G h/o R C 1874-1954 Quin
Edwin W MD d 28 July 1867; age: 38 yrs Quin
Elizabeth w/o N J W; d/o Wm Eichelberger 10 Dec 1837-1 Feb 1917 Quin
Elizabeth 1929-1980 StJo
Elizabeth G w/o N B 30 Mar 1808-4 Nov 1868 Quin
Esther w/o Littleton 28 Mar 1783-12 Oct 1829 Quin
George Hugh 10 Jan 1864-4 Sept 1913 Quin
Hon George W MD h/o M J 1 Aug 1842-12 Mar 1903 Quin
George Walter d 25 Nov 1941; age: 44 yrs Burt
Hampton d 4 Aug 1941; age: 47 yrs Burt
Hugh Thomas s/o L T & C E d 24 Apr 1863; age: 0/11/5 Quin
J Arthur Sr 1921-1981 Quin
James E h/o L L 11 June 1871-21 Feb 1956 Crad-s
James E 26 Sept 1887-22 Nov 1890 Jaco
Jane 29 Aug 1768-4 Mar 1815 Parp
Jane C Mapp w/o Wm R 20 July 1815-8 May 1899 LeCa
Joe Lee 30 July 1928-19 Oct 1980 Onan
John Pvt USA - WWI nd Burt
John M h/o B A 8 Jan 1849-15 Nov 1926 Crad-s
John R d 6 Dec 1843; age: 11 yrs Quin

LeCATO (continued)
John R 1884-1948 Onan
John Walter L s/o Clara 1 Mar 1894-27 Mar 1906 Burt
Kathleen 1910-1960 Onan
Lillian E (w/o W N) 1863-1946 Quin
Lillian L w/o J E; nee Boggs 14 May 1872-17 Apr 1925 Crad-s
Lishia A d 13 Apr 1964; age: 62 yrs Burt
Littleton h/o Esther 21 Mar 1773-23 Oct 1837 (stone badly worn) Quin
Rev Littleton K h/o M C 4 June 1813-4 Jan 1882 (50 yrs a Methodist minister) Coal
Margaret d1965 Shil
Margaret E (Peddie) 20 Oct 1865-17 Jan 1885 Coal
Mary C w/o Littleton K 15 Sept 1815-21 Apr 1859 Coal
Mary J (w/o G W) 25 Mar 1851-29 May 1876 Quin
N J W h/o E E; s/o Nathl B & E W 10 Aug 1835-31 Mar 1911 Quin
Nathaniel B h/o E G 12 Nov 1808-2 Apr 1882 Quin
Ruth Chew w/o E G 13 Dec 1874-27 Feb 1946 Quin
Sallie F 15 Feb 1851-3 Jan 1891 (b in Hertford NC) Quin
Susie C d/o L Thos & Cordellia E 1871-1944 Quin
Susie Walter 29 Nov 1854-14 Feb 1915 Fair
Thomas F d Oct 1884; age: 0/2/2 Quin
Thomas Littleton 5 May 1831-19 Mar 1909 Quin
Virginia Fox w/o A B 1863-1948 Quin
William J 1885-1964 Onan
William Joe 12 Mar 1850-26 Jan 1940 Onan
William N (h/o L E) 15 Oct 1857-27 Jan 1940 Quin
William R h/o Jane C M (ns d1847) LeCa

LEE, Iona P w/o J L 10 Mar 1890-11 Dec 1925 Park

LEE (continued)
James Lawrence h/o I P 28 Nov 1913-29 Mar 1948 Park
Margaret h/o Rev Wm d 13 Jan 1853; age: 77/0/0 Coke
Tifton III 1960-1962 Snea
Rev William h/o Margt (local minister of the M E Church) d 10 Apr 1848; age: 81/0/0 Coke
LEGENDRE, Jacques L 8 May 1889-6 Dec 1973 StGe
LEGG, Daisy C w/o E P 1874-1960 Onan
E Price h/o D C 1865-1927 Onan
LEIGH, Debbie b&d 10 May 1954 Edge
LERBS, John H (h/o M H) 1885-1966 Fair
Mildred H (w/o J H) 1900- Fair
LeROY, Betty C w/o F E 10 Mar 1882-22 Feb 1963 Edge
Fred E h/o B C 10 July 1875-4 Jan 1957 Edge
LESCALLETTE, Alice B 1861-1931 Libe
B Stella 2 Mar 1899-31 Oct 1936 Park
Henry W 1850-1924 Libe
Maggie E (sister) 1890-1934 Libe
LEVIN, Sallie A 21 Apr 1831-10 July 1886 Ward
LEWIS, inf s/o Leonidas & S H nd Libe
inf/o J E & M A b&d 7 Jan 1895 Onan
d/o J H & M S 10-11 July 1899 Edge
d/o A W & D M b&d 13 Sept 1911 Libe
Absolom 2 Aug 1898-4 Apr 1967 Libe
Ada D 1896- Edge
Addie T w/o H N 1888-1949 Park
Addie V, 1st w/o S T 24 Feb 1883-21 Oct 1918 Libe
Albert F (h/o S A) 1878-1949 MtHo-s
Aldon W h/o D B 1877-1937 Libe
Alexander M h/o M R 28 Nov 1834-29 July 1906 Libe

LEWIS (continued)
Alfred J h/o M A; s/o S & Sallie 7 May 1832-19 Nov 1912 Libe
Alfred L h/o C E 1860-1928 Libe
Alice Lee d/o T M & E J 1 May-25 Sept 1865 Libe
Alice W w/o J H nd Edge
Amanda E w/o W D 1845-1930 MtHo
Amanda S w/o H A 1872-1957 Libe
Angela Beth 30 June 1970-25 Oct 1971 Fair
Annie B (w/o A F) 1912-1942 MtHo-s
Annie C w/o W H 1872-1958 Edge
Annie H 1860-1947 Park
Annie V d/o W D & A E 15 Nov 1887-21 May 1898 MtHo
Arinthia J w/o Wm H 10 Feb 1838-15 Mar 1916 Libe
Arthur F (h/o A B) 1909-1967 MtHo-s
Ashton J h/o E V 23 Oct 1880-15 Dec 1959 Libe
Attie F w/o O W 13 Feb 1871-19 Jan 1932 Edge
Audrey B w/o J M 1919- Fair
Ben P 16 Sept 1938-26 May 1956 Park
Bertha 1893-1952 Libe
Bertha J d/o J E & M A 9 Sept 1903-10 May 1904 Onan
Bessie B w/o Wm R Sr 1894- Libe
Bessie P 1884-1918 Edge
Bessie Y w/o S L 1893-1962 Park
Bettie B w/o W E 27 Aug 1868-27 Nov 1954 Edge
Bettie D w/o Capt Saml A 12 Oct 1874-19 Apr 1917 Edge
Bettie F d/o H W & L P 1944-1946 Edge
Bettie S w/o O W 23 Sept 1858-9 Feb 1912 Onan
Burleigh C 1895-1969 Edge
Carlyle W b&d 1918 Libe
Carson R h/o O B 25 Sept 1887-27 July 1949 MtHo-s
Cecie E w/o E M 1888-1976

LEWIS (continued)
Libe
Cecile M w/o R J 1894-1969 Libe
Charlie E 1911-1972 Snea
Charlotte T w/o H C 18 Nov 1835-20 Apr 1903 Edge
Clarence L D 31 Mar 1875-3 June 1932 Mari
Clarence U 16 Feb 1897-24 Dec 1948 MtHo
Coley L s/o J E & M A 9 Mar 1888-31 July 1893 Onan
Comfort S (w/o G T) 2 Sept 1860-4 Oct 1927 MtHo-s
Cora E w/o A L 1866-1937 Libe
Cora M (w/o L E) 1885-1966 Fair
David Ayres 11 June 1920-19 Oct 1979 MtHo-s
DeForest 27 Apr-10 Oct 1894 Libe
Docie E 11 Apr 1858-7 Apr 1932 Libe
Dora Byrd w/o A W 1885-1982 Libe
Dora C w/o J H Jr 1899-1971 Edge
Dorsey E (h/o R W) 1893-1967 Fair
E A d/o L D & M A 26 Oct 1852-11 July 1911 (name cemented; initials from footstone) Mari
E S w/o J D 1865-1946 Libe
Ed Riley h/o EL 1869-1911 Libe
Edith U d/o F C & E C 29 Mar 1883-25 Nov 1920 Libe
Edward C W h/o I V 1867-1942 Libe
Elijah B 10 Feb 1909-14 Mar 1979 Park
Elizabeth; Lena; Thomas; Tully; William nd - all on one stone Onan
Elizabeth A w/o J S 1848-1920 Libe
Elizabeth Johnson w/o M L 1864-1943 Park
Ella Boggs 1 Nov 1875- MtHo-s
Ella D w/o W T 1865-1936 Onan
Ella L w/o R L 1871-1969 Libe

LEWIS (continued)
Ella L b&d 1898 Libe
Elmer M h/o C E 1882-1961 Libe
Elton D 1884-1956 Edge
Emma C w/o F C 19 May 1857-19 Nov 1909 Libe
Emma L w/o E R 1872-1952 Libe
Ester A 1844-1903 Park
Ethel V w/o R J 1871-1940 Edge
Ethel Y (w/o J R) 18 Feb 1872-5 Mar 1945 Edge
Eunice V w/o A J 15 July 1879-10 Feb 1932 Libe
Eva S 1880-1932 Park
Eva S w/o P W 1880-1953 Libe
Fannie E 1910-1912 Edge
Fannie M 1878-1903 Libe
Fletcher M h/o T B 22 Aug 1869-1961 Libe
Frank R 1888-1942 Onan
Franklin C h/o E C 6 Aug 1856-9 Nov 1941 Libe
Fred A 1919-1974 Metr
G Dewey h/o L B 6 July 1896-25 Mar 1976 Park
Gazel B d/o W T & L L 5 Aug-13 Nov 1907 Park
George T (h/o C S) 24 Aug 1849-1 Jan 1935 MtHo-s
George U (h/o P L) 1893-1970 Fair
Geraldine F w/o S J 1 Apr 1853-27 Oct 1933 Park
Gertie Scott (w/o T D) 15 June 1891-30 Apr 1982 Edge
Grace Louise d/o Obed W & A F 10 Oct 1901-7 Aug 1902 Edge
Harry A h/o A S 1870-1961 Libe
Harry W Sr h/o L P 1898-1972 Edge
Harvey J 26 Sept 1912-10 June 1956 MtHo-s
Harvey N h/o A T 1879-1952 Park
Harvey T 26 Feb 1881-4 May 1960 MtHo-s
Hattie E 25 Sept 1884-9 Mar 1966 MtHo-s
Hazel L w/o Winfred 1910-1978 Libe

LEWIS (continued)
Helen T b&d 1902 Libe
Henry C h/o C T 10 Jan 1837-1 Apr 1915 Edge
Henry J (h/o S A) 8 Oct 1840-3 May 1914 Gunt
Herman A 18 Aug 1886-10 Mar 1953 Libe
Herbert C 7 Apr 1924-2 Mar 1976 Fair
Ida C (w/o J H) 5 Jan 1889-2 Jan 1964 MtHo-s
Isabelle R (w/o Walter) 1917- Onan
Isola S 1888- Edge
J D h/o E S 1861-1937 Libe
James E h/o M A 24 June 1866-15 May 1937 Onan
James H 15 Sept 1908-26 Mar 1968 Fair
James H Jr h/o D C 1897-1977 Edge
James H Sr h/o M S 29 Sept 1864-13 June 1938 Edge
James I h/o R G 11 May 1867-19 Dec 1926 MtHo-s
James M b&d 1901 Libe
James R (h/o E Y) 1 Nov 1867-14 Dec 1948 Edge
James S h/o E A 1835-1905 Libe
James W s/o H C & C T 24 June 1858-3 July 1859 Edge
John E (w/o M S) 3 Aug 1832-6 May 1912; age: 80 yrs Edge
John H (h/o I C) 31 Jan 1883-2 Oct 1967 MtHo-s
John Hampton Sr h/o A W nd Edge
John Hampton 10 June 1889-7 Feb 1975 Edge
John Harvey 18 Sept 1884-31 Oct 1958 Libe
John M h/o A B 1908-1978 Fair
John R h/o Josephine 6 Jan 1865-20 Sept 1927 Park
John T h/o L K 1870-1938 Libe
Josephine w/o J R 25 Aug 1866-25 Dec 1927 Park
Ida Virginia w/o E C W 1872-1941 Libe
Julia A T d/o Revil & Polly 18 June 1834-9 Oct 1842; age:

LEWIS (continued)
8/3/22 Lewi
Julia Nelson 20 Apr 1904- Onan
Kate S, 2nd w/o S T 27 Apr 1890-29 Sept 1973 Libe
L Filmore (h/o M H) 16 Feb 1877-10 May 1966 Onan
Laura T w/o Jno R d 21 Aug 1885; age: 18 yrs DrMC
Leatie R 1907-1973 Park
Leemon I 26 Aug 1909-17 Feb 1974 MtHo
Lena Mae (w/o W A) 1902- Fair
Lena S 1908-1968 Park
Lena T 1884-1972 Libe
Lenora S w/o T M 1868-1924 Libe
Leonidas h/o S H 15 Mar 1839-18 Jan 1903 Libe
Levin D (h/o M A) 30 Jan 1818-10 Nov 1886 Mari
Levin J h/o S S 1890-1958 Libe
Levin R h/o V S 10 Feb 1836-nd Onan
Lillian B w/o G D 1 Sept 1895-28 July 1982 Park
Lloyd F 28 Mar 1872-5 Feb 1948 MtHo-s
Lottie L w/o Wm T 1880-1964 Park
Lottie T d/o H C & C T 20 July-22 Aug 1863 Edge
Louise Hill 1919-1956 Snea
Lucille P w/o H W Sr 1 Nov 1903-28 Jan 1945 Edge
Lucy Shrieves 1898- Park
Lula K w/o J T 1872-1950 Libe
Luther E (h/o C M) 1879-1973 Fair
Maggie A 6 Mar 1866-5 July 1934 Libe
Manning D 1896-1939 Park
Margaret R w/o A M 10 Feb 1846-8 Nov 1930 Libe
Margaret S (w/o J E) 25 July 1835-9 Sept 1905 Edge
Margaret S w/o J H Sr 15 Sept 1865-10 June 1960 Edge
Marguerite F w/o M L 1896- Libe
Maria A w/o A J 20 Dec 1837-26 Sept 1901 Libe

LEWIS (continued)
Mark C h/o M F 1887-1970 Libe
Marvin C 20 Feb 1916-29 Apr 1982 Libe
Mary Ann w/o L D; d/o Smith & Annie Melson 27 Aug 1831-4 Mar 1908 Mari
Mary E 1857-1936 Libe
Mary E w/o Capt S A; d/o Capt T S & Sarah Parks 7 Oct 1858-26 Mar 189_ Edge
Matilda w/o Revil J; d/o Jno Spence d 18 Oct 1856; age: 30 yrs (stone missing. Ref: Death Bk p13 Acc Co) Lewi
Mattie A w/o J E 25 Mar 1863-13 Jan 1927 Onan
Maud 3 Nov 1892-17 Apr 1893 Libe
Maude H (w/o L F) 19 Jan 1880-11 Aug 1963 Onan
Maurice L h/o E J; s/o L D & Ann 1863-1944 Park
Melissa C w/o W T 16 May 1872-25 Jan 1904 Libe
Milton P 1898-1962 Libe
Morris s/o M L & E D 20 Oct-15 Dec 1888 Park
Morris D s/o L D & M A 28 July 1855-27 Aug 1861; age: 6/0/29 Mari
Nola Lee w/o W R 1886-1972 Edge
Norman H 1899-1965 MtHo
O W h/o A F 21 Nov 1873-12 Sept 1942 Edge
Olive Bull w/o C R 25 Sept 1894-12 Apr 1971 MtHo-s
Oliver C Sr 1881-1948 Libe
Orris H Jr h/o V S 1898-1945 Park
Orris L 15 Dec 1870-14 May 1907 Libe
Patricia Camper w/o Saml J 1921-1946 MtHo-s
Pearl d/o Stanley J & G F d 13 Dec 1883; age: 0/0/1 Mari
Pearl L (w/o G U) 1895-1973 Fair
Philbert W h/o E S 1875-1944 Libe
Polly M w/o Revil 13 May 1802-

LEWIS (continued)
6 May 1885 Lewi
Randolph U 8 May 1893-30 Sept 1911 Edge
Randolph U 9 Apr 1915-24 Sept 1964 Edge
Raymond R (h/o S G) 14 Aug 1838-27 Feb 1904 Edge
Rebecca H 11 Sept 1873-28 June 1935 MtHo-s
Revil h/o P M 10 Mar 1790-26 Oct 1846; age: 56/7/16 leaving a wife & 11 children Lewi
Capt Revil J 26 Jan 1831-4 Aug 1891; age: 60/6/9 Lewi
Robert J h/o E V 1867-1918 Edge
Robert J h/o C M 1891-1960 Libe
Robert Keith 15 Mar 1955-20 Oct 1973 Fair
Robert L h/o E L 1867-1940 Libe
Roberta B 14 June 1892-9 May 1928 Libe
Rose Gray w/o J I 11 June 1867-20 Apr 1937 MtHo-s
Rosie M 1941-1943 Libe
Rupert Christian 18 Dec 1894-27 Mar 1976 Edge
Ruth W (w/o D E) 1891-1982 Fair
Sallie d 22 Nov 1925; age: 80 yrs Park
Sallie A 21 Apr 1831-10 July 1889 Ward
Sallie A w/o H J 6 Oct 1857-2 Jan 1905 Gunt
Sallie H w/o Leonidas 31 Jan 1842-21 Aug 1901 Libe
Sam Ayres s/o S A & B D 26 July 1903-11 July 1904 Edge
Samuel Absalom h/o M E; s/o Abs & Eliz M 15 Dec 1851-13 Dec 1915 Edge
Samuel J 1859-1891 Park
Samuel Lee h/o B V 1889-1965 Park
Samuel T h/o A V & K S 16 Feb 1883-14 Jan 1969 Libe
Sarah C w/o U D 1889-1970 Park
Sara Elizabeth 1877-1960 Libe

LEWIS (continued)
Sarah G (w/o R R) 12 Jan 1844-9 Jan 1894 Edge
Sarah J w/o W R 4 Dec 1829-22 Aug 1887; mar: 21 June 1849 Onan
Sarah S w/o L J 1897-1973 Libe
Sarah Scott d/o Alfred T unmarked Mont
Sophia S w/o Jno; d/o Shepard & Mary Ann Baker 15 Dec 1839-30 May 1919 Edge
Stanley C s/o Stanley J & G F 18 July 1879-21 May 1882 Mari
Stanley J h/o G F 18 Oct 1850-17 July 1929 Park
Stantley A 8 Oct 1912-26 Jan 1929 Libe
Stella A (w/o A F) 1889-1970 MtHo-s
Sudie E mother/o Wm R Sr 1868-1936 Libe
Sudie R 14 Oct 1895-17 May 1955 Libe
Sue C w/o Wm T J 1881-1956 Libe
Susan M wid/o Wm T 24 Feb 1841-20 Nov 1897; age: 56/8/26 Lewi
Susie F 1894-1932 MtHo
Susie G 1910-1951 Wach
Thelma L 27 Dec 1923-22 Mar 1924 Park
Tibbie B w/o F M 1873-1953 Libe
Thomas J s/o L D & M A 18 June 1861-22 July 1869; age: 8/1/4 Mari
Thomas R s/o L D & M A 12 July 1858-14 Aug 1861; age: 3/1/2 Mari
Tracy Donald (h/o G S) 8 Sept 1900-15 Jan 1978 Edge
Tully M h/o E J Russell; s/o Jas & Cassandra 8 Nov 1839-16 Mar 1866 (drowned in Chesapeake Bay; remains found 27 Apr 1866) Libe
Tully M h/o L S 1866-1944 Libe
Upshur D h/o S C 1887-1942 Park
Vallie S w/o O H 1903-1982 Park

LEWIS (continued)
Veda T (w/o V P) 1907- MtHo-s
Vernetta M w/o Z R Sr 1875-1951 Edge
Vernon P (h/o V T) 1901-1967 MtHo-s
Virginia C 1845-1932 Libe
Virnetta S w/o L R 18 Oct 1840-16 Aug 1913 Onan
W D 1 Sept 1860-5 July 1919 Libe
W Avery (h/o L M) 1904-1965 Fair
Walter (h/o I R) 1921-1981 Onan
Walter D h/o A E 1840-1928 MtHo
Walter T 31 Mar 1892-12 Nov 1959 MtHo
Warren P s/o M L & E J 1892-1964 Park
Warren P 1903-1975 Libe
Webster R h/o N L 1885-1968 Edge
William E h/o B B 25 July 1862-30 Nov 1933 Edge
William H h/o A J 5 May 1837-5 June 1920 Libe
William H h/o A C 1872-1962 Edge
William J 6 Nov 1867-4 Mar 1944 Libe
William J s/o W T & E D 2 Sept 1900-7 July 1902 Onan
William James 20 Sept 1880-29 Sept 1954 Park
William R h/o S J 24 Oct 1827-4 June 1903 Onan
William R Sr h/o B B; s/o S E 1895-1968 Libe
William S s/o A M & M R 3 Oct 1878-27 Feb 1922 Libe
Capt William T h/o S M; s/o Revil & Polly 17 Apr 1837-drowned 17 Mar; found 28 Apr 1866; age: 29 yrs - leaving a wife & 3 children Lewi
William T h/o E D 1866-1941 Onan
William T h/o M C 1871-1939 Libe
William T h/o L L 1878-1956 Park

LEWIS (continued)
William T 1905-1982 Edge
William T 1913-1962 Snea
William T J s/o W R & S J 29 Jan 1853-drowned in Chesapeake Bay 4 Mar 1872 (body revovered 24 May 1872) Onan
William T J h/o S C 1880-1945 Libe
Willie 12 Dec 1924-22 June 1925 Park
Willie H s/o H C & C T 22 Apr 1869-29 Oct 1874 Edge
Willie T 9 Mar 1889-27 Nov 1948 Edge
Winfred h/o H L 1910-1973 Libe
Capt Zadoc C s/o Revil & Polly 30 Aug 1842- drowned 17 Mar (found 25 Apr 1866) age: 23/6/17 leaving a mother, 5 sisters, & 4 brothers Lewi
Zadoc R Sr h/o V M 1872-1959 Edge

LILLISTON, s/o J J & S F 15-22 Aug 1873 Edge
A Delbert h/o M M 1887-1962 Edge
Dr A Herbert s/o A J & E M 13 June 1874-19 Dec 1904 Edge
A Irving h/o V P 1882-1933 MtHo
A W h/o B S 1847-1922 MtHo
A Washington 12 May 1854-22 Feb 1932 Edge
Ada Perry d/o L L & A M d 31 May 1924 Edge
Alfred J h/o E F M; s/o H P 25 Nov 1844-2 May 1933 Edge
Alfred J h/o B B 1894-1932 Edge
Alfred J (h/o M O) 1894-1947 Edge
Alfred T s/o Thos & Charlotte B 7 Nov 1841-9 Dec 1870 Gill
Asbury Bowman (h/o M B) 1904-1979 Fair
Barton K h/o L S; s/o A J & E M 25 Oct 1881-17 Dec 1947 Edge
Bessie S w/o A W 1849-1910 MtHo
Blanche B w/o A J 1894-1978 Edge
Boman B 1878-1952 MtHo-s

LILLISTON (continued)
C Vernon 1897-1964 Libe
Caroline w/o J J 16 Oct 1851-31 Aug 1925 Edge
Daisy W w/o R T 1885-1971 Edge
Earl W h/o E M 1907-1952 Fair
Edith M w/o E W 1913- Fair
Elizabeth A w/o J P 27 July 1840-10 Feb 1897 Libe
Edmond h/o R H 6 June 1810-8 July 1889 Lill
Elizabeth S w/o H P; d/o Seth & Mary A Powell 5 Oct 1837-12 July 1866 Edge
Elizabeth S d/o Edmd & R H 26 Apr 1850-23 July 1874; age: 24/2/27 Lill
Ellen F Melson w/o A J 27 June 1852-10 Nov 1933 Edge
Ellen H w/o Thos d 24 June 1896; age: 76 yrs Gill
Eva C w/o G D 1892-1970 Fair
George D Sr 23 July 1842-24 Nov 1930 MtHo-s
George D h/o E C 1888-1960 Fair
George H 1910-1981 Edge
Georgie L 1880-1934 MtHo
Gordon W 1914-1943 MtHo-s
H Dix s/o A J & E M 21 Sept 1876-20 Nov 1953 Edge
Harold W 1907-1981 Edge
Harriet E w/o S H 1870-1944 Edge
Henry Lee h/o J W 1 Jan 1863-25 Jan 1931 Edge
Henry P h/o M A & E S d 6 July 1866; age: 52 yrs Edge
Herbert D 11 Nov 1918-9 Dec 1980 Edge
I Parker 1909-1966 MtHo
Ida B 1882-1963 MtHo-s
India E 1874-1939 MtHo
James P h/o E A 22 June 1840-18 March 1885 Libe
James T 1897-1955 Wach
James T (h/o S E) 1906-1959 MtHo
Jane T 1857-1930 Edge
John J h/o Caroline d 14 May 1913; age: 64 yrs Edge

LILLISTON (continued)
John W h/o M T 1889-1960 Edge
Junie W w/o H L 17 June 1867-20 Oct 1941 Edge
Kate Baum w/o Wm J 1877-1963 Libe
Kate Parks 1900-1969 Park
Kathryn J w/o L T 1912- MtHo
L Len h/o A M 1885-1946 Edge
L T 12 May 1854-6 Feb 1930 Edge
Leonard T h/o K J 1887-1977 MtHo
Lewis P 1912-1931 MtHo
Lucy Sanford w/o B K 5 June 1887-27 June 1977 Edge
Mamie Ruth (w/o W M) 9 Mar 1883-21 Dec 1946 Edge
Mannie H 1904-1970 Edge
Margaret M (Lynn) w/o A D 1884-1968 Edge
Maria M w/o Tully d Jan 12 1857; age: 17/5/0 Lils
Mary A w/o H P 5 Apr 1926-7 July 1852 Edge
Mary Elizabeth 1837-1929 Edge
Mary T w/o J W 1899- Edge
Mary V 10 Nov 1859-9 Aug 1935 Edge
Mary W w/o Thos d 28 Jan 1862; age: 45 Yrs Gill
Maurice R 1908-1974 Edge
Melvin L h/o N W 1911-1979 Fair
Myrtle Bailey (w/o A B) 1915- Fair
Myrtle Oakley w/o A J 1897-1966 Edge
Nellie W w/o M L 1913- Fair
Peggy Parker b&d-1935 MtHo
R Thomas w/o D W 1884-1959 Edge
Rebecca S 1861-1918 Edge
Robert F 1912- Edge
Roni Elizabeth 1903-1975 Edge
Rosey H w/o Edmd 11 Aug 1817-12 Jan 1885 Lill
Sallie T d age: 87 yrs (nd) MtHo
Samuel H h/o H E 1886-1941 Edge
Sarah F w/o Jno J d/o Chas & E

LILLISTON (continued)
C Booth d 20 July 1874; age: 21/7/17 Edge
Sulie E (w/o J T) 1909- MtHo
Thomas 24 Dec 1799-8 July 1883 Gill
Thomas P s/o Thos & Julia Ann 17 Aug 1831-22 Dec 1881; age: 50/4/15 Gill
Viva P w/o A I 1881-1969 MtHo
William E 1852-1936 Edge
William James h/o K B 1869-1931 Libe
William James Jr b&d-1869 Libe
William M (h/o M R) 8 Oct 1877-1 Apr 1951 Edge
Wilton T 1953-1981 Burt
LIMEBURNER, Adolph p h/o I S 1867-1950 MtHo-s
Ida S w/o A P 1868-1950 MtHo-s
LIND, s/o Raymond & Esther b&d 14 Aug 1946 Libe
LINDSEY, Henry 2 Apr 1831-15 Jan 1922 Edge
LINEBERRY, Mae East 1892-1967 MtHo
LINGO, Benjamin F (h/o M A) d 7 May 1892; age: 50 yrs Ling
Benjamin W 1878-1903 Crad-s
Bennie s/o B F & M A b&d 4 Jan 1883 Ling
Carrie L 1846-1919 Crad-s
Elizabeth S 25 Dec 1845-17 July 1928 StGe
Freddie T s/o Jas E & S R 19 Apr-19 Oct 1878 Linb
George F 1836-1881 Crad-s
George R 1876-1898 Crad-s
Hanna McCann (w/o J F) 1879-1966 StGe
James B Sr (h/o L K) 14 Aug 1877-17 Aug 1971 StGe
James E h/o S R 25 Apr 1834-29 Nov 1904 Linb
John F (h/o H McC) 1872-1960 StGe
John W d 11 May 1885; age: 58 yrs Ling
Lillie Lee w/o W O 29 Nov 1874-4 Oct 1929 MtHo
Lucy Kellam (w/o J B) 1 Nov

LINGO (continued)
1878-21 Dec 1978 StGe
Patience P 25 Apr 1843-17 May 1919 StGe
Mary A (w/o Benj F) 4 Mar 1875-8 Aug 1903; age: 28 yrs Ling
Mary B d/o B F & M A 20 July-19 Oct 1892 Ling
Susan R w/o Jas E 14 Mar 1844-25 Mar 1896 Linb
LINTON, Amy Miles w/o Lilliston E 1907-1979 Park
Harry J 1912-1957 Park
Lilliston E h/o A M 1904-1982 Park
Lola Grace 1898-1978 Libe
Margaret T w/o N H 1938- Park
Norris Hilton h/o M T 7 June 1929-8 Oct 1981 Park
Woodrow 3 Feb 1931-12 June 1972 Libe
LITTLE, Abraham 1911-1976 NewM
Dorothy A 1912-1976 StJo
LITTLETON, Adeline C w/o Saml J 23 Oct 1831-28 Sept 1922 Libe
Bernard 1899-1957 Park
Bessie J w/o F D 1899- Park
Carlton G h/o L R 1917- Park
Caroline S 1908- Park
Carrie F 1893-1940 Park
Clerville h/o M L 1883- Park
Cleveland P h/o O J 1885-1952 Park
Edna w/o Richd 1890-1958 Park
Fletcher D 1908- Park
Flora 1895-1962 Park
Frank D h/o B J 1895-1974 Park
George T h/o S J 9 Sept 1845- 15 Dec 1915 Park
Harold A h/o M W 8 Nov 1887-23 Aug 1956 Park
Harry F h/o K B 1878-1939 Park
Howard J h/o M R 1884-1953 Park
J Wallace 1882-1920 Park
Jimmie 1934-1935 Park
John E 18 Feb 1892-5 June 1931 Park
Kate B w/o H F 1878- Park

LITTLETON (continued)
Lucille R w/o C G 1917- Park
Maggie L w/o Clerville 1880-1950 Park
Manuel J 1919-1954 Park
Mary R w/o H J 1895-1981 Park
May W w/o H A 13 Nov 1895-19 Sept 1972 Park
Oneida M 1904-1908 Park
Orris J w/o C P 1883-1952 Park
Permella A w/o S J 1852-1940 Park
Richard h/o Edna 1887-1963 Park
Roy F 1908-1983 Park
S James h/o P A 1859-1930 Park
Sallie J w/o G T 15 Oct 1853-28 Aug 1917 Park
Scott 1896-1972 Park
Will W 1893-1961 Park
William R 25 June 1881-10 Mar 1913 Park
LLOYD, Elsie d/o R L & M E 9 Apr 1887-30 May 1891 Libe
Larry C 1 Sept 1946-26 Sept 1972 Smit
Lottie Rew s/o N E 1895- Libe
Mary E w/o R L 1861-1948 Libe
Norman Elihu h/o L R 1891-1967 Libe
Reuben L h/o M E 1864-1890 Libe
Frances Billups (w/o J S) 1892-1961 Fair
LODGE, J Shenton (h/o F B) 1889-1962 Fair
LOEBENTHAL, Mary E Wilkins w/o Clarence B d 9 Jan 1962 Onan
LOFLAND, (LOFTLAND),
Able T 1890-1965 Gask
Alfred w/o C W 18 Oct 1815-22 Jan 1897; age: 81/3/4 Lofl
Alfred & William twin sons/o Dr J H A & Kate B b&d 10 July 1880 Lofl
Carrie C 1903-1975 Bagc
Cassandra W w/o Alfred 7 May 1819-2 Apr 1893; age: 75/10/26 Lofl
Cecil A (h/o P B) 1881-1956 Onan

LOFLAND (continued)
Daisy E 1893-1976 Gask
Earle C 1891-1966 Fair
Harry 1918-1972 Shil
James H A MD h/o K R 15 Sept 1849- 29 Feb 1932 Fair
John L d 29 Jan 1971 Bagc
Kate Rose w/o Dr J H A 13 Oct 1850-10 Jul 1903; age: 54/8/27 Fair
Keith b&d 1967 Gask
Mary 1909-1982 Gask
Minnie N w/o S E 1896-1976 Gask
Pamela B (w/o C A) 1893-1980 Onan
Pansy M 1920-1978 Gask
Samuel E h/o M N 1895- Gask
Sarah Ann 15 June 1878-4 Jan 1917 Gask
Sarah Emmeline Frances d/o Alfred and C W 24 Jan 1842-26 Apr 1923 Lofl
Sylvanus Sr 1912-1963 Gask
LOGAN, (LOGON),
Berline d 3 July 1953; age: 68 yrs StLu
Iradella 1941-1976 Snea
Levin T h/o M A 12 Aug 1840-26 Jan 1917 Loga
Mary A w/o L T 26 Oct 1844-23 Dec 1927 Loga
LOMAX, Elizabeth w/o S F 13 Jan 1831-16 Oct 1907 Libe
Fannie A 16 Apr 1868-29 Jan 1940 Libe
George W s/o S F & Eliz d 26 Oct 1881; age: 19/8/4 Libe
Margaret R d/o S F & Eliz 7 Oct 1873-29 Nov 1874 Libe
Robert T s/o S F & Eliz 19 Jan 1870-18 June 1895 Libe
Samuel F 4 July 1856-31 Mar 1913 Libe
Samuel F h/o Eliz d 18 May 1892; age: 67 yrs Libe
Sarah F d/o S F & Eliz 22 Aug 1854- 8 Aug 1855 Libe
LONG, s/o Bob & Rose S b&d 28 Sept 1959 Park
Anna Nichols (w/o C W) 18 Aug 1895-13 June 1958 Fair

LONG (continued)
Anna V 1872-1952 Wach
Benjamin S 1851-1946 Wach
Bruce B 13 Oct 1893-22 Aug 1979 MtHo
Carl W (h/o A N) 19 Jan 1887-6 Dec 1950 Fair
Carl W Jr 4 Mar 1918-5 Sept 1976 Fair
Christine N 1855-1935 MtHo-s
Clayton Tuttle 19 Nov 1894-28 Sept 1963 Fair
Dorothy Parker 1912-1975 Fair
George C Sr 1914-1977 MtHo-s
Marcelline Day 22 Aug 1896-22 Mar 1979 Fair
N Bernard 1860-1946 Fair
LONGWORTH, Adeline Rich 1871-1955 MtHo
Betty Carmine Broughton w/o Danl J 1866-1953 MtHo
LOOKINGLAND, Alice Mister m/o Viola & Geo James 1882-1952 Onan
LOTSPEICH, Alden Ayres 1892-1980 Park
Angela H 1903-1975 Park
Clyde Esmond h/o J R 1889-1962 Park
Jessie Rector w/o C E 1890-1971 Park
LUCAS, Elizabeth E w/o Sylvanus H d 15 Oct 1878; age: 44/0/3 Shir
LUNN, James T Sr h/o M J 1891-1971 Edge
Margaret J w/o J T Sr 1898- Edge
LUPTON, Elizabeth S (w/o S H) 1887-1961 MtHo-s
Samuel H (h/o E S) 1882-1950 MtHo-s
LURTON, Alice J (w/o W L) 11 Oct 1862-2 Feb 1930 MtHo
Earl D 1899-1958 MtHo-s
William L (h/o A J) 20 Aug 1860-23 Jan 1918 MtHo
LUSSIER, Sue C 1915-1958 Wach
LYNCH, I Robert 1892-1965 MtHo
LYTLE, Alice M w/o Wm A; d/o W B & M A Walker 13 Dec

LYTLE (continued)
1848-21 Jan 1903 StGe
Clara M (w/o W W) 1892-1964 StGe
William W (h/o C M) 1878-1946 StGe
MACMILLAN, S Frances w/o S K 1846-1926 Wach
MACNAMARA, Annie Walston w/o Rev Alfred E; d/o J S & R B Tyler 21 June 1869-5 Mar 1949 Onan
McALLISTER, Gladys w/o J W 1919- Park
Joseph W h/o Gladys 1915-1982 Park
McBRIDE, John F h/o L B 1891-1955 MtHo-s
Lottie B w/o J F 1896- MtHo-s
McCONNELL, Harry G s/o Thos & Isabella 1 June 1859- 21 Oct 1892 Onan
McCREADY, A J h/o A J & Josephine 15 Sept 1845-25 Oct 1913 Libe
Altha T (w/o C T) 1882-1957 MtHo-s
Amanda J 1st w/o A J 27 Oct 1851-7 Mar 1882 Libe
Andrew J 27 Mar 1888-15 May 1889 Libe
Andrew J 31 Jan 1891-12 July 1893 Libe
Charles T (h/o A T) 1878-1963 MtHo-s
Charlie W h/o M A 1918- Park
Cynthia T w/o G L 1880-1964 Libe
Dorothy F 1902-1972 Fair
Emma P w/o J Barney 12 Oct 1872-8 Jan 1895 Johc
Eva M 1879-1972 Fair
George Lee h/o C T 1878-1950 Libe
J Barney h/o M V 1870-1950 Park
Josephine 2nd w/o A J 30 Aug 1855-14 Feb 1903 Libe
Josephine w/o S J 21 Feb 1872-3 Dec 1939 Libe
Lee A h/o L B 1899-1949 Park
Lloyd J 1869-1957 Fair

McCREADY (continued)
Louise K d/o J B & M V 12 Apr 1901-20 Mar 1920 Park
Lucille B w/o L A 1905-1972 Park
M Virginia w/o J B 1876-1950 Park
Madeline A w/o C W 1925- Park
Manda Susan d/o C T & A T 1904-1906 MtHo-s
Miriam J 10 Aug 1894-25 July 1895 Libe
Sallie Ann w/o J A S 11 Mar 1808-29 Jan 1886 Libe
Solomon J h/o Josephine 24 Dec 1871-19 Apr 1934 Libe
McCRIMMON, Angus Reginald h/o B H 11 Feb 1878-19 Aug 1944 Edge
Bertha Hand w/o A R 16 Nov 1878-7 Apr 1940 Edge
McCULLOUGH, Ellen R 1917-1970 Park
Margaret E 17 Apr 1917-6 May 1970 Park
McDANIEL, Bessie 1932-1974 Snea
McFARLAND, Irvin C 1900-1972 Onan
McGEE, Edward Joseph (h/o M G) 23 Oct 1873-6 Aug 1959 MtHo-s
Mattie Grinnalds (w/o E J) 4 June 1883-2 Nov 1968 MtHo-s
McHAN, Walter S 1925-1961 Fair
McKAY, Daniel Evans 26 Aug 1927-21 Oct 1982 Fair
Hugh Percy 1885-1965 Fair
Mildred Evans 1897- Fair
McKEAN, Leonett w/o Thos S 1872-1909 Quin
McKENNEY, H Hanson 11 July 1890-29 July 1972 StGe
Margaret 1 Dec 1889-8 Oct 1969 StGe
Mary Read 18 Jan 1856-10 Mar 1934 StGe
McKIM, John Sr 20 Jan 1905-6 June 1981 Edge
McKOWN, Sallie S wid/o Thos; d/o Jno & Elisha Joynes 14

McKOWN (continued)
Feb 1825-22 July 1889; age: 64/5/8 Joyp
McLANE, Claud L (h/o L g) 1881-1952 MtHo-s
McLANE, (McClain), Ellen Bird w/o Jno d 11 Dec 1873; age: 24/1/21 McLa
John h/o Ellen B 27 Oct 1833-17 Aug 1883 McLa
Lena G (w/o C L) 1882-1945 MtHo-s
Linwood C 3 Aug 1906-8 Mar 1907 McLa
Mary E d/o Jno & Ellen d 2 Aug 1873; age: 2/6/1 McLa
Myrtice C 7 Oct 1904-5 Mar 1907 McLa
McLEAN, Amzi Chapin (h/o L M) 1883-1969 StGe
Laura Morford (w/o A C) 1882-1971 StGe
McMATH, d/o A J & B L d 18 July 1900; age: 0/2/0 MtHo
Albert J h/o B L & E C 1859-1926 MtHo
Bessie LeCato 1st w/o A J 10 Dec 1853-16 July 1900 MtHo
Clarence s/o A J & B L 2 June 1886-1 June 1887 MtHo
Edwin T 26 Oct 1884-16 Mar 1913 MtHo
Emma Cordelia 2nd w/o A J 1875-1956 MtHo
George W h/o M D 19 July 1856-11 Sept 1890 MtHo
John P h/o K A 26 Jan 1809-26 Jan 1890 MtHo
Kissia A w/o J P 16 Sept 1820-16 Jan 1908 MtHo
Mabel Byrd 15 Oct 1880-13 Nov 1945 MtHo
Margaret D w/o G W 6 July 1856-6 July 1935 MtHo
Olin LeCato 2 Dec 1882-29 Mar 1908 MtHo
Pearl P 10 July 1886-13 May 1967 MtHo
McMILLAN, s/o Herbert & Grace b&d 30 Oct 1925 StGe
McNABB, Elizabeth Lewis Dabney w/o Rev Jno 16 Mar 1851-

McNABB (continued)
26 Feb 1888 StGe
Hopeton Drake s/o Rev Jno & E L D 23 June 1886-17 July 1888 StGe
Rev John h/o E L D & K A 1841-1914 StGe
Kate A w/o Rev Jno d/o Dr Jno L & Ann Arbuckle Harmanson 1855-1938 StGe
McPHERSON, Catherine J w/o W B 12 Feb 1841-5 Oct 1879 Holl
McTIGHE, Ruth S 11 Dec 1892-21 Sept 1967 MtHo-s
M, W T footstone only Bead
M, H B footstone only Stom
MABIE, Sallie Parramore w/o Harry G 1861-1936 Runn
MADDOX, John W h/o M D 21 May 1891-3 Feb 1967 Park
Julia 1914-1934 NewM
Mary D w/o J W 15 Sept 1903-28 Feb 1970
Raymond W 1927-1952 Park
MADRE, Stanley 1900-1975 Snea
MAJOR, Carolina d/o Wm L & Eliz D d 14 Aug 1844; age: 10/5/0 MajF
Cunie Morris 1895-1971 NewM
Elizabeth D w/o Wm L d 29 July 1854; age: 43 yrs MajF
Elizabeth Purnell d/o Wm Littleton & Eliz Costen Major 1836-1908 MajF
Hezzy 1878-1956 HTri
Horace T 21 May 1893-16 Feb 1945 HTri
John D s/o Wm & Betsy 23 Sept 1803-12 Oct 1819 MajF
John W 1900-1980 Snea
Paul 1893-1959 HTri
Phyllis 17 Feb 1883-4 Sept 1968 HTri
Sarah A 1885-1969 HTri
William L s/o Wm & Eliz d 7 Oct 1848; age: 38 yrs MajF
MANDART, Mabel M 1900-1966 Fair
Michael A 1912-1980 Fair
MANSFIELD, Annie Virginia Jones 1887-1975 Libe

MAPP, s/o & d/o Geo Walter & Georgie Richardson (Quinby) b&d 28 July 1901 Warw
Achsah B w/o R H; d/o Wm & Peggy Bagge 7 Mar 1787-27 Oct 1859 Mapp
Albert 1947-1974 Burt
Ann J 2 Nov 1816- 26 Jan 1895 Mars
Annie 1904-1979 Shil
Annie R 1895- Wach
Annie T (w/o G T) 1870-1935 MtHo
Appy d 1 Nov 1916; age: 73 yrs Snea
Bettie C w/o Jas T 23 Jan 1841-3 Dec 1906 Mars
Brooks J Jr 1927-1969 Burt
Claude Walker s/o G S & S W 17 July 1887-18 Mar 1909 Onan
Cora E d/o J T & B C 10 Mar 1857-17 June 1868 Mars
Daurice 1979-1980 Burt
Edward W 1864-1940 Wach
Edwin L (h/o V S) 1891-1952 MtHo
Edwin L Jr (h/o M P) 1927- MtHo
Edwin T s/o Geo T & Leah 11 Dec 1826-23 Aug 1860; age: 33/8/12 Mars
Elijah T 1913-1967 NewM
Eloise King (w/o J B) 13 Oct 1891-4 Aug 1975 Fair
Emma Dunton w/o N T d/o Jas & Carrie Doughty 1885-1973 Wach
Emma Ray d/o J E & M C 18 Apr-7 July 1895 Wach
Emma S d/o J T & B C 17 Oct 1869-1 Oct 1884 Mars
Fannie P 22 Nov 1864-11 Feb 1926 Wach
Garland JB (h/o L M) 1893-1960 Wach
George B s/o Geo T & Leah 1 Dec 1812-17 Oct 1891 Mars
George H h/o J R 1904- MtHo
George Scarburgh h/o S W 12 Feb 1848-1 June 1916 Onan
George T 3 Apr 1779-13 Aug 1862; age: 83/4/10 Mars

MAPP (continued)
George T (h/o A T) 1870-1942 MtHo
George W 12 Mar 1892-16 May 1950 Snea
George Walter h/o M A s/o J E & M L 25 May 1873-2 Feb 1941 Quin
Georgie Richardson Quinby w/o Geo Walter 8 Feb 1876-31 July 1901 Warw
Hattie T 1905-1974 Burt
Hazel M (w/o J W) 1920-1971 Wach
Henry A W s/o Geo S & S T 19 Jan 1853-22 Jan 1864 (stone missing; 1940 data) MapG
Horace J 1892-1960 JoyC
J Boudoin h/o S F W s/o J T 7 C B 2 Apr 1859-19 Jan 1937 Wach
James 1904-1965 Burt
James C s/o R H & A B 11 Dec 1831-13 July 1864 Mapp
James D Sr 12 Oct 1911-25 Sept 1979 Wach
James S s/o Geo S & Betsy 4 July 1828-16 June 1873 age: 44/11/12 Powe
James T (h/o B C) 12 Feb 1835-1 Dec 1872 Mars
Janie R w/o G H 1900-1968 MtHo
John Brooks (h/o E K) 30 Mar 1887-19 Aug 1969 Fair
John C 1858-1952 Quin
John E h/o M L s/o Geo Bowdoin & Ann J 1 Feb 1846-30 Apr 1927 Quin
John E (h/o M C) s/o Jas B & Bettie C 1860-1943 Wach
John Thomas 1892-1956 Wach
John W h/o H M 1916- Wach
Kate S w/o W E d/o Rev Benj T & Julia A Ames 10 Dec 1843-14 Jan 1927 Mt Ho
Kathryn Ann Arthur 22 Nov 1923-30 Oct 1964 Fair
Leah w/o Geo T 29 Jan 1784-15 Feb 1837; age: 53/0/17 Mars
Lena M (w/o G B) 1912- Wach
Levolia 1957-1968 Burt

MAPP (continued)
Lola d 24 Nov 1967; age: 52 yrs JoyC
Lucille w/o Saml Sr 1900-1975 Burt
Maggie LeCato w/o Dr J E 11 July 1844-20 Sept 1913 Quin
Margaret w/o Geo T d/o Dune & Ann Glenn 31 May 1798-23 Nov 1865 age: 67/5/23 Mars
Margaret F w/o J S 1 Dec 1830-14 Sept 1903 Powe
Margaret P (w/o E L Jr) 1927-1974 MtHo
Margaret T Bell d/o RH & AB 28 Sept 1810-24 Apr 1900 Mapp
Marguerite L 1892-1936 Wach
Mary A d/o Geo T & Annie D 11 Aug 1897-7 Jan 1898 MtHo
Mary C w/o J E d/o Wm & Rachel Richardson 1861-1920 Wach
Mildred Aydelotte w/o G W d 16 Aug 1967 Quin
Missouri M d/o J T & B C 20 Aug 1867-21 May 1882 Mars
Moscoe R 17 Mar 1959; age: 64 yrs Snea
Naomi Mapp 1912- Wach
Norman T h/o E D s/o Jno E & Mary C 10 Oct 1884-7 Dec 1928 Wach
Patricia 1958-1959 Burt
Robbins B s/o R H & A B 10 May 1819-28 Feb 1886 Mapp
Robbins H s/o Houson & Eliz d 3 Sept 1866; age: 84/6/0 Mapp
Sadie 1900-1968 NewM
Sadie A 1865-1952 Wach
Samuel Sr h/o Lucille d 12 Mar 1958; age: 58 yrs Burt
Samuel H Jr 28 Feb 1923-8 Nov 1975 Burt
Sarah F Ward w/o J B 22 Aug 1851-5 Oct 1883 Wach
Sarah Walker w/o G S 5 Nov 1847 Onan
Southey 8 Feb 1905-2 June 1966 Shil
Susan T w/o Geo S 23 Feb 1813-7 July 1867 (stone missing;

MAPP (continued)
1940 data) MapG
Susie Harmon w/o W J 1886-1977 Wach
Virginia P 1919-1920 Wach
Virginia S (w/o E L) 1896-1981 MtHo
William E h/o K S s/o Geo S & Anne J 5 Feb 1844-May 27 1918 MtHo
William J h/o S H 1881-1963 Wach
William R s/o Robbins H 2 June 1813-26 Jan 1897 Mapp
Woody 1920-1972 Burt
MARABLE, Gertrude Wise (1st h Wm E Wise) 1875-1956 MtHo
MARKLAND, John Henry 1866-1929 Park
MARKLEY, Sarah Elizabeth w/o Philip M d/o J D & M A 20 Dec 1848-4 July 1909 Edge
MARSH, Mrs Alice Ailsa w/o W W 14 Apr 1841-6 Oct 1894 Hutc
Alton Henry b&d 1916 Fair
Annie B (w/o E W) 1869-1927 MtHo-s
Annie S w/o L H 1887-1967 MtHo
Arinthia T w/o J R 15 Mar 1854-20 June 1924 Clif
Benjamin F (h/o M N) 1874-1928 MtHo-s
Benson W (h/o B T) 1890-1966 Fair
Bessie G (w/o E D Sr) 1901-1960 MtHo-s
Bettie B 3 June 1869-18 Sept 1896 Fair
Beulah G (w/o R H) 1899- Fair
Blanche T (w/o B W) 1892- Fair
Carrie Lee d/o Jno R & A T 5 Nov 1886- 5 Feb 1897 Clif
Charles A 30 Mar 1920-18 Sept 1980 Fair
Charles R h/o M V 1873-1950 Onan
Charles W (h/o M S) 27 Feb 1861-8 Sept 1899 StGe
Columbus S s/o J R & A T 15 July 1881-25 Jan 1922 Clif

MARSH (continued)

David A h/o M A 12 Aug 1840-20 Dec 1917 Clif
David Wesley h/o S E 1872-1938 MtHo-s
E W (h/o A B) 1864-1922 MtHo-s
Earl S Sr (h/o B G) 1895-1959 MtHo-s
Edward W h/o N W 1867-1955 MtHo
Elizabeth Gray (w/o N R) 1 May 1927- Fair
Eugenia Ellen 26 Sept 1859-20 July 1919 Clif
George Edward 7 Aug 1892-13 Aug 1919 Clif
George F h/o M J 5 Dec 1857-21 Nov 1934 MtHo
Gordon C 10 May 1897-7 Sept 1959 MtHo-s
James R (h/o L E) 17 July 1877-6 July 1930 MtHo-s
Jeter Everette (h/o L S) 1882-1955 Fair
John E h/o V W 1894- StGE
Capt John L (s/o W W & A A) 26 Apr 1873-7 Oct 1892 Hutc
John Randolph h/o A T d 17 Sept 1934; age: 80 yrs (ns Ref: Penisula Enterprise 9/22/34) Clif
John W (h/o MA) 16 Dec 1827-16 Sept 1904; age 77/3/0 Clif
John W s/o J R & A T 5 May 1876-2 Feb 1919 Clif
John W 1890-1963 Fair
Maj L Russell 1917 d near Tan-imbar Island 1945 (bur at sea) Fair
Lena E (w/o J R) 5 Feb 1879-22 July 1959 MtHo-s
Lewis H h/o A S 1883-1959 MtHo
Lewis H Jr 12 Dec 1915-18 Dec 1975 MtHo
Lillian Savage (w/o J E) 1892-1982 Fair
Mabel N 1884-1974 Fair
Maggie Marsh (2nd w/o D A) ns Clif
Mamie E 20 Feb 1897-23 Dec

MARSH (continued)

1953 Fair
Margaret A d/o J W & M A 7 Sept-3 Oct 1876 Clif
Margaret A w/o Capt J W d 3 Nov 1899; age: 68 yrs Clif
Margaret M 15 June 1895-14 Aug 1924 MtHo
Margaret N (w/o B F) 1873-1940 MtHo-s
Margaret P w/o M R 7 Oct 1899-19 Dec 1977 MtHo-s
Marvin E s/o C W & M S 4 Dec 1891-1 July 1900 StGe
Mary Adline d/o J W & M A 28 Oct 1864-9 Sept 1868 Clif
Mary J w/o G F 5 May 1860- 25 Apr 1916 MtHo
Mary V w/o C R 1877-1958 Onan
Matilda A w/o D A 6 Jan 1851-12 Feb 1907 Clif
May Scott 16 July 1877-1 July 1947 Onan
Melissa Sarah w/o C W 21 Sept 1857-2 June 1937 StGe
Merritt R h/o M P 8 Mar 1899-28 Aug 1953 MtHo-s
Nancy Guy 27 Sept 1923-26 June 1957 MtHo-s
Nellie W w/o E W 1867-1932 MtHo
Norris Roland (h/o E G) 23 July 1927-11 May 1973 Fair
Ralph W 1895-1948 MtHo-s
Roland H (h/o B G) 1891-1963 Fair
Sadie Scott w/o W H Jr 4 Apr 1890-29 Apr 1923 MtHo
Sarah Evelyn w/o D W 1872-1948 MtHo-s
Stanley J 1917-1918 MtHo
Violet W w/o J E 1894-1961 StGe
W H 23 Aug 1861-10 July 1948 Clif
Walter H Jr h/o S S 1887-1931 MtHo
William C 25 Dec 1870-20 July 1933 Fair
William G 8 Nov 1891-11 Mar 1972 Fair
William Scott 1913-1976 MtHo

MARSH (continued)
Capt William Walter h/o A A 17 May 1833-10 June 1891 Hutc
MARSHALL, A Douglass h/o E M 1869-1912 Park
Aaron h/o M A 5 Apr 1841-25 May 1919 Park
Alice L w/o J D 9 Jan 1873-28 July 1945 Libe
Charlotte S 1914- Park
Clara M 1880-1971 Park
Doris Bernard 1920-1959 Park
Etta M w/o A D 1878-1955 Park
Frances 1889-1965 Fair
H Webster 1857-1946 Edge
Jefferson D h/o A L 25 June 1863-10 Jan 1926 Libe
John M h/o S F 1873- Libe
Lillian E w/o R F 1900-1974 Park
Lucille Kelly 1913-1964 Edge
Martha Jackson 19 Jan 1925-29 Dec 1940 Libe
Mary A w/o Aaron 31 Jan 1848-7 Dec 1926 Park
Mary M 1879-1982 Shil
Matilda S w/o R E 1916- Fair
Michael T s/o O V & Audrey P b&d 3 Jan 1944 Wach
Otho J h/o P E 1894-1982 Libe
Pauline E w/o O J 1904- Libe
Pearlie L 1887-1932 Park
Roland E h/o M S 1912-1980 Fair
Roland F h/o L E 1901-1972 Park
Sallie F w/o J M 1873-1945 Libe
Stella T 1898-1921 Libe
W Carroll 1919-1941 Quin
Walter E 11 Sept 1891-22 Apr 1964 Park
William C 1894-1924 Quin
William R 1909-1978 Fair
MARSTON, Francis A s/o Geo W & Sarah J d 23 Feb 1859; age: 25/0/15 Tayl
Harvey F h/o M E 16 Aug 1857-16 Aug 1936 Thos
Maggie S d/o Harvey & Missouri 17 Feb 1891-11 Aug 1892; age: 1/5/24 Thos
Missouri E w/o H F 15 May

MARSTON (continued)
1851-10 June 1921 Thos
Willie B s/o Harvey & Missouri 19 May 1893-27 Apr 1894; age 1/1/8 Thos
MARTIN, d/o J W & L B b&d 6 Jan 1893 Mart
Alice L (w/o M T) 1897-1981 Onan
Alva 12 Jan 1921-2 Apr 1922 Onan
Annie w/o J S 7 Oct 1819-7 Sept 1850 Mart
Arthur W s/o Arthur P & Sudie E 15 Sept 1891-7 Sept 1903 Crad
Athelin S 1894-1908 Edge
Basey S d/o Jno & Susan 22 May 1857-9 July 1858 Mart
Bessie W 1894- Onan
Bettie Ames w/o S S 11 Feb 1871-28 Nov 1929 StGe
Beulah M d/o S T & Sallie T d 7 Oct 1890; age: 5 yrs Mart
Birdie S (w/o E F) 1887-1968 Onan
Catheline d/o S T & Sallie T 18 Aug-11 Oct 1893 Mart
Charlotte 3 Aug 1827-17 Dec 1918 Mart
Clara 1902-1977 Burt
Dale Lee nd MtHo
Douglas A h/o M H 1850-1923 MtHo
Edward d 4 Mar 1943; age: 46/-/5 Snea
Edward s/o Edwd & Sally d 4 Apr 1855; age: 65 yrs Cutl
Elexine V 8 July 1845-19 Jan 1872 MarB
Elizabeth M (w/o S W) 27 Jan 1829-26 Apr 1890 StGe
Elizabeth Susan w/o J P 25 Jan 1871-10 Dec 1947 Edge
Ella Susan w/o S K d/o Ezekiel & Margt Smith 19 Feb 1860-16 Mar 1950 MtHo-s
Ernest d 16 May 1964; age 55 yrs Burt
Ernest F (h/o B S) 1884-1971 Onan
Everett 1917-1977 Edge
Frank P h/o S C 1858-1949 Onan

MARTIN (continued)
Fred Douglas 30 Aug 1894-4 Oct 1969 Burt
Fred R 20 May 1864-2 Sept 1916 HTri
G Lynwood Jr (h/o M W) 1908- MtHo-s
George E L h/o Z A 3 Mar 1857-18 Apr 1930 MtHo
Gerald L h/o M C s/o S K & Susan 24 Oct 1886-2 Oct 1929 MtHo-s
Harry d 11 Mar 1953; age: 62 yrs HTri
Henry N s/o W S & Rosey 1 Mar 1828-20 Aug 1850 Mart
Isaac S h/o J I s/o Peter and Rose 4 Jan 1827-7 Jan 1900; age: 73/0/3 Marp
J Dorsey 1890-1935 Park
James 1894-1979 HTri
James 1911-1975 Snea
James Peter h/o E S 1859-1910 Edge
Jane I w/o I S 15 Aug 1831-7 Aug 1908 Marp
Jessie 1884-1969 NewM
John S h/o S A 3 Jan 1818-2 Oct 1891 (moved from Martin-Hatton plot) MtHo-s
John T s/o Wm S & Susan b&d 19 Apr 1870 Mart
John W h/o L B 17 Jan 1854-15 June 1924 Mart
Joseph K s/o Peter & Rosey 18 Dec 1834-15 Feb 1866; age: 32 yrs Hutc
Laurel K d 17 Mar 1946 Onan
Layer d 9 Oct 1860; age: 90 yrs Mart
Lena P w/o R M Jr 20 Dec 1910- MtHo
Lettie A 16 Sept 1875-30 Nov 1958 Onan
Louisa A 1st w/o S K d/o Thos W & Margt Badger 21 Dec 1824-14 July 1856 MarB
Louisa B w/o J W 21 Sept 1857-24 Nov 1924 Mart
Maggie H w/o D A 1860-1920 MtHo
Margaret A d/o Jno S & Annie 24

MARTIN (continued)
May 1845-26 Aug 1849 Mart
Margaret Bull 18 July 1899- Edge
Margaret W (w/o G L) 1907-1973 MtHo-s
Marvin L (h/o M B) 1888-1939 MtHo-s
Mary A w/o Smith K d/o Nathl & Mary Badger 14 May 1819-24 Sept 1842 Badg
Mary A w/o Wm H 15 Jan 1830-28 Sept 1886 Jaco
Mary Ann w/o Wm d 18 June 1908; age: 75 yrs MtHo
Mary Colonna w/o G L d/o Wm Tyler & Va Charnock Colonna 17 Jan 1885-24 June 1958 MtHo-s
Mary E 15 Dec 1870-8 Aug 1915 Burt
Mary S d/o Arthur P & Sudie E 23 Jan 1887- 28 Aug 1903 Crad
Maude B (w/o M L) 1889-1955 MtHo-s
Milton T (w/o A L) 1892-1971 Onan
Noah J 24 May 1926-16 Mar 1945 Onan
Robert M Jr h/o L P 15 Dec 1912-16 May 1981 MtHo
Robert Milton Sr 7 Apr 1885-3 May 1961 MtHo
Rosey A d/o Jacob S & Susan 14 Oct 1797-23 Mar 1876 Mart
Rosey S d/o J S & S A 22 May 1837-9 July 1858 (moved from Martin-Hatton plot) MtHo-s
Rosina W 2nd w/o S K 8 Nov 1834-11 Jan 1892 MarB
Samuel S (h/o B A) 28 Oct 1860-30 Oct 1933 StGe
Sarah C w/o F P 1862-1946 Onan
Sarah E 14 Mar 1853-3 Jan 1917 Libe
Seba Thomas d 7 Aug 1937 Onan
Smith 26 Mar 1756-15 Jan 1832 Mart
Smith K (h/o R W) 7 June 1817-31 Mar 1877 MarB
Smith K h/o E S s/o Smith K & Rosina W 18 Mar 1862-15 May

MARTIN (continued)
1951 MtHo-s
Smith W (h/o E M) 22 Feb 1827-6 Nov 1901 StGe
Sophia w/o Smith d/o Kendal & Rosey Beach 18 Feb 1776-31 May 1822 Mart
Susan A w/o W S 27 Oct 1827-3 June 1895 Mart
Susan A w/o J S 7 Nov 1829-28 Mar 1914 (moved from Martin-Hatton plot) MtHo-s
Thaddeus K 27 Sept 1858-8 Jan 1904 StGe
William H h/o M A 4 Aug 1830-18 May 1907 Jaco
William S s/o Smith 15 Jan 1777-17 Mar 1842 Mart
William S h/o S A s/o W S & Rosa 26 Nov 1821-26 Apr 1879 Mart
William T s/o Wm S & Susan 19 Aug 1871-13 July 1872 Mart
Zippora A w/o G E L 1 Aug 1863-8 June 1930 MtHo
MASON, A Hughlett PhD h/o Mary C s/o A T & B H 3 Feb 1905-31 Jan 1974 StGe
A Ray 5 July 1879-1 Oct 1927 Park
Agnes H 8 Nov 1897-5 Feb 1938 Park
Alfred 1865-1889 Park
Alfred Johnson 25 Feb 1896-22 Aug 1938 Park
Alfred P 24 Mar 1876-7 Dec 1943 Edge
Alice M w/o C C 20 Sept 1875-23 Mar 1946 Edge
Alvin H 19 Jan 1915-18 Mar 1976 MtHo
Alvin Henry h/o W K 27 May 1846-21 Dec 1914 StGe
Alvin T (h/o B H) 27 May 1879-10 Mar 1943 StGe
Ann S 24 Feb 1812-21 July 1852 (erected by her grandmother Hannah Topping) Arli
Anne T w/o H H 1906-1970 Park
Annie B (w/o B D) 1889-1976 MtHo-s
Annie Bailey d 1921 StGe

MASON (continued)
Annie E w/o Stephen E Sr d 26 Jan 1906; age: 86 yrs Chap
Austin R h/o E B 15 Jan 1890-3 Feb 1965 Park
Bertha H 6 Dec 1888-18 Aug 1961 Edge
Bertram D (h/o A B) 1884-1966 MtHo-s
Bessie Hughlett w/o A T 3 Dec 1876-1 Sept 1971 StGe
Bessie L (w/o O H) 23 Feb 1877-26 Feb 1957 StGe
Betsey 17 Jan 1807-8 Aug 1879 JnoP
Beulah Lowe w/o J M 1894- StGe
Bobby Lee 1938-1939 MtHo-s
Burkley 1903-1983 Bays
Carrie R 1883-1886 Park
Carrie W w/o G W 1889-1964 Park
Catherine Nottingham d/o Z C & H A 18 Feb 1856-19 Dec 1908 Onan
Cebie B Sr 1900-1965 Park
Cecil R 23 Oct 1902-16 Feb 1967 Onan
Charles A 31 Oct 1880-26 Mar 1940 Onan
Charles B (h/o M A T) 10 July 1855-25 Feb 1928 Edge
Charles B Jr 24 Dec 1880-23 Dec 1948 Edge
Charles H (h/o M A); s/o Chas H 20 Jan 1819-31 Mar 1878 (moved from Mason Farm) Edge
Charlie C h/o A M 11 Sept 1867-18 Apr 1956 Edge
Clinton L 9 Mar 1889-30 June 1969 Park
D Frank h/o M A 16 June 1872-8 Nov 1939 Libe
Daisey L w/o T A 1880-1925 Park
Duffield h/o E M 1878-1959 Park
Earnest Lee h/o E C 1877-1950 Onan
Edmund C s/o Geo & Sophia d 4 May 1849; age: 55/7/26 Maso
Edward P h/o S E 1850-1928

MASON (continued)
Libe
Dr Edward T (h/o G V) 1870-1928 Onan
Edward T 1908-1966 Onan
Eleanor Custis w/o E L 1874-1948 Onan
Elizabeth w/o H T 1863-1926 Libe
Elizabeth 4 June 1899-28 Aug 1982 Park
Elizabeth J w/o E C; d/o Wm & Patience James 10 Aug 1789-16 Nov 1868 Maso
Elizabeth Lacy w/o L W 14 Aug 1849-9 Mar 1918 Edge
Elizabeth M 26 Oct 1808-28 Apr 1889 StGe
Elizabeth M 25 July 1913-30 June 1953 Park
Ella 1889-1954 Snea
Ella M w/o Duffield 1877-1957 Park
Ella May 6 June 1878-8 Dec 1929 Edge
Ella W 14 Mar 1854-11 Apr 1933 Ling
Elmo H 9 Apr 1895-6 Feb 1939 Edge
Elvin O h/o M S 1876-1953 Edge
Emma d 15 Dec 1961; age: 67 yrs Gask-old
Emma Sue 18 Jan 1883-6 Aug 1948 Edge
Ermon J h/o H C 1906-1956 Onan
Ethel B w/o A R 3 Apr 1891-9 June 1977 Park
Eugene R 1855-1926 Park
Euphemia C w/o S E 3 Apr 1829-18 Feb 1900 Onan
Eva C 1902-1983 Fair
Eva E w/o G H 1894-1964 Bays
Eva L 22 Jan 1872-3 Dec 1912 Libe
Eveline 1 Sept 1841-16 Jan 1924 Park
Fannie 1882-1977 Gask
Fred R h/o N C 1891-1966 Park
Garland L 23 Feb 1900-3 Apr 1939 Park
George B h/o S A 6 Nov 1844-26

MASON (continued)
Nov 1922 Onan
George B 1913-1953 Onan
George H h/o E E 1886-1973 Bays
George W h/o Nancy; s/o Edwd & Eliz 23 Feb 1818-8 Jan 1898 JnoS
George W h/o S T 1855-1907 Onan
George W h/o C W 1887-1973 Park
Gertrude P w/o Wm T 19 Dec 1871-14 July 1955 Park
Grace P w/o S R 6 Jan 1886-23 Feb 1913 Edge
Grace V (w/o E T) 1883-1957 Onan
Grace W w/o R F 1882-1949 Park
H Thomas h/o Eliz 1859-1926 Libe
Harriet A d/o C H & M A 3 May 1853-18 Mar 1878 (moved from Mason Farm) Edge
Hattie R w/o W E 23 Dec 1872-29 Mar 1943 MtHo
Hazel C w/o E J 1906- Onan
Henry P 1842-1898 Park
Herbert H h/o A T 1900- Park
Hester Ann w/o Z C; d/o David & Julia Mears 25 July 1833-4 Apr 1902 Onan
Ivan S (h/o R W) 1914-1939 MtHo-s
J Frank 7 Jan 1859-6 Apr 1939 Park
J Manroe (h/o M E) 1891-1957 MtHo-s
James E 18 June 1837-6 Apr 1924 StGe
James E 1889-1954 Libe
James H h/o M E 12 Dec 1841-5 Oct 1929 Park
James H 20 Feb 1843-7 May 1910 JnoP
James W 10 Aug 1927-10 Apr 1982 MtHo-s
James Walter s/o Geo W & Va S 17 July 1893-22 Jan 1917 MtHo
Jane E 1840-1928 Park

MASON (continued)
John Alan 5 June 1957-17 June 1974 Park
John E 6 July 1847-22 Nov 1902 JnoP
John F h/o K S 1882-1968 Libe
John Milton h/o B L 1893-1960 StGe
John Ralph s/o Brooks & Maggie 29 May 1912-14 Oct 1913 Quin
John T 15 Feb 1850-9 Oct 1921 Ling
John T 11 Nov 1875-4 July 1955 Park
John W h/o L A; s/o Wm & Elizabeth 29 Aug 1835-5 Apr 1909 StGe
Jordon A 15 Jan 1888-29 Oct 1923 StGe
Katie S w/o J F 1884-1968 Libe
L Finney 25 May 1885-25 Aug 1946 Edge
Lee 1904-1972 Snea
Lemuel R h/o L M 1877-1962 Park
Leonard S h/o M B 1884-1964 Park
Levin W h/o E L 30 Aug 1850-7 Feb 1920 Edge
Lillian B w/o R W 16 Apr 1902- MtHo-s
Lillian M 1897-1974 Park
Lillie G w/o R F 1881-1956 Park
Lillie M w/o L R 1879-1948 Park
Lizzie w/o Major 2 June 1851-19 July 1920 Park
Lizzie A d/o Margt H (A?) 14 Feb 1832-11 Feb 1896 Masp
Louisa A w/o Jno W; d/o Saml & Dorenda Coulbourn 20 Mar 1842-30 July 1897 StGe
Louise Douglas 1900-1972 Onan
Lula W 1891-1969 Park
Major h/o Lizzie 29 Aug 1850-14 Feb 1920 Park
Mallissa S w/o W H 8 Sept 1855-31 Dec 1938 Park
Margaret A (H?) d 27 Jan 1888; age: 76 yrs Masp
Margaret E (w/o W T) 16 Oct 1869-22 Dec 1962 Onan

MASON (continued)
Margaret H 1915-1975 Park
Margaret S w/o E O 1880-1952 Edge
Margie E (w/o J M) 1902- MtHo-s
Margie Gibbons 16 Sept 1880-6 June 1977 Park
Marguerite K 1914-1973 Park
Martha A w/o D F 30 Mar 1870-10 Mar 1954 Libe
Mary A w/o C H 10 Jan 1816-6 Mar 1904 (moved from Mason Farm) Edge
Mary A T (w/o C B) 8 July 1854-20 July 1947 Edge
Mary Ann Maria d/o C H & M A 30 Nov 184?-26 May 1852 (moved from Mason Farm) Edge
Mary E w/o J H 24 Aug 1846-21 Feb 1930 Park
Mary K d/o Geo & Scarborough 2 Sept 1807-20 Feb 1892 OldP
Mary Susie d/o Thos & Ann 21 June 1851-30 Dec 1910 JnoP
Mary S 1919-1981 Burt
Mary T w/o Wm D 1871-1936 Park
Mary Virginia d/o C H & M A 7 Mar 1851-24 June 1852 (moved from Mason Farm) Edge
Minnie B w/o L S 1886-1967 Park
Myrtle J 1900-1938 Park
Nancy w/o G W 11 Jan 1814-13 June 1891 JnoS
Nancy G w/o Thos 22 Jan 1809-6 Feb 1889 JnoP
Nansea Rea d/o R W & L B b&d 24 Dec 1927 MtHo-s
Naomi C w/o F R 1897- Park
Nellie M w/o O T 1895-1980 MtHo
Norman O 18 Mar 1904-28 July 1923 Edge
O Harry (h/o B L) 21 Oct 1875-6 Dec 1931 StGe
O Thomas h/o N M 1896-1962 MtHo
Oswald C h/o S E 1864-1942 MtHo

MASON (continued)
Paul T d age: 20 yrs Park
Peanut 1958-68 Park
Preston P s/o T A & D L 1 Jan 1904-1 Feb 1924 Park
R Finney h/o L G 1881-1950 Park
R Norman 15 Sept 1898-21 Dec 1975 Edge
Richard F w/o G W 1867-1946 Park
Robert H Jr d 20 Jan 1955; age: 37 yrs Gask-old
Robert J h/o S E 28 Dec 1862-26 May 1903 Park
Robert J 29 July 1920-12 Nov 1948 Park
Robert Page 31 July 1891-10 Mar 1957 Park
Roland W h/o L B 28 Dec 1899-21 Dec 1973 MtHo-s
Russell P 12 Feb 1908-10 May 1934 Edge
Ruth Ann b&d 1939 MtHo-s
Ruth W (w/o I S) 1919-1939 MtHo-s
Sadie E w/o O C 1870-1962 MtHo
Sallie w/o Southey 27 May 1834-31 Mar 1915 Park
Sallie A w/o G B 10 July 1847-9 Feb 1914 Onan
Sallie E w/o R J 1 July 1867-16 Feb 1933 Park
Sallie T w/o G W 1861-1938 Onan
Sherwood 1906-1958 Park
Sidney R h/o G P 9 Nov 1886-9 Oct 1947 Edge
Southey h/o Sallie 30 Sept 1834-22 Dec 1913 Park
Starr S 22 Mar 1917- MtHo-s
Stephen E s/o Stephen & Esther 23 Dec 1809-20 Nov 1886 Crad-s
Stephen E h/o E C; s/o Stephen 1 May 1843-11 Apr 1907 Onan
Susan E w/o E P 1857-1939 Libe
Susan M w/o T B 20 Feb 1862-9 Oct 1951 Park
Thomas A h/o D L 28 Oct 1875-24 Dec 1960 Park

MASON (continued)
Thorogood B h/o S M 15 Feb 1860-22 Dec 1933 Park
Thurman D 8 Aug 1888-15 Mar 1964 Park
Vernon H 6 Dec 1909-25 June 1970 MtHo-s
W H h/o M S 20 Mar 1853-5 Aug 1930 Park
W Leon 1907-1981 Park
William 1 Oct 1803-3 Dec 1866 StGe
William 1901-1957 Snea
William D h/o M T 1866-1931 Park
William E h/o H R 15 June 1874-5 Feb 1918 MtHo
William T 14 Feb 1835-28 Jan 1912 Edge
William T 15 July 1848-2 Mar 1926 StGe
William T (h/o M E) 8 Apr 1864-19 Mar 1923 Onan
William T h/o G P 13 Sept 1872-14 Dec 1939 Park
William W 1889-1962 Edge
Willianna 1897-1981 Gask
Z L 7 Feb 1865-1 June 1921 Park
Zerobable C h/o H A 24 Sept 1823-27 Feb 1907 Onan
MASSEY, Andrew Bleakley 1925-1954 Onan
Frederick Key 1913-1951 Onan
James Edgar Sr 1897-1959 Onan
Julia Wood 26 Dec 1874-28 Nov 1966 Onan
MATHIAS, Emma S w/o J S 1872-1950 Libe
J Stewart h/o E S 1870-1941 Libe
James W 1-13 Nov 1904 Libe
Ralph Stewart (h/o R P) 1903-1966 Fair
Ruth Polliard (w/o R S) 1913-1959 Fair
MATTHEWS, (MATHEWS),
Addie V 1879-1930 Libe
Albert 1914-1979 Snea
Alfred Jr 29 Apr 1910-16 Mar 1983 Libe
Alfred J h/o L A 30 Aug 1842-2

MATTHEWS (continued)
Dec 1907 Libe
Alfred T h/o E P 25 May 1869-10 Feb 1931 Libe
Alfred T h/o A D 1874-1944 Libe
Alice D w/o A T 1883-1965 Libe
Andrew T s/o A J & L A 8 Aug 1866-11 Aug 1868 Libe
Annie 1909-1979 Metr
Annie B w/o L D 1879-1953 Libe
Annie L 2 Sept 1886-31 May 1957 Park
Arthur d 5 Dec 1983; age: c93 yrs (raised by & served the Carlton Riley family - Parksley) Ross
Avis B 27 Jan 1913- Libe
Barbara S d/o V J & H L b&d 1940 Libe
Beatrice Hall 1903-1967 Park
Beatrice T (w/o W G) 9 Dec 1900- Fair
Bertie S w/o F D 1890-1979 Libe
Bettie J w/o Geo S 20 Mar 1870-12 July 1902 Park
Blanche Parks 6 Jan 1897-16 Oct 1931 Park
Caroline S Copes 12 Dec 1844-5 Mar 1924 Libe
Carrie M S 1906-1982 MtHo
Carroll G h/o J D 1895-1982 Park
Cecil E 1891- Park
Charles J h/o E T 1913-1980 Libe
Clarence E 1894-1967 Snea
Dixie C 1860-1946 MtHo
Dorsey F h/o G B 1878-1951 Libe
Edith S 1931-1979 Metr
Edward s/o A T & E P 28 July 1891-4 May 1894 Libe
Elizabeth H w/o J N 6 Mar 1899- Libe
Elizabeth P w/o A T 12 Sept 1868-30 Aug 1962 Libe
Ella M w/o S J 1881-1943 Libe
Elsie D 1896-1957 Ptea
Elton J 1920-1968 Snea
Elton T h/o I M 1892-1974 MtHo
Elwood T 1911-1965 Park
Eunice J (w/o J E) 1903- Onan
Eva Rolie w/o Wm T 22 May

MATTHEWS (continued)
1869-19 Jan 1933 Park
Eveline T, 1st w/o T J 20 Apr 1846-25 Mar 1910 Park
Evelyn T w/o C J 1920- Libe
Fairy Justis w/o S T 1906-1965 Park
Fletcher L s/o N T & Maggie D 8 Dec 1885-19 July 1903 MtHo
Floyd V 23 Dec 1896-23 Nov 1962 Libe
Frank Jr 22 Jan 1905-7 July 1959 Snea
Frank d 27 May 1961; age: 40 yrs Bays
Frank T h/o S W 1868-1940 Park
Fred D h/o B S 1888-1967 Libe
Frieda B d/o G F & Nora 1929-1930 Libe
G Frank h/o N J 1906-1967 Libe
George C h/o M R 28 Apr 1870-1 July 1929 Park
George Fristoe 1889-1941 Park
George J (s/o Z S & S A E) 7 Oct 1860-5 Jan 1864 Libe
George Socrates 1868-1940 Park
Goldbrough 1864-1937 Libe
Grace 1879-1944 Snea
Grace B w/o D F 1 Feb 1881-2 Apr 1909 Libe
Gracie 1881-1947 Libe
Hadley T 1891-1963 Park
Helen D 1893-1964 Snea
Helen L w/o V J 1909-1965 Libe
Ida M w/o J T 19 Sept 1856-13 Aug 1915 Libe
Inez M w/o E T 1892-1948 MtHo
Isaac 1885-1951 Snea
James A 1915-1977 Metr
James Alfred d 29 Aug 1958; age: 68 yrs StJo
James E (h/o E J) 1901-1949 Onan
James S 1919-1969 Snea
Jennie B w/o S W 16 Jan 1853-6 Feb 1937 Libe
Jesse N h/o E H 23 Feb 1888-23 May 1973 Libe
Jessie D w/o C G 1909- Park
John S h/o S E 1874-1946 Libe
John T h/o I M 17 Nov 1856-22 Oct 1940 Libe

MATTHEWS (continued)
John W h/o M G 1891-1961 Park
Josephine J w/o R W 25 Oct 1847-15 Apr 1888 Park
Laura E 30 Jan 1855-12 Jan 1901 Libe
Laura J (sister) 26 Apr 1858-24 Oct 1891 Park
Lawrence J 31 July 1926-19 Nov 1974 Park
Lelia W 1898- JoyC
Leroy 1911-1977 Snea
Levin F 1838-1916 Libe
Lincy A w/o A J 13 Mar 1844-9 July 1905 Libe
Luther D h/o A B 1875-1951 Libe
M Daisy 19 Feb 1877-22 May 1930 Libe
Manie A w/o Wm S 1865-1957 Park
Manie R w/o G C 5 Jan 1873-11 Sept 1945 Park
Margaret d 12 Oct 1949; age: 31 yrs JoyC
Margaret S 14 Mar 1849-22 Mar 1920 EtDo
Mary 1932-1975 Gask
Mary E 12 Dec 1821-8 Sept 1898 Park
Mary G w/o J W 1900-1973 Park
Mary Wise 1922-1963 Snea
Maude D w/o P S 29 May 1905- Libe
Mazie A Wessells (Addie) 1887-1972 Park
Milton Sye 1904-1966 Snea
Myrtle Ayres w/o Chas W 1895-1939 MtHo-s
Noah T 1850-1933 MtHo
Nora J w/o G F 1905-1980 Libe
Ora B 1912-1971 Snea
Paul S h/o M D 21 June 1899-25 Nov 1976 Libe
Robert W h/o J J 1 Mar 1845-27 Oct 1922 Park
Ronnie 1946-1978 JoyC
Ryland Elton 1812-1967 MtHo
Sadie 1896-1957 Snea
Sallie A E w/o Z S 18 Mar 1833-31 Mar 1903 Libe
Sallie E w/o J S 1879-1943 Libe

MATTHEWS (continued)
Sallie S w/o M W 10 Aug 1860-13 June 1923 Libe
Samuel 1899-1952 Snea
Samuel J h/o E M 1879-1943 Libe
Samuel S Sr 1887-1946 Park
Samuel W h/o J B 7 Mar 1854-10 Aug 1940 Libe
Sarah 1891-1971 StJo
Sarah A (2nd w/o T J) 3 Dec 1868-2 Nov 1922 Park
Sarah J 1899-1980 Libe
Sarah R 1917-1977 Metr
Stanley Thomas h/o F J 1907-1970 Park
Stantley F 4 Sept 1868-28 June 1928 Libe
Susan W w/o F T 1861-1932 Park
Thomas 1880-1956 Snea
Thomas 1914-1974 JoyC
Tully J h/o E T & S A 11 May 1853-17 Mar 1938 Park
Vergie S 22 Nov 1907-20 June 1935 Holl
Vernon J h/o H L 1910-1974 Libe
Virginia T 1846-1928 Libe
Warden 1909-1959 Snea
William Greer (h/o B T) 7 Jan 1890-9 Feb 1978 Fair
William H 29 Dec 1824-2 Aug 1908 Park
William S h/o M A 1862-1941 Park
William T h/o E R 8 Jan 1869-7 Apr 1935 Park
William T h/o L W 1891-1966 JoyC
Willie E 10 Sept 1889-27 Nov 1920 Park
Willye Susan 1920-1942 Park
Zorobabel D (s/o Z S & S A E) 16 May 1865-23 Nov 1872 Libe
Zorababel S h/o S A E 16 June 1832-21 May 1908 Libe
M(EARS), G P footstone only Pitt
M C footstone only Wacb
MEARS, s/o G R & L F 5-10 Nov 1889 MtHo-s
infant b&d 1917 Holl

MEARS (continued)
infant d1921 MtHo
s/o L W & M H b&d 1923 Holl
d/o R W & Eliz b&d 16 Oct 1933 Park
infant b&d 1954 Park
A   Crawley (h/o O E) 1882-1957 Holl
A H Gordon (h/o E F) 7 Mar 1861-1 Feb 1944 Wach
A   Quinton s/o J H & R W 1886-1967 StGe
A T h/o M L 5 May 1861-18 Mar 1941 Libe
A Thomas 1852-1932 MeaB
A   W h/o M E 20 Jan 1859-6 Aug 1938 Oakg
Abel 31 Aug 1804-10 July 1878 MeaB
Adah J 9 Dec 1812-6 Apr 1883 Quin
Adelbert F s/o B F & M T 27 Feb-22 Apr 1911 Libe
Albert A 31 Jan 1831-19 Jan 1889; age: 57/11/19 Meag
Alexander G 1890-1947 Edge
Alfred s/o G D & Rintha b&d 13 July 1911 Libe
Alfred J (h/o J P) 7 Nov 1857-26 Dec 1921 Quin
Alice Marie 9 Aug 1922-31 Jan 1923 Meap
Alice R (w/o C L) 1886-1971 Fair
Alice S (w/o H F) 1896-1932 Meap
Alonzo 1877-1967 Burt
Althea G w/o M J 1906- Libe
Amy 1907-1973 Burt
Anna F, 1st w/o C F 21 Feb 1872-8 Aug 1902 MtHo
Anna P w/o F D 1909- Park
Anne L w/o G P 8 May 1913- Park
Anne Hope 1835-1936 Park
Annie 1889-1953 Holl
Annie A w/o M T 1876-1967 Mitc-w
Annie Coard 9 Nov 1900-15 Jan 1935 MtHo
Annie E, 2nd w/o C F d 5 Oct 1905; age: 31 yrs MtHo

MEARS (continued)
Annie L w/o Oscar M 13 Jan 1880-29 Aug 1904 RodP
Annie M (w/o G W) 1868-1938 Holl
Annie S w/o F W 25 Jan 1893-14 Aug 1974 Park
Annie S w/o K L 1918- Park
Arinthia W w/o G D 1870-1954 Libe
Arthur D 1918-1946 Edge
Arthur R h/o M L 1811-1868 Onan
Arthur R s/o Arthur & Margt 9 Aug 1866-9 Nov 1896 Onan
Arthur T h/o E McM 2 Sept 1839-15 July 1908 Wach
Augustine S 9 Apr 1880-4 Nov 1963 Wach
Austin W 1913- Park
B Bordie h/o J F 8 July 1855-18 Nov 1907 MeaD
B J h/o B S nd Holl
Bagwell G 9 Dec 1817-4 Dec 1892 BMea
Barry Lee 1944-1974 Fair
Benjamin F 1852-1927 Holl
Benjamin F 1906-1967 Holl
Benjamin W (h/o E S M) 17 Oct 1833-2 Dec 1896 Mear
Bernard Lee (h/o B M) 1891-1947 Quin
Bernie 1877-1925 Fair
Bert 1904-1941 Holl
Bertie K 1903- Snea
Bertie L w/o R W 1897-1972 Libe
Bertie S w/o J S 1878-1949 Onan
Bertie V (w/o U T) 1885-1964 Fair
Bessie C 22 Aug 1899-3 Sept 1979 Edge
Bessie J w/o J S B 16 Dec 1877-14 May 1953 Edge
Bessie T (w/o J C) 21 Sept 1890-30 Dec 1966 Wach
Bessie Young w/o W R 29 July 1891-25 Sept 1963 Edge
Betty F (w/o D L) 1884-1983 Fair
Beulah J 1890-1970 Holl

MEARS (continued)
Birdie May (w/o B L) 1895-1969 Quin
Bobby s/o A T & E M 6 May 1865-9 Mar 1872 MeaA
Bransford L 24 Oct 1899-14 Oct 1919 Onan
Buddy 1957-1977 Fair
Burdie S w/o B J 25 Mar 1866-11 July 1904 Holl
Burleigh F h/o M T 1890-1973 Libe
Caroline w/o Thoro 24 Nov 1816-14 May 1895 Thor
Caroline H (w/o J E) 1894-1979 StGe
Carrie A 1857-1895 Edge
Cecil 1882-1920 Edge
Charles B 28 Aug 1880-6 July 1943 StGe
Charles D 16 June 1843-27 Aug 1915; age: 72/2/11 Burt
Charles F h/o A F & A E 6 Feb 1865-16 Dec 1940 MtHo
Charles L (h/o A R) 1881-1952 Fair
Charles T (h/o L C) 1887-1965 Wach
Charlie 1900-1971 Burt
Charlie L 10 Oct 1873-12 Apr 1927 Edge
Charlotte W d/o L C & M W 2-3 Sept 1918 MtHo
Christine d/o R W & India 30 June-8 Dec 1906 Mitc-w
Clara B d 10 Nov 1937; age: 6 yrs Holl
Clara C 9 May 1903-20 May 1962 Edge
Claude V 12 Feb 1900-31 July 1958 Edge
Coley C Jr b&d 1963 MtHo
Cora L w/o R B 1875-1962 MtHo
Daniel W h/o M W 1882-1951 Meap
David (h/o J A); s/o Jas & Hester 27 Aug 1806-16 Nov 1871; age: 65/2/19 Meag
David W 1867-1947 Oakg
Dewey h/o Julia 1899-1954 Wach
Dorsey L (h/o B F) 1882-1958

MEARS (continued)
Fair
Dorsey L 1899-1965 Snea
Dorsey R 1930-1969 Burt
Durwood J (h/o S G) 1907-1959 Edge
E T 20 Jan 1845-4 Feb 1927; age: 82 yrs Oakg
Edward L 1893-1974 Burt
Edward Thomas (h/o G B) 26 Aug 1858-23 Nov 1947 Holl
Edwin Thomas 18 Nov 1899-14 May 1954 MtHo
Elisha A s/o Elisha W & Nancy d 29 Sept 1840; age: 1/10/17 TheG
Elisha W s/o Elisha & Nancy d 17 Dec 1838; age: 37/1/7 TheG
Eliza C w/o J A 1853-1933 StGe
Eliza F w/o A H G 24 Mar 1874-28 May 1963 Wach
Elizabeth C 1881-1952 Park
Elizabeth J w/o J E 6 Jan 1825-7 Nov 1899 Morr
Elizabeth P w/o G J 19 Nov 1834-26 July 1905 Meac
Elizabeth S (w/o G W) 12 Aug 1841-2 Mar 1927 Wach
Elizabeth T w/o T W 1901-1967 Wach
Ella L 1872-1957 Fair
Ella L mother/o Addie Lee 1874-1946 Libe
Ella P d/o B W & E S M 3 Jan-15 July 1858 Mear
Ellen J w/o J T 13 Feb 1845-9 Dec 1913 MtHo
Ellen McMath w/o A T 5 Apr 1844-24 Feb 1922 Wach
Elmer C s/o L T & P A 29 Nov 1921-29 Apr 1922 Oakg
Elva B 1881-1959 Wach
Elwood s/o J K & L E 17 July 1910-10 Sept 1923 Fair
Emily L d/o F W & Annie 16 Apr 1922-17 July 1925 Park
Emma C w/o T R 9 Feb 1864-25 Aug 1938 MtHo
Emma G w/o Columbus; d/o J S & Eliz Bell d 11 June 1896; age: 42/3/22 Anth

MEARS (continued)
Emma Ruth w/o J K 1886-1962 MtHo
Emma S Mapp (w/o B W) 17 Sept 1839-6 Nov 1914 Mear
Ernest H s/o Harvey & Angela 1922-1923 Ptea
Ernest L 1878-1947 Wach
Ernie B w/o W B 21 Dec 1878-1 Oct 1915 MtHo
Essie Barnes 1904-1981 Libe
Essie M d/o M T & A A 1 Aug 1902-11 Dec 1913 Mitc-w
Esther K 20 Apr 1840-7 Oct 1919 StLu
Eva d/o B W & E S M 21 Sept 1872-1 Sept 1873 Mear
Eva M (w/o S S) 1888-1975 MtHo-s
Eva T w/o W T 6 July 1875-5 Aug 1935 MtHo
Evelyn B 1903-1980 Libe
Fletcher H h/o S V 21 Nov 1876-17 Apr 1958 Park
Flora V 1902-1973 Edge
Forest Richard s/o R W & India 12 Apr 1902-28 Oct 1941 Mitc-w
Forrest G 1914-1970 Fair
Fosque D h/o A P 28 Dec 1907-11 Mar 1977 Park
Frances A w/o T A 20 Dec 1830-31 Mar 1918 MtHo
Francis R 1932-1939 Onan
Frank B (h/o M N) 1897-1961 Fair
Frank C s/o J W & M S 4 Feb 1879-23 Mar 1917 MtHo
Frank P h/o M A 9 Oct 1849-21 Oct 1924 Park
Fred C 1869-1938 StGe
Fred T h/o S L 1883-1953 Libe
Frederick h/o Annie 29 May 1884-13 June 1959 Park
Frederick C s/o L C & J C 23 May-15 July 1889 Mear
G Lorenzo 1907-1971 Wach
G Willie (w/o W R) 1910-1942 Davi
Gabrille Beloate w/o E T 11 Mar 1858-5 Mar 1936 Holl
Garfield 1904-1956 HTri

MEARS (continued)
George (h/o Virginia) 1891-1944 Onan
George D h/o A W 1869-1951 Libe
George D (h/o M K) 1893-1976 Onan
George R h/o L F 21 Jan 1865-17 July 1943 MtHo-s
George R 1897-1965 Libe
George T h/o M S d 25 May 1912; age: 82 yrs Wach
George T 1856-1946 Holl
George T h/o H R 1857-1946 Wach
George T h/o Kate d 24 Oct 1918; age: 55 Yrs Snea
George W (h/o E S) 30 June 1830-15 Jan 1912 Wach
George W (h/o A M) 1866-1944 Holl
George W h/o S S 9 Feb 1870-28 Aug 1941 Park
Georgiana S d/o Abel J & Margt 2 June 1844-18 Jan 1846; age: 1/7/16 MeaB
Gilbert J (h/o E P) 3 May 1833-12 Nov 1897 Meac
Gilbert T h/o M B 1902-1964 Edge
Ginnie d/o Jno W & Sue A (Pitts) d (nd); age: 0/4/0 Pitt
Glenwood T s/o H T & Elsie I 22 Sept 1913-14 Feb 1914 Edge
Grayson P h/o A L 10 Oct 1910-4 Jan 1974 Park
Hallie B 17 Oct 1875-21 Aug 1961 StGe
Harry Everett 2 Feb 1875-26 Oct 1935 Mear
Harry R 1898-1963 Edge
Harry T h/o J S 13 Jan 1880-13 Sept 1926 MtHo
Harry T 1881-1939 Onan
Harry W h/o M E 12 May 1900-14 May 1970 Libe
Harvey C (h/o M L) 1884-1952 Fair
Hattie R w/o G T 1866-1941 Wach
Helen A 1891- Edge
Helen E D d/o Noah & Mar-

MEARS (continued)
cielene 14-15 July 1908 Anth
Helen H 1915-1972 Gask
Helen Sara d/o B F & M T 15 Apr 1914-18 Sept 1922 Libe
Hellen M d/o U T & Bertie V 20 Mar-26 Aug 1909 Libe
Hennie 1875-1947 Burt
Henry C D s/o Howard S & Mary B 14 Jan 1878-18 Mar 1879 StoM
Henry S s/o H S & Mary B 16 Jan 1885-10 May 1886 StoM
Herbert T Sr h/o M B 1888-1963 Edge
Herbert T Jr h/o P B 1931- Edge
Herman B 1894-1960 Wach
Hester w/o J A 22 Sept 1822-13 Apr 1895 StGe
Hillas W s/o J L & Margie L 14 Mar-14 Nov 1922 MtHo
Homer Guy 19 Jan 1928-1 Jan 1952 Libe
Howard F (h/o A S) 1888- Meap
Howard S s/o Jas H & Patience 20 Jan 1835-13 Nov 1885 StoM
Indiana (India) w/o R W 12 Feb 1867-1 Dec 1943 Mitc-w
J Alfred Jr (h/o S J) 1900-1968 MtHo
J Carroll (h/o B T) 3 Jan 1891-23 Dec 1951 Wach
J Edward h/o M E 1898-1974 Libe
J Thomas h/o E J 13 Dec 1842-3 Oct 1919 MtHo
James A h/o M E 1862-1930 MtHo
James A III 9 Nov 1927-30 Apr 1970 MtHo
James E h/o V S 13 Feb 1842-10 Mar 1903 Meap
James E (h/o C H) 1884-1975 StGe
James H (h/o P G) 20 Mar 1820-22 June 1891; age: 70/10/2 MeaB
James H (h/o R E) 1859-1914 StGe
James H 1872-1949 Holl
James Leon (surname unclear) 1898-196? Holl

MEARS (continued)
James Oswald h/o M E; s/o J Henry 31 Mar 1847-18 Mar 1906 Holl
Jefferson D 1861-1935 Mitc-e
Jefferson D H s/o Jno W A & Hester 25 Oct 1861-26 June 1897 StGe
Jennie Custis w/o L C d 20 Feb 1942; age: 80 yrs Mear
Jennie F w/o B B 28 July 1857-28 Jan 1935 MeaD
Jennie S w/o H T 20 Feb 1880-19 Sept 1915 MtHo
Joe R h/o M L 1900- Libe
John A (h/o Hester) 4 July 1817-26 July 1862 StGe
John A (h/o E C) 19 Nov 1849-5 Oct 1922 StGe
John B s/o Wm & Bridget (Bull) 7 Sept 1808-10 Dec 1851; age: 43/3/3 Mear
John B S d 23 Feb 1847; age: 10/0/21 Wacb
John Custis s/o L C & J C 29 June 1898-9 Feb 1905 Mear
John E, Capt h/o E J 1 Nov 1834-16 Dec 1897 Morr
John F s/o Wm & Sarah 11 June 1787-20 Sept 1836; age: 49/3/9 Expe
John Golden 7 Apr 1897-9 June 1931 Burt
John H h/o T S 19 Apr 1844-31 Dec 1915 Holl
John H s/o Jno B & Sarah Jane (Ames) 7 July 1852-30 Aug 1879; age: 27/1/23 Mear
John H 20 Nov 1862-8 Jan 1962 Edge
John K h/o E R 1887-1970 MtHo
John L 22 Dec 1889-5 Dec 1959 Edge
John R (h/o N C) 1870-1921 Holl
John S 19 Apr 1797-3 May 1872; age: 75/0/14 Wacb
John S h/o B S 1874-1954 Onan
John Thomas 25 Oct 1873-10 Oct 1946 Wach
John Upshur h/o P S 20 Dec 1878-20 Sept 1931 Holl
John W s/o Joseph T & Ellen I 3

MEARS (continued)
Feb-14 July 1872 Budd
John W 1 Aug 1883-11 Oct 1951 Libe
John W 1922-1940 Edge
John Wesley h/o M S 29 Aug 1848-30 Aug 1913 MtHo
John William (h/o M B) 1879-1943 MtHo
Joseph Wharton s/o Abel 22 Feb 1831-24 Oct 1836 MeaB
Josephine K 1896-1961 Snea
Josiah S B h/o B J 21 Sep 1876-22 Sep 1964 Edge
Judson K (h/oLE)1886-1951 Fair
Julia w/o Dewey 1905- Wach
Julia E 1875-1952 MeaB
Julia M 9 Jan 1866-6 June 1962 Onan
Julia P (w/o A J) 11 Mar 1860-27 July 1925 Quin
Juliet A w/o David d/o Benj & Ann Ames 31 Dec 1808-21 Apr 1868; age: 59/3/20 Meag
Kate Mason 1876-1962 Park
Keith L h/o A S 1914- Park
L Carl h/o W B 1878-1960 Edge
L Winfred (h/o M H) 1892-1969 Holl
Laban J (h/o M A) 12 June 1855-30 Dec 1909 Wach
Laura F w/o G R 15 Nov 1871-25 Apr 1932 MtHo-s
Leah Ann w/o Alfred Jehu d/o Geo B & Ann J Mapp 20 Apr 1837-23 Apr 1911 Oakg
Leola C (w/o C T) 1898-1957 Wach
Leonard Cecil (h/o J C s/o B W) 11 Mar 1861-24 Mar 1935 Mear
Leonard Cecil Jr 20 Dec 1884-5 Sept 1928 Mear
Leonard T h/o P A 4 Apr 1890-7 Dec 1932 Oakg
Lillian W 1920-1959 Wach
Lillie L 1872-1949 Holl
Lillie M 1880-1928 Fair
Lizzie C 19 Oct 1892-27 Sep 1970 MtHo-s
Lloyd K 21 Sep 1848-22 Oct 1934 Edge

MEARS (continued)
Lloyd W h/o M E 11 Sep 1849-21 Feb 1906 Onan
Lock d 1910 (stone missing) Leve
Lola V d/o R W & B L 1922-1933 Libe
Lorenzo D 1 Feb 1858-25 Apr 1935 Onan
Lottie I w/o R W 1899- Edge
Louise E (w/o J K) 1890- Fair
Louise P 13 Sep 1915-19 Apr 1975 Park
Louise V Crockett 1905-1930 Onan
Lucille F 1910-1971 Holl
Luther Carroll h/o M W 1883-1939 MtHo
Lygia Wills d/o D W & M A 6 Feb-17 July 1906 Oakg
M Elizabeth w/o J E 1906- Libe
M Estelle w/o H W 1916- Libe
Mabel Brown (w/o J W) 10 Jan 1881-30 Mar 1951 MtHo
Mabel N (w/o F B) 1899-1965 Fair
Maggie 1869-1964 Burt
Maggie d 1 Dec 1966; age: 72 yrs Burt
Maggie A (Margaret) 1869-1951 Oakg
Maggie H (w/o L W) 1894-1965 Holl
Maggie Sue F d/o Howard S & Mary B 30 Apr 1879-23 May 1880 Stom
Maggie W w/o D W 1888-1971 Meap
Mahaley w/o L K 19 Dec 1845-23 Nov 1922 Edge
Major T h/o A A 1872-1959 Mitc-w
Malissa L w/o A T 6 May 1863-19 Nov 1914 Libe
Manie E 5 July 1875-10 June 1904 MtHo
Manie H w/o S W 10 July 1861-30 Dec 1928 MtHo-s
Mannie E w/o A W 29 Feb 1860-4 Nov 1926 Oakg
Marcie P (w/o N C) 1888-1959 MtHo

MEARS (continued)
Margaret 27 May 1836-1 Nov 1862 Wacb
Margaret 1877-1965 Mitc-w
Margaret Ann w/o Alexander W E 4 Mar 1813-8 Apr 1837 Syca
Margaret B w/o Abel of Abel d 13 Nov 1852; age: 45/0/5 MeaB
Margaret J w/o O M 1884-1943 MtHo
Margaret K (w/o G D) 1894- Onan
Margaret L w/o A R 13 Dec 1832-1 Jan 1918 Onan
Margaret P w/o Wm of A 9 Dec 1805-3 Nov 1877 MeaA
Margaret S w/o G T 25 Apr 1845-1 June 1917 Wach
Margaret S w/o J W 7 Oct 1851-19 Jan 1919 MtHo
Margaret T W d/o Noah & Marcielene 25 Jan 1913-4 Aug 1914 Anth
Margie L w/o O N 1885-1962 Park
Mary w/o Edwd 22 Sept 1820-14 Feb 1899 MtHo
Mary d 25 June 1944; age: 66 yrs Snea
Mary A w/o F P 26 Aug 1849-18 Sep 1914; age: 65 Yrs Park
Mary Ann (w/o L J) 12 May 1861-17 Dec 1924 Wach
Mary B w/o G T 1908- Edge
Mary E w/o Wm Thos 20 Nov 1820-31 Oct 1903 Mear
Mary E w/o J O 13 Dec 1849-6 Feb 1908 Holl
Mary E w/o L W 17 Mar 1853-21 July 1932 Onan
Mary Elizabetrh w/o J A 1863- 1931 MtHo
Mary Swanger d/o Oswald & Mollie Brown 21 Nov 1900-11 Aug 1901 Edge
Mary U 1905-1963 Burt
Mattie W w/o L C 1884-1971 MtHo
Maude L (w/o H C) 1889-1975 Fair
May 1882-1913 Edge

MEARS (continued)
Mazie K (w/o S R) 1901-1969 MtHo-s
Michael 1959-1978 Burt
Mildred V d/o J U & P S 21 Oct 1907-11 June 1908 Holl
Milton J h/o A G 1900-1979 Libe
Minnie B w/o Wm S 1880-1968 Park
Minnie Bradford w/o H T Sr nd Edge
Minnie L w/o J R 1901-1970 Libe
Minnie T w/o B F 1891-1970 Libe
Mollie Lee (nee Chandler) w/o W H 1875-1950 Holl
Mollie M 24 May 1870-21 Nov 1935 Edge
Nancy N w/o Elisha W d 6 Dec 1838; age: 38/1/28 TheG
Nannie C (w/o J R) 1870-1937 Holl
Nannie D (w/o Nathan) 1865- 1948 Fair
Nathan (h/o N D) 1861-1926 Fair
Nathaniel W s/o G J & E P 13 Nov 1871-11 Dec 1895 Meac
Noah C (h/o M P) 1873-1961 MtHo
O S 1872-1959 Edge
Olie Estelle (w/o A C) 1891- 1955 Holl
Oris N h/o M L 1878-1953 Park
Oscar M h/o M J 1876-1940 MtHo
Oscar Prentiss 1916-1971 MtHo
Oswald C 1845-1926 Wach
Otho B 1868-1935 MtHo
Otho Stewart 27 Oct 1893-13 Nov 1973 Park
Page M s/o L C & J C 20 Oct 1890-17 July 1892 Mear
Patience G w/o J H 4 Nov 1816-22 June 1889 MeaB
Patience L 1861-1943 Holl
Patrick B s/o Wm & Bridget 10 Feb 1811-3 Dec 1849; age: 38/9/23 Mear
Paul Connor Jr 24 Oct 1946-15 Sept 1954 Park
Paul Jones 11 Apr 1898-25 Oct

MEARS (continued)
1962 Edge
Pearlie A w/o Wm S 1889-1958 Park
Phillip G s/o Howard S & Mary B 4 Sept 1881-...1882 Stom
Phoebe E d/o Jno W & Margt S 18 Mar-19 Apr 1881; age: 0/1/1 RodP
Phyllis B w/o H T Jr 1927-1964 Edge
Polly Susan w/o J U 10 Aug 1874-2 June 1954 Holl
Priscilla A w/o L T 14 July 1892-8 Aug 1980 OakG
Ralph F 1917-1969 Fair
Ralph T 8 July 1902-20 Dec 1934 Onan
Richard S 1929-1972 Libe
Richard T 1901-1969 Burt
Richard Walter h/o India 23 Jan 1868-6 Jan 1952 Mitc-w
Robert L 1894-1965 Holl
Robert Lee 25 Mar 1929-18 Aug 1944 Edge
Rogers B h/o C L 1877-1933 MtHo
Rose E d/o J A & Hester 22 June 1857-30 Aug 1863 StGe
Rose E w/o Jas H d/o Benj D & Louisa S Wise 1861-1942 StGe
Rosey E B d/o Richd & Margt d 15 Jan 1839 (stone missing; 1940 data) MeaB
Roy W h/o B L 1890-1959 Libe
Russell E 1927-1983 Libe
Russell W h/o L I 1898-1964 Edge
Sadie Virginia w/o F H 6 June 1889-7 Jan 1976 Park
Sally S 13 Dec 1831-7 Feb 1863 Wacb
Samuel Hall s/o S W & Annie E 12 June 1890-12 Apr 1891 Mear
Samuel S (h/o E M) 1885-1960 MtHo-s
Sarah 1901- Onan
Sarah D 5 Jan 1810-16 Aug 1882 Wacb
Sarah Jane Clowes w/o Jno B (Jno B Mears was 1st husband;

MEARS (continued)
Peter J Clowes was 2nd) 25 Aug 1813-25 Oct 1898; age: 85/2/0 Mear
Sarah L w/o F T 1885-1961 Libe
Sarah S w/o Geo 13 Mar 1874-4 Oct 1929 Park
Sewell W h/o M H 25 Feb 1863-24 July 1935 MtHo-s
Sidney U 28 Dec 1903-11 Sept 1968 MtHo
Sophia A B w/o Lorenzo D 31 July 1817-9 Apr 1885 McLa
Southey T 1900-1962 MeaB
Spencer R (h/o M K) 1900-1950 MtHo-s
Stanley 1921-1972 Burt
Stanley P 25 Apr 1894-28 Mar 1909 Onan
Sue A Pitts w/o Jno W (footstone only- "S A P M) Pitt
Susan J d/o Abel & Margt d 24 Feb 1841; age: 6/6/1 MeaB
Susan S 1860-1929 Wach
Susie G (w/o D J) 1905- Edge
Susie J (w/o J A Jr) 1900-1982 MtHo
Tabitha S w/o J H 19 July 1846-27 May 1925 Holl
Ted W h/o E T 1886-1964 Wach
Thelma A w/o Ben F d/o H C & S M Gray 1913-1934 MtHo-s
Thomas A h/o F A 18 Nov 1821-25 May 1905 MtHo
Thomas H 1865-1940 Park
Thomas P 1870-1961 StGe
Thomas R h/o E C 11 May 1861-11 Mar 1936 MtHo
Thoragood (h/o Caroline) s/o Robt & Permelia 25 Nov 1810-15 Oct 1877 Thor
Upshur T (h/o B V) 1887-1953 Fair
Vera V 13 Feb 1886-11 June 1947 Wach
Virginia 1869-1961 Davi
Virginia (w/o Geo) 1891- Onan
Virginia E 20 Jan 1834-27 Nov 1862 Wacb
Virginia H d/o Abel & Margt 21 Dec 1842-4 Aug 1871 MeaB
Virginia J 15 Sept 1860-16 Apr

MEARS (continued)
1940 Park
Virginia S w/o W H P 10 Jan 1847-29 Dec 1930 MtHo
Virginia S w/o J E 7 Dec 1849-30 Aug 1923 Meap
W Rosser (h/o G W) 1887-1941 Davi
Walter B 1901-1942 MtHo
Walter Lee s/o G R & L F 24 Dec 1892-14 Oct 1894 MtHo-s
Warren F 1908-1958 Fair
William of A h/o M P 21 June 1806-4 Aug 1884 MeaA
William B 17 June 1791-1 Oct 1846 (unable to verify) Thos
William B s/o Wm & Bridget 18 May 1820-21 Apr 1849; age: 28/11/3 Mear
William Carlton Sr 1911-1945 Park
William Carlton Jr 1940-1945 Park
William H P h/o V S 30 Nov 1843-20 May 1879 MtHo
William Henry (h/o M L) 1872-1951 Holl
William R 13 Dec 1889-16 Feb 1941 MtHo-s
William S h/o M B 1878-1950 Park
William S h/o P A 1881-1952 Park
William T s/o J W & Margt E 28 Nov 1906-27 Jan 1907 RodP
William Tankard h/o E T 4 June 1869-8 Mar 1920 MtHo
William Thomas (h/o M E) 6 Jan 1828-16 Nov 1888 Mear
Willie 1892-1970 Snea
Willie B h/o E B 3 Feb 1878-28 May 1904 MtHo
Willie Brown w/o L C d/o W R & M E Allen 7 Nov 1886-27 Jan 1917 Edge
Willie L s/o F P & M A 7 May 1876-24 Oct 1878 Park
Willie Rogers h/o B Y 9 Mar 1890- Edge
MEDDARS, Clifton 1924-1975 Park
MEEDAM, Virginia S 1908-1969

MEEDAM (continued)
NewM
MELDRUM, Mary J 1882-1964 Wach
MELSON, s/o Edwd & Mary S b&d 3 May 1879 Lewi
inf s/o Geo W & Mamie S b&d 1917 Crad-s
Algernon J 5 Aug 1870-29 Mar 1936 Edge
Alice Lee w/o G C 1876-1961 Edge
Amanda E d/o Levin J & Sarah J 8 Apr-13 June 1880 ParB
Ann w/o S P 25 Jan 1814-25 June 1906 Edge
Annie F Willet w/o Smith 1 Nov 1798-5 Oct 1872 Mari
Annie R (w/o J H Jr) 19 June 1868-16 July 1944 MtHo
Benjamin T 1851-1932 Edge
Beulah Wessels (RN) (w/o G C) 24 May 1914-14 July 1971 Fair
Carrie E w/o C F 1911- Libe
Clarence Wise h/o V P 24 Oct 1903-12 Dec 1970 Edge
Claude F h/o C E 1907-1973 Libe
Edna Lewis 1855-1940 Libe
Capt Edward-murdered on his vessel *Fannie Soulbeau* 5 May 1882; age: 42 yrs Lewi
Edward S s/o J R & F C S 5 Aug 1865-8 Jan 1886 Edge
Edward S s/o Levin J & Sarah J 6 Aug-1 Oct 1890 ParB
Edward T h/o M A 1874-1938 Libe
Elizabeth S w/o B T 7 Nov 1852-20 Sep 1884 Edge
Elizabeth S 1895-1962 Edge
Emma C w/o Henry 21 Jan 1833-5 Sep 1889 Edge
Essie p (w/o J H) 1889-1970 Fair
Eula J (w/o T H) 1873-1962 Edge
Frances C S w/o J R 27 Dec 1823-18 Apr 1894 Edge
George Arthur s/o Geo W & Mamie S 12 Aug 1907-17 Jan 1908 Crad-s

MELSON (continued)
George Columbus h/o A L 1879-1942 Edge
George Columbus (h/o B W) 5 Feb 1914-17 May 1977 Fair
George T h/o K H 1906-1979 Edge
George W (h/o M S) 1883-1952 Crad-s
George Wesley s/o Geo W & Mamie S 28 Nov 1909-4 Jan 1911 Crad-s
Henry h/o E C 16 Mar 1816-9 Feb 1906 Edge
Henry E 1873-1936 MtHo
Henry W h/o L C 1836-1874 MtHo
Hilton G (h/o P B) 1906-1975 Fair
Ida Virginia w/o Saml C 31 May 1856-18 Jan 1926 Edge
J Bratcher h/o M P 1907-1974 Edge
James C h/o M M 2 Feb 1880-13 May 1927 Edge
James S h/o M A 13 June 1846-22 Jan 1929 Edge
James T h/o M S 1 Nov 1818-28 Apr 1891 Edge
John D h/o M A d 3 June 1868; age: 51 yrs Edge
John H Jr (h/o A R) 15 Aug 1864-25 July 1906 MtHo
John H (h/o E P) 1876-1956 Fair
John H III 1901-1955 MtHo
John R h/o F C S 14 May 1816-22 Apr 1899 Edge
Katherine H w/o G T nd Edge
Kenneth S 1919-1944 Edge
L Thorogood 1885-1954 Edge
Leigh V w/o Jno T d/o Jno T & Margt 30 Mar 1878-23 Dec 1894 (stone missing; 1940 data) Clov
Levin J h/o S J 1847-1925 Edge
Levin J (h/o S Y) 20 Oct 1889-3 Aug 1971 Edge
Levin T (h/o S A) 14 Aug 1851-21 Aug 1920 Edge
Louisa C w/o H W 1841-1918 MtHo
Mabel P w/o J B 1912- Edge

MELSON (continued)
Mamie Pearl d/o Saml C & Ida d 14 Oct 1890; age: 2/1/3 Edge
Marceline P w/o B T 1870-1958 Edge
Margaret A w/o J D d 3 Apr 1877; age: 62 yrs Edge
Margaret A w/o J S 7 June 1854-1 Mar 1931 Edge
Margaret A w/o E T 1875-1950 Libe
Margaret L w/o W H 30 Jan 1875-6 Feb 1949 Edge
Margaret S w/o J T 17 Oct 1827-25 June 1911 Edge
Marie Marhoffer w/o J C 1891-1974 Edge
Mary S (w/o G W) 1886-1963 Crad-s
Olevia W (w/o S S) 1880-1944 Edge
Olivia M 13 Feb 1882-23 Aug 1960 Edge
Ora P (w/o R W) 1919-1973 Edge
Pearl B (w/o H G) 1906-1970 Fair
Ralph W (h/o O P) 1917- Edge
Sallie A (w/o L T) 5 Nov 1852-29 Aug 1948 Edge
Sallie M w/o W T 20 Mar 1855-7 Sep 1929 Edge
Samuel P h/o Ann 13 Sep 1814-15 May 1889 Edge
Samuel S (h/o O W) 1876-1961 Edge
Sarah J w/o L J 1848-1934 Edge
Sarah J d/o Levin J & Sarah J 24 Apr-29 July 1887 ParB
Sarah Y (w/o L J) 20 Feb 1893-18 May 1972 Edge
Smith (s/o Jonathan) 20 Nov 1796-31 Jan 1854 Wilb
Thomas H (h/o E J) 1858-1942 Edge
Thomas W h/o V Y 1884-1973 Edge
Viola Y w/o T W 1882-1963 Edge
Virginia Parker w/o C W 11 June 1912-15 Jan 1973 Edge
Wesley T h/o S M 18 July 1853-

MELSON (continued)
27 Apr 1939 Edge
William E 1866-1941 MtHo
William H h/o M L 1 Oct 1874-21 Dec 1936 Edge
William H Jr 1906-1944 Edge
MELVIN, Elizabeth W wid/o Saml d/o Col T M & M P C Bayly 6 Dec 1815 in Acc Co - 22 Nov 1885 in Halifax Courthouse VA MtCu
Francis J 1860-1923 Wach
MENZEL, Adolf R 1860-1949 Libe
MERKLE, Mrs Ann 1889-1979 Fair
MERRILL, Charlie s/o L H & E A 11 Sep 1860-16 Mar 1861 Onan
Emma Patrick w/o F A 1860-1939 Onan
Esther Ann w/o L H 25 July 1838-4 Apr 1922 Onan
Frank Augustus h/o E P 1860-1945 Onan
Henry F 1915-1944 Park
Levi A h/o M H 24 Aug 1832-1 Aug 1914 MtHo
Levin H h/o E A 3 Nov 1834-28 July 1895 Onan
Levin S s/o L H & E A 1 June 1866-15 Feb 1895 Onan
Lizzie d/o L H & E A 23 July 1863-11 Dec 1883 Onan
Margaret Harris w/o L A 9 Aug 1835-28 Mar 1925 MtHo
MERRITT, Minnie R 1884-1967 Edge
METCALF, (METCALFE), baby boy b&d 1959 OakG
Albert Sidney 9 Aug 1902-12 Apr 1965 Wach
Annie P 1882-1968 Fair
Bernie W 1913-1978 Wach
Edwin W 1907-1968 Wach
Elizabeth D (w/o R T) 1910- Fair
George T 1876-1958 Wach
George T 24 Aug 1915-7 Nov 1974 Wach
James Alfred 1 Aug 1886-28 Jan 1973 Wach

METCALF (continued)
Jesse V 13 1Apr 1921-29 Sep 1966 Wach
Jessie Tapman nd Wach
Mary M w/o R W 1925- Wach
Maude Lee w/o W J 1882-1940 Wach
Robert T (h/o E D) 1902- Fair
Rooker W h/o Mary M 1920-1971 Wach
William J h/o M L 1879-1953 Wach
MICHAEL, Anna T 13 Aug 1889-30 July 1962 Park
Edwin W 7 Mar 1900-24 June 1960 Park
Elizabeth Harmanson w/o Jos J 1 Feb 1900-17 Mar 1979 Onan
Mary W 22 Jan 1871-21 June 1960 Park
MIDDLETON, Alex T 29 Dec 1859-17 Feb 1929 Libe
Annie E 1879-1959 Fair
Annie M 1881-1977 Libe
Bertha W w/o H B 1893- Park
Bertie B 1893-1967 Park
Betsy w/o Wm d/o Stephen & Eliz Drummond 26 July 18092-10 Jan 1875; age: 72/6/16 Clov
Blanche B w/o J A 1 Mar 1893-24 Oct 1975 Libe
Carviller T 11 Oct 1868-8 Sep 1895 Libe
Cora L d/o Capt Jno R & Arinthia B Ewell 29 Dec 1888-4 Oct 1973 Libe
Doris R (w/o S F) 1908- Fair
Edgar T (h/o M L) 1889-1967 Fair
Edward F s/o J E & S S 1908-1944 (killed in action; buried in Arlington Cem) Libe
Ellen w/o R P 1 Sep 1845-9 Aug 1935 Libe
Eveline C w/o G G 12 Mar 1829-27 Feb 1894 Libe
George G h/o E C 4 Jan 1830-10 July 1916 Libe
George L 8 June 1866-1 Feb 1936 Libe
George R s/o G G & E C 6 Oct

MIDDLETON (continued)
1852-3 Dec 1855 Libe
Herbert B h/o B W 1887-1983 Park
Isadora 5 May 1901- Libe
James A h/o B B 9 Jan 1893-7 Sept 1976 Libe
John E 1884-1972 Park
John Emory h/o S S 1880-1950 Libe
John R Sr 1886-1936 Park
John R 29 May 1917-1 Mar 1977 Park
Julia 16 Dec 1898-28 Jan 1910 Libe
L Pearl 1892-1975 Libe
Laura w/o Wm J d/o Annie Fletcher & Wm Pannell 1858-1941 Libe
Mariah 1848-1925 Park
Maura A 1903-1971 Park
Mildred L (w/o E T) 1895-1969 Fair
Nancy J w/o Wm J 1890-1978 Park
Revell P h/o Ellen 13 Apr 1847-5 June 1933 Libe
Sallye Stephens w/o J E 1885-1971 Libe
Samuel T A M s/o G G & E C 9 Feb 1850-25 Nov 1866; age 16/8/17 Libe
Sarah E 16 Apr 1863-19 Mar 1948 Libe
Stanley F (h/o D R) 1906-1959 Fair
William s/o Wm & Eliz 1 May 1794-1 July 1852 Clov
William J h/o Laura s/o Jno & Julia (Shreaves) 1853-1922 Libe
William J h/o Nancy J 1879-1974 Park
MIERS, Francis G (h/o Marguerite) 1891-1976 Fair
Marguerite (w/o F G) 1895- Fair
MIKEL, Maggie B 1907-1971 Burt
MILES, baby boy b&d 1953 Holl
Alicia Barnes w/o J H 1871-1932 Park
Clifford M 14 June 1948-12 Sept

MILES (continued)
1972 Wach
Daniel d 28 Mar 1804; age: 23 yrs SeyS
Earl F 1912-1958 Park
Edward E h/o S P & L B 22 Nov 1861-22 Jan 1926 Onan
Edward T 1876-1963 Edge
Elizabeth D 1909-1950 Edge
Ernest J h/o L P 1878-1953 Park
Eugene T s/o Wm L & Mamie M 25 Sept 1899-6 July 1901 StGe
Evelyn V (w/o U G) 1898- Mt Ho
George 1904-1970 JoyC
George S s/o Wm & Nancy 2 Aug 1865-4 Jan 1923 Mile
Georgia Thomas 1902-1955 Park
John H h/o A B 1859-1932 Park
John Walter 1899-1967 Park
Lawson J 1889-1952 MtHo
Leone P 1893-1981 MtHo
Lillie P w/o E J 1878-1950 Park
Lotta Bagwell 2nd w/o E E 27 June 1879-23 Dec 1912 Onan
Mabel S w/o R J 1909-1974 Park
Maggie Beatrice d/o E T & M E 9 July 1909-19 Nov 1915; age: 6/4/10 Guyp
Nancy R w/o Wm H 24 Dec 1828-26 Jan 1897; age: 68/1/2 Mile
Nonie G 1883- Edge
Pearl Mason w/o R R 1894-1969 Park
Ralph J h/o M S 1909-1978 Park
Robert P s/o E E & S P 20 Oct 1887-23 July 1888 Onan
Roy Reed h/o P M 1883-1950 Park
Susie Pitts 1st w/o E E 2 June 1865-9 Nov 1887 Onan
Thomas b&d 1957 Joyc
U Garner (h/o E V) 1896-1969 MtHo
William G 1917- MtHo
William H s/o Wm & Sally 2 Sep 1833-27 July 1902; age: 68/10/25 Mile
MILLER, Anna D w/o Rev B M (Rector of St Pauls Norfolk VA) d/o Col T M Bayly d 28 Nov 1841; age: 30 yrs (leaving

MILLER (continued)
a child) MtCu
Bertha Krommes 1917-1978 Libe
Beulah B (w/o M U) 12 July 1901-2 Jan 1951 Quin
Charlie L 4 May 1888-5 Oct 1965 Quin
Cleaster 1920-1982 Burt
Daisey E 18 Feb 1894- Quin
Donald Samuel 1953-1977 Libe
John F 5 Dec 1863-21 May 1904 Davi
M Upshur (h/o B B) 4 Apr 1892-22 Aug 1969 Quin
Margaret W (w/o W R) 3 June 1860-18 Feb 1922 Quin
Mary E (w/o W E) 1826-1900 Holl
Maude K 22 Nov 1895-20 Sep 1915 Quin
Sarah d 11 June 1961; age: 74 yrs HTri
Timothy P 1956-1971 Libe
William E (h/o M E) 1828-1901 Holl
William R (h/o M W) 3 July 1858-8 Dec 1917 Quin
MILLIGAN, Hazel Scott 20 Sept 1887-6 Jan 1953 Onan
MILLINER, d/o W F & N Y b&d 28 Jan 1927 Edge
s/o G L & Mildred b&d 1940 Edge
A C H 1872-1962 Edge
Alice S 1883-1955 Edge
Amelia 1890-1963 MtHo
Ann Morris b&d 1957 Fair
Annette L 1923- Edge
Annie P (w/o J H) 1888-1973 Edge
Annie S (w/o Howard) 1888-1975 Edge
Arthur 15 Dec 1907-26 Nov 1965 MtHo-s
Asher Charlie 1894-1963 Edge
Bertie A (w/o E P) 1867-1949 MtHo-s
Burleigh H s/o J J & D A 14 June 1891-14 Jan 1893 Edge
C Smith 5 Oct 1857-11 June 1958 Edge
C W 1865-1922 Edge

MILLINER (continued)
Cary F Sr h/o M M 5 Aug 1888-21 Apr 1982 MtHo-s
Catherine S w/o S S 8 Oct 1836-12 Mar 1913 Edge
Clifton 1916-1982 Edge
Dorothy A w/o J J 25 Jan 1873-12 Jan 1927 Edge
E S 1876-1949 Edge
Edmund F 4 Mar 1851-13 Dec 1920 Edge
Edna B w/o J J 1912- MtHo
Elijah P (h/o B A) 1861-1941 MtHo-s
Elizabeth S w/o J H 9 Apr 1840-5 Dec 1879 Edge
Ella d/o W T & J C 4 Aug 1880-9 Aug 1907 Edge
Emma w/o Herbert 1892-1968 Edge
Emma S w/o R S 1857-1929 Wach
Ernest E 1917-1952 Edge
Estelle (Bell) w/o J R 1889-1950 Edge
Esther w/o Frank ns (moved from Milliner Place) Edge
Esther A w/o T F 9 Dec 1851-27 May 1933 MtHo
Eva D 8 Feb 1892-12 Nov 1936 Edge
Frank h/o Esther ns (moved from Milliner Place) Edge
Fred S 9 Dec 1893-16 Jan 1931 Edge
George L (Rubye) h/o Mildred Milliner Doughty 18 Apr 1901-10 July 1947 Edge
George Wise 10 Mar 1867-26 Mar 1946 Edge
H Irving h/o L H 1886-1952 Libe
Hattie B w/o S B 1908-1945 Libe
Henry Clay 1866-1943 Edge
Herbert h/o Emma 1890-1955 Edge
Herbert 1907-1954 Fair
Howard (h/o A S) 1885-1926 Edge
Ida H 28 Jan 1869-26 Mar 1952 Edge
Ida S (w/o W S) 1872-1938 Edge
Iva M (w/o W J) 17 Dec 1892-16

MILLINER (continued)
Nov 1957 StGe
J H (Budd) (h/o A P) 1885-1972 Edge
James H h/o E S 21 Sept 1835-9 July 1907 Edge
James R (h/o L B) 1867-1932 Edge
James S 1904-1979 Edge
Jane C w/o W T 27 Feb 1846-18 Dec 1922 Edge
Jennie J 7 Nov 1861-8 July 1937 Edge
Jerome P h/o M E 1900-1979 Edge
Jesse J h/o D A 1869-1963 Edge
Joe J h/o E B 1911-1977 MtHo
John J W s/o S S & S E 30 Nov-4 Dec 1862 Edge
John R h/o Estelle 1893-1956 Edge
John W h/o M A 27 May 1851-18 Apr 1927 Edge
John W 15 Mar 1867-9 Feb 1938 Edge
John W (h/o R W) 1886-1971 MtHo-s
L Douglas (h/o M S) 1876-1940 Edge
L L 1874-1954 Edge
Laura L 29 Aug 1870-22 Aug 1960 Edge
Lelia H w/o H I 1878-1960 Libe
Lena B (w/o J R) 1879-1950 Edge
Levin D Jr 7 Dec 1919-13 Sept 1980 Edge
Lula P (w/o O B) 1885-1974 Edge
Maggie A w/o J W 13 July 1855-20 May 1933 Edge
Mamie M 7 Nov 1882-30 Mar 1958 Edge
Manie S 12 Dec 1860-23 July 1940 Edge
Margaret E 9 Aug 1868-3 Oct 1914 Edge
Mary E d/o W S & I S 11 Mar 1903-27 July 1904 Edge
Mary E w/o J P 1905- Edge
Mary Elizabeth w/o L D; d/o Thos A & Laurah F Duncan 15

MILLINER (continued)
Oct 1878-13 May 1913 Edge
Mary H d/o S S & S E 18 June 1859-14 June 1864 Edge
Mary S w/o R S 28 May 1848-22 Apr 1909 MtHo
Maryland F 3 July 1881-24 Apr 1956 MtHo
Maude M w/o C F Sr 11 June 1890-17 Jan 1968 MtHo-s
Maude R (w/o W L) 1891-1976 MtHo-s
Minnie B w/o S S Sr 3 May 1894-13 Feb 1953 Edge
Minnie S (w/o L D) 1880-1953 Edge
Minnie S (w/o S H) 1892-1976 Edge
Nellie Y w/o W F 22 Nov 1898-8 Mar 1977 Edge
Ocia A 2 Sept 1861-28 Oct 1934 Edge
Oscar B (h/o L P) 1887-1965 Edge
Phill T 26 Jan 1880-10 May 1956 Edge
Priscilla A w/o Wm H 25 Nov 1850-21 Nov 1923 Edge
Richmond Irving s/o H I & L H b&d 12 Feb 1916 Libe
Robert S h/o M S 5 Oct 1842-7 Feb 1923 MtHo
Robert S 1 Aug 1863-26 Aug 1942 Edge
Roxie Lee 1913-1921 Edge
Ruby W (w/o J W) 1893- MtHo-s
Ruth A 29-31 May 1943 Onan
S Lee 14 Jan 1863-17 Dec 1933 Edge
Sam S Sr h/o M B 18 Feb 1892-8 Mar 1976 Edge
Samuel 1872-1953 Edge
Samuel S h/o C S 8 Sept 1837-30 Oct 1911 Edge
Sarah J w/o Wm H 17 Mar 1845-18 Apr 1899 Edge
Shelley B 12 Jan 1902-2 May 1961 Edge
Smith H (h/o M S) 1881-1952 Edge
Capt Southey S h/o S E 8 Dec

MILLINER (continued)
1808-13 Dec 1868 Edge
Susan E w/o S S 23 Aug 1825-31 July 1914 Edge
Capt T H 1849-1943 Edge
Thomas F h/o E A 2 June 1859-25 Mar 1894 MtHo
Walter L (h/o M R) 1888-1964 MtHo-s
Wilber J (h/o I M) 25 Mar 1876-6 June 1943 StGe
William C 1848-1925 MtHo
William F h/o N Y 5 Oct 1899-12 Jan 1961 Edge
Wiliam H h/o S J & P A 2 Dec 1842-30 June 1922 Edge
William H 18 Feb 1898-29 June 1899 Edge
William H (Polk) 18 Aug 1899-6 Mar 1981 Edge
William S (h/o I S) 1861-1947 Edge
William T h/o J C 20 Jan 1852-9 Sept 1920 Edge
MILLS, Clifford 1914-1968 Park
Emma Mapp 1928-1980 Burt
Florence S (w/o J S) 1 Nov 1879-8 July 1957 Onan
Hilton 1901-1980 Burt
Joseph S (h/o F S) 3 Sept 1870-17 Nov 1942 Onan
Laura Emma d/o W S & M C 16 Mar-24 July 1879 Onan
Margaret C w/o W S 22 Feb 1837-20 Mar 1910 Onan
Mary S 1910-1970 Burt
Minnie M d/o Wm S & M C 1874-1952 Onan
Sarah A 1897-1959 Gask
Upshur Lee 1891-1969 Park
William S h/o M C 22 Dec 1824-24 Oct 1899 Onan
MISTER, A David 1868-1909 Onan
Albert D 1878-1955 Wach
Alice L (w/o J D) 4 Mar 1865-13 Dec 1923 Wach
Ann D G w/o Wm; d/o Zerrobabel & Bridget Kellam 20 Oct 1801-2 May 1859 Holl
Annie M 1842-1925 StGe
Bettie D 1862-1957 Holl

MISTER (continued)
Charles E h/o M C 1873-1946 MtHo
Charles R 8 July 1865-23 Mar 1935 MtHo-s
Edward Charlie 4 Jan 1824-23 Dec 1910 Onan
Emma A d/o Jno J & Margt A (Joynes) 27 Mar 1867-26 Nov 1879 Joyn
Evelyn W 19 June 1888-5 Oct 1978 MtHo-s
Capt Isaac S 1838-1903 StGe
Jefferson D (h/o A L) 9 July 1861-9 May 1933 Wach
John J (h/o M A) 12 Dec 1834-11 Dec 1911 StGe
Lillian w/o Tully 1895-1977 Park
Margaret Ann w/o J J; d/o Edwd D & Ann C Joynes 21 July 1838-15 July 1906 StGe
Margaret E 1876-1964 Onan
Milton F 1898-1962 Onan
Milton Thomas s/o Thos & Bettie D 15 Oct 1888-1 Jan 1891 Guyb
Minnie C w/o C E 1880-1953 MtHo
Sadie Ray d/o I S & A M 12 Aug 1880-1 July 1899 StGe
Sarah James 1 Mar 1835-15 Apr 1914 Onan
Severn 1871-1973 MtHo
Steven S 25 Jan 1955-4 Mar 1978 Fair
Susan w/o Wm 13 Sept 1773-15 Oct 1836 Snug
Susan E w/o Lorenza D d 26 Aug 1892 (stone missing; 1940 data) Mist
Capt Thomas T 4 Mar 1847-3 Sept 1910 Holl
Tully h/o Lillian 1890-1972 Park
Virginia C A d/o Wm & Ann D G d 11 May 1845; age: 2/4/5 Holl
William h/o Susan d 18 Nov 1829; age: 52 yrs Snug
William (h/o A D G) 8 May 1796-28 Apr 1862 Holl
William H s/o Lorenza Dow &

MISTER (continued)
Susan L 3 Dec 1871-24 Aug 1907 (stone missing; 1940 data) Mist

MITCHELL, s/o prob Annie C b&d 1919 Park
Alfred T h/o E D 1908- Park
Annie C 1898-1965 Park
Elizabeth D w/o A T 1913- Park
Evelyn Wessells w/o W J 1876-1968 Park
Frederick Reybold h/o G B 1879-1924 MtHo
George H d 1891; age: 3 yrs Warw
Goldie Bagwell w/o F R 1884-1943 MtHo
Grace Mae (w/o W R) 1889- Quin
Grant d 25 Dec 1947; age: 48 yrs StLu
James (h/o S E) d 18 Oct 1912; age: 58 yrs Quin
Sarah Elizabeth w/o Jas 16 Dec 1850-18 July 1930 Quin
Steven F 1925-1974 Park
Warren Jackson h/o E W 1874-1923 Park
William Clifton 26 Oct 1906-15 Mar 1964 Quin
William Rufus (h/o G M) 1881-1956 Quin

MOFFETT, John J (h/o T F) 1913-1979 Fair
Thelma F (w/o J J) 1913-1962 Fair

MONROE, Albert 24 Feb 1915-5 Apr 1946 Onan

MOORE, Andrew J (h/o M R) 12 Sept 1887-6 July 1965 Onan
Annie E Kelso w/o W E 1 Dec 1879-17 Mar 1960 Onan
Arnette w/o Horace 1897-1962 NewM
Arron M 1912-1976 Shil
Catherine w/o Jos d 19 Dec 1837; age: 54/4/20 Edge
Charlie Parker (h/o V C) 31 Dec 1897-13 Oct 1961 Onan
Earl B 1906-1978 Onan
Edward A h/o K K 9 Dec 1891-18 Oct 1973 Fair

MOORE (continued)
Forrest Lee 1920-1968 Shil
Francis S eldest s/o Wm P & Mary A 25 Mar 1836-30 Sept 1839 Coal
George 1898-1961 Fair
George L h/o M A 1849-1934 Libe
George W (h/o S Z) 1857-1945 Onan
Harton L 9 Apr 1921-16 Nov 1968 StPa
Haziel B d/o G A & M A 8 Dec 1883-29 Nov 1895 Libe
Horace h/o Arnette 1885-1956 NewM
Isaac s/o Jno & Eliz 31 Dec 1808-10 May 1884 Moor
J H 14 May 1838-30 June 1917 Bogg
James B s/o G L & M A 27 Apr 1891-12 Oct 1918 Libe
John H 1898-1965 - father of Richd, Dorothy, John, Virginia Lee, & Robt Onan
Joseph h/o Catherine undecipherable Edge
Kate w/o L P 21 June 1830-5 Jan 1916 Park
Kathryn K w/o E A 1890-1961 Fair
Lee 1907-1980 Gask
Lena S (w/o W R) 1880-1963 Onan
Littleton P h/o Kate 19 Sept 1825-13 Jan 1916 Park
Lloyd M 28 May 1859-22 Feb 1924 MtHo
Lottie 1882-1963 StPa
Malachi d 5 Sept 1960; age: 50 yrs Gask
Margaret E 3 June 1815-8 Nov 1890 Moor
Margaret S d/o Isaac & Lucy A 10 Apr 1840-21 June 1884 Moor
Maria d1939 MtHo
Mary Ann w/o G L 1859-1916 Libe
Maude V (w/o S W) 1903- Onan
Monnie R (w/o A J) 21 June 1886-17 Apr 1976 Onan

MOORE (continued)
Naomi P 4 Jan 1900- Onan
Stephen J 1 Oct 1819-27 Jan 1880 Moor
Stephen W (h/o M V) 1901-1959 Onan
Sudie Z (w/o G W) 1861-1947 Onan
Susie A d/o W E & A E K 27 Feb 1903-6 Nov 1905 Onan
Tabitha w/o Wm P 29 July 1774-29 Sept 1854 Vaux
Virginia C (w/o C P) 21 May 1900-23 May 1979 Onan
William Edward h/o A E K 16 Sept 1873-8 Sept 1963 Onan
William P Sr s/o Jno & Rebecca 4 Nov 1780-7 Nov 1872; mar: Tabitha Andrews 22 Mar 1801 Vaux
William P s/o Wm P Jr & Mary A 25 Aug 1847-25 July 1873 Vaux
William R (h/o L S) 1874-1935 Onan
MOORMAN, Virginia P 1919-1978 HTri
MORRIS, Alfred M Jr 15 Mar 1905-9 July 1972 Edge
Billy s/o C C & M T 3 Mar 1918-23 Jan 1925 MtHo-s
C Clarence 1899-1938 MtHo
Caroline w/o Capt W J 22 Apr 1824-22 Dec 1907 MtHo
Charlie C h/o M T 1867-1946 MtHo-s
Charlie T (Colombo) 1891-1979 Park
E Burlei h/o H L 1892-1941 Park
Elizabeth B w/o Wm 4 June 1834-20 Sept 1903 Park
Gene 13 Aug 1927- Park
Hilda L w/o E B 1889-1974 Park
John C 1901-1973 Snea
John W 5 Aug 1905-8 Sept 1942 Park
Llewellyn B 1900-1973 MtHo
Manie A w/o Wm F 4 Oct 1869-10 May 1950 Park
Mary T w/o C C 1872-1941 MtHo-s
Sarah w/o Levin d 19 Aug 1920;

MORRIS (continued)
age: 59 yrs NewM
Capt Warren J h/o Caroline - CSA mortally wounded at Battle of Chickamauga (TN) 20 Sept 1863; age: 39 yrs; buried on the battlefield MtHo
William F h/o M A 16 Nov 1853-20 Apr 1938 Park
William J 1922-1940 NewM
William K 11 Oct 1896-5 Oct 1966 Libe
MOSLEY, Rev Pratt Suber h/o Roxie E Miller 1881-1966 Gask
MUIR, Adam Sr (h/o Francina) 5 Nov 1705-29 June 1772 Ever
Ann d/o Adam & Francina 29 Sept 1732-25 Sept 1807; age: 75 yrs Ever
Francina w/o Adam; d/o Geo & Sarah (Preeson) Hack 24 Sept 1706-17 Dec 1784 Ever
James 8 Dec 1778-13 Aug 1796 Ever
Sarah (d/o Adam & Francina) 21 Mar 1741-11 June 1827; age: 86 yrs Ever
MULLEN, Georgianna Dunton 1911-1976 Fair
MULVERHILL, William Boyd 7 Jan 1919-24 June 1981 Quin
MUNNINGS, Maren C 11 Sept 1906-2 Apr 1983 MtHo
MURPHY, Arthur J 1900-1963 Fair
Clara (w/o Edwd) 1890-1933 Onan
Edward (h/o Clara) 1880-1953 Onan
Edward 7 Sept 1920-23 Jan 1928 Onan
George E 1909-1944 (killed in action, WWII) Onan
Howard W 1906-1951 Fair
John N d 3 Jan 1939; age: 65 yrs NewM
Rachel w/o J H 19 Sept 1849-11 Oct 1911 Burt
MURRAY, Annabell 1933-1951 Onan

MURRAY (continued)
Claude Parker (h/o M E) 1903- StGe
Elijah 1910-1956 Snea
Joseph 1912-1965 Onan
Mary Evans (w/o C P) 1905-1979 StGe
William H 1908-1967 Park
MYERS, Gertrude w/o Chas; d/o N J W & Eliz LeCato 1858-1934 Quin
NEAL, James 1897-1970 Burt
Mary C 1900-1980 Burt
NEDAB, Chester M h/o L A 27 Dec 1897-20 Dec 1965 Burt
John F 1904-1982 Burt
John F Jr 1940-1978 Burt
Lucy A w/o C M 28 Jan 1897-12 Jan 1946 Burt
Mazie sis/o Chester M 1900-1984 Burt
Moses 1865-1943 Neda
Robert L 1906-1982 Burt
Sarah 1870-1957 Neda
Theodore s/o C M & L A 1917-1981 Burt
NEEDAM, Annie P 1916-1974 Bail
Upshur 1913-1981 Bail
Virginia T 1915-1978 Shil
NEELY, baby boy b&d 1960 Snea
Amelia W w/o Jno (nee Bailey) 5 Aug 1805-28 Aug 1849 Herm
John h/o Amelia W d 13 Aug 1850; age: 53 yrs Herm
NELSON, Alice E 1875-1968 Onan
Bernice Killmon 1 Sept 1917-18 Sept 1952 Holl
David W h/o M E 1928- Libe
Earl 1897-1981 Libe
Fulton T 12 Oct 1912-29 May 1942 Libe
Hilda L w/o S S 1873-1944 Libe
John Revell h/o M G 20 July 1909-8 Aug 1969 Edge
Lovey H w/o S R 28 Dec 1839-12 Dec 1899 MtHo
Mabel Long w/o M S 3 Jan 1900-25 June 1929 MtHo
Margaret d 29 Dec 1892; age: 65 yrs Onan

NELSON (continued)
Margaret M d/o S S & H L 3 Feb-22 June 1908 Libe
Mary D w/o W S Jr 10 Nov 1898-20 Nov 1969 MtHo
Mary E (Betty) w/o D W 1928-1981 Libe
Merritt S h/o M L 14 Apr 1902-2 Dec 1946 MtHo
Mildred Grant w/o J R 2 Nov 1908-4 July 1968 Edge
Ora Bloxom w/o W S 6 Aug 1869-20 Feb 1934 MtHo
Phillip Harold 1922-1977 Onan
Rachel E 1897-1961 Shil
Samuel S h/o H L 1877- Libe
Spencer R h/o L H 17 Dec 1841-26 Jan 1908 MtHo
T nd Libe
Thomas J 1870-1940 Libe
William C 3 June 1927- Onan
William S h/o O B 30 Oct 1867-8 Feb 1939 MtHo
William S Jr h/o M D 23 Mar 1898-24 Oct 1971 MtHo
NEVILLE, Eric C (h/o S H) 22 Mar 1890- MtHo
George W 10 Mar 1893-8 Aug 1948 MtHo
Margaret E w/o W J II 27 June 1869-26 Mar 1951 MtHo
Mary H w/o W J 26 July 1832-16 Apr 1896 MtHo
Sadie J 1894-1983 Park
Sarah Hazel (w/o E C) 6 Mar 1894-25 Dec 1943 MtHo
William J Sr h/o M H 23 Jan 1819-20 Aug 1899 MtHo
William J II h/o M E 24 Dec 1859-3 Feb 1927 MtHo
William J III 22 Oct 1905-6 Nov 1932 MtHo
NEVIN, Frederick M 1878-1935 Wach
NIBLETT, Linwood W h/o M B 1917-1976 Park
Madelyn B w/o L W 1918- Park
NIBBLETT, Matthew Shrieves b&d 7 June 1984 Libe
NICHOLS, see also NICOLLS, Harrison M h/o N S 1889-1966 Holl

NICHOLS (continued)
Mildred 1877-1960 Fair
Nellie S w/o H M 1897-1970 Holl
NICHOLSON, Joshua L h/o Sadie 1888-1957 Libe
Joshua Lee 1927-1982 Libe
Sadie h/o J L 1906-1983 Libe
NICOLLS, Annie V d/o Chas E & Margie L 29 Nov 1893-13 Jan 1900 Colo
Carroll Meredith s/o Francis E & Mary W 17 June 1905-30 Mar 1910 StGe
Charles C 1901-1948 Onan
Charles E (h/o M C) 1865-1942 Onan
Francis E 1864-1955 StGe
James (h/o J S) 13 July 1838-24 Feb 1908 StGe
Jennie Shaw w/o Jas 28 Apr 1846-20 Dec 1915 StGe
Margaret C (w/o C E) 1872- Onan
Nannie R (w/o W H) 1877-1960 StGe
Willand Reade 1906-1963 Fair
William H (h/o N R) 1871-1953 StGe
Winnie L 1880-1949 StGe
NOCK, baby boy b&d 1980 Snea
Abel Elijah h/o E B 1876-1946 Onan
Amos 19 Oct 1893-5 Aug 1972; age: 78 yrs NewM
Annie Smith 2 Oct 1883-28 Dec 1962 Wach
Annie W 30 Jan 1884-11 Mar 1959 Wach
Aramenia P w/o H P 11 Oct 1864-1 Aug 1925 Edge
Benjamin 25 Apr 1812-1 Jan 1842; age: 29/8/7 OldN
Benjamin s/o Benj & Tabitha d 24 Sept 1843 (unable to verify) OldN
Berry F s/o L W & S C 10 Mar-29 July 1870; age: 0/4/19 Morr
Betsey d 4 Mar 1828; age: 25/0/0 Nock
Bettie d/o L W & S C 1852-1924 Morr
Caroline A w/o E T 8 Jan 1839-

NOCK (continued)
16 Mar 1916 Onan
Dolly B w/o R I 1888-1962 Park
Doris T w/o L W 17 Dec 1899-21 Apr 1934 Park
Dorothy Clair d/o G F & A S b&d 11 Dec 1920 Wach
Edith B (w/o S W) 1886-1977 StGe
Edmund d 27 July 1844; age: 67 yrs Turp
Edward A (h/o F C) 1905-1959 Onan
Edward T h/o C A 23 Jan 1837-1 Jan 1893 Onan
Edwin s/o Edmd & Catherine 23 Oct 1810-28 Sept 1822; age 11/11/6 Turp
Edwin S 1886-1938 StGe
Elijah of G 8 Sept 1804-9 Mar 1849; age: 44/6/1 OldN
Elijah T 1888-1961 NewM
Eliza E d/o H P & A P 10 Aug 1887-5 Apr 1892 Edge
Elizabeth G (w/o G F) 1908-1975 Edge
Ellen James w/o L F d/o Jno & Esther (Marshall) Brittingham 1868-1966 Edge
Ellnora Boggs w/o A E 1881-1972 Onan
Emily J w/o N W 1855-1922 MtHo
Esther W d 29 Aug 1870; age: 76/5/0 Nock
Fannie L w/o J T 1877-1933 Wach
Filmore M 1878-1954 Gask-old
Frances C (w/o E A) 1925- Onan
Frank A 1888-1962 Snea
G Walter s/o Geo & Mary d 10 Nov 1898; age: 22/3/12 OlNp
Garland F s/o S W & S B 21 July 1890-10 Feb 1891 StGe
George s/o Edmd & Catherine 29 Aug 1817-18 Oct 1835; age: 18/1/20 Turp
George of G 5 Oct 1795-6 Oct 1851; age: 56/0/1 OldN
George F (h/o E G) 1882-1959 Edge
George H h/o L M 1865-1930

NOCK (continued)
Onan
George O 29 Nov 1877-24 June 1952 StGe
George R 1925-1974 Snea
George S h/o M E (CSA) 24 Dec 1842-14 June 1916 MtHo
George W h/o M E 12 June 1843-11 Sept 1922 OlNp
Grayson E (h/o M K) 1910-1951 Onan
Harry 1882-1956 Gask-old
Harry A (h/o S E) 1882-1963 MtHo-s
Harry L h/o R K 1878-1949 Park
Herbert s/o N W & E J 1882-1902 MtHo
Horace C 1907-1940 Onan
Horace Colburn s/o Elijah & Margt 25 Sept 1844-29 Oct 1851; age: 7/1/4 Nocp
Horace P h/o A P 13 Nov 1857-10 Feb 1920 Edge
Hyslop E 1911-1978 Onan
Ida C 23 Aug 1866-25 Jan 1966 Burt
Ivory C Jr b&d 21 July 1954 Gask-old
James s/o Jno & Agness 8 Mar 1775-23 Apr 1841; age: 67 yrs Nock
James h/o M C 1908-1977 Gask
James Glenn 21 Nov 1850-20 Mar 1923 Morr
James K h/o M A 25 Feb 1848-12 Feb 1929 Holl
James T s/o Benj & Tabitha d 22 Aug 1844 (unable to verify) OldN
Dr James T h/o M W 1891-1981 Park
Jennie B 1900-1960 Snea
Jesse E 12 Jan 1886-14 Oct 1961; age: 75 yrs Gask-old
Jesse E 1893-1961 Gask-old
Jo 1910-1969 MtHo-s
Joe 1925-1984 Park
John 1892-1956 Snea
John A h/o M B 22 Nov 1912-2 Mar 1983 Burt
John Arthur 10 Mar 1906-16 Feb 1934 Wach

NOCK (continued)
John E (h/o M B) 1894-1954 Onan
John Edward h/o S E 30 July 1836-14 Jan 1908 Oakg
John T h/o F L 1861-1945 Wach
John T (h/o K E) 1866-1942 Onan
John W d 20 Oct 1825; age 22/0/0 Nock
Joseph G (h/o M S) 1895-1970 Onan
Julia Elizabeth (w/o R F) 20 Jan 1916-25 July 1981 Wach
Kate E (w/o J T) 1870-1938 Onan
Kelly L 1980-1981 Snea
Laura C 1884-1983 Gask
Leland E 1902-1960 Onan
Levin Floyd h/o E J s/o Levin W & Sarah Floyd 1853-1920 Edge
Levin W (h/o S C) 10 Sept 1826-27 Feb 1889 Morr
Levin W s/o Jno & Agnes d 17 Dec 1848; age: 59/6/13 OlNp
Levin W h/o D T 4 Jan 1898-20 Apr 1954 Park
Levin W Jr (s/o L W & D T) 3-4 June 1932 Park
Lillian Marie d/o G H & L M 5 July 1899-20 Oct 1900 Onan
Lillie M w/o G H 1875-1957 Onan
Lillie S d/o E T & C A 12 Jan 1871-23 June 1891; age: 20/5/11 Onan
Linwood Awswald 1897-1959 MtHo
Lizzie w/o Abram 30 Nov 1852-18 Jan 1917 Gask-old
Lizzie S w/o S O U nee Boggs 15 Sept 1874-25 Mar 1954 MtHo
Lottie D (w/o N O) 1893-1958 StGe
Louis J s/o L W & Polly W 3 Feb 1823-13 Jan 1855 OlNp
Louise T 1889-1970 Gask
Lucille P w/o W M 1905-1975 Gask
Lynwood Tyson 20 Nov 1924-1 Feb 1964 MtHo-s

NOCK (continued)
Mable B w/o J A 23 Jan 1919- Burt
Madora S (w/o J G) 1898-1972 Onan
Maggie S d/o Jas G & M F d 25 Aug 1888; age: 12/11/22 Wach
Maggie S 1890-1978 Shil
Maggie V d/o S W & S B 26 Jan 1880-4 May 1881 StGe
Mamie 1880-1974 Burt
Mamie H w/o T R 1894- Wach
Mamie K (w/o G E) 1914- Onan
Mamie S 1918-1970 Snea
Margaret 1888-1957 Gask-old
Margaret A w/o Elijah W d/o Nathl & Sarah Fosque 15 Aug 1810-26 Mar 1850; age: 39/7/11 Nocp
Margaret B (w/o J E) 1894-1971 Onan
Margaret F d/o Elijah & Margt 25 Mar-25 Aug 1850; age: 0/5/0 Nocp
Margaret M w/o J Graham 1921-1958 Park
Marie C w/o Jas 1909- Gask
Mary w/o Thos 1836-16 Apr 1907 Snea
Mary A w/o J K 4 May 1848-20 Aug 1912 Holl
Mary E w/o G S 19 Sept 1842-7 Jan 1928 MtHo
Mary E w/o Geo W 18 Mar 1849-19 Aug 1918 OlNp
Mary H 1929-1965 HTri
Matilda Floyd 19 Jan 1850-25 Aug 1923 Wach
Maude White w/o J T 1889-1963 Park
Melvin 1932-1972 Shil
Miriam B d/o L F & E J B 19 Dec 1888-24 Sept 1970 Edge
N J footstone only Nocp
N W h/o E J 1853-1922 MtHo
Nathaniel O (h/o L D) 1882-1955 StGe
Polly Edmonds d/o Jno E & Sarah A 27 Jan 1884-7 July 1891 Oakg
Polly W w/o L W of Jno d/o Jas & Ann Edmonds 2 Dec 1804-2

NOCK (continued)
May 1864; age 59/5/0 OlNp
Rachel w/o Samuel J 20 May 1844-14 July 1912 Burt
Rachel 1884-1957 Gask-old
Ray Floyd (h/o J E) 4 Aug 1917-3 Jan 1955 Wach
Robert I h/o D B 1888-1969 Park
Rose K w/o H L 1892-1927 Park
S W (h/o S B) 31 Oct 1836-6 July 1913 StGe
Sallie A 3 Sept 1827-12 May 1909 OlHp
Sallie Causey 11 Apr 1885-12 Feb 1977 Libe
Samuel Oswald Upshur h/o L S 14 Oct 1868-23 June 1937 MtHo
Samuel W (h/o E B) 1874-1943 StGe
Samuel W 1874-1953 Burt
Sarah 18 Jan 1808-24 Aug 1870 Tayl
Sarah d/o J E & S A 22 Sept-9 Oct 1875 Oakg
Sarah C w/o L W 1 Feb 1830-5 Jan 1904 Morr
Sarah E w/o J E 9 May 1839-1 Aug 1916 Oakg
Sue B w/o S W 3 Mar 1850-22 Mar 1931 StGe
Sue B d/o S W & S B 8-22 Aug 1885 StGe
Susan w/o Thos 27 Apr 1793-13 Nov 1855 Hysl
Susie E (w/o H A) 1885-1963 MtHo-s
Thomas h/o Mary 1839-20 June 1907; age: 68 yrs Snea
Thomas h/o Susan 18Aug 1796-29 June 1857 Hysl
Thomas R h/o M H 1888-1963 Wach
Walter M h/o L P 1905-1981 Gask
William Lofland s/o A E & E A 21 July-31 Dec 1920 Onan
William V s/o Geo W & Mary E 15 May 1870-21 Oct 1876 OlNp
William Stran 26 Sept 1925-17 Dec 1960
Willie May 1897-1965 NewM

NORDSTROM, Bettie Jan 2-3 Oct 1944 StGe
NORFOLK, Indie M 21 Apr 1902-23 Apr 1979 MtHo-s
Parker Foley 19 May 1901-21 Nov 1961 MtHo-s
NORTHAM, Alfred T d June 21 1917; age: 57 yrs Edge
Aline B (w/o R G) 1902- Onan
Annie 26 Sept 1857-6 June 1919 Park
Charles W (h/o K S) 7 Sept 1853-21 Mar 1928 MtHo
Claude L 1876-1941 Onan
David Benson h/o J A 10 May 1819-13 Sept 1864 Onan
Edna S w/o J S 1917-1979 Edge
Elizabeth L 19 Dec 1839-18 May 1918 Park
Ernest D h/o Alberta L 2 Feb 1869-22 Mar 1936 Onan
Ethel N 1883-1966 Edge
Gilley W h/o Annie 12 May 1851-6 May 1916 Park
Gracy Lee 25 Oct 1881-10 Oct 1952 MtHo
Helen Drummond (w/o J B) 1912- Onan
Helen P w/o J E 1916- Edge
Ida P 1874-1964 Park
Isaiah D (h/o L Y) 29 July 1864-12 Dec 1942 Onan
Isaiah David (h/o V L) 25 July 1896-14 Oct 1973 Onan
J Lewis 1897-1984 Libe
J M 1 Oct 1879-30 May 1925 Edge
J Samuel h/o E S 31 Aug 1907-19 Mar 1983 Edge
James C h/o P E d 19 July 1904; age: 58 yrs (no stone) Onan
James M h/o S A 6 Nov 1833-11 Nov 1908 Edge
John Bowdoin (w/o H D) 1896-1981 Onan
John E h/o H P 1914-1979 Edge
JohnH h/o M A 26 Oct 1870-25 Mar 1942 Libe
John L Jr 1920-1950 Libe
Julia A w/o D B 11 May 1825-1 Mar 1909 Onan
Kitty S (w/o C W) 9 Nov 1852-20

NORTHAM (continued)
Mar 1936 MtHo
Lena Y (w/o I D) 20 Sept 1865-2 Mar 1953 Onan
Louise 1912-1933 Edge
Margaret A w/o J H 28 Feb 1867-29 June 1940 Libe
Margie M w/o R L 19 Dec 1893-4 May 1962 Libe
Mary Ann d/o D B & J A 18 Feb 1850-14 Apr 1879 Onan
Nora Lee 20 Aug 1891-10 Dec 1955 Edge
Pauline East d 23 Sept 1905; age: 52 yrs (no stone) Onan
Phoebie E w/o T C 16 Sept 1881-22 Mar 1972 Edge
Pleasie 19 Dec 1866-13 May 1938 Park
R Greenwood (h/o A B) 4 Sept 1898-10 Aug 1961 Onan
Roland L h/o M M 1899-1974 Libe
Samuel L 1898-1956 Park
Sarah A w/o J M 15 Jan 1833-23 Nov 1910 Edge
Sarah J d/o David B & Julia A 1 Aug 1851-23 Mar 1927 Onan
Thomas A h/o V A s/o Col Jas & Sallie D 1 Mar 1824-12 Dec 1887 Onan
Thomas Alfred s/o T A & V A 8 Mar 1857-29 Nov 1875 Onan
Thomas C h/o P E 9 Jan 1879-7 Jan 1950 Edge
Tryphenia A d/o D B & J A 29 Nov 1857-21 Dec 1882 Onan
Virginia Louise (w/o I D) d/o Jas E & Lillian (Boggs) Le-Cato 5 July 1897-24 Feb 1985 Onan
Virnetta A w/o T A 31 Mar 1831-20 Feb 1907 Onan
NORTHAN, Bertie E 18 Nov 1897-25 Oct 1962 SavN
Samuel 1897-1983 SavN
NOTTINGHAM, A Page 1903-1948 Onan
Arthur M h/o C C 17 Mar 1856-30 Aug 1920 Onan
Carlisle L (h/o F P) 1920- Wach
Christine C w/o A M d/o Jno R

NOTTINGHAM (continued)
& Sallie M Burton 2 Mar 1853-16 Sept 1899 Onan
David B h/o L C 17 Feb 1784-1 Aug 1852; age: 68/5/14 Powe
Ethel C 4 July 1898-22 Mar 1975 Onan
Faye P w/o CL 1920-1972 Wach
George Flournoy 2 Oct 1867-21 Aug 1934 Onan
Henry R h/o M M 1855-1936 MtHo-s
Leah C w/o D B 7 Aug 1791-20 May 1866 Powe
Margaret M w/o H R 1861-1938 MtHo-s
Mary H (w/o R L) 1885-1978 StGe
Mildred 18 Feb 1902-14 June 1949 Onan
Richard L (h/o M H) 1885-1964 StGe
Rose Major Custis w/o Julius S; wid/o Jno W Custis; d/o Wm Lyttleton & Eliz (Costin) Major d 1878; age 40 yrs Hedr
Sally Parker w/o Lloyd W 1849-1891 Onan
W Stratton s/o H R & M M 1887-1932 MtHo-s
William Parker s/o Lloyd W & Sally R P 16 Mar-24 Nov 1886 Onan
NUTTALL, Fred D (h/o M C) 1898-19 Fair
Mary C (w/o F D) 1906-1972 Fair
OAKLAND, Marjorie D 20 May 1897-16 Apr 1981 Wach
OBERSEIDER, Grace C w/o Louis 1870-1957 Onan
Louis h/o G C 1881-1942 Onan
O'BRIEN, William d 26 Apr 1918 Onan
O'DELL, Felton C d 14 Nov 1952; age: 24/6/6 Burt
OGBURN, inf/o J A & E E nd Park
Edna E w/o J A Jr 1925- Park
James A Jr h/o E E 1930- Park
O'HARA, Ella J 1904-1976 Park
O'KUSKY, Hank J Jr 1948-1968

O'KUSKY (continued) Fair
Lynn Costin w/o R T 1954-1975 Fair
Richd T h/o L C 1951-1975 Fair
OLDHAM, Lillian Melson w/o R H 1878-1965 Edge
Margaret Powell (w/o R M) 13 May 1094- Onan
Montcalm Jr 15 Feb 1848-15 Feb 1900 StJa
Nancy Elizabeth d/o R H & L M 3 Apr 1907-8 Feb 1931 Edge
Nanie A w/o Montcalm Jr 6 Nov 1850-30 Apr 1903 Edge
Robert H Jr 20 Aug 1901-5 Feb 1902 Edge
Robert Harmanson h/o L M; s/o N A & Montcalm 1874-1957 Edge
Robert Montcalm (h/o M P) 4 Dec 1902-29 Nov 1980 Onan
OLIVE, Catharine J w/o Stephen; d/o Levi & Susan Moore 25 Nov 1829-21 Mar 1894 Bogg
Stephen s/o Jno D & Margt 25 Oct 1824-3 Jan 1867 Bogg
Willie H s/o Stephen & C J 23 Nov 1855-15 Mar 1869 Bogg
OLIVER, Etta S 1895-1959 NewM
Joseph 1883-1937 Edge
Lillie nd Snea
Margie Duncan 1886-1935 Edge
Mollie Collier d/o Wm H & Carrie Mapp 7 Sept 1887-15 Dec 1908 Edge
William E 1878-1917 Edge
William H 1906-1910 Edge
OLSON, Jeannette T 1918-1950 Edge
ONIONS, Edgar T 1886-1965 Park
Laura C d 8 Aug 1939; age: 75 yrs Libe
Revel J d 16 Apr 1914; age: 52 yrs Libe
ONLEY, Azie S 1877-1954 Park
Beulah P (w/o J A) 10 May 1897-25 Feb 1976 Fair
J R s/o Jno H & Mary D 10 Oct 1877-12 Nov 1904 Wate
Joe E 1896-1936 Park
John of Wm 28 Nov 1861-19 May

ONLEY (continued)
1932 Park
John A Sr (h/o B P) 2 Feb 1898-22 Jan 1975 Fair
John H h/o M A 16 Feb 1839-27 Mar 1923 StGe
Josephine H 1876-1955 StGe
Julius F 1868-1941 Park
Maggie R w/o J T 1871-1938 Johc
Mary A w/o J H 14 Dec 1842-27 July 1923 StGe
Minnie H 1890-1962 Park
Trifany d 8 June 1911; age: 77 yrs HicG
O'RAVIS, Andrew John (h/o J H) 14 Nov 1911-2 May 1980 Wach
Julia Hargis (w/o A J) 10 Apr 1917- Wach
OTEY, Jonathan L 1975-1980 Fair
OTTSTADT, Edna Boice 1895-1958 Park
OUTTEN, John Wise 21 Nov 1785-9 Sept 1805 Wise
Mary 14 Oct 1762-11 Aug 1822 Wise
Nettie (w/o R M) 1920-1983 Fair
Richard M (h/o Nettie) 19 Aug 1921-14 Jan 1982 Fair
Sallie M w/o J R d 20 Sept 1936; age: 68 yrs MtHo-s
Trudy V d/o Roy & Jean b&d 6 Mar 1945 Holl
Virgie Churn 1888-1929 MtHo
OVERBY, Ben J h/o S E 1900-1971 Libe
Sarah E w/o B J 1905-1976 Libe
OVERTON, Lester 1889-1953 Wach
OWENS, Annie E 1867-1954 MtHo-s
Caroline Mapp 1856-1941 Edge
Catherine E 1839-1924 MtHo
Gertrude E 1903-1965 Wach
James P 1858-1948 MtHo-s
Mallory C h/o Z S 23 May 1898-19 Aug 1965 Park
Willie Taylor 1880-1941 Park
Zelpha S w/o M C 31 Dec 1899-5 Feb 1982 Park
PADDY, Mrs Blanche L d 20 Oct

PADDY (continued)
1960 MtNe
Edna S 1900-1977 Padd
Justice F 1923-1968 MtNe
Robert O 5 July 1890-23 Feb 1951 Padd
Willard 1883-1978 MtNe
PALMER, Carol B w/o G B 1903-1962 Park
Charlie 1891-1955 NewM
G Burke h/o C B 1888-1971 Park
Levi David 2 Sept 1899-9 June 1909 Snea
Lydia 1902-1927 Snea
Mary A 12 Dec 1899-3 Aug 1973 NewM
Rosa Carline 6 Nov 1903-9 June 1909 Snea
PANNELL, Ann F 1828-1906 MtHo
Claudia 1868-1949 MtHo
PARKE, Julia 1925-1981 NewM
PARKER, d/o G W & J M b&d 7 Nov 1848 (moved from Parker Place) Onan
s/o G W & J M b&d 6 Jan 1852 (moved from Parker Place) Onan
d/o J W & A W 7-15 Sept 1898 Onan
baby boy b&d 1973 Fair
A Boykin h/o M M 20 Aug 1894-6 Apr 1970 Onan
Adah (Bagwell), 1st w/o Geo 12 Sept 1734-26 Aug 1766; age: 31/11/14 PopC
Agnes w/o Henry; d/o Anthony & Elenore West 20 Nov 1768-18 Mar 1839 (moved from Parker Place) Onan
Agnes Wise w/o T W; d/o Wm H & Sarah W Parker 8 Jan 1859-13 Aug 1922 Onan
Alberta 1904-1961 Metr
Alice w/o J W 1902-1953 Wach
Altha H 1921-1970 Burt
Amanda W, 1st w/o B T 28 Sept 1847-1 Feb 1877 Onan
Ann L w/o J R; d/o Levi & Sallie Ward 31 Aug 1801-18 Nov 1868 Onan
Annie Byrd w/o O L 9 Feb 1862-

PARKER (continued)
7 Feb 1915 Onan
Annie Mae w/o F L 1928- Fair
Annie S Gillet w/o J H 29 Dec 1835-14 Jan 1906 Onan
Arthur Bowen h/o I K 1891-1953 Onan
Augustus h/o S R 1840-1918 Onan
Barbara N 1927-1973 Holl
Benjamin M (h/o P H) 25 June 1910- Onan
Benjamin Thomas s/o J R & A L 4 Sept 1836-15 Nov 1897; leaving a widow, Leah S, & children: Edwd B, Wilmer R, Susie F, & Mamie E Onan
Benjamin W h/o E S 16 Apr 1868-11 Apr 1935 Onan
Bessie Evelyn 31 Oct 1914- Wach
Betty Rew (w/o H L) 1894-1944 Onan
Blanche 1897-1926 Wach
Brunette S 8 Nov 1805-24 June 1855 Blen
Brunette S d/o Geo W & Jane M d 16 Apr 1853; age: 15/0/7 (moved from Parker Place) Onan
Catherine Susan w/o R J 16 Aug 1849-13 June 1925 Onan
Charles Calvert s/o T W & A W 6 Dec 1889-10 June 1955 Onan
Charles F s/o G W & J M 27 July 1836-17 July 1838 (moved from Parker Place) Onan
Charlie E h/o M H 1893-1976 Shil
Christopher b&d 1971 MtNe
Clyde Albert h/o L H; s/o Benj W & Eliz D 17 Jan 1913-29 Apr 1978 Onan
Clyde P s/o B T & A W 8 June 1874-8 Sept 1875 Onan
David Augustus 1 June 1915-24 Dec 1962 Fair
Delmas s/o Finney 1907-1929 MtHo
Dollie N w/o N F 1920- Wach
Dorothy Page d/o W H & H L 17 Nov 1888-5 Jan 1891 Onan

PARKER (continued)
Drusilla E w/o G W d 20 Apr 1898 (moved from Parker Place) Onan
E Lee Swanger 19 Jan 1866-22 Oct 1951 Edge
Edna M d/o F L & L A 10 June 1912-11 Nov 1913 MtHo
Edward 1909-1976 Mitc-w
Edward Bagwell h/o Florence Dodson 4 Oct 1872-6 Mar 1931 Onan
Edward T 1914-1975 Bail
Edward W 1892-1972 MtHo
Elizabeth 6 Jan 1831-2 Oct 1902; age: 71/8/26 Burt
Elizabeth A w/o H P; d/o R R & Sarah Riley 15 Jan 1813-17 Sept 1884 Onan
Elizabeth S w/o B W 27 Aug 1872-23 May 1958 Onan
Ella Core w/o G W 1863-1938 MtHo
Elsie B 9 July 1897-15 May 1977 MtHo
Emma d 2 Jan 1962; age: 62 yrs JoyC
Emma S w/o J E 24 Nov 1844-22 Nov 1918 Onan
Emma S w/o G F; d/o Solomon & Ann Phillips 10 Dec 1855-30 Oct 1909 Edge
Estelle B (w/o?) Joseph 1794-1836 Watt
Esther d/o B W & E S 11 Feb 1908-24 Sept 1911 Onan
Ethel d 20 Sept 1963; age: 69 yrs JoyC
Ethel W w/o H R 4 Oct 1886-14 Dec 1943 Edge
Finney 1884-1917 MtHo
Finney Lunelle h/o A M 1918-1976 Fair
Fitzhugh L (h/o L A) 1887-1960 MtHo
Fred 1910-1980 NewM
Freddie R (h/o N L) 1900-1967 Quin
Garland 1917-1977 Snea
George h/o A B (1st wife) 28 Oct 1735-3 Sept 1784; age: 48/10/6 PopC

PARKER (continued)
George 16 July 1890-8 May 1959 Burt
George B s/o Thos & Eliz 5 Dec 1783-13 Mar 1785 Parp
George D 10 Apr 1873-29 May 1937 Onan
George F h/o E S 6 Apr 1843-14 Feb 1923 Edge
George L 2 Dec 1898-1 June 1968 Onan
George T 1842-1928 Mitc-w
George T (h/o V F) 1865-1946 Holl
George T h/o P P 1881-1951 Wach
George W h/o D E 25 Jan 1808-5 Nov 1877 (moved from Parker Place) Onan
George W h/o M A; s/o Jas & Nanie 12 Feb 1826-20 Mar 1858 ParC
George W h/o E C 1853-1928 MtHo
George W 1859-1953 Onan
Gibb Sheperd 1885-1956 Fair
Glauduis P s/o G W & D E 19 Feb 1862-5 June 1871 (moved from Parker Place) Onan
Gustava S 1930-1976 Snea
H Brooks 1890-1953 Wach
Harriet J d/o G W & J M 19 Nov 1832-7 Sept 1838 (moved from Parker Place) Onan
Harry L (h/o B R) 1884-1962 Onan
Harry Lee Jr 1912-1980 Fair
Harry R h/o E W 17 June 1876-21 Aug 1945 Edge
Helen Livingston w/o W H N 17 Jan 1857-23 July 1941 Onan
Helen Livingston 1880-1964 Onan
Henrietta d 8 Jan 1958; age: 40 yrs Gask-old
Henrietta Gillet d/o J H & A S G 4 Jan 1871-5 Aug 1891 Onan
Henry h/o Agnes (West); s/o Jno R & Eliz F 5 Jan 1767-7 Dec 1818 (moved from Parker Place) Onan
Henry s/o G W & J M 23 Mar

PARKER (continued)
1831-14 Sept 1838 (moved from Parker Place) Onan
Henry P h/o E A 2 Feb 1793-2 July 1883 Onan
Henry R 30 Sept 1910-2 Oct 1961 Edge
Ida L d/o Jno W H & S A S 23 July 1854-3 Aug 1863 Oatl
Irene N d/o Jno W H & S A S 28 Apr 1868-20 Aug 1875 Oatl
Irma K w/o A B 1892-1975 Onan
Capt J O h/o K B 1853-1920 MtHo
J Preston 1914-1940 Wach
J S G s/o Geo & Margt 14 Dec 1851 - .... East
James D h/o M M 1886-1956 Edge
James F 1945 Holl
Dr James H h/o A S G 20 May 1830-26 Feb 1887 Onan
James H 1924-1968 Shil
James L 1 June 1921-16 Mar 1946 Shil
Jane M w/o Geo W; d/o Levy & Euphamey Rodgers 29 Feb 1812-1 Sept 1852 (moved from Parker Place) Onan
John E h/o E S; d/o J R & A L 15 Nov 1831-25 Nov 1897 Onan
Rev John E (h/o R W) 1889-1970 MtHo
John F s/o Saml & Mary 17 Sept 1841-23 Feb 1859 Holl
John R h/o A L;s/o Henry & Agnes 9 Mar 1804-5 Dec 1879 Onan
John T s/o B T & M E 27 Oct 1887-18 Mar 1889 Onan
John Thomas (h/o L H) 1887-1953 MtHo
John W s/o B T & M E 21 May 1883-2 July 1886 Onan
John W h/o Alice 1895-1964 Wach
John W H (h/o S A S) 2 Apr 1819-8 Apr 1900 Oatl
John W H h/o O G 27 Aug 1884-MtHo
Julia Guy (1st h: W H Guy) 1865-1950 MtHo

206

PARKER (continued)
Kate B w/o Capt J O 1865-1958 MtHo
Larcenia D 22 Jan 1927-15 Oct 1980 Burt
Larry 1954-1977 Shil
Laura Morris 1891-1974 Fair
Lavinia C 2 Feb 1865-20 Oct 1926 Onan
Leah C d/o Jno W H & S A S 20 Apr 1851-21 Sept 1852 Oatl
Leah S Boggs w/o B D 21 Sept 1849-21 July 1937 Onan
Lena A (w/o F L) 1887-1966 MtHo
Lena Adell d/o B T & M E 16 Sept 1878-18 Oct 1882 Onan
Lena B w/o P H 1907- Wach
Levin 25 Mar 1780-27 Aug 1855; age: 75/5/3 Parg
Lewis B h/o V L 22 Mar 1856-22 Apr 1918 Onan
Lois H w/o C A; d/o Arzie J & Eliz C Hundley 23 Apr 1919- Onan
Lottie Hartman (w/o J T) 1888-1968 MtHo
Louise Nelson d/o W H & H L 6 Oct 1883; age: 0/16/1 Onan
Lucille w/o Major 1900-1969 HTri
Lucinda d/o Thos & Eliz 26 Sept 1785-20 Oct 1786 Parp
Lucy R d/o G W & J M 25 Sept 1834-5 Sept 1838 (moved from Parker Place) Onan
Lynwood B "Buck" (h/o N E) 16 July 1893-23 July 1948 Wach
Mabel H 1911-1982 Shil
Madeline B 1894-1972 Bail
Maggie V 1889-1957 Shil
Maggie Violette 1906-1966 Smit
Major h/o Lucille 1896-1965 HTri
Malcolm H 1888-1964 Onan
Malissa G d/o Josiah & Matilda 20 Apr 1852-14 Dec 1881 Drub
Margaret A w/o G W 15 Nov 1826-11 Sept 1908 ParC
Margaret Susan w/o W L 22 Sept 1835-21 Jan 1911 JamP
Marie H w/o C E 1908- Shil

PARKER (continued)
Martha Emily 1883-1953 Holl
Mary Ann w/o Jno E; d/o Jno S & Sally Mears 19 Nov 1841-30 Nov 1862; mar: 1 Dec 1859 Wacb
Mary D 1874-1960 Druf
Mary E, 2nd w/o B T; d/o Solomon & Ann Phillips 18 June 1851-18 Nov 1889 leaving 2 children: Susie F & Mamie E Onan
Mary M w/o A B 1905-1930 Onan
Mary Margaret d/o A B & M M b&d 1930 Onan
Mattie M w/o J D 1888-1979 Edge
Mollie H 25 Sept 1904-6 Dec 1980 MtHo
Nadine 1934-1960 SHil
Nanie Ellen (w/o L B) 12 Nov 1896-11 Feb 1932 Wach
Naomi L (w/o F R) 1901- Quin
Nettie May (nee Stevens) w/o S T 1880-1974 Mitc-w
Noah 1901-1978 Shil
Norman F "Jake" h/o D N 11 Mar 1919-3 Apr 1977 (photo on stone) Wach
Octavia Geiger w/o J W H 28 Oct 1885-12 Oct 1972 MtHo
Olus d Nov 1936; age: 6 yrs Smit
Oswald D s/o Jas O & Lovey C 11 Feb 1898-29 Sept 1900 MtHo
Otho Lee h/o A B 4 Apr 1862-22 July 1918 Onan
Paul P 1890-1952 MtHo
Pauline H (w/o B M) 5 Sept 1916- Onan
Pearl P w/o G T 1888- Wach
Peggy E (prob d/o Wm O) 29 Jan 1815-15 Dec 1845 (unable to verify) PaBo
Purvies H h/o L B 1898-1961 Wach
Ralph Riley s/o J W & A W 27 Mar 1896-8 Sept 1898 Onan
Richard Lansing s/o Wm H & H L 26 Aug 1892-26 Aug 1894 Onan
Robert J h/o C S 16 Nov 1844-19

PARKER (continued)
Feb 1900 Onan
Robert R 9 Dec 1814-23 May 1880 Watt
Roberta Lee Waples w/o T P 29 Jan 1893-18 May 1970 Onan
Rooker White 1904-1974 Wach
Rose Mary 1864-1941 Onan
Rufus Wise s/o T W & A W 13 May 1907-2 Sept 1979 Onan
Ruth C 1869-1898 Holl
Ruth W (w/o J E) 1883-1967 MtHo
Sallie E b&d 1922 Mitc-w
Sallie R w/o Augustus 1856-1918 Onan
Samuel B 1868-1934 Holl
Samuel H 4 Mar 1847-26 May 1907 Gask-old
Samuel T h/o N M 1876-1940 Mitc-w
Sarah A S w/o Jno W H; d/o N S & L C Topping 19 June 1828-2 Nov 1916 Oatl
Sarah F w/o T H 23 Dec 1865-10 Aug 1914 MtHo
Sarah Natalie Nelson d/o T W & S W 2 Apr 1891-21 Apr 1973 Onan
Sarah Taylor w/o W J 11 Mar 1877-3 Nov 1971 Onan
Sarah W w/o W H; d/o Jno R & Eliz H Nelson West 15 Jan 1819 in Yorktown VA-25 Apr 1883 Onan
Seymour 1902-1973 Smit
Seymour 1925-1981 Shil
Susan C (w/o Wm O) d 1840 (unable to verify) PaBo
Susan J w/o Jas; d/o E C & E J Mason 12 Nov 1816-17 Mar 1891 Maso
Susannah d/o Thos & Eliz 20 Apr 1793-23 Aug 1794 Parp
Tabitha 1847-1933 Mitc-w
Col Thomas (officer in Revolutionary War) 1757-1819 (Ref: VA Mag of H & B Vol 10:318) PopG
Thomas H h/o S F 12 Mar 1844-8 Sept 1926 MtHo
Tully Page h/o R L W 17 Nov

PARKER (continued)
1887-15 Apr 1974 Onan
Tully W s/o Wm O 30 Dec 1816-14 Dec 1856 (unable to verify) PaBo
Tully Wise h/o A W; s/o J W H & Sarah T 5 July 1858-28 Aug 1931 Onan
Vernetta F w/o G T 1873-1937 Holl
Virginia L w/o L B 5 Apr 1863- Onan
W A 31 Aug 1887-3 Dec 1914 Park
Wendy Lynn b&d 27 Jan 1970 Onan
William 1884-1973 Gask
William C 9 Dec 1830-26 Feb 1907 Watt
William H s/o Henry & Agnes (West) 17 Nov 1809-28 June 1883 Onan
William Hancock 1 May 1859-13 Apr 1926 Edge
William Henry Nelson h/o H L 8 Sept 1853-4 Dec 1926 Onan
William James h/o S T 2 May 1878-4 Mar 1927 Onan
William Levin h/o M S 19 July 1832-2 May 1889 JamP
William O h/o S C d July 1820 (unable to verify) PaBo
William T 1908-1967 Fair
Willie N 1885-1903 MtHo
Willis 1915-1977 JoyC
Wilmer R 1882-1956 Onan
Winnie D d/o G W & Ella 29 Dec 1893-28 Nov 1903 MtHo

PARKS, (PARKES),
children/o A T & L K (baby Gene, A T, & Mary E) nd buried with parents Crad-s
child/o P W & N S d Aug 1850; age: 0/0/6 Libe
s/o G P & Elizabeth P b&d 1 Oct 1886 Libe
inf d/o O T & M E d 5 Apr 1897 Libe
inf s/o O T & M E d 23 Dec 1897 Libe
s/o O M & Martha M b&d 21 Mar 1905 Libe

PARKS (continued)
s/o H H & L F b&d 10 Aug 1918 Park
A Pearl w/o B F 1898-1972 Park
A Stuart h/o H L 1889-1973 Park
Addie V w/o S F 22 May 1882-6 July 1962 Park
Alexander B h/o V S 1853-1942 Park
Alexine 1862-1955 MtHo
Alfred N 1900- Onan
Alfred T (h/o L K) 1881-1945 Crad-s
Alice S w/o W T d 4 Feb 1911; age: 55 yrs (moved from Core bur gr - Pastoria) Park
Amanda B w/o J T 10 Mar 1858-20 Sept 1923 Park
Amanda Susan w/o L D 19 Oct 1890-14 Dec 1972 Libe
Amelia J w/o L A 1878-1953 Onan
Anna E d/o O P & T N 14 June-2 Aug 1904 MtHo
Annie E Fox w/o R L 1872-1941 Park
Annie L 1877-1963 Snea
Annie L (2nd w/o W S) 1896- MtHo
Annie M w/o J E 1859-1935 Park
Annie Rippon 6 Dec 1891-1 Nov 1972 Fair
Annie Webb 9 Jan 1891-10 May 1962 Shil
Arinthia P w/o U S 1892-1931 Libe
Arinthia S w/o S D 7 Sept 1859-15 May 1937 Libe
Arinthia S w/o T F 1872-1954 Libe
Arthur W h/o L H 1859-1942 Edge
Ashton E 1900-1955 Park
Augustus J h/o V A 28 Nov 1841-4 July 1921 Park
B F h/o E S 1844-1919 Park
Beatrice P w/o L A 1910-1965 Onan
Belle M 24 Dec 1906-3 Feb 1938 Libe
Ben T h/o E G 1870-1956 MtHo-s

PARKS (continued)
Ben T Jr 1898-1940 MtHo-s
Benjamin F h/o A P 1893-1963 Park
Berlie P w/o H L 1899- MtHo-s
Bernice Y w/o S W 1905-1981 Park
Bernise N d/o O M & Martha M 10 Dec 1901-28 June 1902 Libe
Bessie b&d 1907 MtHo
Bessie S w/o F D 1887-1961 Park
Bettie A (w/o C B) 1888-1948 Onan
Bettie M w/o R F 1883-1956 Park
Bettie S (1st w/o Jno P Justis) 1854-1928 Park
Betty E 1883-1960 Libe
Beulah N w/o L G 29 Oct 1904-17 Sept 1967 Park
Billie 1925-1926 MtHo
Bozman s/o O M & Martha M 23-24 Oct 1903 Libe
Burnice M d/o T F & A S 28 Oct 1909-23 June 1911 Libe
C Braxton h/o E H 1916- Park
Carrie L 1895-1977 Park
Carrie O (w/o H F) 12 Sept 1870-21 Nov 1947 MtHo-s
Cecille M 26 Sept 1890-14 Apr 1970 MtHo-s
Charlene 1926- Park
Charles B h/o Z D 6 Mar 1872-2 Mar 1922 Onan
Charles F (h/o M B) 1885-1920 Ptea
Charles P 17 Nov 1861-16 Apr 1937 Park
Charlie B (h/o B A) 1886-1968 Onan
Charlie E h/o I L 1896-1972 Libe
Clara T d/o P W & N S 22 Dec 1857-May 1861 Libe
Claude M 1904-1973 Park
Claude T 1917-1943 Libe
Cleora C w/o J D 1887-1973 Park
Clifford J h/o M J 16 Dec 1896- Park

PARKS (continued)
Clifton H h/o EP 1918-1957 Libe
Comfort 27 June 1814-7 May 1889 Libe
Cordie E w/o W W 1872-1922 MtHo
Cornelius N 20 Apr 1857-30 Nov 1929 Libe
Deborah Ann 1970-1972 Fair
Dennis Sewell b&d 1976 Libe
Doris May 1926-1949 Onan
Drucella S 13 Dec 1870-11 Nov 1962 Park
E W Jr 17 Apr 1931-14 Mar 1932 Park
Edgar W (h/o M L) 1887-1959 Crad-s
Edgar W h/o V F 1 Nov 1887-26 Feb 1933 Park
Edna B w/o W S 1892-1938 Libe
Edward C (h/o M M) 18 Aug 1831-13 Feb 1898 Mooc
Edward T 12 Mar 1905-9 Feb 1973 Park
Edward Thomas 11 Aug 1848-31 Oct 1909 Libe
Eleanora S w/o B F 12 Oct 1855-11 Sept 1908; age: 53 yrs Park
Elizabeth B w/o Wm D 1860-1945 Park
Elizabeth H w/o C B 1916- Park
Elizabeth M w/o J F 19 Jan 1868-23 Oct 1947 Park
Elizabeth P w/o G P 6 July 1845-5 Aug 1915 MtHo
Elmer S 11 Jan 1903-30 Sept 1947 MtHo-s
Elton 1922-1978 Fair
Elwood T 1884-1947 Onan
Ernest Ross h/o M S 5 Oct 1893-17 Aug 1946 Park
Ethelyne Broughton (w/o J L Sr) 24 Apr 1915-25 Feb 1979 StGe
Etta Mae 1912-1958 Onan
Eudia E d/o Geo & M E 12 Mar 1874-12 Feb 1882 Papl
Eudie L 30 July 1890-27 June 1957 MtHo
Eudith S d/o Geo & M E 11 Oct 1854-7 Oct 1868 Papl
Eugene (h/o G C) 1901-1942

PARKS (continued)
MtHo
Eula J 1893-1975 Libe
Eunice d/o T F & A S 23 Feb 1901-12 Dec 1918 Libe
Eva Groton w/o B T 1873-1936 MtHo-s
Eva P w/o C H 1925- Libe
Eva R (w/o E A) 1911- Fair
Eva West w/o H S 1890-1971 Park
Evalyn D w/o N J 26 Feb 1889-7 Jan 1976 Libe
Evelyn T 18 Aug 1897-21 Sept 1961 Edge
Everett Powell (h/o M K) 20 Sept 1888-25 Nov 1947 MtHo-s
Everette A (h/o E R) 1916-1959 Fair
F Drummond 26 May 1912-21 Nov 1982 Park
F Drummond s/o O F & M F 1918-1972 Park
Flora Ellen 1922-1955 Onan
Floyd V 1876-1896 Libe
Francis Drake h/o S K 29 Feb 1828-11 Apr 1918 Onan
Frank D h/o B S 1880-1956 Park
Frank W (h/o S C) 1895-1972 Onan
Fred P (h/o M O) 1883-1949 StGe
Freddie P 1877-1881 Libe
Garrison G 10 Apr 1887-5 Sept 1945 Edge
Gary H s/o P T & Gladys d 1946 Edge
George h/o Mary E s/o Benjamin 19 Oct 1821-24 Dec 1900; age: 79/2/5 Papl
George Johnson h/o T V 1886-1961 Park
George M h/o L J 22 Aug 1858-4 June 1928 Park
George Parker h/o E P 22 Oct 1845-14 Apr 1911 MtHo
George W 16 June 1899-25 Dec 1937 Libe
Georgie C (w/o Eugene) 1901-1971 MtHo
Granville 1903-1904 MtHo
Grover T 1893-1962 Libe

PARKS (continued)
Harold S h/o E W 1882-1969 Park
Harrison L (h/o I M) 1876-1953 MtHo-s
Harry A 1878-1972 Libe
Harry C (h/o M L) 1885-1950 Edge
Harry C 26 Oct 1904-24 Dec 1967 Libe
Hattie R 1910- Park
Helen L w/o A S 1893- Park
Henry F (h/o C O) 28 Mar 1868-3 Feb 1931 MtHo-s
Henry L h/o B P 1896-1964 MtHo-s
Herbert H h/o L F 1882-1943 Park
Ida Mae (w/o H L) 1877-1944 MtHo-s
Inez L w/o C E 1899- Libe
J Drummond 14 Oct 1889-11 Mar 1921 Onan
J T h/o A B 13 Aug 1847-11 May 1926 Park
James E h/o M A 10 Oct 1855-7 July 1925 Park
James E 1926- Park
James F h/o E M 21 Sept 1864-27 Nov 1920 Park
James H M 15 Feb 1861-3 Nov 1921 Libe
James M h/o M F 1889-1961 Park
James Stewart s/o J F & E M 28 Aug 1891-13 July 1908 Park
Janette B w/o J E 1870-1951 Park
Jay H (h/o S M) 8 Apr 1874-7 Aug 1932 MtHo
Jeanette T w/o Jno T nd Libe
Jennie M 15 Mar 1866-2 July 1946 Onan
Jewell Bloxom 1901-1984 Park
Jewell C w/o M T 1901-1981 Libe
John A b&d 10 Oct 1957 Holl
John Allen (h/o M P) 1891-1964 Fair
John C h/o J T nd Libe
John D h/o C C 1878-1957 Park
John E h/o A M 1860-1934 Park

PARKS (continued)
John E h/o J B 1866-1948 Park
John H 7 May 1891-10 Nov 1912; age: 21 yrs Park
John H Jr s/o J H & Blanche 1922-1925 Libe
John Henry h/o B P Y 1884-1924 Libe
John Lester Sr (h/o E B) 27 June 1906-18 June 1972 StGe
John S 1933-1935 Libe
John T 1852-1933 MtHo
John W h/o M A 1866-1944 Park
Jonah h/o L B 19 June 1861- 19 Nov 1949 Edge
Joseph 1905-1951 Shil
Joshua A 20 Aug 1859-28 May 1939 Onan
Julia H 2nd w/o O T 1880-1958 Libe
Kate R 1st w/o W S 1 Sept 1894-16 Oct 1917 MtHo
Kathleen M w/o R G 1910-1982 Park
Keith B 4 June-20 July 1961 Onan
L Harrison 1908-1948 MtHo-s
Laura H w/o A W 1859-1945 Edge
Lee Gibbons w/o Wm J 16 Sept 1883-10 Jan 1978 Park
Lena J w/o G M 26 Jan 1870-19 Nov 1916 Park
Lena K (w/o A T) 1882-1935 Crad-s
Leonard D h/o A S 27 Aug 1886-22 Oct 1948 Libe
Leslie Gerald h/o B N 13 Oct 1897-29 June 1963 Park
Lester C h/o Lola E 17 Aug 1892-18 Jan 1968 Libe
Lewis A h/o A J 1878-1958 Onan
Lillian J d/o A T & L K 26 Aug 1912-10 Apr 1913 Crad-s
Lois L 1894-1962 Libe
Lola E w/o L C 26 Sept 1898-19 Feb 1960 Libe
Lola S sister/o V W Scott 9 Sept 1894-25 Feb 1956 Park
Lottie B (w/o T L) 1877-1956 MtHo
Louis A h/o B P 1914-1978 Onan

PARKS (continued)
Louisa B w/o Jonah 6 Mar 1859-17 Nov 1924 Edge
Louise H 1909- Onan
Lula F w/o H H 5 Nov 1884-14 Oct 1918 Park
M Blanche (w/o C F) 1888-1935 Ptea
Mabel J w/o C J 9 Apr 1896-30 Nov 1977 Park
Madeline b&d 1895 MtHo
Madeline w/o Ashon d/o G D & A W Mears 27 Mar 1903-23 July 1922 Libe
Madeline L (w/o E W) 1887-1975 Crad-s
Mahalinda Kellam (w/o E P) 5 July 1887-17 Nov 1975 MtHo-s
Manie M d/o Jno E & Emma C 29 Apr 1896-9 Aug 1897 ParB
Marceline d/o P W & N S 10 Aug 1862-1865 Libe
Margaret A w/o J W 1873-1931 Park
Margaret C 1865-1958 MtHo-s
Margaret J d/o P W & N S 22 Dec 1843-14 Sept 1848 Libe
Maria d/o Jno & Tabitha 13 July 1824-19 Apr 1887 Libe
Marion M 1931- Fair
Martha Moore w/o E C 4 Nov 1834-22 Sept 1919 Mooc
Marvin Jackson w/o M W & Ella E 13 Mar 1918-13 Feb 1919 MtHo-s
Marvin W 1889-1962 MtHo-s
Mary A d/o P W & N S 2 Jan 1856-22 July 1900 Libe
Mary A w/o J E 20 June 1856-22 Jan 1932 Park
Mary E w/o Geo 30 May 1833-6 Nov 1903 Papl
Mary E w/o Jno P d/o Wm & Margt Waterfield 5 Sept 1852-17 Jan 1898 Ptea
Mary E 1888-1970 Libe
Mary Ella 1st w/o O T 1874-1920 Libe
Mary F w/o J M 1891-1981 Park
Mary Jewel 8 May 1898-26 July 1979 Park
Mary L (w/o H C) 1883-1975 Edge

PARKS (continued)
Mary O (w/o F P) 1885-1964 StGe
May Finney w/o O F Sr 1886-1951 Park
Merle S (w/o W T) 1908-1972 Fair
Merritt T h/o J C 1898-1952 Libe
Mildred S w/o E R 19 June1896-20 July 1976 Park
Millard G h/o W B 1900-1973 Park
Minnie P (w/o J A) 1895-1974 Fair
Missouri F 1 Apr 1861-21 Nov 1919 Libe
Nancy S w/o P W d/o Seth & Mary Powell 19 Feb 1820-19 June 1884 Libe
Noah J h/o E D 27 Mar 1887-17 July 1980 Libe
Norman H 1882-1970 Libe
Oliver Frank Sr h/o M F 1863-1944 Park
Orris M s/o O M & Martha M 15 May-28 July 1908 Libe
Oscar F 3 June 1890-28 Jan 1932 Park
Oscar P h/o T N 1881-1969 MtHo
Otho Page (Jackie) s/o Otho O 30 Jan 1933-25 Dec 1935 Ptea
Otho T h/o M E & J H 1875-1951 Libe
Otis R 1906-1954 MtHo-s
Parker W h/o N S 10 Sept 1820-30 Apr 1898 Libe
Pauline H w/o T M 1912- Park
Percy R s/o G T & Loys L 30 Aug 1916-2 Nov 1918 Libe
Perry B 1909-1976 Fair
Phoebe w/o T H 1895-1977 Edge
R Carlisle 1902-1984 Park
Rannie S 2 Oct 1890-20 Feb 1973 Fair
Rebecca J 1854-1926 Libe
Richard Lee (Dick) s/o Otho O 11 Oct 1930-15 Mar 1932 Ptea
Robert b&d 1901 MtHo
Robert F 16 Apr 1905-19 Sept

PARKS (continued)
1975 Libe
Robert L h/o A E F 1866-1923 Park
Roxey M d/o T F & A S 20 July 1906-31 July 1907 Libe
Roy F h/o B M 1880-1968 Park
Roy Glenn h/o K M 1908-1981 Park
Sadie Kelly w/o F D 7 May 1867-16 July 1902 Onan
Sadie M w/o W T 24 May 1881-1 May 1927 Libe
Sallie M (w/o J H) 9 Apr 1875-18 Feb 1973 MtHo
Sarah A R 31 Dec 1863-16 May 1924 Libe
Sarah F 7 Mar 1906-22 Feb 1982 Onan
Sarah H 7 Mar 1896-27 Jan 1978 Park
Sarah R w/o Capt T S 17 Dec 1825-2 May 1897 ParB
Sewell D h/o A S 24 Nov 1852-22 Feb 1926 Libe
Shelley W h/o B Y 1901-1976 Park
Socrates F h/o A V 8 Feb 1871-22 Nov 1944 Park
Spencer H 17 June 1898-2 Jan 1947 Libe
Stanley D 6 Feb 1928-6 Nov 1955 Libe
Stephen Thomas 26 Oct 1890-19 Aug 1958 Fair
Suly E 1st w/o Geo W d/o Wm & Jane Shreaves 23 Dec 1861-2 Oct 1881 Papl
Susie C (w/o F W) 1901-1973 Onan
Susie R 1889-1956 Libe
Sylvanus W 1853-1934 Libe
T Moore h/o P H 1910-1983 Park
Tabitha N w/o O P 1877-1962 MtHo
Thelma 1923-1977 Fair
Theresa Veronica w/o Geo 1891-1945 Park
Thomas F h/o A S 1871-1948 Libe
Thomas H h/o Phoebe 1889-1968 Edge

PARKS (continued)
Thomas L (h/o L B) 1877-1960 MtHo
Thomas S h/o S R s/o Arthur & Nancy 1 Mar 1819-18 Jan 1880 Parb
Thomas Smith s/o T S & S R 14 Dec 1854-25 May 1881 Parb
Upshur S h/o A P 7 Mar 1892-9 July 1950 Libe
V Susan w/o A B 1861-1933 Park
Vernie F w/o E W 11 Aug 1889-26 Jan 1972 Park
Vida d/o F D & S K 17 Dec 1901-12 Aug 1902 Onan
Vincent T s/o G T & Loys L 21 Sept-6 Dec 1914 Libe
Virginia A w/o A J 20 June 1847-14 Mar 1933 Park
Virginia M 19 Apr 1908- Park
W Samuel 1883-1952 MtHo-s
Walter S h/o E B 1889-1963 Libe
William D h/o Eliz 1849-1941 Park
William J h/o L G 8 Aug 1878-20 Feb 1927 Park
William Jana s/o J M & M F 1921-1945 (USN died at sea in Asiatic area) Park
William L 18 Sept 1925-2 Apr 1945 Onan
William T (h/o M S) 1904-1971 Fair
William Thomas 23 Dec 1861-6 Apr 1933 Mooc
William W h/o C E 1867-1942 MtHo
Willie B w/o M G 1900-1954 Park
Wilmer b&d 1888 MtHo
Wilson H 1913-1965 Park
Wilson S h/o A L & K R 1888-1961 MtHo
Winnie Kathareen d/o R T & Eva G 30 Nov 1900-21 Jan 1901 Papl
Woody 1927-1979 Fair
Zena D w/o C B 6 May 1872-2 June 1942 Onan
PARMER, Tabitha 1857-1917 Snea

PARRAMORE, Bettie A devoted cousin nd Runn
Elizabeth Custis w/o Wm 23 Apr 1803-20 Dec 1835 Parr
James H (h/o S M) s/o Wm & Margt 22 Feb 1807-10 June 1894 Runn
James H W s/o J H & S M d 9 July 1875; age: 39 yrs Runn
Juliet Ann F w/o T C d/o Miers W & Juliet B Fisher 3 Feb 1836-30 July 1901 Onan
Juliette Bryant Fisher d/o T C & J F 1870-1928 Onan
Lizzie E d/o Southey S & Ellen (Young) 14 June 1857-19 Mar 1956 Runn
Margaret w/o Wm d/o Levin & Ann Teackle d 24 Aug 1824; age: 60 yrs Parr
Mary Darby w/o Thos 24 Jan 1780-17 July 1848; leaving 1 dau Mrs B D (Parramore) Kellam 8 grchildren & 8 gr grchildren Bell
Sarah w/o Wm d/o Digby & Rose Seymour of Northampton d 25 Apr 1802; age: 63 yrs Bell
Sarah Seymour 18 Jan 1801-15 July 1881 Parr
Southey S 1832-1897 Runn
Susan Custis w/o F E 1859-1909 Runn
Susan M w/o J H d/o Wm R & Sarah Custis 16 Jan 1809-1 Aug 1878 Runn
Thomas s/o Col Wm & Sarah 24 Dec 1761-18 May 1832 (He left a wife & 2 daus Mrs Harriet B D Parramore & Mary B Custis & 8 grchildren) Bell
Thomas Custis h/o J A F s/o Wm & Eliz (Custis) 27 Nov 1831-31 July 1892 Onan
William 24 Dec 1767-21 Aug 1841 Parr
William 28 Apr 1798-25 May 1850 mar Elizabeth Custis 25 Nov 1819 Parr
Col William h/o Sarah s/o Thos & Joanna 27 Dec 1741-4 June 1816 leaving 2 sons Thos &

PARRAMORE (continued)
Wm & 8 grchildren Bell
William R devoted cousin nd Runn
PARRISH, Donna T 1949-1983 Park
Humphrey J 1898-1960 Park
PARSONS, Anna E w/o G B 1907- Libe
Elijah H 13 Apr 1848-28 May 1929 Park
Emma P 19 Aug 1877-1 Sept 1950 Park
G Bryan h/o A E 1907- Libe
Helen Burton 1886-1971 Edge
Henry E 1885-1945 Edge
Ina E w/o J S d/o J O & Emma Selby 8 Jan 1872-18 June 1926 Edge
John S h/o I E 29 Jan 1871-27 Jan 1918 Edge
Lillian T 1881-1963 Park
Martha Ann 15 Sept 1851-25 Jan 1940 Park
Mildred Johnson 15 Aug 1887-8 Oct 1917 Park
Vesta S 5 Nov 1875-22 Sept 1965 Park
William Burton 1913-1972 Edge
William Coard 1881-1944 Edge
PARTRIDGE, Fred W h/o G G 20 Sept 1907-30 July 1973 Park
Georgia G w/o F W 25 June 1910 Park
PATE, d/o E C & C C b&d 1 Feb 1894 Park
Clara Blanche d/o E C Jr & C C 1928-1943 Park
Clara C w/o E C Jr d 27 June 1970 Park
Edward Clay h/o E J 5 Jan 1861-5 May 1911 Park
Edward Clay Jr h/o C C 27 Aug 1896-25 Nov 1961 Park
Etta Johnson w/o E C 15 Nov 1867-24 June 1961 Park
PAULEY, Robey 1912-1978 Edge
PAYNE, Annie M (w/o G W) 1889-1946 MtHo-s
Dollie F (w/o J T) 1892-1973 Onan
Edward O d 1954 Fair

PAYNE (continued)
Elwood C 3 July 1928-26 Sep 1981 Fair
Emily C 1913-1962 Park
Florence A d1961 Fair
George 1871-1914 Park
George E 1871-1914 Park
George L 1899-1975 Fair
George W (h/o A M) 1888-1934 MtHo-s
Ira Francis h/o S B 1875-1954 Park
James Carl 22 May 1893-3 Dec 1959 Fair
James H (h/o R F) 3 July 1908- Edge
John T (h/o D F) 1889-1954 Onan
Maude Camper 1890-1963 Fair
Rebecca F (w/o J H) 18 Aug 1916- Edge
Sadie Bevans w/o I F 1880-1966 Park
Vida P 1897-1974 Fair
Wilson 1916-1960 MtHo-s
PEARCE, Henry s/o Gideon & Eliza (Bayne) 1 Oct 1818-15 Oct 1843 JoyB
Calvin Clinton h/o L P 14 Mar 1922-30 Apr 1978 Fair
PEARSON, Lois Payne w/o C C 10 Aug 1922- Fair
PEFFER, Dorothy E (w/o W E) 1911- Fair
Walter E (h/o D E) 1907-1976 Fair
PEIRSON, Orville L 9 Apr 1913-26 July 1983 Fair
PENDERGAST, Agnes M 20 Feb 1911-15 Feb 1983 Park
PENNEWELL, David R 1900-1964 MtHo-s
Elnora S (w/o L S) 7 Dec 1874-17 Jan 1937 MtHo-s
Louis S (h/o E S) 8 June 1869-13 Dec 1924 MtHo-s
Martha E 1847-1923 Onan
Paul J 1901-1960 MtHo-s
R H 13 Nov 1838-12 Apr 1917 Onan
William S 1906-1979 MtHo-s
PENNINGTON, Elizabeth H w/o J

PENNINGTON (continued)
A Sr 1913-1963 Park
James A Sr h/o E H 1890-1966 Park
PEPPLER, Emma L 1881-1963 Edge
Florence E 1900-1965 Wach
George 1886-1956 Edge
Laurie 24 Jan 1909-2 Jan 1968 Edge
Norman H Jr 1 Feb 1924-31 Mar 1980 Wach
Norman Horner 1899-1945 Onan
Rosa May b&d 1954 Wach
Sadie E 1883-1951 Edge
Willard 20 Dec 1909-6 Jan 1974 Edge
PERDEU, Marie Bonniwell 1923-1974 StGe
PERDUE, Claudius Crisfield h/o O P 22 June 1869-23 Aug 1943 Park
Olivia Parsons w/o C C 28 Nov 1869-10 Jan 1951 Park
PERKINS, Amanda 1909-1980 NewM
Louise 1877-1959 StJo
PERRY, Arnold (h/o Henrietta) 1899-1973 Quin
Harold Orlando 1 May 1908-21 Jan 1976 Quin
Henrietta (w/o Arnold) 1917- Quin
PETERS, George W 1885-1944 Quin
PETERSON, John Donald h/o R C 1917-1982 Fair
Rhoda Carson w/o JD 1913- Fair
PETTIT, Llewellyn w/o Thos d/o Jas & Betsy Carmine 17 Aug 1841-5 Feb 1865 MtHo
Robert McGilbert 31 Dec 1946-13 May 1972 Metr
William s/o Wm & Mary of Northampton Co d 11 Dec 1783; age: 22 yrs Bowm
PHILLIPS, inf d/o T B & G C 27-28 Oct 1894 Holl
____ 1901-1968 Gask
Alice Martin 4 Dec 1864-14 Feb 1965 MtHo-s
Ann S w/o Solomon 5 Sept 1815-

PHILLIPS (continued)
21 Nov 1888 Edge
Anna J M 1890-1956 Wach
Augustus h/o M S 20 Feb 1853-11 July 1920 Holl
Augustus W (h/o G B) 10 Nov 1882-6 Nov 1942 Holl
Barton E (h/o M B) 1827-1920 Wach
Benjamin Thomas s/o Soluman & Anne 2 Dec 1844-3 Sept 1904 Edge
Bessie Susan 5 Mar 1881-4 Jan 1956 Fair
Brooks L h/o G T 1884-1967 Wach
Carrie D (w/o W L) 17 July 1899-3 May 1973 Fair
Carson T h/o S E 13 June 1892-12 Mar 1951 Park
Charles A h/o M B 1909-1979 Wach
Charles J (h/o L H) 1919-1981 Onan
Chester A h/o E G 1883-1959 Park
Clifford C 1913-1971 Park
Cordelia Kilmon 1869-1965 Holl
Della M 2 Nov 1887-26 Dec 1982 Park
Dorothy d/o H D & L B 23 Feb-25 July 1917 MtHo
Edward Lee h/o M P 1903-1974 MtHo
Effie Lee 28 Feb 1883-13 June 1980 Fair
Elsie G w/o C A 1887-1974 Park
Elizabeth M C w/o Smith 8 Jan 1805-1 Jan 1872 Bulb
Elizabeth S d/o W S & S A J d 27 June 1852; age: 0/7/18 HaPh
Elmer V (h/o V M) 1907- Edge
Eula M (w/o W A) 1887-1958 Wach
Frank B h/o L M 1883-1924 MtHo
G Custis (h/o O B) 1904-1964 MtHo-s
George Carson s/o L R & A L 17-18 Aug 1903 MtHo-s
George Custis (h/o M A) 9 Oct

PHILLIPS (continued)
1846-5 Nov 1898 (moved from Martin-Hatton) Fair
George E s/o Edwd B & Mary A 1 Dec 1866-12 Dec 1907 Wach
George W (h/o L E) 1869-1958 Wach
Georgia T w/o B L 1888-1918 Wach
Georgie C w/o T B 8 Aug 1864-24 July 1966 Holl
Gertrude B (w/o A W) 20 July 1890-4 Jan 1956 Holl
Harold M (h/o M B) 1889-1977 Fair
Harry D h/o L H 1884-1957 MtHo
Harvey B s/o W A & E M 19 Aug 1911-29 Mar 1912 Wach
Hazel D w/o W E 20 Nov 1910- Quin
Helen 1891-1982 MtHo-s
Holly 1920-1977 NewM
Ida J w/o J D 25 Sept 1887-2 Mar 1916 Onan
Isaac h/o Mary 1858-1954 Wach
Jack R 28 June 1922-10 Oct 1971 Onan
James W 1874-1920 Libe
Jennie Lee d/o Augustus & M S 24 Nov 1880-20 July 1896 Holl
Jesse h/o M H 17 Mar 1798-4 Sept 1873 Wach
Jesse T 1924-1970 Libe
John h/o Nancy 24 June 1762-8 Oct 1848 (on Sunday); age: 86/3/14 JnoP
John D h/o I J 1 Jan 1886-24 Jan 1943 Ona
John E h/o M A 30 Aug 1840-9 Nov 1914 Edge
John R s/o Augustus & Margt (Drummond) 12 Dec 1878-29 Feb 1932 Onan
John S h/o M E 24 May 1861-21 Mar 1948 Park
John W d 28 Sept 1913; age: 77 yrs Wach
John W h/o S E 1848-1932 Onan
Cpl Joseph T s/o T B & G C 8 Nov 1886-11 Oct 1918 (killed in France) Holl
Joseph W s/o G W & L E b&d

PHILLIPS (continued)
23 Mar 1911 Wach
Josie S d/o T B & G C 23 May 1885-20 Mar 1887 Holl
Kitty d 23 May 1940; age: 58 yrs Shil
Laura E (w/o G W) 1874-1958 Wach
Lee Roy 1 Oct 1863-28 Dec 1927 MtHo-s
Levin J (h/o S J) 1896- Onan
Levin W h/o S E s/o Wm & Mary 28 Oct 1816-11 Aug 1891 JnoP
Lillian M w/o F B 1879-1963 MtHo
Lois Logan 25 July 1893-26 Dec 1960 Libe
Lorraine H (w/o C J) 1923- Onan
Louie D 12 Jan 1891-17 Nov 1957 Wach
Louis F 15 Oct 1858-30 Sept 1932 Edge
Louis James h/o O S d 12 Sept 1910; age: 72 yrs Wach
Lula H w/o H D 1885-1955 MtHo
Lula J w/o S V 1886-1967 Libe
Maggie S w/o Augustus 18 may 1859-12 May 1899 Holl
MahalaH w/o Jesse d/o Jodiah & Catherine Bell 15 Jan 1802-10 Nov 1857; age: 54/9/11 Wach
Malinda A w/o J E 28 Oct 1849-5 Apr 1895 Edge
Margaret Ann (w/o G C) 19 July 1852-7 Mar 1928 Fair
Margaret B (w/o H M) 1888-1961 Fair
Mary w/o Isaac 1866-1947 Wach
Mary B (w/o B E) 1835-1923 Wach
Mary B w/o C A 1913-1975 Wach
Mary Emily w/o J S 3 Oct 1861-29 Jan 1941 Park
Mary F 1876-1969 Fair
Mary P w/o W L 1857-1934 Park
Mattie H (w/o Theodore) 1885-1979 Onan
Mattie L w/o S S 1880-1969 Edge
Minnie Lee d/o J S & M E 28

PHILLIPS (continued)
Mar 1886-12 Dec 1888 Park
Minnie Viola (w/o Vernon W; d/o Geo White) 17 Sept 1883-22 May 1948 MtHo-s
Mollie S (w/o W H) 1878- MtHo-s
Myrtle P w/o E L 1903-1980 MtHo
Nancy w/o Jno d 17 June 1791 age: 25/6/19 JnoP
Naomi R (w/o T F) 1904-1968 Wach
Octavius s/o C A & E G 1922-1933 Park
Olevia d/o L W & S E 6 Sept 1856-27 Apr 1883 JnoP
Olevia S w/o L J d/o Wm & Margt Goffigon 23 Jan 1848-6 Dec 1897 Wach
Olga B (w/o G C) 1904- MtHo-s
Pershing L 1 Feb 1919-3 Aug 1965 Libe
Rachel d/o T B & Sallie Floyd 16 Nov 1821-3 Aug 1895 Floy
Ralph L 1914-1978 Libe
Ralph T 29 July 1892-20 Mar 1961 Libe
Robert Coleburn 1861-1953 Holl
Roland W 19 Sept 1874-3 June 1956 Fair
S Vaden h/o L J 1886-1942 Libe
Sallie E 12 Feb 1843-2 Feb 1915 JnoP
Samuel T h/o V S 29 Jan 1857-28 May 1903 Libe
Samuel V Jr 7 Jan 1907-5 May 1945 Edge
Sarah A J w/o W S d/o Wm & Eliz Harman 18 Oct 1822-29 Jan 1899; age: 76/3/11 HaPh
Sarah Ann 31 Aug 1838-31 Oct 1903 Holl
Sarah C d/o Thos F & Susannah Slocome d 27 Dec 1865; age: 80/0/23 Phil
Sarah J (w/o L J) 1895-1975 Onan
Sidney M s/o W A & E M 30 Oct-21 Dec 1912 Wach
Smith s/o Wm & Rachel 13 Mar 1790-31 Aug 1868 Bulb

PHILLIPS (continued)
Solomon h/o A S 17 Jan 1805-14 May 1868 Edge
Southey S (h/o M L) 1871-1945 Edge
Susan E w/o L W d 22 Aug 1879; age: 56/6/0 JnoP
Susie E w/o J W 1837-1920 Onan
Susie E w/o C T 7 July 1906- Park
Tabitha Ann w/o Isaac S 4 Feb 1850-5 Feb 1918 Wach
Tappen F (h/o N R) 1900-1970 Wach
Thelma E 16 Dec 1899-4 Mar 1982 Onan
Theodore 1882-1945 Onan
Thomas B h/o G C 21 Feb 1860-13 July 1930 Holl
Viola M (w/o E V) 1913-1956 Edge
Virnetta S w/o S T 8 Mar 1862-6 Jan 1942 Libe
W Brooks d 3 Mar 1887; age: 30/5/26 HaPh
Walter A (h/o E M) 1878-1956 Wach
Warren L (h/o C D) 16 Jan 1897-30 June 1971 Fair
Wendell Clyde s/o B L & G T 6-11 June 1908 Wach
Wesley F s/o W S & S A J 20 Mar-22 Aug 1855 HaPh
Wesley S h/o S A J 17 FEb 1824-12 Aug 1905 HaPh
Willard E h/o H D 7 May 1907- 16 Mar 1974 Quin
William s/o Wm 13 May 1774- 18 Jan 1854; age: 79/8/5 JnoP
William H (h/o M S) 1877-1963 MtHo-s
William L h/o M P 1853-1926 Park
William O 1913-1967 MtHo-s
William N 1912-1961 Libe
PICKEREL, Clarence A (h/o H L) 1887-1951 StGe
Helen Lee (w/o C A) 1900-1969 StGe
PIELEE, Gilbert h/o Sophia (native of Holland) d 22 Feb 1790;

PIELEE (continued)
age: 50 yrs Tave
Sophia w/o Gilbert mother/o Wm d 11 Mar 1793; age: 42 yrs (monument erected by John Cropper Jr) Tave
William s/o Gilbert (midshipman of the U S Frigate *L'Insurgente*) d 17 Jan 1801; age: 22/2/8 Tave
PIERCE, Emanuel 20 Sept 1869- 11 Mar 1910 Burt
PILCHARD, Doris Frieze 1909- Edge
Francis A w/o S J 24 Jan 1853- 15 Mar 1919 Park
Inez d/o P T & Bessie 1906- 1937 Edge
Kate H w/o M L 1894- Park
Kniles T h/o M A 1881-1950 Park
Manie E w/o Max L d/o Abel W & Jennie Wallace 14 Oct 1886-28 Apr 1906 Smic
Marion A w/o K T 1886-1981 Park
Maurice L h/o K H 1892-1963 Park
Paul T 1878-1957 Edge
Stephen J h/o F A 4 Oct 1850-7 July 1923 Park
PINKSTON, Denny s/o L E & Ina R 1947-1948 Fair
PITTS, s/o T C & E S 15 July 1866- 25 July 1868 Onan
Ann M w/o Wm G 12 Mar 1816-7 Oct 1874; age: 58/6/25 Pitt
Bessie Wescott 18 Dec 1897-31 Aug 1966 MtHo
Carrie 1891-1946 JoyC
Elizabeth S w/o T C 24 Nov 1834-18 Mar 1908 Onan
Ella K Hopkins w/o Wm B 1858-1925 Onan
Gilbert 1927-1970 NewM
Henry 1892-1976 NewM
James 1917-1954 JoyC
Jennie 1890-1956 JoyC
Leah 1906-1979 NewM
P(ITTS), M E footstone only Pitt
Mary Frye 1895-1962 JoyC
Nellie d/o T C & E S 26 Aug

PITTS (continued)
1858-1 July 1863 Onan
Robert s/o Jennie 1906-1949 JoyC
Robert G s/o Wm G & A M 21 Dec 1857-4 Mar 1875; age: 17/2/14 Pitt
Robert Joseph s/o T C & E S 24 Aug 1851-25 Jan 1856 Onan
Thomas C h/o E S 16 Feb 1826-23 Nov 1901 Onan
Thomas C s/o T C & E S 12 Oct 1877-11 May 1890 Onan
Thomas G d 4 May 1892; age: 36 yrs Pitt
William B h/o E K H 1856-1931 Onan
William G h/o A M 28 Dec 1815-3 Dec 1873; age: 57/11/5 Pitt
PLACE, Frank A (h/o G B) 1937-1979 MtHo
Gracie B (w/o F A) 1939- MtHo
PLATT, Charles Paul h/o M P 1885-1936 Libe
Mabel Parks w/o C P 1884-1944 Libe
PLOUSOS, Bertha (w/o Kiriakos) 1896-1968 Fair
Kiriakos (h/o Bertha) 1887-1954 Fair
POLLIARD, Eva K (w/o J L) 1895-1975 Fair
Jno L (h/o E K) 1891-1956 Fair
Merhl A 1903-1961 MtHo-s
Millie K (w/o R H) 1898- MtHo-s
Robert H (h/o M K) 1894-1967 MtHo-s
Robert Henry Jr 1922-1931 MtHo-s
POOLMAN, Elizabeth w/o Jno b 25 Sept 1747 (living in 1799 see Whitelaw: 886) (unable to verify) FoxP
James s/o Jno & Eliz 8 July 1776-4 Mar 1797 FoxP
John (h/o Eliz) b 11 Sept 1744 (living in 1799 see Whitelaw: 886) (unable to verify) FoxP
Lucy M 1885-1963 Metr
POOR, C Wyman (h/o M H)

POOR (continued)
1893-1971 Fair
Martha H (w/o C W) 1896-1982 Fair
PORTER, Joyce Mitchell 17 Nov 1897-19 Jan 1973 Park
POTTS, Martha B (w/o T J) 1874-1931 Quin
Thomas J (h/o M B) 1861-1934 Quin
William R 16 Oct 1920-17 July 1975 Fair
POULSON, inf/o E J & S C b&d July 1830 Poul
Ames Howard d 8 Nov 1942; age: 63 yrs Gask-old
Annie H w/o S L 1897-1977 Holl
Annie M w/o C H 1891-1964 Park
Auburn 1906-1971 Gask
Beatrice 1893-1979 Gask
Catharine P W w/o R J d/o Jno & Tabitha Custis 9 Apr 1813-4 Jan 1896 Poul
Charles H h/o A M 1886-1953 Park
Clarence U (h/o M M) 1906-1968 Fair
Edmund J (w/o S C) 19 June 1801-30 Jan 1884 Poul
Edmund J s/o E J & Susan C 8 Sept 1837-4 Apr 1859 Poul
Elizabeth wid/o Jas 8 Aug 1767-19 Jan 1845 (member of M E church for 60 yrs) Poul
Elizabeth d 7 June 1815; age 0/1/6 Poul
Elizabeth w/o J W 13 Feb 1833-22 Sept 1903 RodP
Elizabeth A d/o E J & Susan C 21 Aug 1825-7 June 1845 Poul
Elizabeth P w/o Jas B 29 Jan 1811-13 Oct 1836 Poul
Elizabeth T d/o R J & C C d 1 Aug 1920; age: 84 yrs Poul
Erastus P h/o N L 22 Oct 1867-24 Feb 1938 Edge
Eula G 1910-1980 Gask
George 1912-1978 Metr
George L 1912-1938 Burt
Herman L 1890-1967 Burt
Hester 1888-1975 JoyC

POULSON (continued)
Howard F 20 Sept 1914-29 July 1964 Gask
J Wallace h/o S M 14 Aug 1930-15 July 1982 MtHo
James Sr h/o Eliza 22 Nov 1768-14 Apr 1840 (member of M E Church for 37 yrs) Poul
James s/o Robt J & Catharine (Custis) 22 Feb 1840-14 Nov 1904 Confederate soldier Poul
James s/o Jno & Eliza 2 Apr 1848-1 May 1880 RodP
James s/o Jno W & Eliz 10-14 Sept 1866 RodP
James B 24 Aug 1803-12 June 1859 Poul
John Custis s/o Robt J & Catharine (Custis) 23 June 1847-16 June 1865 Confederate soldier Poul
John R 24 Oct 1904-7 May 1973 MtHo
John T 1861-1949 Burt
John W h/o Eliz 13 Mar 1838-1 May 1903 RodP
Leah J 1865-1948 Burt
Lester E s/o E P & N L 4 Oct 1889-24 Jan 1964 Edge
M E L Waring w/o Thos H G 15 July 1841-24 Sept 1865 Poul
Major T 1909-1978 Metr
Marcella S (w/o Upshur) 1877-1949 Onan
Martha Ann 1868-1926 Park
Mary D 6 Feb 1838-4 Jan 1908 Poul
Mary D 3 Jan 1894-13 Sept 1904 Burt
Matilda M (w/o C U) 1903-1975 Fair
Maylon R s/o T W & A P 10 Dec 1900-10 Feb 1901 MtHo
Milton R h/o S S 1903-1976 MtHo
Nancy L w/o E P 30 Apr 1871-19 Oct 1954 Edge
Norman S (h/o P P) 1901- Onan
Pearl P 1893-1979 Fair
Pearl P (w/o N S) 1899-1980 Onan
Rebecca G w/o R S 1870-1965

POULSON (continued)
Fair
Richard J 1909-1955 Park
Robert d 10 Oct 1841; age: 89 yrs Poug
Robert 1902-1965 NewM
Robert J 8 Jan 1806-31 Aug 1862 Poul
Robert J s/o R J & C P W 4 Mar 1849-9 Mar 1882 Poul
Robert S h/o R G 1865-1950 Fair
Sarah Custis 16 Mar 1842-17 Apr 1926 Poul
Stanley L 1895-1961 Holl
Sue M w/o J W 8 July 1933- MtHo
Sue S w/o M R 1898-1970 MtHo
Susan C w/o E J 8 Mar1802-14 July 1874; age: 72/4/6 Poul
Susan F d/o E J & S C 28 Sept 1828-1 Apr 1839 Poul
Thomas W h/o A P 8 June 1871-7 Apr 1919 MtHo
Upshur (h/o M S) 1874-1958 Onan
Walter N 1899-1968 JoyC
Wilbert 1888-1952 Snea
William T 1947-1969 NewM
Willie s/o J W & Eliz 13 Feb 1862-13 Sept 1863 RodP
POWELL, Ada d/o H F & E S 22 Dec 1888-26 Mar 1942 MtHo
Alfred 1898-1977 Gask
Alice O d/o G W & M A 2 Mar 1856-20 Nov 1864 Onan
Amanda w/o Wm 22 Feb 1840-22 May 1919 Park
Arinthia S w/o Jno T d/o G P & Eliz Ewell d 31 Jan 1858; age: 26/5/6 Libe
Arthur M 23 Jan 1854-31 July 1936 MtHo
Arthur R s/o Levin & Peggy d 11 July 1842; age: 50/0/28 Powl
Ben D Jr 21 Nov 1926-21 May 1943 MtHo-s
Benjamin D (h/o H L) 1899-1969 MtHo-s
Bettie S d/o G W & M A 13 May 1859-22 Nov 1864 Onan
Bettie W w/o Nathl 1874-1961 Edge

POWELL (continued)
Blanche S (w/o E T Jr) 1899- Wach
Charles Seth s/o H F & N S 26 Aug-16 Dec 1881 MtHo
Charlotte T 1898-1915 Edge
Cecil Carlile III 19 June 1954-15 Oct 1981 Fair
Cecile d/o H F & E S 15 Dec 1878-25 Dec 1964 MtHo
David Jackson s/o J H & S J d Nov 7 1852; age: 3/1/14 Powe
Dorsey S 1884-1972 Edge
Edith T w/o T J 1875-1960 MtHo
Edna Savage w/o E T 25 Dec 1872-19 June 1952 Wach
Edward T h/o S D 1864-1948 Edge
Edwin J (h/o V P) 1904-1968 Edge
Edwin T Jr (h/o B S) 1895-1957 Wach
Edwin Thomas h/o E S 26 Nov 1852-13 Apr 1918 Wach
Elizabeth w/o Arthur R d 10 Feb 1841; age: 53/10/7 Powl
Elizabeth Custis w/o W P 10 July 1860-8 Mar 1922 Onan
Ella S w/o H F 1851-1891 MtHo
Emily E w/o J H 3 Mar 1853-21 Jan 1916 MtHo
Emma S d/o G W & M A 16 July 1852-3 Dec 1853 Onan
Ernest C (h/o M L) 1899-1964 Quin
Ernest H h/o S L 3 Oct 1886-12 May 1930 Edge
Everett J 1904-1979 Park
Everette P h/o N M 1 Dec 1907-4 Oct 1977 Libe
Evie K w/o J W 1877-1954 Park
Fannie w/o E T 8 Jan 1859-19 Oct 1889 Morr
Floyd E 1900-1976 Edge
Frances B (w/o M E Sr) 3 Sept 1911-29 July 1975 Edge
Frederick A 1868-1911 Onan
G William h/o Jannette K 24 Jan 1926-21 July 1979 Park
G William Jr 4 Aug 1955-17 Aug 1974 Park
George H h/o L T s/o J T & R K

POWELL (continued)
2 Mar 1875-20 Jan 1957 Onan
George W 17 Mar 1825-17 July 1885 Onan
George W d 2 May 1918; age: 68 yrs Holl
George W 1925-1936 Holl
Grace L 1918-1920 Holl
Grace M w/o O L 1914- Edge
Grace S (w/o L T) 1894-1971 Quin
Hallie d/o E T & E S 1-2 Apr 1910 Wach
Hattie L 1892- Edge
Hattie L (w/o B D) 1904- MtHo-s
Hattie T 1910-1978 Onan
Henry E 1901-1958 Onan
Henry F h/o E S 1835-1915 MtHo
Herbert S h/o R M 1897-1977 Wach
Ida S w/o W S 25 Sept 1903- Edge
James A h/o L A 1869-1957 Park
James H h/o E E 25 Jan 1845-9 Aug 1922 MtHo
James H (h/o J L) 1865-1934 MtHo-s
Jane Lee (w/o J H) 1859-1938 MtHo-s
Jesse 3 Oct 1884-9 Nov 1917 Park
John H (h/o S J) 24 May 1810-20 Apr 1878 Powe
John T h/o R K 14 Apr 1828-20 Aug 1890 Onan
John Thomas 1897-1937 Onan
John W h/o R F 1854-1916 Edge
John W h/o E K 1877-1962 Park
Julia B d/o J A & L A 10 Oct 1902-29 Oct 1907 Park
L Fletcher (h/o S M) 1891-1945 MtHo-s
L Thomas (h/o G S) 1889-1964 Quin
Larry Dalby 13 Oct 1948-11 June 1984 Park
Laura J 1868-1954 MtHo
Lillie A w/o J A 1874-1909 Park
Louise K 1882-1965 Morr
Lucian Linwood h/o R B 7 Jan

POWELL (continued)
1903-2 Oct 1953 Park
Lucy Thomas w/o G H 15 Aug 1883-7 June 1961 Onan
Mabel S w/o Thos J 16 Aug 1894-4 Jan 1917 Brap
Margaret A 1835-1909 Onan
Marian L (w/o E C) 1897-1975 Quin
Martha J 1896-1976 Hollies
Mary 15 Oct 1862-14 June 1932 Park
Mary Ann w/o Seth d/o Major & Nancy Rayfield d 11 Oct 1845; age: 43/1/6 Libe
Mary E 1907-1979 Park
Mary Mathias (w/o Paul) 12 Oct 1901-25 Oct 1978; age: 77/0/13 Wach
Mildred 1906-1947 MtHo-s
Milton E Sr (h/o F B) 20 May 1905-4 Oct 1950 Edge
Mirty J 1903-1982 Onan
Nathaniel h/o B W 1870-1946 Edge
Nellie M w/o E P 7 Dec 1913- Libe
Oldham L h/o G M 1911-1972 Edge
Oscar L MD (h/o S L) 19 Nov 1875-25 June 1925 Onan
Paul (h/o M M) 26 May 1893- Wach
Percy L 1892-1950 Holl
Reva Byrd Justis w/o L L 2 Jan 1909-7 May 1970 Park
Robert Earle s/o J T & R K 4 Nov 1885-23 Apr 1941 Onan
Roberta Ker w/o Jno Thos d/o Col Robt & Leah Irving Ker Stewart b Wetipquin Md 18 Sept 1840; mar Snowhill Md 28 Feb 1867; d Onancock Va 14 Mar 1932 Onan
Roland H 1897-1973 Quin
Ruberta F w/o J W 1858-1913 Edge
Ruth M w/o H S 1899- Wach
Sallie Bogs (w/o T J) 22 May 1865-17 Feb 1939 Onan
Sallie M (w/o L F) 1897-1973 MtHo-s

POWELL (continued)
Sally D w/o E T 1867-1946 Edge
Sally J w/o J H 21 Oct 1821-2 Feb 1867; age: 46/3/12 Powe
Sarah L w/o E H 1899- Edge
Sarah Long (w/o O L) 27 Mar 1881-24 July 1948 Onan
Seth h/o M A s/o Laben & Polly 18 Jan 1797-29 Dec 1853 Libe
Seth s/o H F & N S 5-19 Nov 1882 MtHo
Stewart Ker s/o J T & R K 15 Mar 1869-25 Apr 1951 (practiced law on E Shore for 60 yrs) Onan
Stuart nd Park
Thomas J (h/o S B) 3 Oct 1864-17 Feb 1914 Onan
Thomas J h/o E T 1883-1934 MtHo
Thomas N s/o J H & S J d 23 Apr 1848; age: 0/1/21 Powe
Vesta P (w/o E J) 1906- Edge
W Henry DDS 9 Nov 1883-15 June 1964 MtHo
Wesley S h/o I S 16 Nov 1892-18 July 1862 Edge
William h/o Amanda 2 Nov 1825-13 July 1909 Park
William H 1892-1975 Gask
William M 8 Jan 1897-10 Mar 1948 Onan
William P h/o E C 11 May 1860-18 Aug 1911 Onan
William R 24 Nov 1894-25 Feb 1938 MtHo

POWERS, Bettie E (w/o T C) 1880-1944 Quin
Eileen Tull 1925-1981 Wach
Ina E (w/o J A) 1873-1946 Wach
Jesse A (h/o Ina E) 1871-1956 Wach
John M 13 Jan 1914-31 Dec 1963 Quin
Lucille D (w/o O D) 1921- Wach
Lynwood (h/o M O) 1897-1972 Quin
Margaret O (w/o Lynwood) 1898-1926 Quin
Otho D (h/o L D) 1920-1981 Wach
Rence Lynn 1965-1973 Wach

POWERS (continued)
Thomas C (h/o B E) 1877-1932 Quin
PRESCOTT, Asa H 1899-1956 Libe
John N 1872-1962 Libe
Nellie C 1901-1981 Libe
Queenie V 1876-1960 Libe
PRESTON, Charlie 24 Aug 1890-1 Jan 1891 (unable to verify) FoxP
PRIER, see PRYOR
PRIESTMAN, Sidney W 8 Feb 1915-14 Dec 1959 Onan
PRITCHETT, Elsie L (w/o E J) nd Wach
Emerson J (h/o E L) 1910-1950 Wach
PROCTOR, Mabel W 1904-1983 Edge
PRUITT, baby girl 22-23 Apr 1949 MtHo-s
Rev 1904-1976 Gask
Amanda W (w/o E C) 1890-1969 MtHo
Beatrice H (w/o E S) 1918-1971 Fair
Bertha M 1900-1971 MtHo
Beulah Evans w/o S D 1907-1982 Fair
Bobbie Reade h/o L G 21 Dec 1920-28 Apr 1979 Fair
Connie b&d 1944 MtHo-s
Elisha C h/o A W 1889-1957 MtHo
Elmer K h/o E F 1914-1964 Park
Elwood S (h/o B H) 1914-1967 Fair
Emily Ruth d/o Thos & Ruth 26 Aug 1940-8 Aug 1941 MtHo-s
Emma J (w/o S T) 1878-1970 MtHo-s
Eva F w/o E K d 1965 Park
Gladys M w/o L H 1918-1972 Park
Rev J B h/o S P 27 Mar 1859-30 Dec 1926 Onan
John P (h/o N C) 14 Oct 1862-9 Mar 1939 MtHo
Leah G w/o B R 1922- Fair
Lee H h/o G M 1913-1973 Park
Maggie C (w/o W H) 1898-1970

PRUITT (continued)
Fair
Margaret W (w/o Thos) 1894-1974 Wach
Mary E w/o W H 1866-1943 MtHo-s
Michael R b&d 1971 MtHo-s
Nellie C (w/o J P) 4 Mar 1870-24 Nov 1942 MtHo
Ona D (w/o S M) 1904- MtHo-s
Sabra Pitts w/o Rev J B 9 June 1870-15 Mar 1919 Onan
Severn T (h/o E J) 1875-1951 MtHo-s
Sid M (h/o O D) 1902-1973 MtHo-s
Spurgeon Dise h/o B E 1890-1971 Fair
Capt Thomas (h/o M W) 1889-1973 Wach
W Stephen 1933-1966 Fair
William H h/o M E 10 Nov 1857-28 May 1930 MtHo-s
Willie H (h/o M C) 1896-1972 Fair
PRYOR, (PRYER, PRIER)
Anna Leona w/o J H 15 Mar 1899-20 Jan 1977 MtHo
Coley W (h/o E E) 1894-1963 MtHo-s
Dollie V w/o J E 1873-1958 MtHo
Dolly Wayne d/o J H & A L 19 Dec 1933-14 Apr 1960 MtHo
Dorothy B (w/o J C) 4 June 1916-31 May 1977 MtHo-s
Ethel E (w/o C W) 1906- MtHo-s
Ethel M w/o J W 1894-1962 Libe
Fred L (h/o S S) 1883-1967 MtHo-s
Inez L (w/o K F) 11 Apr 1919- Fair
J C III 27 Sept 1937-28 Nov 1972 MtHo-s
J Clifford (h/o D B) 27 Jan 1907 MtHo-s
J Harold h/o A L 3 Feb 197-15 Oct 1980 MtHo
James E h/o D V 1872-1961 MtHo

PRYOR (continued)
John W h/o E M 1890-1960 Libe
Kathy Jean d 25 July 1973 Fair
Kenneth F (h/o I L) 16 July 1911-17 Sept 1976 Fair
Levin Riley 17 July 1874-12 Feb 1936 MtHo-s
Mary Alice 16 May 1911-23 Jan 1933 MtHo-s
Mary E w/o J W 1895-1918 Libe
Mary H 19 Nov 1876-6 Nov 1957 MtHo-s
Sue S (w/o F L) 1891-1935 MtHo-s
Vianna F w/o Wm T 28 Apr 1868-14 July 1936 Libe
William T h/o V F 26 May 1866-29 Sept 1925 Libe
PUCKETT, John D (h/o V W) 1884-1921 StGe
Virginia W (w/o J D) 1891-1970 StGe
PURDY, Molly d/o Nathl J & Eliz (Eickelberger) LeCato 1859-1899 Quin
PURNELL, Calvin L h/o I G 1894-1967 Park
Ida G w/o C L 1896-1970 Park
PUTNEY, Gertrude Taylor 1919-1967 Metr
QUILLEN, Cecil H 28 Aug 1904-3 Dec 1978 Edge
QUINBY, Belle 1 Sept 1898-7 Mar 1907 Onan
Elizabeth Upshur w/o Aaron B d/o Littleton Dennis Teackle & wife Eliz 4 Feb 1801-10Mar 1875; age: 74/1/6 Warw
Georgie G w/o Upshur B d/o Thos & Margt B Richardson 14 Nov 1845-30 Nov 1896; age: 51/0/16 Warw
L D Teackle 2 Sept 1915-19 Feb 1975 Onan
Littleton Dennis Teackle 27 Aug 1872-2 Sept 1933 Warw
Lulu Belle Hemphill (organizing regent- E S of Va Chapter, DAR) 1876-1949 Onan
Upshur Balderstone s/o Aaron Balderstone & Eliz Teackle 20 Aug 1841-29 Jan 1898 Warw

QUIVERS, Joseph 23 June 1898-29 July 1966 Snea
RAINEY, Jeneviah 1917-1972 Bays
RALPH, Bessie Fentress w/o T E 1875-1963 Onan
Ray F s/o T E & B F 17 Sept 1900-6 July 1901 Onan
Thomas Edgar h/o B F 1875-1971 Onan
RALSTON, Glancy S 24 Oct 1887-10 Feb 1945 Onan
RAMSEY, Shirley N 1948-1967 HTri
RANDALL, Berbenna 1920-1968 NewM
L (Mother) 1864-1927 NewM
RANSONE, E Dupuy Jr (h/o M C) 1914- Onan
Emmett D (h/o R A) 1878-1961 Fair
Mae Colonna (w/o E D Jr) 1914-1982 Onan
Rita A (w/o E D) 1885-1972 Fair
RAUGHLEY, Mavis 16 Dec 1922-10 Sept 1978 Holl
RAY, James 1923-1980 Snea
RAYFIELD, Infant & twin babies of Major & Betsy nd Rayf
Adell K (w/o H N) 1899-1968 MtHo-s
Annie Lou (w/o J H) 1896- Fair
Arthur J s/o Levi & L A K 13 Mar 1902-12 Nov 1904 MtHo
Betsy w/o Major 24 Feb 1838-10 June 1879 Rayf
Betty E 1873-1956 Park
Buddy (s/o Levi & L A K) 1917- MtHo
Carroll L 10 June 1910-2 May 1974 Fair
Clarence J 1901-1943 MtHo-s
Ella K w/o H T 12 Apr 1864-12 May 1926 Onan
Emily H w/o T J 28 Dec 1820-1 June 1889 Edge
Emma 1872-1896 Croc
Fannie L 1900- MtHo-s
George W 1924-1978 Metr
Gladys Read (w/o J T) 1897-1926 StGe
Harry D s/o Levi & L A K 27 Apr

RAYFIELD (continued)
1903-12 Nov 1914 MtHo
Henry N (h/o A K) 1899-1970 MtHo-s
Henry T h/o E K 3 June 1860-17 Mar 1942 Onan
Howard C 1923-1945 MtHo-s
J Henry (h/o A L) 1890-1948 Fair
John T 30 Oct 1830-12 Jan 1903 Onan
Joseph T (h/o G R) 1890-1972 StGe
Lenoah A K w/o Levi 1880-1958 MtHo
LeRoy F 10 Apr 1880-28 Sept 1899 Onan
Levi h/o L A K 1871-1946 MtHo
Major 15 Dec 1835-3 Apr 1904 MtHo
Martha K 1925-1982 Metr
Martin 1911-1982 Metr
Mary Ann Eliz w/o Geo d 8 July 1909; age: 68 yrs Park
Mary B 1892-1958 Metr
Mary Shaw 27 Sept 1909-13 Nov 1980 Fair
Thomas J h/o E H 24 Mar 1815-18 July 1876 Edge
Thomas T 13 Jan 1905-18 May 1974 Metr
Willie A d/o G S & T W Fisher 26 Aug 1856-26 Aug 1886 Croc
READ, (READE), see also REED,
Alice d 9 Mar 1965; age: 58 yrs StPa
Alma J (h/o V M s/o R P & Sallie) 1849-1912 (moved from Read Plot, Hacks Neck) StGe
Amanda A w/o J D 19 May 1861-8 Nov 1941 Onan
Ann Hack w/o Edmd d/o Peter Hack Sr d 1792; age: 43 yrs Fair
Benjamin A (h/o C L) 1875-1940 StGe
Charles U (h/o M B) 1882-1949 Fair
Clara L (w/o B A) 1870-1949 StGe
E Willard 17 Dec 1870-2 June 1903 StGe

READ (continued)
Edmund s/o Edmd & Absabella d 23 Dec 1836; age: about 78 yrs (leaving 4 daus) Ches
Edmund G s/o Edmd & Nancy 11 Oct 1822-14 May 1829 Ches
Edward Richard Jr 1942-1968 StGe
Elizabeth w/o Edmund (d/o Arthur Teackle) 27 Feb 1760-10 May 1815 Teac
Emily Scarborough w/o Geo S d 26 May 1935 StGe
Eugene J W 9 Aug 1834-12 Mar 1903 StGe
Everett M (h/o N E B) 1909-1976 Fair
G Martyn 1906-1955 StGe
George R s/o Wm & M B 23 Dec 1890-24 Nov 1898 StGe
George Smith (h/o E S) 17 May 1845-18 May 1901 StGe
Henrietta S (w/o L D) 12 Mar 1847-21 Mar 1918 StGe
J Wesley (h/o L B) 1891-1971 MtHo-s
James D 1900-1930 StGe
John D h/o A A 4 Sept 1855-20 Nov 1933 Onan
Littleton D (h/o H S) 23 July 1838-18 Nov 1893 StGe
Ludine B (w/o J W) 1899- MtHo-s
Mrs Margaret A P (w/o Richd P; d/o Richd & Sarah Kendall Rogers) 9 Mar 1809-30 June 1831; age: 23 yrs Ropl
Margaret Sarah 9 Nov 1860-23 Dec 1953 StGe
Margie B 11 May 1869-2 June 1917 StGe
Mary E w/o Richd P footstone MER only remains (ref Whitelaw: 718) Read
Maynard R 1872-1946 StGe
Miles S 1889-1963 Park
Milton H s/o J D & A A 3 Aug 1899-20 Jan 1909; age: 9/5/17 Onan
Minnie B (w/o C U) 1889-1977 Fair
Nina Wise 1879-1967 StGe

READ (continued)
Nola East B (w/o E M) 1901- Fair
Richard Edward 1916-1979 StGe
Col Richard P (h/o S S S s/o Jno) 1808-1884 (moved from Read Plot, Hacks Neck) StGe
Sara S S (w/o R P) 1808-1882 (moved from Read Plot, Hacks Neck) StGe
Tabitha A 7 Apr 1837-7 Jan 1914 StGe
Virginia M (w/o A J nee Martin) 1850-1883 (moved from Read Plot, Hacks Neck) StGe
Wharton b&d 1916 Onan
William K 22 Mar 1858-22 Mar 1925 StGe
REARDON, Madeline R 1887-1964 Onan
REDD, Ora T 1884-1964 Fair
REDMAN, George 1898-1978 Burt
REED, (**REID**), see also **READ**,
Adelaide 1889-1981 Shil
Alonzo E h/o L H 1897-1953 Onan
Ann Teagle nee Parramore m1 Jno B Walker m2 Enoch Reed 29 Nov 1799-31 July 1876 Parr
Enoch 2nd h/o Ann T Parramore Walker 3 Aug1803-6 Aug 1876 Parr
(**REID**?) Faith (Bonniwell) d 1947 StGe
Forrest H 1905-1951 Snea
George 1906-1959 HTri
James Palmer h/o M M 9 Nov 1897-24 Dec 1976 Park
John H 1910-1977 HTri
Kate 1874-1966 Shil
Lillie H w/o A E 1894-1966 Onan
Maggie 1887-1965 Snea
Maggie S 14 Feb 1862-13 Aug 1911 NewM
Mildred M w/o J P 1899-1979 Park
Nora Evans 7 Mar 1887-23 Dec 1931 Onan
Paul L 1901-1977 HTri
Pearl J 1900-1967 Burt
REITEMEYER, Alma A H 1883-

REITEMEYER (continued)
1970 MtHo-s
Maria M C 1877-1976 MtHo-s
REVELL, Annie M w/o B M 1881-1946 MtHo-s
Asher L h/o D C 1885-1959 MtHo
Burton M h/o A M 1879-1955 MtHo-s
Charles E 8 Feb 1835-23 July 1889 Poul
Cora M w/o S J 1859-1944 MtHo
Della C w/o A L 1887- MtHo
Edward S s/o A H & D C 22 Jan 1915-30 Nov 1919 MtHo
George W nd Burf
Levin W h/o S G 1903-1967 MtHo-s
Mary E 1907-1959 Shil
Sallie G w/o L W 1902-1975 MtHo-s
Samuel J h/o C M 1850-1916 MtHo
REVELLE, Paul T Sr 25 Oct 1914-8 Aug 1982 Park
REW, see also **RUE**,
Arlington R 1899-1956 MtHo
Bessie Lee d/o S M & S D 22 Dec 1898-31 May 1899 Park
Betty S w/o Benj T 4 Oct 1881-7 June 1916 Fitz
Carrie d/o Wm & Mary 26 Apr 1883-18 May 1884 Park
Carson L 8 July 1895-18 May 1917 Onan
Charles A h/o S B 1851-1932 MtHo
Charles J h/o L M 1871-1958 Park
Cordelia (w/o Jno) 1863-1934 Onan
Della M w/o Geo E 1882-1951 MtHo
Edith Mason (w/o W P) 6 Jan 1906-21 Jan 1958 Edge
Edward T h/o E Y 1872-1950 Park
Effie Y w/o E T 1873-1933 Park
Elizabeth d/o Wm & Susan 12 Nov 1804-26 Oct 1868 West
Elizabeth R 1900-1962 MtHo
Elton L 3 Oct 1902-8 Apr 1972

REW (continued)
Edge
Eva East w/o G M 1877-1944 MtHo
Eva S w/o F T 12 Sept 1851-9 Feb 1930 Park
Florence E 14 Nov 1875-1 Feb 1961 Park
Francis T h/o E S 18 Aug 1835-28 Apr 1917 Park
George C 1898-1942 Edge
George E s/o Richd & Nancy 10 Nov 1845-27 Feb 1912 Rewp
George E h/o D M 1875-1954 MtHo
George M h/o E E 1875-1952 MtHo
George M 1903-1970 Libe
George R h/o M S 1859-1931 Libe
Harvey E (h/o M S) 1883-1935 Edge
Hazel A w/o R J 1893-1951 Onan
Helen Wright 1886-1945 Park
Herman Clifford 15 Mar 1921-25 Nov 1934 MtHo-s
J Harry 17 Sept 1877-28 July 1933 Park
James A 26 Nov 1896-4 Apr 1962 MtHo
Jennie d/o Wm & Mary 9 Feb 1868-26 July 1870 Park
Jesse K (h/o S C) 24 Nov 1840-27 Jan 1920 MtHo
John (h/o Cordelia) 1855-1943 Onan
John D 1906-1968 MtHo
John R 5 Feb 1874-15 July 1918 Park
Julia w/o Wm 3 May 1810-28 Aug 1857 Coke
Lola M w/o C J 1882-1975 Park
M Jane w/o Revell 1830-1905 Edge
Margaret S w/o G R 1864-1935 Libe
Mary Etta 1874-1952 Edge
Mary G 25 Oct 1821-6 Mar 1901 MtHo
Mary T w/o Wm 1848-1933 Park
Milton T 25 Jan 1904-4 June 1979 Fair

REW (continued)
Minnie S (w/o H E) 1884-1971 Edge
Mollie C w/o T E 14 Oct 1890- Onan
Nancy N (w/o R S) 7 Oct 1813-31 Mar 1890 Rewp
Pansy C 1904-1973 Edge
Pricilla Somers w/o T H 12 Aug 1864-23 May 1950 Park
Rachel T 4 June 1903-11 Apr 1978 MtHo-s
Ralph Ed d 1949 StGe
Rebecca Ann d/o J W & Katherine 25-28 July 1949 Onan
Revell h/o M J 1832-1876 Edge
Richard S (h/o N N) 3 May 1801-17 Sept 1884 Rewp
Robert Paige d 1915 Edge
Rufus J h/o H A 1893-1981 Onan
Ruth M 1917-1965 MtHo
Sallie B w/o C A 1854-1934 MtHo
Sallie D w/o S M 1871-1961 Park
Sallie T Bailey w/o W A 29 June 1856-17 Dec 1905 MtHO
Samuel M h/o S D 1866-1965 Park
Sarah C (w/o J K) 28 Sept 1849-23 Aug 1918 MtHo
Susan Frances d/o Geo S & Margt (Ayres) 2 May 1852-11 Sept 1929 Libe
Thelma M 19 Oct 1912-26 Jan 1914 Onan
Thomas H h/o P S 15 June 1864-16 Oct 1931 Park
Walter Paul (h/o E M) 1917-1969 Edge
Wellington R 1865-1942 Edge
William h/o Julia 23 July 1806-22 Aug 1891 Coke
William h/o M T 1838-1919 Park
William A h/o S T B 11 June 1854-24 Oct 1908 MtHo
William H 1847-1917 Park
William H Jr b&d 1903 Park
William J 30 July 1866-13 Sept 1958 Onan
William J 13 Nov 1911-26 Feb 1983 Fair

REW (continued)
Willie Anna d/o Wm & M T 1866-1884 Park
Willie H B 1881-1963 MtHo
RHEA, Marion B 1911-1972 Quin
RHODES, George W Jr 23 Feb 1859-9 Nov 1939 Wach
George W Sr h/o M E 1837-1908 Wach
Henry Orin 12 Nov 1867-2 Mar 1952 Wach
Mary E w/o G W Sr 1835-1910 Wach
RICE, Ellie Hickman 1884-1971 MtHo-s
Etta Savage (w/o M G) 11 Oct 1898-3 July 1975 Fair
Everal C (w/o W C) 27 Feb 1896-12 July 1969 Fair
Mervin G (h/o E S) 18 Jan 1889-9 Nov 1958 Fair
Walter C Sr (h/o E C) 10 Aug 1897-19 Sept 1969 Fair
RICH, Benjamin S h/o R S 10 Sept 1828-21 June 1901 Super-intendent of 6th Dist US Life Saving Service 1875-1901. Marker erected in his honor by members of the service- 6th Dist. MtHo
N Cornelia Kelly w/o N B 1861-1937 Onan
Newell B h/o N C K 1856-1910 Onan
Rachel S w/o B S 17 Nov 1830-23 May 1908 MtHo
Ralph V 1884-1963 Onan
RICHARDS, Albert A h/o E W M 1881-1959 Onan
Ethel W Marley w/o A A 1888-1977 Onan
Ralph K s/o A A & E W M 18 Oct 1916-26 Sept 1923 Onan
RICHARDSON, Addie H (w/o H G) 1906-1963 MtHo-s
Alec F (h/o M S) 1848-1918 Wach
Alice d/o J W & A B 31 July 1896-31 Oct 1910 Wach
Alice B w/o J W 1857-1939 Wach
Anderson 1886-1936 Holl

RICHARDSON (continued)
Beatrice P (w/o C C) 1915- Wach
Bessie H 29 June 1874-30 Jan 1960 Onan
Bessie S (w/o W L) 18 Sept 1912-9 July 1973 Quin
Bowdoin 18 Jan 1846-13 Mar 1920 MtHo
Catherine nd StPa
Charlotte b&d 1923 Holl
Charlotte S 1899- Holl
Clyde C (h/o B P) 1914-1980 Wach
Colie W s/o G W & S E 27 Aug 1870-16 Sept 1871 MtHo
Danie Chesser 15 May 1893-23 July 1945 MtHo
Fredonia R (w/o H J) 24 June 1894 Arkadelphia AR-6 Mar 1982 Hills Farm Onan
G W h/o M C 1875-1939 MtHo
George W h/o S E 22 Apr 1833-9 Nov 1871 MtHo
Hall G (h/o A H) 1902-1962 MtHo-s
Henry J h/o F R 31 Mar 1895 Maynard AR-21 Aug 1975 Hills Farm, Greenbush VA Onan
Homer C (h/o N D) 1922-1973 Edge
Hugh F 26 Oct 1907-25 Feb 1933 Wach
I Preston 24 Oct 1870-19 July 1952 Onan
R(ICHARDSON?), J T footstone only Warp
Jack A 1923- Holl
James E h/o M H 1879-1931 Wach
James M w/o Saml & Maggie 13 Oct 1876-12 May 1914 MtHo
James S 1903-1975 MtHo
James T 5 Sept 1917-12 Sept 1963 Holl
John Arthur 1904-1968 StPa
John Lloyd 1893-1954 Wach
John W h/o A B 1862-1930 Wach
Joyce Heath nd NewM
Lillie M 1888-1946 MtHo
Linda 1950-1951 Holl

RICHARDSON (continued)
Lola M w/o T G 1885- Wach
Luther E s/o J E & M S 4 Sept 1906-14 Aug 1907 Wach
Mamie E 1894-1960 Onan
Mammie C w/o G W 1882-1938 MtHo
Margaret d 1 Mar 1896; age: 62 yrs MtHo
Margaret w/o Saml 25 Dec 853-2 Feb 1922 MtHo
Mary A 15 Dec 1798-10 Aug 1862 Rich
Mary E w/o Thos d/o Jas & Sallie Walker 15 Sept 1825-28 Apr 1900 Walk
MatildaS (w/o A F) 1866-1936 Wach
Molly H w/o J E 1889-1961 Wach
Nina D (w/o H C) 1925- Edge
R Preston 6 Mar 1898-15 Feb 1963 Onan
Rachel S w/o Wm H 8 Nov 1832-26 June 1898 Wach
Samuel h/o Margt 31 Jan 1856-24 Jan 1917 MtHo
Sarah E w/o G W 1 Aug 1840- nd MtHo
Sophronia 1846-1931 Wach
T Hamilton 1918-1968 Holl
Tank G h/o L M 1874-1954 Wach
Virginia S d/o Wm H & R S 28 Nov 1868-6 Sept 1916 Wach
William H 12 Mar 1828-29 Oct 1868 (leaving a wife & 4 children) Warp
William L (h/o B S) 25Aug 1897-29 Mar 1973 Quin
Yvonne Hall w/o Thos (1st hus Fitchett Dix) 25Sept 1923-6 Apr 1979 Wach
RICKETT, Mary Lizie d/o Louisa Snead nd MtNe (E)
RIDOUT, Frank A (h/o L W) 1867-1929 MtHo-s
Lily W (w/o F A) 1877-1947 MtHo-s
RIGGS, Campsey D w/o J R 1865-1941 Park
Freddie L s/o J R & C D 26 Jan

RIGGS (continued)
1893-28 Jan 1898 Park
John R h/o L S 11 Dec 1874-16 Jan 1940 Park
Joseph R h/o C D 1845-1931 Park
Lula S w/o J R 21 May 1877-23 Nov 1948 Park
Milton C h/o N E 1890-1970 Park
Nora E w/o M C 1891-1948 Park
William J 1876-1938 Park
RILEY, Ann F d/o R R & Sarah 19 Nov 1814-3 June 1880 Onan
Annie G 1892-1960 Park
Beatrice E w/o R A 1895-1967 Libe
Charles T 1851-1909 MtHo
Edward G 1898-1978 Metr
Elizabeth A w/o W M 10 Oct 1805-20 Mar 1896 Rile
Elizabeth J 1840-9 Dec 1919 Libe
Francis S w/o J F 2 Mar 1838-30 Apr 1909 Rile
Frank S h/o I B 1875-1960 MtHo
Fred W 1898-1964 Bays
George T 1872-1946 Libe
Heber J 1886-1951 Park
Henry d 3 Sept 1894; age: 57 yrs Gask-old
Ida d 1955 MtHo
Isabella B w/o F S 1877-1968 MtHo
J Henry 1922-1968 Metr
James R 1919-1978 Metr
John F h/o F S 2 Mar 1842-23 Aug 1923 Rile
John F h/o O M 1874-1957 Onan
John W 1913-1970 Bays
Maggie d/o C T & M E 1 Sept 1879-23 Aug 1885 SeyS
Margaret A w/o Raymond R d/o Chas S & R B 25 Oct 1828-6 Jan 1860 SeyS
Marietta 1859-1935 MtHo
Martha Wise 1799-1870 Scot
Mary (w/o S F) 15 May 1862-17 Apr 1939 MtHo-s
Mary R 1858-1944 Edge
Ola M w/o J F 1888-1963 Onan
Raymond 1826-1910 MtHo

229

RILEY (continued)
Raymond 1890-1940 MtHo
Raymond H 29 Aug 1835-1 July 1912 Libe
Raymond H 1865-1944 Libe
Robert A h/o B E 1893-1970 Libe
Robert J 1910-1966 Bays
Sidney F (h/o Mary) 29 Dec 1868-14 Feb 1927 MtHo-s
Sophia 1897-1983 Metr
Southey d 1938; age: c80 yrs (faithful servant to the Lester O Evans family; ns buried in the yard) Arli
Susan H 1843-1945 Gask-old
Susan R d/o Raymond & Sarah 16 May 1824-2 Oct 1896 Onan
Wellington B s/o J F & F S 30 Mar 1873-2 Dec 1896 Rile
William L 1906-1974 MtHo
William M s/o Geo & Fannie 24 Dec 1804-15 Mar 1875 Rile
William M s/o W M & E A 9 Mar 1845-9 Oct 1891 Rile
William M 26 Apr 1882-19 Feb 1911 Edge
RIPPON, B David Sr (h/o L E) 1917-1965 Edge
Louise E (w/o B D) 1920- Edge
RITTER, Harry F 4 May 1886-18 Nov 1891 (moved from Drumtown Meth Ch) Edge
ROACHE, (ROACH),
Ann May b&d 20 Dec 1971 Edge
Lizzie Sue w/o W J 1894-1967 Edge
Mary Eve b&d 20 Dec 1971 Edge
Priscilla Milliner 1872-1960 Edge
Ralph Woodland 1897-1924 Edge
Ruth Ann Beckett 1916- Park
William J h/o L S 1893-1968 Edge
William J Jr 3 Sept 1917-10 Sept 1965 Park
William L h/o R A B 1908-1955 Park
William M 1858-1909 Edge
ROBBINS, Benjamin C h/o S E 1900- MtHo
John H 1897-1941 MtHo-s

ROBBINS (continued)
Loraine A 1923-1982 Libe
Louis 1920-1984 Libe
Mary d 3 July 1964; age: 68 yrs NewM
Robert W 1923-1980 MtHo-s
Susie E w/o B C 1897-1980 MtHo
ROBERTS, Bettie S 1866-1958 Edge
Betty Jeanice d/o Wm T Jr & J J 9 Nov 1953-1 Apr 1984 Park
Carlie M 1862-1924 Edge
George L h/o M E 16 June 1846-2 July 1928 (moved from Red Bank, North Co) Park
George Leonard s/o W T & Katherine J 22 Aug-16 Sept 1922 (moved from Red Bank, North Co) Park
Hilda R (w/o Z H) 1897-1944 Onan
Jeanice Johnson w/o Wm T Jr 13 Sept 1921- Park
Katherine J 21 Aug 1890-24 May 1971 Park
Margaret E w/o G L 10 June 1853-17 Oct 1933 (moved from Red Bank, North Co) Park
Susie Sparrow 1889-1966 Park
Virginia R w/o Harry J 1 Apr 1868-3 Nov 1904 Onan
William T Sr 10 Oct 1880-4 Feb 1959 Park
William Thomas Jr h/o J J 15 Feb 1919- Park
Zoro H (h/o H R) 1886-1955 Onan
ROBERTSON, Edgar Cornelius s/o E W & Belle B 8 Feb 1895-5 June 1896 Onan
Edgar Marion s/o E W & S F d 23 July 1872; age 0/2/2 Onan
Edgar Waples h/o S F 2 Oct 1845-11 Dec 1923 Onan
Dr John William h/o L P 8 July 1887-28 Sept 1981 Onan
Lula Price w/o J W 2 Jan 1885-26 June 1980 Onan
Mary D w/o Wm d/o Saml & Sa-bra Waples 26 Nov 1827-2 Oct 1862 Onan

230

ROBERTSON (continued)
Sabra M d/o Wm & M D 26 Aug 1851-8 June 1865 Onan
Sue F w/o E W d/o Fred B & Rose Fisher 12 Jan 1848-19 Oct 1878 (or 79) Onan
Sue F d/o E W & S F 26 Sept 1879-25 May 1899 Onan
Sylvester Jr nd Snea
Thomas Britton 1883-1925 Onan
ROBINSON, s/o Jno T & Emma P b&d 18 Apr 1904 Onan
baby boy b&d 1970 Holl
Carrie Lee w/o Wm N 1908-1968 Park
Frances 1921-1969 Metr
John H 1890-1960 Ayre
John T 30 Aug 1876-29 Apr 1919 Onan
Mary S 1900-1978 Shil
Col Tully 31 Aug 1658-12 Nov 1723; age: 65/0/20 (restored by his 3rd gr grdau Henrietta D Ayres Sheppard - 1923) Poul
William 1898-1965 NewM
William N h/o C L 1904- Park
ROSELLE, Ralph V d 23 Jan 1974; age: 74/7/24 HTri
RODGERS, see also **ROGERS**, s/o W T & C F b&d 30 May 1884 Onan
Abel s/o Robt & Tabitha 1778-1845 Ropl
Abel R s/o Robt & Tabitha 25 Mar 1784-1 Feb 1820 Ropl
Alfred B G s/o S F & A T P 13 Apr 1885-1 Apr 1917 Onan
Alice T Pitts w/o S F 3 Jan 1861-8 Dec 1933 Onan
Arthur M 8 Nov 1824-20 Feb 1892 Bogg
Asa J Esq s/o Robt & Tabitha 18 Jan 1794-2 Dec 1845; age: 52 yrs Rodg
Carrie W w/o W F 24 Jan 1860-25 May 1914 MtHo
Cordelia Frances w/o W T d/o Zarobabel C & Hester A Mason 29 Jan 1852-23 Nov 1936 Onan
Edward 1904-1981 NewM
Eliza E w/o J K 8 Oct 1813-20 Nov 1880; age: 67/1/12 RodP

RODGERS (continued)
Elizabeth 26 Apr 1841-26 Feb 1916 Bogg
Elizabeth F w/o W S d/o Thos W & Sally Finney 10 Jan 1825-13 Mar 1883 Onan
Euphamey w/o Levy 19 Mar 1778-10 Mar 1826 Rodc
George M s/o Arthur M & Mary E 18 Mar-27 July 1873 Bogg
George W s/o W S & E F 18 Jan 1855-20 Dec 1856 Onan
John K h/o E E 22 Jan 1823-10 Apr 1879; age: 56/2/18 RodP
John R s/o W F & C W 17 Nov 1886-4 Oct 1918 MtHo
Capt John T s/o J K & E E 31 Mar 1850-8 Sept 1885; age: 35/5/8 RodP
John T 1 July 1900-9 July 1966 Park
John T F 30 June 1887-19 Oct 1958 Onan
Josephine d/o G S & Bell d 10 Oct 1913; age: 28 yrs NewM
Levy h/o Euphamey 1767-21 Apr 1819 Rodc
Lizzie d/o G W & Bell d 15 Feb 1911; age: 26 yrs
Lucy Ann d/o Levi & Euphamey d 2 Apr 1824; age: 16/1/22 Rodc
Peggy S d/o Robt & Tabitha 8 May 1798-5 July 1800 Ropl
Rachael (3rd w/o Wm W) 22 Oct 1784-13 Dec 1858 (Member of M E Church) Bogg
Raymond R w/o Levy & Euphamy 9 Mar 1810-15 Apr 1820 Rodg
Richard s/o Robt & Tabitha 31 Jan 1776-11 Aug 1814 Ropl
Robert h/o Tabitha s/o Abel & Rosey 29 June 1753(or 55)-14 Dec 1827 Ropl
Sarah d/o Robt & Tabitha 27 Nov 1778-28 Jan 1843; age: 64/2/0 Ropl
Smith s/o Robt & Tabitha 15 Apr 1787-18 Nov 1795 Ropl
Spencer h/o A T P 12 July 1856-16 Nov 1939 Onan

RODGERS (continued)
Spencer Finney Jr 9 Jan 1892-20 Sept 1950 Onan
Tabitha w/o Robt 22 Jan 1755-28 Nov 1824; age: 69/10/6 Ropl
Virginia 9 June 1920-13 Nov 1955 Onan
Virginia Nelson w/o W H F 15 July 1889-30 June 1947 Onan
W Harry Finney h/o V N 13 Aug 1886-31 Aug 1929 Onan
W Thomas h/o C F 8 Jan 1851-25 Jan 1914 Onan
William A M s/o Arthur M & Mary E 29 Jan-18 July 1868 Bogg
William F h/o C W 10 Sept 1847-18 Feb 1896 MtHo
William S h/o E F s/o Wm W & Eliz Smith Kellam 9 Dec 1813-26 Oct 1866 Onan
William W (1st wife Susanna Smith, 2nd Eliz Smith Kellam wid, 3rd wife Rachael Boggs) 26 Jan 1785-19 Mar 1856 Bogg
ROGERS, see also **RODGERS**,
s/o W P & L B b&d 23 Dec 1909 MtHo
d/o W P & L B b&d 31 Jan 1920 MtHo
Althia Winder w/o J W 1856-1924 MtHo
Alvin 1954 Shil
Andrew 1890-1965 NewM
Anna T 1909-1974 NewM
Annie C w/o J B 1883-1956 NewM
Arizona J 26 May 1912-15 Dec 1979 NewM
Azie Parks 1901- Onan
Blanch S 1887-1973 StPa
Carl 1902-1981 Shil
Charles Finney 1923-1964 Onan
Charles H h/o M H & M E 5 July 1852-9 May 1923 Onan
Elmer A s/o J W & A W 1 Oct 1882-9 July 1883 MtHo
Emory J "Sam" 1899-1973 Onan
Eula (w/o H J) 25 Apr 1889-3 Feb 1981 Onan
Eva H 1904-1933 NewM
Frank 1880-1957 NewM

ROGERS (continued)
George Augustus s/o Geo S & Margt d 17 Aug 1840; age: 4/0/17 Holb
George E 10 Jan 1891-13 Oct 1961 Ayre
George F 1918-1954 StPa
George S (h/o M J) 10 Jan 1810-24 Jan 1879 Holb
Henry h/o Claris d 17 Sept 1890 Shil
John B h/o A C 1876-1966 NewM
John H 1910-1975 Gask
John Houston s/o Geo S & M J d 18 Dec 1839; age: 7/2/4 Holb
John West h/o A W 1858-1928 MtHo
Lena B w/o W P 7 Dec 1883-15 Jan 1936 MtHo
Lois G 1917-1979 NewM
Louis J 1895-29 Dec 1963; age: 68 yrs Gask
Louis M s/o Geo S & M J 11 Feb 1841-18 Aug 1864 (Ensign C S A) Holb
Louis P 13 Nov 1805-3 Aug 1888 Holb
Margaret J w/o Geo S d 5 Dec 1884; age: 74 yrs Holb
Maria Louisa d/o Geo S & Margt d 13 Aug 1849; age: 19/0/19 Holb
Mary 1905-1958 Shil
Mary S 1903-1966 Shil
Mollie E 2nd w/o C H 6 Oct 1865-3 July 1938 Onan
Monnie H 1st w/o C H d/o Jno R & L M Boggs 9 Jan 1853-15 Sept 1881 Onan
Ralph 1914-1973 Gask
Stella F d/o C H & M E 4 Nov 1891-16 Aug 1892 Onan
W Pitts h/o L B 24 Feb 1883-30 Jan 1946 MtHo
William 1905-1978 NewM
William Perry s/o Geo S & M J d 28 Oct 1849; age: 15/8/18 Holb
William S s/o C H & M E 16 Aug 1890-15 July 1891 Onan
ROLAND, Harold C 1941-1971 MtHo-s

ROLLEY, Elmer Ames (h/o K T) 26 June 1895-2 Nov 1981 Fair
Katherine T (w/o E A) 8 Nov 1896- Fair
Paul Slocumb 13 June 1919-31 Oct 1982 Fair
ROSE, Arinthia S (w/o Wm H) d/o Wm & Rachel Bell d 29 Dec 1893; age: 66/8/3 Thos
William H (h/o A S) 10 Oct 1833-9 Mar 1879 Thos
ROSELLE, Joseph G h/o L S 1861-1946 HTri
Lottie w/o J G 1865-1938 HTri
ROSS, (ROSSE),
baby boy b&d 1964 MtHo-s
Benjamin T 25 Oct 1865-22 Dec 1943 Park
Bettie S 3 June 1854-12 Feb 1932 StGe
Bettye E (w/o J T) 1900- Edge
Bransford M h/o Thelma J 1920-1975 Park
Bruce E w/o W A & D B 20 Mar 1909-19 June 1923 StGe
Charles B h/o M P 1875-1955 Park
Charles K s/o Thos B & Catherine 18 Feb 1884-27 Oct 1903 Evan
Charlie H 1870-1975 MtHo
Charlie H 1907-1965 Onan
Daisey B (w/o W A) d/o Jno & Hester P Bennett 7 Apr 1880-9 Mar 1975 StGe
Dorothy E (w/o Murice) 1921-1978 MtHo-s
Edward B s/o J M & S A d 11 Oct 1841; age: 4 yrs Ross
Edward G 6 Jan 1904-19 May 1947 Wach
Emma Daisey 1884-1980 Park
Emma Evans 1879-1971 StGe
Ernest C 30 Jan 1897-3 Mar 1955 Park
Ida A 1875-1950 MtHo
India Watson w/o L J 10 Feb 1841-25 Jan 1923 Edge
Jack T (h/o B E) 1897-1974 Edge
Jacob M h/o S A 3 Mar 1807-15 Apr 1878 Ross

ROSS (continued)
Jean d/o T R & R W 1922-1928 Park
John H s/o J M & S A 15 Dec 1845-28 Mar 1890; age: 44/3/13 Ross
John J Wise s/o S T & M A 10 Nov 1890-11 Jan 1974 Edge
John P Jr 11 May 1922-12 Aug 1937 Park
Kate B w/o T B 13 Dec 1856-17 Oct 1926 StGe
Kathryn Custis w/o S J 29 July 1896-18 Aug 1968 Edge
LillianWhite w/o W L 19 June 1885-5 Oct 1961 Edge
Lisa Mae b&d 1968 MtHo-s
Lizzie C w/o W H 1894-1968 Fair
Louis J h/o I W s/o Jacob M & Sarah A 29 Sept 1835-14 Feb 1913 Edge
Manie P w/o C B 1880-1977 Park
Margaret Ann w/o S T 2 Aug 1855-4 May 1926 Edge
Murice (h/o D S) 1919-1978 MtHo-s
Novella Baker Anley w/o T R 1912- Park
Roberta A 23 Jan 1872-7 June 1966 Park
Samuel Jacob h/o K C s/o S T & M A 19 Oct 1888-10 Feb 1937 Edge
Samuel Taylor h/o M A 9 Mar 1843-21 Feb 1920 (Judge of Court 1889-1904) Edge
Sarah A w/o J M nee Taylor 20 June 1809-21 Apr 1887 Ross
Terry Lee 1964-1965 Park
Thomas B 1852-1932 StGe
Thomas R Sr h/o N B A 1894-1966 Park
Walter A h/o Daisey B s/o Thos B & Kate B 25 June 1878-8 Nov 1932 StGe
William July 1943-Aug 1980 Park
William B 8 Sept 1898-12 Aug 1937 Park
William H s/o J M & S A d 15

ROSS (continued)
Nov 1858; age: 25 yrs Ross
William H h/o L C 1893-1964 Fair
William L Jr 1919-1983 Edge
William Louis h/o L W s/o L J & I W 10 Aug 1874-22 May 1944 Edge
ROSSEY, Elizabeth J w/o Jacob d 26 Nov 1912; age: 73 yrs MtHo
ROTHAUGE, Sallie d 27 Nov 1895; age: 33 yrs Libe
ROWLES, Elizabeth West w/o Major b 26 Aug 173- (stone broken) OldW
Fannie J w/o Jas C d/o J W & S A Gillespie 8 Aug 1861-24 Aug 1894 Park
Susana w/o John 1 Jan 1743-10 Jan 1790 OldW
ROWLEY, Connie W b&d 1951 Park
Emma Read 1876-1943 StGe
Lawrence E h/o M J 1909-1959 Park
Margaret J w/o L E 1910-1982 Park
Marion B Jr s/o M B & Irene b&d 1949 Park
Noah James 28 Aug 1946-22 Sept 1973 Park
Orris J Jr 1913-1984 Park
ROYAL, Ralph (h/o Jean) 1881-1954 Holb
RUE, see also REW,
Albert J h/o I S 1850-1941 Park
Bessie R w/o T J 1886-1964 Fair
Caressa Scott (1st hus J R Scott) 6 Nov 1882-19 Dec 1963 Edge
Ida S w/o A J 21 Jan 1861-8 Dec 1919 Park
James A 30 Sept 1894-29 Mar 1916 Park
Thomas J h/o B R 1881-1950 Fair
Ziporah M d/o Benj & M A Davis 8 Apr 1837-Apr 1870 TheG
RUEDIGER, (RUDIGER),
Emmeline H 1863-1947 Fair
Ernest (h/o L B) 1890-1954 Fair
Francis C 1917-1973 Fair

RUEDIGER (continued)
Frederick E (h/o E H) 1863-1956 Fair
Irene B 1902-1959 Fair
John H 1911-1967 Fair
Lola B (w/o Ernest) 1893-1958 Fair
RUSSELL, Adeline V b&d 1922 MtHo-s
Annie C d/o Wm J & C A 7 Dec 1877-20 Oct 1894 Libe
Annie Olivia d/o H T K & M E P 4 June 1852-24 Apr 1917 Park
Benjamin H s/o Wm S & M E 18 May 1881-19 Aug 1900 Libe
Benjamin N b&d 1907 Libe
Bernard F 11 June 1918-12 May 1973 Fair
Caroline F C w/o Saml d 19 July 1838; age: 20 yrs Park
Catherine A w/o Wm J 27 June 1841-7 Feb 1924 Libe
Charles F (h/o E C) 11 May 1887-5 Oct 1963 Fair
Charles Hayden 3 Mar 1906-22 Nov 1976 Fair
Claude C h/o G M 1903-1981 Libe
Dianne Louise d/o H L & Bertha L 1961-63 Libe
Dorothy L w/o E W 1895-1959 Park
Edward J h/o V F 1 May 1844-29 Nov 1922 Libe
Edward T s/o E J & V F 7 Feb 1870-12 Oct 1873 Libe
Edward W h/o M E 1872-1907 Libe
Edward W h/o D L 1893-1962 Park
Effie W w/o W T 11 June 1881-11 Sept 1910 Libe
Elizabeth d/o E J & V F 31 Mar-30 Apr 1878 Libe
Elizabeth (w/o G F) 1898- Fair
Elizabeth E w/o S T 27 May 1849-28 May 1913 Libe
Elizabeth J Lewis 25 Sept 1840-16 Sept 1925 Libe
Ella 1904-1950 StJo
Emaline B 1866-1951 Libe
Eva C (w/o C F) 25 Mar 1886-18

RUSSELL (continued)
June 1937 Fair
Fred 21 Sept 1895-26 Jan 1980 Park
Fred L w/o J E & S A 16 Oct 1868-19 May 1895 Park
Garland T h/o Tressa 1907-1979 Libe
George A 1920-1943 Fair
George F (s/o G W & S J) 30 Jan 1881-22 June 1933 Libe
George F (h/o Eliz) 1877-1972 Fair
George W h/o S J 14 Mar 1853-26 July 1921 Libe
George W s/o Wm S & Mary; gr s/o Southey Sherwood 22 July 1870-25 Feb 1902 (grad: Randolph Macon College AB 1892, AM 1893, Johns Hopkins Univ 1897-8) Libe
Gladys M w/o C C 1908-1967 Libe
Gorman Parker h/o P S 1 Dec 1892-14 Feb 1974 Libe
Henry T Kitsun s/o Sarh 24 Mar 1819-25 Nov 1863 Park
Ina Vivian (w/o M R) 9 Aug 1903-22 Jan 1947 MtHo-s
Isabelle W w/o P S 1895- Libe
James A h/o N B 1869-1955 Park
Jennie E w/o W R 10 Aug 1853-22 Feb 1912 Libe
John Dickerson s/o Jno T & Mary S d 17 Oct 1866; age: 0/10/9 Coke
John E h/o S A 15 Apr 1840-18 Mar 1913 Park
John E 1894-1941 Libe
John T d 4 Feb 1873; age: 41 yrs West
John W 1827-1912 Papl
John W h/o P E 24 Dec 1873-19 Oct 1962 On{n
Laura L w/o Wm J 4 May 1873-11 Mar 1936 Park
Leah Dunton Mar 1883-11 Feb 1922 Burt
Lena Johnson w/o Vernon 6 Mar 1896-1 Jan 1959 Park
Lillie May w/o S T 1891-1960

RUSSELL (continued)
Libe
Margaret E w/o E W 1865-1948 Libe
Mary E w/o Wm S 1851-1938 Libe
Mary Ellen Poulson w/o H T K 14 Apr 1830-15 Oct 1907 Park
Milton R (h/o I V) 5 Dec 1903-3 July 1980 MtHo-s
Nora B Albright 1889-1962 Libe
Nora Belle w/o J A 1873-1965 Park
P Stewart h/o I W 1892-1973 Libe
Paul Guy 1904-1969 Libe
Pauline Satchell w/o G P 3 Nov 1895-11 Apr 1976 Libe
Peggy E w/o J W 25 May 1876-5 Dec 1937 Onan
Robert C 17 Apr 1926-16 Feb 1945 Fair
Roy J 1899-1901 Libe
Ruth F 1885-1914 Libe
Sallie A w/o J E 12 May 1840-16 Nov 1926 Park
Sallie J w/o G W 3 Jan 1863-7 Aug 1917 Libe
Sallie J d/o S T & Eliz E 2 Oct 1870-2 July 1916 Libe
Samuel E 1859-1943 Libe
Samuel R 1875-1962 Libe
Samuel T h/o L M 1887-1964 Libe
Sidney P s/o E J & V F 2 Sept-30 Oct 1879 Libe
Susan J 1852-1938 Libe
Sydney Luther s/o Jno T & Mary S d 18 May 1868; age: 4/4/9 Coke
T Frank h/o T J 1868-1956 Libe
Tabitha J w/o T F 1871-1902 Libe
Thomas s/o E J & V F 3-10 May 1881 Libe
Tressa w/o G T 1906- Libe
Vernon (Dink) h/o L J 12 Oct 1900-22 Sept 1971 Park
Vianna F w/o E J 24 Dec 1847-5 Nov 1867 Libe
Vianna F d/o E J & V F 23 Oct 1867-21 Sept 1868 Libe

RUSSELL (continued)
Vinnie L 1878-1950 Libe
W R h/o J E 25 June 1851-14 Aug 1935 Libe
W T h/o E W 24 Nov 1874-12 Sept 1968 Libe
Walter F 1892-1911 Libe
Waren E 1922-1923 Libe
William J h/o C A 1825-6 Feb 1911 Libe
William J h/o L L 17 Nov 1870-2 Oct 1954 Park
William S h/o M E Sherwood s/o Thos & Sally Feb 1849-Oct 1913
William T s/o E J & V F 23 Aug-6 Nov 1874 Libe
Willie N s/o T F & T J 25 Apr 1890-30 May 1911 Libe
Zella B 1883-1950 Libe
Zora T 1879-1958 Libe
RYAN, Clarence Nolen 21 Jan 1891-6 Apr 1970 Fair
S, E footstone only Ches
S, S U footstone only dated 1833 Wapl
SALISBURY, India Watson (w/o W H) 1904- Fair
William Henry (h/o I W) 1903-1964 Fair
SAMPLE, ____ 1927-1967 Shil
inf/o Edith b&d 1955 StPa
Asa 7 Jan 1843-2 Apr 1922; age: 79 yrs NewM
Bedella 1905-1978 HTri
Clifton P 26 Feb 1915-7 Oct 1978 NewM
Edie Aug 1901-July 1904 Burt
Edith 1903-1955 StPa
Edward 1906-1979 Shil
Elijah 1902-1963 Snea
Eliza D w/o L T 1908-1974 Burt
Florie W 1905-1977 Snea
Forrest 1900-1967 Burt
Frank Roger 6 Jan 1896-11 Jan 1978 Shil
Fred D 1895-1969 HTri
George D 1910-1981 Shil
Harriet 1906-1962 Gask
Ida nd (prob d 1977/8) Shil
John 1910-1967 Gask
John Henry s/o Jno T & Racilla

SAMPLE (continued)
31 Dec 1878-14 Apr 1895 Gask
Joseph 22 Oct 1918-19 Sept 1972 Burt
Joshua h/o M L 18 Jan 1890-15 Nov 1972 Snea
Lenora T 1895-1962 Metr
LeRoy 1912-1983 Gask
Levin T h/o E D 1906-1949 Burt
Maggie 26 Oct 1873-13 Nov 1927 Burt
Maggie d/o J T & Pricilla 21 Feb 1887-21 July 1907 Gask-old
Marion H 1879-1967 NewM
Mary Etta d/o Isaac & Maggie 15 Jan 1899-16 Feb 1903 Burt
Mary L w/o Joshua 1885-1968 Snea
Oscar d 6 Dec 1957; age: 63 yrs Burt
Otelia 1894-31 Oct 1961; age: 66 yrs HTri
Patricia Ann 1954-1962 Burt
Tennie S 9 June 1858-18 Dec 1928 NewM
Virginia D 1889-1969 Shil
SANABRIAS, Margline 1908-1959 Snea
SANDIDGE, Ann Powell 1 Sep-7 Nov 1941 Wach
SARENTINO, Louis S 1913-1973 Fair
SARSITIS, Theodore J 1908-1971 Fair
SATCHELL, A M 29 Sep 1874-15 Apr 1951 Libe
Armenda K w/o J H 5 Oct 1853-18 Nov 1936 Park
Bertie J 1885-1965 Libe
Beverly D 25Oct 1884-16 Oct 1918 Holl
C h/o S E 24 Nov 1835-31 Mar 1915 Libe
Carroll 1889-1953 Shil
Charlie 10 Jan 1901-19 Oct 1906 NewM
E B w/o S S 20 Aug 1808-15 Mar 1887 Edge
Elmer T 1910-1962 Libe
Eunice 10 Apr 1929-10 July 1978 NewM

SATCHELL (continued)
George Samuel 1936-1969 HTri
George W 1 Jan 1900-26 Jan 1965 HTri
Georgia M 1903-1959 Shil
Hattie 22 Sept 1862-19 Jan 1923 HTri
J Thomas 24 July 1879-26 July 1942 Park
James Henry h/o A K 21 Oct 1849-10 Apr 1939 Park
James L 1908-1979 Libe
John Sr 1900-1965 Shil
Maniel nd Libe
Margaret Teackle w/o Christopher d 1 Oct 1846 Parr
Mary E w/o T P 4 Nov 1831-4 June 1897 Onan
Morris L nd Libe
Otha T 21 July 1894-15 Sept 1960 HTri
Rachel 1866-6 Nov 1938 Shil
Richard G 1889-1961 Gask
Saida 17 Mar 1895-13 Aug 1911; age: 16 yrs NewM
Sidney 1919-1963 NewM
Dr Southey S h/o E B 20 Sept 1801-21 Nov 1873 Edge
Susan E w/o C 7 July 1841-21 Sept 1919 Libe
Thomas P h/o M E 28 Apr 1838-24 Aug 1921 Onan
Tom nd (probably 1980/1) Shil
William R 1884-1959 NewM
SATCHER, Edward 1882-1953 Fair
Mavis M 1913-1958 Fair
SAULSBURY, Virginia E d/o Henry & Mary 3 Mar 1867-29 July 1885 Onan
SAUNDERS, Joseph d 11 Sept 1962; age: 54 yrs Burt
SAUTTER, Alfred (h/o R L) 6 Aug 1884- Edge
Rebecca L (w/o Alfred) 15 Oct 1874-26 Oct 1955 Edge
SAVAGE, d/o H P & E W b&d 23 Sept 1919 MtHo
baby d 7 Jan 1963; age: 0/2/0 Gask
A Thomas 1889-1919 Onan
Alphonso s/o Betsey dc1917

SAVAGE (continued)
Savs
Amy Frances d/o F H & F T 25 July 1911-20 Sept 1912 MtHo
Ann B w/o Jas K; d/o Jno Harmon 7 Apr 1808-10 Apr 1892 SavH
Anna Kellam w/o G S 1849-1928 Savv
Annie M w/o W S 1886-1950 MtHo
Annie W d/o B W & Reba M 1 July 1915-19 Mar 1921 Park
Arinthia M (w/o E M) 1895-1971 Holl
Bagwell T d 29 May 1878; age: 47 yrs BTSa
Benjamin T h/o N C 1868-1939 Edge
Bertie P Bell w/o W H 8 Feb 1893-3 Feb 1918 Wach
Betsey dc1910 Savs
Beulah A w/o R N 1913- Fair
Bryan W 1890-1962 Park
Catherine J d 2 Mr 1911; age: 84 yrs Oakg
Charles B h/o M C 26 Apr 1850-1 Apr 1912 MtHo
Charles R h/o S H 1882-1968 MtHo
Charlie 1938-1980 Gask
Charlotte Elizabeth 29 Mar 1851-24 Sept 1919 Sava
Cordie D w/o E J 1862-1936 MtHo
David 28 Aug 1920-16 July 1976 Shil
Earl Jackson s/o E S & V E 1925-1944 Park
Earl S h/o V E 1904-1963 Park
Edward 1891-1959 Metr
Edward G s/o Edmond J & Eliz 21 Jan 1820-22 Aug 1881; age: 61/7/1 Sava
Edward G 19 Mar 1881-16 Oct 1959 Edge
Edward J h/o M E 28 Aug 1823-9 May 1873 MtHo
Edward J h/o C D 1848-1929 MtHo
Edward L 1898-1958 HTri
Edward M (h/o A M) 1892-1929

SAVAGE (continued)
Holl
Edward N h/o N M 1889-1955 MtHo
Elijah T 1881-1959 NewM
Elizabeth G w/o E G 16 May 1829-4 Apr 1895; age: 65/10/18 Sava
Elizabeth R (w/o R T) 1846-1930 Onan
Ella H 9 Jan 1862-16 Dec 1952 Edge
Ernest L h/o S S 1892-1968 Shil
Ernest T 1888-1962 Shil
Ethel West 1880-1967 Wach
Evelyn Walter w/o H P 29 Oct 1892-7 Feb 1971 MtHo
Florence Twyford w/o F H 1874-1936 MtHo
Capt Francis d 20 Sept 1823; age: 73 yrs Coal
Frank Howard h/o F T 1876-1941 MtHo
G G 1875-1952 NewM
George 30 Mar 1822-23 Aug 1863 Home
George d 16 Feb 1911; age: 71 yrs Oakg
George 1902-1954 NewM
George 1915-1977 Shil
George 1928-1959 NewM
George B (h/o N B) 1888-1963 MtHo
George L 15 Aug 1893-24 June 1944 NewM
George Lloyd s/o G B & N B b&d 30 Jan 1920 MtHo
George P Bagwell 1891-1982 MtNe
George S s/o Jacob & Mary 6 Sept 1801-13 May 1864 Savv
George S (h/o A K) 1840-1900 Savv
George T h/o M R 1886-1978 Bays
Georgie 1891-1952 HTri
Grace B (w/o J W) 1906-1950 Fair
Grace Drmmond 1872-1959 Fair
Harrison nd NewM
Harry 1908-1971 Metr
Harry W 1909-1969 NewM

SAVAGE (continued)
Hattie T d 17 Jan 1962; age: 76 yrs SavN
Herman Parks h/o E W 13 Feb 1892-23 Aug 1964 MtHo
J Custis 1927-1979 Shil
J Robert h/o L N 1895-1977 Onan
J Walter h/o L E 1899-1967 Edge
James A D 22 Nov 1845-1 Apr 1912 Wach
James B s/o W S & A M 27 Feb 1912-6 Sept 1914 MtHo
James E 6 June 1851-13 Feb 1934 Edge
James I 1900-1945 Libe
James K h/o A B 9 Aug 1808-16 Oct 1853 SavH
James L 12 Apr 1839-17 Dec 1898 Bads
James R (h/o N B) 1897- MtHo-s
James R 29 Feb 1952-13 Oct 1972 Shil
James Robert 17 Sept 1925-10 July 1927 MtHo-s
Jane Ella 1904-1969 Shil
John s/o Major & Susan 1823-1885 Savb
John B 1908-1974 HTri
John Braidwood 9 Apr 1875-12 May 1949 Wach
John E Sr 13 Nov 1885-30 June 1976 Shil
John H (h/o M C) 1890- MtHo-s
John H 1929-1979 Gask
John R h/o Josephine 1869-1961 Onan
John R 14 May 1929-13 Nov 1974 Onan
John T h/o P F 18 July 1851-11 Nov 1924 Park
John T d 17 Mar 1966; age: 76 yrs SavN
John W h/o M M 26 Oct 1879-21 June 1940 Park
John W (h/o G B) 1904- Fair
Joseph Donald Sr 1 Oct 1932-9 Jan 1982 Fair
Joseph H 15 Mar 1841-15 July 1920 Savg

SAVAGE (continued)
Joseph Herman 24 Aug 1909-4 June 1964 Fair
Joseph L (h/o M T) 1877-1964 Fair
Josephine w/o J R 18 Oct 1877-18 May 1911 Onan
Julius 1946-1976 NewM
Karl L 1916-1968 Quin
Lawrence 1918-1978 NewM
Leah d 31 Aug 1823; age: 60 yrs Coal
Lena E h/o T J 1877-1954 MtHo-s
Lena Nock 1899-1971 Gask
Leroy 12 Nov 1934-11 Jan 1972 Gask
Levin 1897-1950 NewM
Lida H 1895-1978 Onan
Lillian E w/o J W 1900-1966 Edge
Lillian N w/o J R 1912-1940 Onan
Liza Cordelia d/o Geo & Anna d 5 Feb 1888; age: 0/6/6 Hero
Lloyd J h/o S D 1859-1936 MtHo
Lloyd Warner s/o L J & S D 23 Oct 1899-23 Dec 1900 MtHo
Lula G 1901-1981 Metr
Maggie 1885-1961 HTri
Maggie Emma 7 Sept 1853-11 June 1938 Wach
Major s/o Roling & Eliz 8 May 1793-1 Oct 1855 Savb
Margaret A 1 Mr 1830-13 Mr 1911 Oakg
Margaret M w/o J W 1 Dec 1885-7 July 1975 Park
Margaret S w/o B T 16 Aug 1825-15 Mar 1911 MtHo
Martha R w/o G T 1896-1965 Bays
Mary C w/o C B 13 Feb 1850-12 May 1921 MtHo
Mary C (w/o J H) 1899- MtHo-s
Mary E w/o E J 25 Dec 1829-18 July 1901 MtHo
Mary E d/o E J & M E 16 Oct 1857-30 Apr 1858 MtHo
Mary Jane d/o Major & Susan 6 Mar 1837-3 Apr 1855 Savb
Mary M w/o Jas T; d/o N B & E

SAVAGE (continued)
G LeCato 26 Sept 1840-31 Aug 1867 (bur with her infant son) Quin
Mary S 1919-1965 Burt
Mason s/o J W & M M 16 Sept 1901-18 Feb 1904 Park
Mattie T (w/o J L) 1881-1963 Fair
Maude 23 Apr 1880-22 Sept 1940 Ptea
Millard J s/o J T & P F 25-31 Nov 1903 Park
Missouri 1896-1960 Guin
Nannie M w/o E N 1893-1978 MtHo
Nellie B (w/o G B) 1888-1962 MtHo
Nola B (w/o J R) 1899-1981 MtHo-s
Nola F d/o E G & E G 8 Oct 1865-20 Aug 1873 Sava
Nonia C w/o B T 1870-1964 Edge
Peggy Ann d/o R N & B A 1 Jan-17 Mar 1939 Fair
Polly F w/o J T 8 Nov 1859-10 Apr 1948 Park
R Thomas (h/o E R) 1839-1916 Onan
Rachel E 1887-1956 HTri
Reion 1911-1959 Bays
Roland T 21 Dec 1890-9 Apr 1975 Edge
Rose J (w/o W L) 1919- Fair
Rosey w/o Wm; (nee Trader) d 25 June 1820; age: 32/2/0 Trad
Roy W s/o J B & M S 16 June 1906-14 Nov 1913 Home
Rufus N h/o B A 1909-1967 Fair
Sadie D w/o L J 1862-1939 MtHo
Sallie 1880-1961 NewM
Sara Hoge d/o L J & S D 5 May 1902-15 May 1918 MtHo
Sarah S w/o E L 1895- Shil
Sudie H w/o C R 1886-1977 MtHo
Suehester 1911-1978 NewM
Susan w/o Major 1803-1872 Savb
Sylvanus 1929-1983 Gask
T Chester 1887-1966 MtHo

SAVAGE (continued)
Thomas J h/o L E 1854-1939 MtHo-s
Veeda T d/o W S & A M 12 Jan-11 July 1905 MtHo
Virginia E w/o E S 1904-1976 Park
W R 18 Nov 1857-7 Nov 1917 Ptea
Warner Thomas s/o L J & S D 2 Nov 1891-8 July 1892 MtHo
Warren L 1884-1953 Park
Wilfred L (h/o R J) 1906- Fair
William (h/o Rosey) d 15 Nov 1815; age: 31 yrs Trad
William J 6 Jan 1832-22 June 1896 Oakg
William J 13 June 1920-3 Mar 1977 Fair
William S h/o A M 1879-1959 MtHo
William T h/o Rosa d 22 Oct 1897; age: 79 yrs Savl
William Wharton 23 Apr 1886-10 June 1911 MtHo
Willie U 1901-1961 Metr
Willmore 1900-1932 HTri
SAWYER, Evelyn M w/o W B 1909- Libe
Willie B h/o E M 1899-1983 Libe
SCARBOROUGH, (SCARBURGH), Alfred 1889-1967 NewM
Americus h/o M J; s/o Americus & Rachel d 6 May 1852; age: 53/1/0 MtHo
Ann P, 1st w/o Wm M; d/o Arthur & Eliz Teackle 8 Jan 1790-4 Oct 1817 Hedr
Bessie M d/o I S & M H 6 Oct 1909-13 July 1915 MtHo-s
Cassey wid/o Geo; d/o Jno & Eliz West 19 May 1777-29 Apr 1859; age: 81/11/10 Fair
Charles 1643-1702 member of Governor's Council (erected by VA Cons Comm 1947) Scam
Charles h/o Eliz; eldest s/o Col Edmd & Mary nd (1643-1702) Scag
Charlotte G 12 May 1912-16 July 1971 StGe

SCARBOROUGH (continued)
Edmund - Govern General of VA 1618-1671 (placed by VA Conservation Comm 1947) Hedr
Edmund B h/o M M 1864-1940 Wach
Edmund B 7 July 1940-10 May 1968 (VA Capt, Co C 60 Inf 9 Div Vietnam) StGe
Eleanor Keaton 1850-1933 Onan
Eliza M, 2nd w/o Wm M 11 June 1797-24 July 1873 Hedr
Elizabeth w/o Chas nd (d1719) Scag
Flora B 1891-1971 Park
George 1902-1976 NewM
George D 1845-1933 MtHo
Harriet Jane d/o Wm M & A P d 31 Jan 1813; age: 3/2/0 Hedr
Harry A h/o R W 1860-1922 Wach
Harry B h/o V L 1909-1947 Wach
Harry Lee s/o H B & V L 1935-1937 Wach
Harry T h/o K B 1883-1958 Park
Haywood 1935-1976 NewM
Helen Tyler 1878-1965 Edge
Henry T s/o Americus & Mary J d 15 June 1856; age: 20/2/7 MtHo
Ina M (w/o I W) 1889-1969 Wach
Ira Stewart h/o M H 1879-1941 MtHo-s
Ira W (h/o I M) 1885-1954 Wach
Jennie F w/o T J 20 Nov 1857-1 Jan 1928 MtHo-s
Jessie C (w/o W H) 1887-1954 Quin
Joseph B 1890-1891 MtHo
Kate B w/o H T 1886-1949 Park
Mamie M d/o W H & J C 25 Nov 1908-12 Jan 1917 Quin
Margaret A d/o Geo & Ann 10 Aug 1803-2 Sept 1881; age: 78/0/22 Fair
Margaret M w/o E B 1871-1945 Wach
Mary D 20 May 1897-31 Oct 1978 Shil
Mary H w/o M F; d/o Jno &

SCARBOROUGH (continued)
Mary Pyle Young 2 Feb 1838-20 Nov 1910 Wach
Mary H w/o I S 3 Dec 1887-9 Feb 1923 MtHo-s
Mary J w/o Americus d 27 Feb 1855; age: 48 yrs MtHo
Minnie R b&d 1880 MtHo
Mitchell F h/o M H; s/o Americus & Mary Turlington 29 May 1834-3 June 1912 Wach
Neta V d/o W H & J C 2-20 Aug 1915 Quin
Rebecca Sarah 1875-1938 MtHo
Rhetta W w/o H A 1864-1944 Wach
Robert W 1933-1969 Wach
Rodney 1970-1972 Burt
Sarah Satchell d/o Geo P & Mary S J 25 June 1838-21 Aug 1853 Bowm
Southey Satchell s/o Geo P & Mary S J 27 Nov-16 Dec 1841 Bowm
Stanley A 1895-1972 Wach
Stewart T 7 Mar 1922-11 Feb 1934 MtHo-s
T J h/o J F 30 Mar 1853-18 Feb 1930 MtHo-s
Thomas Blackstone s/o Dr Geo T & Henrietta (Blackstone) 11 Oct 1875-24 Jan 1935 Edge
Virginia Catherine 1873- MtHo
Virginia E 1844-1890 MtHo
Virginia L w/o H B 1912- Wach
William Edward s/o Wm M & A P d 16 June 1815; age: 0/8/0 Hedr
William H (h/o J C) 1877-1955 Quin
William M (h/o A P & E M) 16 June 1786-29 Mar 1821 Hedr
SCHAEFER, Leo John 19 May 1915-4 Oct 1971 Park
SCHAPER, Kenneth H 28 June 1923-22 May 1973 MtHo-s
SCHERER, Frances w/o Dr Geo; d/o Geo & Margt Hack 29 Aug 1790-17 June 1837 Shir
SCHILLING, Edward J (h/o H P) 1895- Onan
Helen P (w/o E J) 1896-1975

SCHILLING (continued)
Onan
SCHOOLFIELD, Evelyn 1918-1978 Shil
SCHULTZ, Edward P h/o E W 1888-1958 Onan
Elizabeth Westcott w/o E P 1886-1969 Onan
William s/o E P & E W 20 Jan-2 Aug 1914 Onan
SCHUNK, Bessie R (w/o Herman) 1893- MtHo-s
Herman (h/o B R) 1904-1948 MtHo-s
SCHURBY, Florence 1890-1974 Bays
SCOTT, s/o Tully W & Rachel A 30 Mar-6 Apr 1881 Harr
inf/o G R & M J b&d 1887 MtHo
d/o T C & M S b&d 25 Dec 1913 Onan
d/o Geo & Sue b&d 16 Mar 1944 Libe
baby Jacobs b&d 19 Dec 1948 MtHo-s
A T h/o M A 10 July 1845-20 July 1909 Onan
A Thomas (h/o M F) 1899-1975 Edge
Alfred B 1896-1951 MtHo-s
Alfred Henry (h/o B Y) 1875-1967 Onan
Alice C w/o A W 1900-1980 Park
Annie Causey w/o J S 28 Sept 1876-25 May 1970 Libe
Annie Martin w/o I W 5 Jan 1883-5 Aug 1966 MtHo
Annie Milliner w/o Walter 27 June 1895- Edge
SCOTT-ACKLEY, Arinthia J w/o J T 16 Nov 1846-11 June 1901 Libe
SCOTT, Arinthia W w/o J D 1863-1954 Edge
Arnold Parramore s/o Ezer & Margt 11 Sept 1890-3 Dec 1903 Edge
B J 16 Mar 1902-9 May 1918 Edge
Beatrice 1921-1983 Fair
Benjamin T h/o H M 1888-1979

SCOTT (continued)
Libe
Betty S w/o W M 17 Feb 1858-3 Sept 1929 Onan
Blanche H (w/o J T) 1916- Fair
Blanche Young (w/o A H) 1886-1979 Onan
Bobby L 1931-1973 Fair
Brady J 1887-1951 MtHo-s
Carrie G 1902-1952 Shil
Catherine (mother/o Ann C Joynes) d 24 Dec 1865; age: 76 yrs Joyn
Catherine J 1872-1971 Libe
Cecil B 1891-1943 Onan
Charles R h/o M C 22 Feb 1864-4 July 1939 MtHo-s
Charles T (h/o M S) 1874-1953 Onan
Clara E (w/o JT) 1886-1946 Fair
Claude F 1905-1934 MtHo-s
Cora E (w/o J D) 1871-1957 MtHo-s
Daisy H (w/o F B) 1883-1967 Edge
Dallas Hall s/o Woodland & Nina Lee 12 Jan 1936-1938 MtHo-s
Dallas W (h/o L M) 1891- MtHo-s
David Ewell (h/o M B) 7 Oct 1898-2 Aug 1968 Fair
David M (h/o O M) 28 July 1873-14 Aug 1924 MtHo-s
David W h/o M L & I F 20 June 1843-26 July 1911 MtHo
Dorothy J 1911- Fair
Drummond J 1911-1977 MtHo
Edgar R h/o M B 13 Oct 1890-21 Nov 1933 Onan
Edward 1875-1958 MtHo
Edward M s/o J H & Kate J 11 Feb 1907-3 June 1912 Libe
Edward V (h/o L W) 1901-1973 Fair
Effie B 1879-1955 MtHo-s
Elic (h/o K S) 1863-1944 MtHo
Elizabeth w/o J E 1832-9 Oct 1898 ScoB
Elizabeth w/o G W 18 Feb 1810-18 July 1885; age: 75/5/0 StGe

SCOTT (continued)
Elizabeth P (w/o T C) 1846-1921 Onan
Elizabeth P w/o J R 1883-1970 Libe
Ella W (w/o J S) 24 Jan 1882-15 Apr 1945 Onan
Elsie D (w/o J E) 1927- Fair
Elsie Dize b&d 1949 Fair
Emma C Jones (w/o W F) 21 Oct 1880-27 Sept 1967 Fair
Emma L d/o Jno W & Mary B 10 Apr 1887-17 Aug 1888 Onan
Essie C (w/o R J) 24 Mar 1883-5 July 1968 MtHo-s
Ettlemond Winder 1882-1960 MtHo
Mrs Eva S 7 May 1874-27 Aug 1907 Park
F Walter 25 Mar 1893-22 Dec 1917 MtHo
Francis E h/o M H 22 July 1868-26 Apr 1925 Park
Fred B (h/o D H) 1884-1961 Edge
Fred D 1911-1975 Edge
G W (h/o J E Smith) 21 July 1883-10 Mar 1926 Holl
G Farring h/o H E 1893-1971 MtHo
Geneva d/o U M & M L 1906-1908 Onan
George E (h/o M E) 1885-1967 Fair
George H (h/o R A) 1880-1952 Holl
George O (h/o M H) 31 May 1902- Fair
George R h/o M J 20 Mar 1840-12 Mar 1915 MtHo
George R s/o G R & M J June-Aug 1885 MtHo
George R 1896-1969 MtHo
George T h/o M E 26 July 1861-17 Nov 1944 Libe
George T h/o S E 1864- .... Edge
George W (h/o Eliz) 29 Apr 1817-15 Oct 1902 StGe
Grover C 1885-1955 MtHo-s
H Fletcher 1877-1939 Edge
Harry W (h/o M R) 23 Aug 1880-20 July 1968 MtHo-s

SCOTT (continued)
Hazle E w/o G F 1896-1968 MtHo
Hazel M w/o B T 1903-1983 Libe
Henrietta J w/o T M 19 Sept 1843-23 Feb 1915 Onan
Herman W 28 Dec 1891-6 Nov 1920 Edge
Hester A d/o Jas E & Mary d 13 Mar 1882; age: 6/2/10 Bayg
Howard C 1915-1961 Wach
Hurley L (h/o M A) 1891-1959 Onan
Ida Fox, 2nd w/o D W 1857-1924 MtHo
Inez S (w/o J S Sr) 1921-1978 Onan
Ira Weldon (h/o S J) 1889-1955 Fair
Isaiah White h/o A M 11 Nov 1879-3 Mar 1952 MtHo
J Lynwood 1920-1969 Fair
J Talmage (h/o B H) 1907- Fair
James D h/o A W 1861-1953 Edge
James E h/o S E 23 June 1890-1 Sept 1958 MtHo-s
James E (h/o Eliz) d 8 Jan 1907; age: 82 yrs ScoB
James E (h/o E D) 1924- Fair
James Ettlemond 1909-1960 MtHo
James H h/o M A 1962-1950 Onan
John A (h/o P E) 23 Nov 1833-19 Feb 1907 Scop
John D (h/o C E) 1865-1959 MtHo-s
John H 1874-1917 Libe
John H h/o M S 1895- Park
John J h/o L E 24 Aug 1873-11 Oct 1956 MtHo
John R h/o E P 2 Sept 1885-18 Mar 1962 Libe
John Revell h/o C Scott Rue 2 Nov 1886-8 Aug 1949 Edge
John S (h/o E W) 2 Nov 1880-8 June 1957 Onan
John S Sr (h/o I S) 1919- Onan
John Selby h/o A C 13 May 1865-25 Feb 1943 Libe

SCOTT (continued)
John T h/o M S 1838-1899 Onan
John T (h/o C E) 1884-1946 Fair
John Thomas h/o A J 14 Oct 1838-21 Feb 1884 Libe
John W h/o M C 2 June 1849-14 July 1905 Onan
John W (h/o E B Harrison) 27 Mar 1882-23 July 1916 Onan
John W h/o M V 27 Jan 1909- Edge
Joseph A s/o Jno W & Mary B 19-27 Mar 1886 Onan
Joseph D h/o R T 1916-1982 Libe
Kate Parks w/o S T 20 June 1885-12 Oct 1978 MtHo
Katherine H 1860-1903 Onan
Katherine Forrest 1911-1977 MtHo
Kathryn S (w/o Elic) 1870-1954 MtHo
L Fletcher 1876-1945 Edge
Lillie M (w/o D W) 1893-1970 MtHo-s
Lionel C (h/o M D) 1888-1955 Onan
Lizzie H 16 May 1901- MtHo-s
Lottie W w/o W E 1872-1956 Edge
Louise W (w/o E V) 1904- Fair
Lucy E w/o J J 26 Aug 1876-16 June 1943 MtHo
Lucy P 1885-1927 Onan
Lula Mae 1885-1887 Park
Luther D (h/o M E) 1868-1957 Fair
Luther J 1857-1930 Onan
M Etta w/o S T 31 Jan 1893-3 July 1976 Libe
M Jeanette d/o W A & Naomi b&d 1938 Fair
Mae D (w/o L C) 1901-1982 Onan
Maggie A w/o J H 1860-1941 Onan
Maggie Marsh (w/o W S) 1894-1967 MtHo
Maggie R w/o Benj V; d/o A J & Eliz A Killmon 12 Aug 1886-2 Apr 1914 Onan
Maggie T d/o Tully & Rachel 26

SCOTT (continued)
Mar 1884-16 Nov 1898 (moved from Old Scott Farm) MtHo-s
Malinda H 1843-1931 Holl
Malissa H w/o F E 6 Aug 1865-20 Dec 1942 Park
Malissie W w/o O W 27 May 1892-11 Nov 1919 Park
Mamie B w/o E R 16 Jan 1891-13 Nov 1980 Onan
Manie E (w/o L D) 1875-1952 Fair
Manie E (w/o G E) 1888-1960 Fair
Manie V w/o J W 26 June 1912- Edge
Margaret 1848-1902 Park
Margaret C w/o Shalmaneser 29 Sept 1851-24 Aug 1902 Edge
Margaret F (w/o A T) 1900- Edge
Margaret H (w/o G O) 19 Nov 1903-21 Aug 1981 Fair
Margaret J w/o G R 27 Apr 1849-23 May 1899 MtHo
Margaret L, 1st w/o D W 10 Sept 1843-29 Nov 1881 MtHo
Margaret L 1887-1956 MtHo
Margaret S w/o J T 1849-1916 Onan
Margaret S (w/o C T) 1879-1959 Onan
Martha A d/o Jno W & Mary B 29 Apr-8 May 1877 Onan
Marvin M 1910-1963 Fair
Mary A w/o A T 28 Feb 1850-6 Jan 1923 Onan
Mary Ann 19 Aug 1914-26 Apr 1968 Onan
Mary C w/o J W 24 Dec 1853-20 July 1925 Onan
Mary C w/o C R 6 Jan 1866-8 Mar 1937 MtHo-s
Mary E w/o G T 5 Mar 1868-10 Apr 1933 Libe
Mary E d 28 Feb 1906; age: 53 yrs Onan
Mary L w/o U M 1878-1961 Onan
Mary Rebecca (w/o H W) 18 Nov 1882-21 July 1969 MtHo-s
Mary S 1900-1971 MtHo-s
Matilda Sue 20 Nov 1911-18 Mar

SCOTT (continued)
1927 MtHo-s
Messick 1917-1929 Onan
Mildred D (w/o P W) 13 July 1903-3 July 1968 Fair
Miriam Belote (w/o D E) 15 Aug 1898- Fair
Mollie S w/o J H 1894-1976 Park
Monnie A (w/o H L) 1893-1968 Onan
Morris E 1872-1957 Park
Myrtle 3 Aug 1889-27 July 1899 MtHo
Naomi P w/o W A 1908- Fair
Obed D h/o Minnie 22 May 1872-30 Jan 1909 Flet
Olevia B w/o W T 1883-1965 Edge
Olie J s/o W B & Louise b&d 1944 Park
Olie W h/o M W & A C 1888-1962 Park
Olivia M (w/o D M) 18 Aug 1875-15 Oct 1953 MtHo-s
Paul Benjamin 10 Mar 1893-25 Sept 1947 MtHo-s
Paul Winford (h/o M D) 22 Sept 1903-16 Dec 1970 Fair
Peggy 23 Nov 1882-23 Aug 1883 MtHo
Pheobie E 1882-1972 MtHo-s
Polly E w/o Jno A 1 Jan 1830-28 Feb 1896 Scbg
Rachel A (w/o T W) 1860-1936 MtHo-s
Rebecca A (w/o G H) 1882-1961 Holl
Reva T w/o J D 1918- Libe
Robert J (h/o E C) 24 Feb 1872-26 June 1933 MtHo-s
Roland J s/o Alen & Catherine 1 May-8 Sept 1886 MtHo
Roland Lee 25 Sept 1867-8 Apr 1937 Onan
Roxie L w/o Jno R 20 May 1887-18 Feb 1912 MtHo
S Tully h/o K P 8 Sept 1884-9 Jan 1918 MtHo
Sadie E w/o J E 19 Sept 1893-3 Feb 1932 MtHo-s
Sallie Catherine w/o T D 19 Oct 1853-29 Jan 1916 Onan

SCOTT (continued)
Sallie Finney Ashby 9 Oct 1883-18 Mar 1961 MtHo
Samuel S s/o G R & M J 17 Oct 1878-9 Aug 1881 MtHo
Samuel T h/o M E 18 Oct 1891-3 Dec 1947 Libe
Sarah J w/o T E 1919-1946 MtHo
Sarah Jane (w/o I W) 1885-1954 Fair
Shalmaneser h/o M C 4 Feb 1852-7 June 1903 Edge
Spencer L s/o Jno W & Mary B 4 Nov 1893-12 May 1894 Onan
Stella Judefind 14 Dec 1875-8 Aug 1970 Libe
Suddie E w/o G T 1871-1937 Edge
Sue A 6 Oct 1858-1 Jan 1941 Libe
Susie 20 Dec 1896-13 Nov 1906 Fair
T D 3 Feb 1870-6 Sept 1910 Libe
Tabitha 1820-1 July 1898 Onan
Thomas C (h/o E P) 1844-1921 Onan
Thomas E h/o S J 1916- MtHo
Thomas M h/o H J 13 Jan 1836-19 Jan 1913 Onan
Thomas Vaden s/o Ezer & Margt 27 Sept 1884-29 Dec 1887 Edge
Tully J 15 Jan 1860-12 July 1932 Libe
Tully W (h/o R A 1858-1936 MtHo-s
Upshur M h/o M L 1877-1943 Onan
Vernon W bro/o Lola S Parks 16 Aug 1906-8 June 1943 Park
Virginia B 14 Apr-23 June 1906 Onan
Virginia C 1875-1947 Edge
Walter 1843-1901 Park
Walter h/o A M 20 Mar 1895-15 Mar 1981 Edge
Walter 12 Oct 1919-12 Aug 1965 MtHo
Walter B Sr 16 May 1912-29 Sept 1974 Park
Walter F 1880-1953 Onan
Walter J s/o Ezer & M C 14 Sept

SCOTT (continued)
1881-9 Sept 1906 Edge
Walter K 1883-1948 Onan
Warner A h/o N P 1908-1979 Fair
Warner N s/o J D & A W 12 Apr 1909-11 Oct 1941 Edge
Washington B 3 Oct 1847-25 Dec 1916 Holl
Wellington M h/o B S d 25 Nov 1909; age: 59/7/25 Onan
Willard F 1 Oct 1867-25 Mar 1908 Libe
William 1831-1929 Wach
William E h/o L W 1869-1946 Edge
William Fox (h/o E C J) 14 Jan 1877-8 Dec 1957 Fair
William Samuel (h/o M M) 1888-1961 MtHo
William Thomas h/o O B 1880-1958 Edge
Willie 1844-1929 Wach
Winfield A 1845-1914 Holl
SEARS, William Henry 1880-1952 Snea
SEATON, James 1906-1978 Quin
SELBY, Allen T 1888-1981 Libe
David D s/o Zadock & Eliz 21 Nov 1808-11 Apr 1832 Gill
Elizabeth w/o Zadock; d/o David Dickinson & Hannah 23 Aug 1773-3 May 1835 Gill
Elizabeth S w/o Outten d 2 Apr 1874; age: 58 yrs Edge
Emma Marshall w/o J O 20 June 1851-28 May 1943 Edge
G Cleveland (h/o M K) 25 Dec 1892-21 Mar 1959 MtHo-s
John H h/o M V 17 Mar 1845-2 Jan 1918 MtHo
John Lloyd 3 Mar 1891-2 Jan 1947 MtHo
John O h/o E M; s/o Outten & Eliz 10 Oct 1837-30 Apr 1889; age: 51/6/20 Edge
John Soloman s/o J O & Emma E d 20 Mar 1880; age: 1/11/12 Edge
Lester 1917-1977 Gask
Major E h/o T A 1855-1928 Libe
Mary Kate (w/o G C) 8 June

SELBY (continued)
1896-24 Mar 1977 MtHo-s
Mary V w/o J H 15 Feb 1855-10 Sept 1927 MtHo
Onie F d/o J O & Emma F 24 July 1875-8 Aug 1926 Edge
Outten h/o E S 21 Nov 1810-30 Jan 1878; age: 67/2/9 Edge
Tealy Shreves 1886-1967 Libe
Tillie A w/o M E 1856-1928 Libe
Winnie P 1886-1961 Libe
Zadock s/o Zadock & Tabitha 7 Mar 1769-27 May 1833 Gill
SERINI, Trent R 16 Nov 1926-18 Oct 1980 MtHo-s
SEYMOUR, (SEYMORE),
Ada K 1890-1941 Snea
David 1919-1983 Burt
Elizabeth w/o Rev Wm 8 June 1771-18 Jan 1811 SeyS
Dr Hugh Gordon s/o Rev Wm & Eliz of Acco Co VA 22 Sept 1797-30 May 1855; age: 57/8/8 SeyS
John E h/o M F 1902-1978 Gask
Mamie F w/o J E 1903-1977 Gask
Tom 1905-1976 Burt
Rev William (h/o Eliz) 1 Oct 1773-24 Oct 1821 SeyS
SHACKELFORD, C Ray h/o J H 1886-1966 Wach
Johanna H w/o C R 1893-1948 Wach
SHANHOLTZER, Vesta Lewis 1 July 1908-6 Feb 1981 Libe
SHARPLEY, Bertha Tull (w/o E P) 9 Aug 1877-3 Mar 1942 Wach
Edward P (h/o B T) 18 Sept 1876-21 Aug 1956 Wach
SHAW, Willard E 1 Jan 1922-23 Feb 1978 Quin
Willard F 2 Mar 1952-21 Nov 1976 Quin
William E 1900-1973 Quin
SHECKLER, Leta 1913-1982 Fair
SHELLY, Charles F 1909-1981 Fair
SHELTON, Elmer (h/o M K) 4 Oct 1897-26 Sept 1976 Onan

SHELTON (continued)
J C 1874-1928 Onan
Margaret B 12 July 1905-31 Mar 1981 MtHo-s
Mollie K (w/o Elmer) 19 Sept 1895-8 Aug 1966 Onan
SHEPPARD, Jessie 1892-1964 NewM
SHERWOOD, Addie Lee 1910-1970 Libe
Alice L w/o J L 1884-1959 Libe
Elizabeth w/o Revel; m/o South-ey & Jacob Sherwood d 20 Oct 1859; age: 70 yrs Sher
George R s/o Southey & Susan 9 Dec 1852-16 Aug 1853 Sher
Jacob 5 Aug 1817-3 Feb 1902 Sher
John L h/o A L 1882-1957 Libe
John L h/o V C 1912- Libe
Joseph (G or C) h/o S A 5 July 1849-14 Feb 1912 MtHo
Levin F h/o M E 18 Dec 1854-14 Feb 1936 Libe
Margaret E w/o L F 11 Aug 1857-14 Apr 1928 Libe
Sarah A w/o J G (1st hus - Jno H Bradford) 11 Aug 1837-5 June 1915 MtHo
Southey (h/o Susan) 18 Jan 1821-20 Sept 1901 Sher
Southey W s/o Southey & Susan 4 Jan 1855-14 Sept 1864 Sher
Susan w/o Southey 6 Nov 1827-8 Jan 1883 Sher
Viola C w/o J L 1917- Libe
SHETZLINE, Adam 2 Mar 1844-4 Aug 1916 Park
Burnetta Rew 14 Feb 1844-16 June 1920 Park
SHIELD, (SHIELDS),
inf/o L J & R D b&d 20 Feb 1915 Edge
Amy H (w/o T J) 15 Apr 1909-11 July 1962 MtHo-s
Bessie Gean d/o T J & A H 1941-1944 MtHo-s
Billy West s/o F R & M W 22 Feb 1926-9 Feb 1931 MtHo-s
Charles W bro/o N S & E D 9 July 1907-4 Apr 1957 Gask
Dorothy W 1914-1974 Ptea

SHIELD (continued)
Edith D sister/o N S 1902- Gask
Franklin Ray h/o M W 25 Dec 1881-1 Jan 1947 MtHo-s
Helen E 1926-1965 Burt
James B 1860-1926 Wach
James D 19 Mar 1927-4 May 1942 Edge
James David s/o Luther Ray & Nancy (Wessels) 15 Dec 1952-1 Jan 1953 Edge
James H 28 Feb 1893-11 Jan 1868 StPa
James T 1890-1963 NewM
Jerusalem 1871-1942 Burt
Jessie T 10 Jan 1895-4 Oct 1918; killed in Battle of Argonne Edge
John C (h/o M D) 1873-1944 Wach
Littleton L h/o V F 1871-1960 Edge
Lola Mae 5 Dec 1892-19 Sept 1938 NewM
Louise Seymore 1914-1953 Burt
Luther Jacob h/o R D 1885-1959 Edge
Margaret Custis w/o R L; d/o Thos E C & Bettie M 16 Sept 1862-6 Sept 1937 Onan
Margaret West d/o F R 16 July 1889-4 Nov 1960 MtHo-s
Martha B 1863-1956 Edge
Mary D (w/o J C) 1877-1952 Wach
Mary G w/o S K; d/o Jno & Polly Ames 11 Jan 1821-6 Jan 1902 MtPl
Nellie S sister/o E D 1904-1974 Gask
Permelia 1842-1913 Wach
Rebecca Davis w/o L J 1891- Edge
Robert B 22 Nov 1904-5 June 1932 Edge
Robert Clayton only ch/o R L & M C 2 Dec 1896-4 Mar 1910 Onan
Robert Lee h/o M C 18 Apr 1862-11 Dec 1923 Onan
Samuel K h/o Mary; s/o Jas & Ann 25 Aug 1816-27 Oct 1887

SHIELD (continued)
MtPl
Sarah Mae d/o T J & A H 1934-1944 MtHo-s
Silvia w/o Ismael; d/o Peter & Margt Mears 3 Dec 1835-8 Feb 1881 Burt
Sudie 1874-1953 Burt
Thomas B 11 Oct 1800-2 Jan 1842 Onan
Tully J (h/o A H) 16 May 1910-9 Oct 1974 MtHo-s
Virginia F w/o L L 1875-1957 Edge
William E 1867-1924 Wach
SHIPLEY, Alice Lee d 4 Feb 1936 Libe
Manie L 1884-1966 MtHo-s
Mary Elizabeth d 17 Sept 1906 Libe
Robert Pilson nd Libe
Sallie A 24 Dec 1844-22 Feb 1918 Onan
SHIRE, Emily 1902-1978 Onan
SHORES, Harold H (h/o K B) 1899-1966 Onan
Kathleen B (w/o H H) 1911- Onan
SHORT, Alfred W h/o A C 14 Dec 1852-12 Apr 1929 Park
Alice C w/o A W 7 Oct 1856-8 Feb 1925 Park
Hiram J h/o M L 1874-1947 Libe
James W 30 Dec 1908-9 Sept 1974 Libe
Johnnie Thomas 27 Nov 1951-9 Jan 1957 Libe
Mazie L w/o H J 1888-1949 Libe
Tammy Jane b&d 19 Nov 1964 Libe
William Lee b&d 18 Mar 1974 Libe
SHREAVES, (SHRIEVES, SHREVES),
infant b&d 1908 Libe
s/o Chas T & Jennie D b&d 26 Oct 1914 Libe
s/o T P & N B b&d 3 Jan 1929 Holl
baby girl b&d 1972 Libe
Addie B (w/o W L) 1910-1974 MtHo-s

SHREAVES (continued)
Alfred J (h/o M G) 1896-1977 Fair
Alfred M h/o Emma 1876-1942 Onan
Alice B w/o H Lee 16 Dec 1873-5 Sept 1954 Park
Annie M w/o Bowdoin 14 Apr 1849-18 Apr 1918 Park
Augustus D h/o E C 20 Apr 1861-22 Apr 1927 Park
Barton L 3 June 1913-22 May 1973 Edge
Benjamin F 17 May 1871-11 Sept 1903 Ptea
Bessie 1917-1968 Onan
Bessie N w/o U D 1884-1962 Park
Bettie D w/o Wm T 1870-1954 Park
Bowdoin h/o A M 17 Oct 1848-18 Oct 1924 Park
Carrie w/o G C 1890- Edge
Carson J 1907-1966 Onan
Clarence L s/o T W & D H 28 May 1886-28 Aug 1888 Libe
Cora L w/o H F 1876-1946 Libe
D F footstone only - D F S Park
Dallas D 7 Apr 1897-28 Aug 1913 MtHo
Damey H w/o T W 11 Jan 1840-3 Nov 1937 Libe
Danny W 1952-1978 Onan
Dorsie L 13 Mar 1882-6 Nov 1912 Onan
Drummond 1919-1984 Libe
Edgar R h/o R P 1878-1960 Fair
Edna J w/o R L 1891-1969 Park
Edward R h/o S S 1859-1917 Park
Edward T 1915-1968 Edge
Eldridge T s/o J T & M A 3 Apr 1869-30 Jan 1897 Libe
Elizabeth A w/o Jno 14 Feb 1816-30 Mar 1905 Edge
Elizabeth Ann b&d 1945 Onan
Elizabeth F 1914- Onan
Ella D d/o L F & S J 16 July 1871-17 Nov 1886 Park
Elton J 1908-1939 Onan
Emma w/o A M 1879-1964 Onan
Emma C w/o A D 27 Aug 1856-

SHREAVES (continued)
31 Dec 1929 Park
Emma Mae w/o G F 1878-1945 Libe
Esther L w/o J E 1879-1934 Libe
Etta T (w/o L R) 1885-1945 MtHo-s
Eugenia J w/o J W 1845-1930 Libe
Fannie Elizabeth w/o J T 11 June 1843-4 Oct 1908 Holl
Fannie May d/o Jno T & Fannie 12 Apr-2 Aug 1888; age: 0/3/21 Holl
Fletcher W s/o T W & D H 26 Aug 1874-29 Sept 1888 Libe
Florence w/o G T 1912-1977 Park
Frank s/o B F & Ida M 30 May-30 Sept 1902 Ptea
Frederick Louis 5 Oct 1882-24 July 1963 Park
Fulton T 7 Jan 1920-29 Sept 1973 Onan
G Cleveland h/o Carrie 1885-1950 Edge
G Tommy h/o Florence 1914-1968 Park
Garry T h/o M C 1889-1951 Park
George Fletcher h/o E M 1883-1945 Libe
Grayson L 14 Feb 1911-15 Oct 1971 Libe
Grace L 1876-1949 Libe
H Lee h/o A B 17 Apr 1869-23 May 1940 Park
Hanson F h/o M R 1869-1938 Park
Harold E 1900-1977 Onan
Harry A 19 Apr 1896-6 Jan 1945 Park
Henry F h/o C L 1874-1943 Libe
Howard K h/o S L 1903-1981 Libe
Hurbert L s/o J W & M A 1 June 1890-22 Sept 1922 Onan
J T h/o F E 9 July 1840-4 May 1905 Holl
James A h/o G S Duke 1875-1933 Libe
James W h/o M A 21 Jan 1854-

SHREAVES (continued)
11 Feb 1928 Onan
Joe H 1894-1981 Libe
John h/o E A d 16 Mar 1873; age: c59 yrs Edge
John 1873-1938 Park
John E h/o E L 1873-1969 Libe
John T h/o M A 25 June 1840-14 Apr 1907 Libe
John T (h/o R H) 1869-1940 Holl
John W h/o E J 1845-1921 Libe
John W h/o R L 1872-1947 Libe
John W 1923-24 Park
Julia E 1895-1971 MtHo
Juanita Everett 18 Apr 1932- Park
Levin R (h/o E T) 1881-1964 MtHo-s
Lillian J 1907-1932 Park
Lillie Lankford 10 Nov 1884-19 May 1967 Park
Louis F h/o S J 1 Mar 1845-6 July 1920 Park
Louise E 1914- Edge
Lovie T w/o Jno E 29 Mar 1860-10 Feb 1919 Onan
Madora A w/o J W 1864-1950 Onan
Maggie A 1843-1937 Holl
Maine E 1869-1940 Libe
Manie C 1875-1896 Libe
Manie C w/o G T 1892-1973 Park
Marcella M w/o Ww T 1874-1973 Libe
Margaret A w/o J T 30 Sept 1843-19 May 1909 Libe
Margaret R w/o H F 1867-1948 Park
Margaret V (w/o W T) 1902-1969 Fair
Mariah G (w/o A J) 1905-1983 Fair
Mary E w/o T F 1855-1943 Park
Mary F w/o Wm S 1885-1941 Park
Mary Fletcher d/o G F & E M 2 Mar 1905-27 Sept 1923 Libe
Mary Frances w/o T W 1849-1931 Libe
Mary K w/o Shellie 1901- Park
Mary M w/o T F 1902-1970 Libe

SHREAVES (continued)
Melvin Lankford 18 May 1910-3 Aug 1962 Park
Merritt 1903-1970 MtHo
Mollie O 24 Sept 1894-12 Feb 1980 Park
Myrtle d/o Dorsey & Margie 20 Aug 1902-22 Feb 1903 Onan
Nannie B (w/o T P) 1890-1944 Holl
Oscar J 1890-1957 Onan
Pauline T w/o P S 1927- Libe
Preston S h/o P T 1921- Libe
Rinie H (w/o J T) 1870-1951 Holl
Rita Isdell 1940-1970 Libe
Robert J 1945-1967 Onan
Robert L h/o E J 1895-1971 Park
Robert N 14 July 1918-13 Feb 1981 Park
Rose P w/o E R 1880-1975 Fair
Roy F s/o P S & P T 1953-1969 Libe
Ruth Lewis w/o J W 1872-1941 Libe
Ruth M 1911- Edge
S Adrian 14 Oct 1902-27 Mar 1945 Libe
S Susan w/o E R 1861-1945 Park
Sallie R w/o S B 24 Nov 1872-15 Feb 1934 Libe
Sam R 1 June 1842-25 Mar 1904 Holl
Shellie h/o M K 1893-1970 Park
Sidney B h/o S R 22 Mar 1863-2 Mar 1943 Libe
Stanley B 21 May 1899-10 Sept 1930 Libe
Stanley T s/o T W & D H 15 May-22 Aug 1890 Libe
Stella L w/o H K 1900-1984 Libe
Susan J w/o L F 8 Sept 1845-17 Sept 1929 Park
T Purnell (h/o N B) 1878-1973 Holl
Thadeus W h/o D H 11 Oct 1850-2 Aug 1926 Libe
Thomas Wesley h/o M F 1846-1918 Libe
Tully F h/o M E 1856-1925 Park
Tully F h/o M M 1892-1960 Libe
Upshur D h/o B N 1884-1940

SHREAVES (continued)
Park
Vaughn L 1942-1954 Edge
Virginia Odom 11 Dec 1913-26 Sept 1948 Park
W Thomas 1918-1956 Libe
Walter W 22 Aug 1908-28 Mar 1962 Park
William H 1940-1941 Park
William L (h/o A B) 1907- MtHo-s
William S 1871-1926 Libe
William S h/o M F 1882-1958 Park
William T h/o B D 1871-1924 Park
William T h/o M M 1872-1952 Libe
Wilmer T (h/o M V) 1896-1960 Fair
SHULER, Janie Martin 20 Aug 1887-21 Nov 1976 StGe
SIGNER, Joyce Bradford w/o L E 19 Aug 1895- Edge
Lowell Eugene h/o J B 3 Sept 1902-30 June 1968 Edge
SILER, Mrs Bertha d 9 Aug 1954 NewM
SILVERTHORN, (stone broken) 1883-1982 Libe
d/o J R & M C b&d 8 Apr 1912 Libe
Ashton H h/o N T 1886-1948 Libe
Edward T h/o S F 1846-1911 Libe
Emma A w/o J C 7 June 1852-5 June 1934 Libe
John C h/o E A; s/o Wm & Mary 21 Nov 1841-18 Apr 1881 Libe
John R h/o M C 1883-1943 Libe
John Willroy 16 Aug 1871-15 July 1942 Libe
Mattie C w/o J R 1886-1973 Libe
Nona T w/o A H 1890- Libe
S C 7 Jan 1880-12 Dec 1922 Libe
Sallye F w/o E T 1853-1915 Libe
Sammie C Jr 30 May 1919-29 Sept 1972 Libe
Sidney C s/o J C & E A 23 Dec

SILVERTHORN (continued)
1874-6 Mar 1898 Libe
SIMMONS, Charles Okey 13-17 June 1955 Edge
Dreksel L 1976-1977 HTri
SIMPSON, Burley 1890-1975 Edge
Clarence 1881-1930 Edge
Edward 1886-1913 Edge
Fannie M 1902-1973 Libe
John Ray 1929-1968 Edge
John W h/o K W 1898- Edge
Kate W w/o J W 1908-1973 Edge
Larry 1892-1956 Snea
Mary Jane nd Edge
Thomas 1854-1928 Edge
Troy 1858-1937 Edge
SIMS, Elizabeth L w/o R K 1914- Edge
Russell K h/o E L 1913-1973 Edge
SINGLETARY, Angeline H 1865-1948 Libe
Annie L 1897-1970 Gask
SIRMON, G W 2 Dec 1860-18 Apr 1923 Quin
SISCO, Annie M (Deaconess) 1892-1981 Shil
William C (Deacon) 1886-1973 Shil
SKINNER, John 1891-1966 JoyC
SLAVIN, Amelia J 20 Dec 1889-21 Sept 1975 Fair
SLEDGE, Dr J T h/o W A 20 Oct 1852-21 Dec 1915 Park
Willie A w/o J T 24 Mar 1856-15 Jan 1936 Park
SLOCOMB, (SLOCUMB),
Austin Lee 21 Mar 1854-25 Feb 1923 MtHo
Frank Aydelott 4 Sept 1848-25 Mar 1892 MtHo
Guthbert Sewell h/o M S 12 May 1852-8 Feb 1916 MtHo
J Wallace h/o M B 1861-1924 MtHo
Mary Belote w/o J W 1876-1947 MtHo
Mollie S w/o G S; d/o Saml Thos & Mary (Barnes) Schoolfield 23 May 1873-26 Oct 1955 MtHo

SLOCOMB (continued)
Paul h/o Katherine Turner 2 May 1892-20 Nov 1921 (moved from Sycamores) Fair
SLOCOMB-ROLLEY, Paul 13 June 1919-31 Oct 1982 Fair
SLOCOMB, Susan Aydelott 8 Feb 1820-10 June 1906 MtHo
SMALL, Ella E d/o J E & N L 8 Dec 1907-27 Sept 1955 Edge
G Murman s/o J E & N L 17 Nov 1901-3 Mar 1954 Edge
John E h/o N L 20 Apr 1871-14 May 1962 Edge
Nora L Chandler w/o J E 13 Oct 1875-20 Jan 1929 Edge
Stewart F 26 Mar 1895-22 May 1971 Edge
SMITH, A Franklin (h/o M J) 1837-1925 Onan
A Garner s/o A H & Willie S 11 Mar 1900-1 June 1919 Holl
A H 1875-1947 (his children: Virginia Mapp; Myrtle Mears; Fay Penello; Garner Smith) Holl
Alfred 1896-1971 JoyC
Alice P w/o Jos A 6 Sept 1869-26 Apr 1900 RodP
Allen 1902-1980 StJo
Allie M d/o J A & Mattie C 1912-1913 Ptea
Amy C 1921-1969 NewM
Andrew James 9 Nov 1909-13 Mar 1972 Fair
Annie Joynes 1897-1958 Gask
Annie M d 31 July 1892; age: 90 yrs StGe
Annie S w/o W W 1890-1973 Onan
Bernard A 1955-1975 NewM
Bessie M 1905-1966 StJo
Bessie S (w/o J W) 1878-1958 MtHo
Bettie S d/o Jas T C & Georgia A 17 Dec 1860-14 Sept 1887 Crad
Carroll V 1912-1977 Holl
Catharine B w/o Thos H 9 Jan 1780-24 Nov 1853 Unde
Chandler P (h/o M H) 1908-1972 MtHo-s

SMITH (continued)
Charlie 1857-1941 Holl
Charlie 1905-1961 Burt
Donald C 22 Nov 1928-15 Feb 1974 Onan
Donnie 1942-1961 MtHo
Doris Lee b&d 1934 MtHo-s
E S G 23 Mar 1827-24 Feb 1908 Wach
Edgar J h/o J A 13 Sept 1853-5 Jan 1940 Wach
Edith Bull 22 Mar 1902-4 June 1969 Holl
Edith C 1942-1982 Shil
Edwin L s/o F S & E S 20 Nov 1871-7 July 1955 Coal
Effie I w/o Jno T 21 May 1872-6 Feb 1893 East
Effie S 1879-1926 MtHo
Eliza K Mrs d 9 May 1854; age: 65 yrs Hedr
Mrs Elizabeth (w/o Jno; d/o Col Tully Robinson) 25 Aug 1689-15 Dec 1759; age: 70 yrs (see Bible Records Vol. 7 in Clerk's Office, Northampton Co VA) Poul
Elizabeth C 11 Aug 1782-18 Oct 1843; age: 61/2/7 Coal
Elizabeth M w/o J A 1889-1968 Onan
Elizabeth S d/o Jno B & Sally 5 May-28 June 1832 Coal
Ellerson G 24 Nov 1893-22 Nov 1894 Crad
Elsie Hancock w/o J W 1919- MtHo
Emma B d 21 Nov 1962; age: 57 yrs NewM
Emma S w/o F S; d/o Rev L K & Margt Fosque LeCato 26 Sept 1847-22 Jan 1904 Coal
Erastus T h/o F R 25 Dec 1911-9 Dec 1974 Wach
Ethel S w/o G T 25 May 1879-20 June 1916 NewM
Eugene Anthony h/o Margt Scarburgh 26 Apr 1897-29 June 1978 Crop
Eunice S 1908-1951 Gask-old
Eva L 1911-1978 NewM
Ezekiel Y 8 Feb 1825-7 June

SMITH (continued)
1900 Ptea
Fannie 28 Feb 1885-16 Dec 1970 NewM
Fannie F d/o L M & Mary E 29 Dec 1895-29 Nov 1896 Ptea
Fannie R w/o E T 3 Sept 1913- Wach
Floyd L 1870-1949 MtHo
Frances M 1846-1927 Libe
Francis S h/o E S; s/o H G & Margt (Rodgers) 13 Feb 1841-11 July 1920 Coal
Frederick M 29 Oct 1910-15 June 1973 Park
Garland T 1906-1966 NewM
Garland T 1906-1970 Onan
George, MP d 15 Nov 1837; age: 61/2/6 Coal
George F s/o Jno B & Sally 2 Oct 1821-15 Sept 1822 Coal
George Floyd Sr 16 Mar 1919-8 Dec 1979 Fair
George Frank 16 Sept 1822-1874 Coal
George N s/o H G & M E d 31 Dec 1863; age: 20/3/0 Coal
Georgie C w/o Jas T C 2 Feb 1832-17 Oct 1897 Crad
Georgie E 1885-1945 Onan
H D s/o J E & M J 23 Dec 1897-2 July 1899 Coal
H E s/o J E & M J 4 Aug 1895-22 Aug 1898 Crad
Harry C h/o L J' 1887-1966 NewM
Harry W h/o I B 15 Aug 1894-24 May 1975 Libe
Harvey Lee b&d 1928 MtHo-s
Harwood R s/o H G & M E 10 Jan 1855-17 May 1933 Coal
Helen M 1924-1959 MtHo
Henry d 3 May 1912; age: 66 yrs Smit
Henry G 1918-1955 Fair
Herman C 1906-1960 Onan
Hezzie J 1925-1974 NewM
Howard S (h/o L P) 1923-1981 Onan
Hugh G (h/o M E) 18 Aug 1805-19 July 1879 Coal
Ida Belle w/o H W 27 July 1899-

SMITH (continued)
Libe
Capt Isaac 25 Apr 1772-10 July 1833; mar: 17 June 1802 - Margt Doughty Blen
Isaac s/o Wm W & Margt 8 Feb 1823-24 Sept 1878 Harr
James 1907-1946 NewM
James E h/o M S 23 Jan 1864-31 July 1945 Onan
James H s/o H G & M E d 1 Apr 1837; age: 1/8/12 Coal
James H s/o J E & M S 21 May 1898-12 Nov 1921 Onan
James T C h/o G C 15 Aug 1829-1 Nov 1918 Crad
Janie E Scott 2 Mar 1888-16 July 1956 Holl
Jessie L d/o F S & E S 16 Jan-20 July 1879 Coal
John d 12 Mar 1804; age: 64 yrs Coal
John Andrew 1897-1967 Gask
John C 1 Aug 1911-28 Feb 1965 Ayre
John E 1871-1941 MtHo-s
John E 14 July 1918-27 Aug 1966 Shil
John Henry 1884-1947 JoyC
John Henry Jr 1894-1951 JoyC
John L 1916-1981 MtNe
John R 1897-1957 MtHo-s
John S s/o Jno W & Mary Ann d 26 Oct 1850; age: 8 yrs Onan
John S 1842-1850 Onan
John W h/o M A 29 July 1814-6 Nov 1880 Onan
John W h/o M W; s/o Wm & Margt 3 Nov 1816-17 July 1892 Smip
John W (h/o B S) 1869-1944 MtHo
John W h/o M T 1874-1950 MtHo
John W 1892-1963 Fair
John Wilson h/o E H 13 Oct 1916-6 Oct 1977 MtHo
Joseph 1913-1976 NewM
Joseph Allen (h/o M C) 3 Mar 1870-1 Mar 1912 Ptea
Julia A w/o E J 21 May 1857-7 Feb 1915 Wach

SMITH (continued)
Julius A h/o E M 1885-1959 Onan
Julius T h/o M L 20 July 1895-22 Nov 1973 NewM
Kenneth 1949-1972 Burt
Leah d 8 Sept 1802; age: 3 yrs Coal
Lelia d/o H R & Rose L 26 Nov 1878-27 Dec 1897 Coal
Lettie J w/o H C 1888-1973 NewM
Lucille P (w/o H S) 1923- Onan
Lula F (w/o R F) 1876-1941 Onan
Maggie R 1900-1978 NewM
Malinda W w/o J W; d/o Covington & Sally Bennett 1 Feb 1817-6 Mar 1896 Smip
Mamie 1885-1978 JoyC
Manie E 1871-1941 MtHo-s
Margaret w/o Isaac 22 Nov 1779-21 Nov 1861 Blen
Margaret A 15 Nov 1825-2 Dec 1903 Ptea
Margaret E w/o H G 15 Aug 1814-11 June 1897 Coal
Margaret E F d/o H G & M E 17 Nov 1848-22 Apr 1920 Coal
Margaret S 1923-1969 NewM
Margie 1893-1967 Smit
Margie S w/o J E 1 Apr 1870-19 Dec 1939 Onan
Mary d 23 Oct 1820; age: 62 yrs Coal
Mary Ann w/o J W 25 Nov 1820-28 Dec 1858 Onan
Mary Ann 1923-1979 Park
Mary J (w/o A F) 1847-1922 Onan
Mary L w/o J T 12 Oct 1896- NewM
Mattie C w/o J A 11 Mar 1880-14 Nov 1944 Ptea
Mattie T w/o J W d1923 MtHo
Maude E 1900-1961 Gask
Minerva H (w/o C P) 1907- MtHo-s
Nathaniel S 29 July 1803-25 Jan 1872; age: 68/5/26 Coal
Neta C (w/o T E) 1892-1974 Fair
Norman H 1899-1979 Fair

SMITH (continued)
Ocelia A 4 July 1910-24 Nov 1979 Gask
Oran M s/o H G & M E d 15 Jan 1848; age: 2/0/21 Coal
Paul s/o F S & E S 3-11 July 1886; age: 0/0/8 Coal
Peter 1902-1982 Shil
Phillip C 1918-1955 Fair
Rachel M 1895-1975 NewM
Ralph F (h/o L F) 1865-1956 Onan
Rennie Johnson 12 Feb 1927- Libe
Robert 1942-1972 Burt
Rosette d 12 Sept 1961; age: 44 yrs NewM
Ruth C (w/o W S) 1900-1972 MtHo-s
Ruth K 1889- Fair
Samuel 10 Jan 1897-18 Mar 1952 JoyC
Samuel F 1849-1923 Libe
Samuel S 10 Sept 1920-2 July 1942 Libe
Sarah 1891-1979 NewM
Sarah B 1936-1967 HTri
Sarah H d/o Jas & Sally Garrison d 1 May 1838; age: 55/ 5/12 Coal
Spencer W 1824-1906 MtHo
Susan A w/o W S 1871-1924 MtHo
Susan E d/o H G & M E d 31 Mar 1837; age: 4/0/13 Coal
Susan G wid/o T W d 9 Oct 1904; age: 84 yrs ThoC
Susan H w/o Wm P 30 July 1822-20 Sept 1904 StGe
Thomas d 9 Oct 1941; age: 45 yrs Snea
Thomas Berkley s/o Thos Watt & Susan G 25 Aug 1853-11 Aug 1903 ThoC
Thomas E (h/o N C) 1889-1965 Fair
Thomas H h/o C B footstone only; headstone buried under tree roots. (Whl:815 Lt Thos H Smith took part in 1814 in the Battle of Puntoteaque (or Rumley's Gut) near Underhill

SMITH (continued)
Point. This was the nearest thing to a battle on the Shore in the War of 1812) Unde
Thomas W h/o S G 7 May 1801-23 July 1883; age: 82/2/16 ThoC
W Spencer (h/o R C) 1892-1966 MtHo-s
Walter W h/o A S 1888-1958 Onan
Willard T 1875-1958 Onan
William C s/o Jno B & Sally 29 Sept 1825-2 Sept 1829 Coal
William Robinson (s/o Jno & Eliz R) 30 May 1730-17 Dec 1759; age: 29/6/0 Poul
William S h/o S A 1861-1939 MtHo
Willie Ray s/o F S & E S June-26 Dec 1884 Coal
SMULLEN, Elmer C 6 June 1922-10 Dec 1965 Park
Emma T (w/o M F) 10 Jan 1897-14 Apr 1972 Fair
Howard S 5 Oct 1920-6 Dec 1971 Fair
M Frank 1861-1935 Edge
Marion F (h/o E T) 15 Feb 1895-27 May 1965 Fair
SNEAD, Annie R 1895-1977 Shil
Blanche 1897-1973 JoyC
Catherine S d/o Chas S & R B 14 Feb 1830-24 May 1865 SeyS
Charles W s/o Chas S & Rachel B 28 Mar 1837-4 Nov 1888 Scot
Christine 1881-1963 Metr
Clifton (unable to read) Metr
Constance d/o C W & S U 6 Nov 1871-2 June 1874 Scot
Cordie B 1900-1979 NewM
Edna H 1899-1979 Burt
Edward K s/o E K & Mary D 15 Mar-15 Aug 1858 Scott
Col Edward S h/o S U 1 Jan 1793-17 Mar 1853 Scot
Edwood 1921-1973 Burt
Elizabeth 1876-1960 Guin
Ellen 1867-1936 JoyC
Esther W w/o L L 13 Oct 1802-20 Jan 1880 Onan

SNEAD (continued)
Evelyn R 1886-1978 (by nieces Chestina & Sandra) Gask
Ferdinand 1905-1970 JoyC
Fitzroy d 6 Aug 1966; age: 66 yrs Padd
Flossie L 1906-1970 NewM
Frank d1924 StLu
George W 1916-1983 Burt
Georgie d 6 June 1964; age: 80 yrs Gask
Gilbert 1949-1967 Burt
Grover C 1896-1969 Burt
Henrietta A W d/o Thos & Ann 9 July 1803-4 Sept 1854 Recorded in 1940 in Snead fam plot which was moved to Onancock Cem. This stone is not among those moved. Unable to verify.
Rev Horace 1881-1934 Burt
Horace C 1904-1959 Burt
Ishmeal 6 Jan 1821-19 July 1902 Burt
James F 1930-1982 Gask
John A 1907-1974 Burt
John Dennis, MD s/o E S & S U 21 Nov 1830-18 Mar 1866 Scot
John Dennis s/o C W & S U 22 June-3 Sept 1870 Scot
John G s/o E K & Mary D 7 Apr 1863-6 Nov 1864 Scot
Josephine d1941 StLu
Leander 1916-1936 StLu
Leolion S 1896-1980 Gask
Lewis L h/o E W; s/o Tully & Rosetta 9 Mar 1802-3 Aug 1874; age: 71/4/24 Onan
Littleton L s/o Chas S & R B 4 Feb 1839-26 Dec 1857; age: 18/10/2 SeyS
Mrs Louisa nd MtNe(E)
Madeline 1883-1953 Burt
Major 1892-1962 JoyC
Margaret 1920-1951 Metr
Margaret Ker d/o Edwd Smith & Susan Upshur Dennis Snead Sept 1839-9 Apr 1933 Onan
Milton 1895-1925 JoyC
Norman 1906-1975 Burt
Percy Lee 19 Dec 1926-7 Jan 1981 Gask

SNEAD (continued)
Rachel B w/o Chas S 17 Dec 1803-16 May 1866; age: 62/4/29 SeyS
Susan Upshur w/o Col E S; d/o Jno & Eleanor Dennis of Somerset Co MD 20 June 1799-31 Jan 1864 Scot
Susan Upshur w/o Chas W 26 Feb 1838 at Ker Place-3 Feb 1930 Onan
Susan Upshur 26 Dec 1868-26 Dec 1957 Onan
Tabitha S Harmanson d/o L L & E W 15 Dec 1838-7 Jan 1872; age: 33/0/23 (moved from Snead fam plot) Onan
Vernon L 1925-1961 StLu
Vincent 1899-1918 Burt
William 1883-1958 JoyC
William J 1956-1982 Burt
Willie D 1956-1976 Burt
SNELLING, Matilda J 1848-1935 MtHo-s
SNYDER, s/o C L & S A b&d 1923 Edge
Charlie C (h/o M C) 1888-1933 Edge
Cleveland L h/o S A 1884-1962 Edge
Kathleen 1930-1983 Edge
Mary C (w/o C C) 1893-1948 Edge
Stella A w/o C L 1885-1962 Edge
SOMERS, (SOMMERS),
4 infs/o Isaac & D F b&d 1884, 1893, 1901, John - 1903 Park
Albert B h/o M L 13 Mar 1862-14 May 1943 Park
Albert Horsey 1 Oct 1865-10 Apr 1926 Park
Bertie Lewis w/o J H 1895-1971 Park
Bertie W w/o H C 1885-1944 Park
Charlie L 1874-1961 Park
Claude W s/o E T & E S 5 Nov 1890-12 Apr 1915 Park
Deliah F w/o Isaac 10 Feb 1862-21 Nov 1939 Park
Demariah d/o Wm & S C 17 Nov

SOMERS (continued)
1866-20 Nov 1879 Park
Douglas L h/o F L 1874-1938 Park
Douglas Lee s/o Wm & S C d 4 Jan 1872; age: 7/3/28 Park
Edward T h/o E S 22 Oct 1855-19 Jan 1937 Park
Elmer W 12 June 1883-5 Feb 1952 Park
Elvin H 13 Sept 1906-14 Dec 1951 Park
Emily S 8 Apr 1854-14 June 1942 Park
Emma S w/o E T 29 Nov 1857-24 Jan 1949 Park
Eveline W w/o G T 1839-1916 Park
Finney Warren Jr s/o F W & W P 6 June 1915-23 Feb 1917 Park
Finney Warren Jr s/o F W & W P b&d 1920 Park
Florence L w/o D L 12 Mar 1874-13 Nov 1965 Park
G Clifton s/o L J & M W 2 May 1895-28 July 1912 Park
Gay Patterson 1898-21 Oct 1918 (died while serving as volunteer nurse in influenza epidemic, Lynchburg VA) Park
Capt George T h/o E W 1834-1890 Park
Harold Wade s/o WL & Hazel 29 Jan 1925-2 Aug 1930 Park
Harry C h/o B W 1883-1954 Park
Harry Christhilf h/o Mildred Chesser; s/o Wm J & M A 7 June 1894-13 Dec 1933 Park
Hazel B w/o Capt Wm 19 Feb 1896- Park
Horsey h/o N R; s/o Isaac 1762-1852 Park
Capt Isaac h/o D F 14 May 1861-11 May 1929 Park
J Harrison h/o B L 1889-1970 Park
Jeanne d/o H C & M C 22 June 1922-28 June 1926 Park
John s/o Horsey; h/o Betsy Wessells; their sons: Richd, Jno, Wm, Geo, & Saml 1799-

SOMERS (continued)
1856 Park
John H s/o Saml & M W 21 Dec 1869-1 Sept 1905 Park
Capt John Horsey h/o Vianer; s/o J S & Eliz 12 Sept 1828-20 July 1907 Park
John O 17 Dec 1851-3 Dec 1916 Park
Joshua A h/o L E 7 July 1878-21 May 1965 Park
Lloyd J h/o M W 1868-1947 Park
Lula E w/o J A 1 Apr 1883-28 Nov 1952 Park
M Ralph 1920- Park
Manie L w/o A B 7 Jan 1865-11 Feb 1945 Park
Margaret Anna h/o Wm J 28 Aug 1856-26 Mar 1931 Park
Martha C w/o W C 1895-1976 Park
Mary F d/o Saml & M W 14 Aug 1880-8 Mar 1888 (b in Acco Co VA) Park
Mary W w/o Saml 14 Apr 1840-14 July 1917 Park
Mary W w/o L J 1869-1961 Park
Mollie E 1880-1966 Park
Nancy Rew w/o Horsey d1836 Park
Nona L w/o R R 1880- Park
Pearl P w/o W C 15 Apr 1892-13 Oct 1918 Park
Philip N s/o E T & E S 17 Mar 1887-4 Apr 1907 Park
Ralph 22 Sept 1884-6 Mar 1920 Park
Richard R h/o N L 1872-1924 Park
Roland L 19 Jan 1895-4 Aug 1980 Park
Dr Royal Thomas (dental surgeon) 5 Apr 1881-1 May 1964 Park
Ruth L 1905- Park
Sammy s/o A B & M L d age: 4 yrs (also 2 infants) Park
Samuel h/o M W 7 Jan 1836-12 Jan 1913 Park
Serrena C w/o Wm 21 Mar 1832-13 Apr 1907 Park

SOMERS (continued)
Sylvia S d/o F W & W P 10 July 1918- Park
Vernon Lee 1889-1918; USMC (killed in action - Belleau Woods, France on 6 June) Park
Vianer w/o Jno H d 22 Dec 1910; age: 79 yrs Park
W Clarence h/o M C 1891-1975 Park
Capt William h/o S C 30 Sept 1831-21 Feb 1904 Park
Capt William (Jack) h/o H B 4 Feb 1895- Park
William James h/o M A 15 Dec 1853-27 Feb 1929 Park
William Julius 7 July 1877-6 June 1906 (lost at sea enroute to Bahamas - body never recovered) Park
Winifred P w/o F W 19 Oct 1887-8 Nov 1982 Park
SOUTHALL, Ashton Conway 6 Apr 1878-9 Aug 1902 Onan
SOUTHARD, Joshua N 1880-1967 Fair
Mary E 1878-1965 Fair
SPADY, George M (h/o H M) 1927-1980 Onan
Helen M (w/o G M) 1934- Onan
SPANN, Sadie M 1913-1978 HTri
SPARROW, Bettie C 1 Mar 1867-12 Jan 1922 Ptea
C Harmanson (h/o R M) 1893-1958 Fair
Clara S w/o S W 1854-1924 MtHo-s
Collie E (h/o L R) 1891-1968 Edge
Elizabeth w/o Jas H 20 July 1859-8 Sept 1919 MtHo
Ella J d/o F W & E K 5 Feb-16 Aug 1896 Kilp
Ella K w/o F W; d/o L J & S M Killman 20 July 1873-5 Feb 1896 Kilp
Georgie only s/o Geo W & Laura F 10 Jan 1871-29 Oct 1880 Edge
Gershem B (h/o R C) 28 Aug 1888-17 July 1954 Fair

SPARROW (continued)
Harry T 1902-1940 MtHo-s
James W s/o Wesley L & Marian (Hart) 1946-1947 MtHo-s
Joseph J 1858-1934 StGe
Luella R w/o C E 1890-1979 Edge
Lula Mae d/o Jas H & Eliz 15 Sept 1885-11 July 1902 MtHo
Lulie B 1879-1926 StGe
Mamie S (w/o W M) 19 Oct 1893-23 Dec 1973 Fair
Marcellus W (h/o V E) 8 June 1855-25 June 1922 MtHo
Mary Ann d/o Wesley L & Marian (Hart) b&d 1949 MtHo-s
Ruth C (w/o G B) 12 July 1891- Fair
Ruth M (w/o C H) 1895-1970 Fair
Samuel W h/o C S 1850-1926 MtHo-s
Stephanie J 14 Oct 1916- Fair
Virginia E (w/o M W) 11 June 1862-14 Aug 1926 MtHo
W Mitchell (h/o M S) 3 July 1889-10 Aug 1974 Fair
William S 16 June 1884-19 Dec 1974 MtHo-s

SPENCE, Annie M w/o G C 27 July 1882-5 Aug 1902 Quin
Annie M 1888-1952 Quin
Arinthia 1884-1970 MtHo-s
Arthur T (h/o H V) 16 Aug 1904-19 Oct 1976 Quin
Bennie T s/o G C & A M 26 July 1922-8 Dec 1926 Quin
Charlie C 1907-1965 MtHo
Claude C s/o G C & A M 6 June 1911- Quin
Edward T 1894-1961 MtHo-s
Elizabeth Z (w/o G D) 1903- Quin
Geneva B 1913- Fair
George C h/o A M; s/o Joshua T 2 Feb 1881-10 Nov 1962 Quin
George Dewey (h/o E Z) 10 June 1899-26 July 1960 Quin
George H h/o M E 1856-1936 Onan
Hazel V (w/o A T) 1910- Quin
Ida M (w/o W J) 1887-1932 Quin

SPENCE (continued)
Isabel K (w/o M A) 1868-1968 Quin
John D 1900-1970 Fair
John M (h/o M E) 1862-1933 MtHo-s
Joshua T father/o G C 1856-27 Dec 1938 Quin
Lois b&d 1933 Quin
Manuel R (h/o G B) 1910-1970 Fair
Margaret E w/o G H 19 Jan 1857-9 Dec 1903 Onan
Martha E (w/o J M) 1876-1944 MtHo-s
Mary Ella 1899-1960 MtHo-s
Mitchell A (h/o I K) 1870-1937 Quin
Nellie d/o G C & A M 9 Oct 1914-1980 Quin
Norman R 1910-1961 MtHo-s
Richard 1867-1952 MtHo-s
Roosevelt 19 Nov 1904-28 Jan 1980 MtHo-s
Tavie 1903-1968 MtHo-s
Walten James (h/o I M) 1883-1966 Quin
Willie 2 Aug 1893-22 Aug 1968 MtHo-s

SPENCER, (SPENSER),
Annie J w/o G F 1885-1966 Libe
Edna B (w/o K R) 1925- Onan
George F h/o A J 1877-1960 Libe
Harold Stuart 1899-1964 Park
Kenneth R (h/o E B) 1921- Onan
Roberta Watts 1862-1943 Park

SPESSARD, Arlene L 1903-1973 Park
Esther C w/o O T 1914- Park
Orville T h/o E C 1896-1981 Park

SPIERS, Matilda servant, nd Burb
SPIVEY, William 1896-1957 Snea
SPRAGUE, Margaret L w/o S A 1888-1963 Park
S Mason 5 May 1912-2 Nov 1974 Park
Samuel A h/o M L 1885-1973 Park
William A 21 June 1925- Park

SPRY, Rev William itinerant

SPRY (continued)
   minister of the Phila Conf of the M E Church d 29 Nov 1847; age: 42/0/0 Coke
SPURLEY, Estella M 6 Jan 1904-28 Apr 1966 Libe
   William A d 18 Apr 1918 USA-QMC (erected by brother) Libe
STANT, Lemuel E 22 Jan 1896-8 Aug 1925 Edge
   Raymond S h/o S B 23 Mar 1865-10 Mar 1934 Edge
   Sarah B w/o R S 20 Dec 1862-11 Feb 1946 Edge
STAPLETON, M J 1896-1926 Park
STEINMETZ, Charlotte Quinby 10 Sept 1898-10 Jan 1975 Edge
STENGLE, Thomas Harold 4 Sept 1894-4 Sept 1950 MtHo
   Willie G 23 Oct 1872-25 Feb 1897 Onan
STEPHENS, see also STEVENS, Leonard 1894-1962 StJo
   Margaret Ann 1832-5 May 1881 Step
   Rike 1830-May 1883 Step
   Williams H, 1st h/o S S Middleton 1878-1903 Libe
STERLING, Annie J w/o Jno E d 23 May 1914; age: 66 yrs Onan
   C Randolph 1930-1984 Park
   Doris E w/o P J 1909-1966 Park
   Ethel B 1901- Wach
   George M h/o S T 1873-1918 Libe
   Ida Powell (w/o J E) 27 Apr 1872-29 July 1943 Onan
   James B (h/o P N) 1891-1954 Fair
   James H h/o O S 4 Aug 1833-4 Jan 1912 Edge
   John Edward (h/o I P) 18 Oct 1869-18 Feb 1950 Onan
   Capt John M 1 Jan 1881-27 May 1980 Edge
   Kathryn L d/o Mattie M nd Edge
   Lucille C (w/o R F) 25 July 1910-23 Feb 1976 Onan
   Mattie M nd Edge
   Olivia S w/o J H 25 Apr 1855-16 July 1934 Edge

STERLING (continued)
   Paul J h/o D E 1905-1959 Park
   Pearl Bryon d/o J H & O S 22 May 1897-10 May 1914 Edge
   Pearl N (w/o J B) 1894-1975 Fair
   Robert F (h/o L C) 6 Apr 1911-20 June 1979 Onan
   Sandra 1947-1949 Wach
   Sarah T w/o G M 1883-1980 Libe
   Vernon C 20 Nov 1893-5 Dec 1965 Wach
STEVENS, see also STEPHENS,
   Andrew H (h/o M E) 1870-1942 Holl
   Annie M (w/o G C) 1882-1965 Onan
   Arthur G h/o G K 28 Nov 1892-4 Jan 1973 Holl
   Bertha H 1896-1921 Holl
   Bessie 1906-1960 Gask
   Bettie 1904- JoyC
   Beulah L (w/o J T) 1893-1972 Wach
   Brooks L 29 July 1899-20 Sept 1900 Meap
   Charlie (h/o Vinnie) 1886-1970 Holl
   Charlie B 5 Oct 1908-18 Jan 1976 HTri
   Clifton 1913-1970 Holl
   Corrine 1912-1963 NewM
   Emma 10 July 1893-18 Aug 1958 Burt
   Ethel W 1907-1980 Shil
   Etta M (w/o J F) 1906- Holl
   Ettie 6 May 1838-7 Aug 1907; age: 69 yrs MtHo
   Eunice J 1894-1956 Holl
   Eva B (w/o U L) 1902- Wach
   Ewell Thomas (h/o L D) 20 Apr 1896-18 Aug 1960 Wach
   Florence 1909-1963 Shil
   Forrest H Sr 7 Oct 1926-20 Nov 1972 Mitc-w
   George 1892-1958 HTri
   George C (h/o A M) 1880-1967 Onan
   George Tom 1918-1978 Snea
   Gertrude A 1922-1966 Burt
   Gertrude Killmon w/o A G 5 Dec 1898-21 Nov 1972 Holl

STEVENS (continued)
Hattie C 1929-1960 Gask
Henry T 1873-1883 Mitc-w
Hyden 1926-1972 Mitc-w
J Earl 1916-1968 Libe
J Thomas (h/o B L) 1883-1967 Wach
James H 15 Mar 1840-27 Apr 1896 Mitc-e
James Henry h/o M C 1864-1941 Mitc-w
James Lee 1917-1974 Wach
Jeff F (h/o E M) 1891-1975 Holl
John A 1888-1961
John Otho (h/o R E) 1 June 1869-13 Feb 1926 Mitc-w
John T (h/o S A) 20 Nov 1835-23 Mar 1920 Mitc-w
Joseph H h/o M H 1867-1937 MtHo
Kelly d 16 Mar 1973 Mitc-w
Lawrence 1908-1977 Mitc-w
Leonard J 16 Feb 1896-9 Dec 1918 MtHo
Lois Davis w/o E T nd Wach
Madora F 24 June 1891-18 Nov 1927 Holl
Malissa Simpkins (w/o W C) 1886-1979 Mitc-w
Mary C (nee Parker) w/o J H 1867-1953 Mitc-w
Mary H w/o Harold 1894-1969 NewM
Mary J w/o Richd B 20 Oct 1870-4 Nov 1906 Burt
Mary M 1907-1979 NewM
Mary S 1897-1965 Burt
Mollie E (w/o A H) 1876-1968 Holl
Mollie H w/o J H 1870-1940 MtHo
Olevia J (w/o T L) 1876-1967 Wach
Page May 1894-15 Sept 1958 Burt
Robert J 1893-1967 Mitc-w
Rooker F 1915-1962 Holl
Rose E (w/o J O) 15 Oct 1874-6 Feb 1930 Mitc-w
Sallie A w/o J T 1840-1908 Mitc-w
Sarah Ann 1844-1936 Mitc-e

STEVENS (continued)
Sue 1920-1983 Onan
Thomas L (h/o O J) 1873-1933 Wach
Upshur L (h/o E B) 1891-1970 Wach
Vinnie (w/o Charlie) 1887-1975 Holl
Virginia B 1919-1981 Libe
William Columbus h/o M S 1871-1958 Mitc-w
William R 1924-1972 Gask
Wison 1906-1969 Gask
STEVENSON, see Stevenson bur gr in List of Sites,
Annie 15 June 1856-19 Apr 1932 Onan
Emma P 8 Sept 1859- Edge
Florence G 1858-1915 Edge
Isaac K h/o M A 23 May 1817-19 Dec 1890 Edge
John T 1 Jan 1866-29 Aug 1889 Edge
Mollie A w/o I K 6 Jan 1832-29 Nov 1877 Edge
O Milton (h/o R S) 1880-1951 MtHo
Rennie S (w/o O M) 1880-1974 MtHo
STEWART, Albert J d 27 Nov 1869; age: 60 yrs CutS
Alberta A (w/o C A) 1901- Fair
Catherine Sarah w/o P S 24 Dec 1854-19 Dec 1923 Onan
Charles A (h/o A A) 1898-1969 Fair
Charlie H 11 Aug 1923-26 Feb 1968 Gask
Cornelius Colonna 28 Mar 1870-27 Feb 1929 Wate
Elsie Mae 6 Feb 1861-1 July 1936 Onan
Dr Harold J s/o Preston S & Catherine W 1896-1975 Onan
John G s/o P S & C S 18 Apr 1881-11 June 1895 Onan
Levin C 27 Feb 1778-7 Jan 1817; age: 39/10/11 Stew
Margaret M d/o Preston & Catherine W 1875-1957 Onan
Preston S h/o C S 23 June 1850-29 Aug 1916 Onan

STEWARD (continued)
Tabitha S w/o Jas; d/o Tully & Rosella Snead; (wid/o Wm Joynes) 24 Oct 1797-17 Mar 1836 Onan
STILES, Abigal (w/o T W) 1 Nov 1837-4 Feb 1903 Wach
Agnes 16 Oct 1906-26 Jan 1907 Wach
Ayre O 29 Apr 1821-16 Apr 1902 Oakg
Eayre O (h/o E F) 1862-1939 Wach
Elexzine F w/o E O 1864-1939 Wach
Gilbert F (h/o M M) 3 July 1874-6 Nov 1957 Wach
Mattie M (w/o G F) 14 Apr 1879-16 Sept 1942 Wach
Sallie J 24 Oct 1904-3 Jan 1979 Wach
Thomas W (h/o Abigal) 22 Sept 1829-19 June 1909 Wach
Thomas W Jr 5 Dec 1865-11 Apr 1913 Wach
STITELY, Pauline Anderson 1888-1967 Libe
Walter W 1892-1958 Libe
STITES, Eugenia K 15 Sept 1920-17 Dec 1979 Fair
Joseph Durbin III 11 Oct 1946-2 Apr 1972 Fair
STOCKLEY, C Thomas 5 Apr 1846-7 June 1918; age: 72/2/2 Oakg
Francis T (Frank) h/o Mary A 27 Oct 1841-30 Oct 1907 Stoc
Frederick F s/o Sylvester & Margaret 5 Nov 1857-10 Aug 1858 StoM
G Tom 12 Dec 1906-3 Mar 1970 Quin
George Thomas h/o M L 20 May 1868-4 Nov 1906 Quin
George W 30 Dec 1843-6 Apr 1910 Turl
J E 2 Aug 1874-3 July 1930 Turl
John B 1857-1947 MtHo
Madeline LeCato Mapp w/o G T 5 Nov 1870-28 Mar 1948 Quin
Maggie J w/o G W 17 Dec 1864-1 July 1944 Turl

STOCKLEY (continued)
Mary A w/o Francis T; d/o Saml S & Eliza S Coleburn 17 Oct 1838-7 Jan 1886 Stoc
Mary Frances d/o F T & M A 6 Apr 1867-28 Nov 1889 Stoc
Nat Wescott s/o J W & G H W 21 Apr 1900-29 Mar 1901 Turl
Peggy w/o Jeremiah 24 Dec 1792-23 Nov 1868 StoM
Sylvester 26 Dec 1816-20 Sept 1894 StoM
STOKES, Willie d/o Dr P F & S C Browne d 10 Oct 1932 MtCu
STONE, Anna K 23 Aug 1889-25 Feb 1976 Edge
STOTZ, s/o E B & Alice b&d 1935 MtHo-s
Henry (h/o I B) 27 Apr 1857-14 Feb 1934 MtHo-s
Ida B (w/o Henry 26 July 1866-7 June 1955 MtHo-s
STRAND, Abel K 1903-1972 Metr
Cordie 1886-1973 Gask
Edgar 1884-1947 HTri
Edward Peyton 1916-1978 Metr
Ethel Collins 11 Feb 1919-30 Dec 1970 Shil
George E 24 Feb 1912-31 Jan 1963 Gask
Hillie G 1924-1983 Metr
Lizabeth 1913-1964 Metr
Maggie V nd Metr
Margaret S 1881-1974 NewM
Mary A w/o Preston; d/o P Purnell Drummond 1891-1974 Metr
Preston h/o M A 1882-1940 Metr
Robert E 1935-1980 Metr
STRANG, Levie Boggs (i.e., Levinia, h/o A P) 1869-1918 Rodc
STRATTEN, Agnes 1911-1950 Park
STRATTON, Alfred 1895-1978 Gask
Alfred L 1909-1972 Burt
Andrew S 1888-1975 Burt
Baxter 1891-1964 JoyC
Bessie 1901-1972 Burt
Edward d 28 Dec 1963; age: 74 yrs Burt
Hattie 1900-18 Mar 1971; age:

STRATTON (continued)
70/11/4 Gask
Ida J 1887-1976 Burt
John H 1875-1961 Burt
Missouri M 1870-1964 Burt
Thelma 1926-1964 Padd
Thomas A 1881-1945 Burt
STRINGER, Maggie W w/o Benj; d/o Wm & Susan Downing Garrison 6 Aug 1834-1 July 1898 Tayl
STROUD, Katheryne E w/o R S 1900-1950 Park
Robert S h/o K E 2 July 1888-6 Apr 1965 Park
STURGIS, (STURGES), s/o Etheridge S & Lena 27-29 Jan 1905 Sava
baby b&d 1969 NewM
Alexander D s/o G W & M E d 10 Feb 1896; age: 0/0/10 Onan
Annie 1895-1963 Snea
Arinthia Jane w/o J R 10 June 1843-4 Nov 1914 MtHo
Bertie Somers 13 Mar 1885-22 May 1929 Park
Bessie M (w/o C E) 1896-1980 Holl
Cary S 4 July 1876-23 July 1900; age: 24/0/19 Sava
Cary S s/o Etheridge S & Lena 18 Feb 1902-1 Aug 1903; age: 1/5/17 Sava
Catherine K w/o W S 29 July 1814-7 Nov 1901 Stur
Charles T s/o Jno & Margt 11 June 1815-11 May 1875 StuP
Charlotte S w/o J W; d/o Jas & Charlotte Bell 12 Sept 1837-15 Jan 1891 Stub
Clarence E (h/o B M) 1894-1975 Holl
Cleve H 1906-1955 MtHo-s
E Elmer (h/o M F) 1911-1977 Fair
Edith D w/o G B 1892-1937 MtHo-s
Elizabeth A w/o O J 1882-1944 MtHo-s
Ella Hartman 1894-1967 MtHo-s
Elva Waterfield (w/o J C) 15 Sept 1889-26 Jan 1981 Ptea

STURGIS (continued)
Etheridge S (h/o L H) 1874-1946 MtHo-s
Fred 1887-1960 Snea
Frederick T s/o J W & Susan 6 Aug 1867-9 Feb 1873 Stub
George 1912-1982 Snea
George A h/o M A E R 23 Oct 1884-31 Jan 1931 Park
George B h/o E D 1891-1937 MtHo-s
George T 23 Mar 1873-26 Oct 1898; age: 25/7/3 Holl
George W h/o M E 2 Aug 1857-13 Sept 1935 Onan
H H s/o W S & C K 5 July 1852-13 Apr 1888 Stur
Hester 1930-1969 Gask
Indie d 23 Aug 1967; age: 74 yrs StPa
Irving M 4 May 1855-15 Sept 1917 Edge
James 1930-1957 NewM
James Crawley (h/o E W) 31 Oct 1885-23 Feb 1979 Ptea
James T Co F 46 VA Inf - CSA nd Oakg
James T s/o J & E E 6 Aug 1883-9 June 1884 Stur
Jannita B d/o J H & Bessie 14 Aug 1903-4 Nov 1912 MtHo
John E 1870-1944 Onan
John L 1925-1977 Snea
John R h/o A J 28 Apr 1839-22 July 1906 MtHo
John W 24 Dec 1832-4 Dec 1922; age: 89/11/10 Stub
Lena Harris (w/o E S) 1877-1949 MtHo-s
Lennie C s/o O W & Virginia R 20 May 1887-1 July 1899 Tipt
Lenwood nd Tipt
Lillian L d/o J M & Indie E 15 Nov 1872-23 Aug 1885 Stur
Maggie 1883-1964 Shil
Maggie E w/o G W 25 Feb 1867-6 Mar 1913 Onan
Maggie N 1932-1967 Burt
Maggie Nolia 1903-1949 Gask
Margaret E d/o W S & C K 27 Nov 1842-11 Aug 1864; age: 21/8/16 Stur

STURGIS (continued)
Marian F (w/o E E) 1913- Fair
Mary J 17 Mar 1813-9 Dec 1891 StuP
Mary Justis w/o U Q 4 Sept 1880-27 Aug 1960 Onan
Mary Mason w/o Jno W; d/o Wm & Eliz M Mason 4 Apr 1841-9 Apr 1920 StGe
Myrtle 1922-1982 Snea
Otho 1889-1965 Snea
Otho J h/o E A 1878-1964 MtHo-s
Otho R 1911-1975 Burt
Robert 1900-1964 Gask
Stanley 1935-1978 Snea
Upshur Quinby w/o M J 23 Nov 1875-2 Sept 1940 Onan
Vianna S d/o Jno & Margt 18 Nov 1806-11 Sept 1885 Stur
Westley d/o J & Indie b&d 1882 Stur
William S 8 Nov 1808-18 June 1862; age: 53/7/2 Stur
Willie L 1945-1948 Snea
Zinabeth 1963-1964 NewM
SUMMERS, Albert 1922-1982 Snea
SUMMERVILLE, Theodore Jr 1910-1973 Metr
SUNKETT, Isadora J 1889-1970 HTri
SWACKHAMER, Florence M (w/o L F) 1893-1964 Edge
Leon F (h/o F M) 1890-1946 Edge
SWAIN, G Frank (h/o Sue G) 1905-1978 Fair
Sue G (w/o G F) 1907-1986 Fair
SWANGER, Ann Rebecca w/o E B 1 Feb 1829-28 July 1902 Swag
Daisy B w/o Nat 1881-1944 MtHo
Emanuel B h/o A R 25 Mar 1819-12 Apr 1904 Swag
Nat h/o D B 1859-1943 MtHo
SWENSON, Luella I (w/o O P) 1894-1968 Wach
Olie P (h/o L I) 1895-1974 Wach
SWIFT, Daisey A (w/o I W) 1884-1954 MtHo-s

SWIFT (continued)
Ira W (h/o D A) 1880-1924 MtHo-s
TALLAFERRO, d/o Wm & Anne H b&d 3 Dec 1803 Ever
Anne Hatton w/o Wm d 25 Sept 1804; age: 39 yrs Ever
TANKARD, Maggie 1906-1947 NewM
TAPMAN, Isaac Henry 1886-1959 Wach
TAPPAN, Bettie A w/o F M 1859-1946 Park
Donald Jr s/o Donald & Billie b&d 1950 Park
Edna Cole w/o F W 1899- Park
Frank M h/o B A 1869-1938 Park
Frank Webster h/o E C 25 Oct 1892-29 Dec 1958 Park
TARLINGTON, Walter 11 Feb 1917-25 May 1973 Burt
TARR, Elaine E (w/o W A) 1915-1972 Quin
William A 1876-1956 Quin
William A Jr (h/o E E) 1907-1959 Quin
TAWES, Elizabeth Watson Hyslop w/o Henry 2 Apr 1819-24 Nov 1860 Bayb
TAYLOR, chiildren Mary Lou, Harvey R, Mary Ann nd Park
s/o F W & M E b&d 12 Mar 1905 Park
(d/o Jos H & Ella ?) b&d 1911 Park
s/o F W & M E b&d 16 Apr 1917 Park
s/o E A & N D b&d 2 Sept 1917 (stone not located; 1940 data) Syca
s/o W T & C S b&d 17 Aug 1921 Fair
A Jackson h/o H C d 27 July 1894; age: 62 yrs Park
A L h/o E S 1868-1948 Park
A Virginia Ames 23 Aug 1876-23 Nov 1952 StGe
Addie T w/o D W 1903-1949 Libe
Agnes H (w/o H L) 1908- MtHo-s
Alfred 1878-1960 Snea

262

TAYLOR (continued)
Alfred J h/o A R 1881-1958 Park
Alfred R h/o S S 1851-1928 Oakg
Alger J h/o N L 1892- Libe
Amanda A w/o Geo T d 21 July 1868; age: 27/6/11 Syca
Amanda Belote (1st hus - E H Belote) 17 June 1890-5 Mar 1941 Onan
Ann C Bundick (wid/o Jno S Bundick; w/o Saml Taylor) 9 Aug 1794-12 Dec 1850 BunW
Anna Kusian 1887-1913 StGe
Annie 1889-1959 NewM
Annie R w/o R P 14 Dec 1872-6 Oct 1944 Park
Annie R w/o A J 1881-1960 Park
Annie R 1902-1968 Libe
Arcessa 1844-1927 Park
Archie J h/o S S 1906-1975 Libe
Arie D 1925-1974 Park
Arthur T 1919-1964 NewM
Asher C Cpl 1921-1944 (killed in Luxembourg, Germany) Tayl
B Franklin h/o M L 1916- Park
Beatrice P 1910-1945 Libe
Ben F h/o L M 1882-1958 Park
Bertie nd Libe
Bertie L w/o J W 1912-1979 Park
Bertie R w/o Wm H 1884-1968 Libe
Bessie P 1876-1948 Onan
Bessie P 1889-1945 Libe
Bessie W w/o L D 1885-1959 MtHo
Bettie C w/o Wm M; d/o L R & H A Boggs 4 Nov 1854-27 Apr 1886 Rodc
Bettie T w/o C D 1889- Libe
Bettie W w/o W A 1863-1936 Park
Betty w/o E C 6 July 1868-26 June 1931 Libe
Bill Jr 1958-1983 Park
Blanche 1901-1981 NewM
Brantley J h/o M H 1901-1970 Libe
Carolyn F 1927-1982 Libe
Carrie S w/o W T 1891- Fair
Carrie V w/o L T 1917-1978 Park

TAYLOR (continued)
Carson Rodgers (h/o E R) 1879-1962 StGe
Carson Rodgers Jr 27 Dec 1915-7 June 1962 StGe
Cassie S w/o W C 1906- Libe
Charles Samuel h/o J G 1895- Libe
Charles Wm D 1872-1938 Tayl
Charlie B 1889-1953 Quin
Capt Charlie T h/o M F 1876-1938 Park
Charlotte B d/o D C & M S 10 Jan 1848; age: 9/11/12 StGe
Charlote Custis w/o C T 1850-1929 Poul
Clarence L h/o M M 1892-1946 Libe
Cleve M w/o J E; d/o S K & E S Smith 30 Oct 1884-3 Oct 1976 MtHo-s
Clifton h/o G M 25 Sept 1906-5 Oct 1953 Park
Constance S 1878-1955 Onan
Cora Belle w/o E C 1881-1954 Libe
Cordelia F w/o E J 1857-1938 Edge
Cornelius T h/o C C d 21 June 1888; age: 53 yrs Poul
Crippen D h/o B T 1878-1949 Libe
Cristiana E w/o S F 1 Aug 1850-30 Apr 1920 Libe
Custis S (h/o M S) 1874-1935 Tayl
Daniel W h/o A T 1903-1954 Libe
Daniel W 23 May 1925-12 June 1966 Libe
David C d 18 Apr 1855 StGe
David C s/o C T & M F d 5 Sept 1867; age: 6/7/0 StGe
Dawson D h/o M A V 1857-1915 Park
Dewey 1896-1975 Smit
Dora C w/o G D 1900-1976 Edge
Dorothy J w/o R S 16 Apr 1918- Libe
Dorothy Lee b&d 1929 MtHo-s
Dorsey F h/o M F 1888-1947 Libe

TAYLOR (continued)
Mrs Doshia Mae 1891-1965 Park
Drucilla 1862-1942 MtHo-s
Edgar C h/o C B 1884-1958 Libe
Edith H 1884-1970 MtHo-s
Edna Read (w/o C R) 1879-1953 StGe
Edward T 1880-1943 MtHo-s
Edwin G 1909-1936 Libe
Elishee J h/o C F 1867-1954 Edge
Eliza J w/o J S 1876-1953 Libe
Elizabeth Ann w/o Jos B; d/o Jacob & Ann Phillips 1 July 1815-8 Mar 1870 Tayg
Elizabeth C w/o R E 1916-1976 MtHo
Elizabeth East 1904 MtHo
Ella E w/o J H 1872-1923 Park
Elton J 1920-1937 Park
Elwood G s/o J L & N E 15 Dec 1907-26 Feb 1911; age: 3/2/13 Libe
Emily A 8 July 1818-13 Aug 1847 Syca
Emma C d/o Wm & Sallie 4 Dec 1862-8 Sept 1867 Syca
Emma E d/o S C & M W 1 Apr 1881-12 July 1885 Park
Emma Florence w/o E J 8 May 1872-7 May 1928 MtHo-s
Emma G w/o Jos C 20 Aug 1880-5 Feb 1905 Libe
Emma G w/o V D Sr 1890- Park
Emma I 14 Sept 1846-22 July 1847 Syca
Emma S w/o G W 2 Sept 1852-3 Feb 1878 Syca
Emory J 1919-1975 Libe
Erastus C h/o Betty 9 Aug 1867-29 Mar 1918 Libe
Ernest 1880-1966 Metr
Ernest B 1887-1944 MtHo-s
Estella C d/o E C & Bettie 1 Feb 1894-23 Oct 1895 Libe
Esther A w/o Capt Chas K; d/o Jno J & Sarah Garrison Nock 6 Aug 1835-17 Dec 1895 Tayl
Eugenia Hardy (w/o S T) 20 Jan 1857-24 Feb 1923 Syca
Eulalia S w/o A L 1865-1956 Park

TAYLOR (continued)
Evelyn P d/o G L & O A 1913-1920 Libe
Everett T h/o R L 1895-1960 Libe
Ezekiel Jackson h/o E F 9 Sept 1864-27 June 1936 MtHo-s
F Crawford 19 Sept 1887-25 Jan 1910 Syca
Fletcher D h/o M E 4 Feb 1875-21 Feb 1946 Park
Fletcher L Sr h/o L T 1881-1965 Park
Fletcher Lee Jr h/o M T 12 Dec 1908-6 Feb 1972 Park
Florence 1902- Tayl
Frances F 1938-1980 Park
Frances L 1873-1962 Onan
Frank C (h/o M L) 1866- Syca
Frank M s/o C T & M F d 8 July 1866; age: 0/8/0 StGe
Fred W h/o M E 1880-1949 Park
Fred W Jr (h/o K G) 1903-1945 MtHo-s
Frederick Clifton h/o W F 26 Mar 1913-26 Oct 1976 Libe
G Beatrice w/o G T 1906- Libe
G Collier 1898-1964 Fair
Garfield C 1901-1967 Park
Garland E h/o V W 1906-1976 Park
Gay M w/o Clifton 27 Sept 1908- Park
George 1909-1962 NewM
George C (Satch) h/o Rhoda B 11 May 1910-3 June 1967 Edge
George D h/o D C 1891-1963 Edge
George Ed 1907-1982 Park
George K 16 Oct 1801-9 Oct 1836 Syca
George Preston 1904-1975 Libe
George T h/o L K 16 Feb 1838-26 July 1916 Libe
George T h/o G B 1898-1953 Libe
George W (h/o E S) 23 Sept 1849-4 Dec 1875 Syca
George W 22 Oct 1907-8 May 1977 Libe
Georgeanna W d/o Thos & H(?) d 17 Mar 1853; age: 4/11/17

TAYLOR (continued)
Moor
Georgia Ewell w/o H S 31 Jan 1893-18 Nov 1975 Libe
Georgie G 1906-1980 Gask
Gladys G 1907-1952 Libe
Gladys M 1914-1973 Libe
Gloria Lee 1937- MtHo-s
Harold L (h/o A H) 1902- MtHo-s
Harry A 1936-1958 Fair
Harry W 1902-1969 Fair
Helen H (w/o M L) 1907- MtHo-s
Herbert Savage h/o G E 14 Mar 1888-22 Sept 1974 Libe
Hetty C w/o A J 1 Apr 1841-21 Dec 1894 Park
Hilda E 1885-1972 Park
I Clark 4 Sept 1891-25 Dec 1918 Libe
Irene W 1917-1918 Libe
Isabella C w/o Saml T d 17 Nov 1836; age: 22 yrs Amep
J Chandler 1 Jan 1888-22 Jan 1958 StGe
J Selby 1897-1974 MtHo-s
Jake 1889-1977 NewM
James A (h/o M J) 1860-1940 Fair
James H 1882-1966 NewM
James M 1882-1913 Libe
Jerome 1956-1969 Shil
Jesse B h/o G M 1915-1962 Libe
John 12 Oct 1775-15 Oct 1843; age: 68 yrs Syca
John A 1888-1945 Libe
John C (h/o M E) 21 Sept 1846-25 Apr 1903 Syca
John C 1896-1933 Libe
John E 17 July 1912-9 Apr 1974 NewM
John Edwin h/o C M; s/o W M & Eliz C 15 Mar 1882-30 Aug 1947 MtHo-s
John L h/o N E 1871-1927 Libe
John M h/o P A 1842-1916 Libe
John O (h/o S H) 1865-1937 Fair
John S 1870-1928 Libe
John S h/o E J 1872-1912 Libe
John T 1881-1962 Fair
John W 30 Dec 1844-30 Apr 1846

TAYLOR (continued)
Syca
John W 1870-1893 Libe
John W h/o B L 1902-1962 Park
John William 4 Dec 1833-12 June 1916 Libe
Johnie F 16 Mar 1896-24 Feb 1920 Libe
Joseph H h/o E E 1870-1942 Park
Julia Gunter w/o C S 1895-1974 Libe
Julia L d/o Wm & Sallie 11 May 1861-29 Sept 1863 Syca
Katherine G (w/o F W Jr) 1904- MtHo-s
Kathryn June d/o R E & K V 18 Oct 1937-14 Nov 1940 MtHo-s
Kathryn V Kellam w/o R E 17 May 1917-14 Sept 1945 MtHo-s
Kenneth Reed 17 Jan 1925-25 Nov 1975 Libe
L Katharine 17 Nov 1846-21 Mar 1918 Libe
Langston s/o J H & E E 19 Nov 1903-28 Aug 1912 Park
Larry T 23-24 Dec 1949 Park
Laura Carolyn 1945-1958 Park
Laura V w/o W C 1913- Park
Leroy T h/o C V 1920- Park
Lester B 1914-1972 Park
Lewis E 1849-30 Mar 1922; age: 73 yrs Park
Lizzie M w/o B F 1875-1971 Park
Lloyd D h/o B W 1882-1942 MtHo
Lola M 1907-1964 Park
Lola R 1880-1908 Libe
Lorenzo 1917-1967 Metr
Louise W (w/o M T) 1908- Fair
Lucille G 1904-1941 MtHo-s
Lula S 1882-1918 Libe
Lynn Floyd 1861-1919 Edge
Mabel M w/o M S 1915-1977 Edge
Mabel W w/o Robt 1910-1960 Park
Mable C d/o S T & M E b&d 5 Dec 1896 Syca
Mable Lewis w/o B F 1916-

TAYLOR (continued)
Park
Madeline B 9 Feb 1893-8 Nov 1933 Libe
Madeline L 1925-1981 Libe
Mae H w/o B J 1903- Libe
Maggie B w/o Wm B 1898- Park
Maggie E w/o F D 12 Mar 1877-31 July 1938 Park
Maggie E B d/o C T & M F 1 Apr-10 July 1874 StGe
Maggie J w/o W F 1 Mar 1871-16 June 1922 Libe
Maggie M w/o C L 1897-1962 Libe
Maggie S w/o Wm M 23 Feb 1869-22 Jan 1918 Syca
Major d 28 Oct 1820; age: 40 yrs Syca
Manie E w/o F W 1880-1926 Park
Margaret d/o J H & E E 4 Jan 1897-15 Aug 1899 Park
Margaret A 1920-1921 Libe
Margaret A w/o Wm E 1949- Park
Margaret F w/o C T 1880-1946 Park
Margaret S w/o David C d 8 Dec 1861; age: 51 yrs StGe
Margaret S d/o Jno & Ruth 3 Feb 1826-(1915); age: 89 yrs MtHo
Margie P w/o Vaden 1905-1946 Libe
Marie (d/o J L & N E) 31 May-7 Aug 1915 Libe
Marie Lee 1927-1966 Park
Marion E 15 Feb 1906-11 Apr 1951 Gask-old
Mary 1926-1978 Onan
Mary A Vanderslice w/o D D 1867-1943 Park
Mary C w/o Wm McK 1859-1937 Libe
Mary E w/o Augustus C 23 May 1839-24 Jan 1918 Libe
Mary E w/o Jno C d 4 Sept 1907 Syca
Mary G 1908-1967 Libe
Mary J w/o S C 22 Sept 1873-30 Mar 1937 Park
Mary James (w/o J A) 1866-1940

TAYLOR (continued)
Fair
Mary Jane 1857-1938 Park
Mary L (w/o F C) 1865-1945 Syca
Mary M(iddleton) 9 Feb 1895-23 Oct 1971 Libe
Mary S w/o G I; d/o Severn & Lizzie Bevans 26 June 1852-7 July 1886 Gask-old
Mary T w/o F L Jr 1912-1982 Park
Mason 1927-1975 Onan
Mayfield (Annie) 29 Feb 1895-30 Jan 1968 Park
Mazie S 1901-1974 Park
Melinda W w/o S C 22 Feb 1845-10 July 1885 Park
Melvin L (h/o H H) 1909-1974 MtHo-s
Melvin T (h/o L W) 1906-1972 Fair
Merritt S h/o M M 1905-1974 Edge
Merritt S 25 Feb 1909-24 Mar 1968 Libe
Mildred K 1902-1952 Edge
Minnie F w/o D F 1889-1957 Libe
Minnie S (w/o C S) 1879-1962 Tayl
Mitchell Thomas 15 Dec 1921-17 Jan 1977 Libe
Mollie E w/o T B 13 Oct 1860-26 Mar 1937 MtHo-s
Nancy w/o Jno 11 Sept 1783-24 Apr 1832 Syca
Nancy J w/o Chas d 23 Feb 1922; age: 86/8/22 Park
Nannie C d/o Wm & Sallie 4 Dec 1855-11 Sept 1863 Syca
Nannie E w/o J L 1877-1947 Libe
Nellie A w/o R S 1913- Park
Nola L w/o A J 1892-1955 Libe
Norma Henrietta d/o E A & N D 28 Jan 1923-21 Mar 1925 (stone missing - 1940 data) Syca
Norman h/o V G 1919- Park
Ocea Ann w/o G L 1877-1955 Libe

TAYLOR (continued)
Orin Fair 8 Mar 1880-25 Apr 1902 Poul
Orville S 1909-1976 Libe
Oscar M 1891-1954 Park
Oscar W 1882-1959 Libe
Paul B 1923-1979 Park
Pauline B 1918-1977 Park
Permelia A w/o J M 1846-1908 Libe
R Pinkney h/o A R 2 Aug 1872-26 May 1951 Park
R Vernon 1897-1900 Fair
Rachel A (Aunt) 19 Oct 1831-13 Oct 1907 Moor
Richard A C 1903-1935 Fair
Richard Drummond 10 May 1917-3 July 1980 Fair
Robert h/o M W 1908-1961 Park
Robert D Sr 1876-1951 Fair
Robert D Jr 1910-1961 Fair
Robert E h/o E C 1916- MtHo
Robert R s/o S T & M E 25 Oct 1886-4 Oct 1888 Syca
Robert S h/o D J 16 Dec 1915- Libe
Roland S h/o N A 1911-1982 Park
Rosa 1943-1969 Shil
Roy B 1900-1947 Libe
Roy Thomas s/o L T & C V 1947-1950 Park
Royal J 1906-1966 Park
Ruby L w/o E T 1897-1979 Libe
S Crip h/o M J 9 May 1871-2 Oct 1936 Park
Sallie A w/o Wm M 18 Sept 1825-1 June 1910 Syca
Sallie M 1884-1953 Snea
Samuel C h/o M W d 26 Nov 1914; age: 73 yrs Park
Samuel H 1899-1968 Shil
Dr Samuel M h/o S A 17 Sept 1874-11 Feb 1933 Libe
Samuel T (h/o Eugenia 31 Oct 1857-12 July 1921 Syca
Samuel Thomas 12 Jan 1893-8 Apr 1956 Wach
Samuel W 6 Nov 1919-11 Aug 1966 Park
Sarah A w/o S A 24 Sept 1833-29 June 1911 Libe

TAYLOR (continued)
Sarah E 1876-1958 Fair
Sarah S w/o A R 1875-1957 Oakg
Sarah T 1889-1965 Metr
Severn B 18 Mar 1895-22 Aug 1960 NewM
Seymour T 1920-1977 NewM
Shelia S w/o A J 1911- Libe
Stella Scott (w/o W H) 1884-1969 Onan
Sudie A d/o Wm & Sallie 31 July 1851-22 Sept 1863 Syca
Sudie H (w/o J O) 1873-1967 Fair
Susan F w/o T W 1842-1938 Onan
Theodore 1927-1982 Bays
Thomas B s/o C T & M F d age: 3/10/0 StGe
Thomas B h/o M E 18 Jan 1854-27 Feb 1927 MtHo-s
Thomas E 23 Oct 1943-7 Dec 1978 Libe
Thomas Sledge 21 Nov 1893-24 Oct 1926 Libe
Thomas W h/o S F 1842-1912 Onan
Thomas W Jr 6 Apr 1885-16 Aug 1906 Onan
Upshur F h/o V L 1903-1977 Libe
Upshur G s/o C T & M F 26 Sept 1876-29 Apr 1877 StGe
Verna M d/o Wm H & B R 1913-1927 Libe
Vernon C 7 Nov 1891-4 Apr 1981 Edge
Vernon T 1891-1968 Park
Viola L w/o U F 1903-1971 Libe
Virgil D Sr h/o E G 1890-1970 Park
Virginia G 1921-1978 Park
Virginia S d/o Saml & Emily 19 Feb 1843-19 June 1851 Syca
Virginia W h/o G E 1911- Park
W Crippen h/o C S 1902-1972 Libe
W M (h/o M S) 2 Feb 1853-13 Jan 1909 Syca
Walter C h/o L V 1907- Park
Walter D 1912-1926 Tayl
Walter Lee s/o T B & M E 9 Apr

TAYLOR (continued)
1894-3 Aug 1895 MtHo-s
Webster b&d 1941 Libe
Webster A h/o B W 1864-1939 Park
Wilbert C 1901-1969 Park
William 1921-1978 Park
William A 1894-1933 Tayl
William Chandler s/o F C & M L 18 July 1908-24 July 1909 Syca
William Donald 10 Mar 1926-2 Feb 1966 Park
William E 31 Nov 1839-4 July 1841 Syca
William E 19 June 1844-10 Apr 1845 (stone missing - 1940 data) Syca
William E h/o M A 1948-1983 Park
William H h/o B R 1883-1958 Libe
William H 15 Oct 1892-27 Jan 1978 Park
William Hardy 1885-1959 Fair
William Henry (h/o S S) 1876-1950 Onan
William M (h/o S A) 11 Mar 1820-30 Oct 1890; age: 70/7/9 Syca
William McK h/o M C 1857-1942 Libe
William Mason s/o Roy & Sara 11 Jan-20 May 1927 Libe
William S 1893-1917 Libe
William T h/o M B 1888-1966 Park
William T h/o C S 1889-1959 Fair
Willie F s/o C T & M F d 19 Oct 1866; age: 7/4/0 StGe
Willie F 1897-1929 Park
Willie K 1910-1968 Park
Winnie F w/o F C 1912- Libe
TAWES, P Henry s/o Henry & Eliz (Hyslop) 17 Aug 1847-3 Nov 1876 (bur at sea) StGe
TEACKLE, Arthur 28 Feb 1755-31 Jan 1791; age: 36 yrs Teac
Catherine 29 Dec 1748-3 Mar 1765; age: 16/2/0 Faif
Esther Maria Fisher d/o Jno &

TEACKLE (continued)
Eliz of Kegotank, Acc Co VA 30 Mar 1795-18 Oct 1840 Scot
Harriot d/o Arthur & Eliz 31 Jan 1782-5 Oct 1804; age: 23 yrs Teac
Joyce w/o Levin Feb 1735-Dec 1760; age: 26 yrs Teac
Levin (s/o John) d 28 Sept 1794; age: 77 yrs Teac
TEAGUE, Carroll d 29 Jan 1970; age: 84 yrs Burt
Curtis L b&d 1957 Snea
Fannie 1892-1970 Snea
George T s/o Arthur & Rachel 5 Sept 1867-5 Feb 1899 Snea
George Woodrow 9 Jan 1923-18 Nov 1981 Snea
J McKinley 1925-1971 Snea
Rachel w/o Arthur d 23 Mar 1919; age: 72 yrs Snea
TERRELL, Coheste S 18 Oct 1919-6 Jan 1973 NewM
TERRY, Henry M (h/o R W) 25 Mar 1882-26 Aug 1955 Fair
Rachel Wescott (w/o H M) 28 Mar 1883-26 Feb 1974 Fair
THARPE, Everett Spitler s/o Lester Everett & Kathleen (Moore) 27 July 1935-16 Apr 1939 Onan
Kathleen Moore 1907-1965 Onan
THOMAS, ____ 1895-1961 StLu
A LeRoy 1942-1975 MtHo
Absalom J s/o Edwd R & Mary W 20 Jan 1858-drowned 9 July 1867; age: 9/5/19 Lewi
Arinthia E 1863-1949 MtHo-s
Benj Woodall (h/o B G) 1880-1953 Fair
Blanche Grove (w/o B W) 1887-1977 Fair
Calvin Grove 1925-1981 Fair
David 1888-1957 Ayre
Edith C (w/o O J) 1873-1967 Fair
Edward L s/o Edwd R & Mary W 4 Mar 1865-16 Sept 1866; age: 1/6/12 Lewi
Ella 1924-1976 HTri
Elmer B h/o L T 1904-1982 Fair
Emma C 1902-1963 Fair

THOMAS (continued)
Emma N mother/o W W 1871-1968 Fair
Emma S w/o J P 12 Aug 1851-23 Dec 1928 Onan
Florence E (w/o W M) 1902-1950 Edge
Frank F (h/o N J) 1895-1970 Quin
Fred L h/o G D 1873-1964 Onan
Gertrude D (w/o F L) 1879-1937 Onan
Harry Jay (h/o Eula) 7 Apr 1884-11 Feb 1949 Onan
James s/o F L & G T 27 Dec 1905-1 Aug 1907 Onan
Joshua Lester 1897-1951 Onan
Joshua P h/o E S 22 Oct 1844-11 Mar 1907 Onan
Julia Nottingham w/o T B 1902-24 Dec 1982 Onan
Lenard s/o F L & G T 27 Dec 1905-6 Aug 1907 Onan
Lola T w/o E B 1905-1964 Fair
Margaret J d/o Wm H & Sarah C Kellam 23 Dec 1847-28 Nov 1901 Crad
Mary d 8 Oct 1968; age: 75 yrs Shil
Mary 1908-1981 NewM
Nelda K 1909-1980 MtHo
Nellie J (w/o F F) 1900-1978 Quin
Nellie Mae d/o F L & Gertrude 2 May 1907-12 Sept 1913 Onan
Dr O J (h/o E C) 1877-1961 Fair
Robert Charles 1900-1961 Snea
T Brooks h/o J N 1904-1981 Onan
Walter D 1886-1951 StGe
Walter M (h/o F E) 6 Jan 1891-10 Aug 1974 Edge
Walter W 3 July 1893-21 Mar 1956 Fair
THOMPSON, Addeene L (w/o H A) 1920-1963 Fair
Harold A (h/o A L) 1905-1967 Fair
THORNES, (THORNS),
Anna b&d 1931 Libe
B B Jr 1933-1945 Libe
Betsey S w/o Wm H 6 May

THORNES (continued)
1838-10 June 1922 Park
Rev Brantley B h/o M S 1903-1978 Libe
Cecil C 1884-1932 Libe
Dorsey W 1910-1964 Park
E C 1935-1951 Libe
Edna M 1894-1952 Quin
Edward D 1923-1978 Libe
Gertrude A 1896-1920 Libe
Gertrude M b&d 1944 Libe
Gillie T h/o M F 1883-1948 Libe
Harry D Jr 12 Dec 1927-9 Sept 1928 MtHo-s
Iva B mother/o Ralph & Carl 1896-1972 Park
J Berkley 1900-1963 Libe
J Berkley Jr 1940-1973 Libe
Jerry T b&d 1944 Libe
John C h/o L J 26 Aug 1851-8 Apr 1938 Libe
John H h/o M A 1879-1965 Libe
Lavinia J w/o J C 15 May 1861-27 July 1935 Libe
Leuvenia J 25 July 1866-6 Oct 1897 Libe
Maggie M 1875-1938 Libe
Mannie F w/o G T 1886-1947 Libe
Margaret A w/o J H 1889-1914 Libe
Margie R 1903-1936 Libe
Mary Susan w/o B B 1905- Libe
Miriam M d/o J H & M A 11 July 1913-15 Apr 1914 Libe
Miriam Sue Wessells w/o R T 31 Aug 1931- Park
Paige W 10 Sept 1922- Libe
Teresa Lynn d/o Ralph T & M S 20 May 1967-1 Feb 1969 Park
Viola 1926-1930 Libe
Viola L 15 July 1913- Libe
W R 30 Mar 1880-19 Feb 1929 Libe
William H h/o B S 26 Nov 1854-19 Nov 1925 Park
William L s/o R W & Dorothy 11-12 Sept 1943 MtHo
William R 1865-1925 Libe
Willie E 24 Apr 1883-16 Apr 1951 Libe
Woodrow W 1936-1954 Libe

THORNTON, Beatrice White 4 Apr 1895-4 June 1966 Quin
Calhoun J 1867-1917 Park
Charles H 1884-1970 Edge
Edward A 1896-1931 Park
Elizabeth S (w/o H L) 1900- Wach
Ella T (w/o J W) 1862-1937 Wach
Emma F 1898-1900 Park
Emory h/o M R 1902-1955 Wach
Evelyn M 1909-1913 Park
Garland J 1929-1979 Park
George T h/o M B 8 Mar 1899-26 July 1978 Park
Gertrude L w/o H W 1921- Park
Gladys M w/o H R 2 May 1902- Park
H Austin 1906-1955 Park
H Wendell h/o G L 1918-1968 Park
Harvey L (h/o E S) 25 Aug 1898-9 May 1977 Wach
Hayward R h/o G M 8 Aug 1895-8 Jan 1968 Park
James h/o M A 22 Feb 1817-30 Oct 1906 Park
James L h/o S C 1876-1941 Park
John W (h/o E T) 1888-1973 Wach
Lillian M d 8 Jan 1943; age: 35/0/9 Wach
Mamie J 1886-1964 Edge
Margaret R w/o Emory 1907-1935 Wach
Marie B w/o G T 1905-1968 Park
Mary A w/o Jas d 10 Sept 1913; age: 84 yrs Park
Michael E 20 Oct 1972-5 Jan 1973 Wach
Miles Burt Sr (h/o S A) 1907-1967 Wach
Sallie Ann (w/o M B) 1903-1979 Wach
Samuel T b&d 1895 Park
Sarah C w/o J L 1876-1965 Park
Willie F 1873-1947 Park
THORPE, Margaret L 1922-1984 Libe
THRASHER, Elizabeth Ann b&d 16 Mar 1962 MtHo
TIDBALL, Mary Josephine

TIDBALL (continued) Browne w/o Rev Thos Allen 7 June 1847-12 Feb 1903 MtCu
TIFFANY, Evelyn May w/o Dr Louis McLane; d/o T H & E H M Bayly 13 Apr 1851-25 May 1929 MtCu
TIGGS, James 1915-1975 Snea
TIGNALL, (TIGNAL),
Alfred Thomas h/o C M 1873-1965 Onan
Catherine Maude w/o A T 1875-1956 Onan
George M 14 July 1890-2 Oct 1974 MtHo
George Maddux s/o Saml & Eliz 13 May 1852-2 Nov 1860; age: 8/5/19 Coke
George S h/o M N 1869-1931 Onan
Mary A w/o Saml 1841-1928 Onan
Mary N w/o G S 31 Oct 1871-13 Feb 1922 Onan
Samuel h/o M A 1808-1895 Onan
TILGHMAN, Danny R 14 June 1955-11 Apr 1973 Fair
Ernest L 21 Oct 1928-12 Dec 1980 Fair
George S h/o S J 1922-1951 Libe
Manie S w/o S C 5 Aug 1966-7 Jan 1921 Onan
S Carroll h/o M S 1 June 1894-13 Oct 1901 Onan
Sarah Jane w/o G S 1921-1951 Libe
TINDALL, see TYNDALL,
TIPPETT, Mary Lang 31 July 1894-17 July 1958 Edge
TIPTON, J T h/o R S 26 Mar 1850-24 Jan 1924 Tipt
Rachel Stevens w/o J T 20 Apr 1850-31 Dec 1898 Tipt
TITLOW, D Jemison (h/o S G) 1877-1965 Fair
Daniel J 1854-1908 Onan
Elizabeth 1856-1933 Onan
Elizabeth A 19 July 1894-20 Dec 1926 Onan
Elizabeth S 1834-1906 Onan
Milton R 1880-1906 Onan
Sallie G (w/o D J) 1880-1954

TITLOW (continued) Fair
TODD, baby boy b&d 16 Jan 1950 Onan
TOPPING, (TOPPIN),
Bessie Sue 1910-1969 Gask
Brantley 1932-1957 Gask-old
Brantley Lee 1896-1969 Gask
Danny O 1940-1966 Gask
Effie d1964 Metr
Gladys F 1916-1981 Metr
John H Sr 1909-1981 Gask
Leah C w/o N S; d/o Jno & Susan Riley 1 Sept 1788-29 Aug 1877 Oatl
Leland E 1914-1983 Metr
Maggie 1914-1964 Metr
Nathaniel S s/o Garret & Scarborough 15 Nov 1792-20 July 1866 Oatl
TOWNSEND, Mary Ella w/o N T; d/o J R & M F 22 Nov 1863-23 Oct 1886 Hero
TOYE, Annie 1903-1935 Neda
TRADER, Almer U (h/o P R) 1893-1967 Fair
Alonzo T h/o N E 1879-1961 Park
Bertha 1896-1976 Metr
Cornelius T h/o M P 1887-1961 Park
Dawson J 1868-1946 Park
Dorsey J 1901- Park
Drucilla T 1888-1976 Park
Frank h/o O F 1860-1942 Park
George T Jr h/o M J 1900-1971 Park
James T (h/o M H) 1896-1976 Fair
Laura T 1873-1903 Park
Manie Y 1905- Park
Margaret H (w/o J T) 1898- Fair
Maude J w/o G T Jr 1905- Park
Mollie P w/o CT 1889-1967 Park
Nena E w/o A T 1879-1970 Park
Olivia F w/o Frank 1862-1942 Park
Patience (w/o Saml; wid/o Bartholomew Taylor) 1 Dec 1755-23 Sept 1835; age: 79 yrs Trad
Pearl R (w/o A U) 1899-1978

TRADER (continued) Fair
Samuel s/o Saml & patience 1 Dec 1793-(sailed in schooner *Wm & Henry*) lost at sea 15 Apr 1818; age: 25 yrs Trad
Samuel (w/o Patience) d 19 Feb 1810; age: 47 yrs Trad
Samuel h/o Susie 1885-1942 Holl
Susie w/o Saml 1873-1930 Holl
Timothy P s/o Wm b&d 1955 Fair
TREAGER, ELizabeth (w/o Ernest) 1869-1943 Quin
Ernest (h/o Eliz) 1871-1944 Quin
TREAHERNE, Leonard 1883-1970 NewM
TROWER, Ann W w/o T L; d/o Levin W & Polly W Nock 12 Oct 1839-4 July 1885 (moved from Old Nock Plot) Oakg
Annie L 15 Oct 1871-18 Dec 1956 Oakg
Catherine K (w/o H W) 1913- MtHo-s
Delitha d/o Thos & Ann 14 Dec 1856-31 May 1858 OldN
Douglas W 16 Sept 1860-29 Sept 1921 Oakg
Elva T 9 Dec 1869-17 Feb 1951 Oakg
George Nock 13 Oct 1862-10 Dec 1941 Oakg
Herbert W (h/o C K) 1909- MtHo-s
John L s/o Thos L & Annie W 23 Oct 1858-1 Feb 1922 Oakg
Louisa S w/o Thos L; d/o S M & E R Turlington 19 Mar 1833-25 Feb 1854 Turp
Louisa T d/o T L & L S 14 Feb-9 May 1854 Turp
Sadie B 1884-1944 StPa
Thomas L(ittleton) h/o A W; s/o Jno & Delitha 1 July 1827-8 Jan 1888 Oakg
Thomas L Jr s/o T L & A W 20 Sept 1866-6 July 1885 (moved from Old Nock Plot) Oakg
Thomas L III 21 Sept 1889-6 Aug 1958 Oakg
William T 29 Oct 1893-16 Sept

TROWER (continued)
1961 Oakg
TURITT, s/o C W & E E b&d 27 Dec 1901 MtHo
Charles W h/o E E 1855-1917 MtHo
Elizabeth E w/o C W 12 Oct 1862-3 July 1906 MtHo
Madeline W 1897-1976 Park
Margie B 20 Sept 1893-14 Mar 1949 MtHo
TRUSS, Tyrone P 1938-1972 Gask
TULL, Catherine J (w/o G C) 1894-1966 Wach
Clarence B h/o E J 1881-1961 Wach
Clifford H 17 Jan 1921-19 May 1974 Libe
Elizabeth C w/o Wm H 28 June 1847-2 July 1915 Wach
Elizabeth Jane w/o C B 1883-1969 Wach
George C (h/o C J) 1883-1967 Wach
John H 1878-1955 Wach
John Richard "Jack" 5 Jan 1917-18 May 1964 Wach
Virginia C w/o Jno S 21 Mar 1846-25 Jan 1915 Park
TUNNELL, d/o W D & E B b&d 21 July 1871 Shab
s/o W D & E B 11-17 May 1889 Shab
inf/o W D & E B b&d 6 Aug 1894 Shab
Edward J h/o E C 1872-1951 Fair
Elizabeth B w/o W D; d/o Edwin T & Indianna F Mapp 17 May 1853-8 Aug 1894 Shab
Elizabeth S d/o J D & M A W 5 Oct 1834-6 Oct 1853 Tunn
Eva C w/o E J 1873-1966 Fair
Georgie S d/o T H & T A 3 July 1846-23 July 1866; & her inf son MtHo
Indie Jones d/o W D & E B 22 Aug 1881-12 Oct 1885 Shab
Jackson D h/o M A W; s/o Wm & Eliz 22 May 1807-5 Oct 1881; age: 74/4/13 Tunn
Kate B d/o J D & M A W 1844-

TUNNELL (continued)
1912 Tunn
Margaret A W w/o J D; oldest d/o Jno B & Sarah P Burton 20 June 1809-9 Jan 1885 Tunn
Mary T d/o J D & M A W 1846-1912 Tunn
Nannie 22 June 1879-9 Oct 1908 Onan
Nehemiah d 23 Dec 1795 at sea; mariner on schooner *Fair American* of the Port of Folly Landing. Buried in Jamaica. The F
William D h/o E B 25 June 1843-28 May 1902 Shab
TURLINGTON, inf d/o S Z & E K nd Edge
twins/o Saml C & Mary E b 31 May 1892 son lived 1 day; dau lived 10 weeks Turf
s/o R L & M J 19 Dec 1905-7 Feb 1906 Turf
Alice S d/o O J & E A 1902-1975 MtHo-s
Ann d/o S M & E R 20 Jan 1838-19 June 1857 Turp
Annie B 1901-1964 Fair
Annie W Mapp w/o Wm M 16 Jan 1868-13 Feb 1945 Turf
Bessie Parks 1893-1970 MtHo-s
Carrie D 1919-1973 Gask
Catherine w/o Jno d 10 July 1822; age: 32 yrs Turf
Catherine A w/o P S 5 June 1827-1 Feb 1876 Turl
Charlie L h/o F L 1896-1931 MtHo
Delmar 1938-1982 Gask
Devon K b&d 1982 Snea
Elizabeth R w/o S M; d/o Edmund & Catherine Nock 13 Sept 1806-6 May 1854 Turp
Emma Kate w/o S Z 23 July 1853-27 Dec 1896 Edge
Eugene 1910-1968 Gask
Fannie D w/o T W 1 Sept 1864-1 Sept 1949 Wach
Fannie Lee w/o C L 1897-1958 MtHo
Florence Bayly w/o S J; d/o Thos H Bayly & Anna Fletcher

TURLINGTON (continued)
Browne 27 June 1877-22 June 1947 (memorial stone also at MtCu) Edge
George E h/o M E G 25 May 1879-2 Apr 1915 Edge
George T h/o W C 1 Dec 1904-6 July 1978 Fair
George W h/o M A K 24 Feb 1828-17 Feb 1911 Holl
George W h/o L S 1867-1947 Home
Helen Heath w/o Dr Wm E 25 Sept 1900-19 July 1982 Fair
Irene 1925-1971 Burt
James H Sr 1892-1956 MtHo-s
James H 1916-1939 MtHo-s
James N h/o L T 25 June 1828-7 Aug 1903; age: 75/1/8 Turf
John h/o Catherine d 21 Aug 1838; age: 50 yrs Turf
John A s/o J N & L T 24 Oct 1858-24 Feb 1859 Turf
Dr John A h/o Y D 1887-1965 MtHo
John E (s/o S M & E R) 21 July 1840-21 Apr 1866 Turp
John H s/o Jno & Rachel S 4 Nov 1851-1 Mar 1878 TurJ
John H s/o W T & S A 10 Apr-29 July 1865 Home
John T s/o Jos & Eliz 6 Sept 1819-20 Dec 1853 TurJ
Johnny s/o S Z & E K nd Edge
Julia S w/o Wm M 1894-1972 Edge
Lauretta Trower w/o J N 17 Oct 1829-1 June 1911 Turf
Leah Susan w/o G W 1870-1955 Home
Leon 1922-1981 Burt
Leona East 15 Aug 1912- Fair
Dr Leonard J 23 Aug 1855-3 Mar 1933 Turf
Leonard R 1901-1963 Fair
Leonard S s/o Saml C & Mary E 29 Mar-17 Aug 1896 Turf
Louis J 1853-1935 TurJ
Margaret Susan w/o Saml Z; d/o A J & S A Bird 19 Sept 1849-30 June 1922 MeaB
Martha A Kilmon w/o G W 15

TURLINGTON (continued)
Dec 1836-17 Oct 1932 Holl
Mary E w/o R A; d/o Robt & Navilla Ashby 1872-1936 Edge
Mary E Godwin w/o G E 14 Jan 1878-12 July 1964 Edge
Mary Elizabeth w/o S C 1854-1905 MtHo
Mary L d/o S Z & E K 28 Apr 1877-25 Nov 1891 Edge
Mary Louise 1888-1967 MtHo
May Joynes (w/o R L) 25 May 1875-9 May 1933 Turf
Milton Mapp 1889-1971 MtHo-s
Nathaniel J h/o P I; s/o Jno & Nancy 18 May 1829-19 May 1893 Home
Norma B 11 July 1922-2 Oct 1939 MtHo-s
Peter S (h/o C A) 22 Feb 1811-5 June 1873 Turl
Polly I w/o Nathl J 17 Mar 1829-15 Dec 1898 Home
Rachel S w/o Jno; d/o Jacob & Eliz Jester 17 Mar 1828-29 Sept 1893 TurJ
Richard A h/o M E A; s/o Saml Z & Emma K 1873-1937 Edge
Richard Vernon s/o R A & M E A 14 July 1897-17 Oct 1902 Edge
Robert Lee (h/o M J) 19 June 1862-3 Dec 1951 Turf
Salley S w/o Jno; d/o Jno & Eliz Walker d 20 June 1858; age: 80 yrs OlWa
Samuel C h/o M E 1856-1942 MtHo
Samuel J 10 May 1907-23 Feb 1974 Oakg
Samuel James s/o S Z & E K 19 Jan 1875-30 Jan 1926 Edge
Samuel M (h/o E R) 28 Apr 1804-5 May 1862; age: 58/0/7 Turp
Samuel Z h/o E K 23 June 1847-19 July 1928 Edge
Sarah A d/o S Z & E K nd Edge
Sarah A w/o W T 22 Dec 1832-5 Dec 1901 Home
Sarah G d/o G W & L S 3 Feb 1899-17 Mar 1901 Home
Stella C 1903-1972 Wach

TURLINGTON (continued)
Susan C 1853-1937 TurJ
Thomas W h/o F D 8 May 1859-15 June 1931 Wach
Valeria Louisa d/o J N & L T 22 Mar 1865-8 Feb 1889 Turf
Virginia M d/o W T & S A 4 Apr 1851-17 Sept 1863 Home
Walter M 1902-1970 Wach
Wessie W (w/o W B) 1913- Wach
William 1919-1984 Burt
William B (h/o W W) 29 Nov 1910-26 Jan 1972 Wach
William Brodas s/o G H & M A 20 Mar 1855-14 July 1857; age: 2/2/25 Holl
Dr William E 15 Dec 1893-10 July 1972 Fair
William M h/o J C 1884-1956 Edge
William Milton h/o A W M 10 May 1860-8 Feb 1845 Turf
William T h/o S A 9 Jan 1827-26 Nov 1901 Home
Willyeanna C w/o G T 12 June 1909- Fair
Yula Dix w/o J A 1889-1972 MtHo
TURNER, Ada L 1899-1953 MtHo-s
Albert Rudolph 8 Sept 1926-19 June 1948 NewM
Alice D w/o G T 1876-1966 Park
Allen E (Jack) h/o L W 1911-1964 MtHo-s
Annie 16 Mar 1892-7 Oct 1942 Shil
Annie Eliza 1877-1951 JoyC
Bert L d 25 Sept 1962 Shil
Catherine A w/o J E d 7 Oct 1906; age: 73/3/16 Turn
Catherine S d/o J E & Ann 6 Nov 1860-1 Aug 1864 Turn
Charles F 1860-1938 Holl
Clarence d 20 Oct 1964; age: 68 yrs Gask
Cleve Mears s/o J H & E K 1892-1950 Fair
D J d 1 Aug 1864; age: 0/6/26 Turn
E Florence (w/o W U) 14 July

TURNER (continued)
1898-29 July 1980 MtHo-s
Elizabeth B (w/o O S) 1880-1936 StGe
Elizabeth S w/o G K 20 July 1828-28 Nov 1873; age: 45 yrs Turn
Elsie G d/o Margt F Bagwell 1878-1953 MtNe(E)
Emma Kate w/o J H 8 Dec 1867-12 Apr 1937 Fair
Emma S 1892-1911 Holl
Fairy W (w/o J E) 1905- Quin
Fletcher 1908-1969 JoyC
Frederick D 19 Mar 1870-23 May 1947 Edge
Garland L (h/o S C) 1902-1966 Wach
George G s/o Geo & Kate Susan 11 July 1885-Sept 1890 Chbg
George H (h/o L E) 1886-1976 MtHo-s
George K h/o E S d 26 June 1884; age: 73/6/2 Turn
George O 1904-1979 Metr
George T (h/o K S) 1858-1940 MtHo-s
George T h/o A D 1871-1946 Park
Grace Stevenson (h/o H L) 1896-1974 Fair
Harold Lynwood (h/o G S) 1887-1956 Fair
Inez Gertrude d/o J H & E K 30 Sept 1894-18 Oct 1895 (moved from Sycamores) Fair
James Sr 1891-1967 Shil
James 1913-1979 NewM
James A 1915-1974 Metr
James E (h/o C A) d 3 Nov 1864; age: 33/2/6 Turn
James E s/o Wm J & Sarah 1 Dec 1878-11 Sept 1909 SmiC
James E (w/o F W) 10 Mar 1898-30 Jan 1974 Quin
James Edward s/o J H & E K 1888-1945 Fair
James Louis 17 Dec 1925-14 Mar 1965 Park
James S s/o Jas & Catherine 28 Nov 1858-21 Sept 1886 (moved from Lawrence cem) MtHo

274

TURNER (continued)
John E s/o Jas S & Margt A 26 Dec 1866-11 May 1891 MtHo
John E 1877-1880 MtHo
John H d 17 July 1971; age: 86 yrs Shil
John R h/o Susan 14 Jan 1811-6 July 1890 (moved from Burckard bur gr) Onan
John T (h/o V A) 5 Jan 1835-22 Sept 1895; age: 60/8/12 Turn
John T d 1 Feb 1940; age: 68 yrs Negr
John T h/o L S 1873-1968 NewM
John T (h/o M M) 13 Nov 1888-8 June 1972 MtHo-s
Johnie s/o Geo T & Kate S 18 Sept 1882-28 Aug 1890 Chbg
Joseph S s/o Jas & Catherine 25 Dec 1877-10 June 1880 Lawr
Joshua s/o Jno & Mary 1 May 1802-31 May 1876; age: 74/1/0 Nock
Joshua H h/o E K 21 Dec 1864-6 Jan 1915 (moved from Sycamores) Fair
Kate S (w/o G T) 1868-1945 MtHo-s
Leah 1898-1976 JoyC
Leibig Morse 15 Mar 1895-9 June 1960 MtHo-s
Lenora E (w/o G H) 1886-1958 MtHo-s
Lillian S (w/o R J) 1901-1982 Fair
Lillian W w/o A E 1912- MtHo-s
Lizzie S w/o J T 1888-1971 NewM
Margaret D d/o Jno & Tabitha d 13 Jan 1825; age: 20/8/11 OlCu
Margaret E d/o J T & V A 30 Apr 1866-8 Dec 1872; age: 6/2/8 Turn
Margaret S 1863-1948 Holl
Margaret Sue b&d 1956 Onan
Mary E d/o J E & Ann 20 Oct 1862-1 Aug 1864 Turn
Mary H (w/o P C) 1891-1977 Holl
Mary M (w/o J T) 16 Feb 1881-

TURNER (continued)
11 Jan 1946 MtHo-s
Nathaniel Benjamin 12 June 1923-6 Nov 1981 NewM
Otho S (h/o E B) 1872-1953 StGe
Paul C (h/o M H) 1893-1953 Holl
Ralph J (w/o L S) 1898-1978 Fair
Robert 1902-1980 NewM
Sallie A d/o J H & E K 21 Mar 1890-27 Sept 1895 (moved from Sycamores) Fair
Sarah E 19 July 1909-16 Jan 1969 JoyC
Mrs Susan (w/o J R) 1 Sept 1820-1 Feb 1887 (moved from Burckard bur gr) Onan
Susie B 28 Sept 1890-21 July 1965 Edge
Susie C (w/o G L) 1910- Wach
Swansie May d/o Geo T & Sallie V 1 Nov 1909-28 Aug 1910 MtHo
Vinalt s/o G T & A P 31 Aug 1897-18 Dec 1908 Park
Virginia A w/o J T 6 Nov 1834-15 Mar 1901 Turn
W Upshur (h/o E F) 7 Feb 1892-16 July 1946 MtHo-s
Will 1894-1970 Metr
Willie L 22 July 1908-8 Apr 1962 NewM
TUSKAN, Stephan T 11 May 1915-9 Oct 1950 Edge
TUTTLE, Dolly Dell d/o J M & Myrtle b&d 1948 Fair
TWOMEY, Patrick B h/o Madeline 1903-1983 Libe
TWYFORD, (TWIFORD),
bro & sister (J R W plot) nd Libe
d/o Roland R & Va L b&d 16 Jan 1917 Lofl
Ames 1924-1984 Park
Annie R w/o D N 7 May 1883-15 Oct 1939 Libe
Annie T w/o R J 14 Mar 1880-14 Sept 1961 MtHo
B Chandler 21 Jan 1911-28 June 1948 Fair
Bernard H 31 Dec 1889-25 Jan 1944 Edge
Carrie Lee 30 May 1875-17 Dec

TWYFORD (continued)
1962 Libe
Catharine E J d/o Jas W & Levenia A Ann d 6 Sept 1839; age: 6/4/20 Coke
Clarence adopted s/o L E & M C 5 Sept 1897-26 Sept 1910 Libe
Daniel U 2 Mar 1896-9 Aug 1978 Libe
Dorsey N h/o A R 15 Apr 1881-21 Nov 1966 Libe
Edmonia I d/o J H & K L 13 Apr 1872-3 Feb 1874 Lofl
Elizabeth A w/o R T 10 Jan 1842-17 Apr 1915 MtHo
Elizabeth B w/o Obed P 10 Dec 1804-27 Jan 1836 Ames
Elizabeth S 1845-1920 Libe
Elizabeth Watson w/o P B 1883-1969 MtHo
G Dennie 18671896 Libe
Gayle Fox 24 Apr 1938-28 June 1948 Fair
George D 1835-1905 Libe
George R 1864-1890 Libe
George T h/o M W 1884-1946 MtHo-s
H Watson 1915-1966 Fair
Harvey C h/o L M 1875-1968 Libe
J W 12 Jan 1867-18 Aug 1927 Libe
James H (h/o Kate) 5 May 1835-29 Jan 1908 Lofl
Jane E w/o W H 23 Apr 1852-13 Jan 1928 Edge
John B (h/o L B) 1877-1948 MtHo-s
John E h/o N T 25 Sept 1892-17 Mar 1970 Libe
Julius Rever W h/o M A 19 Nov 1829-14 Dec 1916 Libe
Kate w/o J H 17 Sept 1844-11 Dec 1922 Lofl
Lela M w/o H C 1872-1937 Libe
Lena C h/o O D 23 Dec 1881-6 Nov 1947 MtHo
Lola B (w/o J B) 1881-1961 MtHo-s
Luther E h/o M C 1872-1948 Libe
Maggie R 1929-1978 NewM

TWYFORD (continued)
Margaret Annie w/o J R W 19 Dec 1830-12 Nov 1913 Libe
Margaret Fox 1894-1936 Park
Margaret Parker w/o P R 13 Mar 1854-28 May 1919 Edge
Margie S w/o S R 1913- MtHo-s
Mary C w/o L E 1877-1969 Libe
Mary E (w/o P M) 1880-1947 MtHo-s
Mary S w/o O P; d/o Thos & A B Edmunds 18 Jan 1832-12 Feb 1855 Edmu
Mattie W h/o G T 1891- MtHo-s
Mildred Lee d/o O D & L C 10 July-30 Nov 1910 MtHo
Millie d/o Jas H & Kate 1866-1940 MtHo
Mitchell T 26 Mar 1905-9 Nov 1981 Fair
Nellie T w/o J E 7 Aug 1897- Libe
Nettie T 1898-1932 Libe
Nora C (w/o R J) 1894- MtHo
Nora w/o T W; d/o Jno W & Margt Nock Kelly 12 Nov 1880-8 Mar 1967 Edge
Obe D h/o L C 28 July 1873-24 July 1931 MtHo
Obed P d 5 Jan 1852; age: 65 yrs Joyp
Oscar A s/o R T & E A 26 Oct 1853-17 Jan 1881 MtHo
P O 21 Mar 1844-16 Oct 1917 MtHo
Perry M (h/o M E) 1878-1957 MtHo-s
Philander Riley h/o M P 13 Jan 1852-14 May 1928 Edge
Phillip Beauregard h/o E W 26 June 1881-8 Aug 1906 MtHo
Revell J (h/o N C) 1883-1957 MtHo
Revel T h/o E A 29 Dec 1842-30 Mar 1883 MtHo
Robert J (h/o A T) 19 Jan 1872-28 Oct 1931 MtHo
S Russell h/o M S 1905-1979 MtHo-s
Tabitha (w/o Robt) 30 Jan 1751-12 July 1801 Twyf
Tabitha W w/o Robt; d/o Jas H

TWYFORD (continued)
& Margt W Dix 29 Apr 1827-22 Oct 1848 Dixf
Thomas O s/o T O & Sarah E 5-6 Apr 1911 Lofl
Thomas Wise h/o N K; s/o Wm H & J E 4 Aug 1873-22 June 1936 Edge
William H h/o J E 9 Apr 1842-24 Sept 1926 Edge
Zipporaii d/o Robt & Tabitha 29 Apr 1784-1 Apr 1800 Twyf
TYE, James E b&d 1948 MtHo-s
TYLER, Charlotte Thomas d/o G C & M A A A 1853-1930 Onan
Dr George C h/o M A A A 1816-1888 Onan
H C King 1885-1965 Edge
James Dennis s/o Jno D & M R 2 Aug 1876-5 May 1877 Onan
Jesse T 1896-1978 Gask
John d 31 Sept 1834; age: 51/9/17 Coke
John Dennis s/o Severn & S R d 19 July 1894; age: 80/5/0 Onan
John S nd Park
John Severn h/o R B & Marguerite 16 Aug 1840-20 Nov 1921 Onan
Lear Geneva 1915-1948 MtNe
Mary A A A w/o G C 1829-1895 Onan
Mary Ann d/o G C & M A A A 1858-1875 Onan
Mary R w/o Jno D d 27 Apr 1869; age: 55/3/21 Onan
Oscar 1884-1959 JoyC
Rosie B w/o J S; d/o Wm & Annie Walston d 10 Jan 1894; age: 47/9/25 Onan
Samuel C s/o J S & R B 5 Oct 1882-26 Jan 1945 Onan
Sarah E d/o Jno D & M R d 3 Sept 1846; age: 7/7/17 Onan
Sarah R w/o Severn 31 Aug 1797-6 Nov 1872 Onan
Sarah Reaston d/o G C & S A A A 1855-1860 Onan
Capt Thomas R s/o Severn & S R d 16 Dec 1878; age: 60/5/7 Onan

TYLER (continued)
Thomas Severn s/o J S & Marguerite b&d 28 Feb 1906 Onan
TYNDALL, (TINDALL),
Anne D (w/o J W) 1876-1944 MtHo-s
Catherine 1893-1926 Edge
Daniel T h/o O P 1889-1969 Park
Edward 1917-1963 Park
John H 16 Sept 1838-1 May 1933 Holl
John W (h/o A D) 1871-1944 MtHo-s
John W (h/o M F) 1878-1942 MtHo-s
Mollie F (w/o J W) 1888-1968 MtHo-s
Olevia P w/o D T 1897-1979 Park
Randolph W 2 July 1905-22 Dec 1967 MtHo-s
S S h/o S T 1850-1932 MtHo
Samuel 1887-1959 Holl
Sarah T w/o S S 2 Dec 1850-21 Oct 1924 MtHo
Stanley 25 Mar 1902-22 Mar 1920 Holl
Tabitha Lang w/o S S 1857-1924 Edge
UBER, Carlton E h/o N F 1873-1942 Park
John Carlton 27 Nov 1911-9 Dec 1983 Park
Nan 1915-1916 Park
Nellie F w/o C E 1887-1971 Park
Thelma D 1912-1978 Park
UFFELMAN, Meryle Edwin d 19 Oct 1978 Fair
UNDERHILL, Alonzo G (h/o B K) 12 Mar 1875-14 Feb 1941 Holl
Alonzo G Jr 27 June 1903- Holl
Ann d 8 Apr 1862; age: 77 yrs (50 yrs a Methodist) LeaW
Birdie K (w/o A G) 16 July 1877-7 Feb 1921 Holl
Matilda W 31 Jan 1908-9 Aug 1976 Holl
Nancy w/o Thos 13 Nov 1783-22 Dec 1856 Bogb

UNDERHILL (continued)
Thomas (h/o Nancy) 7 Dec 1771-8 Apr 1855 Bogb
UPSHUR, Abel d 30 Oct 1753; age: 51 yrs Warw
Abel (h/o Eliz) d 25 Mar 1790; age: 34 yrs Warw
Arthur d 15 Jan 1784; age: 58 yrs Warw
Arthur (h/o Mary) b in County Essex England-d 26 Jan 1709; age: 85 yrs Warw
Arthur Wilson h/o E P B b "Pear Plain", Northampton Co VA 8 Feb 1817-d 2 Sept 1844 at sea - Purser on the *Falmouth* (no stone; ref: Mrs Jno Upshur) Hill
Bertha 1913-1972 NewM
Caleb d 17 Oct 1778; age: 34 yrs Warw
Charlie 1890-1972 Smit
Elizabeth w/o Abel d 15 Jan 1794; age: 31/10/0 Warw
Esther Parramore Bayley w/o A W b1821 "Cedar Grove", Northampton Co VA-d 19 Sept 1843; age: 23 yrs (stone missing - ref: Mrs Jno Upshur) Hill
George W 1941-1957 NewM
James T 1941-1982 Burt
John d 5 Sept 1799; age: 58 yrs Warw
Dr John h/o Lucy; s/o Littleton & Jane d 15 May 1818; age: 26 yrs Parp
Leah d 24 Apr 1792; age: 61 yrs Warw
Littleton 20 Apr 1788-27 Aug 1811; age: 25 yrs Warw
Lucy w/o Jno; d/o Thos & Eliz Parker d 29 Apr 1818; age: 22 yrs Parp
Mary w/o Arthur b in County Warwick England-d 3 July 1703; age: 85 yrs Warw
Moses 1899-1968 Gask
Rachel w/o Abel d 25 Dec 1749; age: 47 yrs Warw
Virginia 1890-1961 NewM
VALENTINE, Robert H 17 July 1904-15 Feb 1980 Edge

VANDERGRIFT, Mark W 5-14 Sept 1956 Holl
VANDERSLICE, Walter H 19 Aug 1927 Onan
VanDEXTER, Kathryn S w/o N R 7 Oct 1906- Libe
N Roland h/o K S 25 Mar 1901-4 Jan 1982 Libe
VanKESTEREN, John (h/o Lamberdina) 1878-1959 Fair
John Jr h/o M P 1906- Oatl
Lamberdina (w/o Jno) 1883-1965 Fair
Mary Puffer w/o Jno 1915-1982 Oatl
VanKLEEF, Gerard 1901-1981 Fair
Henry A 1929-1939 Fair
Maria 1896-1983 Fair
VanNESS, Florentine Gill (w/o W H) 9 Feb 1880-9 Dec 1968 Onan
Wade H 24 Oct 1916-24 Sept 1934 Onan
Wade Hampton (h/o F G) 21 Sept 1882-27 Feb 1947 Onan
VanNORTWICK, Joseph L h/o M M 6 Mar 1893-26 Dec 1970 Park
Marie M w/o J L 28 Sept 1888- 21 Aug 1977 Park
VanPELT, Rev J Clarence h/o Mabel VanPelt Finney 8 Nov 1865-29 Feb 1916 MtHo
VanRAEMDONCK, G (Belgium) 7 July 1899-26 June 1972 MtHo-s
Nell w/o G 3 Sept 1907-5 June 1979 MtHo-s
VAUGHAN, Alice B (w/o W J) 1911- Onan
Charles Sidney s/o W J & Alice b&d 23 July 1936 MtHo
W Jeff (h/o A B) 1909-1963 Onan
VENNIE, Mabel 1938-1977 NewM
Ricardo 1862-1970 NewM
VERNON, Emma d 8 Dec 1951; age: 55 yrs Burt
VINCENT, Lacy Gordon 1891- 1965 MtHo-s
Martha Emma 1869-1946 MtHo-s

VINCENT (continued)
Mary Eliza 1899-1977 MtHo-s
Otis William 1894-1972 MtHo-s
Samuel James 1861-1914 MtHo-s
William T s/o W T & Annie (Carbaugh) 25 Dec 1893 in Granite VA-10 Sept 1969 Onan
WADDY, Roberta K w/o E D 15 Sept 1873-11 Oct 1891 (moved from Wilkins bur gr) Edge
WAGART, Margaret A (w/o R A) 1865-1947 MtHo-s
Robert A (h/o M A) 1865-1937 MtHo-s
WAGNER, Jeanne M (w/o M A) 1893-1962 Fair
Melvin A (h/o J M) 1898-1968 Fair
WALENTA, Elizabeth Parks w/o Rev P H 29 Mr 1895 MtHo-s
Rev Paul H h/o E P 6 Nov 1894-3 July 1981 MtHo-s
WALKE, Annie 1903-1979 Gask
WALKER, baby girl b&d 1942 Edge
Annie d 23 Nov 1916; age: 49 yrs Snea
Arenthia E d/o R W & L M 10 Apr-24 Oct 1918 Park
Bessie T w/o M G 1886-1964 Park
Carroll R 1914-1981 Edge
Cecelia d/o H C & M E 25 Sept 1858-19 Oct 1861 StGe
Charles C (h/o E H) 1 Nov 1882-17 Feb 1971 Onan
Charles W 1881-1971 Edge
Charlie 11 Mar 1890-3 Aug 1962 HTri
Elton R 1914-1983 Gask
Emma S w/o R W 14 Feb 1865-6 July 1927 Park
Emory 1877-1960 Edge
Etta M w/o R W 14 Aug 1894-31 Aug 1913 Park
Eva Hopkins (w/o C C) 8 Sept 1883-18 Apr 1968 Onan
Florence G w/o T H 1876-1958 Park
Fredrick Kellam 9 Feb 1915-21 Mar 1967 Walf

WALKER (continued)
George 1924-1980 Gask
George B s/o R W & E S 17 Aug 1899-1 Oct 1919 Park
George W 27 Jan 1829-30 May 1907 Walf
Helen S 1927-1930 Park
Henry C (h/o M E) 6 Jan 1832-18 Mar 1905 StGe
J Seph 1893-1954 HTri
Capt James h/o Sallie; s/o Jas & Eliz 21 Sept 1793-26 Oct 1875 Walk
James s/o Jas & Sally 6 Feb 1840-24 Sept 1842 Walk
James 1924-1973 Gask
James G 1881-1953 Park
John B, 1st h/o Ann T Parramore; s/o Levin & Eliz 26 Apr 1796-7 July 1826 Parr
John Harry h/o M B 1863-1955 MtHo-s
John R s/o Jas & Sallie 15 Dec 1835-4 May 1918 Walk
John S h/o S A 1780-29 Jan 1853 OlWa
John W P d 21 Aug 1825; age: 1/6/26 Parr
Joseph C 23 Mar 1893-7 Oct 1954 HTri
Lavinia 1910-1975 Gask
Lovelace 1928-1983 Gask
Lucinda Parker 3 Apr 1828-1 Feb 1921 Onan
Lula Mears w/o R W 19 July 1896-2 Oct 1934 Park
Margaret E w/o H C 11 June 1836-9 Mar 1923 StGe
Margaret E 1842-1926 Walf
Marguerite W 5 Feb 1896-24 Dec 1980 MtHo-s
Mary A 18 July 1844-13 Apr 1912 StGe
Mary Ann Winder w/o Wm B 30 Jan 1827-19 Mar 1906 StGe
Mary Beach w/o J H 1865-1939 MtHo-s
Mary Kellam 1 Apr 1884-3 Apr 1963 StGe
Mary T w/o R W 31 May 1850-19 Nov 1885 Park
Mollie G 1889-1961 Gask

WALKER (continued)
Muscoe G h/o B T 1879-1941 Park
Page C 1917-1979 Park
Paul W s/o H C & M E 20 Apr-15 Sept 1875 StGe
Percy G Sr 1875-1959 Walf
R Lee s/o R W & M T 22 Nov 1877-6 Dec 1908 Park
Robert 29 Jan 1895-21 Feb 1964 Gask
Robert C 1939-1943 Edge
Robert W h/o E S 9 Oct 1844-13 Feb 1923 Park
Roland W h/o E M & L M 29 May 1890-2 Mar 1954 Park
Sallie w/o Jas; d/o Mayor & Susannah Hornsby 4 Feb 1799-5 Oct 1843 Walk
Sallie B d/o Jas & Sallie 10 June 1832-27 Dec 1899 Walk
Sarah J 1886-1966 Metr
Susan d/o Jas & Sallie 26 Apr 1828-27 Feb 1917 Walk
Susan Ann w/o J S 1792-19 May 1822 OlWa
Thomas H h/o F G 1875-1953 Park
William 1905-1976 Gask
William P d 3 Sept 1821; age: 2/3/12 Parr
WALLACE, Albert C h/o J G 1909- Wach
Anzele w/o Wm; d/o Wm & Anzele Elliott 8 Oct 1790-20 Aug 1865 Brad
Arintha J (w/o F W) 1868-1948 Quin
Cora E w/o R C 1873-1948 MtHo-s
Daniel h/o M B nd Walp
Elizabeth w/o G B 28 Oct 1834-9 July 1915 Walp
Frederick W (h/o A J) 1868-1943 Quin
G Milton (h/o M L) 29 Mar 1903-31 Dec 1976 Edge
George B (h/o Eliz) 6 Jan 1833-17 Sept 1893 Walp
Georgie M w/o J D 1877-1963 Quin
Harry R (h/o V J) 1910- Wach

WALLACE (continued)
J Edward Jr 20 Oct 1924-10 Dec 1946 Quin
Janie M (w/o S F) 1897-1941 Quin
Jeanette G w/o A C 1923-1981 Wach
John D h/o G M 1870-1945 Quin
John O (h/o L R) 1873-1941 Quin
Lela Mae 1922-1924 Quin
Lena R w/o J O 1883-1958 Quin
Louise Bell 1919-1976 Edge
Margaret 1908-1980 Wach
Margaret Boothe w/o Danl nd Walp
Margaret L (w/o G M) 6 July 1908- Edge
Robert C h/o C E 1868-1946 MtHo-s
Ruth A (w/o S C) 1904- Wach
Stanley C (h/o R A) 1901-1958 Wach
Stanley C Jr 1921-1975 Wach
Stanley F (h/o J M) 1895-1965 Quin
Susan w/o Jno 17 Nov 1839-17 May 1912 Wach
Ursula Parks 22 Oct 1902-11 Dec 1980 Quin
Violet J (w/o H R) 1916- Wach
William h/o Anzele 30 Sept 1781-8 Oct 1858; age: 77/0/8 Brad
William Naaman 1905-1943 (photo on marker) Wach
William Naaman s/o A G & J G 1944-1968 Wach
WALLER, George R h/o L G 1876-1935 Oakg
Lola G w/o G R 1883-1974 Oakg
WALLS, s/o L R & M W b&d 1915 Park
LeRoy h/o M W 1893-1965 Park
Mary W w/o L R 1893-1961 Park
WALSTON, Catherine Teakle d/o Wm & Anna G 16 Apr 1839-26 Aug 1840 Wals
Margaret A d/o Wm & Anna G 22 Jan-24 Oct 1845 Wals
Mary w/o Saml 28 Oct 1773-27 Dec 1827 Wals
Samuel 19 Mar 1778-16 June

WALSTON (continued)
1833 Wals
Samuel s/o Wm & Anna G 1 Jan 1834-25 Sept 1841 Wals
Samuel I s/o Wm & Anna G 18 Apr 1843-18 Apr 1880 Seve
Thomas s/o Wm & Anna G 16 Nov 1810-25 Sept 1811 Wals
William s/o Saml & Mary 7 Jan 1806-4 Oct 1868 Wals
William B 28 May 1836-7 Sept 1866 Wals
WALTENBERG, Romaine G 1889-1980 MtHo-s
WALTER, Ann d 24 Jan 1856; age: 34 yrs (moved from Walter grave) Fair
Audrey Winder (w/o J F) 24 May 1903-20 July 1954 MtHo
Edwin LeCato s/o J S & L S 24 May 1870-14 Oct 1892 Fair
G Smith (h/o L B) 25 Dec 1859-17 Sept 1921 Onan
George 1883-1958 Shil
George Edwin (h/o M C) 19 Dec 1900-23 Mar 1974 MtHo
George W 31 Aug 1820-4 Jan 1844 Quin
J Harry 25 Nov 1887-19 Jan 1934 MtHo
Jackson L s/o J S & L S 20 May 1872-10 Apr 1889 Fair
James B s/o J S & Ann 19 Sept 1850-8 Jan 1890 Fair
Jefferson Davis s/o J S & L S 2 Jan 1862-11 Jan 1884 Fair
Jefferson F (h/o A W) 18 June 1890-11 June 1966 MtHo
John Richard h/o R T; s/o Jno S & Mary 13 Aug 1841-4 Oct 1888; age 47 yrs StGe
John Savage (h/o L S); s/o Richd & Polly 10 Dec 1812-19 Dec 1874 Fair
Lena B (w/o G S) 16 Apr 1871-10 Feb 1950 Onan
Dr Littleton Thomas; s/o J S & L S 22 Mar 1860-17 May 1884 Fair
Lydia S w/o J S 23 July 1843-28 Nov 1881 Fair
Mabel Cathey (w/o G E) 17 Oct

WALTER (continued)
1903- MtHo
Mary A w/o Jno S; d/o Jno S & E B Beach 30 July 1813-1 Feb 1847 Beac
Mary Belote (w/o N F) 3 Jan 1862-4 Mar 1960 MtHo
Mary Benson w/o Richd Sr d 20 Sept 1836; age: 52 yrs Quin
Nathaniel F (h/o M B) 22 Jan 1856-26 July 1934 MtHo
Richard (h/o M B) d 26 Jan 1840; age: 66/0/8 Quin
Roland Elwood 14 June 1920-28 Aug 1976 HTri
Rose T w/o Jno R 13 July 1847-19 May 1915 StGe
William H 1913-1960 Shil
Willie Hugh s/o J S & L S d 5 Oct 1870; age: 3/0/0 Fair
WALTERS, Sarah A (w/o W J) 1876-1947 MtHo-s
William J (h/o S A) 1876-1932 MtHo-s
WAPLES, s/o Wm & Virginia b&d 2 Sept 1944 Onan
Alice Woodward d/o Jno S & Lizzie T 14 Mar 1888-11 Dec 1898 Onan
Anna D w/o S T 28 May 1854-27 Apr 1915 Onan
Charles S (h/o M F) 1865-1957 Onan
Mrs E Agnes d/o Revell & Eliz West 12 Dec 1843-2 Jan 1929 Onan
Edward B h/o S A F; s/o Saml & S P 17 Jan 1825-8 Nov 1912 Onan
Edward B Jr h/o M E; s/o E B & S A F 19 Jan 1855-2 May 1938 Onan
Edward Jennings s/o O Jennings & Emma S 16 Aug 1892-27 Aug 1893 Onan
Elizabeth Woodward w/o J S 4 Aug 1856-30 Apr 1939 Onan
Eva Gray w/o E B 4 July 1869-29 July 1939 MtHo-s
Fletcher R 11 June 1886-26 Feb 1887 Onan
George P s/o J S & E T 31 July

281

WAPLES (continued)
1885-1 Mar 1892 Onan
John Scarbrough h/o E W 23 Jan 1857-14 June 1944 Onan
Maggie Finney (w/o C S) 1866-1946 Onan
Martha W d/o Saml & S P 26 Nov 1827-4 Feb 1867 Onan
Mary E w/o E B Jr; d/o S R & Mary Chandler 1 Apr 1858-12 Nov 1894 Onan
Sabra P w/o Saml; d/o Henry & Sallie Townsend 9 May 1791-23 Dec 1856; mar: 20 Aug 1822 Onan
Sallie F d/o E B & S A 12 July 1859-18 May 1863 Onan
Capt Samuel h/o S P 9 June 1755-11 Aug 1834 (Rev soldier) Onan
Samuel T h/o A D 10 Sept 1852-5 Aug 1934 Onan
Sarah A w/o E B; d/o T W & Sally Finney 24 Jan 1823-13 June 1886 Onan
Sarah Elizabeth 1883-1950 Onan
Sarah T d/o Saml & S P 13 Dec 1823-25 Sept 1870 Onan
WARD, Alex J (h/o P E) 22 Jan 1826-31 May 1892 Ward
Alice A w/o Louis F; d/o J E & M E Bell ns LeCa
Alice B w/o G W 28 Aug 1896-2 Mar 1920 MtHo
Alice S 8 Sept 1833-14 Apr 1919 MtHo
Andrew L 26 Nov-2 Dec 1849; age: 0/0/11 Ward
Annabelle D w/o G H 1906- Gask
Annie M 1851-1933 Onan
Arthur J s/o A J & P E 22 Mar 1856-1 Sept 1891 Ward
Bernard S (h/o M S) 1901-1981 Fair
Bettie J (w/o J C) 1874-1960 Quin
Dial s/o Lancelot & M A d 25 Jan 1852; age: 35/3/24 Warp
Ethan Allen 6-14 Sept 1853 Ward
George G s/o Jno L & Susan J d 23 Aug 1866; {ge: 2/8/29 JnoS
George H h/o A D 1900-1983 Gask

WARD (continued)
Gask
George W h/o W L 14 Jan 1872-7 Nov 1933 Onan
George W (h/o M M F) 10 Mar 1894-22 Sept 1948 Fair
George William s/o G W & Alice 28 May 1917-28 Apr 1918 MtHo
Harvey J (h/o R S) 1853-1910 Fair
Hattie M w/o J H 1885-1973 Burt
James H h/o H M 1875-1951 Burt
James N s/o Wm & Margt S; (faithful husband) Apr 1826-June 1887 Warb
Jennie H (w/o W D) 17 May 1856-14 Oct 1917 Quin
John 1876-1956 Snea
John Cutt (h/o B J) 1875-1962 Quin
John G s/o Jno L & Malinda 26 Mar 1855-30 Sept 1873 JnoS
John L 25 May 1826-9 Oct 1898 JnoS
John Lester s/o Jno L & Annie M 30 Sept 1884-20 Oct 1918 Onan
John Thomas 1903-1936 Quin
Lancelot h/o M A 15 Jan 1791-30 Dec 1856 Warp
Langylot s/o Lancylot & M A 11 July 1829-15 Sept 1882; age: 52/2/4 Warp
Letty R w/o Albert D; d/o Nathl & Mary Badger 14 Sept 1807-2 July 1855; age: 47/9/18 Badg
Letty S 2 June 1842-9 Dec 1858 Warp
Lillian W (w/o W F) 1888-1954 Quin
Mae Gaskins w/o P P 1897-1964 Quin
Margaret M Finney (w/o G W) 25 July 1900-13 Mar 1964 Fair
Margaret S w/o W P 15 Sept 1800-10 May 1835 Warb
Margaret S (w/o B S) 1914-1970 Fair
Mary A w/o Lancelot (d/o Jas East) 7 Sept 1799-9 July 1861;

WARD (continued)
age: 61/10/2 Warp
Mary E w/o Jas N; d/o Jas K & Eliz Shield 13 Dec 1833-20 Aug 1852 Shie
Paul P h/o M G; s/o Jas 1898-1963 Quin
Peggy E w/o A J 4 Oct 1830-19 Dec 1869 Ward
R Susan (w/o H J) 1860-1942 Fair
Sarah A w/o Wm M; d/o Bagwell C & Margt Mason d 18 Oct 1859; age: 27/1/29 Warp
Susan J w/o J L 26 July 1819-13 Jan 1881 JnoS
W Frank (h/o L W) 1884-1943 Quin
W Frank Jr nd Quin
William D (h/o J H) 24 June 1856-11 Sept 1917 Quin
William P h/o M S 24 Mar 1800-6 May 1885 Warb
Winiferd L w/o G W 13 July 1882-17 July 1963 Onan
WARNER, Emily J w/o G J 31 July 1825-28 July 1883 BunW
George J h/o E J 2 May 1823-1 Aug 1881 BunW
J Harry (h/o M R) 1906-1981 Fair
Lorenzo G 21 June 1857-11 Jan 1882 BunW
Mollie R (w/o J H) 1911- Fair
Willie s/o G J & E J 21 Feb 1846-27 June 1866 BunW
WARREN, inf/o Geo & Ella b&d 1900 Quin
Ada Lee d/o L D & E M d 16 Nov 1909 MtHo
Anna J 1856-1940 Holl
Annette Vickers d/o L D & E M 1887-1924 MtHo
Bettie D (w/o J G) 1883-1961 Onan
Caroline Alice d/o L D & E M 1875-1923 MtHo
Charles Laws 4 Feb 1894-30 Aug 1967 StGe
Don s/o Frank & Margt 1948-1969 Quin
Elizabeth Scott 1818-1884 Onan

WARREN (continued)
Ella G w/o G W 1883-1951 Quin
Emma C 1866-1959 Holl
Emma Morris w/o L D 1848-1920 MtHo
Ethel M (w/o J M) 1915- Quin
Finney W h/o W P; s/o A B & M L 10 May 1888-8 May 1977 Park
Gaston s/o Geo & Ella b&d 1903 Quin
George W h/o E G 1877-1966 Quin
Hebard L (h/o M D) 10 Mar 1861-1 Oct 1913 Onan
J Garland (h/o B D) 1884-1964 Onan
James M (h/o E M) 1906-1947 Quin
John (h/o T M 3 Mar 1822-2 May 1899 Holl
John Laws (h/o S T) 28 Oct 1851-18 Mar 1934 StGe
John Laws 1905-1967 StGe
Laws nd StGe
Levin Dix h/o E M 18 Aug 1843-15 July 1902 MtHo
Lynwood G 25 Apr 1892-15 Oct 1957 Onan
Mary D (w/o H L) 14 Dec 1867-10 Nov 1934 Onan
Rev Patrick 22 Dec 1816 Northampton Co VA-12 Mar 1871 Washington DC Onan
Randall s/o Geo & Ella 1910-1912 Quin
Ryland R 1 Sept 1901-17 Aug 1938 Onan
Sarah T w/o J L 18 Aug 1862-11 Sept 1915 StGe
Susan Frances 1841-1907 StGe
Tabitha M w/o Jno 24 Jan 1825-18 Feb 1896 Holl
William Otho 1871-1887 StGe
WARRINGTON, John T s/o Jno K & Sarah 7 Mar 1817-29 Apr 1852; age: 34/11/22 (moved from Burckard bur gr) Onan
WASHBURN, Edna Savage 1906-1945 Wach
WASHINGTON, Cordelia V 1921-1981 Shil

WASHINGTON (continued)
E Goldie 1899-1963 NewM
Gladys 1910-1967 Gask
WATERFIELD, d/o W T & Anne E nd age: 0/7/0 Leve
Annie E (w/o W T) 20 June 1862-24 July 1958 Ptea
Annie N (w/o C I) 1901- StGe
Carroll I (h/o A N) 1899-1979 StGe
Emma Sue d/o J T & M E 31 May-3 Nov 1898 Onan
Fred J (h/o J L) 1878-1953 StGe
J S 17 Nov 1832-10 Aug 1909 Holl
James T h/o M E 1872-1950 Onan
James W h/o S L 1849-1921 Onan
Janie E (w/o L T) 1889-1966 Fair
Jennie L (w/o F J) 1879-1953 StGe
John T 10 Apr 1841-18 Jan 1916 Holl
Leland T (h/o J E) 1884-1969 Fair
Manie E w/o J T 1873-1942 Onan
Margaret S (mother) 4 May 1826-26 July 1884 Warb
Maude H (w/o W B) 26 June 1897-7 Mar 1971 StGe
Ralph V 1 Jan 1887-17 Jan 1962 Ptea
Rossetta Anne w/o Jas P Haley & Wm H Waterfield d 21 Feb 1910; age: 87/5/26 MtHo
Susan L w/o J W 1853-1932 Onan
W Benson (h/o M H) 4 May 1896- StGe
William H, 2nd h/o R A 17 Apr 1825-9 Aug 1907 MtHo
William T (h/o A E) 14 June 1857-9 Nov 1918 Ptea
William T 1922-1971 Fair
WATERHOUSE, Frank L h/o R S 28 Oct 1866-28 Oct 1935 Park
George W 1907-1944 Park
H L s/o F L & S B W b&d 1890 Park

WATERHOUSE (continued)
John W 1869-1953 Park
Len 1910-1929 Park
Len F h/o V M 1890-1971 Park
Mary F 1879-1960 Park
Nellie 1922-1923 Park
Rebecca S w/o F L 1 Mar 1868-5 Mar 1959 Park
Susie b&d 1920 Park
Virgie M w/o L F 1895- Park
WATERS, Charles B 1923-1938 Burt
E Thomas h/o T J 1 Nov 1874-13 Jan 1949 Onan
Edwin Lee 1920-1976 Fair
Edwin T s/o Wm C & Margt W d 12 May 1875; age: 30/4/10 LeaW
Estella P (w/o W E) 1895-1964 MtHo-s
George E s/o Geo C & Malinda d 13 Nov 1873; age: 27/3/27 Bogb
Heyward R 20 Sept 1922-29 Nov 1944 MtHo-s
Margaret W d 30 Sept 1886; age: 70/7/0 (50 yrs a Methodist) LeaW
Tibbie J w/o E T 11 Oct 1880-6 Apr 1971 Onan
William E (h/o E P) 1883-1942 MtHo-s
WATKINSON, s/o F H & M E b&d 16 Dec 1906 Edge
A Cora w/o W T 1881-1943 Edge
Alfred B 24 Apr 1908-22 Dec 1925 Edge
Almer R s/o B E & A M 2 Oct 1905-5 June 1934 MtHo-s
Annie E w/o J T 13 Feb 1840-17 Feb 1927 Edge
Annie J d/o W T & A C 13 Sept 1902-30 May 1904 Edge
Annie M (w/o B E) 1874-1942 MtHo-s
Benjamin E (h/o A M) 1869-1960 MtHo-s
Benjamin F 19 July 1859-8 Oct 1924 Edge
Bessie E (w/o W E) 1892-1970 MtHo-s
Bessie W 1926-1982 Edge

WATKINSON (continued)
Blanche M 30 Sept 1885-17 May 1941 Edge
Cathrine J w/o J W 16 Apr 1841-2 Apr 1909 MtHo
Cecil E 1909-1972 Fair
Charles J (h/o N M) 1896-1971 Fair
Clarence I 1894-1961 Edge
Cornelious S h/o J A 30 Oct 1854-7 Dec 1919 Edge
David W 1856-1934 MtHo
Dudley P 1916-1976 Edge
Edith May 1912-1929 Park
Edward T h/o L G 1878-1939 Edge
Emaline 1907-1971 MtHo-s
Fletcher 1891-1972 MtHo-s
Floyd L 1890-1944 MtHo
Frank H h/o M E 1883-1935 Edge
George 1872-1939 Edge
George H h/o W A 28 May 1843-12 Aug 1935 Edge
Gertie A 1916- MtHo
Gilbert J 1893-1963 MtHo
Golden F 1855-1908 Edge
Haywood K b&d 1928 MtHo-s
Jackie Lee s/o R S & S H 1947-1975 Onan
Jennie West w/o Wm C 1886-1970 Park
John R h/o L E 1926-1980 Fair
John T h/o A E d 28 June 1910; age: 75 yrs Edge
John W h/o M L 1871-1952 Libe
Julia A w/o C S 12 July 1856-6 July 1933 Edge
Lella Mae 1883-1961 MtHo
Lester E 4 Apr 1895-9 Sept 1981 MtHo-s
Levin h/o S A 5 Mar 1838-22 Jan 1919 Edge
Lizzie R 1895-1976 MtHo
Lois E w/o J R 1928- Fair
Lola Gertrude w/o E T 29 July 1880-19 Oct 1968 Edge
Luther B 1889-1965 Edge
Maggie L w/o J W 1882-1955 Libe
Mamie J w/o R L 1887-1940 Park

WATKINSON (continued)
Margaret A w/o Geo 25 Oct 1825-16 May 1903 Edge
Margaret E 1862-1932 MtHo
Mary E w/o F H 1882-1955 Edge
Meadie Martin 1899-1966 Park
Mildred E w/o R V 1897-1978 MtHo-s
Myrtle Lee w/o R E 1911-1982 MtHo-s
Nellie M (w/o C J) 1901-1961 Fair
Phillip D 7 Dec 1923-10 Sept 1928 Edge
Ralph V h/o M E 1898-1947 MtHo-s
Reede S h/o S H 1919- Onan
Robert L h/o M J 1888-1966 Park
Roy E h/o M L 1910- MtHo-s
Ruth M w/o W T; (d/o E H & V S Young) 1910-1965 Edge
Sallie A w/o Levin 7 Jan 1837-25 May 1904 Edge
Samuel S 1866-1958 Edge
Samuel W 1910-1965 Edge
Sarah E 1850-1932 Park
Sue H w/o R S 1924- Onan
Thelma Northam w/o Wm F 1903- Park
Walter E (h/o B E) 1887-1946 MtHo-s
Walter F 1901-1963 Libe
Wellington T h/o A C 1879-1965 Edge
Wesley B s/o C S & J A 27 Jan 1891-26 May 1914 Edge
Wesley J 1852-1935 Edge
William Coley h/o J W 1876-1954 Park
William F h/o T N 1906-1979 Park
William T h/o R M 1907-1977 Edge
Willie A w/o G H 11 Feb 1861-10 Sept 1908 Edge
WATSON, s/o W T & M H nd footstone - C B W MtHo
s/o Rev J C & H J b&d 15 Jan 1880 Onan
d/o W G b&d 27 Oct 1942 MtHo-s

WATSON (continued)
Addie Allen w/o M F 1888- Edge
Albert Thomas (h/o L B) 1877-1956 Fair
Allen Ray s/o O D & R N 5 Aug 1898-15 Oct 1918; killed in France Edge
Alpheus Hill s/o J A & S E d1872; age: 0/1/0 Grot
Annie 1924-1980 Snea
Annie B w/o Thos P 20 July 1823-14 Apr 1896 Wats
Annie B d/o J R & Ida W 12 Dec 1904-25 Apr 1911 MtHo
Annie Bundick w/o Jas R; d/o Geo W & Nancy Mason 6 Feb 1851-13 Oct 1889 Wats
Annie V w/o H O 28 Feb 1854-27 June 1904 MtHo
Arthur d 17 Apr 1819; age: 51 yrs Onan
Arthur, MD h/o M H 6 July 1817-24 Feb 1900 Onan
Arthur H h/o L T 1895-1958 Wach
Benjamin (h/o Susan) 28 May 1767-10 Mar 1838; age: 71 yrs Wate
Benjamin F h/o M C 1879-1934 Wach
Benjamin L 17 Apr 1867-17 Nov 1873 Edge
Bessie B d/o J C & M R 18 Jan-1 July 1892 MtHo-s
Bessie E w/o S R 1883-1964 MtHo
Blanche Rich 1893-1956 Edge
Bobby 1943-1974 MtHo
Burleigh W h/o L S 1 May 1879-24 May 1943 Park
Carrie Flora w/o Thos B 1 Dec 1865-8 Dec 1904 NewM
Carrie W w/o H C 1881-1962 MtHo
Charles Fletcher h/o M M 1858-1942 MtHo
Charlie Bagwell s/o W T & M H 5 Nov 1885-5 Oct 1886 MtHo
Charlie Oscar s/o W T & M H 1 Oct 1882-30 June 1884 MtHo
Charlie R s/o Jessie & Jennie M 23 Jan-28 July 1912 MtHo

WATSON (continued)
Cornelia F 1868-1948 Edge
Corra d/o Jos & Georgia d 30 Jan 1875 Park
E Corbin (h/o J J) 15 Feb 1873-19 May 1917 MtHo
Edward R h/o E W 1804-1896 Onan
Elizabeth w/o Jno 7 Feb 1781-24 July 1859 Coke
Elizabeth M w/o Jos C 27 Sept 1822-6 Feb 1883 Coke
Elizabeth S w/o J E 23 Jan 1829-14 Feb 1908 Edge
Elizabeth S w/o J E 17 Feb 1854-27 Dec 1925 Edge
Elizabeth W w/o E R 1813-1893 Onan
Elmer T 1905-1961 MtHo
Ethel Nock w/o Wm H 1892-1973 Park
Eunice L w/o M C 14 May 1902- Park
Fitzhugh L 1905-1981 Edge
Florence Crippen d/o J A & S E d1871; age: 0/1/0 Grot
George C h/o S C 1847-192 MtHo
George Granville (h/o M D) 28 Apr 1893-14 Feb 1972 Wach
George S 16 Aug 1840-7 Jan 1911 MtNe(E)
Georgie A 21 Dec 1850-9 Mar 1902 Park
Gillet d 9 Apr 1819; age: 23 yrs Onan
Golden F h/o R A 10 Apr 1858-4 Apr 1931 Onan
Harriet S w/o W F 24 Nov 1860-23 Apr 1924 Edge
Henry O h/o A V 21 Oct 1845-28 June 1921 MtHo
Herman C h/o C W 1882-1968 MtHo
Ida B w/o J R 1866-1955 MtHo
J Hughes (h/o M H) 1906-1964 Fair
J W (Bill) 1919-1981 Wach
James Alfred h/o S E K 9 Nov 1847-29 Sept 1883; mar: 19 Dec 1867 Grot
James H 19 Oct 1816-1 Jan 1863 Coke

WATSON (continued)
James R h/o Ida W 2 Feb 1854-23 July 1927 MtHo
James S 14 Jan 1864-26 Sept 1870 Edge
James T 1872-1959 MtHo
James T (h/o L E) 26 July 1884-10 July 1910 MtHo-s
Jessie W 1876-1954 MtHo
Jimmie d1876; age: 0/4/0 Grot
John 22 Dec 1782-5 June 1843 Coke
John s/o A H & L T b&d 4 July 1917 Wach
John C 4 May 1813-18 Nov 1896 Wate
John E h/o E S 23 Aug 1822-15 May 1885 Edge
John E h/o E S 5 Jan 1851-24 July 1934 Edge
John E (h/o M S) 1887-1951 MtHo-s
John E 1900-1967 NewM
John Frank s/o Thos P & Annie B 23 Dec 1846-14 Aug 1872 Wats
John H d 4 Dec 1911; age: 51 yrs NewM
John J 26 Apr 1874-24 Oct 1950 Park
John M (1st h/o S Parker Heath) 29 Dec 1791-19 June 1835 OldP
John M h/o M H 28 Dec 1874-24 Feb 1937 MtHo
Joseph C 24 Aug 1826-24 May 1862; age: 35/9/0 Coke
Joseph C h/o M R 5 Aug 1862-23 Jan 1957 MtHo-s
Julia J (w/o E C) 20 Aug 1877-26 Oct 1928 MtHo
L O h/o M E 1850-1926 MtHo
Levenia S w/o B W 16 May 1883-10 Oct 1964 Park
Lillian E (w/o J T) 1 Sept 1886-30 June 1933 MtHo-s
Lizzie Neville, 2nd w/o W T 7 Dec 1855-22 Dec 1912 MtHo
Lizzie S d/o W F & H S 20 July 1887-15 May 1898 Edge
Lottie Budd (w/o A T) 1883-1979 Fair

WATSON (continued)
Louise W 1887-1974 NewM
Lucille T w/o A H 1895-1977 Wach
Lucy (Pitts) w/o Arthur J d 18 Feb 1887; age: 76 yrs Pitt
M Clifton h/o E L 3 Feb 1905-9 Oct 1982 Park
Maggie Davis (w/o G G) 28 June 1899- Wach
Maggie R w/o J C 11 Oct 1859-28 Mar 1925 MtHo-s
Major Fosque h/o A A 1886-1965 Edge
Margaret 1949-1981 Snea
Margaret S (w/o J E) 1889- MtHo-s
Mary C (w/o B F) 1880-1967 Wach
Mary E w/o L O 1853-1925 MtHo
Mary H, 1st w/o W T 2 June 1853-16 Mar 1895 MtHo
Mary Mason w/o C F 1859-1939 MtHo
Mary Nixon w/o Dr Arthur 14 Apr 1827-25 May 1865; age: 38/1/11 Onan
Mary V 1888-1954 MtHo
Mildred H (w/o J H) 1913- Fair
Minnie H w/o J M 23 Dec 1872-8 Mar 1953 MtHo
Nannie E A 1892- MtHo
Olive Hazel d/o O D & R N 8 Sept 1905-6 July 1908 Edge
Olivia E 1879-1923 MtHo
Oscar D h/o R N 1875-1966 Edge
Oscar W 1901-1976 MtHo
Otho Lee 1904-1956 MtHo
Peter L h/o S G 1877-1957 MtHo
Rachel A w/o G F 15 Jan 1858-1 July 1906 Onan
Rebecca Norman w/o O D 1874-1961 Edge
Rodger Bruce s/o S R & B B 2 Feb 1915-14 Sept 1916 MtHo
Roger G 1914-1948 Park
Sallie G w/o P L 1890-1974 MtHo
Spencer R h/o B E 1880-1937 MtHo
Susan w/o Benj d 14 Apr 1837; age: 62 yrs Wate

WATSON (continued)
Susan C w/o G C 1849-1921 MtHo
Susan Elizabeth w/o J A; d/o Thos & Tabitha Kellam 18 Feb 1845-14 Jan 1927; age: 82 yrs Grot
Thomas d 4 Oct 1946; age: 30 yrs NewM
Thomas P h/o A B 11 Mar 1821-7 Aug 1907 Wats
Trevie D 1898- MtHo
Urbany Vassa d/o J A & S E 1869-1870; age: 0/1/0 Grot
Vernon 1 May 1879-3 Dec 1960 Fair
Virginia Susan 1897-1971 MtHo
Weldon 1910-1977 MtHo
Wilber J s/o Jno & Maggie 31 Jan 1916-1 Apr 1918 MtHo
William 1902-1979 Fair
William Columbus s/o Jos & Georgie 20 Nov 1875-1 Dec 1880 Park
William F h/o H S 20 Nov 1862-26 Apr 1923 Edge
William G 13 Oct 1902-29 Nov 1979 Fair
William H h/o E N 1883-1956 Park
William Jeter s/o Rev J C & H J 4 Nov 1878-15 July 1880 Onan
William T h/o M H & L N 1849-1946 MtHo
Willianna Olive d/o J A & S E K 9 Nov 1873-2 June 1893; age: 19/6/23 Grot
Willie G 1903-1973 MtHo
WATTS, s/o Robt & Janice b&d 20 Feb 1963 Park
Edwin h/o M R 1902- Libe
Evelyn Justis 8 Feb 1893-15 Feb 1967 Park
Howard h/o J M 18 Sept 1893-8 Aug 1964 Park
John David 24 May 1852-22 Aug 1917 Park
John R 15 Mar-31 July 1957 Park
Julia M w/o Howard 28 May 1893-7 Oct 1967 Park
Madeline Riley w/o Edwin 1905-1976 Libe

WATTS (continued)
Madeline S 31 Jan 1898-26 Nov 1900 Park
Mary E 20 Feb 1872-24 Jan 1962 Park
WEAL, Major 1895-1982 Snea
Mollie 1905-1974 Snea
WEAVER, Etta d/o J C & M S d 5 Sept 1881; age: 10 wks Onan
James C h/o M S 25 Dec 1822-30 June 1900 Onan
Martha Snead w/o J C 23 Nov 1839-16 July 1899 Onan
WEBB, Annie K 1905-1908 Park
Catherine A w/o S R 1871-1928 Park
Claude A (h/o Carrie) 24 Dec 1912-2 July 1975 Wach
Dorsey L 1 July 1901-6 Aug 1932 Park
Dorty L h/o E M 5 June 1892-7 May 1949 Park
Ella H (w/o R H) 1881- StJo
Essie Mae w/o D L 1894-1976 Park
G Blanding h/o H M 1898-1964 Quin
George 1904-1968 Shil
Hilda M w/o G B 1901- Quin
James 1912-1979 Gask
John T 15 June 1875-20 Jan 1915 Park
Lettie R 1889-1959 NewM
Lillie S 1895-1978 Gask
Mary E d/o Jno & Emma 27 July 1885-11 Sept 1903 StJo
Randolph s/o G B & H M 22 Oct 1924-9 Jan 1925 Quin
Robert H (h/o E H) 1879-1963 StJo
Southey R h/o C A 1855-1918 Park
WEBSTER, Bertha 1903-1972 Gask
WEEKS, Dean S 1883-1959 Wach
Elizabeth S 16 July 1858 in London England-21 Jan 1890 Wach
WEIR, Mabel M (w/o T M) 1917- Onan
Thomas M (h/o M M) 1915-1979 Onan

WELCH, Helen J w/o Wm M Jr 1923- Quin
May F (w/o W M Sr) 1883-1936 Quin
Sarah H d/o Wm & Eliz d 9 July 1847; age: 37/6/15(13?) GeoH
William M Sr (h/o M F) 1882-1944 Quin
William M Jr (h/o H J) 1916-1979 Quin
WELLS, Alan Kelso s/o Richd B & Etruria 6 Dec 1924-1 Jan 1925 Onan
WERNER, Harry 1887-1959 Onan
Margaret Melson w/o Henry 1891-1929 Edge
WESCOTT, Alice E (d/o Hester C) 1892-1924 StGe
Annie Copes 21 June 1869-4 May 1945 MtHo
Carrie Tunnell 5 May 1891-26 Aug 1969 MtHo
E D h/o V S 1 Jan 1838-30 May 1908 Holl
George Homer 1 Apr 1923-15 Feb 1944; age: 20 yrs MtHo
George J h/o N S 31 July 1891-3 Dec 1975 MtHo
George T s/o Rev G C & M A 8 Jan 1833-28 Dec 1891 Oakg
Gustave H 12 Feb 1901-9 Apr 1977 Edge
Gustave T (h/o J A) 6 June 1862-6 Sept 1934 Edge
Hester Catherine 1850-1923 StGe
J Clayton s/o J C & S P 1889-1931 Onan
John L 20 Nov 1889-3 May 1913 StGe
Joseph Clayton h/o S P 1856-1923 Onan
Julia A (w/o G T) 12 Jan 1873-8 May 1939 Edge
Lean McAllen Powell w/o N B 16 July 1857-27 Sept 1948 Edge
Lottie V w/o Jos C; d/o L T & E K James 20 Feb 1860-1 Sept 1884 Leve
Lucy Anderson (w/o W C) 6 Nov 1889-7 Apr 1974 MtHo
Major Joseph (h/o R A) 24 Apr

WESCOTT (continued)
1888-16 Dec 1973 Onan
Major T 24 June 1844-24 Sept 1879; age: 35/3/0 Pitt
Mary A w/o Rev Geo C d 30 Aug 1879; age: c70 yrs Oakg
Nathaniel B h/o L McA 14 Sept 1856-18 Mar 1930 Edge
Nina S w/o G J 1895- MtHo
Robert Lee 23 Apr 1890-14 Sept 1958 MtHo
Rubie Ann (w/o M J) 11 Apr 1897- Onan
Sallie Polk w/o J C 1853-22 June 1944 Onan
Virginia S w/o E D 15 July 1839-28 Apr 1917 Holl
William Copes (h/o L A) 28 Nov 1888-30 May 1951 MtHo
William W 23 Dec 1852-22 May 1904 StGe
Willie Joynes W W & H C Wescott 1 Mar 1881-9 Jan 1900 StGe
WESSELLS, infs 3 stones marked "infant" - prob ch/o Thos & Carrie Wess
inf/o E J & M E d 25 June 1886 Park
inf (prob of E & N R) b&d 1890 Libe
inf/o E J & M E d 3 Oct 1890 Park
s/o Thos & Carrie 23 Oct-25 Dec 1890 Wess
d/o W B & L E b&d 27 Oct 1916 Park
A J h/o Georgianna 24 Sept 1842-22 Nov 1906 Wess
Ada Mayfield nd Libe
Addie Annis 1904-1969 Libe
Addie Mae w/o Beauregard 30 Jan 1885-5 Jan 1977 Libe
Agustus F h/o Elisha nd Park
Alfred H h/o L C 1876-1965 Edge
Alice H w/o K D 1910- Fair
Amanda H 23 Aug 1901-2 Aug 1969 Libe
Andrew J 1867-1947 Park
Anna E w/o Wm T 1970-1942 Park

WESSELLS (continued)
Annie B w/o O L 1877-1951 Libe
Annie L nd Park
Arinthia C 1868-1953 Libe
Arthur h/o M A 2 Apr 1839-1 Sept 1915 Park
Arthur J h/o B C 1871-1941 Park
Asa C 3 Dec 1879-11 Mar 1917 Park
Ashton Percelle s/o A D & Lula 2 May 1899-25 July 1900 Park
Augustus D s/o A F & Alishia 14 June 1877-16 Feb 1907 Park
Beauregard h/o A M 17 Mar 1883-29 May 1949 Libe
Belle d/o Jas T 1877-1924 Park
Bertie C w/o A J 1875- Park
Bertie L (w/o S E) 1887-1946 Edge
Betsy nd Park
Bettie W w/o Wm J 1855-1933 Park
Caroline G (w/o G T) 18 Feb 1872-7 Oct 1930 Edge
Carrie J w/o H C 1903- Park
Carroll H 1913-1974 Park
Cecil M s/o W B & L E 26 Aug 1901-25 Feb 1905 Park
Clara H d/o A J & Georgianna 30 Oct 1885-13 May 1891 Wess
Columbus 1848-1924 Park
Daisy B w/o H L 1893-1977 Park
David Calvin h/o L W 12 Mar 1899-15 Jan 1975 Edge
Dixie T 1899-1946 Park
Dorsey H h/o E R 20 Nov 1889-8 Jan 1941 Park
E Jackson h/o M E 15 May 1862-13 Jan 1947 Park
Earl J h/o J M 22 Oct 1893-15 Oct 1961 Park
Edward nd Park
Elisha w/o A F 12 Nov 1855-29 Dec 1914 Park
Emily L w/o J D 1863-1934 Park
Ephraim h/o N R 3 Aug 1857-21 Nov 1908 Libe
Essie M w/o S M 1894-1966 Onan
Estolia 1911-1981 Libe
Eudie G 1882-1955 Park
Eva B 1874-1927 Park

WESSELLS (continued)
Eveline T w/o G C 8 Dec 1847-26 Oct 1906 Libe
F Lee (h/o M L) 1885-1962 Fair
Frederick W (h/o N L) 14 Sept 1888-30 Sept 1975 Edge
George 1922-1959 Metr
George C h/o N R 1867-1946 Park
George T (h/o C G) 27 Nov 1866-10 Jan 1954 Edge
Georgiana (w/o A J) 11 Nov 1848-11 Oct 1934 Edge
Graham E 1936-1953 Park
H Blanche d/o Wm J & B W 1897-1913 Park
Harold Webster 14 Nov 1917-10 Oct 1958 Fair
Harry A 1896-1964 Park
Harry C h/o C J 1898-1974 Park
Henry L h/o D B 1891-1961 Park
Iva Lee 1899-1951 Park
J Ephraim (h/o D J) 1879-1948 Park
J W 4 May 1854-6 Nov 1915 Park
James F h/o Vianna 11 Dec 1872-4 May 1917 Park
James T 1840-1929 Park
Jane R 12 Apr 1852-3 May 1910 Park
Jeff D h/o E L 1861-1946 Park
Jennie M w/o E J 5 May 1910-18 Sept 1978 Park
Jerry Wayne s/o H Carlton & Louise 1943-1952 Fair
Jewel C d/o E J & M E 21 Aug-19 Nov 1889 Park
John W 6 Sept 1887-31 Oct 1948 Park
John W (h/o M L) 15 July 1890-10 May 1937 Fair
Julia Elizabeth d/o W B & L E 5 Oct 1896-21 May 1915 Park
Kermit D h/o A H 1908- Fair
L Bates h/o Mary E 12 Jan 1860-18 Sept 1929 Park
Lee Etta w/o Wm B 1876-1953 Park
Lillian w/o Wm 6 May 1880-6 June 1962 Park
Lillie R w/o O T 1904-1984 Libe

WESSELLS (continued)
Lina Pearl 10 June 1891-7 July 1966 Libe
Louise m/o Jerry & Barry 1924-1970 Fair
Louise C w/o A H 1881-1940 Edge
Louise Wright w/o D C 17 Jan 1905- Edge
Lucy Matthews w/o Harry C; m/o Page F 1900-1920 Libe
Luther E h/o S S 25 July 1872-28 Sept 1937 Edge
Manie E w/o E J 7 May 1864-19 Sept 1937 Park
Manie L (w/o F L) 1887-1952 Fair
Marcella T 20 Aug 1911-10 Nov 1980 Edge
Mrs Marian 1891-1968 Libe
Marion E d/o J E & D J 25 June 1910-27 Jan 1915 Park
Marvin J 1893-1961 Park
Mary A w/o Arthur 24 Apr 1853-1 Apr 1917 Park
Mary E w/o L B 15 Apr 1863-9 Dec 1945 Park
Mary J w/o O F 3 Mar 1853-21 Nov 1939 Park
Mary J d/o A F & Elisha 27 Aug 1889-9 Aug 1907 Park
Minnie Lewis (w/o J W) 3 May 1893-3 Jan 1933 Fair
Nannie R w/o Ephraim 7 Feb 1866-8 Aug 1936 Libe
Nettie L (w/o F W) 6 Apr 1894- Edge
Nona Ray w/o G C 1887-1958 Park
Norman 15 Nov 1889-21 June 1967 Park
Norman E 6 Mar 1908-6 June 1961 Edge
Oliver Ernest 1879-1960 Park
Oliver F h/o M J 12 Mar 1851-5 Apr 1933 Park
Oscar T h/o L R 1884-1969 Libe
Otho L h/o A B 1873-1949 Libe
Pauline 1938-1969 Gask
Ralph M 1928-1957 Park
Sadie S w/o L E 18 Apr 1877-10 May 1959 Edge

WESSELLS (continued)
Serissa P w/o Dorsey W 15 Sept 1894-27 Jan 1920 Park
Shella D 1891-1953 Park
Sherman M h/o E M 1892-1948 Onan
Sidney E (h/o B L) 1884-1957 Edge
Stella B 1896-1902 Park
Stewart Alfred (h/o V P) 28 Sept 1899-8 Jan 1975 MtHo
Stuart A 1906-1946 Park
Vera Parker (w/o S A) 12 Mar 1900- MtHo
Vianna w/o J F 19 Feb 1870-6 Dec 1942 Park
Virgil L 17 Sept 1923-11 June 1964 Park
Virgil L 1950-1978 Park
William h/o Lillian 9 Oct 1873-20 Mar 1960 Park
William B h/o L E 1878-1953 Park
William C 5 May 1914-22 Nov 1944 Park
William Herbert 19 Dec 1880-28 May 1917 Park
William Howard h/o W C 1889-1928 Park
William J h/o B W 1857-1926 Park
William T h/o A E 1869-1943 Park
Willie A w/o Roy G 25 July 1881-20 Oct 1918 Park
Winnie C w/o Wm H 1889-1963 Park
WEST, inf/o M W & Mary A b&d 15 Aug 1868 GenW
(or possibly Wise) A W, N W 1785, W R W Deep
Abel 30 May 1734 at this place-30 May 1816; age: 82 yrs OldW
Annie M 31 Oct 1860-4 Dec 1937 Onan
Anthony s/o Anthony of... stone broken Wepl
Beatrice Riggs w/o G W 1897-1955 Park
Berkley L (h/o E S) 1873-1938 Holl

WEST (continued)
Carlton James 2 Dec 1927-9 Feb 1967 Onan
Cecil 1928-1956 StPa
Major Charles d 28 Feb 1757 (stone originally on Lot #30, Onancock. Removed to cellar of Kerr Place, Onancock) Kerr
Charlotte Ann 1946-1962 Onan
Clara 1876-1957 Bays
Clara B w/o Wm J 1882-1941 Park
Claudious A Jr 2 July 1948-6 Mar 1975 Gask
Daisey 1880-1939 Gask-old
E Thomas h/o M P 2 Nov 1851-22 May 1920 Onan
Egbert Bayly s/o M W & Mary A 7 Feb 1872-30 Jan 1873 (moved to St George's) GenW
Edward T (h/o L F) 1874-1930 Holl
Edwin N 1861-1934 Park
Eliza d 5 Sept 1962; age: 64 yrs Gask-old
Elizabeth w/o N M d Nov 1833 & 3 children (erected by James H West-1869) Wesl
Elizabeth S (w/o B L) 1876-1961 Holl
Elizabeth Smith (w/o W J) 12 Feb 1907- Fair
Frank A (h/o N L) 25 Feb 1854-2 June 1936 Onan
Frank M 1879-1946 Onan
G Bowdoin (h/o J G) 1871-1958 Onan
George D 1900-1983 Metr
George R 1826-1901 Park
George S h/o M S 31 Jan 1825-16 July 1898 Crad
George T 1878-1977 Gask
George William h/o B R 1895-1972 Park
Harold Parker 1884-1949 Fair
Harris A 1889-1977 Fair
Howard G 1924-1974 Onan
Ida A 1867-1959 Park
Jane w/o Jno W 7 Dec 1827-26 June 1881 Onan
John d 12 Feb 1964; age: 71 yrs Gask-old

WEST (continued)
John 20 Dec 1696-12 Oct 1773 OldW
John M s/o Mitchell & Margt A 9 June 1848-4 Apr 1892 MtWi
John T s/o Salathiel M & Eliz 16 May 1833-26 Nov 1868 Pitt
John W 12 Jan 1887-29 Dec 1951 Onan
John William 18 July 1890-23 July 1964 Shil
Joseph J 1895-1976 Onan
Joseph T nd (prob dc1965) Shil
Josie G (w/o G B) 1876-1968 Onan
Julia Evans w/o W E Sr 24 Oct 1897-13 Jan 1979 Edge
Laura F 1 Aug 1915- Fair
Louise 1929-1965 Metr
Lula J 1878-1936 Park
Lydia F (w/o E T) 1876-1944 Holl
Margaret 1872-1969 StGe
Margaret Ann w/o Mitchell Wellington 2 Jan 1815-2 Mar 1854 GenW
Margaret C w/o Revel 7 Oct 1820-21 Dec 1901 Onan
Margaret G 1908- Park
Margaret H w/o M S; (d/o Peter Rogers) 4 Sept 1791-19 May 1837; age: 45/9/15 GenW
Margaret Susan w/o G S 27 Feb 1830-23 Nov 1893 Crad
Marie J 1930-1973 Metr
Mary Ann Bayly w/o Gen M W 1832-1915 (moved from Gen West Place) StGe
Mary Patrick w/o E T; d/o Jos & Margaret Patrick of Phila, PA; mother of Margt J, Emma P, Gertie M, & Mamie A 1851-1903 Onan
May 1900-1961 Metr
Melvin 1909-1967 NewM
Mitchell Scarborough h/o M H; s/o Salathiel 10 Oct 1784-8 Sept 1846; age: 61/10/29 GenW
Mitchell W 1882-1963 Onan
Gen Mitchell Wellington h/o Mary Ann Bayly; s/o Mitchell

WEST (continued)
Scarborough & Margt Rogers West 13 Mar 1815-17 July 1899 StGe
Nancy 1893-1980 Shil
Nancy L (w/o F A) 21 Nov 1855-28 Jan 1930 Onan
Nanney 23 Oct 1738-20 Dec 1805 OldW
Nathaniel M h/o Eliz d June 1833 (erected by James H West-1869) Wesl
Noah s/o Wm dc1981; age: c70 yrs Wesg
Lieut Otha K s/o Gen M W & Margt Ann 26 Nov 1838-23 July 1864 Wise's Bgd, CSA; wounded battle at Petersburg, 12 June 1864. (Moved from Gen West Place) StGe
Paige d 5 Jan 1970; age: 69 yrs Snea
Peter Rogers b&d 1868 StGe
R Henry h/o S E 1869-1941 Holl
Richard N 19 July 1835-23 May 1922 Holl
Rudolph 1925-1974 Gask
Russell E 17 Sept 1922-21 Nov 1976 Gask
Ruth E 7 Jan 1929-1 Mar 1977 Onan
Sallie E 17 May 1835-20 May 1909 Holl
Sarah E w/o R H 1861-1941 Holl
Susanna 4 July 1766-9 July 1806 Parp
Thomas nd Gask
Timothy R b&d 1957 Onan
Upshur 1919-1976 Gask
Viola James 26 June 1862-26 May 1948 Onan
William d 7 Sept 1953; age: 52 yrs Wesg
William 1944-1972 Metr
William C 28 Feb 1859-7 July 1951 Onan
William Edwin Sr h/o J E 10 May 1894-26 Nov 1961 Edge
William J h/o C B 1883-1964 Park
William Jesse (h/o E S) 17 Sept

WEST (continued)
1906-4 Feb 1979 Fair
WHALEY, Donald C 1895-1916 Ptea
Grace Eloise w/o Wm; d/o W H A & Mary Ellen (Johnson) Hopkins 1 Nov 1871 in Onancock-17 Dec 1930 in Charleston SC Onan
Hance L 1913-1916 Onan
Margaret T S (w/o W W) 1878-1951 Onan
Martin C (h/o S M) d1946 Ptea
Mary Alice d/o M C & S M 1897-1912 Ptea
Sadie M (w/o M C) d1959 Ptea
William h/o G E 25 Oct 1856-21 Apr 1934 Onan
William W (h/o M T) 1878-1963 Onan
Comdr Zedekiah, US Navy-Maryland 30 Nov 1782-killed in the Battle of the Barges (DAR marker) Scot
WHARTON, Eula Sarah 1907-1965 Gask
John C 17 Sept 1898-9 Sept 1923 Gask-old
John E 1862-1929 Gask-old
Kate M 1864-1937 Gask-old
Louise A w/o Jas L 1905-1951 StJo
William B 29 Nov 1936-15 Feb 1978 Gask
WHEALTON, Burford C 1942-1974 Park
Emory W 1903-1974 Park
Mollie Burton 1885-1961 MtHo
WHEATLEY, James R (h/o M V) 26 Nov 1933- Wach
Marie V (w/o J R) 30 Mar 1934- Wach
WHEELER, Azalee Martha 1904-1971 Park
WHITE, s/o A P & S A b&d 16 Jan 1891 Libe
s/o Booker & Fairy b&d 7 Feb 1909 Quin
d/o Ray & Margt b&d 9 May 1912 Edge
d/o Ray & Margt b&d 23 Aug 1913 Edge

WHITE (continued)
Alfred K 4 June 1883-26 June 1948 Park
Alfred P h/o S A: s/o Henry B & Hettie 21 Jan 1835-22 Dec 1906 Libe
Alfred P Jr h/o N C 1876-1932 Libe
Alfred T h/o E K 21 Dec 1855-22 June 1933 Park
Alice P 1881-1959 Park
Andrew J h/o T H 1870-1949 MtHo
Ann Hack d/o H E & E W b&d 1914 Park
Annie Pearl d/o O F & T W 29 July-6 Aug 1904 Whit
Arthur C beloved hus; s/o Jas & Matilda 6 June 1822-14 Sept 1859; age: 37/4/8 JoCu
Barbara C d/o Paul H & Emma C b&d 10 Apr 1942 MtHo
Beatrice d 2 Feb 1968; age: 41 yrs Bays
Bernard T (h/o E Y) 1884-1978 Edge
Betty E d/o E C & E E 1880-1967 Edge
Bronzie J 1898-1974 Park
Caroline Jones d/o Saml C & Mary E 8 Aug 1834-23 July 1842 WhiB
Catherine D w/o Harry T 1850-1921 Park
Charlie W 9 Sept 1880-20 Apr 1882 Park
Charlie s/o D F & D S 23 Feb 1888-30 Aug 1890 Edge
Charlotte 15 Aug 1820-30 Apr 1882 Whie
D Frank h/o D S; s/o David C & Hettie 8 May 1850-31 Dec 1897 Edge
D Rowland 14-28 Mar 1948 MtHo
David F 8 Sept 1885-29 May 1956 Edge
Dennard Corbin s/o A T & E K 30 July 1892-9 June 1908 Park
Dora S w/o D F 1855-1914 Edge
Earl Thomas 1908-1970 Bays
Edgar J 31 Oct 1878-28 Oct 1879 Park

WHITE (continued)
Edward B f/o Louise, Eva Sue, & Edwd 1896-1967 Fair
Edith C 1918-1978 Park
Edith W w/o H E 1887-1978 Park
Eleanor Price 11 Dec 1905-16 July 1979 Fair
Elizabeth 1906-1984 Park
Elizabeth E w/o E C 1847-1926 Edge
Ella M w/o G W 1882-1950 Park
Ellen d 4 Dec 1904 Shil
Ellen Major w/o W W 8 Oct 1848-3 Aug 1927 Holl
Elva Y (w/o B T) 1886-1974 Edge
Emily K w/o A T 3 May 1856-27 Oct 1933 Park
Emma C w/o J H 27 Aug 1872-29 Nov 1958 Onan
Emory S 1848-1940 Onan
Ephraim C h/o E E 1839-1901 Edge
Ernest C (h/o J M) 28 Nov 1892-7 June 1974 Onan
Frank 1892-1958 Shil
Garland O 19 Apr 1899-28 Dec 1918 Onan
George F h/o G H 1906-1977 Libe
George H h/o L G 1872-1958 Metr
George W h/o M E d 9 Mar 1900; age: 70/10/0 (moved from Bradford-White bur gr) Fair
George W h/o E M 1888-1966 Park
Gladys H w/o G F 1913-1981 Libe
H Warren s/o W F & N H 9 Feb-12 July 1899 MtHo
Harry C s/o J M & C E 21 Mar 1898-29 Jan 1902 Edge
Harry E h/o E W 1885-1965 Park
Harry E Sr (h/o V P) 1918-1980 Wach
Harry L 1901-1980 Quin
Harrye Cleves d/o Saml & M M 7 Aug-3 Dec 1899 Onan
Helen Blanche d/o W T & M D

WHITE (continued)
1894-1896 Wach
Henrietta w/o R A; d/o Benjamin Pruitt 18 Sept 1800-4 July 1874 Clov
Henry B 1798-1869 Park
Henry T h/o M T 25 Aug 1831-18 Aug 1882 MtHo
Henry Thomas s/o T E & Henrietta H 1851-1934 Park
Herbert E 1905-1924 Quin
Hetty 1801-1961 Park
Hiden M 1 Nov 1867-25 Dec 1951 MtHo
Hugh G (h/o M L) 26 Sept 1859-16 Feb 1943 Quin
I Linwood (h/o L M) 1899-1966 MtHo-s
India A w/o L H d 12 Apr 1905 Onan
Ira G (h/o M E) 1882-1969 Quin
J Edward 1875-1956 Onan
J Myers h/o C E (French) 1 Nov 1860-28 Mar 1902; drowned off Cape Hatteras NC Edge
James H h/o M C d 8 Oct 1887; age: c50 yrs MtHo
James H h/o E C 4 May 1871-23 Feb 1929 Onan
James J Sr 1874-1950 Park
Jodie A d/o L H & I A 8 Jan 1880-17 July 1899 Onan
Joe III b&d 20 July 1946 Edge
John A s/o Elijah & Rosa A 12 Sept 1812-11 Apr 1886 Onan
John E h/o Sally G; s/o Jno & Ann U 14 Jan 1831-18 Dec 1883 KelG
John F 1923-1940 MtHo-s
John W 20 Sept 1850-18 Apr 1913 JnoS
Joseph L Sr h/o L A 1896-1969 Edge
Julia M (w/o E C) 16 Aug 1896-27 Mar 1946 Onan
Julius C H/o M C d 28 Mar 1863; age: 36/10/18 (leaving a wife & son) Park
Kamela Darice d/o Stuart F & Wanda C 6-7 May 1966 Park
Katherine M d/o W C & Katherine M d 6 Feb 1921 MtHo-s

WHITE (continued)
Kathryne T 1897-1970 MtHo-s
Leona M (w/o R B) 1908- Quin
Levin J 1873-1952 Park
Levin W 1932-1971 Fair
Lillie G w/o G H 1889-1966 Metr
Lola V d/o E C & E E 1871-1944 Edge
Lona M (w/o I L) 1897- MtHo-s
Louis H h/o I A 11 Oct 1844-14 Sept 1924 Onan
Lucy D 1896-1968 Burt
Lyde Ashby w/o J L Sr 1896-1968 Edge
Maggie L (w/o H G) 16 July 1854-13 June 1940 Quin
Margaret C w/o J C 5 Aug 1827-22 July 1911 Park
Margaret E (w/o Ira G 1883-1979 Quin
Margaret Lilliston, 1st w/o R D 26 Oct 1885-30 Mar 1926 Edge
Marie Somers 12 Feb 1899-2 Aug 1983 Park
Marteia d 6 June 1852; age: 66 yrs Drmc
Martha 1786-6 June 1852; age: 66 yrs (50 yrs-a Methodist) Edge
Mary w/o Louis H; d/o Jas & Harriet Drummond 9 July 1844-23 Sept 1874 Drub
Mary 1918-1983 Bays
Mary C w/o J H 10 Mar 1846-2 Dec 1904; age: 58/8/22 MtHo
Mary Della w/o W T 1872-1959 Wach
Mary Ellen w/o Geo W; (d/o Mrs Rachel Bradford) d 17 Apr 1887; age: 25/3/0 (d nr Fair Oaks VA) BraW
Mary J w/o J W 1861-1938 MtHo
Maud w/o S H; d/o Wm S & M C Mills 3 July 1872-5 Aug 1932 Onan
Millard F 1 Jan 1897-31 Mar 1967 Fair
Miranda T w/o H T 23 Dec 1838-13 Oct 1926 MtHo
Nancy C w/o A P 1877-1951 Libe
Napoleon Oswald s/o O F & T W

WHITE (continued)
30 Mar 1897-24 Apr 1904 Whit
Nealy Custis 1881-1968 Holl
Nellie W w/o Capt Pete 1933-1982 Park
Oswald Finney h/o T W 26 Feb 1852-16 Aug 1926 Whit
Otho J h/o S A 16 Mar 1866-12 Mar 1934 Onan
Paul d 24 Mar 1962; age: 62 yrs JoyC
Capt Pete h/o N W 1923-1979 Park
Peter 1838-24 June 1930 Shil
Ray D h/o M L & V D; s/o Frank & Dora 1 May 1875-8 Apr 1938 Edge
Rebecca Coston 1873-1954 Holl
Richard A h/o Henrietta; s/o Levin & Sally 31 Dec 1797(5?)-29 Mar 1869 (stone broken) Clov
Ronald B (h/o L M) 1904-1958 Quin
Rosey 14 Feb 1779-19 Oct 1867 Onan
Roy R 1900-1956 Bays
S Claud 1877-1953 MtHo-s
Sally A 1875-1967 Park
Samuel H s/o A P & S A 14 Oct 1867-23 June 1899 Libe
Sarah Virginia 22 Sept 1865-27 Feb 1963 Fair
Shelley s/o Wm J & Margt J 12 Aug 1881-31 July 1886 Park
Sudie A w/o O J 1 Nov 1869-4 July 1948 Onan
Susan w/o Henry d 16 Aug 1927; age: 83 yrs StLu
Susan A w/o A P 28 Oct 1845-17 July 1931 Libe
Susie d/o W T & M D 1890-1979 Wach
Sallie G w/o Jno E 1844-1930 Wach
Tabatha W w/o O F 16 July 1864-15 Dec 1929 Whit
Tabitha H w/o A J 1865-1945 MtHo
Thomas 20 Apr 1891-3 Aug 1959 Snea
Thomas A 1879-1941 MtHo

WHITE (continued)
Thomas E w/o M C 6 Oct 1890-28 Mar 1955 Onan
Timothy R 3 Feb 1894-29 Jan 1919 Onan
Vera V 1900-1954 Park
Virginia Dudley, 2nd w/o R D 9 Apr 1887-3 Feb 1966 Edge
Virginia P (w/o H E) 1920-1974 Wach
W Carroll 1895-1971 MtHo-s
Wallace 1908-1964 Gask
Walter Rowland, 1st h/o A G W Hoenshel 1903-1944 MtHo
Wardella Mapp 1920-1975 Gask
William C 1912-1962 Park
William C Jr 1923-1940 MtHo-s
William F 11 Feb 1862-4 Feb 1932 MtHo
William J 22 Apr 1835-29 July 1901 Park
William Thomas h/o M D 1867-1950 Wach
William W h/o E M 13 Sept 1841-9 July 1890 Holl
WHITTINGTON, Ira T 1897-1978 Edge
WIDGEON, Blanche Zember (w/o D C) 11 Mar 1899-7 June 1970 Quin
D Crockette (h/o B Z) 8 Dec 1895-9 Sept 1958 Quin
WIKSTROM, Carl E 1900-1983 Libe
WILDY, Edgar A (h/o G H) 22 May 1903- Fair
Gertrude H (w/o E A) 20 Feb 1903-24 Jan 1971 Fair
WILEY, Sherman b&d 1956 Wach
WILKERSON, Alice J w/o S D 1882-1956 MtHo-s
Bertie W (w/o H T) 1895-1973 Onan
Dora R w/o N T 1873-1954 Onan
Fred W 1884-1972 Onan
Harold T (h/o B W) 1892-1947 Onan
Noah T h/o D R 1870-1923 Onan
Preston G 8 Aug 1891-30 Apr 1950 Park
Sewell D h/o A J 1882-1930 MtHo-s

WILKINS, Annie E 1916-1958 Metr
George Douglas h/o S W 23 Oct 1875-10 Mar 1924 MtHo-s
John Wise 1 Aug 1906-7 Apr 1972 MtHo-s
Langdon Cheves h/o M B H; s/o Gilbert Aspinwall & Emma (Cheves) 28 Feb 1881 in Savannah GA-9 Mar 1932 in New York City Onan
Mary Battaile H w/o L C; d/o Dr Chas L & Ann Hay Harmanson 14 Mar 1887-29 June 1963 Onan
Mary E w/o Wm B 13 Dec 1850-20 Feb 1885 (moved from Wilkins bur gr) Edge
Sarah West w/o G W 15 Nov 1882-13 July 1973 MtHo-s
Susan Bayly d/o Jno & Susan 23 May 1803-5 July 1842 Wise
WILL, Nora Tyler 1873-1962 Edge
WILLETT,.... d 15 Dec 1940 Park
WILLETT, Alva E 18 May 1880-13 Mar 1951 Libe
Betty nd Libe
Charles C h/o Mary;'s/o Wm & Gertrude 6 Jan 1789-6 July 1859 Wilb
Charles W d 31 Oct 1912; age: 24 yrs Libe
Clara W (w/o H F) 1897- Edge
Clarence W 1901-1946 Libe
Dasy 31 Dec 1883-31 Dec 1885 Libe
Elicia 14 Nov 1870-7 Aug 1872 Libe
Elicia A Lewis w/o T R 19 Nov 1842-31 July 1916 Libe
Frank O d 4 Mar 1913; age: 57 yrs Park
George nd Libe
Gertrude d/o C C & Mary 4 Sept 1820-19 Mar 1891 Wilb
Harold F (h/o C W) 1892-1966 Edge
Harry T h/o M K 28 Jan 1898-17 Jan 1976 Libe
John W s/o C C & Mary 11 May

WILLETT (continued)
1826-10 Aug 1843 Wilb
John W h/o P H 24 May 1835-1 Sept 1920 Park
Libby B 25 Nov 1857-19 Feb 1935 Libe
Mabel S 1898-1958 Libe
Mary w/o C C; d/o Wm & Elizabeth Turner 2 Aug 1789-2 Oct 1828 Wilb
Mary A d/o C C & Mary 19 Apr 1828-19 Dec 1832 Wilb
Myrtle K w/o H T 1904- Libe
Obadiah W h/o S H 25 May 1877-16 Nov 1939 Libe
Oscar L 1890-1949 Onan
Polly nd Libe
Polly H w/o J W 5 Mar 1838-3 July 1922 Park
Sarah H w/o O W 11 Sept 1885-5 Sept 1941 Libe
Thomas R h/o E A L 20 May 1833-22 Dec 1900 Libe
Thomas R 11 Apr 1861-4 Oct 1937 Libe
Virginia Etta 12 June 1864-20 Mar 1929 Libe
Waitman W s/o C C & Mary 6 Nov 1814-7 Aug 1870 Wilb
William J 6 July 1874-23 Jan 1941 Libe
WILLIAMS, Adron T (h/o R D) 7 Apr 1925-14 Mar 1948 MtHo-s
Alma C (w/o R T) 1886-1962 Holl
Anna S, 2nd w/o E W 22 Sept 1896-1 Nov 1938 MtHo
Barbara Ann 1933-1934 MtHo-s
Benjamin T s/o Thos H & Margt 8 Nov 1861-13 July 1881 Meac
Bessie L (w/o W H) 1881-1951 MtHo
Bettie S d/o Thos H & Margt 15 Apr 1867-13 May 1876 Meac
Bobby S 1953-1957 Onan
Carlisle Mister (h/o E L) 11 May 1914- Fair
Charlotte 1931-1982 Metr
Clarence 1895-1982 Snea
Cora Virginia w/o Benja F d 25 July 1913; age: 52 yrs Holl
Dickie s/o O M & D P 13 Dec

WILLIAMS (continued)
1937-15 Sept 1940 MtHo-s
Donna J b&d 1953 MtHo-s
E W h/o M L & A S 4 Apr 1873-24 Nov 1933 MtHo
Edward M (h/o R W McC) 1928-1974 Fair
Elizabeth nd Holl
Evelyn Louise (w/o C M) 10 Oct 1917 Fair
Florence E (w/o H T) 1882-1960 MtHo-s
Florence M w/o R L 1894- MtHo-s
George H 1900-1963 Holl
George W 8 June 1856-31 Jan 1914 Holl
Gregory M b&d 1947 MtHo-s
Hattie A 1902-1978 Fair
Hiram T (h/o F E) 1878-1956 MtHo-s
Ira F s/o J C & M E 21 June 1892-20 Aug 1901 Ptea
James nd Holl
James O (h/o M S) 1862-1926 StGe
James O (h/o M C) 1901-1975 Fair
Jimmy L 25 May 1952-17 May 1980 Fair
John H h/o M F 12 Mar 1867-26 Aug 1941 MtHo-s
Johnathan Stacy b&d 1973 MtHo-s
Julia F 25 Oct 1833-23 June 1919 Onan
Leslie H 4 Aug 1901-28 Oct 1981 Fair
Lloyd T (h/o S G) 1889-1958 StGe
Lyda V w/o N F 20 Mar 1907- MtHo-s
Mae Marshall 1911-1981 Fair
Margaret L, 1st w/o E W 15 Sept 1880-2 Sept 1929 MtHo
Margaret S w/o T H 24 Aug 1838-13 Dec 1911 Onan
Margaret S (w/o J O) 1862-1956 StGe
Marvin 1908-1977 MtHo-s
Mary C (w/o J O) 1905-1981 Fair
Mary E w/o Octavious 1890-1962

WILLIAMS (continued)
MtHo-s
Mrs Missouri d 7 Feb 1947 Holl
Moses 1911-1978 NewM
Norman F h/o L V 18 May 1904-24 Dec 1970 MtHo-s
Octavious h/o M E 1885-1969 MtHo-s
Ollie M h/o D P 1907-1964 MtHo-s
Oscar 1888-1946 Ayre
Pansy Leigh Killmon w/o C Edwd 1897-1938 MtHo
R Tankard (h/o A C) 1884-1953 Holl
Ralph L 1911-1966 Fair
Raymond F 23 Dec 1902-5 Aug 1977 Quin
Robert L h/o F M 1892-1950 MtHo-s
Roland H 2 Mar 1895-17 May 1960 MtHo
Roxie W McCabe (w/o E M) 1931-1979 Fair
Ruth D (w/o A T) 1925-1948 MtHo-s
Ruth V (w/o W L) 1920- MtHo-s
Samuel B 7 Mar 1918-31 Jan 1980 MtHo-s
Susie G (w/o L T) 1891-1974 StGe
Thomas H h/o M S 25 Feb 1841-14 Apr 1901 Onan
William H (h/o B L) 1879-1945 MtHo
William L 14 Dec 1918-26 Dec 1944 MtHo
William Lewis s/o David C & Mary Ann d 30 Sept 1853; age: 3/6/29 (moved from Burckard bur gr) Onan
William Lewis (h/o R V) 26 Sept 1917-9 Feb 1980 MtHo-s
WILLING, May 1890-1960 Wach
WILLIS, Ann C w/o Zorobabel d 26 July 1851; age: 61/2/12 MtWi
Calton V (h/o S A) 1856-1913 Wach
Edward L h/o J E 25 Dec 1822-3 July 1887 MtWi
Edward L s/o E L & J E 13 Dec

WILLIS (continued)
1860-15 Apr 1861 MtWi
Emily P T d/o Custis & Sally H d 13 Nov 1903; age: 74 yrs Wilg
Emma G d/o H G & Cordia 17 May 1888-1 Sept 1906 NewM
James C 11 July 1817-25 Aug 1853; age: 36/1/14 MtWi
Jane d/o Elliott & Minnie 26 Feb-9 Oct 1920 Wach
Jesse h/o Maggie d 21 July 1910; age: c65 yrs NewM
John C 23 May 1917-23 Apr 1960 Wach
John Elliott 1889-1950 Wach
John H s/o Zorobabel & Nancy 17 June 1832-8 Oct 1866 MtWi
Joice E w/o E L 20 Oct 1827-20 Oct 1890 MtWi
Littleton s/o Custis & Bridget d 28 Aug 1856; age: 62 yrs Dunt
Littleton T s/o Littleton & S W 7 Apr 1836-7 July 1864 Dunt
Maggie w/o Jesse d 16 Oct 192_ NewM
Margaret w/o Jno H d/o Abel & Margt Edmonds Mears 7 Feb 1839-7 Nov 1925 MtWi
Mary A w/o Littleton 18 Jan 1794-3 Feb 1828 Dunt
Michele Quintina 18-30 July 1954 Gask-old
Minnie P 1891-1974 Wach
Molly B (d/o Littleton & Sarah) 4 Dec 1831-10 Sept 1833 Dunt
Robert C 1897-1915 Wach
Robert T s/o Zorobabel & Ann (Spiers) d 16 Sept 1846; age: 16/8/16 MtWi
Rosa W 1856-1936 MtWi
Sadie D s/o E L & J E 10 Nov 1863-21 Oct 1892 MtWi
Sarah Ann (w/o C V) 1867-1936 Wach
Sarah W w/o Littleton; d/o Jno & Catherine Coleburn 13 Apr 1798-29 June 1877 Dunt
Thomas 1919-1983 Gask
Virginia Joyce 1892-1975 Wach
William H s/o H G & Cordia 2 Sept 1891-30 Dec 1916 NewM

WILLIS (continued)
Zorobabel d 5 Jan 1842; age: 49/1/23 MtWi
Zorobabel 14 Jan 1853-22 July 1901 MtWi
WILLS, Jennie D 1859-1943 StGe
WILSON, Edd T (h/o M L) 1885-1941 Quin
Alton M h/o D S 1896-1964 Park
Dorothy S w/o A M 1897-1975 Park
Helen Diane 11 Nov 1960-18 July 1967 Onan
James Fisher h/o M E B b Inverness, Scotland d 5 Oct 1821; age: 36 yrs Tave
Jennie 1921-1959 Snea
Judith G 30 Jan 1930-5 Feb 1975 Onan
Kitty d/o AM & D S Feb 1954-15 Sept 1955 Park
Marion d 27 Mar 1964; age: 29 yrs Gask-old
Marion 1955-1956 Gask-old
Melanie Elizabeth Bringier w/o Jas F mar in New Orleans 5 June 1816; d...leaving 3 inf children to mourn Tave
Minnie L (w/o E T) 1889-1965 Quin
Robert E 1920-1983 Fair
Willie H 1901-1974 Fair
WILTBANK, Horace s/o Horace & Nita 2 May-12 Aug 1909 Libe
WIMBOROUGH, Annie M d/o Geo & Margt Parker 27 Apr 1855-2 Sept 1888 ParC
WIMBROW, Fred H 1889-1947 MtHo-s
Frederick Jr 24 Apr 1917-28 Nov 1972 MtHo-s
Grace K 1891-1967 Holl
Larry W 1886-1950 Holl
M N h/o Susaner 15 May 1855- Park
Mildred W 1924- MtHo-s
Sallie W 1891-1975 MtHo-s
Susaner w/o M N 17 Dec 1856-6 July 1915 Park
William W 1908-1966 Holl
WINDER, Alexander M s/o Wm

WINDER (continued)
T & Birtannie 5 Apr 1893-3 May 1894 Onan
Annie Ayres 1857-1936 StGe
Annie D 1866-1867 Onan
Bertha C (w/o E A) 1896-1973 MtHo
Crawford C 1891-1892 Onan
Edith J w/o Jno L 8 Apr 1856-6 Sept 1883 Crad-s
Edward A (h/o B C) 1891-1966 MtHo
Elkanah 1856-1859 Onan
Elkanah J 1862-1866 Onan
Ellen D w/o Wm S; d/o E D & A C Joynes 9 Feb 1842-7 Sept 1880 Joyn
Ernest N s/o Wm S & Ellen D 9 Sept 1871-19 May 1882 Joyn
Frances A w/o J E T 30 June 1834-4 Jan 1896 Onan
Hessy D w/o J D 1806-1884 Onan
James A (h/o M D) 1837-1913 StGe
James E 1870-1871 Onan
John 1865-1914 Onan
John D h/o H D 1806-1876 Onan
John E h/o S A 17 Oct 1829-27 July 1874 Onan
John E T h/o F A 16 Oct 1830-9 Oct 1887 Onan
Lucetta F b&d 1898 Onan
Mable S 1921-1952 Burt
Mary D w/o J A 1843-1926 StGe
Mattie E w/o E J 1861-1885 Onan
Dr Samuel 28 Sept 1790-16 Aug 1831 Ande
Sarah A w/o J E 13 Aug 1832-7 July 1901 Onan
Wilbur 1858-1939 Onan
WINDSOR, Ida S 1867-1931 MtHo-s
Margaret w/o R B 11 Sept 1907-12 Mar 1978 MtHo
Margie L 30 Oct 1893-1 May 1925 MtHo
Mary Virginia 1920-1978 Fair
Nell C (w/o W L Sr) 1886-1966 MtHo-s
Robert B h/o Margt 26 Aug 1905-

WINDSOR (continued)
24 July 1957 MtHo
Shirley V 1942-1962 Fair
William L Sr (h/o N C) 1889-1966 MtHo-s
WISE, s/o Edwd S & Eliz S 19 Feb-3 July 1897 Jaco
(or possibly West) A W, N W 1785, W R W Deep
Abbot Ridout 1898-1973 MtHo-s
Andrew h/o B N 28 Dec 1902-20 July 1979; age: 76/6/22 Park
Ann Jennings w/o H A; d/o Rev Obadiah & Ann (Wilson) Jennings of Nashville TN 31 Dec 1808-4 May 1837; mar: 23 Oct 1828 Wise
Annie M 1910-1971 Smit
Annie Sue 1937-1982 MtNe
Arthur Tucker h/o E L F 1881-1945 Onan
Benjamin A 1904-1964 Bays
Bertie B 1890- MtHo-s
Bessie L 17 Dec 1904-16 Sept 1976 Metr
Bettie G w/o Jno H; d/o G J & E J 16 July 1843-12 Sept 1877 BunW
Bettie G w/o Geo D d 20 Nov 1874; age: 24/4/10 (moved from Core bur gr-Pastoria) Park
Bettie T 1847-1942 JoyC
Beulah N w/o Andrew 1907-1960 Park
Carrie L d/o J E & Bettie C 16 Mar 1875-11 Dec 1920 Park
Carroll E 1915-1935 MtHo-s
Charlie A h/o W A 1891-1968 Bays
Charlie M 1892-1983 MtHo
Charlie P 1890-1978 Snea
Clara T B 1 Oct 1903-20 July 1914 Wise
Clarence S h/o E J 1888-1933 Libe
Clinton T 1908-1969 JoyC
Cordelia Bailey 1861-1937 Shil
Dorothy E 1917-1936 MtHo-s
Elizabeth w/o Jno Jr 18 Sept 1727-27 Dec 1753; age: 26/3/9 Wise

WISE (continued)
Elizabeth d/o Jno & Margt 4 Mar 1758-24 May 1812 Wise
Elizabeth Bagwell 13 Jan 1881-31 May 1966 Onan
Elizabeth Douglas 1795-1871 Scot
Elizabeth S w/o Jno E 14 July 1820-16 Nov 1887 Wisp
Elsie J w/o C S 1892-1961 Libe
Emma Littleton Finney w/o A T 16 Dec 1889-15 July 1984 Onan
Emma Susan 1902-1967 Gask
Etta d 22 Mar 1943; age: 68 yrs JoyC
Eva w/o J S; d/o Hugh & Nancy (Hamilton) Douglas of Nashville TN 21 Feb 1851-13 Apr 1925 Wise
Frank 1917-1975 Metr
George d 19 Nov 1934; age: 69 yrs JoyC
George 1903-1965 Burt
George D h/o R P 19 May 1849-9 Oct 1929 Park
George Douglas s/o Jno & Mary (Henry) 5 Nov 1790-9 Jan 1821 Wise
George Douglas s/o Jno Jas & Harriet A W 17 Sept 1831-5 July 1864 (CSA Captain; killed at Petersburg) Wise
Capt George G h/o M S 1874-1942 Onan
George Robert 16 Mar 1894-25 Oct 1969 Gask
George T 2 July 1910-18 Feb 1960 JoyC
Hannah w/o Jno; d/o Capt Edmund & Hannah (Butler) Scarburgh b in England-d at Clifton Wise
Harriet A Wilkins w/o Jno J 15 May 1807-12 Jan 1883 Wise
Harry A h/o L P 1884-1934 Park
Harvey E 1885-1945 MtHo-s
Helen d/o C S & E J 3 July 1913-1 July 1918 Libe
Henrietta E B w/o H A 6 Jan 1876-1 Apr 1957 Wise
Henry A s/o Jno & Sarah Corbin

WISE (continued)
(Cropper) 3 Dec 1806-12 Sept 1876 (VA Congressman; Minister to Brazil; Gov of VA; Br Gen CSA 1861-5) Wise
Henry A s/o Jno E & E S 9 Dec 1859-5 Feb 1882 Wisp
Henry A h/o H E B 6 Apr 1874-15 Aug 1968 Wise
Howard d 13 Aug 1952; age: 54 yrs Burt
Hugh Douglas s/o Jno S W & Eva (Douglas) 10 Oct 1871-28 May 1942 (US Military Acad-1894; San Juan Hill-1898; Philapme Insurrection-1899-1901; France WWI 1917-18. Ret Col) Wise
Ida w/o H D; d/o Richd S & Adell (Babcock) Hungerford of Watertown NY 11 Nov 1880-26 Oct 1956 Wise
J Robert (h/o M W) 1876-1959 Fair
James T 1877-1955 JoyC
Jennings C s/o Jno S & Eva (Douglas) 10 Sept 1881-20 Feb 1968 Wise
Col John 1617 in England-1695 at Clifton (Justice; Col in militia) Wise
John s/o Jno & Matilda W 8 Aug 1699-9 Aug 1763; (Justice) Wise
John s/o Jno & Hannah (Scarburgh) d1717 (Burgess, Justice) Wise
Col John 27 July 1723-Mar 1769 Wise
John s/o Jno Jr & Eliz 30 Oct 1749 (Mon night)-31 Oct 1760 (age 11 yrs lacking 10 dys. Died at Nottingham ye grammar school in PA under the care of Saml Finley) Wise
John 1895-1976 Snea
John 1907-1974 JoyC
John A 1899-1962 Bays
John E s/o Isiah & Ann 5 June 1816-17 Jan 1911 Wisp
John E (h/o M C) 1922- MtHo-s
John Evans 1896-1966 MtHo-s

WISE (continued)
John F 1883-1949 MtHo-s
John H s/o Jno E & Eliz S 9 Nov 1842-12 Dec 1923 Park
John H s/o Henry & Annie 16 Dec 1863-19 Jan 1912 Snea
John H 1875-1944 JoyC
John J h/o H A W; s/o Jno & Mary (Henry) 8 Sept 1794-6 Apr 1834 Wise
John J 1924-1969 Shil
John James Henry s/o Jno J & H A W 11 Jan 1830-1896 (Surgeon-CSA) Wise
John S (h/o M A) 9 Aug 1853-21 Dec 1918 MtHo
John S 11 Nov 1905-26 Sept 1974 Wise
John Sergeant s/o Henry A & Sarah (Sergeant) 27 Dec 1846-12 May 1913 (VA Congressman; US Attorney; wounded in battle at New Market VA; Prov Lt CSA 1864-5) Wise
Joseph L 1900-1959 Fair
Lee 15 May 1896-14 Aug 1956 Burt
Lillian Parks w/o H A 1887-1970 Park
Lizzie d/o Geo D & B G d 14 Dec 1874; age: 0/7/11 Park
Louise D 1908-1977 Snea
Mabel 1913-1974 Metr
Major John s/o Jno & Margt (Douglas) bc1765-30 Mar 1812 (Speaker of House, Clerk of Acc Court) Wise
Margaret w/o Jno; d/o Col Geo & Tabitha (Drummond) Douglas 1736-1808 Wise
Margaret A (w/o J S) 18 July 1857-4 Oct 1929 MtHo
Margaret S w/o G G 1879-1952 Onan
Marguerite C (w/o J E) 1925-1959 MtHo-s
Marietta d/o Geo Douglas & Marietta (Atkinson) 30 Jan 1862-23 June 1928 Edge
Marietta A w/o Geo D 24 Dec 1837-13 Feb 1894 Wise
Marita E 28 Jan 1916-23 Oct

WISE (continued)
1918 JoyC
Mary w/o Jno; d/o Judge Jas & Sarah (Scarburgh) Henry d 9 Aug 1796 Wise
Mary Elizabeth w/o H A; d/o Dr Peter & Sarah (Waugh) Lyons 12 Dec 1817-17 July 1901; mar: Nov 1853 The beloved foster mother of the children of Ann Jennings & Sarah Sergeant Wise Wise
Mary Etta 1907-1965 Bays
Mary M 1891-1953 JoyC
Mary P 1908-1978 JoyC
Matilda w/o Jno; d/o Col Jno & Matilda (Scarburgh) West d1722 at Clifton Wise
Mattie J 1880-1967 JoyC
Mattie W (w/o J R) 1882-1968 Fair
Nannie E d/o Jno H & B G d 3 Nov 1870; age: 3/3/26 BunW
Norman W 1937-1981 Snea
Obadiah Jennings s/o H A & Ann (Jennings) 12 Apr 1831-9 Feb 1862 (Sec't U S Embassies in Paris & Berlin, Editor of Pictorial Enquirer. Capt in Wise's Legion, CSA. Killed in Battle of Roanoke Is) Wise
Rachel Ballard 1889-1972 Shil
Rekial b&d 1973 Gask
Rennie P w/o G D 30 Oct 1857-1 Sept 1925 Park
Richard Alsop s/o H A & Sarah (Sergeant) 2 Sept 1842-21 Dec 1900 (Lt CSA; MD-Prof of Chem at Wm & Mary; member VA Gen Ass; Congressman 2nd Dist) Wise
Robert 1 Jan 1895-17 Dec 1964 Snea
Robert L 1916-1972 Metr
Robert W 9 Nov 1886-9 Oct 1930 JoyC
Rosa 1880-1971 Park
Ruth E 1886-1948 MtHo-s
Sadie P Bagwell (w/o W T) 4 July 1857-22 Aug 1951 Onan
Sarah w/o H A; d/o Hon Jno & Margaretta (Watmaugh) Ser-

WISE (continued)
geant of Phila PA 24 Sept 1817-4 Oct 1850; mar: 26 Nov 1840 Wise
Sarah Corbin w/o Jno; d/o Gen Jno & Margt (Pettitt) Cropper 21 Mar 1777-21 Jan 1813 Wise
Sarah Crippen m Robert Russell 9 May 1818; mar: Wm E Wise 12 June 1827; d 24 Aug 1856; age: 72 yrs Park
Scarburgh w/o Jno; d/o Col Tully & Sara (West) Robinson 16 Apr 1691-29 Jan 1770 Wise
Susan (Mrs) 31 Mar 1770-23 Sept 1849 Coke
Susie E 1901-1961 Metr
Thomas 1889-1969 Metr
Thomas I 1889-1958 Bays
Victoria d 22 May 1958; age: 53 yrs Gask
Virgie d 26 Aug 1945; age: 45 yrs JoyC
William 1895-1973 Metr
William E (h/o G Marable) 1879-1912 MtHo
William Gillet s/o Jno J & Harriet 16 Nov 1833-21 Jan 1840 Wise
William T (h/o S P B) 19 Jan 1853-30 May 1934 Onan
William T s/o Jno E & E S 4 May 1840-18 Sept 1850 (unable to locate; 1940 data) Wisp
Willie A w/o C A 1893-1974 Bays
WISER, Fannie (w/o J L) 1898-1962 Quin
John L (h/o Fannie) 5 Aug 1886-2 Feb 1952 Quin
WITMER, Robert H (h/o V S) 1917-1977 MtHo-s
Virginia S (w/o R H) 1912- MtHo-s
WOLFE, David F 1918-1969 Wach
John W (h/o M B) 1893-1946 Wach
Millie Blackwell (w/o J W) 1892-1975 Wach
WOOD, Austin Flint MD 1876-1936 Park

WOOD (continued)
Estelle Tyler 1917-1937 Park
Capt John Bennett 1942 MtHo-s
Maria Catherine w/o W W 1848-1924 Park
Mary Elizabeth 1945 MtHo-s
William Woodford h/o M C 1848-1921 Park
WOODS, Roger L 5 Jan 1944-2 May 1980 Park
WOOLLEY, Melvin W 19 Apr 1894-26 Apr 1909 Wach
William H 13 Aug 1850-21 Jan 1908 Wach
WORKMAN, Kate F w/o Chas B 7 Mar 1859-19 Feb 1926 StGe
WRENCH, Sarah L 22 Dec 1910-16 Mar 1982 NewM
WRIGHT, A Vernon 1906- Park
Alfred J h/o M A 1849-1927 Libe
Annie Bundick w/o Wm T 1863-1950 Park
Bessie C w/o J T 1890-1931 Libe
C Webster h/o N L 1871-1950 Park
Dorsey F h/o M C 1889-1954 Libe
Edna M 1912-1982 Park
Edward h/o V S 27 Sept 1871-13 Apr 1945 Park
Edward W 11 Oct 1849-27 Oct 1914 Libe
Elijah W (h/o M T); s/o Isaac & Mary 5 Nov 1809-20 June 1880 Onan
Emma E 11 Jan 1840-4 Oct 1911 LocM
Emma Katherine w/o Edwin S 12 Feb 1859-1 May 1914 DrDi
Ethel G 28 Feb 1905-26 May 1982 Park
Fannie Lee (w/o J T) 15 Mar 1885- Onan
Isaac (h/o R B) 13 Oct 1801-7 Feb 1873 Stur
Isaac T 1844-1896 Onan
J Thomas h/o B C 1886-1944 Libe
James E h/o L M 1892-1968 Park
John B h/o K S 10 June 1864-5

WRIGHT (continued)
Aug 1933 Park
John Tully (h/o F L) 7 Dec 1885-3 Mar 1959 Onan
Katherine Somers w/o J B 1867-1961 Park
Levin J h/o M G 1878-1937 Park
Lillie M w/o J E 1894-1984 Park
Malinda A w/o A J 1853-1925 Libe
Margaret T (w/o E W) 28 June 1807-19 Mar 1891 Onan
Mary C w/o D F 1899- Libe
Mary G w/o L J 1884-1977 Park
Mary T w/o O J 1914- Park
Mattie Hazel 1897-1982 Park
Nancy L w/o G W 1878-1957 Park
Norma C d/o D F & M C 1930-1941 Libe
Orville J h/o M T 1914- Park
Rachel B w/o Isaac 19 Dec 1813-26 Nov 1877; age: 63/11/7 Stur
Samuel W s/o J B & K S 1897-1959 Park
Viana Somers w/o Edwd 19 July 1871-5 Aug 1940 Park
Virginia Hickman 1863-1952 Onan
William s/o Denis & Nancy 29 June 1822-12 Apr 1883; age: 60/9/3 Budb
William H 25 July 1896-4 Oct 1916 Park
William Thomas h/o A B 1861-1942 Park
WYATT, Fletcher 1904-1968 NewM
Florence B 1892-1960 HTri
James 1901-1968 NewM
James W 1879-1953 Fair
Lydia N (w/o R E) 1910-1971 MtHo-s
Robert E (h/o L N) 1904-1971 MtHo-s
Willie P 1881-1958 Fair
WYNNE, Thomas A (h/o G D) 1901-1974 Fair
YORK, A Blaine 1882-1945 Edge
Rose W 1897-1979 Edge
Y..., J T This could be the

Y... (continued)
footstone for a Yardley whose family owned land at Underhill Point. See Whitelaw:815 Unde
YOUNG, inf/o G H & N R b&d 1908 Libe
A Lela w/o E T 1885-1978 Edge
Adelene B w/o Wm E 1879-1971 Park
Alice Lee 21 Mar 1875-27 Apr 1954 Park
Allie T h/o M G 1881-1947 Libe
Andrew J h/o Eliz 1856-1933 Park
Anita 1932-1972 MtHo
Annie Lee w/o Gillie Sr 1874-1948 Park
Audrey C (w/o B R) 1917- Fair
B F h/o E S 2 Dec 1856-22 Mar 1920 Park
Benjamin F s/o B F & E S 10 Oct 1879-17 Nov 1891 Park
Benjamin Franklin 18 Mar 1895-19 Mar 1983 Park
Bernice May 1899-1920 Libe
Betty Lea 6 May 1922- Crad-s
Blanche Parks 1889-1983 Libe
Broadus R (h/o A C) 1909-1977 Fair
Carrie 1904-1980 Wach
Carrie H w/o S B 1895-1983 Libe
Charles H h/o J S 1889-1960 Edge
Clara E w/o G W 1895-1951 Edge
Clarence D h/o N L 1 July 1897-30 May 1952 Park
Dewey F 1900-1971 Fair
Dora Susan 7 Oct 1886-15 Feb 1982 Park
Earl W 21 May 1911- Park
Ed Tom h/o A L 1882-1941 Edge
Edith B 1889-1961 MtHo
Edith Raab 1920-1960 Wach
Edward s/o Dr E J & S E 1 May 1838-29 Sept 1841 Seve
Edward J s/o Dr E J & S E 11 Mar 1844-14 Mar 1852 Seve
Edward S Sr 4 Dec 1890-1 Feb 1958 Edge
Edward S Jr 5 Oct 1923-15 Sept

YOUNG (continued)
1971 Edge
Edward Samuel 4 Dec 1890-1 Feb 1958 Edge
Effie May w/o Wm T 1879-1959 Libe
Elisha Sarah d/o S J & M L 22 Aug 1860-10 Sept 1863; age: 3/0/18 Joyp
Eliza C d/o S J & M L 16 July 1868-10 Oct 1877; age: 9/3/15 Joyp
Eliza E w/o G R 1875-1954 Libe
Eliza S w/o B F 12 Sept 1856-15 July 1917; age: 60/10/3 Park
Elizabeth S w/o R W d 23 Feb 1918; age: 68 yrs Libe
Elizabeth S w/o A J 1860-1930 Park
Elizabeth S d/o J E & M E b&d 11 Oct 1879 Edge
Ellen w/o W D 1864-1943 Metr
Emma Edna w/o J H Sr 7 Dec 1874-24 Dec 1922 Wach
Essie E w/o Wm T 1896- Park
Etta Cleveland 17 June 1892-15 Jan 1978 Park
Everett M h/o M T 1908-1981 Libe
Florence D d/o Gillie & Annie 9 July 1906-26 Jan 1915 Park
Florida M (w/o R F) 1913- Onan
Francesca Kratz w/o J S 21 July 1928-8 July 1982 Libe
George R h/o E E 1870-1971 Libe
George T h/o McC T 16 Feb 1866-28 May 1908 Park
George Washington s/o Jno T & M E b&d 19 Sept 1875 Edge
Gillie Sr h/o A L 1867-1952 Park
Gillie H h/o N R 1889-1945 Libe
Gillie W Jr 7 Apr 1896-5 Nov 1974 Park
Grace M 12 Sept 1925- Park
Grayson W h/o C E 1891-1971 Edge
Grover H 1875-1940 Edge
Harvey F h/o T M 25 Feb 1901-24 Aug 1963 Park
Hazel E 10 Jan 1900- Crad-s
Henry E 15 July 1897-7 Mar 1978

YOUNG (continued)
Crad-s
Ida May 20 Aug 1890-18 Mar 1983 Park
Irving S 1876-1953 Wach
J Littleton 1897-1967 Libe
J Thomas 1909-1970 Libe
James H (h/o P F) 16 July 1865-6 Oct 1944 Edge
James H Jr 22 Mar 1904-13 Feb 1948 Edge
James R h/o M E 1889-1949 Park
Jennie S (nee Turlington) w/o C H 1892-1961 Edge
Jewell M w/o P W 1911- Park
John 1820-1898 Edge
John E h/o M E 7 Oct 1851-5 Aug 1930 Edge
John H Sr h/o E E 20 Jan 1861-8 July 1939 Wach
John L 1908-1967 Wach
John S h/o M L 1889-1948 Park
John T h/o S J 1877-1944 Park
John W s/o J E & M E 4 Nov 1871-16 Jan 1894 Edge
John W D s/o Jno T & M E 1 Sept 1861-25 May 1885 Edge
Joseph Samuel h/o F K 25 Dec 1922-3 Dec 1979 Libe
Julia w/o W B 14 Oct 1851-22 Jan 1917 Edge
Kelly Thomas b&d 1961 Edge
Krandel B h/o M R 1913-1983 Libe
Lee W h/o L C 15 Jan 1889-17 Jan 1981 Park
Leonard h/o M C 1882-1965 MtHo-s
Leonard Cifton h/o M S 1901-1963 Park
Lillie B 1896-1944 Edge
Lola P d/o Wm & Margt E 21 Aug 1886-31 Aug 1896 Majo
Louis A (h/o M L) 1871-1935 MtHo
Lula B 2 Aug 1896- Edge
Lula C w/o L W 12 June 1890-15 Jan 1965 Park
Lurline T w/o R S 1879-1948 MtHo
McCartie L w/o G T 11 Sept

305

YOUNG (continued)
1870-30 Mar 1902 Park
Maccrina G w/o A T 1881-1965 Libe
Madeline P d/o J H & Blanche Parks 1912-1969 Libe
Maggie 1888-1948 Wach
Margie L w/o J S 1889- Park
Margie P (w/o S T) 1911- MtHo
Martha J w/o O S 1888-1927 Libe
Mary Anna 1851-1940 Park
Mary C w/o Saml 30 Aug 1863-4 Mar 1953 Edge
Mary C w/o Leonard 1892-1973 MtHo-s
Mary E w/o Jno T 25 May 1838-1 July 1915 Edge
Mary E w/o J E 8 Sept 1856-18 May 1928 Edge
Mary E w/o J R 1896-1968 Park
Mary Josephine d/o Wm & Susan 9 Dec 1858-24 Feb 1875 Edge
Mary Lavenia w/o S J 15 Mar 1830-20 Aug 1904; age: 74/5/5 Joyp
Mattie Hartman 1868-1938 MtHo
Melvin S s/o O S & M J 1908-1939 Libe
Mildred T w/o E M 1908-1984 Libe
Minnie L (w/o L A) 1877-1955 MtHo
Miriam R w/o K B 1913- Libe
Myrtle Susan w/o L C 1902-1977 Park
Nancy Lee w/o C D 15 Oct 1884-13 Feb 1950 Park
Nina R w/o G H 1892-1937 Libe
Oliver S h/o M J 1884-1961 Libe
Paul W h/o J M 1910-1979 Park
Polly F (w/o J H) 16 Apr 1873-17 Apr 1937 Edge
Ralph W 13 Oct 1919-29 Aug 1970 Park
Richard F (h/o F M) 1912- Onan
Richard W h/o S M 24 Feb 1830-11 Sept 1910 MtHo
Robert B 1896-1963 StLu
Robert S h/o L T 1876-1965 MtHo
Robert W h/o E S d 14 Dec 1914;

YOUNG (continued)
age: 74 yrs Libe
Ronald W 1935-1954 Libe
Royal J 1949-1975 Park
Russell W 1909-1982 MtHo
Ruth E 1891-1974 Wach
Sallie M w/o Isaac 5 Sept 1848-14 Jan 1919 Park
Sallie P d/o Dr E J & S E 7 Nov 1839-16 Apr 1856 Seve
Sally J w/o J T 1878-1951 Park
Sally T w/o Dr E J; d/o Wm & Eliz C Parramore 21 Sept 1821-23 June 1861 Seve
Samuel h/o M C 14 Mar 1863-27 Apr 1934 Edge
Samuel Crippen 2 Feb 1878-13 Dec 1946 Park
Samuel T (h/o M P) 1911-1976 MtHo
Samuel Thomas 1859-1930 Libe
Sarah A d/o Jno & Susannah 1 Mar 1819-21 Dec 1889 Will
Sarah E w/o Dr E J; d/o Jno & Sally Parramore 7 Jan 1816-23 May 1857 Seve
Severn J h/o M L 7 Dec 1833-27 Oct 1900 Joyp
Stanley A 1885-1956 Libe
Stuart B h/o C H 1890-1967 Libe
Susan w/o Wm 6 Aug 1830-20 Oct 1909 Edge
Susan M w/o R W 5 Mar 1842-5 Sept 1902 MtHo
Thelma M w/o H F 2 Mar 1907- Park
Warner A 1906-1955 MtHo
Warner S 1906-1977 Fair
Wayne Lee 5 Dec 1936-2 Oct 1938 Wach
William 8 Apr 1820-1 Nov 1900 Edge
William B h/o Julia; s/o Wm & Susan 22 Jan 1854-12 Jan 1907 Edge
William D h/o Ellen 1866-1947 Metr
William E h/o A B 1881-1956 Park
William T h/o E E 1893-1954 Park
William Thomas h/o E M 1876-

YOUNG (continued)
1947 Libe
William Thomas 11 Feb 1883-29 Mar 1955 Park
Wilson Robert 1915-1940 Libe
Woodrow Wilson 1913-1914 Libe
ZEMBER, baby boy b&d 1962 Quin
Elizabeth B (w/o H L) 1904- Quin
Hundley Lee (h/o E B) 18 Mar 1895-2 Feb 1969 Quin
John H (h/o M E) 1870-1931 Quin
Margaret E (w/o J H) 1875-1951 Quin
Page W 1926-1927 Quin
Sharon Lee 27-28 July 1950 Quin
ZIEGLER, Jo Ann Milliner 1947-1980 Onan

ADDENDUM

ABDELL, John s/o Jno & Mary 19 Nov 1794-2 Jul 1872; age; 77/7/13 MattW

AMES, Elizabeth S Sturgis w/o O W b 28 Apr 1864- ns (ref-family) Stub

AYRES, George Wilbert Sr 12 Mar 1924-2 Nov 1991 Ayrp
George Wilbert Jr 3 Sep 1942-1 Aug 1991 Ayrp

*BROWN Norris L s/o Wm A & Josephine mar Mary W Matthews 1 Dec 1880; 21 Jun 1855-11 Sep 1892 MattW
*Mary W w/o N L; d/o Wm K & Elizabeth Ann Matthews 21 May 1855- MattW
*(Only the footstones: MWB & NLB show beside a pile of rubble covering the headstones. Data from Clerk's Office, Northampton Co.)

BULL - monument to Amelia Bull Ayres, Charlie Bayly Bull, John Thomas Bull, Mary Elizabeth Bull. nd (All names on one stone.)
Bettie d/o Thos W & Lizzie M d 17 Jul 1855; age: 0/0/4 Bull
Edward s/o Thos W & Lizzie M d 28 Mar 1867; age: 0/4/15 Bull
Lizzie M (Neeley) w/o Thos W 29 Apr 1832-5 Apr 1868 Bull
Thomas W h/o L M 14 Sep 1818-13 Jan 1884 Bull

BUNTING, Juliet L w/o Thos; d/o Geo & Eliz Smith d 17 Oct 1836 Coal

CHURN, Eliza w/o Jno; d/o Jos & Eliz Abdell 22 Feb 1808-3 Sep 1874; age: 66/0/11 MattW
George F s/o Jno & Eliza 3 Feb 1845-9 Jun 1865 MattW

COWARD, Margaret w/o Saml; d/o Edmd & Jane (Kerr) Scarburg 6 Mar 1772-4 Aug 1800; leaving 2 daus - Jane & Margt Vale
Margaret d/o Saml & Margt 15 Mar 1798-9 Oct 1818 Vale
Samuel s/o Wm & Margt. 29 Mar 1771-31 Aug 1821; leaving a wife & 4 children. Monument by Jane O Bayly, his eldest dau. Vale

GUY, Claud H d age: 23 yrs nd Lawr

HICKMAN, Vernon Cecil s/o Randall C & Bettie A 10 Oct 1905-18 Sep 1906; age: 0/11/7 Lawr

MASON, Charlotte w/o J O; d/o Jno W & C Sturgis ns (dc1933; ref-family) Stub
James O h/o C S ns (d bef 1922; ref-family) Stur
Lyde d/o Jas O & Charlotte ns (dc1934; ref-family) Stub

MATTHEWS, Mary A E d/o Wm K & Eliz Ann 11 May 1853-20 Jul 1854 MattW
Susan A d/o Wm K & Eliz Ann 17 Aug 1846-29 Jul 1854 MattW
William R s/o Lewis R & Ader T 24 Nov 1821-12 Feb 1853 MattW

MOORE, Terese d/o Will & Lizzie (Sample) Thomas dn (dc1936; ref-family) Samp

NOCK, John s/o Edmd & Catherine 7 Oct 1813-19 Oct 1842; age: 29/0/12 OldN

PARKES, inf/o Jno & Bessie of Tangier Is) ns (dc1940; ref-family) Stub

READ, Sarah S d/o Edmd & Anne d 13 May 1790; age: 7/0/0 Fair

REW, Julia w/o Wm 31 May 1810-28 Aug 1857; in her 47th yr Coke

SAMPLE, Annie w/o J A nd (dc1938; ref-family) Samp

John Alfred h/o Annie nd (bef 1936; ref-family) Samp

SMITH, James P 5 Aug 1808-12 Apr 1853; age: 44/8/7 MattW

Margaret A R 24 Jun 1813-11 Aug 1888 MattW

TURNER, Mrs Ann 29 Jul 1783-25 Jan 1857 MattW

Nathel B 13 Dec 1778-5 Jun 1850; age: 71/5/22 MattW

WYATT, Arthur M mar Emory V Downing 8 Dec 1852; 7 Oct 1827-28 Sep 1853; age: 26/0/121 MattW

E V w/o Arthur; d/o Dr E W P Downing 30 Jun 1832-13 Jun 1866 MattW

Isme G s/o Isme & Polly; mar Margt B Thompson 11 Jan 1854; 18 Sep 1822-21 Jul 1870 MattW

INDEX

This cross-index lists names buried in the text. First check the alphabetically arranged text for the surname(s) of interest and then use the index to find others with the same surname(s) mentioned elsewhere in the text.

ABDELL, Eliz 309 Eliza 309 Jos 309
ABRAMS, Elizabeth 134 Jno 134 Margaret Susan 134 Mary H 1 Saml J 1
ADAIR, Mary 9
ADAMS, Alice 136 Helen 8
ADDIE, Mazie 181
ADDISON, Jane O 13 Jas H 2 Kendall 13 Lucille 128 Sue 110
AILWORTH, Lottie 58 101
ALBRIGHT, Nora B 235
ALLEN, Addie 286 Gertie 18 M E 189 W R 189 Willie Brown 189
AMES, A Virginia 262 Ann 186 Ann Priscilla Hornsby 132 Annie 115 Benj 186 Benj T 171 Catherine 148 Charlotte (Downing) 71 Eliz 76 J S 148 Jno 247 Jno Stephen 71 Julia A 171 Juliet A 186 Kate S 171 Lela 71 Levin S 4 132 Louisa Taylor 71 M S 148 Maggie E 71 Margt 138 Mary F 76 Mary G 247 Matilda A 138 Minnie 12 Polly 247 Rebecca 124 Richd 86 Richd Thos 71 Rose 80 Saml 138 Sarah Jane 185 Wm C 76
ANDERSON, Lucy 289 Pauline 260
ANDREWS, Florence 116 Tabitha 197
ANLEY, Novella Baker 233
ANNIS, Addie 289 Major 26 Polly 26 Sarah E 145 Susan 26

ARBUCKLE, Ann 117 170 Anne C 117
ARLINGTON, Ann S 84 Jno 84 Rosey (Ann) 94
ARMISTEAD, Tully 142
ARTHUR, Kathryn Ann 171 Laura 70
ASHBURNE, Mary F 138
ASHBY, Lyde 295 Mary 156 Mary E 273 Navilla 273 Robt 273 Sallie Finney 245
ATKINSON, Marietta 302
AYDELOTT, Susan 76 251
AYDELOTTE, Mildred 172
AYERS, Fern 44 Henrietta D 18 Margt 227
AYRES, Amelia 309 Annie 300 Jno J 62 Laura 55 Margareta A 58 Margt 62 Myrtle 181 Nancy 58 Thos 58
BABCOCK, Adell 301
BADGER, Letty R 282 Louisa A 174 Margt 174 Mary 174 282 Mary A 174 Nathl 174 282 Thos W 174
BAGGE, Achsah B 171 Peggy 171 Wm 171
BAGWELL, Adah 204 Elizabeth 301 Goldie 196 Lotta 192 Margt F 274 Sadie P 302
BAILEY, Amelia W 198 Annie 175 Cordelia 300 Myrtle 166 Sallie T 227
BAITY, Alice 62
BAKER, Mary Ann 164 Novella 233 Shepard 164 Sophia A 164

BALEY, see BAILEY 11
BALLARD, Rachel 302
BARNES, Alicia 192 Annie M 152 Arinthia T 152 Arthur 152 Ellsworth 17 Essie 184 Kate 140 Mary 250
BASSET, Charlotte 72
BATTAILE, Adelaide 9 Adelaide Rogers 124 Ann Hay 117 Ellen 124 Henry 9 124
BAUM, Kate 166
BAYLEY, Annie 79 Esther Parramore 278
BAYLEY, see BAILEY 11
BAYLY, Anna D 192 Chas 7 E H M 270 Edmund 13 Elizabeth W 191 Evelyn May 270 Florence 272 Jane O 309 M P 36 M P C 191 Margaret Ann 151 Margaret P 68 Margt 68 Mary Ann 292 Richard 13 Richd 151 Rose 13 Sally 36 Sarah 7 151 Susan 297 T H 270 T M 36 191 192 Thos 68 Thos H 12 272
BAYLY, see BAILEY 11
BAYNE, Eliza 215
BEACH, E B 20 281 Elizabeth 57 Jno S 20 281 Kendal 175 Mary 279 Mary A 281 Mollie 56 Molly 57 Reuben 57 Rosey 175 Sophia 175 Virginia 25
BEARD, Renova 77
BECKETT, Ruth Ann 230
BECKETT, see BECKET 19
BELL, Alice Ann 20 Anne 141 Arinthia S 233 B J 34 Catherine 217 Charlotte 21 261 Cordie 89 Eliz 183 Elizabeth C 84 Emma G 183 Estelle 193 G H 84 Geo W 34 Georgia 75 J S 183 Jas 261 Jas H 21 Jodiah 217 Katy 34 Keturah Garrison Glenn 105 Louise 280 M R 84 Mahala H 217 Margaret 45 138 Margaret T 172 Mary J 21 Rachel 34 233 Robin 21 Sadie 34 92 Sally A 21 Sarah E 21 Wm 34 233
BELOATE, Eliza 134 Gabrille 184

BELOTE, Amanda 263 E H 263 Jas 94 Mary 250 281 May 16 Miriam 244 Sarah 125 Susie 149
BENNETT, Covington 253 Daisey B 233 Hester P 233 Jno 233 Malinda W 253 Sally 253
BENSON, Annie W 25 Mary 281
BETTY, Mary E 198
BEVANS, Lizzie 266 Mary S 266 Sadie 215 Severn 266
BILLUPS, Frances 167
BIRD, A J 47 273 Annie 47 Ellen 170 Margaret Susan 273 S A 273 Sarah Mears 47 Wm 47
BLACKSTONE, Ann 27 Henrietta 241 Margaret 60 Margaret Douglass 21 Rachel 58
BLACKWELL, Millie 303
BLAND, May 135
BLEN, Margt Doughty 252
BLOXOM, Bettie S 36 Caroline W 137 Irene 15 Jewell 211 Ora 198
BLOXSOM, Gertd 64 Missouri 87
BOGGS, Agnes 30 Amelia 18 Bettie C 263 Eliz 58 Eliz P 142 Elizabeth M 11 Ella 161 Ellnora 199 Emma S 93 Francis 30 58 H A 263 Jas S 142 Jno R 232 Jos P 93 L M 232 L R 263 Leah M 30 Leah S 207 Levie 260 Levinia 260 Lillian 153 202 Lizzie S 200 Lolita 46 Mary 149 Monnie H 232 Pearl 94 Rachael 232 Sarah A 58 Sarah S 142 Susan E 93
BOGS, Sallie 222
BOICE, Edna 204
BOND, Lelia 100
BONNIVIL, Nannie 53 Thelma 14
BONNIWELL, Faith 226 Marie 215
BOOTH, Chas 166 E C 166 Sarah F 166
BOOTHE, Margaret 280
BORUM, Maude 103
BOWCOCK, Lillie 102
BOWDOIN, Amanda 139 J B 139 Virginia 94 139

BOYCE, Vercie 33 139
BOYETT, Louisa 116
BOYKIN, Celeste 120
BRADFORD, Alica 46 Elcy 86
  Elcy T 86 Ella D 35 78 Geo 33
  J E 35 78 Jas 21 Jno H 246
  Joyce 250 Lucretia 21 Mary
  Ellen 295 Minnie 187 Page 9
  Polly 46 Rachel 21 295 S A 35
  78 Sarah A 246 T A 86 Thos 46
BRINGIER, Melanie Elizabeth
  299
BRITTINGHAM, Ellen James 199
  Esther (Marshall) 199 Jno 199
BROADWATER, Eliz 96
  Elizabeth 35
BROUGHTON, Betty Carmine 168
  Ethel 121 Ethelyne 210
BROWN, Lula 65 Mabel 186 Mary
  Swanger 187 Mollie 187 Oswald 187 P F 260
BROWNE, Anna Fletcher 273
  Mary Josephine 270 S C 260
  Wille 260
BRYON, Pearl 258
BUDD, G W Jr 37 Lottie 287
  Nellie 119 Sallie 60
BULL, Ann B 86 Annie 107
  Bridget 185 Edith 27 251 Esther E 29 Harriet E 83 Jno R
  83 Julia A 83 Margaret 174
  Mary 82 Olive 163 Virginia 122
BUNDICK, Ann C 263 Annie 286
  303 Clara 32 Elizabeth 81
  Evelyn 20 Geo 21 Jane 81 Jno
  S 81 263 Junita 46 Lucretia 21
  Lula 16 Nancy 21 V A 47
BUNTING, Hennie E 48 J C 48
  Mary 48
BURLEY, Indiana 67
BURTON, Alice T 6 Esther 11
  Helen 214 Jno B 272 Joshua 6
  Maggie 148 Margaret A W 272
  Mollie 293 Polly 6 Sallie M
  203 Sarah P 272
BUTLER, Hannah 301
BYRD, Alice 81 Annie 75 204
  Dora 161 Ephrim 154 Mabel
  170 Malinda A 154 Mariah 154
  Ruth 145 Sarah 21 Susan 41
CAKE, Eloise 39

CAMPBELL, Julia 63 Rose 44
  Sallie 47 Susie 56
CAMPER, Maude 215
CANNON, Elizabeth A 48 Wm 48
CARBAUGH, Annie 279
CARMINE, Betsy 215 Ellenora 62
  Jas 215 Jno T 27 Llewellyn
  215 May H 27
CARSON, Rhoda 215
CATHEY, Mabel 281
CAULT, Harriet 102
CAUSEY, Annie 241 Sallie 201
CHANDLER, Amy 112 Catharine
  Angelica 29 Elisha 112
  Elizabeth 29 Jno W 29 Margaret 76 Margt 30 Mary 282
  Mary E 282 Mitchel 41
  Mitchell 55 Mollie Lee 187
  Nancy B 55 Nora L 251 Rose D
  89 S R 282 Susan (Byrd) 41
  Susan A 30 Susan Reeston 41
  Tabitha 112 Wm D 30
CHARNOCK, Melinda F 123
CHASE, Gloria June 45
CHERRIX, see CHERRICKS 54
CHESSER, Lillie 16 Mildred 255
CHEVES, Emma 297
CHEW, Ruth 159
CHEWNING, Elizabeth 124
CHRISTIAN, Susanna 48
CLAMPITT, Elizabeth 81
CLAYTON, Jas A 148 Lydia M
  148 Sarah 148
CLEVELAND, Etta 305
CLOWES, Peter J 188 Sarah Jane
  188
COARD, Annie 182 Elizabeth 118
  Mattie 26
COATES, Lula 32
COBB, Sulie 65
COLBOURN, see COLEBURN 56
COLE, Edna 262
COLEBURN, Catherine 299 Eliza
  S 260 Jno 299 Mary A 260
  Saml S 260 Sarah W 299
COLLINS, Ethel 260 Mary 4
COLONNA, Elizabeth E 126 139
  Mary 174 Va Charnock 174
  Wm Tyler 174
CONQUEST, Emma V S 67
  Euphemia M 67 Wm 67

CONWAY, Estelle 17
COOPER, Nancy 14 Rebecca 99
COPES, Ann P 60 Annie 289
  Caroline S 180 Etta 99 Isabelle
  15 Susan N 149 Thos P 60
CORBAN, Leah 93
CORBIN, Agnes Drummond 151
  Anna 63 Annette 22 Barbara 64
  Coventon 64 Eliz (Revell
  Horsey) 151 Mae 51 Sabra 64
CORE, Ella 205 Lola 120 Mary W
  138 Sarah 46
CORGIN, Geo 151
COSTEN, Eliz 170
COSTIN, Lynn 203
COSTON, Rebecca 296
COULBOURN, Dorenda 178
  Louisa A 178 Saml 178
COULBOURNE, see COLEBURN
  56
COWARD, Eliza 147
COXTON, Bessie B 114
CRIPPEN, Sarah 303
CROCKETT, Evelena 88 Louise
  V 186 Sallie D 90
CROPPER, Alice B 126 Ann J B
  63 Anna 120 Anne 120
  Catherine 102 Eliza
  Washington 102 Jno 12 102
  303 John 13 John Jr 218 Margaret 12 Margt 12 13 Margt
  (Pettitt) 303 Margt P 13 Pearl
  45 Sabra 112 Sally 36 Sarah
  Corbin 301 303 Thos 112 Thos
  B 63
CROWN, Jesse 69
CROWSON, Ivy 88
CURTIN, Alice 69
CUSTIS, Alice E 69 Ann 112 Ann
  (Kendall) 112 Anne 112 Bettie
  134 Betty 3 Catharine 220
  Catharine P W 219 Charlote
  263 Eleanor 176 Eliz 214
  Elizabeth 214 221 Florence
  109 Henry 112 Jane H 69 Jas
  W 114 Jennie 185 Jno 219
  Kathryn 233 M P B 114 Margaret 114 Mary B 214 Rose
  Major 203 Sarah 220 Susan 214
  Susannah 141 Tabitha 219
CUTLER, Isabel 48
DABNEY, Elizabeth Lewis 170

DAVIS, Annie Louise 59
  Elizabeth 132 151 Emma E 20
  Gladys 18 Lois 259 Maggie
  287 Marion 36 Rebecca 247
DAY, Marcelline 168
DEAN, Ella 35
DEEBLE, Jane 128
DENIS, Charlotte J 112
DENNIS, Eleanor 255
DENNIS, Elizabeth 11 Ella 97 Jno
  255 Sallie 65 Susan Upshur 254
DERBY, Harriet 8 Mary Charlotte
  9
DEWES, Cheryl 70
DICKERSON, Mary 31
DICKEY, Lelia Bond 100
DICKINSON, David 245 Elizabeth
  26 245 Hannah 245
DIX, Ann 27 Fitchett 229 J Morgan 73 Jas H 276 277 Margt W
  277 Martha 37 Rose 27 Tabitha
  W 276 Yula 274 Yvonne Hall
  229
DIZE, Elsie 242
DODSON, Etta 156 Florence 205
DOUGHTY, Ann 18 Annie P 92
  Carrie 82 171 Carrie V 93
  Emma Dunton 171 Helen D 82
  Jas 171 Jas A 82 93 Margaret
  79 Mary 141 Mildred Milliner
  193
DOUGLAS, Eleanor 67 Elizabeth
  301 Eva 301 Geo 302 Hugh 301
  Louise 178 Margaret 11 302
  Margt 302 Nancy (Hamilton)
  301 Tabitha (Drummond) 302
DOUGLASS, Dorothy 77 Margaret
  21 27 Rebecca 77
DOWNING, Alice E 146 Bessie
  Jane 146 Charlotte 71 E V 310
  Emory V 310 Indie 1 J R 146
  Jno B 116 Mildred D 116 Polly
  W 116 Susan 261 W P 310
DRMMOND, Grace 238
DRUMMOND, Alice Lee 98 Ann
  11 13 Anna 35 Betsy 191
  Elecia A 98 Eliz 191 Elizabeth
  C 67 Harriet 67 295 Helen 202
  Jas 67 295 Jno R 98 Maggie 76
  Margaret Sarah (Sadie) 76
  Margt 216 Mary 141 295 Mary
  A 260 P Purnell 260 Raymond

DRUMMOND (continued)
  80 Richd 11 Robert A 76
  Stephen 191 Tabitha 302
DUDLEY, Virginia 296
DUNAWAY, Julia 84
DUNCAN, Laurah F 194 Margie
  203 Mary Elizabeth 194 Thos
  A 194
DUNFORD, Lois 66
DUNKLEY, Hamner 42
DUNTON, Carvey 80 Elizabeth 65
  Georgianna 197 Leah 235
  Margt 80 Mary R 80
EARL, Edna 78
EAST, Annie 49 Elizabeth 264
  Eva 227 Jas 282 Mary A 282
  Pauline 202
EDMONDS, Ann 201 Anna 86
  Annie 3 Jas 201 Polly 201
  Polly W 201
EDMUNDS, A B 276 Mary S 276
  Thos 276 see also EDMONDS
  84
EDWARDS, Annie B 11 Jas 11
  Sarah R 11
EICHELBERGER, Elizabeth 159
  Wm 159
EICKELBERGER, Eliz 224
ELLIOT, Sarah 82
ELLIOTT, Anzele 280 Wm 280
EMERY, Mary 80 May 84
ENGLISH, Mitylene 81
EVANES, see EVANS 87
EVANS, Ann 151 Benj M 151
  Beulah 223 Charlotte 151
  Cordie 22 David 153 Elizabeth
  E 153 Emma 233 Julia 292
  Lester O 230 Maria Melson
  102 Mary 198 Nora 226 Rachel
  153
EVERETT, Juanita 249 Laura H
  128
EWELL, Amey 91 Arinthia B 191
  Arinthia S 220 Arithia 101 Bernice 10 Cora L 191 Daisey 6
  Doris L 10 Eliz 220 G P 220
  Georgia 265 Jno R 191 Louise
  S 43 Margaret 62 Mark 91 Oveless E 10 Polly 91
FAIRBANKS, Emma 132
FENLEY, Mary 18
FENTRESS, Bessie 224

FIELD, Evelyn Harrison 12 Margt
  12
FINLEY, Saml 301
FINNEY, E B 3 Elizabeth F 231
  Emma Littleton 301 Ethel 3
  Lucy 30 Mabel VanPelt 278
  Maggie 128 282 Margaret M
  282 May 212 Rosanna 69 Sallie
  129 245 Sally 231 282 Sarah A
  282 Susan 129 T W 282 Thos
  W 231 V B 3 Wm W 6
FISHER, Anne F 109 Elizabeth 67
  Ellen 110 Fenwick 67 Fred B
  231 Geo 149 154 Jas A 109
  Juliet Ann F 214 Juliet B 214
  Kissier E 154 Miers W 214
  Patience 149 Rachel 149 154
  Rosannah 67 Rose 13 231 Sue
  46 Sue A 109 Sue F 231
FITCHETT, Mattie 82 Susie 129
FITZGERALD, Chas 49 Elizabeth
  F 49
FLETCHER, Anna 35 Annie 122
  192 Edith 122 Elisha A 78
  Elishea 94 Elizabeth 78
  Elizabeth Broadwater 35
  Frances 4 Jas Henry 35 Mary
  80 Sarah 94 Thos 78 Thos W
  94
FLOYD, Lynn 265 Margaret E 43
  Matilda 201 Rachel 217 Sallie
  217 Sarah 200 T B 217
FLUHART, Emmie 20
FOGLE, Margaret 65
FONTAINE, Elizabeth 104
FORREST, Katherine 243
FOSQUE, Lee 89 Margaret A 201
  Margt 251 Nathl 201 Sarah 201
FOX, Annie E 209 Gayle 276 Ida
  243 Margaret 276 Virginia 159
FRENCH, C E 295 Hannah 56
FRIEZE, Doris 218
FRYE, Mary 218
FULCHER, Prudie 68
GARDNER, Clara L 146 Coli W
  146
GARRISON, Abel 157 Adah 21
  Arinthia G 110 Eliz 15
  Elizabeth 15 Elizabeth A 110
  Elizabeth S 157 Isabelle 80
  Isaiah 21 Jacob 80 Jas 253 Jno
  15 Keturah 21 105 Maggie W

GARRISON (continued)
  261 Margaret R 157 Margt 157
  Mary J 80 Matilda E 109 O S
  110 Rachel 96 Sally 253 Sarah
  264 Susan Downing 261 Wm
  261 Sarah H 253
GASKINS, Mae 282
GEIGER, Octavia 207
GIBB, Anna Cropper 120 Anne 120
  E W 120 Eliza W 150
  Elizabeth Washington 150 Jos
  120 Jos W 150
GIBBONS, Ida 64 Lee 211 Margie
  178
GIDDINGS, see GIDDENS 103
GIDDINS, see GIDDENS 103
GILDEN, May 132
GILL, Florentine 278
GILLESPIE, Fannie J 234 Hattie
  1 J W 234 S A 234
GILLET, Annie S 205 Henrietta
  206 Mary 9
GILLETT, Ayres 68 Elizabeth 26
  Henrietta 26 27 64 Margt 68
  Sarah T 64 Tabitha 68 Wm 26
  27 64
GLADSTONE, Catherine 22
GLENN, Ann 172 Dune 172 Jas 21
  Keturah 21 Keturah Garrison
  105 Lizzie 97 Margaret 172
GODWIN, Ann 114 Mary E 273
GOFFIGAN, Wm 217
GOFFIGON, Margt 217 Olevia S
  217 Victoria 41
GOLDEN, Kathryn 106 Matthew
  106
GOLDIE, Cathrine 10
GORDON, Lacy 278
GRANT, Mildred 198
GRAY, Elizabeth 173 Eva 281
  Lillie 94 Mattie 48 Rose 163
GREENE, see GREEN 107
GREY, see GRAY 106
GRINNALDS, Lena 116 Mattie
  169
GRINNOLDS, see GRINNALDS
  107
GROTON, Eva 210 Tabitha Ann
  Marian 149
GROVE, Blanche 268
GUNTER, Julia 265 May 84

GUY, Beatrice 57 Bessie 54
  Carrie 14 Emma 18 Julia 206
  Margt T 74 Mary E 74 Nancy
  173 R P 74 W H 206
HACK, Ann 225 294 Elizabeth 18
  122 Frances 241 Geo 241
  Margt 241 Mary 124 Matilda 7
  Peter 7 18 122 149 Peter Sr
  225 Sallie B 149 Sallie B U
  149 Sally 9
HALEY, Jas P 284 Rossetta Anne
  284 Sarah 120
HALL, Beatrice 180 Priscilla 71
  Yvonne 229
HALLETT, Anna 10
HAMILTON, Nancy 301 Sally 11
HANCOCK, Elsie 251
HAND, Bertha 169
HARDY, Emma J 69 Esther 69
  Eugenia 264 Wm H 69
HARGIS, Etta 83 Julia 204
HARMAN, Eliz 217 Margt Kellam
  146 Sarah A J 217 Wm 217
HARMANSON, Ann Arbuckle 170
  Ann Hay 297 Chas L 297 Eliza
  18 Eliza A R 18 Elizabeth 191
  Jno L 170 Kate A 170 Mary
  Battaile 297 Matthew 18
  Tabitha S 255 see also HAR-
  MONSON 117
HARMON, Ann B 237 Jno 237
  Margaret A 21 Susie 172
HARRIS, Lena 261 Margaret 191
HARRISON, E B 243 Elizabeth V
  105 Evelyn 12 J E 69 M A 69
  Willianna S 69
HART, Geo H 2 Marian 257 Sallie
  2
HARTE, see HART 118
HARTMAN, Ella 261 Lottie 207
  Mattie 306
HATTON, Anne 262 Margt 148
HAY, Battaile 117
HEATH, Emily 50 Helen 273
  Joyce 228 Juliet Grace 4 S
  Parker 287
HEMPHILL, Lulu Belle 224
HENRY, Jas 302 Mary 301 302
  Sarah 22 Sarah (Scarburgh) 302
HICKMAN, Alice 77 Ellie 228
  Mildred B 28 Virginia 304

HIDEN, Elizabeth Chewning 124
HILL, Jane O 13 Louise 162 Mary 8 Saml Coward 13
HINMAN, Minnie 73
HOGE, Sara 239
HOLLAND, Geo E 115 Lelia K 115 Rebecca 48
HOLLOWAY, see HOLLAWAY 126
HOLT, E R 139 Elizabeth E 126 Elizabeth E Colonna 139
HOPE, Anne 182 Annie L 122
HOPKINS, Elizabeth 109 Ella K 218 Eva 279 Grace Eloise 293 J L 120 Jane 95 Jos 109 Margaret A 95 Mary Ellen (Johnson) 293 Mollie M 109 S J 120 Sallie J C 120 Stephen 95 Sudie 135 W H A 293
HORNSBY, Ann Priscilla 132 Mayor 280 Sallie 280 Susannah 280
HORSEY, Eliz (Revell) 151
HUGHLETT, Bessie 175
HUME, Jessie 41
HUNDLEY, Arzie J 207 Eliz C 207 Lois H 207
HUNGERFORD, Adell (Babcock) 301 Ida 301 Richd S 301
HURST, Kate 19
HUTCHINSON, Ella 137 Josephine 40 Mary 19 Pearl 89
HYSLOP, Eliz 268 Elizabeth Watson 262 see also HYSLUP 133
HYSLUP, Elizabeth 139 Jane 34
IRONMONGER, Virginia 25
ISDELL, Rita 249
JACKSON, Annie 56 Iva 63 Martha 174
JAMES, E K 289 Elizabeth J 176 Grace 12 Ida 81 L T 289 Lottie V 289 Mary 120 Patience 176 Sarah 195 Viola 293 Wm 176
JAMISON, Anita 65
JENKINS, Helen 45
JENNINGS, Ann 300 302 Ann (Wilson) 300 Obadiah 300
JESTER, Eliz 273 Jacob 273 Rachel S 273
JOHNS, Emma 156

JOHNSON, Bertha 124 Catherine 75 109 Elizabeth 161 Emily 27 Etta 214 Isabelle 71 Jeanice 230 Kasiah 8 Lena 235 Margt S T 76 Mary 128 Mary Ellen 293 Mary W 123 Mildred 214 Rennie 253 Sarah 103 Vercie Boyce 33
JOHNSTON, Sallie Campbell 47
JONES, Annie Virginia 170 Elizabeth E Colonna 126 Emma C 242 Helen 113 Margaret 58
JONSTON, see JOHNSTONE 139
JOYNES, A C 300 Ann 18 Ann C 195 242 Annie 251 E D 300 Edwd D 195 Elias D 68 Elisha 169 Elizabeth 7 Ellen D 300 Harriet E R 18 Jno 169 Jno G 18 Louisa Ann 72 Malisha 40 Margaret Ann 195 Margaret T 5 Margt 68 Margt A 195 May 273 Pamelia A 68 Ruben 7 Sallie S 169 Tabitha S 260 Thos R 72 Virginia S 5 Wm 260
JUDEFIND, Stella 245
JUNE, Jane 154
JUSTICE, see JUSTIS 142
JUSTIS, Bettie S 209 Evelyn 288 Jno P 209 Mary 262 Reva Byrd 222 Sam Revel 65 Vianah 65
KEATON, Eleanor 240 Margaret 144 Ruth 21
KELLAM, Ann 40 81 Ann D G 195 Anna 237 B D 214 Bettie 81 Bridget 195 Chas 116 Custis 79 Dorothy Douglass 77 Edith 72 Eliz 79 Eliz Smith 232 Eliza 27 Elizabeth S 75 Etrula 156 F C A 27 Frederick 148 149 Geo A 40 81 Gloria 95 Harriet 79 Hulton 34 Jno W 133 Julietta 133 Kathryn V 265 Lincoln 75 Loletia 107 Lucy 166 Mahalinda 212 Margaret 28 116 Margaret J 269 Margaret W 148 Margt W 133 Maria 157 Mary 279 Mary A 40 Minnie Ames 12 Sallie 75 Sallie A 34 Sarah A 27 Sarah C 269 Sarah S 149 Susan 34 Susan Elizabeth

KELLAM (continued)
  288 Tabitha 288 Thos 288
  Willianna 150 Wm H 269 Yula
  77 Zerrobabel 195
KELLEY, Hannah French 56 Jas
  W 56 Martha K 56 see also
  KELLY 150
KELLUM, Mary 34 see also
  KELLAM 146
KELLY, Jno W 276 Mabel 138
  Margt Nock 276 Nora 276
KELSO, Annie E 196 Margaret 89
KENDALL, Ann 112 Sarah 225
KER, Sarah 151
KERR, Jane 309
KILLMAN, C L 80 Ella K 256
  Exckiel 80 L J 256 Pearlina J
  80 S M 256 see also KILLMON
  152
KILLMON, A J 243 Bernice 198
  Caroline 15 E H 63 126 Eliz A
  243 Ethel E 88 Gertrude 258
  Hattie 123 Isabella T 15 J S 75
  K S 75 Kate L 63 Maggie D
  126 Maggie R 243 Manie J 75
  Mary 63 126 Mary W 65 Myrtle
  144 Pansy Leigh 298 Thos 15
  see also KILLOM 152 see also
  KILMON 152
KILMON, Cordelia 216 Gertrude
  39 Hazel 49 Margaret 75 Martha A 273
KIMMERLE, Mamie 92
KING, Eloise 171
KINGSLEY, Orvis 5
KNIGHT, Mary 105
KRATZ, Francesca 305
KROMMES, Bertha 193
KUSIAN, Anna 263 Mary 149
LANG, Mary 82 270 Mollie 94
  Tabitha 277
LANKFORD, Lillie 249 Lulie 118
  Suzanne 82
LeCATO, Beatrice 86 Bessie 170
  E G 239 E J 140 Eliz 198 Eliz
  (Eickelberger) 224 Emma S
  251 Fanny 153 J C M 21 Jas E
  153 202 L K 251 Lillian 202
  Lillian (Boggs) 153 Madeline
  260 Maggie 172 Margt Fosque
  251 Mary Ester 21 Mary M 239
  Molly 224 N B 239 N J W 198

LeCATO (continued)
  Nathl 224 Virginia Louise 202
  W R 21
LEE, Alice 22 Lena 23 Martha
  Lowry 76 Maude 40 Virginia 38
LEIGH, Sarah 61
LEONARD, Ellen 20
LEWIS, Bertie 255 Betsy 17 Edna
  189 Elicia A 297 Elizabeth J
  234 Eulalie (Martin) 52 Julia T
  128 Mabel 72 Mable 265 Maj
  17 Martha Arminda 52 May 155
  Minnie 291 Ruth 249 S J 26
  128 Sarah 83 Sarah Emma 26
  Sarah J 17 Vara 58 Vesta 246
  W R 26 128 Wm Oscar 52
LILLISTON, Annie 42 Bertha 19
  Clara Teresa 108 Ellen 11
  Emma 96 Jane T 14 Laura 81
  Margaret 295 R S 42 W E 42
LIVINGSTON, Helen 206
LODGE, Margaret B 60
LOFTLAND, see LOFLAND 167
LOGAN, Lois 217
LOGON, see LOGAN 168
LONG, Jean 86 Mabel 198 Sarah
  222
LOWE, Beulah 175
LUKER, Luke 48 Susan 48
  Susanna (Christian) 48
LYDE, Mary Lee 54
LYNN, Margaret M 166
LYONS, Mary Elizabeth 302 Peter
  302 Sarah (Waugh) 302
McALLEN, Lean 289
McCABE, Roxie W 298
McCANN, Hanna 166
McCLAIN, see McLANE 170
McMATH, Ellen 183 Margaret 12
  Mary 30 Rebecca 35
McNEILE, Capt 117
MAJOR, Eliz Costen 170 202
  Elizabeth Purnell 170 Ellen
  141 294 Margaret 52 Wm Littleton 170
MAPP, A B 21 Ann J 186 Ann T
  126 Annie W 272 Bette G 127
  Bettie (Thomas) 71 Bettie V
  75 Caroline 204 Carrie 203
  Catherine C 29 Edwin T 272
  Elizabeth B 272 Emma 47 195
  Emma S 3 184 Gabriella

MAPP (continued)
Scarburgh 140 Geo B 186 Geo S 29 Geo T 71 126 Hester A 29 Howson 71 Indianna F 272 J C 76 Jane C 159 Jas C 75 Jas T 127 Katherine 66 Leah 71 126 Leah Ann 186 Madeline LeCato 260 Maggie A 127 Manie C 76 Margaret 21 94 Mary 75 138 Mollie Collier 203 Peggie 71 R H 21 Rebecca Douglass 77 Saphronia 76 Sophronia 75 Virginia 251 Wardella 296 Wm H 203
MARHOFFER, Marie 190
MARLEY, Ethel W 228
MARROW, Ella 15
MARSH, Maggie 85 173 243 Pearl 2
MARSHALL, Emma 106 245 Esther 199 Frances 158 Jenifer 67 MaBel Selby 106 Mae 298 Sarah E 145
MARTIN, Agnes 66 Alice 215 Annie 241 Eulalie 52 Janie 250 M B 66 Virginia M 226
MARTON, Callie 73
MASON, Annie Bundick 286 Bagwell C 283 Cordelia Frances 231 E C 208 E J 208 Edith 226 Eliz M 262 Eveline 108 Geo W 286 Hester A 231 Kate 186 Mae 53 Maggie N 47 Margt 283 Marian 32 Mary 262 287 Nancy 286 Pearl 192 Sallie 58 Saml 108 Sarah A 283 Susan J 208 Wm 262 Zarobabel C 231
MATHEWS, see MATTHEWS 179
MATHIAS, Mary 222
MATTHEWS, Charlotte 110 Cora B 137 Elizabeth Ann 309 Floyd V 110 Lucy 291 Marian Mears 110 Mary W 309 Wm K 309
MAY, Evelyn 12
MEARS, A W 212 Abel 299 Amanda 14 Annie 3 5 Benj W 3 Benja W 47 Bertie 19 115 Betty A 96 David 176 Dorothy 126 E Cora 47 Edna 38 Eliza 20 Ella 150 Ellen 44 Emma 47 Emma S 3 G D 212 Grace 78 Hester Ann 176 J H 150 Janie

MEARS (continued)
79 Jeff 121 Jno 77 Jno B 188 Jno S 207 Julia 176 Kate 121 Lula 148 279 Madeline 212 Margaret 1 80 299 Margt 247 Margt Edmonds 299 Marian 110 Martha 116 Mary 77 Mary Ann 207 Mary E 34 Maude 117 Myrtle 251 Nola 114 Pearl 43 Peter 247 R W 150 Ruth 89 S Earnestine 156 Sadie 133 Sally 207 Sarah 47 Sarah Jane 55 188 Sarah Jane Clowes 188 Silvia 247
MELLON, Rose 114
MELSON, Annie 163 Ellen F 165 J T 154 Jane 128 Lillian 203 Manie A 154 Margaret 289 Mary Ann 163 Smith 163 Sophia 154
MERRILL, Lida K 138
METCALFE, see METCALF 191
MIDDLETON, Mary 266
MIERS, M E Missouri 40 Wm 40
MILES, Amy 167 Anna Lee 90
MILLER, Grace 50 Roxie E 197
MILLINER, Annie 241 Jo Ann 307 Mary 19 Mildred 76 Priscilla 230
MILLS, M C 295 Maud 295 Wm S 295
MITCHELL, Elizabeth 137 Joyce 219 Mary 49
MOORE, Catharine J 203 Kathleen 268 Levi 203 Martha 212 Susan 203 Susan P 150
MORFORD, Laura 170
MORRIS, Ann 193 Emma 283 Kathryn 154 Laura 207
MUIR, Adam 120 Franconia 120 Margaret 120
MURRAY, Alethea R 106
NEELEY, Lizzie M 309
NELSON, Eliz H 208 Julia 162 Louise 207 Margaret 32 Mrs 69 Sarah Natalie 208 Virginia 232
NEVILLE, Lizzie 287 Lora 43 Mary 146 Nita 148
NEWTON, Andrew 10 Beatrice 35 Cathrine 10 Christina 10
NICHOLS, Anna 168
NIXON, Mary 287

NOCK, Ann W 271 Catherine 272 E W 69 Edmund 272 Elijah W 69 Elizabeth R 272 Esther 20 Esther A 264 Ethel 286 Jno J 264 John Edward 82 L W 71 Laura C 102 Lena 239 Levin 71 Levin W 271 Margaret S 71 Margt 71 Margt A 69 Mary Taylor 69 Mollie 117 Polly W 271 S C 71 Sarah Elliot 82 Sarah Garrison 264 Virginia 142 Virginia M 69 Wessie 82
NORMAN, Rebecca 287
NORTHAM, Blanche 141 Henrietta 108 Sallie Wright 142
NOTTINGHAM, Alice 54 Catherine 175 Frances 150 Julia 269 Ruth 30
NOWELL, Annie 62
OAKLEY, Myrtle 166
ODOM, Virginia 250
PANNELL, Annie Fletcher 192 Laura 192 Wm 192
PARAMORE, Sarah E 306
PARKER, Agnes West 121 Agnes Wise 204 Annie M 299 Betty 38 Dorothy 168 Eliz 278 Geo 151 299 Harriet 47 Henry 121 Jno W H 68 96 Julia Guy 112 Lucinda 279 Lucy 278 Margaret 276 Margt 299 Mary C 259 Peggy 166 Phoebe S 68 Roxanna C 5 Rufus 49 S A S 96 Sally 203 Sarah 151 Sarah A 68 Sarah R 121 Sarah W 204 Susan 101 Susan C 96 Thos 278 Vera 291 Virginia 190 Wm H 204
PARKES, B S 144 Virginia 157 see also PARKS 208
PARKS, Ada 136 Bertha 106 Bessie 272 Blanche 180 304 Elizabeth 279 Esther 118 Geraldine 104 Kate 166 243 Lillian 302 Lola S 245 Mabel 219 Marcie 40 Mary E 163 Maude 6 Otho Page 57 Richd Lee 57 Sarah 163 Sharon 102 T S 163 Thelma 158
PARRAMORE, Ann T 279 Ann Teagle 226 Eliz C 306 Elizabeth 13 Esther 11 278 Jno

PARRAMORE (continued) 306 Louisa 127 Mary 11 Mrs B D 214 Nellie 3 Sallie 170 Sally 306 Sally T 306 Thos 11 Wm 13 306
PARSONS, Helen 156 Nancy 31 Olivia 215 Sarah 31 Winnie 121 Wm 31
PATE, Sarah 101
PATRICK, Jos 292 Margaret 292 Mary 292
PATTERSON, Gay 255
PAYNE, Lois 215 Nancy 43
PEDDIE, Margaret E 159
PENELLO, Fay 251
PERDEW, Marie 32
PERROW, Sallie 54
PETTIT, Hester 114 Margt 12
PETTITT, Margaret 64 Margt 303 Mary 64 Wm 64
PHILLIPS, Ann 205 207 264 Arinthia 115 Elizabeth Ann 264 Emma S 205 Harriet E 39 Jacob 264 Mary E 207 Minnie 70 Sally V 7 Smith 39 Solomon 205 207
PILCHARD, Bessie P 108 Doris 99
PITTS, Alice T 231 Bessie S 117 Lucy 287 Sabra 223 Sue A 184 188 Susie 192
POLK, Sallie 289
POLLIARD, Ruth 179
POULSON, Annie B 84 Eliza 85 Jno 85 Kate 96 Martha W 85 Mary Ellen 235
POWELL, A Sarah 98 Ann 236 Arithia Ewell 101 Arthur 58 Clara E 101 Eliz C 141 Elizabeth 58 Elizabeth F 141 Elizabeth S 165 Ida 258 Jno T 101 Katherine 36 Lean McAllen 289 Leila 128 Margaret 203 Margaret E R 58 Mary 212 Mary A 165 Mary S 111 Nancy S 212 Nellie 68 Seth 165 212 Wm P 141
PREESON, Sarah 197
PRICE, Eleanor 294 Lula 230 Otelia 155
PRIER, see PRYOR 223
PRUITT, Benj 295 Henrietta 295

PRYER, see PRYOR 223
PURNELL, Elizabeth 170
PUSEY, Jane 149
PYLE, Mary 241
QUINBY, Charlotte 258 Elise 20 Georgie Richardson 171 Margaret Upshur 99 Upshur 262
QUINTINA, Michele 299
RAAB, Edith 304
RAYFIELD, Major 222 Mary A 111 Mary Ann 222 Nancy 111 222 Saml 111
READ, Edna 264 Emma 234 Gladys 224 Henrietta 131 Mary 169
READE, Kathryn 148 see also READ 225
REASTON, Annie Sue 28
RECTOR, Jessie 168
REED, Enoch 226 Helen Margt 4
REESE, Virginia 53
REESTON, Susan 41
REID, Faith 31 see also REED 226
REVELL, ___h 60 Eliz 151 Nina 12
REVILL, Jno B 11 Rosey D 11 Rosey S 11
REW, Bettie 90 Betty 205 Lillie 157 Margaret Katherine 136 Nancie 55 Nancy 55 256 Richd 55 Sallie 65 Sallie Dennis 65
RICH, Adeline 168 Blanche 286
RICHARDSON, Georgie G 224 Grace 23 Mamie 148 Margt 148 Margt B 224 Mary C 172 Rachel 172 Thos 224 Wm 172
RIGGS, Beatrice 291
RILEY, Carlton 180 Elizabeth A 205 Jno 271 Leah C 271 Madeline 288 Mae 58 R R 205 Sarah 205 Susan 271
RIPPON, Annie 209
ROACH, see ROACHE 229
ROACHE, Sally 54
ROBB, Rebecca 58
ROBERTS, Evelyn 127
ROBERTSON, Sue 72
ROBINS, Edwd 31 Esther 31 Letty 10 Margt 31 Mary 10 Thomas 10

ROBINSON, Elizabeth 251 Sara (West) 303 Scarburgh 303 Tully 251 303
RODES, Hardenia 96 Jennie 96 Robt 96
RODGERS, Elizabeth P 29 Elizabeth S 29 Euphamey 29 206 Jane M 206 Levi 29 Levy 206 Margt 252 Rachael 29 Wm 29
ROGERS, Adelaide 9 124 Adelaide M 17 Elizabeth 62 Eunice 84 Euphaney 132 Geo S 17 Harriet T 132 Levi 132 M J 17 Margaret A P 225 Margaret H 292 Margt 293 Mary 40 Peter 292 Richd 225 Sarah Kendall 225 Susan 17 Suzette 124
ROSSE, see ROSS 233
ROWLES, Elizabeth 112 Helen 77
RUDIGER, see RUEDIGER 234
RUE, C Scott 243
RUSSELL, Carrye 51 E J 164 Eleanor 73
SAMPLE, Lizzie 310 Polly 117
SANDE, Kristine 46
SANFORD, Lucy 166
SATCHELL, Ann 141 Anne 141 Anne Bell 141 Charlotte Bell 141 Christopher 141 E B 101 Eliza Frances 101 Estella 39 Pauline 235 S S 101
SAULSBURY, Henry 3 Mary 3 Sallie E 3
SAVAGE, C 154 Edna 221 283 Elizabeth 64 Etta 228 Jewel 88 Jno 64 L 154 Lena 134 Lillian 173 Margaret 43 Margaret S 154 Mary Ann 64 Mary Julia 54 Willie Anna 51
SCARBOROUGH, A P 67 Eleanor D 146 Elizabeth A P 67 Emily 225 Wm M 67
SCARBROUGH, Mary 21
SCARBURG, Edmd 309 Jane 309 Margaret 309
SCARBURGH, Edmund 301 Gabriella 140 Hannah 301 Hannah (Butler) 301 Margt 251 Matilda 302 Sarah 302 Tabitha 68

SCHERER, Frances 1 112 Geo 1 112 Margaret H 112
SCHOOLFIELD, Mary (Barnes) 250 Mollie S 250 Saml Thos 250
SCOTT, Caressa 234 Dimariah 106 E Blanche 118 Elizabeth 283 G W 25 George-Anna 25 Gertie 161 Hazel 193 J R 234 Jane 52 Janie E 252 Jno W 118 Lotta 33 May 173 Nellie 68 Sadie 173 Sallie J 151 Sarah 14 Stella 142 V W 211 Winfield 114
SELBY, Elizabeth 104 Emma 214 Emma Marshall 106 Harriet Fleming 112 Henritta 104 Ina E 214 J O 214 Jno Outten 106 Sally T 112 113 Zadock 104
SERGEANT, Jno 302 303 Margaretta (Watmaugh) 302 303 Sarah 302
SEYMORE, Louise 247 see also SEYMOUR 246
SEYMOUR, Digby 214 Rose 214 Sarah 214
SHAW, Jennie 199 Mary 225 Millie H 115
SHEA, Cordie E 99
SHEPPARD, Henrietta D 18 Henrietta D Ayres 231
SHERWOOD, Elizabeth 246 Jacob 246 S A 33 Southey 235 246
SHIELD, Annie P 44 Eliz 283 Elizabeth 44 Jas K 44 283 Mary E 283
SHIELDS, see SHIELD 246
SHORT, Mae Mason 53
SHREAVES, Geneva 81 Jane 213 Julia 192 Suly E 213 Wm 213
SHREVES, Addie 136 see also SHREAVES 247
SHRIEVES, Lucy 162 Veeda E 41 see also SHREAVES 247
SIMPKINS, Malissa 259
SIMPSON, Shirley 44
SKIDMORE, Mollie 109
SLOCOMB, Susan Aydelott 76 Susan Britann 76 Wm Corbin 76
SLOCOME, Sarah C 217 Susannah 217 Thos F 217

SLOCUMB, see SLOCOMB 250
SMITH, Ann 141 Annie 199 Bessie 66 Cleve M 263 Cordie E 159 E S 263 Eliz 112 309 Eliza K 20 Elizabeth 18 82 292 Ella Susan 174 Emily 20 Ezekiel 174 Garner 251 Geo 82 309 Jno 20 141 Josephine 85 Juliet L 82 309 Margaret 141 Margt 174 Minnie Viola 217 Nancy 63 S K 263 Sarah 141 Susanna 232 Susannah (Custis) 141
SNEAD, Agnes 109 Anna 48 Jno 109 Louisa 229 Martha 288 Mary Lizie 229 Millie 109 Peter 48 Rachel 48 Rosella 260 Tabitha S 260 Tully 260
SNELL, Alice 92
SOMERS, Bertie 261 Josephine 23 Katherine 304 Marie 295 Pricilla 227 Viana 304
SOMMERS, see SOMERS 255
SPARROW, Sadie V 145 Susie 230
SPENCE, Jno 163 Matilda 163
SPENSER, see SPENCER 257
SPICER, Katherine 84
SPIERS, Ann 299
STANT, Raymond S 106 Sarah B 106
STEPHENS, Sallye 192
STERLING, Frances Nottingham 150
STEVENS, M S 33 Manie 83 Nettie May 207 Rachel 270 W C 33
STEVENSON, Grace 274
STEWART, Alice 141 Alice Ann 20 Leah Irving Ker 222 Mary 80 Roberta Ker 222 Robt 222
STILES, Margaret 61
STINSON, Marie Warfield 129
STITELY, P A 5
STOCKLEY, Sarah 68
STRINGER, Comfort 146
STRUGIS, Chas T 133
STURGES, see STURGIS 261
STURGIS, Bettie S 133 C 309 Charlotte 309 Eliz M 97 Emma 101 Esther W 97 F M 134 Geo A 6 Jno W 309 Lillian 76 Margt 59 Mary J 133 Thos 97

SWANGER, Sarah 46
TANKARD, Jno 101 Sallie 101 Susan 101
TAPMAN, Jessie 191
TAYLOR, A B 22 Ann C 43 Bartholomew 271 Batholomew 7 Bertha 139 Eugenia 10 Gertrude 224 Louisa 4 71 Margaret 7 111 Mary 69 Patience 7 271 S 43 Sally 155 Sarah A 233
TEACKLE, Abel 11 Ann 214 Ann P 240 Arthur 225 240 Eliz 224 240 Elizabeth 225 Elizabeth Upshur 224 Levin 214 Littleton Dennis 224 Margaret 214 237 Margaret G 11 R Gascins 11
THOMAS, Annie 3 Bernice 10 Bettie 71 Eva 37 Kelly 305 Lizzie 310 Lucy 222 Margaret J 148 Margaret Sarah 76 Mary 43 Miranda 28 Seba 174 Susan 27 Terese 310 Will 310
THOMPSON, Margt B 310
THORNS, Martha 144 see also THORNES 269
THORNTON, Anna 49
TIGNAL, see TIGNALL 270
TINDALL, see TYNDALL 277
TOPPING, Hannah 175 L C 208 N S 208 Sarah A S 208
TOWNSEND, Henry 282 Rosey 129 Sabra P 282 Sallie 282
TRADER, Rosey 239
TRAVIS, Josephine 48
TROWER, A N 78 Lauretta 273 Lena Elva 4 Polly 78 T L 78
TULL, Bertha 246 Eileen 222
TUNNELL, Carrie 289
TURLINGTON, E R 39 60 271 Effie 153 Elizabeth R 39 Jennie S 305 Kate 40 Leah J 60 Louisa S 271 Mary 241 S M 39 60 271
TURNER, Belle S 146 Cattrine 38 Eliz 297 Elsie G 12 Esther 63 Geo 63 J T 146 Katherine 297 Mary 297 Pansy G 12 Susan E 63 V A 146 Wm 297
TWIFORD, see TWYFORD 275
TWYFORD, Anna E 77 Elizabeth 108 Florence 238 Geo D 108 Roberta Sarah 108

TYLER, Annie Walston 169 Estelle 303 J S 169 Mary R 21 Nora 297 R B 169
TYSON, Va 80
UNDERHILL, Nancy 30 Susan E 30 Thos 30
UPSHUR, Bettie 8 John 11 Margaret 99 Mrs Jno 278 Pearl 12 Rachel 11 Sally 9 Sally B 112 Susan 255 Thos 112
VAN PELT, Mabel 93
VANDERSLICE, Mary A 266
VARLETT, Anna 112 Casper 112 Judith 112
VAUGHAN, Anna 10
WALKER, Ann T Parramore 226 Ann Teagle 226 Eliz 273 Jas 229 Jno 273 Jno B 226 Mary E 229 Mattie 140 Salley S 273 Sallie 229 Sarah 172
WALLACE, Abel W 218 Jennie 218 Manie E 218
WALSTON, Annie 277 Rosie B 277 Sarah P 27 Wm 277
WALTER, Ann 134 Evelyn 238 Jno S 134 Matilda 97 Matilda A 134 Mildred 149 Richd 97 Sarah 41 Susie 159
WAPLES, Mary D 230 Roberta Lee 208 Sabra 230 Saml 230
WARD, 'Annie' Lillian 141 Ann L 204 Esther 122 Levi 204 Margt 120 Minnie 126 Sallie 204 Sarah F 172
WARFIELD, Marie 129
WARNER, Marion Lee 54
WARREN, Lela 104
WASHINGTON, Martha 66
WATERFIELD, Elva 261 Margt 212 Mary E 212 R A 113 Wm 212
WATMAUGH, Margaretta 302
WATSON, Elizabeth 262 276 Grace 88 India 233 236 Mabel 35 Rebecca Anne 49
WATTS, Mary 127 Roberta 257
WAUGH, Sarah 302
WEAVER, T Lee 13
WEBB, Annie 209
WELCH, Elizabeth 21 Margaret R 21 Wm 21
WESCOTT, Bessie 218 Betsy E

WESCOTT (continued)
  77 E D 80 Elsie 39 Jos J 77
  Mamie 77 Margaret 134 Maude
  36 Nan 80 Rachel 268 Va
  Tyson 80
WESSELLS, Anne E 114 B W 112
  Betsy 255 Evelyn 196 Mazie A
  181 Melisha G 6 Miriam Sue
  269 Ruth 9 W J 112 Winnie W
  112
WESSELS, Beulah 189 Nancy 247
WEST, Agnes 121 204 206 208
  Annie 47 Anthony 112 204
  Caroline 50 Cassey 240 E
  Agnes 281 Elenore 204 Eliz
  240 281 Eliz H Nelson 208
  Elizabeth 234 Elizabeth
  Rowles 112 Ethel 238 Eva 210
  James H 292 Jennie 285 Jno
  240 302 Jno R 208 Lois 136
  Margaret 247 Mary 127 Matilda
  112 302 Matilda (Scarburgh)
  302 Rachel 102 Revell 281 S
  Wallop 104 Sara 303 Sarah 297
  Sarah W 208
WESTCOTT, Elizabeth 241
WHARTON, Ann 84 Catherine 66
  Jas 84 Polly 78 Susan 84
WHEELER, Harriet J 74 Henry 74
  Margaret A 74
WHITE, Beatrice 270 Cordie E
  Shea 99 Ellen Major 141 Geo
  217 Georgia 153 Grace 86 Henrietta 108 Lillian 233 Margaret
  T 108 Mary 141 Maude 201
  Nora 52 53 R A 108 Rooker 208
  Wm W 141

WHITEHURST, Addie 136
WILKINS, Harriet 8 Harriet A 301
  Mary E 167
WILLET, Annie F 189
WILLIAMS, Eliza C 56 Henrietta
  W 102 Jas O 102 Peter 56
  Sabra C 102
WILLIS, Virginia 129
WILLS, Carrie 90
WILSON, Ann 300
WINDER, Althia 232 Annie 158
  Audrey 281 Frances Cathrine
  35 Mary Ann 279
WISE, Annie 93 Catherine C 11
  Dorinda 132 E Spencer 94 Edna
  70 Eleanor Douglas 67
  Elizabeth E 11 Gertrude 172
  Jno R 11 Martha 229 Mary 67
  181 Nina 225 Sally 11 Sarah
  Sergeant 302 Tabitha Scarburgh
  68 Tully R 67 Wm E 172
WOOD, Julia 179
WOODWARD, Elizabeth 281
WRIGHT, Helen 227 Louise 291
  Sallie 142
YERBY, Sallie 76
YOUNG, Bessie 182 Blanche 242
  Catherine 91 Daisey 88 E H
  285 Elizabeth C 91 Ellen 214
  Gilly 91 Jno 240 Mary H 240
  Mary Pyle 241 Ruth M 285 V S
  285
ZEMBER, Blanche 296

www.ingramcontent.com/pod-product-compliance
Lightning Source LLC
Chambersburg PA
CBHW050330230426
43663CB00010B/1807